THE FATE OF THE DEAD

SUPPLEMENTS TO
NOVUM TESTAMENTUM

VOLUME XCIII

THE FATE OF THE DEAD

Studies on the Jewish and Christian Apocalypses

BY

RICHARD BAUCKHAM

BRILL
LEIDEN · BOSTON · KÖLN
1998

This book is printed on acid-free paper.

Library of Congress Cataloging-in-Publication Data

Bauckham, Richard.
  The Fate of the Dead : Studies on the Jewish and Christian Apocalypses
/ by Richard Bauckham.
     p. cm. — (Supplements to Novum Testamentum, ISSN 0167-9732 ;
v. 93)
  Includes bibliographical references and index.
  ISBN 9004112030 (cloth : alk. paper)
     1. Apocalyptic literature—History and criticism.   2. Eschatology—
History of doctrines—Early church, ca. 30-600.   3. Future life—
Christianity—History of doctrines—Early church, ca. 30-600.
  4. Eschatology, Jewish—History of doctrines.   5. Future life—
Judaism—History of doctrines.   I. Title.   II. Series.
  BL501.B38   1998
  291.2'3—dc21   98-16848
                                                                              CIP

Die Deutsche Bibliothek - CIP-Einheitsaufnahme

Bauckham, Richard:
The Fate of the Dead : Studies on the Jewish and Christian Apocalypses /
by Richard Bauckham. – Leiden ; Boston ; Köln : Brill, 1998
     (Supplements to Novum testamentum ; Vol. 93)
     ISBN 90–04–11203–0
[Novum Testamentum / Supplements]
  Supplements to Novum testamentum – Leiden ; Boston ; Köln : Brill
     Früher Schriftenreihe
     Fortlaufende Beiheftreihe zu: Novum testamentum
     Vol. 93. Bauckham, Richard: The Fate of the Dead. – 1998

ISSN   0167-9732
ISBN   90 04 11203 0

PRINTED IN THE NETHERLANDS

CONTENTS

DETAILS OF PREVIOUS PUBLICATION OF CHAPTERS

Note: In most cases previously published articles have been revised for this volume.

1 *Anchor Bible Dictionary*, ed. D. N. Freedman (New York: Doubleday, 1992) vol. 2, pp. 145-159.

2 *JTS* 41 (1990) 355-385.

3 *Proceedings of the Irish Biblical Association* 18 (1995) 78-93.

4 *NTS* 37 (1991) 225-246.

5 not previously published.

6 *Apocrypha* 1 (1990) 181-196.

7 not previously published.

8 *Apocrypha* 5 (1994) 7-111.

9 *Revue de Qumran* 59 (1992) 437-446.

10 J. H. Charlesworth and C. A. Evans ed., *The Pseudepigrapha and Early Biblical Interpretation* (Studies in Scripture in Early Judaism and Christianity 2; JSPSS 14; Sheffield: JSOT Press, 1993) 269-291.

11 not previously published.

12 *Apocrypha* 4 (1993) 141-175.

13 not previously published.

14 not previously published.

PREFACE

The studies collected in this volume reflect some fifteen years of study of the extra-canonical Jewish and Christian apocalypses. Those which have been previously published (nine of the fourteen chapters) were published in the years 1990-1995, but many incorporate work done in the 1980s, as do some of the previously unpublished studies. I should like to acknowledge the circumstances in which some of them originated.

Chapter 6 originated as a paper delivered to an International Colloquium held to celebrate the Centenary of the Section des Sciences Religieuses (Vème Section) de l'École Pratique des Hautes Études (of the Sorbonne), in Paris, in September 1986. The session in which it was given ('Les Littératures Apocryphes') reflected the lively interest in and pioneering research on the Christian apocryphal literature which characterize the Section and its research centre, CANAL (Centre d'analyse pour l'histoire du Judaisme hellenistique et des origines chrétiennes). It also introduced me to the work and many of the members of the Association pour l'Étude de la Littérature Apocryphe Chrétienne (AELAC), which is responsible for the research for and ongoing publication of the volumes of the Corpus Christianorum Series Apocryphorum, and to which I was later admitted as a member. Like all who study apocryphal literature, I am much indebted to the work of the members of this Association. Further fruitful contact with the circle of its members in Paris came when I was invited by Pierre Geoltrain to be a visiting Director of Studies at the École in the spring of 1991. The lectures I gave then on 'The Apocalypse of Peter in its Literary and Historical Contexts' formed the basis of chapter 8 of the present volume. I am grateful to those who discussed them with me and entertained me at that time, especially Pierre Geoltrain, Jean-Daniel Dubois (President of AELAC), Alain Desreumaux, Jean-Claude Picard and Pierluigi Piovanelli. Chapter 12 of the present volume was also written at the invitation of CANAL, and these three chapters (6, 8, 12) were first published in the excellent journal *Apocrypha*, which was launched by the Paris members of AELAC in 1990, and has become an invaluable repository of new research on the apocryphal literature.

Chapter 7 originated as a paper given to a conference of the Historical Theology group (now the Christian Doctrine group) of the Tyndale Fellowship at Tyndale House, Cambridge, in 1983. Chapter

11 was originally planned as an appendix to my commentary on *Jude, 2 Peter* (Word Biblical Commentary 50; Waco: Word Books, 1983), but had to be excluded for reasons of space and has only reached publishable form in the preparation of the present volume. Chapter 3 originated as a lecture to the annual meeting of the Irish Biblical Association in Dublin in April 1995. I am most grateful to Michael Maher for inviting me on that occasion and for his and Martin McNamara's hospitality. Chapters 4 and 10 originated as papers read to the Ehrhardt Seminar in the Faculty of Theology (now the Department of Religions and Theology) in the University of Manchester. This biblical studies research seminar, which flourished under the chairmanship of the late Professor Barnabas Lindars, S.S.F, and then of Dr George Brooke, was a regular source of academic stimulation during the period (1977-1992) when I was Lecturer and then Reader in the History of Christian Thought in the Department of Historical and Contemporary Theology at Manchester. The contents of this present volume must also be indebted in countless ways to the almost continuous conversation, on all matters Jewish and apocalyptic, in which I engaged with my friend Philip Alexander during the many years when we were colleagues in Manchester.

Other scholars who have contributed to my studies in this volume by generously supplying me with their own published or unpublished work include Antonio Acerbi, Philippe Gignoux, Julian Hills, Johan de Jong, Martin McNamara, Paolo Marrassini, Enrico Norelli, Mauro Pesce, Jean-Marc Rosenstiehl and Ben Wright. I should especially like to mention the late Roger Cowley, with whom I had begun to collaborate in work on the Apocalypse of Peter not long before his untimely death in 1988. I am also grateful to Mark Bredin for undertaking the complex and laborious task of compiling the indices.

December 1997

RICHARD BAUCKHAM

ABBREVIATIONS

The following list provides a key to the abbreviations used in this volume for Jewish and Christian apocryphal works, and other Jewish, early Christian and Gnostic works. Where possible, the abbreviations conform to those used in J. H. Charlesworth ed., *The Old Testament Pseudepigrapha*, 2 vols. (London: Darton, Longman and Todd, 1983, 1985).

Not listed here are abbreviations for biblical works, which follow SBL style, and abbreviations for journals and series, which also follow SBL style.

ActsJn	Acts of John
ActsThom	Acts of Thomas
G, Syr	Greek, Syriac
ApAb	Apocalypse of Abraham.
ApEl	Coptic Apocalypse of Elijah
ApElfrag	Apocalypse of Elijah: Latin fragment
1ApJas	First Apocalypse of James (CG V, 3)
ApMos	Apocalypse of Moses
ApocrJas	Apocryphon of James (CG I,2)
ApPaul	Apocalypse of Paul.
P	Paris Latin text
StG	St Gall Latin text
ApPaul Red I	Apocalypse of Paul Latin Redaction I
ApPaul Red IV	Apocalypse of Paul Latin Redaction IV
ApPaul Red V	Apocalypse of Paul Latin Redaction V
ApPaul Red VII	Apocalypse of Paul Latin Redaction VII
ApPaul Red VIII	Apocalypse of Paul Latin Redaction VIII
ApPaul Red X	Apocalypse of Paul Latin Redaction X
ApPet	Apocalypse of Peter
A	Akhmim Greek text
B	Bodleian Greek fragment
E	Ethiopic version
R	Rainer Greek fragment
ApSedr	Apocalypse of Sedrach
ApZeph	Apocalypse of Zephaniah (Coptic texts)
ApZeph (Clem)	Apocalypse of Zephaniah: quotation in Clement of Alexandria, *Str.* 5.11.77
ArApPet	Arabic Apocalypse of Peter
AscenIs	Ascension of Isaiah
b. 'Abod. Zar.	Babylonian Talmud tractate 'Aboda Zara
2 Bar	2 (Syriac Apocalypse of) Baruch
3 Bar	3 (Greek Apocalypse of) Baruch
G, Sl	Greek, Slavonic

4 Bar	4 (The Rest of the Words of) Baruch, or Paralipomena Jeremiae
b. ʿArak.	Babylonian Talmud tractate ʿArakin
Barlaam	History of Barlaam and Josaphat
Barn	Epistle of Barnabas
b. Ber.	Babylonian Talmud tractate Berakot
b. Giṭṭ.	Babylonian Talmud tractate Giṭṭin
b. Ḥag.	Babylonian Talmud tractate Ḥagiga
b. Ket.	Babylonian Talmud tractate Ketubot
BkThom	Book of Thomas (CG II, 7)
BohDormMary	Bohairic Account of the Dormition of Mary
BohHistJos	Bohairic Account of the Death of Joseph
b. Sanh.	Babylonian Talmud tractate Sanhedrin
b. Shab.	Babylonian Talmud tractate Shabbat
b. Soṭ.	Babylonian Talmud tractate Soṭa
b. Sukk.	Babylonian Talmud tractate Sukka
b. Taʿan.	Babylonian Talmud tractate Taʿanit
CantRab	Midrash Rabbah on Canticles
CD	Damascus Covenant
ChrJerah	Chronicles of Jeraḥmeel
1 Clem	1 Clement
2 Clem	2 Clement
CopApJn	Coptic apocryphal Apocalypse of John
CopApPaul	Apocalypse of Paul (Coptic version)
CopLifePach	Coptic Life of Pachomius
3 Cor	'3 Corinthians' (part of the Acts of Paul)
Did	Didache
DidascLord	Didascalia of our Lord Jesus Christ
EcclRab	Midrash Rabbah on Ecclesiastes
1 En	1 (Ethiopic Apocalypse of) Enoch
2 En	2 (Slavonic Apocalypse of) Enoch
3 En	3 (Hebrew Apocalypse of) Enoch
EncJnBapt	Encomium on John the Baptist by John Chrysostom
EpApp	Epistle of the Apostles
EpPetPhil	Epistle of Peter to Philip (CG VIII,2)
EthApMary	Ethiopic Apocalypse of the Virgin
EthBkMyst	Ethiopic Book of the Mysteries of Heaven and Earth
ExodRab	Midrash Rabbah on Exodus
4 EzraArm	Armenian version of 4 Ezra
GBart	Gospel of Bartholomew = The Book of the Resurrection
GedMos	Gedulat Moshe
GenRab	Midrash Rabbah on Genesis
GkApEzra	Greek Apocalypse of Ezra
GkApJn	Greek apocryphal Apocalypse of John
GkApMary	Greek Apocalypse of the Virgin
GNic	Gospel of Nicodemus
GPet	Gospel of Peter
HebApEl	Hebrew Apocalypse of Elijah

HebVis II	Hebrew Vision II (Revelation of Moses) (Gaster)
HebVis V	Hebrew Vision V(Gaster)
HebVis VII	Hebrew Vision VII (Gaster)
JosAsen	Joseph and Aseneth
Jub	Jubilees
LAB	Pseudo-Philo, *Liber Antiquitatum Biblicarum*
LadJac	Ladder of Jacob
LAE	Life of Adam and Eve
LetAris	Letter of Aristeas
LevRab	Midrash Rabbah on Leviticus
2 Macc	2 Maccabees
3 Macc	3 Maccabees
4 Macc	4 Maccabees
m. Soṭ.	Mishnah tractate Soṭa
MystJn	Mysteries of John the Apostle and Holy Virgin
NHApPaul	Nag Hammadi Apocalypse of Paul (CG V, 2).
NHApPet	Nag Hammadi Apocalypse of Peter (CG VII, 3)
OdesSol	Odes of Solomon.
PistSoph	Pistis Sophia
PrJos	Prayer of Joseph
Ps-Phoc	Pseudo-Phocylides
PsSol	Psalms of Solomon
4QBer[a]	Blessings from Qumran Cave 4 (4Q286)
4QEn	Aramaic Enoch from Qumran Cave 4
1QH	Hodayot (Thanksgiving Hymns) from Qumran Cave 1
1QM	War Rule from Qumran Cave 1
QuesBart	Questions of Bartholomew
QuesEzra	Questions of Ezra
A, B	Recensions A and B
SahDormMary	Sahidic Dormition of Mary (fragments I, II)
SahHistJos	Sahidic Account of the Death of Joseph (fragments I-III)
SahLifeMary	Sahidic Life of the Virgin (fragments I–IV)
SephRaz	Sepher ha-Razim
SibOr	Sibylline Oracles
Sifre Deut	Sifre on Deuteronomy
Sifre Num	Sifre on Numbers
Sir	Ben Sira (Ecclesiasticus)
SophJesChr	Sophia of Jesus Christ (CG III,4 and BG 8502,3)
SyrHistMary	Syriac History of the Virgin
SyrTransMary	Syriac Transitus Mariae
TAb	Testament of Abraham
A, B	Recensions A and B
TDan	Testament of Dan
TeachSilv	Teachings of Silvanus (CG II,4)
Tg Neof	Targum Neofiti
TIsaac	Testament of Isaac
TJac	Testament of Jacob
TLevi	Testament of Levi

TLord	Testament of our Lord
TMos	Testament of Moses
t. Sanh.	Tosefta tractate Sanhedrin
VisEzek	Visions of Ezekiel (Re'iyyot Yehezkiel)
VisEzra	(Latin) Vision of Ezra
B	MS B
L	MS L
Wis	Wisdom of Solomon
y. Ber.	Palestinian Talmud tractate Berakot
y. Sanh.	Palestinian Talmud tractate Sanhedrin
y. Ḥag.	Palestinian Talmud tractate Ḥagiga
y. Ta'an.	Palestinian Talmud tractate Ta'anit

TEXTS AND TRANSLATIONS

The following lists editions and translations of some of the apocryphal works cited in this volume. In the case of works which appear in the major collections of Jewish, Christian and Gnostic apocryphal works in translation—J. H. Charlesworth ed., *The Old Testament Pseudepigrapha*, 2 vols. (London: Darton, Longman and Todd, 1983, 1985); F. García Martinez, *The Dead Sea Scrolls Translated* (tr. W. G. E. Watson; Leiden: Brill, 1994); E. Hennecke, W. Schneemelcher, and R. McL. Wilson ed., *New Testament Apocrypha*, 2 vols. (Cambridge: James Clarke, 1991, 1992); J. M. Robinson ed., *The Nag Hammadi Library in English* (Leiden: Brill, 1977)—details of editions can be found in those collections. Such works do not appear in the following list except in a few cases where the edition cited is significant and not referred to in the collections.

Apocalypse of Elijah: Latin fragment
M. E. Stone and J. Strugnell, *The Books of Elijah Parts 1-2* (Missoula, Montana: Scholars Press, 1979) 14 (trans.), 15 (text).

Apocalypse of Paul (Armenian)
L. Leloir, '*L'Apocalypse de Paul* dans sa teneur arménienne,' *Revue des études arméniennes* 14 (1980) 234-285 (trans.);
L. Leloir, *Écrits Apocryphes sur les Apôtres: Traduction de l'Édition Arménienne de Venise*, vol. 1 (CCSA 3; Turnhout: Brepols, 1986) 87-172 (trans.).

Apocalypse of Paul (Coptic)
E. A. W. Budge, *Miscellaneous Coptic Texts in the Dialect of Upper Egypt* (London: British Museum, 1915) 534-574 (Coptic text), 1022-29 (trans.).

Apocalypse of Paul (Latin)
Paris Latin text: M. R. James, *Apocrypha Anecdota* (Texts and Studies 2/3; Cambridge: University Press, 1893) 11-42;
St Gall Latin text: T. Silverstein, *Visio Sancti Pauli* (Studies and Documents 4; London: Christophers, 1935) 131-147.
(See now also T. Silverstein and A. Hilhorst, *Apocalypse of Paul: A New Critical Edition of Three Long Latin Versions* [Cahiers d'Orientalisme 21; Geneva: Cramer, 1997].)

Apocalypse of Paul Latin Redaction IV
3 texts:
PL 94, cols. 501-502;
F. Meyer, 'La descente de saint Paul en enfer: poème français composé en Angleterre', *Romania* 24 (1895) 365-375;
H. Brandes, 'Über die Quellen der mittelenglischen Versionen der

Paulus-Vision', *Englische Studien* 7 (1884) 44-47 = H. Brandes, *Visio S. Pauli* (Halle: Niemeyer, 1885) 75-80.

Apocalypse of Paul Latin Redaction V
T. Silverstein, *Visio Sancti Pauli* (Studies and Documents 4; London: Christophers, 1935) 196-203.

Apocalypse of Paul Latin Redaction VII
T. Silverstein, *Visio Sancti Pauli* (Studies and Documents 4; London: Christophers, 1935) 204-208.

Apocalypse of Paul Latin Redaction VIII
T. Silverstein, *Visio Sancti Pauli* (Studies and Documents 4; London: Christophers, 1935) 209-213.

Apocalypse of Paul Latin Redaction X
T. Silverstein, 'The vision of Saint Paul: new links and patterns in the Western Tradition', *Archives d'Histoire Doctrinale et Littéraire du Moyen Age* 34 (1959) 244-247.

Apocalypse of Peter
D. D. Buchholz, *Your Eyes Will Be Opened: A Study of the Greek (Ethiopic) Apocalypse of Peter* (SBLDS 97; Atlanta, Georgia: Scholars Press, 1988) (Ethiopic text and trans.).

Arabic Apocalypse of Peter
A. Mingana, *Woodbrooke Studies* 3/2: *Apocalypse of Peter* (Cambridge: Heffer, 1931) (text and trans.).

Bohairic Account of the Dormition of Mary
F. Robinson, *Coptic Apocryphal Gospels* (Texts and Studies 4/2; Cambridge: University Press, 1896) 44-67 (trans.).

Bohairic Account of the Death of Joseph
F. Robinson, *Coptic Apocryphal Gospels* (Texts and Studies 4/2; Cambridge: University Press, 1896) 130-147 (trans.).

Coptic apocryphal Apocalypse of John (part of the Discourse on Michael the Archangel by Timothy of Alexandria)
E. A. W. Budge, *Miscellaneous Coptic Texts in the Dialect of Upper Egypt* (London: British Museum, 1915) 513-520 (Coptic text), 1022-1029 (trans.).

Coptic Life of Pachomius
L. Th. Lefort, *Les vies coptes de saint Pachôme et de ses premiers successeurs* (Bibliothèque du Muséon 16; Louvain: Bureau du Muséon, 1943).

Didascalia of our Lord Jesus Christ
F. Nau, 'Une Didascalie de Notre-Seigneur Jésus-Christ (ou: Constitutions des saints apotres),' *Revue de l'Orient Chrétien* 12 (1907) 225-254 (Greek text and trans.).

Encomium on John the Baptist by John Chrysostom
E. A. W. Budge, *Coptic Apocrypha in the Dialect of Upper Egypt* (London: British Museum, 1913) 128-145 (Coptic text), 335-351 (trans.).

Ethiopic Apocalypse of the Virgin
  M. Chaîne, *Apocrypha be B. Maria Virgine* (CSCO: Scriptores Aethiopici: Ser I, 8; Rome: de Luigi, 1909) 45-68 (Latin trans.), 53-80 (text).

Ethiopic Book of the Mysteries of Heaven and Earth
  J. Perruchon and I. Guidi, *Le Livre des mystères du ciel et de la terre* (PO 1/1; Paris: Librairie de Paris, 1907).

Gedulat Moshe
Three versions:
  M. Gaster, *Studies and Texts*, vol. 1 (London: Maggs, 1925-28) 125-141 (trans.);
  L. Ginzberg, *The Legends of the Jews*, vol. 2 (Philadelphia: Jewish Publication Society, 1910) 304-315 (trans.);
  A. Netzer, 'A Midrash on the Ascension of Moses in Judeo-Persian,' in S. Shaked and A. Netzer ed., *Irano-Judaica II: Studies Relating to Jewish Contacts with Persian Culture Throughout the Ages* (Jerusalem: Ben-Zvi Institute, 1990) 112-141 (text and trans.).

Gospel of Bartholomew (= The Book of the Resurrection)
  E. A. W. Budge, *Coptic Apocrypha in the Dialect of Upper Egypt* (London: British Museum, 1913) 1-48 (Coptic text), 179-215 (trans.).

Greek apocryphal Apocalypse of John
  C. Tischendorff, *Apocalypses apocryphae* (Leipzig: Mendelssohn, 1866) 70-94.

Greek Apocalypse of the Virgin
  M. R. James, *Apocrypha Anecdota* (Texts and Studies 2/3; Cambridge: Cambridge University Press, 1893) 115-126;
  H. Pernot, 'Descente de la Vierge aux Enfers d'après les manuscrits grecs de Paris,' *Revue des Études Grecques* 13 (1900) 233-257.
  (See chapter 13 of this volume for other editions of this text.)

Hebrew Apocalypse of Elijah
  M. Buttenweiser, *Der hebräische Elias-Apokalypse und ihre Stellung in der apokalyptischen Litteratur des rabbinischen Schrifftums und der Kirche* (Leipzig: Pfeiffer, 1897) (text and German trans.);
  G. W. Buchanan, *Revelation and Redemption: Jewish Documents of Deliverance from the Fall of Jerusalem to the Death of Naḥmanides* (Dillsboro, North Carolina: Western North Carolina Press, 1978) 426-440 (trans.).

Hebrew Vision II (Revelation of Moses)
  M. Gaster, 'Hebrew Visions of Hell and Paradise' in *Studies and Texts*, vol. 1 (London: Maggs, 1925-28) 141-143 (trans.).

Hebrew Vision V
  M. Gaster, 'Hebrew Visions of Hell and Paradise' in *Studies and Texts*, vol. 1 (London: Maggs, 1925-28) 152-158 (trans.).

Hebrew Vision VII
  M. Gaster, 'Hebrew Visions of Hell and Paradise' in *Studies and Texts*, vol. 1 (London: Maggs, 1925-28) 160-161 (trans.).

History of Barlaam and Josaphat
   PG 96, cols. 859-1246.

Mysteries of John the Apostle and Holy Virgin
   E. A. W. Budge, *Coptic Apocrypha in the Dialect of Upper Egypt* (London:
   British Museum, 1913) 59-74 (Coptic text), 241-257 (trans.).

Pistis Sophia
   V. MacDermot, *Pistis Sophia* (Nag Hammadi Studies 9;
   Leiden: Brill, 1978) (Coptic text and trans.).

Sahidic Dormition of Mary (fragments I, II).
   F. Robinson, *Coptic Apocryphal Gospels* (Texts and Studies 4/2; Cambridge:
   University Press, 1896) 2-41 (text and trans.).

Sahidic Account of the Death of Joseph (fragments I-III)
   F. Robinson, *Coptic Apocryphal Gospels* (Texts and Studies 4/2; Cambridge:
   University Press, 1896) 147-159 (text and trans.)

Sahidic Life of the Virgin (fragments I–IV).
   F. Robinson, *Coptic Apocryphal Gospels* (Texts and Studies 4/2; Cambridge:
   University Press, 1896) 2-41 (text and trans.).

Sepher ha-Razim
   M. A. Morgan, *Sepher ha-Razim: The Book of Mysteries* (Chico, California:
   Scholars Press, 1983) (trans.).

Syriac History of the Virgin
   E. A. W. Budge, *The History of the Virgin Mary and the History of the Likeness
   of Christ*, vol. 2 (London: Luzac, 1899) (trans.).

Syriac Transitus Mariae
   A. Smith Lewis, *Apocrypha Syriaca: The Protevangelium Jacobi and Transitus
   Mariae* (Studia Sinaitica 11; London: Clay, 1902) 12-69 (trans.);
   W. Wright, 'The Departure of my Lady Mary from the World,' *Journal of
   Sacred Literature* 7 (1865) 129-160 (trans.).

Testament of our Lord
   J. Cooper and A. J. Maclean, *The Testament of our Lord* (Edinburgh: T. &
   T. Clark, 1902) (trans.).

Vision of Ezra (*Visio Beati Esdrae)*
   B MS B: P.-M. Bogaert, 'Une version longue inédite de la "Visio Beati
   Esdrae" dans le Légendier de Teano (Barberini Lat. 2318),' *RBén* 94
   (1984) 59-64.
   L MS L: O. Wahl, *Apocalypsis Esdrae: Apocalypsis Sedrach: Visio Beati Esdrae*
   (Pseudepigrapha Veteris Testamenti Graece 4; Leiden: Brill, 1977) 49-
   61.

Visions of Ezekiel (Re'iyyot Yehezkiel)
   L. Jacobs, *The Jewish Mystics* (London: Kyle Cathie, 1990) 27-31 (trans.).

INTRODUCTION

The ancient apocalypses are a literature of revelation. In visions, auditions, and cosmic and otherworldly journeys, the seers to whom they are attributed receive, by heavenly agency, revelations of the mysteries of creation and the cosmos, history and eschatology. The kinds of secrets that are disclosed are quite wide-ranging and vary from one apocalypse to another, but prominent among them is the fate of the dead. This is what has come to be known in Christian theology as personal eschatology, as distinct from historical and cosmic eschatology, which concern the future of human history and of the cosmos at the end of this age when God's kingdom comes. Personal eschatology concerns the future of individuals beyond death. It was mainly in the apocalypses that Jewish and then Christian understandings of life after death developed: the expectation of judgment and resurrection for all the dead, the two final destinies of eternal life and eternal condemnation, and the 'intermediate state' of the dead between death and the general resurrection. Such personal eschatology was not for the most part divorced from historical and cosmic eschatology, since the hope of individuals was to share in the corporate future of God's people in God's kingdom and in the cosmic future of new creation for the world. Hence resurrection and judgment are typically expected to occur not at death but at the end of the age. Only at a rather late date did attention in some apocalypses which focused on the fate of the dead concentrate on their state immediately after death to such an extent as to neglect historical and cosmic eschatology altogether. Conversely, apocalypses whose main interests lie elsewhere rarely neglect personal eschatology altogether.

There are very few apocalypses which make no reference at all to the fate of the dead, but some give much more attention to this topic than others, providing, in particular, extensive accounts of the blessings of paradise and the punishments of hell. Apocalypses of this kind have been comparatively neglected. This is partly because most attempts to study the ancient apocalypses as a corpus have limited their scope to the Second Temple period (ending c. 100 C.E.), excluding Jewish apocalypses of later date and all Christian apocalypses except the New Testament Apocalypse of John. Even some apocalypses, such as 2 Enoch and the Apocalypse of Zephaniah, in which the fate of the dead is prominent and which probably originated within this period, have been marginalized because of uncertainty about their date. Some Christian apocalypses concerned with the fate of the dead, such as the Apocalypse of Paul, have been studied for the sake of their influence on Christian beliefs about and images of life after death in the ancient and medieval periods, but have not been treated as part of the continuous literary tradition of the Jewish and Christian apocalypses which extends from the third century B.C.E. to the middle ages. In this book, we shall be concerned with the study of particular apocalypses whose main subject-matter is the fate of the dead and which have been largely neglected, such as the Apocalypse of Peter, the Apocalypse of the Seven Heavens, and the Apocalypses of the Virgin, works which date from the early centuries C.E. We shall also be concerned with themes that recur throughout the corpus of apocalypses, both those which set the fate of the dead within a range of wider cosmic or eschatological interests and those which focus largely or solely on the fate of the dead. On the chronological range of works we consider relevant there is no strict lower limit, though the main emphasis is on the period down to the third century C.E. We shall not be excluding later works from our view, both because some apocalypses are difficult to date, but also because the whole tradition of Jewish and Christian apocalypses, down to the late middle ages, retains very important elements of continuity with the apocalypses of the Second Temple period. Studying the tradition as a whole can sometimes illuminate the earlier apocalypses.

We treat the Jewish and Christian apocalypses as a continuous tradition.[1] The extra-canonical Jewish apocalypses of the Second Temple period were copied and read by Christians, and, since they were not eventually preserved in rabbinic Judaism, in almost every case they have come down to us only because Christians read them as Christian religious literature. The Christian apocalypses which were written from the late first century onwards continue and develop both the content and the literary forms of the ancient Jewish apocalypses (as do the later Hebrew apocalypses, though the historical means of continuity are in their case more obscure[2]). Many of them are much closer to the extra-canonical Jewish apocalypses than to the canonical apocalypses of Daniel and the Apocalypse of John. Only very rarely did the latter provide the model for a later Christian apocalypse. In

---

[1] Cf. R. Bauckham, 'The Apocalypses in the New Pseudepigrapha,' in C. A. Evans and S. E. Porter ed., *New Testament Backgrounds: A Sheffield Reader* (Biblical Seminar 43; Sheffield: Sheffield Academic Press, 1997) 84-86.

[2] P. S. Alexander, 'Later Hebrew Apocalyptic: a Preliminary Survey,' *Apocrypha* 1 (1990) 212-216.

some cases, it is very difficult to tell whether an apocalypse was originally Jewish or Christian, or whether the clearly Christian elements in
an apocalypse have been added to an originally Jewish work. Even
when we find it impossible to decide such an issue or to date a
particular apocalypse in the least precisely, such apocalypses can still
make important contributions to our understanding of the tradition
as a whole.

The corpus of apocalypses to which the studies collected here refer
is thus quite large. Its most important members are: Daniel, 1 Enoch
(a collection of Enochic apocalypses), the fragments of the ancient
Apocalypse of Elijah, 2 Enoch, the Apocalypse of Zephaniah, 2
Baruch, 4 Ezra, the Apocalypse of Abraham, 3 Baruch, the Greek
Apocalypse of Ezra, the Latin Vision of Ezra, the Apocalypse of
Sedrach, the Questions of Ezra, the Apocalypse of the Seven Heavens, the (canonical) Apocalypse of John, the Ascension of Isaiah, the
Apocalypse of Peter, the Apocalypse of Paul (and its several versions
and redactions), the four Apocalypses of the Virgin Mary, the Coptic
apocryphal Apocalypse of John, the Mysteries of John the Apostle,
the Greek apocryphal Apocalypse of John, the Questions of
Bartholomew, the Ethiopic Apocalypse of Baruch, the Apocalypse of
Gorgorios, the Hebrew Apocalypse of Elijah, the Gedulat Moshe and
other Hebrew visions of heaven, paradise and hell. (Since I have
devoted two other books to the canonical Apocalypse of John,[3] it does
not feature prominently in this book, except in chapter 10.)

Reference will, of course, also frequently be made to related material in works which are not generically apocalypses. The worldview
and the ideas to be found in the Jewish and Christian apocalypses are
certainly not confined to the apocalypses. They were written and
read by people who also read other genres of Jewish and Christian
literature. Their distinctiveness is as the literature of revelation of
otherworldly mysteries. Therefore they contain extended accounts of
these revealed mysteries. It was to apocalypses that people turned for
such accounts (though such accounts sometimes also occur in apocalyptic subsections within works of other genres), but they found frequent reference to the same images and concepts in the other types of
Jewish and Christian literature they read. Whereas, for example,
some of the apocalypses describe the punishments in hell at length,
paraenetic works refer much more briefly to punishment in hell as
sanction for their ethical requirements. Study of the apocalypses

---

[3] R. Bauckham, *The Theology of the Book of Revelation* (Cambridge: Cambridge University Press, 1993); idem, *The Climax of Prophecy: Studies on the Book of Revelation* (Edinburgh: T. & T. Clark, 1993).

should not therefore restrict itself to the apocalypses, and some of the chapters in this book employ the apocalypses to explain and to illuminate passages in other kinds of literature, including the Gospel of Luke and the Letter of James.

(In common with some other recent writers, I use the terms 'apocalypse' and 'apocalyptic' to refer to the literary genre of the apocalypses. This seems to be the only way to avoid the conceptual confusion that has come to surround the use of these terms and to restore some useful precision to their use.[4] I have tried to avoid the common but misleading use of 'apocalyptic' or 'apocalypticism' to describe the kind of worldview or the kind of eschatology to be found in the apocalypses. This is misleading—especially when the range of apocalypses studied is extended beyond the very narrow range to which studies of Second Temple Judaism usually confine themselves—because it may suggest too much uniformity in worldview and eschatology among the apocalypses, because the worldview and the kind of eschatology to be found in the apocalypses is not what distinguishes them from other literature, and because apocalyptic revelations concern a variety of topics besides eschatology.)

The fourteen studies collected in this book (five of which have not previously been published) have been written as independent units, but many of them are closely interconnected in their subject-matter.

The first three chapters treat a particularly important theme in our apocalypses and related literature: a visit to the places of the dead which enables the visitor to reveal their character and contents to the living. Such revelations of the fate of the dead by means of otherworldly journeys are to be found in several cultural traditions of the ancient world, which parallel and in some cases must have influenced the accounts of such journeys in the Jewish and Christian apocalypses. Chapter 1 ('Descents to the Underworld') therefore places an initial overview of this theme in our literature in the context of a survey of the theme in the cultures of the ancient Middle Eastern and Mediterranean world. (Literature which locates the places of the dead elsewhere than in the underworld, as many of the apocalypses do, is also included in the survey.) Chapter 2 ('Early Jewish Visions of Hell') deals with the origin and development of visions of hell or

---

[4] For recent discussions of the definitions, see D. S. Russell, *Divine Disclosure: An Introduction to Jewish Apocalyptic* (London: SCM Press, 1992) 8-13; J. J. Collins, *Seers, Sibyls and Sages in Hellenistic-Roman Judaism* (Supplements to *JSJ* 54; Leiden: Brill, 1997) chapter 2; W. Adler in J. C. VanderKam and W. Adler ed., *The Jewish Apocalyptic Heritage in Early Christianity* (CRINT 3/4; Assen: Van Gorcum/Minneapolis: Fortress, 1996) 2-13.

'tours' of the punishments in hell within the apocalypses of the Second Temple period especially. It takes the discussion beyond Martha Himmelfarb's pioneering treatment of the apocalyptic 'tours of hell' by attending also to early visions of hell to which the texts refer only briefly. These provide strong evidence that the genre of tours of hell (as also of visits to paradise) originated within the more comprehensive cosmic tour apocalypses, and that an important transition in the literary development of the tradition came with a changed view of the fate of the dead. It was only when the dead came to be seen as already being either actively punished or granted the blessings of paradise immediately after death, prior to the resurrection and final judgment, that it became possible for seers to see the dead being punished or enjoying their rewards. While chapter 2 argues from the texts a detailed case on the origin and development of tours of hell, chapter 3 ('Visiting the Places of the Dead in the Extra-Canonical Apocalypses') provides a more straightforward account which summarizes and synthesizes the material on this theme, locating all the apocalyptic visits to the places of the dead in their appropriate place within the tradition as it developed from the earliest Enochic literature to the medieval period.

There are no visits to the places of the dead in the New Testament, but the literature discussed in our first three chapters can illuminate the New Testament, as chapters 4 ('The Rich Man and Lazarus: The Parable and the Parallels') and 5 ('The Tongue Set on Fire by Hell [James 3:6]') demonstrate. The parable of the rich man and Lazarus employs the well-known motif of a dead person who returns from the place of post-mortem punishment in order to reveal to the living what they may expect unless they repent. It employs the motif in order to subvert it. Lazarus is not permitted to return to this world, because the rich man's brothers, who have Moses and the prophets to instruct them, do not need the kind of apocalyptic revelation which visits to the places of the dead were held to provide. Understanding the way hell is portrayed in the apocalypses and related literature also shows that the usual interpretation of the last four words of James 3:6 is wrong. This text draws on the apocalyptic tradition of punishments in hell as measure-for-measure retribution applied to the part of the body which committed the sin in question.

Chapter 6 ('The Conflict of Justice and Mercy: Attitudes to the Damned in Apocalyptic Literature') treats the tradition of the Jewish and Christian apocalypses as a whole and illustrates the fruitfulness of studying themes as they recur throughout the tradition, even when it is not possible to plot a chronological development. It studies the attitudes to the damned which are expressed in the apocalypses, showing that they provided a vehicle for exploring some profound theological concerns, albeit in a popular and dramatic way. In various ways and to varying extents they find ways not only of affirming the justice of the punishment of the damned, but also of giving effect to compassion for their plight. In the final section of this chapter the Apocalypse of Peter is prominent, and the suggestion is made that it influenced those Christians whom Augustine, at the beginning of the fifth century C.E., reported as claiming that the damned will be saved by the intercession of the saints at the day of judgment. Chapter 7 ('Augustine, the "Compassionate" Christians, and the Apocalypse of Peter') argues in detail that the Apocalypse of Peter was indeed the main source of these Christians' view, and highlights the clash of theological principles in Augustine's debate with them.

The Apocalypse of Peter, already prominent in chapters 6 and 7, is the subject of chapters 8, 9 and 11, and plays a part in chapter 10. It is probably the most neglected of Christian writings from before 150 C.E., despite its considerable influence in the early Christian centuries. The extended study of this apocalypse in chapter 8 ('The Apocalypse of Peter: A Jewish Christian Apocalypse from the Time of Bar Kokhba') aims to remedy this neglect. It situates the Apocalypse of Peter in the Palestinian context of Jewish Christianity at the time of the Bar Kokhba revolt (132-135 C.E.). As such, the Apocalypse of Peter is rare evidence of early second-century Palestinian Jewish Christianity, and also exemplifies perfectly that continuity of Jewish and Christian apocalyptic tradition which this volume as a whole asserts. The Apocalypse of Peter is shown to be, to a large extent, a compilation of Jewish apocalyptic traditions about the fate of the dead, but this chapter also shows how they have been assembled and redacted in such a way as to address the situation of its Jewish Christian readers.

Chapter 9 ('A Quotation from 4Q Second Ezekiel in the Apocalypse of Peter') argues that the scriptural quotation about resurrection in Apocalypse of Peter 4:7-9 is not based directly on Ezekiel 37:1-14, but is taken from the apocryphal Ezekiel whose text is now known in fragments from Qumran. Chapter 10 ('Resurrection as Giving Back the Dead') also studies one of the traditions about resurrection found in Apocalypse of Peter 4, in this case one which is also found in the New Testament Apocalypse of John and in a series of Second Temple Jewish and rabbinic texts. This is the idea that the places of the dead to which God has entrusted the dead will give back the dead when God requires them. Study of the various forms and uses of this particular image of resurrection reveals a good deal about the understanding of resurrection in early Judaism which the New Testament shares. Chapter 11 ('2 Peter and the Apocalypse of Peter') is the first study of all the evidence which can be adduced for a literary relationship between these two works, arguing that there is some probability that the Apocalypse of Peter is dependent on 2 Peter.

Other neglected apocalypses are the subjects of chapters 12, 13 and 14. Chapter 12 ('The Apocalypse of the Seven Heavens: The Latin Version') is a full study of a short text which is extant in an incomplete Latin version, as well as in Old Irish and Anglo-Saxon. Its rather distinctive account of the passage of the dead through the seven heavens on their way to judgment, hell or paradise, has some parallels in other apocalypses which demonstrate that it is a Jewish or Christian work of some antiquity (perhaps second century C.E.).

Chapter 13 ('The Four Apocalypses of the Virgin Mary') studies the four Christian apocalypses which attribute visits to the world of the dead to the Virgin Mary. It is the first extended study which properly distinguishes these four apocalypses, investigates the distinctive characteristics of each, and reconstructs the history of their composition within the broader tradition of Jewish and Christian apocalypses depicting the fate of the dead (as sketched in chapter 3).

Chapter 14 ('The Ascension of Isaiah: Genre, Unity and Date') takes the extensive and important recent studies of this early Christian apocalypse by a research group of Italian scholars as its point of departure. Agreeing with them that the work is a wholly Christian one, it goes further in arguing for the unity of the work on the basis of consideration of its genre. A fresh examination of the evidence for date concludes that the Ascension of Isaiah very probably dates from c. 70-80 C.E., a conclusion which must make its relevance to the study of the New Testament and earliest Christianity indisputable.

CHAPTER ONE

DESCENTS TO THE UNDERWORLD

I INTRODUCTION

In most of the ancient world, as in many other cultures, the realm of the dead was located in the underworld (Hades, Sheol, sometimes Gehenna) and a descent to the underworld was a way of visiting the dead. There were also other locations for the dead. An old alternative to the underworld placed the realm of the dead at the furthest extremity of the world in the west, where the sun goes down. Sometimes the righteous dead were placed in an earthly or heavenly paradise, whereas the underworld was reserved for the wicked dead, as their place of punishment. During the early centuries C.E., there was a tendency among pagans, Jews and Christians to relocate even the place of post-mortem punishment in the upper atmosphere or the lower heavens. Thus journeys to the world of the dead were not always descents. While this chapter will focus on descents, it will not be possible to avoid referring sometimes to other kinds of journeys to the world of the dead when they are closely related to descents to the underworld. The regular descent to the underworld by all who die (without returning) will not be discussed, but only cases of those who descend alive and return still alive, or who descend in death but escape death and return to life.

Descents to the underworld occur in the myths and traditions of many cultures. They may be attributed to the gods and heroes of myths and legends. Attitudes to the loss of loved ones in death may find expression, for example, in stories of those who braved the terrors of the underworld in order to rescue a relative who had died. The cycle of the seasons may be represented in myths of gods who periodically descend to and return from the underworld. Myths of heavenly gods descending to the world ruled by the infernal deities may serve to emphasize the power of death which cannot be overcome or alternatively to define the limits of the power of death. Descents may also occur as unusual psychological experiences, in trance, vision or temporary loss of consciousness, when the soul seems to leave the body and finds itself in the other world as described in the traditions of the culture. Such descents may be chance occurrences, or they may be deliberately cultivated and undertaken, as by the shamans of central Asia. Very often accounts of descents to the underworld, either attributed pseudonymously to great heroes or seers of the past, or else actually reported by those who have experienced visions and trances, serve as revelations of the secrets of death and the life to come, preparing their hearers or readers for the journey of death, or seeking to influence their lives by warning of the future rewards and punishments consequent on behaviour in this life. Descents of all these kinds and more are found, to varying extents, in the various cultures of the biblical world. The following survey will show, by contrast, how remarkably lacking they are in the biblical literature itself, though the particular forms which descents to the underworld took in the environment of the biblical tradition will also illuminate aspects of it.

II MESOPOTAMIA

Several Sumerian myths include descents to the netherworld by divine or human beings, which are the oldest known examples of such stories. All make clear that a descent to the world of the dead is extremely perilous. The netherworld is 'the land of no return,' guarded by seven walls, each with a gate and a gatekeeper whose role is to let only the dead enter and to let noone leave. To descend and to return to the land of the living is possible only on exceptional terms. Indeed (as the story of Inanna's descent will make clear) even a god cannot descend without dying.

In the myth of *Enlil and Ninlil*, the god Enlil is banished to the netherworld by the gods as punishment for his rape of Ninlil. Ninlil, who is pregnant with Enlil's child Nanna-Sin, the moon god, follows Enlil. Since the moon god belongs in the sky, Enlil does not want his child doomed to live in the netherworld. He adopts a remarkable stratagem to prevent this. As Ninlil leaves the city of Nippur and travels to the netherworld, Enlil disguises himself three times: first as the gatekeeper of Nippur, then as the gatekeeper of the netherworld, then as the ferryman who rows the dead across the river in the netherworld (the Sumerian equivalent of the Greek Charon). On each occasion he makes love to Ninlil and fathers a child. These three new offspring, who become three of the gods of the underworld, are exchanged for the moon god, who is thus free to take his place in heaven. Enlil thus conforms to an inflexible rule of the netherworld: noone who enters can leave except by providing a substitute. (For a much later survival of this idea, see Lucian, *Catapl.* 10.).

The same rule comes into play in the fullest account of a descent, that of the goddess Inanna, the morning star. This is known both in a Sumerian version and in a slightly different Akkadian version (the *Descent of Ishtar*). The motive for Inanna's descent is not entirely clear, but it seems that not content with being the queen of heaven she suddenly felt the desire to rule also the lower world of which her sister Ereshkigal is queen. On a false pretext she gains admittance, but the process by which she passes each of the seven gates is in fact the process of death. At each she is made to relinquish items of her jewellery and clothing, until when she enters the presence of Ereshkigal and the Anunnaki, the seven judges of the dead, she is naked, as the dead are when they reach the netherworld. There she is condemned, killed and hung up as a decaying corpse. However, Inanna had given instructions to Ninshubur her servant to appeal to the gods on her behalf if she did not return. Only Enki is able to help. He fashions two strange creatures who slip unnoticed into the netherworld, ingratiate themselves with Ereshkigal, and are able to use the water of life and the grass of life they have brought with them to revive Inanna. However, Inanna may leave only on the condition she find a substitute. Accompanied by a troop of terrible demons she ascends to earth and seeks a substitute. Eventually she comes to her consort, the young shepherd Dumuzi. Enraged by the fact that he is not mourning for her, she allows the demons to seize him. He temporarily escapes, his sister Geshtinanna comes to his aid, and Inanna consents to an arrangement whereby Dumuzi's fate is to be shared with his sister: each year he will spend half the year in the netherworld and Geshtinanna the other half of the year. This conclusion (cf. the Greek myths of Persephone and Adonis) makes it certain that the myth has some connexion with the cycle of the seasons. In fact the theme of the disappearance and renewal of fertility is more obvious in the Akkadian version, in which Ishtar's rescue is prompted by the concern of the gods about the infertility of the earth which has resulted from her descent and death. But Jakobsen's highly ingenious and detailed explanations of such myths in terms of the events of the agricultural year[1] are debated.[2]

A Sumerian story of a hero's unsuccessful descent to the netherworld is told in *Gilgamesh, Enkidu, and the Netherworld*. (An Akkadian version of this story also forms tablet 12 of the Gilgamesh Epic, where it did not originally belong.) When a chasm opens in the

---

[1] T. Jacobsen, *The Treasures of Darkness: A History of Mesopotamian Religion* (New Haven: Yale University Press, 1976) 62-63 on this story.
[2] Cf. G. S. Kirk, *Myth: Its Meaning and Functions in Ancient and Other Cultures* (Cambridge: Cambridge University Press/ Berkeley: University of California Press, 1970) 88-118.

ground and two treasured objects belonging to Gilgamesh drop into
the netherworld, his friend Enkidu offers to retrieve them. Gilgamesh
gives him careful instructions on how to behave in the netherworld so
as not to attract attention to himself. Enkidu fails to follow the instructions and is held there, as dead. Gilgamesh appeals to the gods
but the most they can do for him is to enable Enkidu's ghost to
ascend temporarily to speak with Gilgamesh. Enkidu tells Gilgamesh
about life in the netherworld: how his own corpse is decaying there,
and how various categories of the dead fare better than others. The
account is of great interest as the earliest instance of a description of
the state of the dead given by someone returned from the realm of
the dead. It was to have many successors in other cultures.

The Akkadian *Epic of Gilgamesh* (*ANET* 72-998, 503-507), whose
account of Enkidu's death is different, recounts a dream which
Enkidu had when his death was near (7.4.11-55). It seems to be a
premonition of his approaching death. A fierce psychopomp seizes
him and leads him down to the 'house of darkness,' where he sees the
kings of old. The text breaks off at the point where Ereshkigal asks,
'Who has brought this man here?' Possibly, as in stories in Greek and
Roman literature (see section VII below), the story continued by dis-
closing that Enkidu had been brought to the netherworld too soon, so
that he had to be sent back, though with the knowledge that his real
death was fast approaching.

An Akkadian text from the seventh century B.C.E. (*ANET* 109-110)
tells another story of a visit to the netherworld in a dream by a living
human being. An Assyrian crown prince called Kummâ (perhaps
Assurbanipal[3]) prays to Ereshkigal and Nergal, the rulers of the
netherworld, to be allowed to see the netherworld. His prayer is
answered in a dream in which he describes the terrifying appearance
of the various guardians and gods of the netherworld. Like the dead,
he is arraigned before Nergal and the Anunnaki. He is spared death
at the hands of Nergal only so that, when he returns to the upper
world, he may persuade his father to follow the will of the gods of the
netherworld.

III Egypt

The myth of Osiris cannot be included here, since his resurrection
does not mean his return to the world of the living: he remains in the
realm of the dead, as its ruler. More properly a myth of descent and

---

[3] J. Bottéro, 'Le "Pays-sans-retour,"' in *Apocalypses et Voyages dans l'Au-delà*, ed. C.
Kappler (Paris: Editions du Cerf: 1987) 68.

return is that of the sun god Re, who every evening, after travelling in his boat across the sky, descends to the world of the dead through an entrance in the far west, and during the night passes through the underworld before ascending into the sky again every morning. The *Book of What is in the Other World (Am-Tuat)* and the *Book of Gates* describe in detail Re's passage through the world of the dead during the twelve hours of night.[4]

Two stories of human beings visiting the world of the dead are known. One is reported by Herodotus (2.122), who says that king Rhampsinitus (Ramses III) descended alive into the realm of the dead, where he played dice (probably draughts) with Demeter (i.e. Isis) and returned to earth with a golden napkin she had given him. He describes an annual ritual supposed to commemorate the event.

The other story is that of Setme and his son Si-Osiris.[5] The story is extant in a Demotic text written probably in the second half of the first century C.E., but, since Setme Khamuas was high priest of Memphis c. 1250 B.C.E., it is likely to be based on an older Egyptian tale. An Egyptian in Amente, the realm of the dead, was allowed to return to earth in order to deal with an Ethiopian magician who was proving too powerful for the magicians of Egypt. He was reincarnated as the miraculous child of a childless couple, Setme and his wife, and called Si-Osiris. When he reached the age of twelve he vanquished the Ethiopian magician and returned to Amente. But before this there was an occasion when father and son observed two funerals, one of a rich man buried in sumptuous clothing and with much mourning, the other of a poor man buried without ceremony or mourning. The father declared he would rather have the lot of the rich man than that of the pauper, but his son expressed the wish that his father's fate in Amente would be that of the pauper rather than that of the rich man. In order to justify his wish and demonstrate the reversal of fortunes in the afterlife, he took his father on a tour of the seven halls of Amente. The account of the first three halls is lost. In the fourth and fifth halls the dead were being punished. In the fifth hall was the rich man, with the pivot of the door of the hall fixed in his eye. In the sixth hall were gods and attendants, in the seventh a scene of judgment before Osiris. The pauper was to be seen, elevated to high rank, near Osiris. Si-Osiris explained to his father what they saw, and the fate of the three classes of the dead: those whose good

---

[4] E. A. W. Budge, *The Egyptian Heaven and Hell*, 3 vols. (London: Kegan Paul, Trench, Trübner, 1906).

[5] F. Ll. Griffith, *Stories of the High Priests of Memphis: The Sethon of Herodotus and the Demotic Tales of Khamuas* (Oxford: Clarendon Press, 1900) 42-66, 142-207.

deeds outnumber their bad deeds (like the pauper), those whose bad deeds outnumber their good deeds (like the rich man), and those whose good and bad deeds are equal. (This account accords with ancient Egyptian concepts.[6]) The story is of special importance, both because it is an example of the genre of conducted tours of the underworld (also to be found in Greek, Jewish and Christian literature) and because it passed into Jewish religious folklore (see section VIII) and has been claimed as the original of the parable of the rich man and Lazarus (Luke 16:19-31).

IV Syria and Palestine

Among the mythological texts from Ugarit, the Baal cycle includes a notable divine descent to the netherworld (*ANET* 138-142). After his victory over Yam, the god of the waters of chaos, Baal, at the summit of his power, saw signs of the power of Mot, the god of death, encroaching on his rule. So he sent messengers to Mot in the netherworld to demand his submission to Baal's power, but Mot's reply was to summon Baal to admit defeat and come down to him in the netherworld. Baal sent a message of capitulation ('I am your slave') and then descended to the netherworld. In fact, he died. His sister Anat found his body and buried it on the summit of mount Zaphon. Then, driven by her love for her brother, she sought out Mot in the netherworld and vanquished him. Baal revived, returned and resumed his rule. But seven years later Mot again challenged Baal and they engaged in a fierce struggle. The outcome is not preserved: presumably Baal won a finally decisive victory over Mot. If so, the descent of Baal differs significantly in its final outcome from that of Inanna. Both are first obliged to submit to the power of the netherworld in dying and then escape the power of death with the help of other gods. But whereas in the myth of Inanna's descent the power of death remains intact, in that of Baal it is eventually subjected to Baal's power.

The myth has commonly been connected with the annual cycle of the seasons, and there are elements of the text which suggest this. Baal, the storm god who brings clouds and rain and therefore fertility, would descend to the netherworld at the end of spring, when the scorching heat of summer begins, and return to life in the autumn, bringing the autumn rains and plenty after the summer drought. However, the final battle with Mot in the seventh year is hard to

---

[6] J. Zandee, *Death as an Enemy according to ancient Egyptian conceptions* (SHR 5; Leiden: Brill, 1960) 297-302.

explain in this way, and may indicate that the agrarian elements have been subsumed into a larger mythical design. Xella[7] sees the myth as expressing the eternal dialectic between life and death. Baal defends the cosmic order against the power of death, not abolishing it but forcing it to observe limits. Mot's attempt at unlimited power—killing gods and threatening the extinction of humanity—is foiled, and death becomes a power subdued and kept in its place by Baal. Xella's further supposition that Baal's resurrection includes representatively some kind of transcendence of death by the great ancestors of the people seems more speculative.

Tammuz, for whom the women of Jerusalem in the sixth century B.C.E. observed a ceremony of mourning (Ezek 8:14), was the Sumerian Dumuzi (see section II). There is much later evidence about his cult in Phoenicia and Syria, centred at Byblos (Gebal) in hellenistic times, when he was also called in Greek Adonis (from Semitic *Adonî*, 'my lord'). But since this Syrian cult of Tammuz was the intermediary between Mesopotamia and the Greek cult of Adonis, well established in Greece by 600 B.C.E., it must have flourished already in Old Testament times, while the myths of Dumuzi (section II above) and Adonis (section VII below) are sufficiently similar to show that some such myth about Tammuz, descending to and returning from the netherworld annually, must have been current in Syria and Palestine.

V Hebrew Bible

Cooper[8] argues that Psalm 24:7-10 is a fragment of a descent myth in which a high god (now identified with Yahweh) descends to the netherworld to confront the powers of death. The verses describe either the divine Warrior's entry into the netherworld to combat death or his victorious emergence from the netherworld after subduing death. The doors are the gates of the netherworld, barred against God's entry or exit. The gatekeepers, commanded to open, challenge him for his identity. This is an attractive interpretation (especially as it would make the early Christian interpretation of these verses with reference to the descent of Christ to Hades a reactivation of their original mythical sense: see section X below), but unfortunately there are no extant parallels to precisely such a fragment of myth. Baal's entry into the netherworld (section IV above) is not triumphant, but a

---

[7] P. Xella, 'Baal et la mort,' in *Apocalypses et Voyages dans l'Au-delà*, ed. C. Kappler (Paris: Editions du Cerf, 1987) 83-100.

[8] A. Cooper, 'Ps 24:7-10: Mythology and Exegesis,' *JBL* 102 (1983) 37-60.

submission to death. In the fragmentary narrative no account of his subsequent re-emergence from the netherworld is preserved, and we cannot tell whether his final conflict with Mot involved a descent.

Ancient Israel shared the conviction of the Mesopotamian peoples that 'he who goes down to Sheol [the underworld] does not come up' (Job 7:9; cf. 10:21; 16:22; 2 Sam 12:23). No exceptions were known: there is no Old Testament instance of a true descent to and return from the underworld by a living human being, though there is one case of the calling up of a shade from Sheol by necromancy (1 Sam 28:3-25) and other references to this practice, which was rejected by the law and the prophets (Lev 19:31; Deut 18:10-12; Isa 8:19; 65:2-4). However, the *idea* of descending to Sheol and returning alive to the land of the living does occur as a way of speaking of the experience of coming very close to death and escaping. When the psalmists feel themselves to be so close to death as to be virtually certain of dying they speak of themselves as already at the gates of the underworld (Ps 107:18; Isa 38:10; cf. 3 Macc 5:51; PsSol 16:2) or even already in the depths of the underworld (Ps 88:6). They have already made the descent to the world of the dead and only Yahweh's intervention brings them up again (Ps 9:13; 30:3; 86:13; Isa 38:17; cf. Sir 51:5). The picture of descent and return is more than a poetic fancy. For the psalmists to be already in the region of death means that they are in death's power. The experience of Yahweh's power to deliver them was a step towards the belief that his sovereignty over the world of the dead would in the future be asserted in bringing the dead back to the world of the living in eschatological resurrection. The assertion that Yahweh 'kills and makes alive' (Deut 32:39; 1 Sam 2:6; 2 Kgs 5:7; cf. 4 Macc. 18:18-19), later found in the form, 'he leads down to Hades and brings up again' (Tob 13:2; Wis 16:13), originally referred to the kind of experience the psalmists expressed but became the basis of the later Jewish confession of faith in 'the God who makes the dead live' (JosAsen 20:7; Rom 4:17; 2 Cor 1:9; *Eighteen Benedictions*).[9]

Jonah 2:2-9 is a psalm of thanksgiving for deliverance from death by drowning, which uses the kind of language just discussed in a specially strong form: 'I went down to the land [Sheol] whose bars closed upon me for ever; yet thou didst bring up my life from the Pit' (2:6). It has been appropriately incorporated by the author of the book of Jonah, who wished to represent Jonah's miraculous escape from drowning as his rescue by God from the world of the dead

---

[9] R. Bauckham, 'God who raises the Dead: The Resurrection of Jesus in relation to Early Christian Faith in God,' in Paul Avis ed., *The Resurrection of Jesus Christ* (London: Darton, Longman & Todd, 1993) 136-143.

itself.[10] Jonah's descent into the sea was a descent to the depths of the underworld, and the great fish was the means by which God delivered him from Sheol and brought him back to dry land. That the fish does not itself represent Sheol but the means of ascent from Sheol is shown by the reference to 'three days and three nights' (1:17). The use of this phrase in the *Descent of Inanna* (see section II above) shows that it was the time it took to travel from the earth to the underworld. In Jonah's case it was the time the fish took to bring him back from Sheol to the world of the living.[11] In later Jewish interpretation, however, the belly of the fish came to be seen as representing the belly of Sheol from which God delivered Jonah (Jon 2:1-2, 7-8 LXX; 3 Macc 6:8; Matt 12:40).

VI IRAN

Three visits by living human beings to the world of the dead are known from the Zoroastrian tradition: the legend of a visit to paradise by Zoroaster's royal patron Vištāsp, the long and detailed vision in the *Ardā Virāz Nāmag*, and the journey of Kirdīr. The last is of great importance, since it is related in an account by the high priest Kirdīr himself (third century C.E.) in two inscriptions from Iran. It is therefore a historical event, which took place in the reign of the Sassanid king Shapur I (c. 240-270 C.E.).

Kirdīr relates how he prayed for a vision of the other world, as a special favour from the gods in reward for his outstanding piety and religious service, and in order to increase his confidence in Zoroastrian teaching about the afterlife. He also expresses the wish that his account of it should aid its readers' belief in heaven and hell, so that the vision has in fact the function of a revelation of the fate of the dead, confirming the revelation given in Zoroastrian traditions. The vision itself is not narrated by Kirdīr in the first person; rather he reports the way it was narrated by a group of people (designated in the text by an unknown word) who were presumably visionaries who went into trance, after the performance of a ritual, and told Kirdīr what they were seeing as they experienced it.[12] (For a partial parallel from Jewish Merkavah mysticism, see *Hekhalot Rabbati* 18:4: the mys-

---

[10] Cf. R. Couffignal, 'Le Psaume de Jonas (Jonas 2,2-10): Une catabase biblique, sa structure et sa function,' *Bib* 71 (1990) 542-552.

[11] G. M. Landes, 'The "Three Days and Three Nights" Motif in Jonah 2:1,' *JBL* 86 (1976) 446-450; idem, 'The Kerygma of the Book of Jonah: The Contextual Interpretation of the Jonah Psalm,' *Int* 21 (1976) 3-31.

[12] For this interpretation of the text, see P. O. Skjærvo, '"Kirdīr's Vision": Translation and Analysis,' *Archaeologische Mitteilungen aus Iran* 16 (1983) 294.

tic during his ascent to heaven speaks about what is happening and
scribes record it.) The visionaries themselves travel through the other
world and as they do they see a man who looks like Kirdīr (his soul)
following the route which the souls of the dead take. Most of the
account (some of which is fragmentary in the extant texts) conforms
closely to the traditional Zoroastrian features of the world of the
dead: a beautiful woman (who is Kirdīr's *daēna*, a personification of
his conscience) comes to meet him and they travel together on a
luminous road towards the east; they pause before a judge with scales
to weigh the sins and merits of the dead; they come to the bottomless
pit of hell, full of reptiles, and must cross it on the perilously narrow
bridge (called Činwad in other sources) which widens for them; they
ascend to a succession of palaces in paradise.

The account of the vision of Ardā Virāz, though the pseudo-
historical introduction to it seems to date it at about the same time as
Kirdīr's vision,[13] only reached the written form in which we have it
much later, in the tenth or eleventh century C.E. It has no doubt been
through a number of redactions,[14] but whether it has a historical
core, originally preserved in oral tradition, is very uncertain. Besides
the traditional Zoroastrian features, such as the bridge Činwad, the
bulk of the text describes in detail the many different punishments
suffered in hell by specific classes of sinners. Both the general concept
and some of the specific details (such as those punishments in which
people are suspended by some part of their body) of the description of
the punishments in hell are paralleled in the Jewish and Christian
apocalyptic tradition of descriptions of hell (see section VIII below).
The direction of dependence has been disputed, but the presence of
motifs which are also paralleled in ancient Greek accounts of Hades[15]
makes it fairly certain that the *Ardā Virāz Namāg* is indebted to the
Judaeo-Christian apocalyptic tradition, which has mediated to it features borrowed from the Greek Hades. Thus the distinctively Zoroastrian features of the other world in *Ardā Virāz Namāg* have been
augmented, probably at a relatively late date, by borrowings from
other traditions.

However, there are features which link *Ardā Virāz Namāg* with
Kirdīr's account. The magi seek a vision of the other world for

---

[13] F. Vahman, *Ardā Wirāz Nāmag: The Iranian "Divina Commedia"* (Scandinavian
Institute of Asian Studies Monograph Series 53; London/Malmo: Curzon, 1986)
227-228, but cf. 233.

[14] P. Gignoux, *Le Livre d'Ardā Vīrāz* (Institut Français d'Iranologie de Téhéran:
Bibliothèque Iranienne 30/Paris: Editions Recherche sur les Civilisations, 1984) 14-17.

[15] M. Tardieu, 'L'Ardā Vīrāz Nāmāg et l'eschatologie grecque,' *Studia Iranica* 14
(1985) 17-26.

propaganda purposes: in order to verify Zoroastrian teaching and the efficacy of the cult with regard to the fate of souls after death.[16] Virāz is selected for his outstanding piety and righteousness, just as Kirdīr attributes his vision to his exceptional worthiness. Ritual preparations precede his trance which he experiences in the presence of others. However, unlike Kirdīr he experiences the journey to the other world himself and unlike Kirdīr's visionaries he does not narrate it while experiencing it, but only when he returns after seven days of apparent sleep. This apparent sleep is a feature which is shared with the legend of Vištāsp's visit to paradise, as is the drink of wine mixed with henbane—presumably a drug to induce trance—which is given to both before their experiences.

Gignoux[17] detects an ancient Iranian tradition of shamanistic experience (for shamanism, see section VII below) in the three features preserved as a literary tradition in the later sources: a drug conducive to ecstatic experience, the state of apparent death and the journey to the other world. It is unfortunate for this argument that in the earliest account, Kirdīr's, the drug is not mentioned and the state of the visionaries is certainly not apparent death (they speak). However, it is possible that the accounts do reflect, very remotely, the experiences of an early period. Lucian's satirical account (from the second century C.E.) of a Babylonian magus who conducted Menippus to Hades (see section VII below) suggests that Kirdīr's experience, though exceptional by his own account, was not unique among the Zoroastrian magi. Menippus had been told that Zoroaster's disciples the magi 'by means of certain incantations and initiation rites could open the gates of Hades, take down anyone they wished in safety and afterwards bring him back again' (*Men.* 6).

VII Greece and Rome

Many descents to the underworld were known in the classical Greek and hellenistic cultures.[18] A number of different influences and concerns are needed to account for them. But two particular kinds of

---

[16] On this feature in all three accounts, see P. Gignoux, 'La signification du voyage extra-terrestre dans l'eschatologie mazdéenne,' in *Mélanges d'histoire des religions offerts à Henri-Charles Puech*, ed. P. Lévy and E. Wolff (Paris: Presses Universitaires de France, 1974) 63-69.

[17] P. Gignoux, '"Corps osseux et âme osseuse": essai sur le chamanisme dans l'Iran ancien,' *JA* 267 (1979) 41-79; idem, 'Les Voyages chamaniques dans le Monde iranien,' in *Monumentum Georg Morgenstierne I* (Acta Iranica 21; Leiden: Brill, 1981) 244-265.

[18] A faily complete listing can be found in R. Ganschinietz, 'Katabasis,' *PW* 10/2 (1919) 2359-2449.

origin may be mentioned at the outset. One is the mythical representation of the cycle of nature as a descent to and return from the
underworld. This appears in the myth of Demeter and Persephone,
on which the Eleusinian mysteries were based, and which it is difficult
not to suppose was connected with the cycle of the seasons in its
origins.[19] At any rate the connexion is clear in the earliest extant
source, the *Homeric Hymn to Demeter* (seventh or early sixth century
B.C.E.). Persephone was gathering flowers when the earth opened and
the god Hades carried her off to the underworld. When her mother
Demeter, after searching for her, discovered the truth, she wandered
the earth disguised as an old woman and came to Eleusis. Eventually
she brought about a famine which threatened to put an end to humanity and to their sacrifices to the gods. Zeus succeeded in pacifying
her only by sending Hermes to persuade Hades to let Persephone
return to her mother. The compromise which resulted was that
Persephone was to spend two-thirds of each year with her mother on
Olympus and one-third with her husband Hades as queen of the
underworld. When Demeter consented to this arrangement, she
made life return to the fields. She also taught her secret rites to the
princes of Eleusis. This was the myth that was somehow enacted in
the ceremonies of the Eleusinian mysteries, but again the *Hymn to
Demeter* already makes clear that in these the theme of the renewal of
the fruitfulness of the natural world was linked with the promise of a
blessed afterlife in the underworld. Although the annual descent and
return of Persephone is unmistakably parallel to that of Dumuzi in
the Sumerian myth, the Greek myth, unlike the Sumerian, acquired a
significance for personal fate. However, precisely how the assurance
to initiates that they would be happy in Hades after death was linked
to the myth and to the secret rites of the mysteries remains obscure.

Not only parallel to, but actually derived from the cult and the
myth of Dumuzi was the Greek cult and myth of Adonis, though as
the name itself indicates (= Semitic *adonî*, 'my lord') the Greek Adonis
was more immediately the Tammuz of Phoenicia, Syria and Cyprus.
As Dumuzi was linked with Inanna and Tammuz with Astarte, so
Adonis was linked with Aphrodite. The old form of the Greek myth
seems to have been that Adonis as a child was so beautiful that
Aphrodite hid him in a coffin and gave him to Persephone. Later,
when she wanted him back, Persephone, who also loved him, refused.
The deal, arbitrated by Zeus, was that Adonis was to belong for one
third of the year to Aphrodite, one third to Persephone, and one third

---

[19] But cf. W. Burkert, *Structure and History in Greek Mythology and Ritual* (Berkeley:
University of California Press, 1979) 138.

to himself. He added his own share to Aphrodite's and so spends two-thirds of the year on Olympus and one third in the underworld. More popular than the odd form of Adonis' death in this version was the story that he dies from a wound by a wild boar during hunting. A later version, attested only by Christian authors, has Aphrodite herself go down to Hades to ask Persephone to give Adonis back. It is doubtful whether in Greece the Adonis myth retained any agrarian association, while the festival in July at which Adonis' death was mourned by women seems to have put no particular emphasis on his return from the underworld.

Secondly, a number of scholars have argued for a decisive influence of 'shamanism' on certain Greek religious traditions. Shamanism is a type of religious practice characteristic of the central Asian tribes, but also found in many other societies. The shaman is an ecstatic whose soul leaves his or her body and goes on journeys, including journeys to the underworld. His or her ritual initiation typically involves a ritual death and rebirth experienced as a descent to the underworld. He or she may also travel to the underworld to conduct the soul of a dead person there or to encounter the dead and other supernatural beings. Since the shaman also enjoys a privileged relationship with animals and the natural world, Orpheus, to whose music the whole natural world responded and who visited Hades to rescue his wife, seems an obviously shamanistic figure. Moreover Orpheus came from Thrace, where the shamanistic practices of central Asia penetrated.[20] Certainly shamanism seems to illuminate the story of Orpheus better than the theory that this myth represents the cycle of the seasons, for which there is no evidence. Shamanistic features have also been seen in the figures of Hercules[21] and Odysseus, while Pythagoras, who also visited Hades, can be seen as an historical Greek shaman.[22]

Many of the descents (*katabaseis*) in Greek mythology are for the purpose of rescuing from death someone who had recently died. The classic instance is Orpheus' rescue of Eurydice (in some versions of the story successful, in others not[23]). Theseus and Pirithous descended to bring Persephone back from Hades, but were unsuccessful. They themselves (or, in one version of the story, only Theseus) were later

---

[20] M. L. West, *The Orphic Poems* (Oxford: Clarendon, 1983) 4-7.

[21] Burkert, *Structure and History*, 78-98.

[22] W. Burkert, *Lore and Science in Ancient Pythagoreanism* (trans. E. L. Minar, Jr.; Cambridge, Massachusetts: Harvard University Press, 1972) 162-163.

[23] See I. M. Linforth, *The Arts of Orpheus* (Berkeley: University of California Press, 1941) 16-21; M. O. Lee, 'Orpheus and Eurydice: Myth, Legend, Folklore,' *Classica et Mediaevalia* 26 (1965) 402-12.

rescued by Heracles (who had not descended for this purpose, but in
order to bring up the hound of Hades, Cerberus). On another occasion Heracles descended in order to rescue Alcestis, the wife of his
friend Admetus. Dionysus descended to bring back his mortal mother
Semele.

A different motive is represented in the story of Heracles' descent
to capture and to bring to earth the dog Cerberus: this was the last of
the twelve heroic exploits he was obliged to perform at the command
of Eurystheus. A rather similar instance occurs in the story of Cupid
and Psyche (Apuleius, *Met.* 4.28-6.24). One of the tasks imposed on
Psyche by Aphrodite was to descend to Hades and to ask Persephone
to fill a box with beauty for Aphrodite (6.16-21).

Such motives apply only to the gods and heroes of myth. But the
desire to obtain oracular advice from the dead was a motive in the
myths which could also be shared and followed by ordinary humans.
Odysseus, in the best known of all the literary accounts of journeys to
Hades, went there to consult the famous dead seer Teiresias, who
gave him prophetic advice about his future. (Compare Saul's similar
motive for consulting the dead Samuel: 1 Samuel 28:6-25. The story
is comparable to the extent that Odysseus not only travelled to
Hades, but also employed a necromantic ritual to summon the spirits
of the dead.) Virgil later imitated Odysseus' motive when he made
Aeneas visit Hades in order to consult his father Anchises, who
prophesies the future history of Rome (*Aen.* 6). It was also imitated by
Lucian in his satirical dialogue *Menippus* (probably based on the *Nekyia*
of the Cynic philosopher Menippus), in which Menippus visits
Teiresias in Hades to seek advice on the best form of life. In Lucian's
account Menippus returns to earth by way of the famous oracular
shrine of Trophonius at Lebadea in Beotia, where visitors were able
to make a ritual descent to the underworld to consult the hero
Trophonius (probably originally a chthonic deity). After ritual preparations, the inquirer descended a narrow shaft, feet first like the dead,
into an underground cave (sometimes called the *katabasion*), where he
or she might spend several days and where Trophonius would appear
to him or her (Pausanias 9.39; Lucian, *Dial. Mort.* 3).

Another reason why the living might attempt, through trance or
dream, a journey to the underworld is suggested by the legend of
Leonymus of Athens (Pausanias 3.19.11-13), who was wounded in
battle and, seeking means of recovery, was advised by the Delphic
oracle to go to the White Isle (Elysium[24]). Another motive is uniquely

---

[24] See Burkert, *Lore and Science*, 152-153; A. T. Edwards, 'Achilles in the Underworld: Iliad, Odyssey, and Aethiopis,' *GRBS* 26 (1985) 215-227; I. P. Culianu,

attested in a fragment of a poetic account of a descent to Hades, undertaken by a man who blames his dead wife or mistress for his ruin and seeks her out among the dead in order to upbraid her.[25] While such references suggest the availability of magical and ritual means of descent for various purposes, the most important function of such descents was in initiation into the mysteries (see below).

The means of descent to Hades were various. The Greeks knew numerous places which in local tradition were supposed to be entrances to the underworld: springs, rivers, lakes, caves, chasms and volcanoes.[26] These were used by the gods and heroes of the myths. Heracles, for example, descended by way of Taenarum and ascended by way of Trozen, while Lucian's Menippus took a boat to the mouth of the Euphrates, where the earth opened, and returned by way of the cave of Trophimus. Such descents, however, encountered the obstacles which normally only the dead could pass. There was the dog Cerberus (variously supposed to have two, three or fifty heads) who guarded the gate of Hades, the Acherusian lake (or, later, the river Styx), across which the ferryman Charon would willingly row only the dead (Virgil, *Aen.* 6.392-393), and other monsters beyond. Heracles was conducted to Hades by Athene and Hermes (the latter the psychopomp who led down the souls of the dead); Orpheus charmed the guardians and the rulers of Hades with his music; Aeneas bore the golden bow as his passport and tribute to Persephone; Lucian's Menippus dressed up as Heracles, Orpheus and Theseus at once, in order to fool Charon and the guards; Apuleius's Psyche managed to get through with only the usual fare for Charon and sops of bread to throw to Cerberus. But in normal circumstances a living person could not for a moment expect to be able to make the journey before death (Euripides, *Alc.* 357-364).

However, since the obvious way to reach Hades was to die (cf. Heracles' advice to Dionysus in Aristophanes, *Frogs* 120-135), it was also possible to visit Hades and return during a temporary experience of death. Stories were told of people who had been dead or at least taken for dead but revived after a few days and recounted their experiences in the world of the dead. Such stories correspond to the very frequent modern testimonies of people who have 'died' and been resuscitated and report visionary experiences of reaching the thresh-

---

Psychanodia I: A Survey of the Evidence concerning the Ascension of the Soul and its Relevance (EPRO 99; Leiden: Brill, 1983) 38-39.

[25] D. L. Page, *Literary Papyri, Poetry* (vol. 3 of *Select Papyri*; LCL; London: Heinemann, 1941) 416-421. The description of the descent is unusual, and the account of Hades focuses on gruesome description of mutilated corpses.

[26] Lists in Ganschinietz, 'Katabasis,' 2379-2387.

old of the next life before being send back. So, although most of the
stories we have from antiquity belong to a literary tradition, it is likely
that the literary tradition had its origins in stories actually told by
people who had had near-death experiences. The earliest example,
and a model for others, is already a conscious literary creation: Plato's
story of Er the Pamphylian (*Resp.* 10.614B-621B), who was killed in
battle, but several days later revived on his funeral pyre and recounted what he had seen as a disembodied spirit in the realm of the
dead before being returned to his body. The no longer extant *Peri
physeōs*, one of the Greek works supposed to have been written by
Zoroaster, actually identified Zoroaster with Plato's Er (like Er, he is
described as 'the son of Harmonius, the Pamphylian'; cf. also
Arnobius, *Adv. Gent.* 1.52) and began with an account of how
Zoroaster visited Hades between death and resuscitation.[27] Plutarch
(*De sera* 22-33) tells a similar story of Thespesius, who became unconscious and was taken for dead but revived on the third day: the story
is no doubt modelled on Plato's, for the same purpose of depicting the
author's view of the fate of souls in a myth.

Other accounts of temporary death probably bring us closer to
popular storytelling. Aristotle's disciple Clearchus of Soli (fragment 8)
told of Cleonymus, an Athenian, who revived from apparent death
and reported that he had seen the rivers of Hades and souls being
judged and punished and purified. He also met another temporary
visitor to Hades and the two agreed to try to get in touch when they
returned to earth. The same motif appears in Cornelius Labeo's story
of two men who died on the same day, met each other at a cross-
roads (the cross-roads in Hades: cf. Plato, *Grg.* 524A), were commanded to return, and resolved to live as friends thereafter
(Augustine, *De Civ. Dei* 22.28). The soldier Gabienus, while dying
from his wounds, was able to bring a prophetic message (which
turned out to be misleading) from the gods of the underworld before
he expired (Pliny, *Hist. Nat.* 7.178).

Pliny reports from Varro the story of the two brothers Cerfidius, of
whom one, taken for dead, returned from Hades with the news of the
other brother whom he had met in Hades and was then found to be
dead (Pliny, *Hist. Nat.* 7.177). Evidently the wrong brother had initially been taken to Hades by mistake. This motif of mistaken identity
(found also in Hindu and Chinese folklore) occurs also in Plutarch's
story of Antyllus (*apud* Eusebius, *Praep. Evang.* 11.36) and later in sto-

---

[27] J. Bidez and F. Cumont, *Les mages hellénisés*, vol. 1 (Paris: Société d'Editions 'Les
Belles Lettres,' 1938) 112-113; but cf. J. D. P. Bolton, *Aristeas of Proconnesus* (Oxford:
Clarendon Press, 1962) 159, 203 n. 26.

ries reported by Gregory the Great (*Dial.* 4.36). Lucian parodied it in the character of Cleomenes (*Philops.* 25) who claims that he went to Hades temporarily during an illness because his psychopomp came to fetch him by mistake. He was sent back when Pluto declared he was not to die yet, whereas the man who was due to die was Demylus the coppersmith who lived next door to Cleodemus. As usually in these stories, Cleodemus authenticates his tale by reporting that Demylus did in fact die not long after Cleodemus had brought the news from Hades. The fact that Cleodemus also mentions seeing the well-known sights of Hades indicates again that such stories were often the framework for descriptions of Hades, especially its punishments. Plato and his successors were probably making their own use of a less sophisticated tradition of such stories, which was to continue in Christian use (ActsThom 51-59; Gregory, *Dial.* 4.31, 36; Bede, *Hist. Eccl.* 5.12; *Preaching of Andrew;*[28] *History of the Contending of St Paul*[29]).

A variant on the theme of temporary death is that of the recently dead person temporarily recalled by necromancy. Lucan, *Pharsalia* 6.569-830, relates in fascinating detail how the Thessalian witch Erichtho recalled the soul of one of Pompey's soldiers only recently dead and still on the journey to Hades. Though he is reluctant to return, she obliges him to reenter his body. He tells what he has seen and prophesies the future before the witch allows him finally to die.

For those who wished to visit Hades without dying dreams, visions and trances were the available means. Pindar (fragment 116/131) apparently considers that the future life in Hades is frequently revealed in dreams, since the occult power of the soul is released while the body sleeps (cf. Xenophon, *Cyr.* 8.7.21). Perhaps it was in dreams that some of those who were initiated in the mysteries experienced the underworld (see below). Empedotimus, a fictional philosopher-seer in a lost work of Plato's disciple Heraclides Ponticus, 'saw the truth about the fate of souls as if witnessing a drama' on a vision of Pluto and Persephone,[30] though Heraclides (like Plutarch and others later) located Hades in the air. The possibility of seeing Hades in a vision without even descending into it is parodied by Lucian in the character of Eucrates who claims to have seen everything in Hades through a chasm in the earth (*Philops.* 22-24; cf. Virgil, *Aen.* 8.243-246).

---

[28] A. Smith Lewis, *The Mythological Acts of the Apostles* (Horae Semiticae 4; London: C. J. Clay, 1904) 7-8; E. A. W. Budge, *The Contendings of the Apostles* (Oxford: Oxford University Press, 1935) 147-148.

[29] Budge, *The Contendings*, 552-554.

[30] Bolton, *Aristeas*, 151-153.

A close equivalent to the experience of temporary death through illness could be had in the form of cataleptic trance, in which the subject appears to be dead and in which therefore the soul could be thought to experience places distant from the body. Catalepsy for the purpose of shamanistic experience seems to have been cultivated in Greece.[31] One way in which it could be achieved seems to be suggested by the demonstration of hypnotism which allegedly convinced Aristotle that the soul could separate from the body (reported by his disciple Clearchus of Soli, fragment 7).[32] The magician guided the soul from the body with a wand, leaving the body as insensitive as a corpse, and when the soul returned to the body it reported all it had seen. It was surely a cataleptic trance that Timarchus in Plutarch's story (*De gen.* 21-22) experienced in the cave of Trophonius: unsure whether he was awake or dreaming, his soul left his body and travelled above the earth to a position from which he was able to look down on Hades. Since Timarchus was unconscious for two days, this was not the incubation and dreaming associated with other oracles. Clark suggests that visitors to the cave of Trophonius may have been given an hallucinatory drug.[33]

When Lucian's Menippus wished to visit Hades he travelled to Babylon to consult the Chaldean magus Mithrobarzanes, who put him through an elaborate ritual preparation lasting a month, including ritual purification and spells to protect him from the dangers of the journey, before conducting him to Hades by boat and copying Odysseus' necromantic ritual (*Men.* 6-9). Behind Lucian's somewhat tongue-in-cheek account must lie the practice of ritual and magical means of visiting the dead. It also indicates that by the second century C.E., the Chaldean magi had a reputation in the Roman world as shamanistic psychopomps for living visitors to the other world. The firsthand account of the magus Kirdīr, a century later (see section VI above), gives some clues as to how it was done.

Of the famous mythical descents there were literary accounts, not many of which have survived. That of Odysseus in book 11 of the *Odyssey* is not, in the strict sense, a descent (but cf. 11.475), since Odysseus reaches the environs of Hades by sailing to the edge of the world beyond the river Oceanus. There he conjures the spirits of the dead by a necromantic ritual. Only at the end of the account, in a

---

[31] Bolton, *Aristeas*, 139-141, 148-149, 153-156; Culianu, *Psychanodia I*, 37-39.

[32] H. Lewy, 'Aristotle and the Jewish Sage according to Clearchus of Soli,' *HTR* 31 (1938) 205-235.

[33] R. J. Clark, 'Trophonios: The Manner of his Revelation,' *TAPA* 99 (1968) 63-75.

passage which has often been thought a later addition (11.565-627), does Odysseus seem, without explanation, to view the sights within 'the house of Hades': Minos sitting in judgment and several of the famous dead engaging in the activities which occupy them in the realm of the dead. Whatever the origin of this passage, it is notable that, more than the rest of the account, it resembles the genre of other accounts of visits to Hades, in relating, one after another, the sights which the visitor saw and, in particular, specific types of punishment taking place. Most of Homer's dead are neither happy nor suffering punishment, but the exceptional cases of Tityos, Tantalus and Sisyphus (11.576-600) point the way that other influential accounts would follow.

Besides the *Odyssey,* two other old epic poems, now lost, included journeys to Hades: the *Minyas* seems to have recounted the descent of Theseus and Pirithous (Pausanias 10.28.2), while the *Nostoi* (on the return of the heroes from Troy) included a *nekyia* whose subject is unknown (Pausanias 10.28.7). A lost poem of Hesiod also described the descent of Theseus and Pirithous (Pausanias 9.31.5). There was probably an old epic poem on the descent of Heracles to seize Cerberus. Aristophanes' comedy *The Frogs* (only one of many Greek dramas which portrayed a descent to Hades) recounts a descent of Dionysus, who explicitly follows the example of Heracles, and seems to be a parody of a well-known account of the descent of Heracles. A poem, perhaps by Pindar, on this theme survives in fragments.[34] There was a *Descent to Hades* (Εἰς Ἅιδου κατάβασις) attributed to Orpheus,[35] in which presumably he described in the first person his own descent to rescue Eurydice and what he saw in the underworld. This may have been only one of several accounts of Orpheus' descent, which seems to have been important for various mystery cults. One reference to a description by Orpheus of the descent of Heracles[36] may indicate that there was a *Descent of Heracles* ascribed to Orpheus, but may only mean that Heracles' earlier descent was mentioned in Orpheus' account of his own descent. It is noteworthy that, in the second century c.e., Lucian's *Menippus* (8) takes it for granted that Heracles, Orpheus and Odysseus were the three heroes whose descents to Hades were well-known.

These descents probably provided Greeks of the classical period and later with much of their information about the world of the dead.

---

[34] H. Lloyd-Jones, 'Heracles at Eleusis: P. Oxy. 2622 and P.S.I. 1391,' *Maia* 19 (1967) 206-229.

[35] O. Kern, *Orphicorum Fragmenta* (Berlin: Weidmanns, 1922) 304-306.

[36] Kern, *Orphicorum Fragmenta*, no. 296.

The accounts of the blessedness of the happy dead in Pindar and the accounts of the underworld, its geography and the fate of the dead in Plato's dialogues (*Phd.* 112A-114C; *Grg.* 523A-526D; *Resp.* 614B-621D) and in the pseudo-Platonic *Axiochus* (371 ff.) may well derive in large part from them. So did the famous painting of Hades by Polygnotus at Delphi, which Pausanias describes in detail (10.28-31). Although it depicts the descent of Odysseus, many of its details must derive from other accounts. The lost descents have probably also left their mark on later versions modelled on them. Lucian's satirical works *Menippus,* an account of Menippus' visit to the underworld, *Vera historia,* which includes a visit to the islands of the dead beyond the ocean, and *Cataplus,* which describes the journey of the dead to Hades and their judgment (cf. also *Philops.* 22-25), are probably parodic imitations of the manner and content of the great mythical descents to which he alludes in the *Menippus,* as well as making fun of those claimed for historical persons such as Pythagoras. The sources of book 6 of Virgil's *Aeneid* have been much debated and cannot be reconstructed with any certainty, but they probably included descents of Orpheus and Heracles. Certainly Virgil was consciously writing in the already ancient and well-known genre of descents to Hades and took not only Odysseus as the model for Aeneas in his descent. A Bologna papyrus of probably the third or fourth century C.E. contains a very fragmentary text of a *katabasis* which described both various categories of sinners undergoing punishment and the state of the blessed dead. Some close parallels with Virgil's account have been observed in it.[37]

Such literary accounts of descents to Hades functioned as *revelations* (apocalypses) of the world of the dead. It is important to distinguish between the motives of the heroes themselves in the stories and the function of the literary accounts. Orpheus and Odysseus did not go to Hades in order to see it (though Arnobius, *Adv. Gent.* 5.28 does attribute this motive to Heracles, probably reflecting a literary account in which the motive of the writer and the readers was attributed to the hero). But accounts of their descents were able to describe what they saw in Hades and could function for their readers as apocalypses—revelations of the geography of Hades, its monsters and rulers, the journey the dead will have to take in order to reach it and the judgment they will face when they arrive, and especially the fate of the various classes of the dead. This function became more explicit

---

[37] See R. Turcan, 'La catabase orphique du papyrus de Bologne,' *RHR* 150 (1956) 136-172; R. Schilling, 'Romanité et ésotérisme dans le Chant VI de l'Enéide,' *RHR* 199 (1982) 363-380.

when the role of the guide, who conducts the visitor to Hades, is no longer simply to show the way, as Hermes presumably did for Heracles, but also to explain what the visitor sees in Hades, as the Sibyl does for Aeneas in *Aeneid* 6 (see also the role of guides in Plutarch, *De gen.* 22; *De sera* 27-30). If *Odyssey* 11.565-627 already forms a little apocalyptic revelation of Hades, *Aeneid* book 6 is the fullest such revelation that survives. It must reflect the apocalyptic form and function of older accounts. The revelatory function of descents to Hades was also exploited by Plato and Plutarch, who used the genre to express in mythical form their own understandings of the fate of the soul (Plato, *Resp.* 10.614B-621B; Plutarch, *De sera* 22-33; *De gen.* 21-22).

What the tradition of descents to Hades seems especially to have revealed is the fate of souls after death. The old Homeric view was that the existence of the dead is undifferentiated: all share the same joyless gloom. The exceptions—on the one hand, Tantalus, Tityos and Sisyphus, who are punished eternally for their crimes against the gods, and, on the other hand, a very few heroes of divine descent, like Menelaus, who are exempted from the common lot and dwell in blessedness in Elysium—are exceptions that prove the rule. But the descents to Hades, so far as we can tell, reflected and encouraged a growing belief in retribution after death. The damned, who may be regarded either as those guilty of heinous crimes or as those who have not been initiated in the mysteries, suffer punishments,[38] while the blessed enjoy themselves in a sunlit paradise. Although Plato already consigns the souls of the blessed to the sky and sends only the wicked below ground, the common view in the early period, which still survives in Virgil, is that the place of happiness after death is also in the underworld. In Aristophanes' *The Frogs* Dionysus sees in Hades both the eternal mud in which various types of criminals are plunged and the sunlit myrtle groves in which the initiates of the Eleusinian mysteries dance (145-158). It is mistaken to regard such views as peculiarly 'Orphic,' though they do seem to have been especially associated with the mysteries. The well-known accounts of descents to Hades must have played an important part in making retribution in the afterlife a very common belief in the hellenistic world.

Depictions of the punishments in Hades (both literary and visual) often focused on the famous individual sinners, all allotted imaginatively eternal forms of punishment. These included the three mythical persons mentioned by Homer (Tantalus, Tityos and Sisyphus) and

---

[38] Cf. Kern, *Orphicorum Fragmenta*, nos. 293, 295.

some others: 'the ceaseless fetching of water by the Danaids' (Ps-
Plato, *Axiochus* 371E; cf. Pausanias 10.31.11), 'the thirst of Tantalus'
(*Axiochus* 371E; cf. Pausanias 10.31.12; Lucian, *Men.* 14), 'the entrails
of Tityos eternally devoured and regenerated' (*Axiochus* 371E; cf.
Lucian, *Men.* 14; Virgil, *Aen.* 6.595-600), 'the never-resting stone of
Sisyphus, whose end of toil is again the beginning' (*Axiochus* 371E; cf.
Lucian, *Men.* 14; Pausanias 10.31.10), the wheel of Ixion (Lucian,
Men. 14; Virgil, *Aen.* 6.601), Ocnus continuously plaiting a cord which
is eaten by a donkey as soon as it is plaited (Pausanias 10.29.1), and
Theseus and Pirithous chained to their chairs (Pausanias 10.29.9;
Virgil, *Aen.* 6.601, 617-618). Even historical individuals can sometimes be seen undergoing infernal punishment (e.g. Pythagoras in his
descent to Hades saw the soul of Homer hanging from a tree:
Diogenes Laertes 8.21; and cf. the parodic example in Lucian, *Vera
hist.* 2.26). These individual examples now served not as exceptions so
much as warning examples to all who might suffer a similar fate after
death (thus, e.g., Sisyphus' punishment is generalized in Virgil, *Aen.*
6.616 and Ixion's in 6.617).[39] More general descriptions of the types
of punishments of the damned, often infernal versions of earthly punishments, appear (Plato, *Grg.* 525C; Lucian, *Catapl.* 28; *Men.* 14;
Virgil, *Aen.* 6.556-557, 616-617; Ps-Plato, *Axiochus* 372; Plutarch, *De
sera* 30). Some are represented as purgatorial (Virgil, *Aen.* 6.740-742).
Specific categories of sinners are listed (Plato, *Phaedo* 113-114; Lucian,
Vera hist. 2.31; *Men.* 11; Virgil, *Aen.* 6.608-613, 621-624) and punishments appropriate to specific kinds of sins are depicted (Pausanias
10.28.4, 5; Lucian, *Vera hist.* 2.26). Especially detailed and systematic
in its specification of categories of sinners is the Bologna papyrus.[40]

The descents seem to be linked with the mysteries, though it is
impossible to be precise on this point. According to the account of his
descent, Heracles was initiated at Eleusis before going down to Hades
and was presumably thereby protected from the dangers of the
underworld. The chorus of Eleusinian initiates who constitute the
blessed dead in Aristophanes' *The Frogs* also suggest a link between

---

[39] For these typical individuals in funerary art, see F. Cumont, *After Life in Roman
Paganism* (New Haven: Yale University Press, 1922) 85; cf. 171.

[40] See Turcan, 'La catabase.' The evidence cited in this paragraph, and especially
the Bologna papyrus, show that Cumont, *After Life*, 170-176; idem, *Lux Perpetua* (Paris:
Geuthner, 1949) 219-234, is unjustified in claiming that the detailed classifications of
sinners and their punishments, found in the Jewish and Christian apocalypses, *cannot*
have derived from Greek and Roman sources, since the latter refrain from such
detail. Apart from the evidence just cited, Cumont neglects the currency of now no
longer extant literary accounts of descents to Hades (listed above).

Eleusis and the descent of Heracles, on which the play is based. At least by the fourth century B.C.E., the Eleusinian mysteries were held to have been founded by Orpheus, who was also associated with Bacchic mysteries, as well as with specifically Orphic groups and with the Pythagoreans.[41] All such groups taught initiation in the mysteries as a means of attaining a happy afterlife rather than punishment. The *Descent to Hades* attributed to Orpheus cannot be securely associated with any one mystery cult. It was ascribed by some in antiquity to Cercops the Pythagorean or Herodicus of Perinthus: if it did not originate in Pythagorean circles, at least it was taken over by them.

How far initiation into the mysteries involved a ritual enactment or trance experience of a descent to the underworld is uncertain, though it is clear that it did in some cases. There is no evidence that the Eleusinian mysteries included a descent to the underworld. A fragment included in one of the Greek magical papyri (PGM LXX, lines 5-19) refers to a mystical initiation in an underground chamber, where the initiate was shown objects associated with the goddesses of the underworld. Presumably this was a symbolic descent to the underworld. The initiate is to be protected by appeal to this initiation from the hostile powers of the realm of the dead, perhaps on a subsequent descent in trance or dream[42] or after death (cf. the many Egyptian spells for protecting the dead from the demons and other dangers of the underworld[43]). Probably many of the caves and underground chambers associated with shrines were ritual equivalents of Hades and could be used for ritual descents. Apuleius, in his description of initiation into the mysteries of Isis, recounts, as all that can be divulged of the most secret part of the process:

> I approached the boundary of death and treading on Proserpine's threshold, I was carried through all the elements, after which I returned. At dead of night I saw the sun flashing with bright effulgence. I approached close to the gods above and the gods below and worshipped them face to face.[44]

This may refer to the fact that in Egyptian mythology the sun-god travels through the underworld during the twelve hours of the night

---

[41] West, *The Orphic Poems*, 7-29.

[42] H. D. Betz, 'Fragments from a Catabasis Ritual in a Greek Magical Papyrus,' *HR* 19 (180) 287-295, who suggests the fragment is from a ritual of the Idaean Dactyls.

[43] J. Zandee, *Death as an Enemy according to ancient Egyptian conceptions* (SHR 5; Leiden: Brill, 1960) 253-259.

[44] Apuleius, *Met.* 11.23, translated by J. G. Griffiths, *Apuleius of Madauros: The Isis-Book (Metamorphoses, Book XI)* (EPRO 39; Leiden: Brill, 1975) 99.

(see section III above). The initiate may undergo a ritual death and resurrection in identification with Osiris.[45]

One of the few historical individuals about whom an account of a descent to Hades was current was Pythagoras, though only a few allusions to it survive.[46] The satirical account given in a fragment of Hermippus (*apud* Diogenes Laertes 8.41) describes how Pythagoras built an underground cellar in his house, disappeared into it for several years, and when he emerged claimed he had been to Hades. Burkert regards this as a rationalized version of a story in which Pythagoras' descent to Hades took place in the subterranean chamber of a sanctuary of Demeter (since Hermippus' account refers to Pythagoras' mother). He takes Pythagoras' famous golden thigh as a sign of his initiation into the cult of the Great Mother which enabled him to travel to the underworld with impunity. The Pythagorean doctrines of blessed immortality and metempsychosis were closely related to this initiatory descent into Hades.[47] Hermippus' account of Pythagoras' descent to Hades is curiously parallel to the story reported by Herodotus (4.94-96) about the god Zalmoxis worshipped by the Getae of Thrace, and it is clear that the Greeks themselves associated the two.[48] The cult of Zalmoxis was also a mystery cult conferring blessed immortality.[49] Finally, it seems that Parmenides describes his philosophical journey (fragment 1) in terms of a journey, like that of Odysseus, to the distant edge of the world where the sun goes down to the underworld. If not exactly a *descent* to Hades, it is as much one as that of Odysseus, and to be understood as in the tradition of Pythagoras' descent.[50]

Thus, for the Greco-Roman world, descents to Hades were more than stories about the gods and heroes. They were also apocalypses, revealing the fate of souls in the netherworld, and they were models which could in some sense be imitated, especially in the experience of initiation in the mysteries, which dispelled the terrors of the underworld and secured a blessed immortality.

---

[45] Griffiths, *Apuleius*, 296-308.

[46] The elaborate attempt of I. Lévy, *La Légende de Pythagore de Grèce en Palestine* (BEHE.H 250; Paris: Librairie Ancienne Honoré Champion, 1927) 79-128, to reconstruct it is highly speculative.

[47] Burkert, *Lore and Science*, 155-163.

[48] Cf. also Gregory Nazianzus, *Or.* 4.59; and Bolton, *Aristeas*, 144-146.

[49] M. Eliade, *Zalmoxis: The Vanishing God* (trans. W. R. Trask; Chicago: University of Chicago Press, 1972) 21-61.

[50] J. S. Morrison, 'Parmenides and Er,' *JHS* 75 (1955) 59-68; W. Burkert, 'Das Proömium des Parmenides und die Katabasis des Pythagoras,' *Phronesis* 14 (1969) 1-29.

VIII JEWISH AND CHRISTIAN APOCALYPSES

In the Jewish tradition descents to the underworld are found largely within the apocalyptic tradition, in which they are ascribed to seers of the past such as Enoch, Elijah and Moses. The Christian apocalyptic tradition of visionary descents to the world of the dead is entirely continuous with the Jewish tradition. In both Judaism and Christianity the tradition spans at least a thousand years.

The earliest visits to the world of the dead in Jewish apocalypses take place in the context of a cosmic tour in which the secrets of heaven and earth are revealed to the seer by angelic guides.[51] The oldest is that of Enoch (1 Enoch 17-36), dating from the third or early second century B.C.E. Enoch is taken to the far extremities of the earth. In keeping with the widespread ancient tradition which located the realm of the dead, or at least the entrance to it, in the far west, where the sun goes down, Enoch is taken to a mountain on the western edge of the world, in which he sees four 'hollows' where the four categories of the dead are kept, separate from each other, until the day of judgment (1 Enoch 22 = 4QEn^a 1:22; 4QEn^d 1:11:1-3). This classification of the dead into four categories, instead of merely the two categories of the wicked and the righteous which later prevailed universally in Jewish descriptions of the world of the dead, indicates the archaic character of this account. 1 Enoch 17:1-8, while not expressly mentioning Sheol (the world of the dead), describes its environs in the mythical west in terms which resemble both the Greek mythical geography of *Odyssey* book 11 and the Mesopotamian geography which is described most fully in the *Epic of Gilgamesh*. The latter, which alone includes the mountain, is the more probable source.[52] Besides the realm of the dead, Enoch's tour also included the fiery abysses where the erring stars and the fallen angels are punished (1 Enoch 18:10-19:2; 21).

Later versions of the cosmic tour (from the first century C.E. onwards) take the form of an ascent through the seven heavens, and the realms of the dead are sometimes located within the seven heavens. Thus Enoch in 2 Enoch 8-10 sees paradise and hell in (or perhaps from: cf. 40:12; 42:3) the third heaven. (These are not the places which the dead inhabit yet, but the places of reward and punishment ready for them to enter after the last judgment). In this tour Enoch also sees the fallen angels confined in the second and fifth heavens (2

---

[51] See, in more detail, chapter 2 below.

[52] P. Grelot, 'La géographie mythique d'Hénoch et ses sources orientales,' *RB* 65 (1958) 33-69.

Enoch 7; 18). According to the later, probably Christian Testament of Isaac, Isaac saw in the heavens the hell in which the wicked dead are presently being punished (TIsaac 5). But in other forms of the tour through the seven heavens, visits to hell and paradise take place only after the ascent to the seventh heaven, and hell retains its traditional place beneath the earth. This was probably the case in the original ending of 3 Baruch (summarized in the Slavonic version of 16:4-8), although secondary additions to the text in the Greek version locate Hades in the third heaven (4:3, 6; 5:3) and the souls of the righteous in the fourth heaven (10:5). The pattern of a visit to the subterranean hell, as well as to paradise, after a tour of the seven heavens also occurs in the Hebrew apocalypse of Moses, known as the Gedulat Moshe, which in its present form is probably quite late but reflects an ancient model. From cosmic tours with a strong interest in the fate of the dead developed apocalypses exclusively concerned with the fate of the dead, such as the Apocalypse of Zephaniah and the Apocalypse of Paul, which take their seers on journeys around the heavens, the underworld and the extremities of the earth, but only in order to see sights concerned with the judgment, punishments and rewards of the dead.

It seems that during the first two centuries c.e. a gradual change took place in Jewish and Christian belief about the fate of the wicked after death, from the older view that the wicked are not actively punished immediately after death, but held in detention awaiting punishment at the last judgment, to the later view that the eternal punishment of the wicked begins already after death. This change was very important for apocalyptic descents to the underworld (where increasingly only the wicked were located). The older view allowed for visits to the place of detention in Sheol (1 Enoch 22), visits to the hell which is already prepared for but not yet inhabited by the wicked (1 Enoch 26:3-27:4; 2 Enoch 10; 40:12; 2 Bar 59:10), and prophetic visions of the casting of the wicked into Gehenna at the last judgment (1 Enoch 41:2; 2 Bar 59:11). But only the later view enabled a seer to see and to describe in detail the punishments actually being inflicted on the wicked in hell. The later view therefore spawned a long tradition of 'tours of hell,' in which a variety of different punishments appropriate to different categories of sinners is described.

The oldest extant 'tour of hell' of this kind is probably that found in a Latin fragment of the ancient Apocalypse of Elijah,[53] which was

---

[53] M. E. Stone. M. E. and J. Strugnell, *The Books of Elijah: Parts 1-2* (SBLTTPS 8; Missoula, Monatna: Scholars Press, 1979) 14-15.

a Jewish work dating from no later than the first century C.E. It
features the 'hanging punishments' (in which the sinners are hung up
by the part of the body with which they had sinned). They are also
found in a whole series of later tours of hell, the most important of
which are the Apocalypse of Peter, Acts of Thomas 51-60, the Apocalypse of Paul, the Greek Apocalypse of Ezra, the Greek Apocalypse of
the Virgin, the Gedulat Moshe, and the Hebrew texts which describe
visits to hell by Isaiah and Rabbi Joshua ben Levi. Most of these
apocalypses, along with others which do not include the hanging
punishments (such as the Apocalypse of Zephaniah, the Latin Vision
of Ezra, and Testament of Isaac 5), describe a wide variety of other
punishments, such as immersion in a river of fire or a burning furnace, impalement on wheels of fire, and tantalization. The main concern is to show how a wide range of particular sins[54] is specifically
punished by appropriate forms of judgment in the afterlife. Some of
these tours of hell (such as the Apocalypse of Paul and the
Apocalypses of the Virgin) were extremely popular in the medieval
period. Together with the parallel descriptions of paradise, they form
a literary tradition whose greatest product was Dante's *Divine Comedy*.

Especially since Dieterich's argument[55] to this effect, these tours of
hell have been thought to be heavily indebted to the Greek and
Roman descents to Hades (see section VII above).[56] Himmelfarb[57]
has shown that they developed within the tradition of Jewish
apocalypses, as is shown by the important formal features they share
with the cosmic tour apocalypses. This does not, of course, preclude
Greek influence on them, especially since the Jewish and Christian
apocalyptic tradition frequently borrowed from other cultural traditions. While the tours of hell make use of features which were already
traditional characteristics of the Jewish Gehenna, especially its fiery
quality, some of the punishments in the tours of hell closely resemble
those found in Greek and Roman descriptions of the punishments in
Hades,[58] where also the idea of differing punishments for various

---

[54] Categories of sinners in or bound for hell can also be listed without the concern
for assigning specific punishments: 2 En 10; TJac 5:7-9; QuesBart 38.

[55] A. Dieterich, *Nekyia: Beiträge zur Erklärung der neuentdeckten Petrusapokalypse* (Stuttgart: Teubner, 1913).

[56] See also S. Reinach, 'L'Apocalypse de St Pierre' (Paris; Alcan-Lévy, 1893); E.
Norden, *Kleine Schriften zum klassischen Altertum* (Berlin: W. de Gruyter, 1966) 218-233.

[57] M. Himmelfarb, *Tours of Hell: An Apocalyptic Form in Jewish and Christian Literature*
(Philadelphia: University of Philadelphia Press, 1983); cf. also R. Bauckham, 'The
Apocalypse of Peter: An Account of Research,' ANRW 2/25/6 (1988) 4712-4750;
and chapter 8 below, section III.7.

[58] See Himmelfarb, *Tours of Hell*, 84, 92-96, 107-108, 119.

categories of sinners can be found. It may be that, not only specific
punishments in hell, but also the very idea of punishments inflicted on
the wicked immediately after death, so that they can be seen on a
visionary visit to the underworld, was the result of Greek influence, in
particular the influence of the descents to Hades, in which the Greek
view of punishment in the afterlife would have been most vividly
accessible. Thus the Jewish and Christian tours of hell are probably to
be seen both as developing out of the cosmic tours of Jewish
apocalypses, with their strong interest in the fate of the dead, and also
as incorporating ideas and images available in their cultural environment in the Greco-Roman world. Not only Greek but also Egyptian
(see section III above, for the story of Setme and Si-Osiris) descents to
the underworld may have influenced the tours of hell, while Zoroastrian influence is possible but more problematic in view of the dates
of the literature (see section V above: the distinctively Zoroastrian
features are missing from the Jewish and early Christian texts, though
the infernal bridge later became a feature of medieval Christian visions of hell).

The means by which the apocalyptic seer descends to the underworld are not usually specified more closely than by saying that an
angel took him or her. Although medieval Jewish texts refer to specific entrances to the underworld, as in Greek tradition,[59] these are
not used in the tours of hell, nor is there often any reference to
obstacles to be passed. Enoch shudders at the sight of the gatekeepers
of hell (2 Enoch 42:1). Ezra passes without difficulty, like the righteous dead, the two fiery lions who guard the gates of hell (VisEzra 3).
Paul, like Odysseus, has to cross the river Oceanus to reach hell in the
far west, but it is not said how he does so (ApPaul 31). In the Gedulat
Moshe, the fire withdraws before Moses as he enters hell, but when
he fears to descend to the abyss of fire and snow, the Shekinah goes
before him to protect him from the angels of punishment. The angelic guides (or, in the case of Joshua ben Levi, the prophet Elijah,
and, in the apocalypses of the Virgin, Christ himself) are a constant
feature of the tours: they lead, guide, explain and answer questions.

The Apocalypse of Zephaniah (which is probably of Jewish but
may be of Christian origin) has a particular interest in that the seer
seems to follow the path of a dead person through Hades to paradise.
The fragmentary beginning of the Akhmimic text (1:1-2) seems to
describe the body of Zephaniah appearing to be dead. Evidently he
has gone into a cataleptic trance like those in which some descents to
Hades in the Greek tradition took place (see section VII above; and

---

[59] Ganschinietz, 'Katabasis,' 2387.

for cataleptic trance in the Jewish and Christian apocalyptic tradition, see AscenIsa 6:17; 4 Bar 9:7-14). In this state his soul could leave his body and be taken by an angel through the other world. His angelic guide protects him from the angels of punishment who seize the souls of the wicked when they die (4:1-10). He perhaps passes the gates of Hades (5:1-6) and the sea of fire in Hades (6:1-3), and is threatened by both. He encounters the angel Eremiel (= Remiel) who is in charge of the souls in Hades and whom he mistakes for God (6:4-7, 10-15), and another terrifying angel who he discovers is Satan in his traditional role of judicial accuser (8:5). Satan reads out all Zephaniah's sins from a scroll; Zephaniah prays to God for mercy; he is told that he has triumphed over the accuser and come up from Hades; another angel apparently reads out the record of his righteous deeds; and he travels out of Hades in a boat accompanied by myriads of angels. He finds himself, presumably in paradise, with the patri-archs (7-9). Evidently he has passed through the experiences of a righteous person's soul after death. The closest analogy seems to be that of Kirdīr (see section VI above), though in Zephaniah's case he himself goes into trance and recounts his experience afterwards (cf. 8:5). This apocalypse, like so many descents to the underworld, serves the purpose of revealing what people can expect after death and warning them to be prepared.

Another feature of the Apocalypse of Zephaniah recurs in many of the tours of hell: when Zephaniah sees the wicked in torment in hell, he is moved to pray for God's mercy for them (2:8-9). So do Ezra (GkApEzra; VisEzra), Baruch (3 Bar 16:7-8 Sl), Paul (ApPaul 33; 40; 42; 43), and the Virgin Mary (in her several apocalypses). Zephaniah and others also see the patriarchs and the righteous dead in paradise praying for the damned (ApZeph 11; TJac 7:11), while Paul is joined in his intercession by other saints and angels (ApPaul 43-44). These pleas for mercy are sometimes rebuffed, but sometimes win a conces-sion from God, such as the Sabbath or Sunday rest of the damned, a day's respite each week from the pains of hell (ApPaul 44). The motif of intercession for the damned was clearly important in the tradition. By attributing it to ideal, exemplary figures of Jewish and Christian piety, the authors were allowing an authoritative mode of expression to the natural compassionate reaction which they and their readers felt, when faced with the horrors of hell. This desire for mercy coex-ists with the emphasis on the justice of hell in the same apocalypses.[60]

Jewish and Christian tours of hell are found not only in apocalypses, but also in narrative contexts in which a character visits

---

[60] See chapter 6 below.

hell in a vision or a dream or an experience of temporary death. The detailed descriptions in such cases are no doubt drawn from the tours of hell in the apocalypses. Significant examples are the Jewish story of the rich wicked man and the pious poor man, which is probably related to the Egyptian tale of Setme and Si-Osiris (see section III above) and which incorporates two different tours of hell in the version in the Palestinian Talmud (y. Ḥag. 77d; y. Sanh. 23c) and in the version in *Darkhei Teshuvah*;[61] the story in the Acts of Thomas 51-60, of a girl who dies, sees hell and is brought back to life by the apostle (cf. other stories of temporary death in section VII above); Isaac's vision of hell in the Testament of Isaac; and Pachomios' vision of hell in the Coptic life of this fourth-century Egyptian saint.[62] In the Testament of Abraham, Abraham is taken to see not hell itself but the place in the east (or by the river Oceanus: B8:3) where the dead are judged after death and two entrances lead to their respective destinies (A11-14; B8-11): the scene is strongly reminiscent of that visited by Plato's Er (see section VII above).

IX CHRIST'S DESCENT TO HADES (NEW TESTAMENT)

Since the commonest Jewish view in New Testament times was that all the dead descend to Sheol (Hades), Jesus' descent to Hades was simply the corollary of his death, just as it was implied in his resurrection 'from the dead.' But rarely in the New Testament is his descent to Hades given any attention. Paul's adaptation of Deuteronomy 30:13 in Romans 10:7 simply describes resurrection as being brought up from the realm of the dead, while Ephesians 4:9-10 may indicate Christ's descent in death to Hades (cf. Pss 63:9; 139:15), though it is often taken to refer only to his descent from heaven to earth (but cf. TDan 5:10-11 for Ps 68:18 used with reference to the descent to Hades).

More significant are two passages which apply to Jesus' resurrection the Old Testament notion of deliverance from Sheol by God (see section V above). In Acts 2:24-32 (cf. 13:34-37), a quotation from and allusion to psalms (vv 25-28, 31: Ps 16:8-11; v 24: Ps 18:4-5; 116:3; 2 Sam 22:6; cf. Polycarp, *Phil.* 1:2) interpret the resurrection as God's deliverance of Jesus from the power of Hades, as well as from the

---

[61] J.-M. Rosenstiehl, 'Les révélations d'Elie. Elie et les tourments des damnés,' in *La Littérature Intertestamentaire: Colloque de Strasbourg (17-19 Octobre 1983)* (Paris: Presses Universitaires de France, 1985) 99-107
[62] Himmelfarb, *Tours of Hell*, 28-29.

physical corruption of death. Matthew 12:40 takes up the tradition of Jewish interpretation of Jonah for which the belly of the fish represented the underworld, so that Jonah's emergence from the fish was God's deliverance of him from death (see section V above). Thus 'the belly of the whale' in Jonah's case corresponds to 'the heart of the earth' (cf. Jon 2:3-4 LXX), i.e. Hades, in Jesus' case. Jonah's virtual death and resurrection prefigures Jesus' actual death and resurrection.

Revelation 1:18 ('I have the keys of Death and Hades') presupposes that the gates of Hades, which release noone who has entered them, have been for the first time opened for a man to leave. The divine prerogative of releasing from the realm of death (cf. Wis 16:13) now belongs to Christ. That in his death and resurrection he has gained power over death and Hades is implied, but not the later notion of a victory won in Hades.

Thus in the New Testament Christ's descent to and sojourn in the realm of the dead seems to have no independent interest or significance beside his death and resurrection. Such significance has often been found in 1 Peter 3:19; 4:6, understood to refer to a preaching of Christ to the dead during his sojourn in Hades. However, it is now widely recognized that in 3:19 the proclamation to the spirits follows the resurrection (v 18: 'made alive in the spirit'), while 'the spirits in prison' are most probably angels (cf. v 22). A reference to the idea, widely attested from the beginning of the second century, that Christ after his death preached the salvation he had achieved to the saints of the Old Testament period, is more probable in 4:6, but on the other hand 'the dead' may there refer to those who heard the Gospel while alive, but subsequently died.

Matthew 27:52-53 seems to be related to the widespread early extra-canonical tradition that Christ released the Old Testament saints from Hades, especially as this was evidently understood as a real resurrection (see section X below). The Matthean passage probably draws on that tradition, but makes no explicit reference to Christ's activity in Hades. Instead the motif is used to express the eschatological significance of the death of Christ, by which the power of death has been broken. It is striking that in perhaps the New Testament's closest contact with the development of the theme of the descent to Hades in other early Christian literature, the interest is exclusively in the significance of the death of Christ, not in any activity of Christ in Hades.

X CHRIST'S DESCENT TO HADES (EARLY CHURCH)

As well as retaining the fundamental notion that Jesus Christ's soul
had to descend to Hades in order for him fully to share the human lot
in death (SibOr 8:312; Irenaeus, *Adv. Haer.* 5.31.2; Tertullian, *De
anima* 55.2; Hilary, *Enarr. in Ps.* 53, 138), Christians from a very early
date saw in the descent to Hades an event of soteriological significance for the righteous dead of the period before Christ, whose souls
were in Hades. This significance was expressed in three main motifs:
(1) that while in Hades Christ preached to the dead, announcing and
conferring on them the benefits of the salvation he had achieved; (2)
that he brought the righteous out of Hades and led them into paradise or heaven; (3) that he defeated the powers of death or Hades
which keep the dead captive in the underworld. The second of these
motifs is usually combined with the first or the third, as its consequence. Only rarely (OdesSol 42:11-14) are the first and third combined.

The idea of Christ's preaching to the dead is found from the
beginning of the second century onwards (GPet 41-42; Ignatius,
Magn. 9.2; EpApp 27; SibOr 1:377-378; 8:310-311; the elder quoted
in Irenaeus, *Adv. Haer.* 4.27.1-2; Hippolytus, *Antichr.* 26; 45; *Song,* fr.
1). An apocryphal fragment attributed to Jeremiah was current
(quoted in somewhat varying forms in Justin, *Dial.* 72.4; Irenaeus,
Adv. Haer. 3.20.4; 4.22.1; 4.33.1; 4.33.12; 5.31.1; *Dem.* 78)[63]: it is
possible that one form of this (Irenaeus, *Adv. Haer.* 4.33.1; 4.33.12;
5.31.1) was a Jewish text prophesying the resurrection of the righteous at the last day, whereas the version which mentions the preaching to the dead (Justin, *Dial.* 72.4; Irenaeus, *Adv. Haer.* 3.20.4; 4.22.1;
Dem. 78) is a Christian adaptation of the text referring it to Christ's
descent to Hades. The recipients of Christ's preaching in these early
references are the righteous people of the Old Testament period who
hoped for Christ (Ignatius, *Magn.* 9:2). When he proclaimed to them
the good news of the salvation he had won, they believed in him and
received forgiveness of sins through his death (Irenaeus, *Adv. Haer.*
4.27.1-2). The idea met the problem of the fate of the righteous who
died before Christ, and most probably arose in a Jewish Christian
context where this would be a natural concern. According to the
Epistle of the Apostles 27, Christ not only preached but baptized the
righteous dead (cf. also GNic 19)—a natural corollary of the idea that

---

[63] See also K. Gschwind, *Die Niederfahrt Christi in die Unterwelt* (NTAbh 2/3/5;
Münster: Aschendorff, 1911) 199-227; W. Bieder, *Die Vorstellung von der Höllenfahrt Jesu
Christi* (ATANT 19; Zürich: Zwingli-Verlag, 1949) 135-141.

he brought Christian salvation to them. The idea of the baptizing of the dead is also found in Hermas, *Sim.* 9:16:2-7, where it is not Christ but the apostles and teachers of the first Christian generation who preached Christ and administered baptism to the dead. This unique notion is otherwise found only in Clement of Alexandria, who quotes it from Hermas (*Str.* 2.43.5; 6.45.4).

The scope of the preaching was extended beyond the Old Testament saints by Clement of Alexandria and Origen, who were also the first to refer to 1 Peter 3:19 in connexion with the descent to Hades.[64] Clement included righteous pagans alongside the Old Testament saints (*Str.* 6.6.37-53), while Origen thought also of the conversion of sinners in Hades (*Princ.* 2.5), as 1 Peter 3:19 must imply, if taken seriously as a reference to the descent. Some other Greek Fathers followed Origen,[65] but the prevalent view in the Latin church continued to limit the soteriological benefit of the descent to those who were already believers before Christ.

It was widely believed that Christ brought the Old Testament saints out of Hades and led them up to paradise or heaven, though this was denied by Tertullian in the interests of his view that before the last judgment only the Christian martyrs go to heaven, while the rest of the righteous dead remain in Abraham's bosom in Hades (*De anima* 58). The primitive view was that the dead left Hades along with Christ at his resurrection (OdesSol 42:11) and ascended to heaven with him at his ascension (AscenIsa 9:17; ApPet 17; Origen, *Comm. in Rom.* 5:10). As it was sometimes put, he descended alone but ascended with a great multitude (Acts of Thaddeus, *apud* Eusebius, *Hist. Eccl.* 1.13.20; Melito, new fr. 2.17; Armenian Acts of Callistratus 9). There is also good evidence that originally the thought was of an actual resurrection of the dead: language normally reserved for bodily resurrection is used (Ignatius, *Magn.* 9:2; Melito, *Peri Pascha* 101; new fr. 2.12, 15; Origen, *Comm. in Rom.* 5.10; cf. also the Jeremiah apocryphon mentioned above), and Matthew 27:52 was sometimes connected with this resurrection of the saints (Irenaeus, fr. 26).[66] Since Christ's death and resurrection were the eschatological saving event, entailing the resurrection of all who believe in him, the Jewish hope of the resurrection of the righteous was thought to be fulfilled when Christ brought them out of Hades. After all, to be brought

---

[64] W. J. Dalton, *Christ's Proclamation to the Spirits: A Study of 1 Peter 3:18-4:6* (AnBib 23; Rome: Pontifical Biblical Institute, 1965) 16-20.

[65] Dalton, *Christ's Proclamation*, 18-19.

[66] Cf. J. A. MacCulloch, *The Harrowing of Hell* (Edinburgh: T. & T. Clark, 1930) 289-291.

out of Hades was to be raised from the dead, as it was for Jesus himself.

Using the picture of Hades as a stronghold in which the dead are held captive by the angelic rulers of the dead, Christ's descent could be seen as a conquest of Hades. Often this was portrayed in images derived from Old Testament texts considered prophetic of the descent. Thus the gatekeepers of Hades trembled when they saw Christ approach (Job 38:17 LXX; cf. Hippolytus, *Pasch.*; Athanasius, *C. Ar.* 3.29; Cyril of Jerusalem, *Catech.* 4.11; Creed of Sirmium, *apud* Athanasius, *Syn.* 1.9).[67] He broke open the gates of bronze and the iron bolts (Ps 107:16; Isa 45:2; cf. OdesSol 17:9-11; TeachSilv 110:19-24; Tertullian, *De Res. Carn.* 44; Eusebius, *Dem. Evang.* 8.1; QuesBart 1:20; GNic 21:3). He released the captives from their chains and led them out of their prison (Ps 68:18; 107:14; Isa 49:9; 61:1; for releasing captives, cf. OdesSol 17:12; 22:4; Melito, fr. 13; new fr. 2.12; ActsThom 10; GNic 21:3; for Ps 68:18, cf. TDan 5:10-11). Psalm 24:7-10 was understood as a dialogue between Christ's angelic forces and the powers of death at the gates of Hades (GNic 21). Also influential was Jesus' parable about binding the strong man and plundering his goods (Mark 3:27; cf. Melito, *Peri Pascha* 103; fr. 13; Origen, *Comm. in Rom.* 5.10; for plundering Hades, cf. AscenIsa 9:16; TLevi 4:1; Cyril, *Hom. Pasch.* 6.7; for binding Hades, cf. GNic 22:2; QuesBart 3:20). Christ is also often said to have conquered or destroyed death or Hades (Melito, *Peri Pascha* 102; fr. 13; TLord 1:23).[68]

There are traces of the view that, as one of the dead, Christ was initially bound in Hades and had to break free before also freeing others (OdesSol 17:10; TeachSilv 110:14-16; Irenaeus, *Adv. Haer.* 5.21.3), but generally the picture of Christ entering Hades by storming its fortifications seems to have prevailed. In the fullest and most dramatic portrayal of the scene, in the Gospel of Nicodemus (Acts of Pilate), he is accompanied by an army of angels (21:3). It is important to notice that in the early period the defeated powers are the angelic rulers of the dead (cf. AscenIsa 9:16; ActsThom 10; 143; 156), often Death or Hades personified (OdesSol 42:11), but not Satan and the forces of evil. In Jewish and early Christian thought Satan was not located in the underworld, but in the lower heavens. (A very exceptional case in which Beliar is the power Christ defeats, plundering the dead from him, is TDan 5:10-11.) However, the more Hades was thought of as an enemy whom Christ defeated, the more natural it

---

[67] Cf. MacCulloch, *The Harrowing*, 217-218.
[68] Cf. MacCulloch, *The Harrowing*, 230-232.

would be to see him as an ally of Satan (cf. Origen, *Comm. in Rom.* 5.10), as he is in the Gospel of Nicodemus and Ephrem Syrus.[69] In these and some other later Fathers, the result of the descent is that Satan is chained in the abyss.[70] Here the descent has become a mythical portrayal of Christ's triumph over all evil.

The influence of pagan myths of descent to the underworld on Christian ideas of Christ's descent to Hades was probably minimal. The parallels with Orpheus and Heracles were noticed and exploited in minor ways by some later Christian writers, but there is no indication that they account for the origin of any of the Christian ideas. It is the theme of the conflict with and defeat of the powers of the underworld which has most often been claimed to have a broad mythological background in the religious cultures of the ancient world,[71] but it is extremely difficult to identify a suitable myth which was available in the environment of early Christianity. Of the myths surveyed in the earlier sections of this chapter, it is only in the Ugaritic account of Baal's victory over Mot (section IV above) that the motif of a god who descends to the world of the dead and defeats the powers of death occurs. This parallel is far too chronologically remote to count as an influence on early Christianity. In fact, the idea of Christ's defeat of the powers of Hades is sufficiently explained from the Jewish apocalyptic expectation that at the last day God would 'reprove the angel of death' (2 Bar 42:8), command Sheol to release the souls of the dead (2 Bar 42:8), abolish death (LAB 3:10), close the mouth of Sheol (LAB 3:10) or seal it up (2 Bar 21:23; cf. TeachSilv 103:6-7). In the expectation of resurrection there was a sense of death and its realm as a power which had to be broken by God (cf. also Matt 16:18; 1 Cor 15:44-45; Rev 20:14; 4 Ezra 8:53). These ideas were transferred to the context of Christ's descent to Hades because of the early Christian belief that Christ's death and resurrection were the eschatological triumph of God over death. The details, as we have seen, derived from that process of christological exegesis of the Old Testament which supplied so much of the phraseology and imagery of early Christian belief.

The idea of Christ's descent to Hades was powerful and important for early Christians not just because it met the problem of the salvation of the righteous of the Old Testament (and only occasionally because it opened salvation to good pagans of the past), but also

---

[69] MacCulloch, *The Harrowing*, 111-113.
[70] MacCulloch, *The Harrowing*, 232-233.
[71] See especially J. Kroll, *Gott und Hölle: Der Mythos vom Descensuskampfe* (Leipzig, 1932; reprinted Darmstadt: Wissenschaftliche Buchgesellschaft, 1963).

because it represented that definitive defeat of death from which
Christian believers benefit. If it tended to take precedence over the
resurrection of Jesus in this respect,[72] this was because it showed
Christ delivering others from death. His rescue of the Old Testament
saints and taking them to heaven was the sign of what he would also
do for Christian believers (EpApp 27-28), who experienced salvation
as release from the chains of Hades (OdesSol 17:4). If there is truth in
the suggestion (too strongly asserted by Daniélou[73] and Ménard[74])
that in the Odes of Solomon baptismal immersion is conceived as a
descent into Hades and an experience of Christ's deliverance of the
dead from Hades, then perhaps at this point Christianity came closest
to the significance of the Greek descents to Hades in the mysteries
(see section VII above).

However, a final point at which the Christian tradition of the
descent took up Jewish motifs is in the prominence which the raising
of Adam from Hades to paradise gains in Gospel of Nicodemus 19,
24-25.[75] Even Adam's baptism (19; cf. 24:2) has a precedent (ApMos
37:3) in the Jewish tradition of Adam's translation to paradise. The
release of Adam from Hades gave a universal significance to the myth
of the descent. In this form especially, the 'harrowing of hell' became
for medieval Christians a powerful dramatization of the *Christus victor*
theme in soteriology.

XI Bibliography

I *General*

F. Bar, *Les Routes de l'Autre-Monde: Descents aux Enfers et Voyages dans l'Au-delà*
    (Paris: Presses Universitaires de France, 1946).
H.R.E. Davidson ed., *The Journey to the Other World* (Folklore Society Publica-
    tions 2; Cambridge: Brewer/ Totowa, NJ: Rowman & Littlefield, 1975).
C. Kappler ed., *Apocalypses et Voyages dans l'Au-delà* (Paris: Editions du Cerf,
    1987).
J. Kroll, *Gott und Hölle: Der Mythos vom Descensuskampfe* (Darmstadt: Wissen-
    schaftliche Buchgesellschaft, 1963 reprint of 1932 edition).

---

[72] Thus Bieder, *Die Vorstellung*, 202-203, ascribes it to a flagging of faith in Christ's
victory in death and resurrection.
[73] J. Daniélou, *The Theology of Jewish Christianity* (trans. J. A. Baker; Philadelphia:
Westminster, 1964) 244-248.
[74] J. Ménard, 'Le "Descensus ad inferos,"' in *Ex Orbe Religionum: Studia Geo
Widengren*, eds. C. J. Bleeker, S. G. F. Brandon, M. Simon, J. Bergman, K. Drynjeff,
H. Ringgren, vol. 2 (SHR 22; Leiden: Brill, 1972) 303-304.
[75] See also MacCulloch, *The Harrowing*, 337-339.

II *Mesopotamia*

J. Bottéro, 'Le "Pays-sans-retour,"' in *Apocalypses et Voyages dans l'Au-delà*, ed. C. Kappler (Paris: Editions du Cerf, 1987) 55-82.

G. Buccellati, 'The Descent of Inanna as a Ritual Journey to Kutha?,' *Syro-Mesopotamian Studies* 4/3 (1982) 3-7.

T. Jacobsen, *The Treasures of Darkness: A History of Mesopotamian Religion* (New Haven: Yale University Press, 1976).

G.S. Kirk, *Myth: Its Meaning and Functions in Ancient and Other Cultures* (Cambridge: Cambridge University Press/ Berkeley: University of California Press, 1970).

S.N. Kramer, 'Dumuzi's Annual Resurrection: An Important Correction to "Inanna's Descent,"' *BASOR* 183 (1966) 31.

S.N. Kramer, '"Inanna's Descent to the Nether World": Continued and Revised,' *JCS* 4 (1950) 199-211; 5 (1951) 1-17.

I. Loucas, 'La déesse de la prospérité dans les mythes mésopotamien et égeen et la descente aux enfers,' *RHR* 205 (1988) 227-244.

III *Egypt*

E.A.W. Budge, *The Egyptian Heaven and Hell*, 3 vols. (London: Kegan Paul, Trench, Trübner, 1906).

F.Ll. Griffith, *Stories of the High Priests of Memphis: The Sethon of Herodotus and the Demotic Tales of Khamuas* (Oxford: Clarendon Press, 1900).

J. Zandee, *Death as an Enemy according to ancient Egyptian conceptions* (SHR 5; Leiden: Brill, 1960).

IV *Syria and Palestine*

N. Robertson, 'The Ritual of the Dying God in Cyprus and Syro-Palestine,' *HTR* 75 (1982) 313-359.

P. Xella, 'Baal et la mort,' in *Apocalypses et Voyages dans l'Au-delà*, ed. C. Kappler (Paris: Editions du Cerf, 1987) 83-100 .

V *Hebrew Bible*

A. Cooper, 'Ps 24:7-10: Mythology and Exegesis,' *JBL* 102 (1983) 37-60.

G.M. Landes, 'The Kerygma of the Book of Jonah: The Contextual Interpretation of the Jonah Psalm,' *Int* 21 (1967) 3-31.

G.M. Landes, 'The "Three Days and Three Nights" Motif in Jonah 2:1,' *JBL* 86 (1967) 446-450.

VI *Iran*

P. Gignoux, '"Corps osseux et âme osseuse": essai sur le chamanisme dans l'Iran ancien,' *JA* 267 (1979) 41-79.

P. Gignoux, 'Der Grossmagier Kirdir und seine Reise in das Jenseits,' in *Orientalia J. Duchesne-Guillemin Emerito Oblata* (Acta Iranica 23; Leiden: Brill, 1984) 191-206.

P. Gignoux, 'La signification du voyage extra-terrestre dans l'eschatologie mazdéenne,' in *Mélanges d'histoire des religions offerts à Henri-Charles Puech*, ed. P. Lévy and E. Wolff (Paris: Presses Universitaires de France, 1974) 63-69.

P. Gignoux, *Le Livre d'Ardā Vīrāz* (Institut Français d'Iranologie de Téhéran: Bibliothèque Iranienne 30; Paris: Editions Recherche sur les Civilisations, 1984).

P. Gignoux, 'Les Voyages chamaniques dans le Monde iranien,' in *Monumentum Georg Morgenstierne I* (Acta Iranica 21; Leiden: Brill, 1981) 244-265.

P.O. Skjærvo, '"Kirdir's Vision": Translation and Analysis,' *Archaeologische Mitteilungen aus Iran* 16 (1983) 269-306.

M. Tardieu, 'L'Ardā Vīrāz Nāmāg et l'eschatologie grecque,' *Studia Iranica* 14 (1985) 17-26.

F. Vahman, *Ardā Wirāz Nāmag: The Iranian 'Divina Commedia'* (Scandinavian Institute of Asian Studies Monograph Series 53; London/Malmo: Curzon, 1986).

VII *Greece and Rome*

H.D. Betz, 'Fragments from a Catabasis Ritual in a Greek Magical Papyrus,' *HR* 19: (1980) 287-295.

J. Bidez and F. Cumont, *Les mages hellénisés*, vol. 1 (Paris: Société d'Editions 'Les Belles Lettres,' 1983)

J.D.P. Bolton, *Aristeas of Proconnesus* (Oxford: Clarendon Press, 1962).

W. Burkert, 'Das Proömium des Parmenides und die Katabasis des Pythagoras,' *Phronesis* 14 (1969) 1-29.

W. Burkert, *Lore and Science in Ancient Pythagoreanism* (trans. E. L. Minar, Jr.; Cambridge, Massachusetts: Harvard University Press, 1972).

W. Burkert, *Structure and History in Greek Mythology and Ritual* (Berkeley: University of California Press, 1979).

R.J. Clark, 'Trophonios: The Manner of his Revelation,' *TAPA* 99 (1968) 63-75.

I.P. Culianu, *Psychanodia I: A Survey of the Evidence concerning the Ascension of the Soul and its Relevance* (EPRO 99; Leiden: Brill, 1983).

F. Cumont, *After Life in Roman Paganism* (New Haven: Yale University Press, 1922).

F. Cumont, *Lux Perpetua* (Paris: Geuthner, 1949).

A.T. Edwards, 'Achilles in the Underworld: Iliad, Odyssey, and Aethiopis,' *GRBS* 26 (1985) 215-227.

M. Eliade, *Zalmoxis: The Vanishing God* (trans. W. R. Trask; Chicago: University of Chicago Press, 1972).

R. Ganschinietz, 'Katabasis,' PW 10/2 (1919) 2359-2449.

F. Graf, *Eleusis und die orphische Dichtung Athens in vorhellenistischer Zeit* (RVV 33; Berlin/New York: de Gruyter, 1974).

J.G. Griffiths, *Apuleius of Madauros: The Isis-Book (Metamorphoses, Book XI)* (EPRO 39; Leiden: Brill, 1975).

P. Lambrechts, 'La "résurrection" d'Adonis,' *Annuaire de l'Institut de Philologie et d'Histoire Orientales et Slaves* (Brussels) 13 (1953) 207-240.

M.O. Lee, 'Orpheus and Eurydice: Myth, Legend, Folklore,' *Classica et Mediaevalia* 26 (1965) 402-412.

I. Lévy, *La Légende de Pythagore de Grèce en Palestine* (BEHE.H 250; Paris: Librairie Ancienne Honoré Champion, 1927).

H. Lewy, 'Aristotle and the Jewish Sage according to Clearchus of Soli,' *HTR* 31 (1938) 205-235.

I.M. Linforth, *The Arts of Orpheus* (Berkeley: University of California Press, 1941).

H. Lloyd-Jones, 'Heracles at Eleusis: P. Oxy. 2622 and P.S.I. 1391,' *Maia* 19 (1967) 206-229.

J.S. Morrison, 'Parmenides and Er,' *JHS* 75 (1955) 59-68.

R. Schilling, 'Romanité et ésotérisme dans le Chant VI de l'Enéide,' *RHR* 199 (1982) 363-380.

R. Turcan, 'La catabase orphique du papyrus de Bologne,' *RHR* 150 (1956) 136-172.

M.L. West, *The Orphic Poems* (Oxford: Clarendon, 1983).

VIII *Jewish and Christian Apocalypses*

R. Bauckham, 'The Apocalypse of Peter: An Account of Research,' ANRW 2/25/6 (1988) 4712-4750.

A. Dieterich, *Nekyia: Beiträge zur Erklärung der neuentdeckten Petrusapokalypse* (Stuttgart: Teubner, 1913).

M. Gaster, 'Hebrew Visions of Hell and Paradise,' *JRAS* 2 (1893) 571-611, reprinted in M. Gaster, *Studies and Texts in Folklore, Magic, Medieval Romance, Hebrew Apocrypha and Samaritan Archæology* (London: Maggs, 1925-1928), vol. 1, 124-164.

P. Grelot, 'La géographie mythique d'Hénoch et ses sources orientales,' *RB* 65 (1958) 33-69.

M. Himmelfarb, *Tours of Hell: An Apocalyptic Form in Jewish and Christian Literature* (Philadelphia: University of Philadelphia Press, 1983).

J.-M. Rosenstiehl, 'Les révélations d'Elie: Elie et les tourments des damnés,' in *La Littérature Intertestamentaire: Colloque de Strasbourg (17-19 Octobre 1983)* (Paris: Presses Universitaires de France, 1985) 99-107.

IX, X *Christ's Descent to Hades*

W. Bieder, *Die Vorstellung von der Höllenfahrt Jseu Christi* (ATANT 19; Zürich: Zwingli-Verlag, 1949).

J. Chaîne, 'La descente du Christ aux Enfers,' DBSup 2 (1934) 395-430.

W.J. Dalton, *Christ's Proclamation to the Spirits: A Study of 1 Peter 3:18-4:6* (AnBib 23; Rome: Pontifical Biblical Institute, 1965).

J. Daniélou, *The Theology of Jewish Christianity* (trans. J. A. Baker. Philadelphia: Westminster, 1964).

M.M. Gatch, 'The Harrowing of Hell: A Liberation Motif in Medieval Theology and Devotional Literature' *USQR* 36 (1981) 75-88.

K. Gschwind, *Die Niederfahrt Christi in die Unterwelt* (NTAbh 2/3/5; Münster: Aschendorff, 1911).

R.J. Hoffman, 'Confluence in Early Christian and Gnostic Literature: The Descensus Christi ad Inferos (Acta Pilati XVII-XXVII),' *JSNT* 10 (1981) 42-60.

F. Loofs, 'Christ's Descent into Hell,' in *Transactions of the Third International Congress for the History of Religions*, vol. 2 (Oxford: Clarendon, 1908) 290-301.

J.A. MacCulloch, *The Harrowing of Hell* (Edinburgh: T. & T. Clark, 1930).

J. Ménard, 'Le "Descensus ad inferos,"' in *Ex Orbe Religionum: Studia Geo Widengren*, ed. C. J. Bleeker, S. G. F. Brandon, M. Simon, J. Bergman, K. Drynjeff, H. Ringgren, vol. 2 (SHR 22; Leiden: Brill, 1972) 296-306.

M.L. Peel, 'The "Descensus ad Inferos" in "The Teachings of Silvanus" (CG II,4),' *Numen* 26 (1979) 23-49.

P.-H. Poirier, 'La Prôtennoia trimorphe (NH XIII,1) et le vocabulaire du Descensus ad inferos,' *Muséon* 96 (1983) 193-204.

B. Reicke, *The Disobedient Spirits and Christian Baptism: A Study of 1 Pet. iii. 19 and its Context* (ASNU 13; Copenhagen: Ejnar Munksgaard, 1946).

R.V. Turner, 'Descendit ad Inferos: Medieval Views on Christ's Descent into Hell and the Salvation of the Ancient Just,' *JHI* 27 (1966) 173-194.

CHAPTER TWO

EARLY JEWISH VISIONS OF HELL

I Introduction

A rather neglected but historically important group of Jewish and Christian apocalypses contain what Martha Himmelfarb has called 'tours of hell.'[1] These are visionary visits to the place of punishment

---

[1] M. Himmelfarb, *Tours of Hell: An Apocalyptic Form in Jewish and Christian Literature* (Philadelphia: University of Pennsylvania Press, 1983). The apocalypses she discusses are the Apocalypse of Peter, the Apocalypse of Zephaniah, the Apocalypse of Paul, the Ethiopic Apocalypse of Mary, the Ethiopic Apocalypse of Baruch, the Apocalypse of Gorgorios, the Greek Apocalypse of Mary, the Greek Apocalypse of Ezra, the Vision of Ezra, the Latin fragment of the Apocalypse of Elijah, the Gedulat Moshe, and the Hebrew accounts of visits to hell by Isaiah and Joshua ben Levi, together with the tours of hell in the Acts of Thomas, the Testament of Isaac, the Life of Pachomios, and the story of the rich wicked man and the pious poor man which appears in different forms in the Palestinian Talmud and *Darkhei Teshuvah*. Studies of these apocalypses which have appeared since Himmelfarb wrote, include the translations and introductions in J. H. Charlesworth ed., *The Old Testament Pseudepigrapha*, vol. 1 (London: Darton, Longman & Todd, 1983) (Apocalypse of Zephaniah, Greek Apocalypse of Ezra, Vision of Ezra, Testament of Isaac), and in H. F. D. Sparks ed., *The Apocryphal Old Testament* (Oxford: Clarendon, 1984) (Testament of Isaac, Apocalypse of Zephaniah, Greek Apocalypse of Ezra, Vision of Ezra); also E. Lupieri, 'Poena aeterna nelle più antiche apocalisse cristiane apocrife non gnostiche,' *Augustinianum* 23 (1983) 361-72; D. D. Fiensy, 'Lex Talionis in the Apocalypse of Peter,' *HTR* 76 (1983) 255-258; P.-M. Bogaert, 'Une version longue inédite de la "Visio Beati Esdrae" dans le Légendier de Teano (Barberini Lat. 2318),' *RBén* 94 (1984) 59-64; J.-M. Rosenstiehl, 'Les révélations d'Élie: Élie et les tourments des damnés,' in A. Caquot et al., *La Littérature Intertestamentaire: Colloque de Strasbourg (17-19 octobre 1983)* (Bibliothèque des Centres d'Études Supérieures Spécialistes; Paris: Presses Universitaires de France, 1985) 99-107; M. Tardieu, 'L'Arda Viraz Namag et l'eschatologie grecque,' *Studia Iranica* 14 (1985) 17-26; R. Bauckham, 'The Two Fig Tree Parables in the Apocalypse of Peter,' *JBL* 104 (1985) 269-287; E. G. Chazon, 'Moses' Struggle for His Soul: A Prototype for the Testament of Abraham, the Greek Apocalypse of Ezra, and the Apocalypse of Sedrach,' *SecCent* 5 (1985-86) 151-164; B. J. Diebner, 'Die Söhne des Priesters Jo(a)tham: Anspielung auf ein Stück verlorener Heiliger Schrift?,' *Dielheimer Blätter* 16 (1982) 40-49; M. Himmelfarb, 'The Experience of the Visionary and Genre in the Ascension of Isaiah 6-11 and the Apocalypse of Paul,' *Semeia* 36 (1986) 97-111; C. Kappler, 'L'Apocalypse latine de Paul,' in C. Kappler ed., *Apocalypses et Voyages dans l'Au-delà* (Paris: Éditions du Cerf, 1987) 237-266; D. D. Buchholz, *Your Eyes Will Be Opened: A Study of the Greek (Ethiopic) Apocalypse of Peter* (SBLDS 97; Atlanta, Georgia: Scholars Press, 1988); R. Bauckham, 'The Apocalypse of Peter: An Account of Research,' in W. Haase ed., *Aufstieg und Niedergang der römischen Welt*, 2.25.6 (Berlin/New York: de Gruyter, 1988) 4712-4750; J.-M. Rosenstiehl, 'L'Itinéraire de Paul dans l'Au-delà: Contribution à l'étude de

of the wicked after death, in which the seer is shown a variety of punishments being inflicted on various categories of sinners. Though most of these apocalypses contain material other than the tour of hell, such as a visit to paradise, a revelation of what happens to a soul at death or a dialogue about the justice and mercy of God in relation to hell, nearly all of them are overwhelmingly concerned with the fate of the dead.[2] Himmelfarb's important study of the tours of hell in these apocalypses has done much to sort out the relationships between these works.[3] She has also illuminated the origins of the tradition of tours of hell. She has shown that the earliest Jewish tours of hell must have been already known in the first century C.E., though these earliest tours are probably not extant as such. But the Apocalypse of Zephaniah, the Latin fragment of the Apocalypse of Elijah, the Apocalypse of Peter, a passage in the Palestinian Talmud, and Isaiah's tour of hell which is preserved in medieval Hebrew sources, all bring us close to the earliest tours. She also argues that a distinctive formal feature of the tours, the 'demonstrative explanations' in which the seer's guide explains, usually in response to questions, what he sees ('These are those who...' or similar), links the tours of hell to the tour apocalypses, of which the earliest is Enoch's cosmic tour (1 En 17-36) in the Enochic Book of Watchers. The questions and demonstrative explanations are there used with reference to the sights the angels show Enoch, and subsequently appear in other tour apocalypses, such as 2 Enoch, 3 Baruch and the Ascension of Isaiah, which belong in some sense to the tradition initiated by the Book of Watchers. Moreover, both the Book of Watchers and some of these other works show an interest in reward and punishment after death (both for fallen angels and for humans), and although the demonstrative explanations are not confined to matters connected with this interest, they nearly always occur in this connexion, not always in others.[4] Himmelfarb concludes that the 'tours of hell represent one

---

l'Apocalypse apocryphe de Paul,' in P. Nagel ed., *Carl-Schmidt-Kolloquium an der Martin-Luther-Universität Halle-Wittenberg 1988* (Martin-Luther-Universität Halle-Wittenberg Beiträge 1990/23 [K9]; Halle, 1990) 197-212; R. Bauckham, 'The Conflict of Justice and Mercy: Attitudes to the Damned in Apocalyptic Literature,' *Apocrypha* 1 (1990) 181-196 (= chapter 6 below); idem, 'Virgin, Apocalypses of the,' in *The Anchor Bible Dictionary*, ed. D. N. Freedman, vol. 6 (New York: Doubleday, 1992) 854-856; idem, 'The *Apocalypse of Peter:* A Jewish Christian Apocalypse from the Time of Bar Kokhba,' *Apocrypha* 5 (1994) 7-111 (= chapter 8 below).

[2] The Gedulat Moshe also has an independent interest in the cosmology and angelology of the seven heavens.

[3] For a summary of these results, see the chart in Himmelfarb, *Tours,* 170.

[4] Himmelfarb, *Tours,* chap. 2.

stream in the development of tour apocalypses in the centuries after the Book of Watchers.'[5] This important conclusion serves to place the tours of hell firmly within the tradition of Jewish apocalyptic (and the tradition of Christian apocalyptic continuous with it), in opposition to Dieterich's influential argument[6] that the tour of hell in the Apocalypse of Peter (and therefore derivatively all the others) was a christianized version of a Greek (Orphic-Pythagorean) account of the punishments in Hades.

I reached independently some of the same conclusions as Himmelfarb on the relationship between these apocalypses and on the origin of the tradition in Jewish apocalyptic,[7] though I did not anticipate her use of the evidence of the 'demonstrative explanations' or much of the detail with which she has argued her case. In this article I intend to support and to make more precise the connexion she establishes between the tours of hell and the broader tradition of tour apocalypses. To a large extent, her argument for this connexion hinges on the demonstrative explanations, together with the interest in the subject of reward and punishment after death which the Book of Watchers and some other tour apocalypses show. Her argument that the Apocalypse of Zephaniah is particularly close in certain respects to the Book of Watchers and forms a kind of bridge between it and the apocalypses in which the tour of hell is more prominent than in the Apocalypse of Zephaniah is not very persuasive.[8] In the end, her argument leaves a gap between the cosmic tours, like that of Enoch, which do not include tours of hell, and the apocalypses exclusively concerned with the fate of the dead, which do include tours of hell. The main argument of this article is that the gap may be narrowed, perhaps even bridged, by closer attention to visions of hell which are not tours of the punishments in hell and to references to visions of hell which are not described.

Himmelfarb's work perhaps pays insufficient attention to the fact that the tours of hell presuppose a particular view of the fate of the wicked after death which was not always held in early Judaism and was far from universally held even in the first century c.e. This is that

---

[5] Himmelfarb, *Tours*, 169.

[6] A. Dieterich, *Nekyia: Beiträge zur Erklärung der neuentdeckten Petrus apokalypse* (2nd edition 1913, reprinted Stuttgart: Teubner, 1969).

[7] Bauckham, 'Apocalypse of Peter.'

[8] Himmelfarb, *Tours*, 151-153. These arguments are perhaps of some value in indicating a relatively early date for the Apocalypse of Zephaniah, but as similarities with the Book of Watchers they are outweighed by large differences, e.g. in the cosmography.

the active punishment of the wicked begins not at the last judgment, but already at death. Only because this is so can the seer in a tour of hell view the various punishments taking place at the time of his vision. In order to locate the origin of tours of hell within the tradition of tour apocalypses, it will therefore be necessary to pay close attention to the view of the fate of the wicked in the cosmic tour apocalypses. It may be that this will explain the absence of tours of hell from the most important cosmic tour apocalypses, and that the appearance of tours of hell is closely connected with belief in the punishment of the wicked immediately after death.

For this purpose we shall look closely at the visions of hell which are not tours of hell in the cosmic tour apocalypses. In the process we shall make a small contribution to the larger subject of the history of tour apocalypses (which has not yet been written in even the most preliminary way). Conclusions about the relation of cosmic tour apocalypses and tours of hell will then be drawn before we also consider two interesting references to visions of hell which are not in the context of tour apocalypses.

II Enoch's Cosmic Tours

The Enoch literature which we now know as 1 Enoch and 2 Enoch preserves five versions of Enoch's tour of the secrets of the cosmos: (1) 1 Enoch 17-19; (2) 1 Enoch 21-36; (3) 1 Enoch 41; 43-44; (4) 2 Enoch 3-22; (5) 2 Enoch 40-42. The first two of these, both now belonging to the Book of Watchers (1-36), from the third or early second century B.C.E., and separated by the list of the seven archangels in chapter 20, overlap and were probably originally alternative versions of Enoch's tour of the cosmos.[9] The third version (1 En 41; 43-44) forms part of the first of the Parables of Enoch. This first parable (1 En 38-44) seems as a whole to be parallel to the Book of Watchers: chapter 38 parallels the introductory prophecy of the day of judgment in 1 Enoch 1-5; chapter 39:1-2 briefly summarizes the story of the Watchers (1 En 6:1-14:7; 15-16); chapters 39:3-40:10 are an alternative account of Enoch's ascent to heaven (1 En 14:8-25); and chapters 41; 43-44 are an alternative account of Enoch's tour of the cosmos (1 En 17-19, 21-36). The third parable also contains fragments of a tour of the cosmos (1 En 59; 60:11-23) which could perhaps count as yet another version (cf. also 71:3-4). In 2 Enoch there is, first, an account

---

[9] M. Black, *The Book of Enoch or I Enoch* (SVTP 7; Leiden: Brill, 1985) 15-16.

of Enoch's ascent through the seven heavens[10] (3-22).[11] This is an adaptation of the tradition of Enoch's tour to the new cosmology of seven heavens. The sights which in the versions in 1 Enoch he sees at the furthest extremities of the earth are now distributed among the seven heavens, and his admission to the presence of God in heaven, which in 1 Enoch precedes the tour (1 En 14:8-25; 39:3-40:10), now becomes the culmination of his tour through the heavens. The second account of the tour in 2 Enoch is given when Enoch afterwards describes it to his sons (2 En 40-42). It is not just a summary of chapters 3-22, but a relatively independent account.

In keeping with the interests of the Enoch literature, all five of these versions of the tour have, along with the interest in cosmological and meteorological secrets, some degree of reference to the final judgment, but they are by no means all equally concerned with the fate of wicked people after death. The first version (1 En 17-19) has no reference to the dead at all,[12] but continues the main theme of the Book of Watchers by climaxing in Enoch's view of the place where the seven erring stars and the Watchers are punished until the day of judgment (18:10-19:2). The second version (1 En 21-36) begins with two distinct places for punishment for the seven stars and the Watchers (21), but continues with a visit to Sheol, the first in Jewish literature (22). Sheol, with its four chambers for different classes of the dead, seems to be portrayed as, for the wicked, not a place of punishment,[13] but a place of detention, where they await their punishment at the day of judgment. In this second version of the tour, Enoch also sees the place of punishment for the wicked after the last judgment (located literally in the valley of Hinnom: 26:3-27:4), though the pun-

---

[10] The extension of the scheme to ten heavens in some manuscripts of the longer recension (20-22J) must be regarded as secondary: cf. F. I. Andersen in Charlesworth ed., *Old Testament Pseudepigrapha*, vol. 1, 135 n., 136 n.

[11] References to 2 Enoch are to the translation by F. I. Andersen in Charlesworth ed., *The Old Testament Pseudepigrapha*, vol. 1, 102-221, and use the letters J and A to refer to his translations of the longer and shorter recensions respectively, which are represented by manuscripts J and A. An exclusive preference for either the longer or the shorter recension as more original would probably be mistaken.

[12] There is probably not even a passing explicit reference to Sheol in 17:6 (cf. Black, *Enoch*, 157), though the mountain of 17:2 seems to be that in which the four hollows of Sheol are situated according to 22:1-2.

[13] The phrase, 'for this great torment' (εἰς τὴν μεγάλην βάσανον), in 1 Enoch 22:11 is difficult. It has often been taken to mean that the wicked are already suffering punishment in Sheol, but no fire or other means of punishment are mentioned: the 'hollows' for the souls of the wicked are simply dark. It may mean that the wicked have already been set apart for torment at the last day. If it refers to present torment, the reference must be to the kind of anguished fear of the judgment to come to which 4 Ezra 7:79-87 refers.

ishment itself is not described, and the future paradise around the earthly throne of God and the tree of life, where the righteous will dwell after the judgment (24:3-25:7). In the third version (1 En 41; 43-44), an obscure reference to the judgment of the wicked seems to be a vision of their removal from the presence of the righteous for punishment at the last day (41:2; cf. 38:3). There is no interest in their fate after death prior to the judgment.

In the account of Enoch's tour of the seven heavens (2 En 3-22) both paradise and hell (not so called) are located in the third heaven, or at least are viewed from there (8:1J; 10:1; cf. 40:12J; 42:3J). They are presented in parallel as, respectively, the place prepared for the righteous as an eternal inheritance (9:1) and the place prepared for the wicked as an eternal reward (10:4, 6).[14] There is no indication that either has any human occupants as yet, when Enoch views them, though both are furnished with appropriate angelic occupants. The account of hell mentions 'all kinds of torture and torment' and 'dark and merciless angels, carrying instruments of atrocities torturing without pity' (10:1, 3J; cf. the angels of punishments with scourges and fetters in 1 En 53:3; 56:1; 62:11; 63:1).[15] If this might seem to suggest that there must be prisoners being tortured, they are pointedly not mentioned. The place 'has been prepared for those' who practice sins which are listed in detail (10:4-5). The account seems on the brink of becoming a description of the various punishments meted out to various types of sinners, but it does not. Since the punishments are not yet taking place, a vision of this Gehenna as it now is, merely awaiting the wicked, can hardly describe them. Sheol, the place of detention until the judgment, is not included in the tour.

Enoch's account of his tour to his sons (2 En 40-42) also describes hell (now so called: 40:12-42:2)[16] and paradise (42:3-5). Hell seems now to have its traditional location in the abyss (40:12J) and the wicked are now mentioned: 'And I saw how the prisoners were in pain, looking forward to endless punishment' (40:13J), or, 'and I saw

---

[14] For the angels of punishment in tours of hell, see Himmelfarb, *Tours,* 120-121.

[15] Note also the parallelism between Enoch's exclamation on seeing paradise—'How very pleasant is this place!' (8:8)—and his exclamation on seeing hell—'How very frightful/terrible is this place!' (10:4); cf. 1 Enoch 21:9; 24:5; 32:5. For the parallelism of the accounts of paradise and hell, see also U. Fischer, *Eschatologie und Jenseitserwartung im hellenistischen Diasporajudentum* (BZNT 44; Berlin/New York: de Gruyter, 1978) 48-49.

[16] Fischer, *Eschatologie und Jenseitserwartung,* 51, takes 40:12-42:2 to refer to the place of judgment of the fallen angels. This is mistaken, as 41:2 shows.

there a certain plain,[17] like a prison, an unbounded judgment'
(40:13A). Enoch records their deeds and their sentences.[18]

Despite the obscurity of the text in the light of the two versions, it
seems that the wicked dead are not in hell, but observe it, knowing
they are condemned to it, and suffer the pain of anticipating their
future punishment. This meaning seems confirmed by other accounts
which offer a similar picture. In the extended account of the intermediate state in 4 Ezra 7:75-101, it is explained that after death the souls
of the dead have seven days of freedom, during which they see the
rewards awaiting the righteous and the torments awaiting the wicked.
The wicked are therefore sad in anticipation and the righteous rejoice
in anticipation of the destiny awaiting them, but the rewards and
punishments themselves are reserved for the last day. After the seven
days the righteous enter into their chambers, where they rest in
quietness until the end, but the wicked, it seems, do not have chambers, but continue to wander around in tormented awareness of their
doom (7:80, 93). The same conception is found in the *De universo*,
which has been frequently ascribed to Hippolytus but according to a
recent study should be attributed to Tertullian.[19] In any case, it certainly preserves Jewish ideas about the intermediate state.[20] It recounts how both the righteous and the wicked are taken, after death,
to Hades, but assigned to different parts of Hades. The wicked are
dragged down to the environs of Gehenna, where they see the fire
and smoke of their future punishment, and suffer in fear and anticipation of it.

Even more interesting, however, is the survival of the same notion
in a Christian apocalypse contained in the final section of the Syriac
Transitus Mariae,[21] which in its present form must date from about

---

[17] But cf. the reading of *Merilo Pravednoe*, 'I saw there something more, like a
prison': Andersen in Charlesworth ed., *The Old Testament Pseudepigrapha*, vol. 1, 220
and n. x2.

[18] The explicit statement in 41:1J that Enoch sees all his ancestors there seems to
be a Christian addition, along with 42:5, which predicts their removal to paradise,
presumably by Christ at his descent to hell.

[19] C.E. Hill, 'Hades of Hippolytus or Tartarus of Tertullian? The Authorship of
the Fragment *De Universo*,' *VC* 43 (1989) 105-126.

[20] It is notable that while the account of the state of the dead in Hades alludes to
the parable of the rich man and Lazarus, it differs from the parable in denying that
the wicked are as yet in torment in fire. Their present suffering is only in antiicpation
of the fire of Gehenna.

[21] Translations in A. Smith Lewis, *Apocrypha Syriaca: The Protevangelium Jacobi and
Transitus Mariae* (Studia Sinaitica 11; London: C. J. Clay, 1902) 64-69; W. Wright,
'The Departure of my Lady Mary from the World,' *Journal of Sacred Literature* 7 (1865)
156-169; and cf. E. A. W. Budge, *The History of the Blessed Virgin Mary and The History
of the Likeness of Christ which the Jews of Tiberias made to mock at* (London: Luzac, 1899)

the fifth century C.E. It describes how the Virgin Mary, whose body after her death has been transported to the earthly paradise, is there raised up by Christ and taken by him on a tour of the heavens, in which she sees the treasuries of rain, winds, lightnings and so on, the angelic hierarchies, and then, in the highest heaven, the heavenly Jerusalem where God dwells. This has such close resemblances to such tours of the heavens as those of Levi (TLevi 3), Enoch (2 En 3-22) and Baruch (3 Baruch), that it must derive from the tradition of Jewish apocalyptic tours of the heavens. After the heavenly Jerusalem, the Virgin is shown the mansions of the righteous and the fires of hell. (It is worth noting that here there are the questions and 'demonstrative explanations' that Himmelfarb has identified as formal characteristics of the genre of tour apocalypses, including the tours of hell.[22]) The mansions are those which the righteous do not yet inhabit but will inherit on the day of resurrection. Similarly Gehenna is not yet inhabited by the wicked. Mary sees a place of darkness and roaring flames, and people standing near it, weeping. 'What are these?,' she asks, and receives from Christ the reply, 'This that is roaring is Gehenna, which is kindled for the wicked; and these who are standing and looking upon it are the sinners; and from a distance they are beholding their torment, and knowing for what they are reserved at the last day; for the day of judgment is not yet come, that they should receive the inheritance of darkness; and at the time of the judgment, those who have neglected my commands ... shall be tormented in this Gehenna.'[23] It must have been a similar scene that Enoch witnessed in 2 Enoch 40:13.

Thus the tradition of Enoch's cosmic tour acquired, in 2 Enoch, a strong emphasis on the horror of the torments of Gehenna prepared for the wicked in the future, but since these are not conceived as occurring before the day of judgment, a description of the wicked being punished in hell is not possible within the genre of the tour apocalypse, where the seer views the sights of the cosmos as they are in his time.

---

131. There are also Arabic and Ethiopic versions: Arabic translated in M. Enger, *Ahbār Yūhannā assalīh fī naqlat umm almasīh, id est Ioannis Apostoli de Transitu Beatae Mariae Virginis Liber* (Elberfeldae: Friderichs, 1854) 88-107; Ethiopic translated in M. Chaîne, *Apocrypha de Beata Maria Virgine* (CSCO 39-40; Rome: de Luigi, 1909) Latin section 39-42. Other forms of the assumption narrative contain a quite different apocalypse at the same point: for details, see chapter 13 below.

[22] Himmelfarb, *Tours*, chap. 2.

[23] Translation from Wright, 'Departure,' 159.

III ELIJAH'S COSMIC TOUR

The Hebrew Apocalypse of Elijah (Sefer Eliyahhu), which in its present form seems to date from the early Byzantine period,[24] consists largely of a prophecy of the last days, but it begins with a brief cosmic tour:

> The Spirit of God took me up and brought me[25] to the south of the world, and I saw there a high place, burning with fire, and no created being was able to enter there.
>
> Again the Spirit took me up and brought me to the east of the world, and I saw there [seven][26] stars fighting one against the other, and none of them resting.
>
> Again the Spirit took me up and brought me to the west of the world, and I saw there souls undergoing judgment in torment, each one according to his deeds.[27]

This tour is surely an abbreviated version of a once longer account. Such a brief account could hardly have been written for its own sake, while as an introduction to the prophecy which follows it serves no purpose. It should be remembered that apocalyptic literature was often transcribed with no great respect for its exact form. Scribes would abbreviate or omit material that was of no interest to them. It seems credible that an apocalypse which once consisted of a longer cosmic tour and an eschatological prophecy has been preserved for the sake of the latter, which has been expanded and updated, whereas the former has been abbreviated. The tour, in resembling Enoch's tours to the extremities of the world, has an archaic character. From at least the second century C.E. this form of tour was replaced by tours of the (usually seven) heavens (TLevi 2-5; 2 Enoch; 3

---

[24] M. Buttenwieser, *Der hebräische Elias-Apokalypse und ihre Stellung in der apokalyptischen Litteratur des rabbinischen Schrifttums und der Kirche* (Leipzig: Pfeiffer, 1897) 68-82; idem, *Outline of the Neo-Hebraic Apocalyptic Literature* (Cincinnati: Jennings & Pye, 1901) 30, argued that the original apocalypse was written in 261 C.E., but that the extant form of the work incorporates additions from the sixth and early seventh centuries C.E.

[25] This formula (based on Ezek. 11:1, 24 etc) is also used in a cosmic tour apocalypse (seven heavens apocalypse) in the fragment of an Apocalypse of Zephaniah quoted by Clement of Alexandria, *Strom.* 5.11.77; cf. also the NHApPaul 19:20-23.

[26] 'seven,' not in Buttenwieser's text, is in the variant text published by Ibn Schmuel, translated by G. W. Buchanan, *Revelation and Redemption: Jewish Documents of Deliverance from the Fall of Jerusalem to the Death of Nahmanides* (Dillsboro, North Carolina: Western North Carolina Press, 1978) 428.

[27] My translation of the Hebrew text in Buttenwieser, *Der hebräische Elias-Apokalypse*, 15. Buchanan, *Revelation and Redemption*, 427-28, also translates a variant text published by Y. Ibn Schmuel: the biblical quotations in the latter are clearly secondary additions.

Baruch; Syriac Transitus Mariae; Gedulat Moshe; cf. ApAb 19; b. Ḥag. 12b).

The sights Elijah sees on his tour can be identified from Enoch's tours in the Book of Watchers, though the points of the compass do not correspond and the descriptions notably differ. The high place in the south must be the central of Enoch's seven mountains (1 En 18:6-8; 24-25), which do not themselves burn with fire but are protected by mountains of fire (18:9; 24:1). On this mountain is God's earthly throne (25:3) and the tree of life which no flesh will be allowed to touch until the day of judgment (25:4). The stars Elijah sees in the east must be the seven erring stars of 1 En 18:13-16; 21:3-6. In 1 Enoch they are bound in an abyss of fire. Their perpetual warfare in the Apocalypse of Elijah is perhaps an alternative form of punishment.[28]

The place of the dead which Elijah sees is in the west, like Enoch's Sheol (1 En 22), but in Elijah's case he sees the souls of the wicked already being punished in it. Very signicant is the phrase, 'each one according to his deed,'[29] which suggests that in a fuller account Elijah would have seen a variety of torments corresponding to the various sins of the souls. Precisely such an account is attributed to Elijah in a quotation in the apocryphal Latin Epistle of Titus:

> The angel of the Lord showed me a deep valley, which is called Gehenna, burning with sulphur and pitch, and in that place are many souls of sinners, and there they are tormented with various tortures. [A list of punishments, mostly by hanging, follows.] By these various tortures the acts of each are shown forth. [An explanation of which sins are punished by which torments follows.][30]

The sentence in the Hebrew Apocalypse of Elijah is a neat and precise summary of this account. It should be noted that, as well as the correspondence in substance, both refer to the wicked in hell as 'souls' (נפשות, *animae*). This is very unusual in tours of hell,[31] though it is also found in the Apocalypse of Zephaniah (2:8; 10:3).

The Latin quotation has been widely regarded as taken from an early Jewish Apocalypse of Elijah,[32] from which several other quota-

---

[28] For the idea that the powers of evil are engaged in constant fighting with each other, see AscenIs 7:9-12; 10:29-31.

[29] For the phrase with reference to punishments in Gehenna, see ApPet 13:3.

[30] Translation from M. Stone and J. Strugnell, *The Books of Elijah: Parts 1-2* (SBLTT 18; Missoula, Montana: Scholars Press, 1979) 14 (the Latin text is on p.15). Probably even this quotation is abbreviated: the explanations of the torments would probably have originally been given by the angel in response to questions by Elijah.

[31] Note the use of 'souls' in 1 En 22:3-13.

[32] M. R. James, *The Lost Apocrypha of the Old Testament* (London: SPCK, 1920) 53-61; M. E. Stone, 'The Metamorphosis of Ezra: Jewish Apocalypses and Medieval

tions are known.[33] Didymus the Blind seems to refer to this Apocalypse when he writes, with reference to the parable of Dives and Lazarus, that 'in Hades there are different regions. There is a place of rest there and another of condemnation. This is said in the Apocalypse of Elijah.'[34] (Didymus naturally speaks of Hades because it is a question of the state of souls after death and prior to the last judgment.) This reference shows, what we would in any case expect, that Elijah saw the place of the righteous dead as well as the place of punishment for the wicked.

Vision,' *JTS* 33 (1982) 7 n. 3; 9; Rosenstiehl, 'Les révélations d'Élie'; Himmelfarb, Tours, 34-36, 131-32, 169. D. Frankfurter, *Elijah in Upper Egypt: The Apocalypse of Elijah and Early Egyptian Christianity* (Studies in Antiquity and Christianity; Minneapolis: Fortress Press, 1993) chapter 2, is right to hold that the Coptic Apocalypse of Elijah (which he argues was written in Egypt in the third century C.E.) is quite distinct from the work or works attributed to Elijah in other sources and from the Hebrew Apocalypse of Elijah. But he is too cautious in thinking of a variety of such Elianic works and traditions, rather than a single ancient Apocalypse of Elijah (first century C.E. at the latest), from which the Letter of Titus quotes, to which Origen (*Comm. Matt.* on Matt 27:9) Didymus (*Comm. Eccl.* 92.5) and Jerome (*Comm. Is.* 17, on Isa 64:4; *Ep.* 57) refer (and cf. the further references to a cosmic tour by Elijah in Frankfurter, *Elijah* , 60-61), and from which the Hebrew Apocalypse of Elijah later developed. The coherence of the material provides a strong case for this.

[33] Collected in Stone and Strugnell, *Books of Elijah*; and in E. Schürer, *The History of the Jewish People in the Age of Jesus Christ (175 B.C.—A.D. 135)*, ed. G. Vermes, F. Millar, M. Goodman, vol. 3/2 (Edinburgh: T. & T. Clark, 1987) 799-803. Surprisingly, Stone and Strugnell miss the fact the third fragment for which they collect testimonies ('What no eye has seen nor ear heard...') finds a trace in the Hebrew Apocalypse of Elijah: 'But the eye cannot see the greatness and glory which the holy One blessed be he will provide for his sons' (trans. Buchanan, *Revelation and Redemption*, 438).

[34] Didymus, *Comm. Eccles.* 92.5-6 on Eccles 3:16 (in M. Gronewald ed., *Didymos der Blinde: Kommentar zum Ecclesiastes (Tura-Papyrus)*, vol. 2 [Papyrologische Texte und Abhandlungen 22; Bonn: Rudolf Habelt, 1977] 130): καὶ γὰρ ἐν τῷ ᾅδῃ διάφορα χωρία ἐστίν· καὶ ἔστιν ἀναπαύσεως ἐκεῖ τόπος καὶ ἄλλος καταδίκης. τοῦτο ἐν τῇ ἀποκαλύψει Ἠλία φέρεται. Elsewhere (*Comm. Eccles.* 235.27-28 on Eccles 8:4b-5a) Didymus refers to the Prophecy of Elijah. This latter reference is certainly to the extant Coptic Apocalypse of Elijah, as is another reference by Didymus to 'an apocryphal book' (*Comm. Zech.* 77.19 [342] on Zech 4:11-14). Although the editors of Didymus' commentary on Ecclesiastes assume that he referred to the same apocryphon of Elijah in all three cases (J. Kramer and B. Krebber ed., *Didymos der Blinde: Kommentar zum Ecclesiastes (Tura-Papyrus)*, vol. 2 [Papyrologische Texte und Abhandlungen 16; Bonn: Rudolf Habelt, 1972] 159-161), Frankfurter, *Elijah*, 24, 43, 46, rightly argues that only the latter two are to the Coptic Apocalypse of Elijah, which is, in fact, more appropriately described as a Prophecy of Elijah, the title Didymus gives it in *Comm. Eccles.* 235.27-28. A revelation of the places of the dead, to which Didymus, *Comm. Eccles.* 92.5-6, must refer, would not belong in the extant Coptic Apocalypse of Elijah, but is precisely the content of the aprocryphon of Elijah which is quoted in the apocryphal Epistle of Titus.

The account of the hanging punishments in hell in the quotation in the apocryphal Epistle of Titus is close to that in the Apocalypse of Peter. It is an important early example of that genre of tours of hell which Himmelfarb has studied. If we are correct in seeing it as part of a cosmic tour of Elijah which the Hebrew Apocalypse of Elijah summarizes, then we have discovered a point at which the tradition of tours of hell emerges within the genre of cosmic tours. Moreover, it emerges in a cosmic tour which is closely related to the earliest versions of Enoch's cosmic tour, in the Book of Watchers, and must date from a relatively early period, before a tour of the heavens replaced a tour of the extremities of the earth as the standard form of a cosmic tour.

IV Moses' Cosmic Tours

Although no full ancient apocalypse survives describing a cosmic tour by Moses, there are two summary accounts of such tours in works of the first century c.e. One is in the *Liber Antiquitatum Biblicarum* of Pseudo-Philo (LAB) 19:10,[35] which expands the account of Deuteronomy 34:1-4, according to which God showed Moses the promised land from the top of mount Nebo before his death, into a revelation of the secrets of the heavens:

> And he showed him the place from which the clouds draw up water to water the whole earth, and the place from which the river takes its water, and the land of Egypt, and the place in the firmament from which the holy land drinks. And he showed him the place from which the manna rained upon the people, even unto the paths of paradise. And he showed him the measurements of the sanctuary and the number of sacrifices and the signs by which they are to interpret the heaven.'[36]

It is notable that several of these items are found in cosmic tours. The place from which the clouds draw water was seen by Baruch in the fourth heaven (3 Bar 10:6-8). Enoch saw the mouth of all the rivers in the far West (1 En 17:8). According to rabbinic tradition, manna was produced in the third heaven (b. Ḥag. 12b). On the whole this looks like a visit to the lower heavens (not reaching the throne of God in the highest heaven) rather than to the extremities of the earth. The

---

[35] On this passage, see M. Stone, 'Lists of Revealed Things in the Apocalyptic Literature,' in F. M. Cross, W. E. Lemke, P. D. Miller, Jr., ed., *Magnalia Dei: The Mighty Acts of God: Essays on the Bible and Archaeology in Memory of G. Ernest Wright* (Garden City, New York: Doubleday, 1976) 418.

[36] Translation by D. J. Harrington in J. H. Charlesworth ed., *The Old Testament Pseudepigrapha*, vol. 2 (London: Darton, Longman & Todd, 1985) 327-328.

specifically Mosaic items are 'the measurements of the sanctuary' (cf. Exod 25:9; 26:30; LAB 11:15) and 'the number of sacrifices,' though both show the concern for measuring and numbering that is characteristic of some tour apocalypses (e.g. 2 En 40:2-12). It is curious to find these items revealed to Moses at this point, rather than on mount Sinai (cf. LAB 11:15). From their recurrence in 2 Baruch 59:4, 9 (see below) they would seem to be traditional items of revelation to Moses.

It is doubtful whether this is a summary of an actual apocalypse. Rather it is probably an attribution to Moses of the kind of revelation of the contents of the heavens which the author knew in tour apocalypses of which the subjects were other seers. Later Jewish exegetical tradition (Sifre Deut 357) also interpreted Deuteronomy 34:1-4 as an apocalyptic revelation to Moses, but of a quite different kind. Instead of a tour of the heavens, Moses is given a vision of future history and eschatology. An elaborate interpretation of the names in vv 1-3 makes out of them a revelation of the future history of Israel until the end, while 'the city of palm trees' (v 3) is understood to be paradise and 'Zoar' (v 3) is taken to be Gehenna. But this interpretation, which unlike LAB 19:10 attributes to Moses a vision of hell before his death, cannot be traced to an early period.

The second early account of a cosmic tour attributed to Moses is in 2 Baruch 59:4-11.[37] This tour takes place at the time of the revelation on Sinai, when God 'took Moses to him' (59:3). Presumably, therefore, this is a tour primarily of the heavens. It has only two items in common with LAB 19:10: the measurements of the heavenly sanctuary[38] (59:4) and 'the number of offerings'[39] (59:9). Significantly, these specifically Mosaic items of revelation are placed respectively at the beginning[40] and about half way through the list of revealed things, while the last item is also a specially Mosaic one: 'the investigations of the law.' These strategically placed items give a Mosaic character to what is otherwise mainly a list of the kind of things

---

[37] On this passage and its links with other 'lists of revealed things' in the apocalypses, see Stone, 'Lists of Revealed Things,' 414-419.

[38] Here the Arabic version seems to be preferable: 'the shape of Zion with its appearance so that the holy temple could be made according to its measure' (translation from F. Leemhuis, A. F. J. Klijn, G. J. H. van Gelder, *The Arabic Text of the Apocalypse of Baruch edited and translated with a parallel translation of the Syriac text* [Leiden: Brill, 1986] 90).

[39] Translations of the Syriac of 2 Baruch are from Leemhuis, Klijn and van Gelder, *Arabic Text*.

[40] Preceded by 'the manners of the laws and the termination of time' (59:4a). The latter is also paralleled in the LAB's account of the revelation to Moses before his death (19:14-15).

revealed in other tours of the cosmos.[41] Another significant feature, however, is that some items are not cosmic but eschatological secrets, i.e. they could not have been seen by Moses in a tour of what there is now to be seen in the cosmos, but only in prophetic visions of the future. The list therefore goes beyond the Enochic tours to include visions of the future such as can be found in other parts of the Enoch literature, such as the Apocalypse of Weeks and the Animal Apocalypse. A parallel to the combination of the tour of the cosmos and visions of the eschatological future can be found in the Parables of Enoch, especially the third (1 En 58-69).

Many of the items in the earlier part of the list correspond to those which in a tradition of Wisdom origin are listed as hidden things that only God knows. This wisdom tradition seems to have partly influenced the phrasing and arrangement of the list. But such items are also paralleled in the tour apocalypses as secrets which are revealed to the apocalyptic seer.[42] In the following table references are given only to Enoch's tours and closely related passages in the Enoch literature. The Enochic eschatological visions are not included.

2 Baruch 59:4-11	*Hidden wisdom*	*Enoch's tours*
the manners of the laws		
the termination of times		[LAB 19:14-15]
the likeness of Zion...		[LAB 19:10]
the measures of fire	2 Bar 48:4; 4 Ezra 4:5	
the depths of the abyss	Sir 1:3; 2 Bar 48:5[43]	2 En 40:12
the weight of the winds	2 Bar 48:2; 4 Ezra 4:5[44]	1 En 60:12; 2 En 40:11
the number of raindrops	2 En 47:5; Sir 1:2[45]	1 En 60:21-2; 2 En 40:8
the suppression of wrath		
the multitude of long-suffering		1 En 71:3; 1 En 41:1
the truth of judgment		

---

[41] The form of the list—phrases composed of nouns in a genitival relationship—finds a parallel in the much briefer list in 2 En 23:1: cf. Stone, 'Lists of Revealed Things,' 416.

[42] For the correspondence between the hidden secrets of wisdom and the secrets revealed in apocalyptic literature, see Stone, 'Lists of Revealed Things,' 414-439; I. Gruenwald, *Apocalyptic and Merkavah Mysticism* (AGJU 14; Leiden/Köln: Brill, 1980) 6-16.

[43] Cf. also Job 38:16.

[44] Cf. also Job 28:23.

[45] Cf. also 4 Ezra 5:36; 2 Bar 21:8; 2 En 47:5.

the root of wisdom[46]	Sir 1:6	⎫
the richness of understanding[47]		⎬ 1 En 48:1 (?)
the fountain of knowledge[48]		⎭
the height of the air	Sir 1:3; 1 En 93:14[49]	2 En 40:12
the greatness of paradise	cf 4 Ezra 4:7	1 En 70:3
the end of the ages	Sir 1:2(?) [Wis 7:18]	
the beginning of the day of judgment		
the number of offerings		[LAB 19:10]
the earths that have not yet come		
the mouth of hell	cf 4 Ezra 4:7	2 En 40:12
the standing-place of vengeance	2 En 40:12 (?)	
the place of belief		⎫
the region of hope		⎬ 1 En 22:9 (?)
the likeness of the coming torment		⎭ 2 En 40:12J (?)
the multitude of angels that have no number[50]		1 En 40:1; 71:8-9
the powers of the flame		1 En 17:3 (?)
the splendour of lightnings		⎫ 1 En 17:3; 41:3; ⎬ 43:1; 59:1-3; 60:13-⎭ 15; 2 En 40:9
the voice of the thunders		
the ranks of the archangels		1 En 40:2-10; 2 En 19-20
the treasuries of light	Job 38:19,24 (?)	1 En 41:5 (?)
the changes of the times	[Wis 7:18]	2 En 13; 23:1; 40:6
the investigations of the law		3 En 11:1 (?)

The arrangement of items in the list is not as haphazard as it might first appear. Most items clearly fall into groups. The earlier part of the list is especially related to the tradition of secret wisdom and shares its emphasis on measuring and counting, which is also reflected in the tour apocalypses, especially 2 Enoch (e.g. 40:2-12).[51]

---

[46] For the phrase, cf. Wis 3:15; Sir 1:20; 2 Bar 51:3.
[47] For the phrase, cf. 2 Bar 61:4.
[48] For the phrase, cf. Bar 3:12; 4 Ezra 14:47.
[49] Cf. also Armenian 4 Ezra 5:36A.
[50] Cf. 2 Bar 48:10; 56:14.
[51] For this emphasis in 3 Baruch, see M. Dean-Otting, *Heavenly Journeys: A Study of the Motif in Hellenistic Jewish Literature* (Judentum und Umwelt 8; Frankfurt am Main/Bern/New York: Peter Lang, 1984) 153-155.

This earlier part of the list begins and ends with groups of measured items; between them come a group of items referring to the divine qualities of mercy and judgment, and a group referring to the divine wisdom. The 'greatness [i.e. large measurements] of paradise' ends this part of the list, but also leads into the middle section which is especially concerned with eschatological matters. The final section concerns the angels and the meteorological phenomena and calendrical matters which they control. This analysis highlights the fact that the three specially Mosaic items ('the likeness of Zion,' 'the number of offerings,' 'the investigations of the law') are unrelated to the rest of the list but placed in such a way as to frame it.

The meaning of the sequence of five items beginning with 'the mouth of hell' is not entirely clear, but almost certainly indicates that the wicked are not yet suffering punishment in hell, as the eschatology of 2 Baruch would in any case suggest (cf. 30:5). Probably Moses sees the open mouth of the abyss, like Enoch in 2 Enoch 40:12. The 'standing-place of vengeance,' perhaps equivalent to the 'place of condemnation' in 2 Enoch 40:12, may be the place where the souls of the wicked await the judgment, and in that case 'the place of faith' and 'the region of hope' may be the chambers of the souls of the righteous in Sheol, where they await their future reward.

Of particular interest is the last item: 'the likeness of the coming torment.' This must indicate a vision of the future punishment of the wicked in Gehenna after the judgment. In the Apocalypse of Peter Christ shows Peter 'in his right-hand palm the image which will be fulfilled in the last day; and how the righteous and the sinners will be separated and how the upright of heart will do and how the evildoers will be rooted out forever and ever. We saw how the sinners will weep in great affliction...' (3:2-3).[52] Similarly, Abraham's symbolic vision of the history of the world from the beginning to the end is called a 'picture' of creation (ApAb 22:1; 23:1, 4; 24:3; 26:7; 27:1).

There are a few recorded visions of the punishment of the wicked in Gehenna at the end, attributed to Enoch (1 En 54:1-2; 90:26-27), Abraham (LAB 23:6; Tg Neof Gen 15:17: see section VII below) and Elijah (Hebrew Apocalypse of Elijah[53]). They are all brief; none describes a variety of punishments as the tours of hell do. The Apocalypse of Peter is somewhat different, since chapters 7-12 describe in detail the various punishments of the wicked in Gehenna in the form of a prophecy spoken by Christ to the apostles. It is not clear whether

---

[52] Translation from Buchholz, *Your Eyes Will Be Opened*, 177.

[53] Buttenwieser, *Der hebräische Elias-Apokalypse*, 66. See also the apocryphal Greek Apocalypse of John, especially the ending according to MS.E.

this prophecy is intended to spell out the content of the vision Peter and the apostles saw according to 3:3 (quoted above), but it is not presented in the form of a vision. The prophecy is very closely related in content to the tours of hell in the Elijah fragment, the Apocalypse of Paul and the other texts studied by Himmelfarb, but it is not in the form of a tour of hell (and therefore lacks questions by the seer[54]). It is clear that it must be closely based on one of the tours of hell, but has transposed what in its source a seer saw as now taking place in hell into a prophecy of what will take place in Gehenna after the judgment.[55] Apocalypse of Peter 7-12 is a unique case which is not likely to represent what the author of 2 Baruch had in mind.

So it is likely that the author of 2 Baruch conceived 'the likeness of the coming torment' which Moses saw as a vision of the consigning of the wicked to Gehenna at the last judgment, but not as a detailed description of a variety of punishments in Gehenna. It is not possible to be sure whether in 59:4-11 he was summarizing the contents of an actual apocalypse of Moses, modelled on the tour apocalypses of Enoch, or whether he simply himself attributed to Moses a cosmic tour like that of Enoch, perhaps out of hostility to the Enoch literature and a desire to exalt the figure of Moses instead of Enoch.[56] The arrangement of the list probably favours the latter alternative.[57] In that case, it is probable that he had Enoch's visions of the future judgment of the wicked in mind.

In the medieval Hebrew Gedulat Moshe[58] Moses is taken through the seven heavens with Metatron (Enoch) as his guide, and then tours the punishments in hell and visits paradise, but rather few of the contents of this work correspond to the list in 2 Baruch 59:4-11.[59] If

---

[54] Noted, but not correctly explained, by Himmelfarb, *Tours*, 56.

[55] The Akhmim Greek fragment of the Apocalypse of Peter restores the account of hell to the form of a vision ('I saw': vv 21, 25, 26). But this is a later, adapted form of the original apocalypse (see Bauckham, 'Apocalypse of Peter,' 4713-4718). That the visionary form here is secondary can be seen from the fact that the seer (Peter) asks no questions, while the 'demonstrative explanations' are not ascribed to his guide (Christ) but are simply part of the narration.

[56] So R. H. Charles, *The Apocalypse of Baruch* (London: A. & C. Black, 1896), 101.

[57] As Stone, 'Lists of Revealed Things,' 414-419, shows, this and similar lists in apocalyptic literature have a common form. But the items included in such lists vary. It is therefore unlikely that 2 Bar 54:5-11 reproduces precisely a list already fixed in tradition.

[58] Texts listed in J. T. Townsend, 'Minor Midrashim,' in Y. H. Yerushalmi ed., *Bibliographical Essays in Medieval Jewish Studies* (New York: Ktav, 1976), 375; translation in M. Gaster, 'Hebrew Visions of Hell and Paradise,' in *Texts and Studies*, vol. 1 (London: Maggs, 1925-28) 125-141.

[59] The following parallels are perhaps worth noting: in the fourth heaven Moses sees the heavenly temple; in the seventh he sees two chained angels who are wrath and anger; paradise is immeasurably great.

the latter does describe an actual apocalypse, this is not likely to have been either the Gedulat Moshe or even an earlier form of it.[60] However, the Gedulat Moshe is important for our purposes because its hell is one in which the wicked are already punished, and Moses' visit to it belongs unequivocally to the genre of tours of the punishments in hell which Himmelfarb has studied. Moreover, the Gedulat Moshe as a whole is a genuine cosmic tour. The major sections on hell and paradise give it a strong emphasis on the fate of the dead, but Moses' ascent through the seven heavens resembles the tours of the seven heavens in 2 Enoch and 3 Baruch, and is occupied with the cosmological and angelological concerns typical of tour apocalypses.[61] The particular structure of this apocalypse—an ascent through the heavens to the throne of God, followed by visits to hell and paradise, which are not placed within the scheme of seven heavens—is found also in the apocalypse in the Syriac Transitus Mariae, which we discussed in relation to 2 Enoch, and in the original form of 3 Baruch, as we shall see shortly.[62] Whatever its date in its present form,[63] the Gedulat Moshe must be based on a relatively early model, as is also suggested by some demonstrably early traditions within it, such as the hanging punishments in hell. Its importance for us is that, like the Hebrew Apocalypse of Elijah, it demonstrates the emergence of the tour of the punishments in hell within the genre of the cosmic tour. Unfortunately, it does not help us to date that emergence.

V BARUCH'S COSMIC TOUR

The work known as 3 Baruch, an apocalypse in the form of a tour of the heavens, is extant in Slavonic and Greek versions. There seems good reason for supposing that the Slavonic version, which shows less Christian reworking than the Greek, represents the original work in important respects better than does the extant Greek text.[64] In particular, it is likely that the references to the wicked and the righteous

---

[60] Contra I. Lévy, *La Légende de Pythagore de Grèce en Palestine* (BEHE.H 250; Paris: Librairie Ancienne Honoré Champion, 1927) 154-155.

[61] The strongly angelological interest in both 2 En 3-22 and Gedulat Moshe shows the tour of the seven heavens moving in the direction of the Hekhalot literature.

[62] This correspondence to the structure of other apocalypses indicates that S. Lieberman, 'On Sins and their Punishments,' in *Texts and Studies* (New York: Ktav, 1974) 29, may be wrong to call the Gedulat Moshe 'nothing but a collection from several different works.'

[63] I am not convinced by Lieberman's argument ('On Sins and their Punishments,' 29-30) for Muslim influence on it.

[64] H. E. Gaylord in Charlesworth ed., *The Old Testament Pseudepigrapha*, vol. 1, 657.

dead in the Slavonic version, which are quite different from those in the Greek version, are the more original.

The two versions agree on one curious and unique feature: in the first and second heavens Baruch sees two distinct groups of the people who built the tower of Babel, punished by being transformed into composite animal forms. These are perhaps substituted for the two groups of angelic Watchers which Enoch saw in the second and fifth heavens (2 En 7; 18).[65] It is remarkable that 3 Baruch, which throughout chapters 2-5 is preoccupied with the stories of Genesis 2-11, makes no reference to the Watchers. The author is perhaps engaged in a polemical rejection of the Enoch traditions, so that as well as substituting Baruch for Enoch he also substitutes the human builders of the Tower for the angelic Watchers. Instead of deriving evil on earth from the fall of the Watchers, he emphasizes its origin in the Garden of Eden (ch. 4).

The builders of the Tower are a special category of the wicked dead. About the location of the rest of the dead the two versions differ. According to the Greek, Hades is in the third heaven (4:3, 6[?]; 5:3), but this seems to be a secondary development of the information in the Slavonic that the belly of the serpent is as large as Hades (5:3). The Greek version interprets the birds which Baruch sees in the fourth heaven as the souls of the righteous (10:5), but again this seems to be a secondary interpretation. In the Slavonic the birds which praise God without ceasing (10:5) are not identified with human souls; they are probably heavenly creatures (like the phoenix which accompanies the sun in chapter 6). When the endings of the two versions are compared, it looks as though these secondary references to the dead in the Greek version are compensations for the omission of a full treatment of the righteous and the wicked dead which originally concluded the apocalypse.

In the Greek version Baruch ascends no further than the fifth heaven; he is not admitted through the door which leads to the heavenly temple beyond (presumably in the sixth or seventh heaven),[66]

---

[65] Probably the Watchers in the second heaven are those who sinned, while those in the fifth heaven did not sin but mourn for their brothers who did: W. J. Dalton, *Christ's Proclamation to the Spirits: A Study of 1 Peter 3:18-4:6* (AnBib 23; Rome: Pontifical Biblical Institute, 1965) 182.

[66] Even the Greek version clearly implies that there are more than five heavens, and since there is no parallel to the idea of six heavens, the usual number of seven heavens should probably be assumed. There is therefore no great difficulty in supposing that Origen's reference (*Princ.* 2.3.6) to a book of Baruch which clearly indicates seven heavens is to our 3 Baruch. But Origen's reference would have greater support from the longer ending of the apocalypse which our argument postulates in the following paragraphs.

but is rather abruptly returned to earth (17:1-2). However, the Slavonic has, before Baruch's return to earth, the following passage:

> And the angel said to me, 'By the command of the Ruler I say to you, Baruch, stand on the right side and you will see the glory of God. And you will see the resting-place of the righteous, glory and joy and rejoicing and celebration. And you will see the torture of the impious, wailing and groans and lamentations and the eternal worm. Their voice goes up to heaven and implores, "Have mercy on us, God."'
> And I Baruch said to the angel, 'Lord, who are these?'
> And he said to me, 'These are the sinners, having despised the command of God.'
> And I said to the angel, 'Permit me, Lord, to cry on their behalf.'
> And the angel said to me, 'You also may cry for them; perhaps the Lord God will hear your voice and have mercy on them.' (16:4-8)[67]

This passage is plainly an abbreviation of a longer account. The angel promises Baruch that he will (1) see the glory of God, presumably in the highest heaven; (2) see the abode of the righteous; and (3) see the torment of the wicked. The fulfilment of the first and second promises is unrecorded, and the account jumps from the third promise into the midst of its fulfilment. The account which has been summarized must have told of Baruch's further ascent to the throne of God in the seventh heaven, and then of visits to paradise and hell.

Several considerations favour the view that the Slavonic here abbreviates the original ending of the apocalypse, which the Greek has completely omitted. (1) The angel's promise 'you will see the glory of God' (16:4) takes up the promise which has been repeatedly made to Baruch since his arrival in the third heaven (4:2S; 6:12; 7:2; 11:2), usually in the form, 'Wait and you will see the glory of God' (6:12G; 7:2; 11:2). This promise is to be finally fulfilled when Baruch enters the heavenly throne-room of God in the seventh heaven, and sees God, as Enoch did (2 En 21-22). The earlier promises were not, as has been suggested,[68] fulfilled in Baruch's seeing the glory of the sun and the glory of Michael. Rather the command to 'Wait and you will see the glory of God' warns Baruch against confusing the glories of the lower heavens with the glory of God[69] which he will see only when he reaches the highest heaven. This is shown by the parallel

---

[67] Translation by Gaylord in Charlesworth ed., *The Old Testament Pseudepigrapha*, vol. 1, 678.

[68] Gaylord in Charlesworth ed., *The Old Testament Pseudepigrapha*, vol. 1, 678 n.

[69] Cf. Dean-Otting, *Heavenly Journeys*, 109-110, 135-137, 155-157. Her thesis of a polemic against sun-worship is hampered by her acceptance of the ending of the Greek version as original.

motifs which are used in the Ascension of Isaiah to direct Isaiah on from the glories of the lower heavens to the greater glory and his real goal in the seventh heaven (AscenIs 7:7-8, 17, 21-22; 8:7-9). (2) An ascent through the heavens which does not reach the presence of God in the seventh is unparalleled, and 3 Baruch's especially close resemblance to 2 Enoch leads one to expect Baruch to have seen God. (3) The Slavonic suggests that the original structure of 3 Baruch was: ascent through the seven heavens, visit to paradise, visit to hell. This structure, with paradise and hell not located within the seven heavens but outside and visited subsequently to a journey to the highest heaven, is paralleled in the apocalypse in the Syriac Transitus Mariae (where paradise precedes hell, as in 3 Bar 16) and in the Gedulat Moshe (where hell precedes paradise). (4) 16:5-6 use the question by the seer and the 'demonstrative explanation' by the angelic guide which are characteristic of the tour apocalypses and the tours of hell. (5) Baruch's prayer for mercy for the wicked in hell is a frequent feature of the tours of hell,[70] and is found in the apocalypse in the Transitus Mariae which is the closest parallel to the structure suggested for the original 3 Baruch.

In the apocalypse in the Transitus Mariae, the damned who cry for mercy are not yet tormented in hell, but only see and anticipate with dread their coming punishment at the last day. The Virgin Mary's plea on their behalf is for Christ to have mercy on them at the last judgment.[71] If the Slavonic summary of the original end of 3 Baruch can be trusted, Baruch, by contrast, saw the torments of hell already in progress. This would be consistent with the apocalypse's almost complete lack of reference to the day of judgment and the eschatological future (cf. 1:7).

We cannot tell whether Baruch's visit to hell was a real tour, viewing a variety of punishments, but at least we see once again, as in the Hebrew Apocalypse of Elijah and the Gedulat Moshe, a visit to a hell in which the wicked are already being punished taking its place within a cosmic tour apocalypse.[72]

---

[70] Cf. Bauckham, 'The Conflict of Justice and Mercy' (= chapter 6 below).

[71] Wright, 'Departure,' 159.

[72] Unfortunately it was not until after I had revised this chapter for this volume that I was able to see the important study of 3 Baruch by D. C. Harlow, *The Greek Apocalypse of Baruch (3 Baruch) in Hellenistic Judaism and Early Christianity* (Leiden: Brill, 1996): he dissents from my argument in this section.

VI Cosmic Tours and Tours of Hell

The preceding four sections have shown how, within the tradition of tour apocalypses, a transition from the belief that the punishment of the wicked will begin after the last judgment to the belief that it is already taking place in the intermediate state before the last judgment coincides with the emergence of visions of the punishments taking place in hell. Before that transition interest in the fate of the wicked was expressed in three forms: (a) a visit to the place where the wicked await their judgment (1 En 22; 2 En 40:13); (b) a visit to the hell which is already prepared for the wicked (1 En 26:3-27:4; 2 En 10; 40:12; 2 Bar 59:10); (c) a prophetic vision of the casting of the wicked into hell at the last judgment (1 En 41:2; 2 Bar 59:11). In none of these cases is there a description of the various punishments assigned to the various sins, such as is found in the tours of hell. A transition to belief in the punishment of the wicked immediately after death is indicated by visits to the place where the wicked are now being tormented (Hebrew Apocalypse of Elijah; 3 Bar 16:4-8; Gedulat Moshe). If we are correct in identifying the Latin Elijah fragment as the fuller version of Elijah's visit to hell as recounted in the Hebrew Apocalypse of Elijah, then the transition in this case gave birth to a tour of hell within the context of a cosmic tour apocalypse, as has also happened in the Gedulat Moshe. The full account of Baruch's visit to hell may well also have been a tour of the punishments.

The texts we have studied are also evidence of another transition: from the older form of cosmic tour in which the seer was taken to the extremities of the earth (1 Enoch; Hebrew Apocalypse of Elijah) to the later form in which the same sights are located within the seven heavens (2 Enoch; 3 Baruch; Gedulat Moshe). This transition cannot be dated precisely,[73] but it had certainly occurred by the second century c.e. and was most likely taking place during the first century c.e. The cosmic tour in the Hebrew Apocalypse of Elijah can scarcely originate later than the first century c.e.; it could be earlier. This makes the tour of hell in the Latin Elijah fragment probably the oldest extant tour of hell, and its context within a tour apocalypse all the more significant. But the transition from the older to the later view of the fate of the wicked does not correspond with the transition from the older to the later form of tour apocalypses: the older view of the fate of the wicked is still found in the tour of the seven heavens in

---

[73] The matter is complicated by a few possible references to a scheme of three heavens: Testament of Levi 3-4 seems to have undergone modification to increase an original three heavens to seven; cf. also Midrash Tehillim 114:2.

2 Enoch.[74] This confirms other evidence that belief in the punishment of the wicked in hell before the last judgment grew gradually. It was probably a minority view until well into the second century C.E.[75] Thus the first cosmic tour to include a tour of hell (Hebrew Apocalypse of Elijah) will have antedated some which did not (2 En 3-22; 2 Bar 59:4-11) as well as others which did (3 Baruch; Gedulat Moshe).

The link between the emergence of tours of hell and the transition to belief in the punishment of the wicked now suggests that the question of Greek influence on the tours of hell should be reopened. Himmelfarb's argument, against Dieterich, that the tours of hell were not simply borrowed from pagan Greek sources but developed within the Jewish apocalyptic tradition has been confirmed by our study. But, of course, this does not exclude Greek influence on the tours of hell. Jewish apocalyptic borrowed freely from many other cultural traditions. Some of the punishments in the Jewish and Christian tours of hell have clear precedents in Greek and Roman descriptions of punishments in Hades,[76] while there is also one striking parallel to a punishment in the tour of hell in the Egyptian story of Setme and Si-Osiris.[77] But it should also be noted that the Jewish and Christian tours of hell have in common with the Greek descents to Hades the assumption that the punishments of the wicked are taking place now. This assumption would have been most easily and vividly available in the form of the accounts of descents to Hades in which the various different punishments there were described, as seen by a visitor to Hades.[78] So it may be that Jewish apocalyptic borrowed from Greek (and perhaps Egyptian) sources both the idea of punishment immediately after death and also along with it some of the actual punishments depicted in the Jewish tours of hell. These did, of course, take up already traditional features of the Jewish Gehenna (fire, smoke, brimstone, worms), but precisely because the latter had never been described in detail, as consisting in a variety of specific punishments

---

[74] Cf. also the apocalypse of the Virgin in the Syriac Transitus Mariae, which has a tour of a plurality of heavens.

[75] Only one passage in the New Testament (Luke 16:19-31) refers to the punishment of the wicked immediately after death. Josephus, *Ant.* 18.14, claims the Pharisees believe there are post mortem rewards and punishments under the earth, but LAB, 2 Baruch and 4 Ezra all postpone the active punishment of the wicked until the last judgment. 4 Macc 18:5 (probably first century C.E.) refers to punishment immediately after death.

[76] Himmelfarb, *Tours*, 84, 92-93, 94-96, 107-108, 119.

[77] Himmelfarb, *Tours*, 79-81, 93-94, 111.

[78] On the Greek and Roman descents to Hades, see R. Bauckham, 'Descent to the Underworld,' in *The Anchor Bible Dictionary*, ed. D. N. Freedman, vol. 2 (New York: Doubleday, 1992) 145-159 (= chapter 1 above).

for specific sins, it did not provide sufficient material for a tour of hell. Thus it was in the development of the tours of hell that Greek and Egyptian accounts of the world of the dead would have proved useful sources of images for Jewish apocalyptists.

We now turn to two references to visions of hell outside the context of cosmic tours.

VII ABRAHAM'S VISION OF HELL

Abraham must rank with Enoch as a seer who might well have been given a tour of the punishments of hell but in fact was not. A tradition which goes back to the first century C.E. (LAB 23:6-7; 2 Bar 4:4; 4 Ezra 3:14; Apocalypse of Abraham)[79] and was continued in the Targums (to Gen 15:17) and rabbinic literature (GenRab 44:21; Pirqe de-Rabbi Eliezer 28; Pesikta Rabbati 15:2; Midrash Tehillim Ps 16:7; Mekilta Baḥodesh 9:24) interpreted Abraham's vision in Genesis 15 as an apocalyptic revelation of the future. In this context, although other aspects of the interpretation vary, the 'smoking furnace' of Genesis 15:17 was naturally and almost always understood to be Gehenna. The earliest extant example of this tradition, in LAB 23:6, takes the furnace and the torch of Genesis 15:17 to be respectively Gehenna and paradise: '[I] set before him the place of fire where the deeds of those doing wickedness against me will be expiated, and I showed him the torches of fire by which the just who have believed in me will be enlightened.'[80] There can be no doubt, within the eschatological outlook of LAB, that the reference is to the final destiny of the wicked and the righteous after the last judgment. The same reference is clear in Targum Neofiti, according to which Abraham saw seats being arranged and thrones erected—for the last judgment—immediately before he saw Gehenna. In the same Targum Abraham sees the wicked being cast into Gehenna. This vision is perhaps the kind of 'likeness of the coming torment' that Moses saw, according to 2 Baruch 59:11. Such an interpretation of Genesis 15:17 was not likely to produce an apocalypse describing the torments in Gehenna as seen by Abraham.

The Apocalypse of Abraham is a fullscale apocalypse based on Genesis 15, but it stands outside the tradition of interpretation we have described in not taking the furnace of 15:17 (ApAb 15:1) to be

---

[79] Two of these passages (LAB 23:6-7; Apocalypse of Abraham) are discussed in C. T. Begg, 'Rereadings of the "Animal Rite" of Genesis 15 in Early Jewish Narratives,' *CBQ* 50 (1988), 36-46, but with little reference to the visions of hell.

[80] Translation by Harrington in Charlesworth ed., *The Old Testament Pseudepigrapha*, vol. 2, 333.

the place of punishment for the wicked. It may be intended to symbolize the expanse of fire in the seventh heaven which envelops the angels and the throne of God (cf. 15:3, 6-7; 17:1; 18:1-3, 13; 19:1, 4). Admittedly, elsewhere the river of fire which flows from the heavenly throne is said to flow into Gehenna and become the fire in which the wicked are punished, but there is no trace of this concept in the Apocalypse of Abraham. Gehenna is mentioned later when Abraham looks down from the heavens and sees the whole of the earthly creation below, including 'the abyss and its torments,[81] and its lower depths and the perdition in it' (21:3). We cannot be sure that the punishments in hell are going on at the time of Abraham's ascent to heaven, because this is part of a visionary 'picture' of creation (22:1; cf. 21:1) in which a symbolic history of the world from creation to the judgment unfolds (cf. 31:2-5 for hell as the destiny of the wicked after the judgment).

It has been argued that another version of Abraham's vision in Genesis 15 is to be found in the Testament of Abraham (A10-14; B8-12).[82] This account of Abraham's journey above the earth and to the place of the judgment of souls in the far east may well have been inspired by aspects of the tradition of interpretation of Genesis 15, but it cannot be intended to be the vision of Genesis 15, since it is dated very shortly before Abraham's death (A15:1). In it Abraham does not see hell itself, only the judgment of souls after death and the consigning of some to eternal punishment.

VIII HEZEKIAH'S VISION OF HELL

Ascension of Isaiah 1:2b-4 refers to a vision of hell seen by king Hezekiah:

> ...the words of righteousness which the king himself had seen, and the judgments of this world [v.l. 'the eternal judgments'], and the torments of Gehenna, and the prince of this world [MSS 'and the place of punishment of this world,' 'which is the place of punishment of this world,' 'which is the eternal place of punishment'], and his angels, and his authorities, and his powers, and the words concerning faith in the Beloved which he himself had seen in the fifteenth year of his reign during his sickness. And he [Hezekiah] handed to him [his son Manasseh] the written words which Samnas the secretary had written out.[83]

---

[81] R. Rubinkiewicz in Charlesworth ed., *The Old Testament Pseudepigrapha*, vol. 1, 699 n., suggests that 'the abyss and its torments' may be a gloss.

[82] M. Delcor, *Le Testament d'Abraham* (SVTP 2; Leiden: Brill, 1973) 39-42.

[83] Translation adapted from that of M. A. Knibb in Charlesworth ed., *The Old Testament Pseudepigrapha*, vol. 2, 156.

Even though the last phrase in this description of Hezekiah's vision ('the words of faith in the Beloved') indicates that the reference is to a Christian composition, since 'the Beloved' is used throughout the Ascension of Isaiah to refer to the pre-incarnate Christ, it will be appropriate to consider it here. Himmelfarb's study shows how the Jewish and Christian traditions of visionary tours of hell are really a single tradition. Certainly at the time of writing of the Ascension of Isaiah (late first or early second century c.e.)[84] any sharp distinction between Jewish and Christian apocalypses is artificial.

The passage quoted has not usually been recognized as describing a vision of hell. This is largely due to the influence of R. H. Charles' interpretation of Ascension of Isaiah 1:2b-5,[85] which formed part of his source-critical theory of the composition of the Ascension of Isaiah.[86] The passage quoted above, describing Hezekiah's vision, is followed in v 5 by a description of the vision which Isaiah saw in the twentieth year of Hezekiah's reign and the written record of which Hezekiah also handed to his son Manasseh:

> concerning the judgment of the angels, and concerning the destruction of this world, and concerning the robes of the saints, and concerning the

---

[84] Cf. M. Erbetta, *Gli Apocrifi del Nuovo Testamento:* vol. 3: *Lettere e Apocalissi* (Casale Monferrato: Marietti, 1983), 180; Knibb in Charlesworth ed., *The Old Testament Pseudepigrapha*, vol. 2, 149-150; A. Acerbi, *Serra Lignea: Studi sulla Fortuna della Ascensione di Isaia* (Rome: Editrice A.V.E., 1984), 14-20; idem, *L'Ascensione di Isaia: Cristologia e profetismo in Siria nei primi decenni del II secolo* (Studia Patristica Mediolensia; Milan: Vita e Pensiiiero, 1989) 277-282; J. M. Knight, *Disciples of the Beloved One: The Christology, Social Setting and Theological Context of the Ascension of Isaiah* (JSPSS 18; Sheffield: Sheffield Academic Press, 1996) 33-39; E. Norelli, *Ascensio Isaiae: Commentarius* (CCSA 8; Turnhout: Brepols, 1995) 65-66. For an argument that the Ascension of Isaiah should be dated 70-80 c.e., see chapter 14 below.

[85] R. H. Charles, *The Ascension of Isaiah* (London: A. & C. Black, 1900), xiii-xiv, xxxix, xlii, 2, 29. Charles' view is criticized by James, *Lost Apocrypha*, 81-85; Knibb in Charlesworth ed., *The Old Testament Pseudepigrapha*, vol. 2, 147-148; M. Pesce, 'Presupposti per l'utilizzazzione storica dell'Ascensione di Isaia: Formazione e tradizione del testo; genere letterario; cosmologia angelica,' in M. Pesce ed., *Isaia, il Diletto e la Chiesa* (Testi e ricerche di Scienze religiose 20; Brescia: Paideia, 1983), 24-28, 40-45; Norelli, *Ascensio Isaiae: Commentarius*, 51-53; idem, *L'Ascensione di Isaia: Studi su un apocrifo al crocevia dei cristianesimi* (Origini NS 1; Bologna: Centro editoriale dehoniano, 1994) 45-49, 229-234.

[86] Charles' source-critical division of the Ascension of Isaiah, though still broadly followed by Knibb in Charlesworth ed., *The Old Testament Pseudepigrapha*, vol. 2, has been rejected by the Italian research team responsible for the new edition of the Ascension of Isaiah (CCSA 7-8), who see the whole work as originally Christian. See Pesce, 'Presupposti,' 22-29. E. Norelli thinks of different authors, from the same circle of Christian prophets, for chapters 6-11 and chapters 1-5 (Norelli, *Ascensio Isaiae: Commentarius*, 36-52; idem, *L'Ascensione*, 59-67), while A. Acerbi has a more complex theory of three Christian sources (Acerbi, *L'Ascensione*, chapter 8).

going out, and the transformation, and the persecution and ascension of the Beloved.[87]

The Ascension of Isaiah contains two reports of Isaiah's vision (3:13-4:22 and chapters 6-11). Charles supposed that the introduction to the book described the first of these as Hezekiah's vision (1:2b-4) and the second as Isaiah's (1:5). He thought that 3:13-4:22 had originally, before its incorporation in the Ascension of Isaiah, been part of a Testament of Hezekiah. This title (ἡ διαθήκη Ἐζεκίου) is given by the Byzantine chronicler George Cedrenus to a work in which he evidently read the passage which is now Ascension of Isaiah 4:12-18 and from which he quotes 4:12. Charles supposes that Cedrenus knew the work from which the compiler of the Ascension of Isaiah drew 3:13-4:22.

However, against Charles' theory, it must be said that this is not the most plausible interpretation of Cedrenus' evidence. That a work entitled the Testament of Hezekiah ever existed Cedrenus, writing in the eleventh century, is our only evidence. It is unlikely that one of the sources of the Ascension of Isaiah survived long enough to feature in Cedrenus' source[88] but left no other record of its survival. Moreover, Cedrenus himself places his quotation of 4:12 in the mouth of Isaiah, not Hezekiah.[89] The probability is that Cedrenus knew the whole of the Ascension of Isaiah under the title Testament of Hezekiah, since 1:1-6 could easily give the impression that the whole work is a testament of Hezekiah to his son Manasseh (cf. also 11:42-43). Indeed, this impression is by no means unjustified, since these verses describe how Hezekiah gave his son, as a kind of testament, a record of his own vision and a record of the vision of Isaiah which occupies much of the rest of the Ascension of Isaiah. The question remains, however, whether the vision of Hezekiah is recounted elsewhere in the book.

Charles' view that 1:2b-4 describes the vision recounted in 3:13-4:22 is implausible for two reasons: (1) The final editor of the Ascension of Isaiah, to whom Charles attributes 1:1-6, does not attribute 3:13-4:22 to Hezekiah, but very emphatically to Isaiah (3:13, 31; 4:1, 19-22). If he intended 1:2b-4 to refer to 3:13-4:22, he did his work

---

[87] The Ethiopic text of this verse ('their going out' and 'their transformation') should be corrected according to the Greek Legend 1:2: cf. Knibb in Charlesworth ed., *The Old Testament Pseudepigrapha*, vol. 2, 157 n., and cf. AscenIs 3:13.

[88] Cedrenus is probably reproducing a source: see Pesce, 'Presupposti,' 25; Acerbi, *Serra Lignea*, 64.

[89] Cf. Pesce, 'Presupposti,' 26; Knibb in Charlesworth ed., *The Old Testament Pseudepigrapha*, vol. 2, 147.

very incompetently. (2) The contents of 3:13-4:22 do not correspond to the description in 1:2b-4. The latter's reference to 'the torments of Gehenna'—which Hezekiah saw—is not satisfied by the brief reference to Gehenna in 4:14. We have enough descriptions of the torments of Gehenna in apocalyptic works to know what a second-century reader would have expected from that phrase. Moreover, as we shall see, the explanation that Hezekiah saw this vision during his sickness (1:4) indicates a quite different kind of vision from that recounted in 3:13-4:22.

However, there is no need to see in 1:2b-4 a description of 3:13-4:22, because the latter passage is adequately included in the description of Isaiah's vision in 1:5. Chapters 6-11 satisfy parts of that description well: the date in the twentieth year of Hezekiah (6:1), the vision of the garments of the saints (9:24-26), the vision of the going forth, transformation, persecution and ascension of the Beloved (10:17-11:32). On the other hand, 'the judgment of the angels' and 'the destruction of this world' receive only very brief mention in 10:12. Chapter 4 conforms better to this part of the description. It looks as though the author of 1:5 regards 3:13-4:22 and 6-11 as two complementary accounts of the same vision of Isaiah, each of which focusses on aspects of the vision which are only briefly mentioned in the other. This is confirmed by the order in which he lists the contents of the vision, corresponding to the order in which their fullest treatment occurs in the Ascension of Isaiah: the judgment of the angels and the destruction of this world (4:2-19), the garments of the righteous (9:24-26), the going forth, transformation, persecution and ascension of the Beloved (10:17-11:32).

Thus the major visionary contents of the whole book are adequately described in 1:5. Nothing in the book requires the description of Hezekiah's vision in 1:2b-4. It seems that these verses must describe another work which was known to the author and his community.[90] That this work is no longer extant and seems to be nowhere else mentioned in ancient literature is not especially surprising. The 'words of the righteous Joseph' (4:22) is presumably a reference to the Prayer of Joseph, of which we have only three short quotations by Origen, though it is mentioned in the ancient lists of apocryphal works. The type of Christianity reflected in the Ascension of Isaiah is, by any account, unusual. It would not be surprising if one of the works produced in this community (the Ascension of Isaiah) gained a wider circulation, while another (the Vision of Hezekiah) did not.

---

[90] *Contra* Norelli, *Ascensio Isaiae: Commentarius*, 79-82.

The sickness of Hezekiah during which he had his vision (1:4) is that of Isaiah 38, which records a psalm Hezekiah wrote after recovering (38:9-20). In this he says that he was consigned to the gates of Sheol (38:10), but that God brought back his soul from the pit of destruction (38:17). According to that trend of Jewish exegesis which found in Old Testament texts allusions to apocalyptic revelations granted to the great men of the past,[91] these verses could easily have been interpreted as referring to a visionary descent to the underworld, in which Hezekiah saw the torments of Gehenna, before being returned to this world. Such a vision would correspond to and complement Isaiah's visionary ascent through the seven heavens. Presumably, just as Isaiah saw in vision the Beloved's future descent and ascent through the heavens, so Hezekiah would have seen the Beloved's future descent to and ascent from Sheol (to which AscenIsa 4:21; 9:16; 10:8, 10, 14; 11:19 allude, without describing). This would explain the last item in the description of Hezekiah's vision: 'the words concerning faith in the Beloved' (1:4).

According to the cosmic geography of the Ascension of Isaiah, Sheol is below this world and Abaddon[92] below that (10:8). Christ descended to Sheol, whence he brought the righteous dead up with him to the seventh heaven (9:16-18), but he did not descend to Abaddon (10:8), where presumably the wicked dead are and which is presumably the same as the Gehenna into which the devil and his angels will be cast at the last day (4:14). Sheol has an angel in charge of it (9:16; 10:8; 11:20), as well as other angels (10:10). But Satan and his angels are not now in Sheol or Gehenna, but in the firmament (7:9; 10:29; 11:23). He is 'the prince of this world' (1:3; 10:29; cf. 2:4; 4:2; 10:12), ruling it from the firmament, but not of the underworld.

This creates some difficulty in understanding the account of Hezekiah's vision in 1:2b-4. The reference to it as 'the words of righteousness' (1:2)[93] would be an appropriate description of a vision of divine judgment on the wicked dead. The 'judgments of this world' and 'the torments of Gehenna' would both describe the punishments of the wicked (those who belong to 'this world,' frequently a pejorative term in the Ascension of Isaiah[94]) and indicate, presumably, that Hezekiah toured the punishments in hell like many another seer in the apocalyptic tours of hell. But it is less easy to understand why he

---

[91] Two examples in LAB have already been discussed (Moses: 19:10; Abraham: 23:6-7). Another is the vision of Kenaz in LAB 28:6-9, which is based on Judg 1:15.

[92] Ethiopic *Haguel* ('Perdition') in 10:8 doubtless renders Abaddon.

[93] For the expression, cf. 1 En 13:10; 14:1.

[94] 2:4; 3:25; 4:2, 4; 6:13; 10:12, 29.

saw, in the same vision, 'the prince of this world, and his angels, and his authorities, and his powers.' Not only does the Ascension of Isaiah not locate Satan and his angels in the world of the dead. Ancient Jewish literature never does so, and with hardly any exceptions nor does the Christian literature of the first three centuries.[95] Not until later was Satan commonly seen as the lord of the underworld, presiding with his angels over the punishment of the damned. The only tour of hell in which the seer encounters Satan in the underworld is the Apocalypse of Zephaniah (6:16-7:9), but there Satan appears in no other role than as judicial accuser of the dead, reading out a record of their sins.

At first sight it is tempting to reject Dillmann's emendation of the Ethiopic text (*makuannen* for *makuennân*),[96] which has been universally accepted, and retain the manuscript reading: 'and [or "which is"] the place of punishment of this world, and its angels, authorities and powers.' On other hand, 'the place of punishment of this world', though coherent with what precedes, would be rather redundant. Moreover, the fragmentary Coptic text of this verse (the only witness to it besides the Ethiopic) has the word 'prince' (the Greek ἄρχων preserved in the Coptic). However, the Coptic does not have 'the prince of this world,' but 'the prince of his/its[...'[97] Gehenna, in the preceding phrase, may be the antecedent of the possessive. Thus the text may originally have referred in some way to the ruler of Gehenna,[98] and 'his angels, authorities and powers,' and has been altered in the Ethiopic to the more familiar 'prince of this world' (10:29; cf. 2:4; 4:2; 9:14; 10:12).[99] These would be, not Satan and his rebel angels, but the angels of punishment who serve God by tormenting the wicked in Gehenna.

If we do read 'the prince of this world,' there are two possibilities. One is that Hezekiah saw a prophetic vision of Satan and his angels being cast into Gehenna at the last day (4:14). The other is that he saw Satan and his angels in Gehenna. This would be contrary to the view of the Ascension of Isaiah itself, but there is no reason why the work which recounted the vision of Hezekiah should have been con-

---

[95] J. A. MacCulloch, *The Harrowing of Hell* (Edinburgh: T. & T. Clark, 1930) 227-234, 345-346.

[96] A. Dillmann, *Ascensio Isaiae Aethiopice et Latine* (Leipzig: Brockhaus, 1877) 62.

[97] P. Bettiolo, A. Giambelluca Kossova, C. Leonardi, E. Norelli, and L. Perrone eds., *Ascensio Isaiae: Textus* (CCSA 7; Turnhout: Brepols, 1995)162-163.

[98] The 'prince of Gehenna' is mentioned in b. Sanh. 52a; b. Shab. 104a.

[99] In the Slavonic and one Latin version, which should perhaps be preferred to the Ethiopic at this point, 9:16 refers to the angel of Sheol as 'the prince of death' and to 'all his power(s).'

sistent in every respect with the Ascension of Isaiah. It would also be contrary to the general view in Judaism and Christianity at that time. But there is at least one early exception to the general view: Testament of Dan 5:11 (an undoubtedly Christian verse) refers to Christ's descent to Hades: 'he shall take from Beliar the captives, the souls of the saints.' It should be noted that the name Beliar is used for 'the prince of this world' in the Ascension of Isaiah (1:8, 9; 2:4; 3:11, 13; 4:2, 4, 14, 16, 18; 5:1), which also sees Christ's descent to Hades as a plundering of the souls from the ruler of Hades (9:16), though it does not identify Beliar and the ruler of Hades. The name Beliar is also used in one of the few visions of Satan himself in apocalyptic literature, in the Questions of Bartholomew, where Beliar is dragged up from hell and displays the punishments with which he and his angels torture the damned (3:7-47). It is possible that this section of a relatively late text, much preoccupied with the seven heavens and angelology (3:28-35, 45-47), preserves early material to which the lost vision of Hezekiah was related.

Speculation aside, Ascension of Isaiah 1:2b-4 certainly provides evidence to confirm the supposition[100] that there must have been more visionary accounts of the punishments in hell than have survived.

IX CONCLUSION: THE DEVELOPMENT OF TOURS OF HELL

The development of the genre of tours of hell may be sketched as follows:

(1) Cosmic tours, like those in 1 Enoch, displayed from an early date an interest in the fate of the dead, among other cosmic secrets. With the emergence of belief in the punishment of the wicked immediately after death, a tour of the punishments in hell was included in such apocalypses. The Apocalypse of Elijah was evidently an example of this development. It may even have been the earliest.

(2) Within the genre of tours of the seven heavens, there may have been apocalypses which included a tour of hell located (as in 2 Enoch) within one of the heavens, but no such apocalypse has survived. Instead, we have apocalypses in which an ascent through the seven heavens is followed by a visits to paradise and hell: 3 Baruch (Slavonic) and the Gedulat Moshe. (Since this pattern is also followed in the apocalypse in the Syriac Transitus Mariae, where hell, as in 2 Enoch, is only reserved for the wicked in the

---

[100] Himmelfarb, *Tours*, 137, 144.

future, the pattern probably pre-dated its use in apocalypses which included a tour of hell.)

(3) Some cosmic tour apocalypses developed a particularly strong emphasis on the fate of the dead. Thus the Gedulat Moshe, while retaining a tour of the seven heavens with cosmological and angelological concerns independent of the fate of the dead, gives most space to the visits to hell and paradise, while even within the tour of the heavens Moses encounters the angel of death in the sixth heaven. The transition is then not great to apocalypses exclusively concerned with the fate of the dead, such as the Apocalypse of Zephaniah and the Apocalypse of Paul, which while they range quite widely over the heavens and the underworld and even the extremities of the earth, are interested only in matters concerned with the fate of the dead. In fact, the Apocalypse of Paul may well have developed from basically the same pattern as that of 3 Baruch and the Gedulat Moshe: ascent through the heavens, visit to paradise, visit to hell (see chapter 11). With the belief that the souls of the dead are first taken up to the throne of God for judgment before being taken to paradise or hell (ApPaul 14-18), this pattern became the way the seer could follow the path of souls after death and observe their fate.

(4) The vision of Hezekiah seems to have been solely a descent to the world of the dead below: to Sheol and the abyss. The Greek Apocalypse of Mary is a much later example of this type.

(5) The Apocalypse of Peter is a unique case of the transformation of a tour of hell into a prophecy of the punishments of the wicked after the last judgment. It undoubtedly reproduces the contents of a tour of hell, but the visionary form has been eliminated to create a prophecy of the future. This may indicate that the writer had not himself adopted the view of the fate of the wicked which the tours of hell reflect. It certainly indicates that, with his imminent eschatological expectation, he was not interested in the fate of the wicked before the last judgment.

(6) Finally, a tour of hell could take its place within a narrative of events on earth. This is the case in the Testament of Isaac, in the Acts of Thomas (51-60), the Life of Pachomios, and in the various versions of the Jewish story of the wicked rich man and the pious poor man. These are cases of apocalyptic traditions, already no doubt well established within the apocalypses, being borrowed, as blocks of tradition, for insertion into narratives which are not themselves apocalypses.

CHAPTER THREE

VISITING THE PLACES OF THE DEAD IN THE EXTRA-CANONICAL APOCALYPSES

I INTRODUCTION

The purpose of this chapter is to survey a major theme in the extra-canonical apocalypses, both Jewish and Christian. Most people who have studied biblical studies know that these apocalypses exist. Most biblical scholars have read some of them, or have studied texts of particular relevance to the biblical texts. But those who approach this literature only out of interest in its relevance to biblical texts rarely understand it very well. There is a natural tendency to think first of the apocalypses we know well—the canonical ones: Daniel and Revelation—and to suppose that the extra-canonical apocalypses are simply non-canonical examples of the same kind of thing. Looking at these works for the sake of specific parallels and comparisons with the biblical texts inevitably has the same kind of result. Our sense of what the extra-canonical apocalypses are like is heavily biased towards their resemblances to the biblical literature. From this arises, for example, the view—unchallenged until recently, and still common— that apocalyptic literature is entirely concerned with a certain kind of eschatology: with the future and final outcome of history. Since Daniel and Revelation are concerned with this, it has seemed natural to suppose that this is what apocalypses are about, and therefore to treat apocalypses which are not about this or parts of apocalypses which are not about this as marginal to our perception of apocalyptic literature.

Both the form and the contents of the extra-canonical apocalypses are quite diverse, and in many respects they differ markedly from anything within the canon of Scripture. Biblical scholars need to be much more aware of this than they commonly are, even for the sake of the study of the biblical literature, because negative comparisons can be as illuminating as positive ones. In other words, to recognize that many important features of Jewish apocalyptic literature are absent from the Christian literature, even the Christian apocalypses, of the earliest period of Christianity, is to begin to ask questions one would not otherwise be able to ask.

Moreover, if we are interested in the currently much discussed question of early Christianity's relationship to Judaism, there is another important reason for studying the extra-canonical apocalypses in their own terms, not just as a quarry for parallels to the biblical apocalyptic texts. Thinking about the indebtedness of Christianity to Judaism often seems to assume an unexamined and inaccurate model of that indebtedness, according to which all Jewish influence on Christianity passed through the New Testament. We study Jewish literature as background to the New Testament, and the New Testament as the source from which later Christians were working. What they owed to Judaism (apart from their direct indebtedness to the Old Testament) reached them via the New Testament. However, even if we leave out of account channels of influence and indebtedness other than literary ones, this model is misleading. It ignores the fact that early Christians throughout and long after the New Testament period continued to read extra-canonical Jewish literature, especially the extra-canonical Jewish apocalypses. They even read and valued Jewish apocalypses written during and after the New Testament period (such as 4 Ezra, 2 Baruch, 3 Baruch, and the Apoocalypse of Abraham). In fact, of course, almost all pre-rabbinic Jewish literature which we know, apart from the Dead Sea Scrolls, we know only because Christians preserved it.

As far as apocalyptic literature is concerned, the literary tradition of the apocalypses, Jewish and Christian, needs to be understood as a continuous tradition surviving and developing in both Judaism and Christianity over the course of many centuries. It was a tradition which continued from pre-Christian Judaism into both the Christianity and the Judaism of the Christian era. Christians read the extra-canonical Jewish apocalypses; they revised, adapted and interpolated them; and they wrote new apocalypses which were very often modelled on and indebted to the extra-canonical Jewish ones much more than they were to the canonical apocalypses of Daniel and Revelation. It is only a small exaggeration to say that the apocalyptic tradition was a literary tradition which in passing from Judaism into Christianity by-passed the New Testament. The result is that many themes which have exerted a strong influence on the Christian tradition, including those we shall examine in this chapter, have their roots in early Judaism not via the New Testament, but independently of the New Testament.

A major concern of the whole apocalyptic tradition from beginning to end was the fate of the dead. Given that this literature is visionary literature, in which the apocalyptic seers are often transported into various parts of the cosmos, it is not surprising that one form which interest in the fate of the dead took in the apocalypses was that of visits to the places of the dead. The visionary is taken to view either the places where the dead are now or (sometimes) the places where the dead will be after the last judgment. These are not visions of the future, and so the prophet John's vision of the New Jerusalem in chapters 21-22 of the book of Revelation does not fall within our definition of a visit to the places of the dead. Whereas John sees in vision what will happen after the last judgment, the theme of the present chapter is visits by apocalyptic seers to the places of the dead as those places exist now, prior to the last judgment. No such visits are described in the biblical literature, but they are frequent in the extra-canonical apocalypses.

II Forms of Cosmic Tour in the Apocalypses

Visits to the places of the dead have their origin in the apocalyptic genre I shall call the cosmic tour. Apocalyptic literature is about the revelation of mysteries: the secrets of the cosmos and the secrets of the divine purpose. To be shown such secrets the apocalyptic seers are often taken on guided tours, accompanied by angels, of those parts of the cosmos which are otherwise inaccessible to mortals. There they see not only what we would readily consider matters of religious interest—such as the throne of God, the angels engaged in praising God or preparing to execute judgment, the fallen angels in prison, the places of the dead and so on—but also matters which we would consider rather of scientific interest, especially matters of meteorology and astronomy: where the snow, the dew and the winds come from, how the sun travels across the sky, and so on. All such things belong to the mysteries of how God governs his world, both nature and history, and are knowable only as they are revealed to the apocalyptic seers.

The first cosmic tourist, so far as we know, was Enoch. By this I mean not that he was the most ancient of the figures to whom apocalyptic revelations were ascribed, belonging to the antediluvian age, but rather (though the point is not unconnected) that the narrative of Enoch's cosmic tour is the oldest such narrative we have. In fact, we have five distinct versions of Enoch's cosmic tour,[1] but the two earliest of these both belong to the oldest part of the Enoch literature (1 En 1-36) and date from the third or early second century B.C.E. Here we are at the origins of apocalyptic literature and here, as we shall see

---

[1] They are (1) *1 Enoch* 17-19; (2) *1 Enoch* 21-36; (3) *1 Enoch* 41; 43-44; (4) *2 Enoch* 3-22; (5) *2 Enoch* 40-42. See R. Bauckham, 'Early Jewish Visions of Hell,' *JTS* 41 (1990) 358-362 = chapter 2 above, section II.

shortly, are the oldest Jewish accounts of visits to the places of the dead.

Before considering these visits themselves, we need to note several different forms which cosmic tours in the apocalypses take. In 1 Enoch the inaccessible places to which Enoch is taken by angels all lie at the furthest extremities of the earth, not below or above the earth. Enoch does visit the throne-room of God in heaven (1 En 14), but that ascent to heaven is quite distinct from his cosmic tour. The cosmic tour itself presupposes the very ancient notion, to be found also in early Greek literature, such as the *Odyssey*, and in Mesopotamian literature, such as the *Epic of Gilgamesh*, which locates such mysterious places as the places of the dead at the furthest extremities of the earth. Only one other cosmic tour in Jewish apocalyptic literature known to us seems to have taken this form. There was an ancient Apocalypse of Elijah, from the first century C.E. at the latest, which is no longer extant, except in a few fragments.[2] However, the opening section of the medieval Hebrew Apocalypse of Elijah, which describes in very summary form a tour of the extremities of the earth by Elijah closely resembling Enoch's tour (in 1 En 17-19, 21-36), most probably derives from the ancient Elijah apocalypse.[3] As we shall see in other instances, apocalyptic literature is such that we can often detect very ancient forms in much later apocalypses.

In the first and second centuries C.E., a new cosmology altered the form of the cosmic tour. Above the earth's atmosphere rose a series of seven heavens, of which the uppermost, the seventh, was the throne-room of God. Now the apocalyptic seers were escorted by angels in an upward journey through the seven heavens, viewing on the way the fascinating contents of each heaven, before coming into God's own presence in the seventh heaven. Most of the cosmic secrets which Enoch (in 1 En 17-19, 21-36) had seen beyond the ends of the earth were now relocated above the earth, in the seven heavens. Indeed, Enoch's own cosmic tour was rewritten as a tour of the seven heavens—in 2 Enoch (the Slavonic Apocalypse of Enoch), which is most likely a work of the first century C.E.[4] The places of the dead

---

[2] Texts and translations in M. Stone and J. Strugnell, *The Books of Elijah: Parts 1-2* (SBLTT 18; Missoula, Montana: Scholars Press, 1979).

[3] Bauckham, 'Early Jewish Visions of Hell,' 362-365 = chapter 2 above, section III.

[4] Introduction and translations: F. I. Anderson, '2 (Slavonic Apocalypse of) Enoch,' in J. H. Charlesworth ed., *The Old Testament Pseudepigrapha*, vol. 1 (London: Darton, Lonman & Todd, 1983) 91-221. Enoch's tour of the seven heavens is narrated twice: in *2 Enoch* 3-22 and 40-42.

could themselves be relocated within the seven heavens, which is where Enoch sees them in 2 Enoch (8-10, 42).

However, a third form of the cosmic tour apocalypse also developed, in which the seer ascends through the seven heavens to the throne of God, and is only then taken to see hell and paradise, though in none of these cases is it clear where hell and paradise are located. There are three examples of this form of tour: in 3 Baruch,[5] the Gedulat Moshe ,[6] and the Syriac Transitus Mariae.[7] 3 Baruch, which dates from the early second century C.E., has this form in the Slavonic version, though not in the Greek version. In my view, the Slavonic is more original in this, as in other respects.[8] The Gedulat Moshe (also known in other versions as the Ascension of Moses) is a medieval Jewish apocalypse in Hebrew; whether or not it is a medieval version of an ancient apocalypse, it certainly preserves an ancient apocalyptic form and ancient apocalyptic traditions. Finally, an early Christian text, the final section of the Syriac Transitus Mariae,[9] must also be based on an old Jewish apocalyptic model.[10] In it the virgin Mary is conducted through the heavens by an angel, and after reaching the highest heaven , she is then shown the places of final destiny for the righteous and the wicked respectively.

The cosmic tours mentioned in the previous three paragraphs all include visits to the places of the dead. (There are other tours of the seven heavens which do not refer to the places of the dead.) Moreover, the tours mentioned also share the common characteristic that the places of the dead occur, more or less prominently, among many

---

[5] Introduction and translations: H. E. Gaylord, '3 (Greek Apocalypse of) Baruch,' in Charlesworth ed., *The Old Testament Pseudepigrapha*, vol. 1, 653-679.

[6] Translation in M. Gaster, 'Hebrew Visions of Hell and Paradise,' in Gaster, *Texts and Studies*, vol. 1 (London: Maggs, 1925-28) 125-141.

[7] Translations in A. Smith Lewis, *Apocrypha Syriaca: The Protevangelium Jacobi and Transitus Mariae* (Studia Sinaitica 11; London: C. J. Clay, 1902), 64-69; W. Wright, 'The Departure of my Lady Mary from the World,' *Journal of Sacred Literature* 7 (1865), 156-169; and cf. E. A. W. Budge, *The History of the Blessed Virgin Mary and The History of the Likeness of Christ which the Jews of Tiberias made to mock at* (London: Luzac, 1899) 131. There are also Arabic and Ethiopic versions: Arabic translated in M. Enger, *Ahbar Yuhanna as-salih fi naqlat umm al-masih, id est Ioannis Apostoli de Transitu Beatae Mariae Virginis Liber* (Elberfeldae: Friderichs, 1854), 88-107; Ethiopic translated in M. Chaîne, *Apocrypha de Beata Maria Virgine* (CSCO 39-40; Rome: de Luigi, 1909), Latin section 39-42.

[8] Bauckham, 'Early Jewish Visions of Hell,' 371-374 = chapter 2 above, section V.

[9] For full discussion of this text (the Six Books Apocalypse of the Virgin), see chapter 13 below.

[10] Bauckham, 'Early Jewish Visions of Hell,' 361-362 = chapter 2 above, section II.

other cosmic secrets which the seers see on their tours. Baruch, Moses and the Virgin Mary, like Enoch, all seem to be as interested in meteorology and angelology as they are in the fate of the dead. Cosmic tours concerned exclusively with the fate of the dead we shall consider later.

III Changing Views of the Intermediate State

The cosmic tours that have been mentioned constitute some of the evidence for a very important change in ideas about the dead.[11] In the earliest of our literature the dead are conceived as in a state of waiting for the day of judgment, when the righteous will be rewarded and the wicked punished. Later literature depicts the dead as already either enjoying the delights of paradise or suffering the punishments of hell. The transition from one view to the other apparently took a long time. The two views overlapped. The later view seems already to have been known in the first century C.E., but did not become at all popular until the second century C.E., while the older view can still be found as late as c. 200 C.E.

Clearly, these two views about the present state of the dead, prior to the last judgment, affect what it is possible for an apocalyptic seer to see when he or she visits the places of the dead. On the older view, a seer can see the dead in the places in which they await the judgment—the chambers of the souls, as they came to be called. He or she can also see paradise and hell, the places of final destiny for the righteous and the wicked after the judgment, but can only see them without human inhabitants, ready and prepared for those who *will* be assigned to them after the judgment. On the later view, on the other hand, a seer can see the righteous already enjoying their reward in paradise and the wicked already suffering their punishments in hell.

1 Enoch 22 contains the oldest account we have in the Jewish apocalyptic literature of a visit to the place where the dead are. In the furthest west, where the sun goes down, Enoch is shown a great mountain containing four hollows or pits, in which four different categories of the dead are kept. The language used is that of imprisonment or detention awaiting judgment, even though this may hardly seem appropriate for the righteous. All that distinguishes the place where the righteous wait is that it is light rather than dark, and has a spring of water to relieve the thirst from which the dead tend to suffer. The archaic character of this account, which preserves ideas

---

[11] Bauckham, 'Early Jewish Visions of Hell,' 357-358, 375-376 = chapter 2 above, sections I, VI.

very close to the origins of Jewish belief in post-mortem judgment, appears in the description of the other three categories of the dead. The wicked are those who had sinned and had not been judged for their sins in their lifetimes: therefore they must await a reckoning at the end of history. Another compartment contains those who had suffered murder and are waiting to act in the role of prosecuting witnesses against their murderers at the judgment. Whether they were themselves righteous or not seems beside the point: what is due to them after death is the opportunity to seek the justice they did not have the opportunity to obtain in this life. Finally, there is an obscure category of people who seem to be not wicked enough to be raised for judgment at the end; their punishment is simply to remain in Sheol for ever. This is the first and only time we find the dead categorized in this fourfold way; thereafter in the apocalypses there are only ever two categories of the dead—wicked and righteous.

Enoch not only sees Sheol where the dead are detained awaiting judgment; he also sees the places in which they will be rewarded and punished at the judgment. Again the very archaic nature of this account is clear, for Gehenna is here literally the valley of Hinnom beside Jerusalem (1 Enoch 27), and the blessed place from which the righteous will observe the punishment of the wicked in the valley of Hinnom is mount Zion, the temple mount in Jerusalem, to which the tree of life (which Enoch sees at the ends of the earth) will be transplanted in the last days (1 En 24-25).

Matters are rather different when Enoch's cosmic tour is rewritten as a tour of the seven heavens in 2 Enoch. Just as Paul was taken up to paradise in the third heaven, though he refused to divulge anything else about the experience (2 Cor 12:4), so it is when Enoch reaches the third heaven that he sees paradise and hell. Both are described in ways that were or became standard. Paradise has wonderfully fragrant and fruitful trees, with the tree of life at their centre, and is watered by four rivers of honey, milk, oil and wine. Angels guard it, praising God, but no human inhabitants are mentioned (2 En 8). Hell is dark, with a river of fire and ice, and staffed by cruel angels with instruments of torture. We might suppose that there must be people being tortured, but in fact these are pointedly unmentioned (2 En 10). This, we are told, is the place that has been *prepared* for sinners (10:4), just as paradise is the place that has been *prepared* for the righteous (9:1). Both categories are elaborated in lists of the kinds of things the righteous do and the kinds of things the wicked do (2 En 9; 10). Clearly, this revelation of the places of final destiny for the righteous and the wicked is intended to function paraenetically—to encourage and to warn.

What of the dead themselves? In 2 Enoch Enoch never sees the righteous dead, but in an obscure passage he sees the wicked dead, apparently not in hell, but observing it, knowing themselves condemned to it, suffering the pain of anticipating their future punishment (40:13). They are not yet being actively punished, but suffer the expectation of it.[12] Similarly, in the Syriac Transitus Mariae, when the Virgin Mary sees Gehenna, with the smoke rising from it, and the stench of sulphur and the roar of flames coming from it, she also sees the wicked standing and viewing it from a distance. They are weeping, 'knowing for what they are reserved at the last day; for the day of judgment is not yet come, that they should receive the inheritance of darkness.'[13] Mary's vision is more symmetrical than Enoch's, because she also sees the righteous viewing their future reward from afar. She sees the tabernacles of the just, with lights shining and trumpets sounding in their honour, but the righteous themselves 'beholding their happiness from a distance, until the day of resurrection, when they shall inherit their mansions.'[14]

We find similar pictures in works which do not belong in our category of visits to the places of the dead, but which give an account of the state of the dead, and which can fortunately be more securely dated than our apocalypses. 4 Ezra (the Apocalypse of Ezra), a Jewish work of c. 100 c.e.,[15] and the De universo, a Christian work of c. 200 c.e.,[16] depict the righteous awaiting their future reward in restful joy, while the wicked wait in anguished fear of their coming punishment. This conception has the advantage of making the righteous dead already happy and the wicked dead already miserable, while keeping the emphasis on a future day of judgment as the point at which fates are assigned. Both paradise and hell can be described—even visited by apocalyptic seers—and so function paraenetically for readers of apocalypses, but they remain a future destiny, not yet actualized for anyone. However, the potential for vivid and extended descriptions would certainly increase if it were possible to describe the righteous already enjoying the delights of paradise and the wicked already suffering the punishments of hell.

---

[12] For this interpretation of the text, see Bauckham, 'Early Jewish Visions of Hell,' 360-361 = chapter 2 above, section II.

[13] Translation from Wright, 'Departure,' 159.

[14] Translation from Wright, 'Departure,' 158.

[15] The relevant passage is 4 Ezra 7:75-101.

[16] For the latest study, see C.E. Hill, 'Hades of Hippolytus or Tartarus of Tertullian? The Authorship of the Fragment De Universo,' VC 43 (1989) 105-126, who attributes it to Tertullian.

The new conception which made that possible makes perhaps its earliest appearance in literature known to us in the Apocalypse of Elijah, which, as we have noticed, contained a cosmic tour to the extremities of the earth, like Enoch's original tour. A substantial fragment[17] of this lost apocalypse survives as a quotation in the apocryphal Epistle of Titus. Whereas Enoch saw the souls detained in Sheol (1 En 22), Elijah sees them already being actively punished in Gehenna. He sees a variety of different kinds of sinners suffering a variety of appropriate punishments. These include the so-called hanging punishments which are to be a feature of almost all subsequent detailed descriptions of the punishments in hell. People are punished by being hung up eternally by an appropriate part of the body. For example, those who have blasphemed or borne false witness hang by their tongues, while adulterers hang by their genitals. The hanging punishments in this fragment of the ancient Apocalypse of Elijah are the first appearance in our literature of the notion that every sin must have its own appropriate punishment in hell, since the justice of hell consists in the punishment of each according to his or her deeds. Hanging punishments are one form of appropriate punishment; in other apocalypses many other kinds of appropriate punishments also appear. Visits to hell become tours of the punishments, enabling the seer to observe in each case what kind of sinner is suffering what kind of punishment.[18] Clearly the paraenetic potential of an apocalyptic visit to hell is now enhanced enormously. Adulterers can be warned precisely what horrifying fate is awaiting them, and so on. The description of different forms of punishment allotted to different categories of sin never developed within the old-fashioned view that the wicked will only be punished after the last judgment. It apparently depended on the capacity to describe the punishments actually going on now, as seen by an apocalyptic seer visiting the places of the dead.

At this point we should comment briefly on the origin of the new view of the condition of the dead in intermediate state. The apocalyptic visits to the places of the dead developed within the tradition of the Jewish apocalypses. They were a Jewish theological development and show literary features derived from their Jewish apocalyptic origins.[19] But it is also true that there were many Greco-Roman pagan literary

---

[17] Text and translation in Stone and Strugnell, *The Books of Elijah*, 14-15.

[18] See M. Himmelfarb, *Tours of Hell: An Apocalyptic Form in Jewish and Christian Literature* (Philadelphia: University of Pennsylvania Press, 1983); R. Bauckham, 'The Apocalypse of Peter: A Jewish Christian Apocalypse from the Time of Bar Kokhba,' *Apocrypha* 5 (1994) 60-71 = chapter 8 below, section III.7 (b).

[19] Himmelfarb, *Tours of Hell*.

accounts of descents to Hades, many of which described the delights
enjoyed by the blessed and the punishments endured by the damned.
These too were apocalypses of a kind, revealing the fate of the dead
in order to warn the living.[20] In these Greco-Roman accounts, there
was no question of a future day of judgment: the dead enjoyed
paradisal bliss or suffered infernal punishments now. Moreover, it
was in these Greco-Roman descents to Hades that the specification of
a variety of particular punishments, even specific punishments appropriate to particular crimes, seems first to have appeared. The Jewish
and Christian descriptions of the punishments in hell undoubtedly
borrowed some such specific punishments from pagan sources,
though others were elaborated within the Jewish and Christian
apocalyptic tradition. (Punishments by fire, for example, were characteristic of the Jewish and Christian hell, not of the Greco-Roman
Hades). It seems likely that not just particular punishments, but the
very idea of describing the bliss of the righteous and the punishments
of the wicked already experienced immediately after death was borrowed by Jewish apocalyptists from the pagan descents to Hades.[21]

The Gedulat Moshe is a good example of the way the traditional
structure of the cosmic tour could accommodate, not only the new
view of paradise and hell, but also the considerably more extensive
descriptions of both which the new view facilitated. In some thirty
sections of the work (as divided in Moses Gaster's edition) Moses
views the contents of the seven heavens. In a further twenty-one
sections he views hell, with its various different punishments assigned
to different kinds of sinners, and in a further seventeen sections he
views paradise, whose main feature is the various different kinds of
thrones, made of different kinds of precious materials, assigned to
different categories of the righteous. But the new view of the intermediate state also made possible another literary development of major
significance for the history of apocalyptic literature. It enabled the
apocalyptic interest in the fate of the dead to break out of the confines
of cosmic tours which had other subjects and interests besides the fate
of the dead, and to flourish in the form of apocalypses solely concerned with revealing the fate of the dead.

---

[20] R. Bauckham, 'Descent to the Underworld,' in D. N. Freedman ed., *The Anchor
Bible Dictionary*, vol. 6 (Garden City, New York: Doubleday, 1992) 149-154 = chapter
1 above, section VII.

[21] Bauckham, 'Visions of Hell,' 376-377 = chapter 2 above, section VI;
Bauckham, 'The *Apocalypse of Peter*,' 58, 66-67 = chapter 8 below, section III.7.

IV Cosmic Tour Apocalypses Concerned Exclusively with the Fate of the Dead

The oldest of these may be the Apocalypse of Zephaniah, which survives in Coptic in a rather fragmentary condition.[22] It may be a pre-Christian Jewish apocalypse, though some detect indications of a Christian origin. Its special interest lies in the fact that it seems to depict an apocalyptic seer following the path of the soul of a dead person through the other world.[23] As in some of the Greco-Roman descents to Hades, Zephaniah apparently falls into a cataleptic trance, which enables his soul to leave his body and to be conducted by an angel through the experiences of a soul after death, but then to return to his body and to recount what he has seen. The angel conducts him through the air and through Hades to paradise. The angel protects him from the angels of punishment who seize the souls of the wicked after death. In Hades he encounters the terrifying figure of Satan. But Satan appears here solely in his ancient traditional role of judicial accuser. He reads out all Zephaniah's sins from a scroll; Zephaniah prays to God for mercy; another angel reads out the record of his righteous deeds; and Zephaniah is told that he has triumphed over the accuser. He travels out of Hades in a boat and finds himself in paradise with the patriarchs. From here it is possible to look back into Hades and down into the pit of Hades, the abyss, where the wicked are punished. Zephaniah describes the various punishments endured by various categories of sinners. The fact that the righteous can see the wicked suffering in hell does not in this text, as in some others, mean that they rejoice to see God's justice done. It means that they pray for God's mercy for the damned. Apparently for at least some of the wicked repentance and forgiveness are still possible until the day of judgment, which therefore functions not to initiate punishment but to seal the fate of the wicked. This idea of the possibility of repentance and deliverance from hell is rare in the apocalypses, but the motif of prayer for mercy for the damned, either by the righteous in paradise or by the apocalyptic seer who sees the sufferings of the wicked in hell, is common in many of the apocalyptic descriptions of visits to hell.[24] Sometimes it is merely rebuffed, but

---

[22] Introduction and translation in O. S. Wintermute, 'Apocalypse of Zephaniah,' in Charlesworth ed., *The Old Testament Pseudepigrapha*, vol. 1, 497-515; see also the comments in R. Bauckham, 'The Apocalypses in the New Pseudepigrapha,' *JSNT* 26 (1986) 100-103.

[23] Bauckham, 'Descent,' 155 = chapter 1 above, section VIII.

[24] See R. Bauckham, 'The Conflict of Justice and Mercy: Attitudes to the Damned in Apocalyptic Literature,' *Apocrypha* 1 (1990) 181-196 = chapter 6 below, section III; Bauckham, 'Descent,' 155 = chapter 1 above, section VIII.

sometimes it wins some kind of concession from God, such as the famous Sabbath or Sunday rest of the damned, a day's respite each week from the pains of hell.

The longest, most detailed and elaborate, as well as the most influential, of the apocalypses concerned exclusively with revealing the fate of the dead, is the Apocalypse of Paul.[25] Here the basic pattern of the apocalypse—though the text sprawls somewhat beyond this pattern—is that of our third type of cosmic tour apocalypse, in which an ascent through the heavens to the throne of God is followed by visits to the places of the dead. Paul first ascends through the heavens (though he seems to reach only the third, owing to this apocalypse's biblical basis in 2 Cor 12:2-4) and is then taken to see paradise and hell, located not within the heavens, but, rather remarkably, still at the furthest extremities of the earth. The pattern is that of a complete cosmic tour, but the sights to be seen concern exclusively the fate of the dead. In fact, in a rather less precise way than Zephaniah, Paul follows the path of the dead.[26] His initial ascent through the heavens enables him to see how souls, leaving their bodies at death, are conducted by guardian angels up to the throne of God, who then consigns them either to paradise or to hell. (There are other accounts which elaborate this notion further, assigning specific experiences to the souls in each of the seven heavens as they travel up to be judged by God in the seventh heaven, and then assigned either to paradise or to hell.[27]) Paul's cosmic tour is a vast compendium, not wholly consistent, of traditional apocalyptic material about the fate of the dead and the places of the dead. As such it transmitted such material from its older, often Jewish apocalyptic origins, to millions of later Christians.

The real significance of the Apocalypse of Paul lies in its vast popularity over the course of many centuries. People evidently wanted to know about the afterlife, and the Apocalypse of Paul told them, in more detail than any other available source. It was popular through most of the Christian world, except the Greek-speaking

---

[25] Introductions and translations: H. Duensing and A. de Santos Otero, 'Apocalypse of Paul,' in W. Schneemelcher ed., *New Testament Apocrypha*, vol. 2 (trans. R. McL. Wilson; revised edition; Cambridge: James Clarke, 1993) 712-748; J. K. Elliott, *The Apocryphal New Testament* (Oxford: Clarendon Press, 1993) 616-644.

[26] Cf. J.-M. Rosenstiehl, 'L'itinéraire de Paul dans l'au-delà: Contribution à l'étude de l'Apocalypse de Paul,' in *Carl-Schmidt-Kolloquium an der Martin-Luther-Unioversität 1988 (Wissenschaftliche Beiträge* 1990/23 [K9]; Halle, 1990) 197-212.

[27] *Questions of Ezra* A14-20; *Apocalypse of the Seven Heavens:* see R. Bauckham, 'The *Apocalypse of the Seven Heavens:* The Latin Version,' *Apocrypha* 4 (1993) 141-175 = chapter 12 below.

churches of the east, since, though it originated in Greek, it was supplanted there by the Greek Apocalypse of the Virgin, to which we shall return. But in the other churches of the east—Coptic, Syriac, Armenian—the Apocalypse of Paul was well known, while in Ethiopia the Ethiopic Apocalypse of the Virgin is nothing but a version of the Apocalypse of Paul, with the protagonist for some reason changed.[28] But it was in the Latin west that the Apocalypse of Paul had its greatest success, not only in its original form, but transmuted into a whole series of abbreviated and otherwise adapted later redactions in Latin, and translated into the European vernaculars.[29] Medieval Christian conceptions of the other world, the fate of the dead, paradise and hell, came from the Apocalypse of Paul probably more than from any other source.[30] It exerted its influence on a whole series of medieval western visions of paradise and hell (such as the visions of Wetti, Tundale, Adamnán, the Monk of Evesham, Thurkill, and St Patrick's Purgatory).[31] These constitute, in effect, a new genre of cosmic tour apocalypses exclusively concerned with the fate of the dead. Finally and climactically, Dante's *Divine Comedy* is the great work of art which arose miraculously out of this long tradition of works of indifferent literary merit.

V   Apocalypses Concerned Exclusively with Hell

From cosmic tour apocalypses concerned exclusively with the fate of the dead we pass to a further development of the tradition: apocalypses concerned exclusively with the fate of the wicked dead, the damned in hell.[32] The Apocalypse of Paul in its original form has an extensive description of hell, but also an even more extensive description of paradise; in fact, the account of hell is sandwiched between two different accounts of paradise. But later abbreviations of the Apocalypse of Paul in the western church—especially the so-called Latin Redaction IV, which was the most popular, with its translations into the European vernaculars—tend to reduce the

---

[28] See chapter 13 below, section II.

[29] See T. Silverstein, *Visio Sancti Pauli* (Studies and Documents 4; London: Christophers, 1935); and other literature in Elliott, *The Apocryphal New Testament*, 616-619.

[30] Cf. D.D.R. Owen, *The Vision of Hell* (Edinburgh: Scottish Academic Press, 1970).

[31] A collection of some of these visions in English translation is E. Gardiner ed., *Visions of Heaven and Hell Before Dante* (New York: Italica Press, 1989).

[32] Some of the medieval visionary literature, such as the vision of Charles the Fat, belongs in this category.

apocalypse to an account of the punishments in hell. In the east, the
work which came to function much as the Apocalypse of Paul did in
the west, as the most popular revelation of the after-life, vastly influential on the Christian imagination, was a work which in most of its
forms consists entirely of a tour of the punishments in hell. This is the
Greek Apocalypse of the Virgin, or (its usual title in the manuscripts)
the Apocalypse of the Holy Mother of God concerning the Punishments.[33] In it the Virgin is conducted around the many different
punishments (some twenty-five different kinds) assigned to different
categories of sinners in hell, and then, moved with compassion for the
damned, like Paul in the Apocalypse of Paul, she prays for mercy for
them, joined by the archangel Michael and various saints. Her intercession wins for the damned a respite from punishment for fifty days
each year.

The popularity of this work must be due to the facts that it both
portrays hell in vivid imaginative terms as a warning against a whole
series of specific sins and also expresses a natural compassionate reaction to the sufferings of the damned. Other works which combine
these features—emphasizing the justice of hell in vividly warning
terms and at the same time voicing the issue of mercy and compassion—are the Greek Apocalypse of Ezra[34] (whose contents are not
entirely limited to hell) and the Latin Vision of Ezra.[35] These works
belong to a tradition in which Ezra has become the apocalyptic seer
who argues with God about the problem of damnation and has to be,
as it were, convinced of the justice of hell. There is a good deal of
wrestling with the problem of hell and the issues of justice and mercy
going on in these works. Hell, we must suppose, tended increasingly
to crowd paradise out of our tradition both because it was thought
pedagogically more effective to warn people with pictures of punishment in hell than to attract them with pictures of reward in heaven,
but also because hell was to some degree a theological problem which
was felt to be such at the relatively popular level to which these
apocalypses appealed.[36]

---

[33] See chapter 13 below, section I.

[34] Introduction and translation in M. E. Stone, 'Greek Apocalypse of Ezra,' in
Charlesworth ed., *The Old Testament Pseudepigrapha*, vol. 1, 561-579.

[35] Introduction and translation in J. R. Mueller and G. A. Robbins, 'Vision of
Ezra,' in Charlesworth ed., *The Old Testament Pseudepigrapha*, vol. 1, 581-590; but see
also the longer text published in P.-M. Bogaert, 'Une version longue inédite de la
"Visio Beati Esdrae" dans le Légendier de Teano (Barberini Lat. 2318),' *Revue
Bénédictine* 94 (1984), 59-64.

[36] Bauckham, 'The Conflict of Justice and Mercy' = chapter 6 below.

VI Reports of Visits to the Other World in Narrative Contexts

So far we have considered visits to the places of the dead which occur in full-scale apocalypses and are attributed to the apocalyptic seers, the kind of ancient revered persons—Enoch, Ezra or the Virgin Mary—to whom apocalypses were attributed. But there is another category of visits to the places of the dead, which are stories told in narrative contexts. Here the visit to the places of the dead is made not by a seer but by an ordinary person, the account of paradise and/or hell is typically much briefer, and the story may either exist as a kind of anecdote in its own right or belong in a larger narrative context. There is, for example, the story in the apocryphal Acts of Thomas (51-60), in which a girl dies, goes to hell, is brought back to life miraculously by the apostle, and narrates what she had seen of the punishments in hell as a warning to the living. There is the Jewish story of the rich man and the poor man, which exists in several versions, in which, after the death of both men, a friend of the poor man visits the other world in a dream and sees his pious friend in paradise, while the rich tax-collector suffers torment in hell (y. Sanh. 23c; y. Ḥag. 77d).[37] Such stories are known already in Egyptian and Greco-Roman antiquity and have a long history in Christian literature. The means by which the visit to the places of the dead is made and then reported to the living are varied in such stories.[38] Many of them, including pagan ones and the influential anecdotes told by Gregory the Great (*Dialogues* 4.36), draw on the notion of temporary death, which we now call near-death experience: a person dies, reaches (usually) the threshold of hell, sufficiently to see what would be in store for them if they stayed, but is sent back to the world of the living.[39] In other cases, a permanently dead person returns as a ghost or in a dream to warn the living of what lies in store for the wicked. Or a living person may visit the other world in dream or vision. These stories deserve mention here primarily because, though significantly different as a literary tradition from the apocalypses, they frequently draw on the apocalyptic tradition for the way in which they describe the visit to the places of the dead.

---

[37] See R. Bauckham, 'The Rich Man and Lazarus: The Parable and the Parallels,' *NTS* 37 (1991) 226-227 = chapter 4 below, section I.

[38] Bauckham, 'Descent,' 150-151, 155 = chapter 1 above, section VII; Bauckham, 'The Rich Man and Lazarus,' 236-242 = chapter 4 below, section III.

[39] Cf. C. Zaleski, *Otherworld Journeys: Accounts of Near-Death Experience in Medieval and Modern Times* (New York: Oxford University Press, 1987).

With these stories our subject makes interesting contact with the
New Testament, which contains one story that belongs in its own
distinctive way to this category.[40] This is the parable of the rich man
and Lazarus (Luke 16:19-31). We should note that this is the only
New Testament text which adopts the later rather than the earlier
view of hell, i.e. it envisages the rich man already suffering punishment immediately after death prior to the last judgment. The genre
of stories to which it belongs always takes this view and depends for
its effectiveness on it. But Jesus' parable gives the motif of a visitor to
the places of the dead returning to report on them a novel twist. The
rich man proposes that Lazarus should be such a person: either
Lazarus should be sent back alive to the world of the living (he would
then be one of those characters who dies temporarily and returns to
life) or Lazarus should return as a ghost to communicate with the
living. It is not clear which form of the motif is envisaged, but in
either case it is envisaged in order to be refused. Lazarus does not
return. The parable's account of the places of the dead is not brought
to the living by a person who visits the other world and returns. By
employing this motif in order to reject it the parable subverts its own
revelation of the places of the dead. The rich man's brothers have
Moses and the prophets. They do not need an apocalyptic report of a
visit to the places of the dead.

---

[40] See the detailed discussion in Bauckham, 'The Rich Man and Lazarus' = chapter 4 below.

CHAPTER FOUR

THE RICH MAN AND LAZARUS:
THE PARABLE AND THE PARALLELS

The interpretation of the parable of the rich man and Lazarus (Luke 16:19-31) shows both how misleading extra-biblical parallels to biblical motifs can be when misused, and also how enlightening they can be when correctly used. The parable makes use of two major narrative motifs which can be paralleled in other ancient literature: (1) a reversal of fortunes experienced by a rich man and a poor man after death; (2) a dead person's return from the dead with a message for the living. Since Gressmann's monograph[1] drew attention to one important example of (1)—the Egyptian story of Setme and Si-Osiris (together with later Jewish stories derived from it)—much discussion of the parable has been dominated by this one parallel. Both the way in which this parallel has been used in the interpretation of the parable and the restriction of interest to this one parallel have had unfortunate consequences.[2]

I THE EGYPTIAN PARALLEL

The story of Setme and his son Si-Osiris[3] is extant in a Demotic text written probably in the second half of the first century C.E., but, since Setme Khamuas was high priest of Memphis c. 1250 B.C.E., it is likely to be based on an older Egyptian tale. An Egyptian in Amente, the realm of the dead, was allowed to return to earth in order to deal with an Ethiopian magician who was proving too powerful for the magicians of Egypt. He was reincarnated as the miraculous child of a childless couple, Setme and his wife, and called Si-Osiris. When he

---

[1] H. Gressmann, *Vom reichen Mann und armen Lazarus: eine literargeschichtliche Studie* (Abhandlungen der königlich preussischen Akademie der Wissenschaften: Philosophisch-historische Klasse, 1918 no.7; Berlin: Verlag der königlich Akademie der Wissenschaft, 1918).

[2] For a survey and critique of scholarship on the parable since Gressmann, see R. F. Hock, 'Lazarus and Micyllus: Greco-Roman Backgrounds to Luke 16:19-31,' *JBL* 106 (1987) 448-455. References to recent literature can be found in Hock's notes and in V. Tanghe, 'Abraham, son Fils et son Envoyé (Luc 16,19-31),' *RB* 91 (1984) 564-565 nn.14-16.

[3] F. Ll. Griffith, *Stories of the High Priests of Memphis: The Sethon of Herodotus and the Demotic Tales of Khamuas* (Oxford: Clarendon, 1900).

reached the age of twelve he vanquished the Ethiopian magician and returned to Amente. But before this there was an occasion when father and son observed two funerals, one of a rich man buried in sumptuous clothing and with much mourning, the other of a poor man buried without ceremony or mourning. The father declared he would rather have the lot of the rich man than the pauper, but his son expressed the wish that his father's fate in Amente would be that of the pauper rather than that of the rich man. In order to justify his wish and demonstrate the reversal of fortunes in the afterlife, he took his father on a tour of the seven halls of Amente. The account of the first three halls is lost. In the fourth and fifth halls the dead were being punished. In the fifth hall was the rich man, with the pivot of the door of the hall fixed in his eye. In the sixth hall were gods and attendants, in the seventh a scene of judgment before Osiris. The pauper was to be seen, elevated to high rank, near Osiris. Si-Osiris explains to his father what they saw, and the fate of the three classes of the dead: those whose good deeds outnumber their bad deeds (like the pauper), those whose bad deeds outnumber their good deeds (like the rich man), and those whose good and bad deeds are equal.

It should be noticed that the story of the two funerals and the visit to Amente (the section of the narrative which parallels Luke 16:19-26) is included within a longer narrative from which it is relatively distinct. The fact that Si-Osiris is not an ordinary child, but a reincarnated soul from Amente, makes it possible for him to take his father on a visit to Amente. But provided some other means of learning of the fate of the rich man and the poor man after their deaths could be substituted for this, the story could easily exist independently of the longer narrative in which it now stands. It may well have existed as a story in popular folklore before becoming part of the story of Setme and Si-Osiris.

The seven Jewish versions of the story[4] to which Gressmann drew attention are therefore not necessarily directly derived from the story of Setme and Si-Osiris as such. Although the story of the funerals of a rich man and a poor man, followed by a revelation of the reversal

---

[4] Gressmann, *Vom reichen Mann und armen Lazarus*, 70-86 (texts A-G). On these stories see also M. Gaster, *The Exempla of the Rabbis* (London/Leipzig: Asia Publishing Company, 1924) 119-20 (no.332), 243; S. Lieberman, 'On Sins and their Punishments,' in *Texts and Studies* (New York: Ktav, 1974) 33-48; M. Himmelfarb, *Tours of Hell: An Apocalyptic Form in Jewish and Christian Literature* (Philadelphia: University of Pennsylvania Press, 1983) 29-31, 78-82; J.-M. Rosenstiehl, 'Les révélations d'Élie: Élie et les tourments des damnés,' in A. Caquot et al., *La Littérature Intertestamentaire: Colloque de Strasbourg (17-19 octobre 1983)* (Bibliothèque des Centres d'Etudes Supérieures Spécialisés; Paris: Presses Universitaires de France, 1985) 103-107.

of their fortunes after death, is recognizably the same story, the Jewish versions are not indebted to the longer narrative of Setme and Si-Osiris or to features of the story as it is told about Setme and Si-Osiris which link it with the longer narrative. They could be versions of the story as it may have existed independently of its incorporation in the narrative of Setme and Si-Osiris.

It will be useful to summarize the earliest of the Jewish versions, which occurs in the Palestinian Talmud (y. Sanh. 23c; y. Ḥag. 77d).[5] It tells of a rich taxcollector named Bar Ma'yan and a poor Torah scholar in Ashkelon. They die on the same day, but whereas the taxcollector is buried in style, the poor pious man is unmourned. A friend of his is troubled by the contrast, until in a dream he sees the poor man in paradise and the taxcollector tormented in hell. His punishment is tantalization: he continually tries to drink from a river but cannot. The friend of the poor man also sees a certain Miriam being punished in hell (according to one report she hangs by her breasts, but according to another the hinge of the gate rests in her ear: compare the punishment of the rich man in the Egyptian story). He learns that the poor man sinned once in his life, while the rich man performed one good deed in his life. The splendid funeral of the rich man was his reward for his one good deed, while the poor man's one sin was punished by his dying neglected. The story illustrates the principle that the righteous are punished for their few sins in this world, so that in the next world they may enjoy only bliss, whereas the wicked receive in this world the reward for their few good deeds, so that in the next world they may justly receive only punishment.

If the Jewish version in the Palestinian Talmud is recognizably the same story as the Egyptian, the same cannot be said of the parable. If the Jewish and Egyptian stories are to prove enlightening for interpretation of the parable, then not only its resemblances to both, but also its differences from both must be given close attention. Against the parable, the Egyptian story and the story in the Palestinian Talmud agree on three points.[6] First, the story begins with the burials of the rich man and the poor man. It is on the contrasted manner of their burial that the story hinges. It is not so much that the state of the two men after death is found to be the opposite of their state during *life* in this world, but rather that they are treated quite differently in the next world from the way they were treated at their *burials* in this

---

[5] Translation in *Sanhedrin Gerichtshof* (trans. G. A. Wewers; Übersetzung des Talmud Yerushalmi 4/4; Tübingen: Mohr [Siebeck], 1981) 148-149.

[6] The first and third points are pointed out by R. Bultmann, *The History of the Synoptic Tradition* (trans. J. Marsh; 2nd edition; Oxford: Blackwell, 1968) 204.

world. While the parable may contain a hint of this motif in mentioning the burial of the rich man, while failing to refer to the burial of
Lazarus (Luke 16:22),[7] it does not give the burials the key role they
have in the Egyptian and Jewish stories. Its emphasis is on the respective conditions of life of Lazarus and the rich man, which are reversed
after death.

Secondly, in both the Egyptian and the Jewish stories a revelation
of the fate of the two men after death is given to a character in the
story who has observed their burials. This does not happen in the
parable. The hearers or readers of the parable learn what happens to
Lazarus and to the rich man after death, but there is no character in
the story who does. However, the contrast at this point is not so
simple, because in the parable the *possibility* of a revelation of the post-
mortem fates of Lazarus and the rich man, to be given to the rich
man's brothers, is raised and rejected (Luke 16:27-31). Thus the real
parallel in the parable to Setme's visit to Amente and to the dream of
the man of Ashkelon is not Luke 16:22-26, but Luke 16:27-31. The
parable envisages a different means of revelation from those which
are employed in the Egyptian and the Jewish stories, but the more
important contrast is that in the Egyptian and the Jewish stories a
revelation to a character in the story happens, whereas in the parable
such a revelation is requested but refused.

Thirdly, in both the Egyptian and the Jewish stories the poor
man's post-mortem fate is due to the fact that his good deeds outnumber his evil deeds, whereas the rich man's fate is due to the fact
that his evil deeds outnumber his good deeds. The Jewish story re-
fines the theme by making the rich man's burial the reward for his
one good deed, and the poor man's burial the punishment for his one
sin. In neither case is it because the rich man is rich that he suffers
after death or because the poor man is poor that he is compensated
after death. In the parable, however, there is no reference to the good
deeds of Lazarus or the evil deeds of the rich man. The reason for the
reversal of fortune is clearly stated but different. It is simply that the
rich man has received 'good things' during his life, whereas Lazarus
has received 'evil things' (Luke 16:25).

If we consider what the parable shares with the Egyptian and the
Jewish stories, the story-line common to all three is: a rich man and a
poor man die and their fortunes are reversed in the next world. We
may add that in all three there is reference to a revelation of the

---

[7] In a Jewish context it is not likely that even the body of a beggar would go
unburied, but the burial would be unceremonious. A rich man's burial would be a
much more notable feature of the end of his earthly life.

differing fates of the two men in the next world, made or to be made to a character or characters in the story (but this revelation, by different means and for different purposes, is given in the Egyptian and Jewish stories, requested and refused in the parable). This analysis must leave it in considerable doubt whether the Egyptian story was actually the source of the parable, as Gressmann argued and many[8] have followed him in asserting. The common story-line, as we shall see, can also be found in Lucian. It is not really in itself a story, but a folkloric motif, around which many different stories could be built. The additional theme—the revelation of the fate of the dead to the living—is also, as we shall see, a common motif found in many stories. The Egyptian and the Jewish stories are the same story, not simply because they use these two motifs, but because they use them in the same way: they make the point about reversal of fortune by emphasizing the contrasting burials of the two men; they explain the reversal in the same way; they use the motif of a revelation to the living in similar, if not quite identical ways. The parable, on the other hand, uses both motifs differently. It does not tell the same story.

It is quite plausible that a version of the Egyptian and Jewish story was current in first-century Palestine and that Jesus would have known it.[9] Thus (assuming the parable to be authentic) he could have borrowed the two motifs from it. On the other hand, he may well have known other stories which used one or both motifs. He could have known the motifs without consciously borrowing them from any one particular story. In any case, he has used them to construct a new story, which as a whole is not the same as any other extant story. The important consideration for the meaning of the parable is how these motifs now function within this new story. But comparison with the way they function in other stories can help to highlight their function in the parable. In this sense, the parallels and contrasts with the Egyptian and Jewish story of the rich man and the poor man can be instructive, but it would be a mistake to give them a privileged role in the interpretation of the parable. Parallels and contrasts with the same motifs as used in other stories may be equally enlightening.

Exclusive concentration on the Egyptian story as a parallel to the parable and the frequent view that it can be confidently treated as the

---

8 Listed in Hock, 'Lazarus and Micyllus,' 449 n.7.

9 J. Jeremias, *The Parables of Jesus* (trans. S. H. Hooke; 2nd edition; London: SCM Press, 1972) 178-79, 183, thought that Jesus must have known the Jewish version in the Palestinian Talmud because the Parable of the Great Supper (Matt 22:1-10; Luke 14:15-24) also shares a narrative motif with it. But again, this is a question precisely of a narrative *motif* which could occur in more than one story.

actual source of the parable have had at least two seriously detrimental effects on the interpretation of the parable. In the first place, they have fostered the impression that the parable has two very distinct parts—the story of the reversal of fortune (vv 19-26) and the discussion of the question of Lazarus's return (vv 27-31)—of which the second part is in some sense secondary (whether as Jesus' addition to a traditional Jewish story,[10] or as the early church's addition to a traditional Jewish story,[11] or as the early church's or Luke's addition to a parable of Jesus[12]). Because the Egyptian story has been thought to parallel only the first part, a distinction has been drawn between what is traditional in the parable and what is novel, with the first part regarded as traditional, the second as novel. As we have already noticed, this distinction is not entirely valid even in terms of comparison with the Egyptian story. The motif of a revelation of the fate of the dead to the living—which is central to the second part of the parable—is integral to the Egyptian story. It is used very differently in the parable, but this observation may help us to see that the second part of the parable is neither wholly novel nor lacking in real relationship to the theme of the first part. However, when we cease to give the Egyptian story privileged status as a parallel, we shall be able to appreciate the relevance of closer parallels to the second part of the parable, and the question of what is traditional and what is novel can be reexamined.

Secondly, treatment of the Egyptian story as the source of the parable has encouraged the supposition that a criterion for the judgment of the rich man and the poor man rather like that in the Egyptian story must be implicit in the parable. Because commentators have found it difficult to stomach the idea that the rich man suffers just because he has been rich, while Lazarus is compensated simply for having been poor, they have been glad of the way out of the difficulty which the Egyptian story appears to offer them. If the Egyptian story was wellknown, Jesus could take its explanation of the reversal of fortune of the two men for granted.[13] However, this is a misuse of the parallel. Because the Egyptian story has interpreted the motif of reversal of fortune in a particular way, we cannot assume

---

[10] Gressmann, *Vom reichen Mann und armen Lazarus*, 54-59; Jeremias, *The Parables of Jesus*, 186.

[11] Cf. D. L. Mealand, *Poverty and Expectation in the Gospels* (London: SPCK, 1980) 48.

[12] L. Schottroff and W. Stegemann, *Jesus and the Hope of the Poor* (trans. M. J. O'Connell; Maryknoll, New York: Orbis, 1986) 25.

[13] So Jeremias, *The Parables of Jesus*, 185.

that this interpretation is implicit in Jesus' use of the same motif. On the contrary, we must take seriously the difference between the Egyptian story and the parable at this point.

II THE REVERSAL OF FORTUNES

The first part of the parable (vv 19-26) is solely concerned with the reversal of fortunes of the rich man and Lazarus.[14] The point is that the rich man's luxurious lifestyle in this life is replaced by suffering in the next, while Lazarus's destitution and suffering in this life are replaced by exaltation in the next. Whereas the Egyptian and Jewish stories, as we have seen, focus the theme of reversal on the burials of the two men, the parable makes it much clearer that it is what they enjoyed or suffered during their lives that is to be contrasted with their fates after death. Thus the three opening verses (19-21) juxtapose the luxury of the rich man and the pitiful existence of Lazarus in such a way that their proximity makes the contrast all the more stark.[15] The reversal of fortune is twice stated in parallel chiastic arrangements:

rich man in this world	poor man in this world	poor man in next world	rich man in next world
v. 19	vv 20-21	v 22a	vv 22b-23a
v 25aα	v 25aβ	v 25bα	v 25bβ

The final verse of this section (26) makes clear the finality of the reversal. Since the reversed fortunes of the two men after death are a necessary consequence of their respective conditions in this life, nothing can happen after death to change them.

It is sometimes said that the parable does not explain why the fortunes of the two are reversed after death, and so some implicit criterion of judgment must be supplied.[16] It must be assumed that the rich man is condemned because he was not only rich but misused his

---

[14] For a semiotic analysis of the reversal of fortunes in the parable, see W. Vogels, 'Having or Longing: A Semiotic Analysis of Luke 16:19-31,' *Eglise et Théologie* 20 (1989) 43-45: the rich man moves from *having* to *not having* and *longing*, while Lazarus moves from *not having* and *longing* to *not longing* and *having*.

[15] Cf. Tanghe, 'Abraham,' 565-567.

[16] E.g. K. Grobel, '...Whose Name was Neves,' *NTS* 10 (1963-64) 374.

wealth,[17] or because he acquired it unjustly,[18] or because he neglected to give charity to the poor man at his gate.[19] Similarly, it must
be assumed that Lazarus was not only destitute but pious.[20] But the
claim that the parable does not explain the reversal of fortunes is
untrue. The reason is clearly stated in verse 25, where Abraham
justifies the reversal to the rich man. Of course, there is something
implicit even in verse 25. It is assumed that the state of affairs in the
next world is due to God's justice. The common Jewish eschatological
assumption that the next world exists to put right the injustices of this
world can be taken for granted. What has to be put right is the fact
that one man lived in luxury while another was destitute. The next
world compensates for this inequality by replacing it with a reverse
inequality. The rich man has already received his good things (τὰ
ἀγαθά σου: v 25): it is now his turn to suffer. Lazarus has already
suffered enough; he should now be 'consoled' (παρακαλεῖται).

For this view of the matter, it is not relevant to condemn the rich
man for over-indulgence, dishonesty or even neglecting his duty of
charity to the poor (if that means he should have relieved Lazarus'
suffering while remaining rich himself). What is wrong with the situation in this world, according to the parable, is the stark inequality in
the living conditions of the two men, which is vividly and memorably
conveyed simply by the juxtaposition of the rich man's expensive
luxury and the poor man's painful beggary (vv 19-21). This is why
there is no mention of the moral qualities of the two men. The injustice which God's justice in the next life must remedy lies in the mere
facts which are stated in verses 19-21. To try to base the fate of the
two men in the parable on considerations other than these stated facts
is to evade the parable's clear-sighted view of the flagrant injustice of
the situation it sketches. What is not stated is not relevant.

In effect, therefore, it is true that the rich man suffers in the next
life just because he was rich in this life, while the poor man is blessed
in the next life just because he was poor in this life. The reasons why

---

[17] E.g. A. Plummer, *A Critical and Exegetical Commentary on the Gospel according to S.
Luke* (ICC; Edinburgh: T. & T. Clark, 1901) 390; J. A. Fitzmyer, *The Gospel According
to Luke (X-XXIV)* (AB 28B; New York: Doubleday, 1985) 1132. W. O. E. Oesterley,
The Gospel Parables in the Light of their Jewish Background (London: SPCK, 1936) 208,
argues that, if he feasted every day, the rich man could not have obeyed the commandment to work six days a week.

[18] E.g. J. D. M. Derrett, *Law in the New Testament* (London: Darton, Longman &
Todd, 1970) 90.

[19] E.g. Plummer, *Luke*, 392; Fitzmyer, *Luke*, 1128.

[20] E.g. Oesterley, *The Gospel Parables*, 209; Jeremias, *The Parables of Jesus*, 185; I. H.
Marshall, *The Gospel of Luke* (NIGTC; Exeter: Paternoster, 1978) 632.

scholars have been so reluctant to accept that the parable teaches this, even though it so explicitly does, are no doubt various. Probably some do not themselves see the inequality described at the beginning of the parable as in itself unjust. But then it is characteristic of the Gospel parables to shift our perspective on things. Others perhaps object to the notion that the eternal destiny of individuals should be determined solely by this one consideration. But this would be the teaching of the parable only if we understood it to be a systematic statement about human destiny after death, whereas in fact it is a parable concerned with the single issue of wealth and poverty. Finally, it may be objected that the notion of justice involved in the reversal of fortunes is unacceptably crude. The inequality of the two men's position in this life is not satisfactorily remedied by the imposition of a reverse inequality in the next life (especially if the brevity of this life is contrasted with the eternity of the next).

If the theme of eschatological reversal were taken as a literal description of how God's justice will operate after death it would be morally intolerable. However, if it is taken as a popular way of thinking which the parable uses to make a point, it can be seen as serving primarily to express and to highlight the intolerable injustice of the situation where one enjoys luxury and another suffers want. The motif of the eschatological reversal of fortunes for rich and poor[21] surely belongs properly to the religious folklore of ordinary people, the poor. It is their hope in the justice of God against the injustice of this life as they experience it. Jesus in the parable takes up that perception, that hope and a popular way of expressing it. The parable is one of many indications that Jesus was close to both the religious folklore and the concerns of ordinary, poor people.

By contrast, the Egyptian story is not. The way it uses the motif of the reversal of fortunes is far from suggesting that the rich because they are rich now will suffer hereafter or that the poor because they are poor now will be exalted hereafter. Its message is rather that one's destiny in the next world is determined solely by one's good or evil deeds in this world, to which social position is irrelevant. It should be read against the background of the strongly hierarchical assumptions of Egyptian tradition. It counters the expectation that the social hierarchy of this world will be reproduced in the next. This is why the theme of the burials is central. Setme naturally assumes that a man whose splendid funeral shows him to be of high social status, esteemed by the whole community, will occupy an equally enviable

---

[21] On the theme, see Mealand, *Poverty and Expectation in the Gospels,* 41-52; Schottroff and Stegemann, *Jesus and the Hope of the Poor,* 19-32.

position in Amente. The theme of reversal is used to shatter this view with an extreme case—the righteous poor man who is highly honoured in Amente, contrasted with the wicked rich man who is humiliatingly punished in Amente. But it is not meant to turn Setme's assumption on its head. The point is that moral worth is not related to social status in this world, but moral worth in this world is what will determine social status in Amente. It is perhaps not difficult to see why many scholars would like to make Jesus' parable more consistent with such a view. In fact, the comparison of the two stories shows that they use the motif of reversal with quite different aims.

In a recent article[22] Ronald Hock has tried to direct attention away from the Egyptian story as a parallel to the parable and instead to compare the latter with the contrast between rich and poor in Lucian's two dialogues *Gallus* and *Cataplus*. He is probably wrong to argue that the latter are *more* relevant to the interpretation of the parable than the Egyptian story is, but right to argue that they are *also* relevant. The 'comparative net,' as he puts it, must certainly be cast 'wide enough to include ... the traditional culture of Greco-Roman society.'[23] Lucian in fact shows that the motif of the reversal of fortunes of rich and poor belonged to the common culture of the Mediterranean world.

It is the *Cataplus* which partly parallels the plot of the parable, but because the poor man in it, Micyllus, also appears along with rich men in the *Gallus*, Hock uses the latter to fill out our understanding of Lucian's approval of the poor and disapproval of the rich. The *Cataplus* depicts, in dialogue form, a journey of the dead to Hades—conducted by Hermes, rowed across the Styx by Charon, judged and consigned to their destinies of punishment or bliss by Rhadamanthus. The story is told with Lucianic humour, but about the virtues of the poor and the evils of the rich Lucian is certainly serious. The dialogue focusses on three souls who make the journey: those of a Cynic philosopher, the shoemaker Micyllus (who is poor but not destitute like Lazarus), and the rich tyrant Megapenthes. Examined for sins, the philosopher and the poor man are both found spotless and sent to the isles of the blessed, whereas the tyrant is found deserving of a punishment designed especially for his case. The contrast of rich and poor is somewhat complicated by the fact that Megapenthes is not only rich but also a tyrant, so that abuses of political power loom large among his crimes, as well as the immorality Lucian associates with wealth. It should also be noticed that Lucian employs (here as elsewhere) the

---

[22] Hock, 'Lazarus and Micyllus.'
[23] Hock, 'Lazarus and Micyllus,' 456.

theme of death as the great leveller, which puts rich and poor on the same footing. Megapenthes is reluctant to die because he has so much to lose; Micyllus welcomes death because he has nothing to lose (*Cat.* 14-15). But it is also true (as Hock stresses) that Lucian associates wealth with morally reprehensible lives and poverty with morally blameless lives. The rich are likely to have amassed their wealth by dishonest means, to live by violence and injustice, and especially to live hedonistically, indulging their appetites with banquets and sexual promiscuity. Megapenthes is damned for his lack of self-control. Poverty, on the other hand, promotes hard work, simple living, self-control. Micyllus is blameless because his poverty protects him from the corrupting opportunities for self-indulgence that ruin Megapenthes.

Lucian's use of the motif of reversal seems closer to Jesus' parable than is that in the Egyptian story. He does not make wealth and poverty in this life irrelevant to the judgment after death. But on the other hand he does not preserve, as the parable does, the stark simplicity of the motif in its basic form: that it is the inequality of rich and poor as such which is unjust and must be remedied. In his own way. Lucian moralizes as much as the Egyptian story. The rich are condemned because riches make people wicked, especially hedonistic, and the poor are approved because poverty makes them virtuous. Hock, who like most scholars cannot accept Luke 16:25 as sufficient explanation for the reversal of fortunes in the parable,[24] reads into it Lucian's Cynic perspective. The rich man is supposed to be condemned 'not merely because of what he failed to do, that is, feed Lazarus. but because of what he habitually did, that is, live hedonistically and immorally.'[25] But this is to misuse the parallel in Lucian in the same way as others have misused the Egyptian story. The parable does not condemn the rich man because his lavish feasts are self-indulgent and associated with sexual immorality, but because he is living in luxury while Lazarus is destitute. The *juxtaposition* of the rich man's luxury and Lazarus' painful poverty expresses the parable's point of view without any moralizing between the lines.

In another respect Hock's argument is very puzzling. He points out that the Egyptian story, by providing a parallel only to the first part of the parable, has encouraged scholars to divide the parable into two distinct parts and impeded a perception of its unity.[26] But

---

[24] He calls the rationale for the reversal of fortunes 'opaque': 'Lazarus and Micyllus,' 452-453, 455.

[25] Hock, 'Lazarus and Micyllus,' 462.

[26] Hock, 'Lazarus and Micyllus,' 449, 454.

Lucian's *Cataplus* provides no parallel to the second part of the parable, to which Hock in fact scarcely refers.[27] It is not at all clear how the parallel with Lucian is supposed to make clear the unity of the parable. This will be better approached by way of other, neglected and unnoticed, parallels to the motif of a dead person's return with a message for the living.

III The Proposed Return of Lazarus

The ancient world was familiar with a variety of methods by which the living might know what happens in the world of the dead. One such method, which the Egyptian and Jewish stories of the rich man and the poor man employ, was a visit by a living person to the world of the dead (usually in a dream or a vision). Sometimes such a visit could fulfil the purpose for which the rich man in the parable requests that Lazarus be allowed to return to the world of the living: to warn the living of the torment which awaits them after death unless they repent. The late Jewish story which Bultmann[28] preferred to the Egyptian story as a source for the parable of the rich man and Lazarus is an example. It tells of a rich and godless married couple. In the man's house is a door leading to hell. Though warned never to enter, the wife cannot resist her curiosity, looks in and is dragged into hell from which there is no escape. A giant offers to take the husband to hell in search of her. A young man goes with the giant on the husband's behalf, sees the wife in torment, and brings back a message urging her husband to repent and so avoid sharing her fate. He does so.[29] This strange story is unlikely to be as old as the New Testament, but it preserves an old motif (a wicked person suffering in hell sends a warning message to a relative who repents) which the parable of the rich man and Lazarus also uses.

However, as well as the idea of a living person visiting hell the notion of a dead person returning soon after their death to the world of the living was also common. It took two forms, and since examples of both could throw light on the parable both will be considered here. The first is the notion of temporary death. Stories were told of people who had been dead or at least taken for dead but revived after a few days and recounted their experiences in the world of the dead. Such stories correspond to the frequent modern testimonies of people who

---

[27] Hock, 'Lazarus and Micyllus,' 462.

[28] Bultmann, *The History of the Synoptic Tradition*, 197.

[29] I. Lévi, 'Un receuil de contes juifs inédits,' *REJ* 35 (1897) 76-81 (story XI); cf. Gaster, *The Exempla of the Rabbis*, 122 (no.338), 245 (list of parallels).

have been clinically 'dead' through cardiac arrest and then have been resuscitated and report visionary experiences of out-of-the-body journeys, in which they reach the threshold of the next life and glimpse its joys (or, occasionally, its terrors), before being sent back.[30] These so-called 'near-death experiences' often seem to be clothed in the imagery of the next life which is familiar from the subject's religious tradition. Whatever their explanation, some (though far fewer) people in ancient cultures must have had similar experiences. Most of the stories we have from antiquity belong to a literary tradition, but it is reasonable to suppose that the literary tradition had its origins in stories actually told by people who had had near-death experiences, and also that there was an oral folklore tradition of such stories on which the literary tradition sometimes draws.

The earliest example, which became a model for some others, is Plato's story of Er the Pamphylian (*Resp.* 10.614B-621B). This is already a conscious literary creation, though whether Plato borrowed and reworked some existing story, perhaps of oriental origin, has been inconclusively discussed. Er was killed in battle, but several days later revived on his funeral pyre and recounted what he had seen as a disembodied spirit in the realm of the dead before being returned to his body. When he first arrived at the place where departed souls are judged he was told to observe all that went on in the realm of the dead and report it to the living on his return. The story is a vehicle for Plato's own views on the fate of souls after death: blessedness in heaven for the good, punishment in Hades for the wicked, and a choice of lives in which to be reincarnated. But it is told as a kind of revelation which will help people live well and wisely with their future destiny in view.

Other writers followed Plato's example. The no longer extant *Peri physeos*, told how Zoroaster (apparently identified with Plato's Er)[31] visited Hades between death and resuscitation.[32] Plutarch (*De sera* 22-33) tells of Thespesius, who was knocked unconscious and taken for

---

[30] R. A. Moody, Jr., *Life After Life* (New York: Bantam, 1975); J. C. Hampe, *To Die is Gain: The Experience of One's Own Death* (trans. M. Kohl; London: Darton, Longman & Todd, 1979); and a large literature listed in C. Zalesky, *Otherworld Journeys: Accounts of Near-Death Experience in Medieval and Modern Times* (New York: Oxford University Press, 1987) 257-266. Zalesky's book summarizes the critical discussion so far, and makes a valuable contribution to it from the perspective of comparison with medieval visions of the same type.

[31] Like Er, he is called 'the son of Harmonius, the Pamphylian'; cf. also Arnobius, *Adv. Gent.* 1.52.

[32] J. Bidez and F. Cumont, *Les mages hellénisés*, vol. 1 (Paris: Société d'Editions "Les Belles Lettres,' 1938) 112-113; but cf. J. D. P. Bolton, *Aristeas of Proconnesus* (Oxford: Clarendon, 1962) 159, 203 n.26.

dead but revived on the third day. The story is no doubt modelled on
Plato's, for the same purpose of depicting the author's view of the fate
of souls in a myth. Plutarch reports that Thespesius reformed his life
after seeing the horrors of punishment in the next life, and he may
well have hoped his readers would similarly respond to the story.
Probably of the same type was the story told by Aristotle's disciple
Clearchus of Soli (fragment 8) of Cleonymus, who revived from apparent death and reported that he had seen the rivers of Hades and
souls being judged and punished and purified.[33] But another feature
of this story reveals its closeness to popular storytelling: Cleonymus
met another temporary visitor to Hades and the two agreed to try to
get in touch when they returned to earth. The same motif appears in
Cornelius Labeo's story of two men who died on the same day, met
each other at the crossroads in Hades, were commanded to return,
and resolved to live as friends thereafter (Augustine, *De civ. Dei* 22.28).

A popular motif to explain the experience of temporary death
seems to have been that of mistaken identity. Pliny reports from
Varro the story of the two brothers Cerfidius, of whom one, taken for
dead, returned from Hades with news of the other brother whom he
had met in Hades and was then found to be dead (Pliny, *HN* 7.177).
Evidently the wrong brother had initially been taken to Hades by
mistake. This motif of mistaken identity occurs also in Plutarch's story
of Antyllus (*ap.* Eusebius, *Praep. Evang.* 11.36). Lucian parodied it in
the character of Cleomenes (*Philops.* 25) who claims that he went to
Hades temporarily during an illness because his psychopomp came to
fetch him by mistake. He was sent back when Pluto declared he was
not to die yet, whereas the man who was due to die was Demylus the
coppersmith who lived next door to Cleodemus. As usually in these
stories, Cleodemus authenticates his tale by reporting that Demylus
did in fact die not long after Cleodemus had brought the news from
Hades.[34]

The folkloric character of such stories is unmistakable. No doubt
sometimes they were just good stories. Their claim to be true anecdotes about named people was an important part of their appeal. But
the fact that Lucian's Cleodemus mentions seeing the wellknown
sights of Hades suggests it was not only in the sophistated literary
tradition of Plato and Plutarch that such stories were the framework
for revelations of Hades, especially its punishments.

---

[33] Probably the Coptic Apocalypse of Zephaniah should also be understood as
belonging to this literary tradition.

[34] The theme of mistaken identity continues in later Christian stories: Augustine,
De cura pro mortuis gerenda 15; Gregory the Great, *Dial.* 4.36. Even modern instances
are reported from India: Zalesky, *Otherworld Journeys,* 239 n.45.

Two variants of the motif of temporary death may be mentioned. One is that of the recently dead person temporarily recalled by necromancy. In Lucan's *Pharsalia* 6.569-830, the witch Erichtho recalls to his body the soul of one of Pompey's soldiers only recently dead and still on the journey to Hades. He tells what he has seen and prophesies the future before the witch allows him finally to die.[35] Another special form of the motif of temporary death, found only in Christian stories, is that of a person who dies and is miraculously raised from the dead by an apostle. In stories of this kind in the Acts of Thomas (51-59) and the Preaching of Andrew[36] the resurrected person tells of what he or she has seen in hell, with a salutary effect on those who hear. A story in the History of the Contending of St Paul[37] is unusual in that the dead man not only sees the punishments in Gehenna but actually begins to be punished himself, until an angel rescues him so that Peter and Andrew can restore him to life.

The second way in which a dead person was believed to be able to return to visit the living was as a ghost or in a dream. This possibility was very widely believed in the ancient world.[38] Many instances— legendary, fictional and purportedly historical—occur in ancient literature. The dead might either appear by their own volition or be called up by magical practices.[39] Most often it was the recently dead who appeared to those who had known them. Their appearances served a wide variety of purposes. They might come to comfort mourning relatives.[40] Since the dead were thought to be able to foresee the future, they might appear to warn someone of impending

---

[35] For this kind of necromancy (reviving a corpse), see also Apuleius, *Met.* 2.28-29; F. Cumont, *Lux Perpetua* (Paris: Librairie Orientaliste Paul Geuthner, 1949) 101-102.

[36] Arabic translated in A. S. Lewis, *The Mythological Acts of the Apostles* (Horae Semiticae 4; London: C. J. Clay, 1904) 7-8; Ethiopic translated in E. A. W. Budge, *The Contendings of the Apostles* (Oxford: University Press, 1935) 147-148.

[37] Budge, *The Contendings of the Apostles*, 552-554. Cf. also an incident in the *History of John*: Lewis, *The Mythological Acts of the Apostles*, 161-164; W. Wright, *Apocryphal Acts of the Apostles*, vol. 2 (London: Williams & Norgate, 1871) 19-25.

[38] See L. Collison-Morley, *Greek and Roman Ghost Stories* (Oxford; Blackwell, 1912); Cumont, *Lux Perpetua*, 78-108. Rabbinic examples are in Strack-Billerbeck 1.148-149, 225; 4.1142.

[39] On necromancy, see W. O. E. Oesterley, *Immortality and the Unseen World: A Study in Old Testament Religion* (London: SPCK, 1921) 124-140; Cumont, *Lux Perpetua*, 97-108; R. Garland, *The Greek Way of Death* (London: Duckworth, 1985) 2-3, 133; Collison-Morley, *Greek and Roman Ghost Stories*, 33-44.

[40] Quintilian, *Declam.* 10; cf. F. Cumont, *After Life in Roman Paganism* (New York: Dover, 1959; reprinted from 1922 edition) 61. This constitutes motifs nos. E324-327 (cf. E361) in Stith Thompson, *Motif-Index of Folk-Literature* (2nd edition; Copenhagen: Rosenkilde & Bagger, 1955-1958).

catastrophe[41] or their oracular powers might be consulted by necromancy.[42] Victims of murder might appear in order to inform on their
murderers,[43] or appear to their murderers in order to menace them.[44]
The unburied or inadequately buried might request burial rites.[45]
Wives might request husbands to make their clothes available to them
in the next life by burning them.[46]

For our purposes the most relevant examples are those few cases
where the dead person reveals his or her own fate or that of others in
the next world. A very ancient example of this type occurs in the
Sumerian poem *Gilgamesh, Enkidu and the Netherworld*,[47] where Enkidu
descends to the underworld on a mission from his friend Gilgamesh,
fails to escape alive but is allowed to return temporarily as a ghost to
speak to Gilgamesh. He speaks in some detail about the fate of the
dead in the world of the dead, which is not a place of reward and
punishment for good and evil, but in which various categories of the
dead fare more or less better than others. An example from the
Roman period is a Latin epitaph which describes how a young man
recently deceased appears to his mother. He tells her not to mourn
for him, because he is not in Tartarus, the place of punishment, but
among the stars where he enjoys the blessedness of an apotheosised
hero.[48] In several rabbinic stories (collected in EcclRab 9.10.1-2) of
dead rabbis appearing to living rabbis in dreams, details of the status
of specific people in paradise, such as which rabbis were worthy to sit
next to which, are said to have been reported.

The most interesting case for our purposes occurs in the Jewish or
Christian Book (or Penitence) of Jannes and Jambres, which survives
in very fragmentary texts.[49] It is impossible to be certain whether the

---

[41] Pliny, *Ep.* 5.5; Valerius Maximus 1.7.6.

[42] 1 Sam 28:7-25; Herodotus 5.92.

[43] Apuleius, *Met.* 8.4; Aelian, fragment 82; Cicero, *De divin.* 1.27.57; Gaster, *The Exempla of the Rabbis*, 130-131 (no.353). This is motif no. E231 in Stith Thompson, *Motif-Index*.

[44] Plutarch, *Cimon* 6; Suetonius, *Nero* 34.

[45] Homer, *Iliad* 23.65-107; Alcaeus, fragment 38; Suetonius, *Calig.* 59; Pliny, *Ep.* 7.27; Augustine, *De cura pro mortuis gerenda* 12; cf. Suetonius, *Gaius* 59. This is motif no. E235.2 in Stith Thompson, *Motif-Index*.

[46] Herodotus 5.92; Lucian, *Philops.* 27; cf. *b. Ber.* 18b.

[47] Sumerian text translated in C. J. Gadd, 'Epic of Gilgamesh, Tablet XII,' *Revue d'Assyriologie* 30 (1933) 127-143; Akkadian version (which forms tablet 12 of the Gilgamesh epic) translated in A. Heidel, *The Gilgamesh Epic and Old Testament Parallels* (2nd edition; Chicago: University Press, 1949) 93-101.

[48] Cumont, *Lux Perpetua*, 93.

[49] The Latin fragment, the Vienna papyrus fragments and the larger of the Chester Beatty papyrus fragments are translated by A. Pietersma and T. R. Lutz in J. H. Charlesworth ed., *The Old Testament Pseudepigrapha*, vol. 2 (London: Darton, Longman

work was originally Jewish or Christian,[50] though the former seems more probable,[51] or whether it was already written by the time of Jesus (though it cannot be later than the early third century C.E.).[52] However, it seems clear that a *story* of Jannes and Jambres, the names given in Jewish tradition to the Egyptian magicians who opposed Moses, was already current in some form in pre-Christian Judaism (cf. CD 5:19; 2 Tim 3:8-9). There is a reasonable probability that at least the outline of the story to be found in the Book of Jannes and Jambres was known in pre-Christian Judaism.

The relevant part of the story is as follows. As divine punishment for his opposition to Moses, Jannes dies, as does his mother soon afterwards. Jambres buries his mother next to his brother's tomb, and then uses the books of magic which his brother had entrusted to him to call up his brother's shade from Hades. (The fragmentary text does not allow us to tell what his motive may have been.) When the soul of Jannes appears, he acknowledges that his death was just punishment for his opposition to Moses and Aaron. He is now in the underworld 'where there is great burning and the lake of perdition, whence no one ascends.' He urges Jambres to lead a good life so as not to share his fate in Hades: 'take heed in your life to do good to your sons and friends, for in the netherworld no good exists, only sadness and darkness.'[53] Only fragments of the rest of Jannes' evidently long communication to his brother survive, but it is clear that he described the torture he and those like him were suffering in Hades ($23f^r = 6{\rightarrow}23$-26).[54] He described Hades as a place where noone, not even kings, get favoured treatment because of their social status ($22j^v = 7{\downarrow}25$-27). There seems to have been reference to a variety of sins which had

---

& Todd, 1985) 437-442. Texts, facsimiles and translations of all fragments except the two Papyrus Michigan fragments (which remain unpublished) are in A. Pietersma, *The Apocryphon of Jannes and Jambres the Magicians* (Religions in the Graeco-Roman World 119; Leiden: Brill, 1994).

[50] The possible indications of a Christian origin which Pietersma and Lutz, in Charlesworth ed., *The Old Testament Pseudepigrapha*, 2.433, point out are not at all conclusive.

[51] Pietersma, *The Apocryphon*, 58.

[52] Pietersma and Lutz in Charlesworth ed., *The Old Testament Pseudepigrapha*, 2.432. Pietersma, *The Apocryphon*, 58, 133-134, thinks it was known to the author of 2 Timothy.

[53] Latin fragment translated by Pietersma, *The Apocryphon*, 281; cf. Pietersma and Lutz in Charlesworth ed., *The Old Testament Pseudepigrapha*, 2.440-441; M. R. James, *The Lost Apocrypha of the Old Testament* (London: SPCK, 1920) 32-33.

[54] References to the Chester Beatty fragments give, first, the numbers of the fragments used in the translations in Charlesworth ed., *The Old Testament Pseudepigrapha*, 2.441-442, and, secondly, the frame numbers and line numbers of the reconstructed texts in Pietersma, *The Apocryphon*.

brought people to punishment in Hades ($22a^v = 7\!\downarrow\!1\text{-}6$, $22b^v = 7\!\downarrow\!12\text{-}$
13, $22c^v = 7\!\downarrow\!14\text{-}15$). Significantly, he seems to have said that there
could now be no forgiveness for him and others like him in Hades
($23f^v = 6\!\downarrow\!23\text{-}26$). Unfortunately, the texts do not preserve the rest of
the story. We do not know whether Jambres heeded his brother's
warning, repented and obtained forgiveness. A reference to the story
in the Penitence of Cyprian seems to imply that he was not forgiven,
but is not conclusive on the point.[55]

The idea of a message from a dead brother, tormented in Hades,
to his living brother, revealing his fate and urging his brother to
repent and thereby to avoid the same fate, is clearly close to Luke
16:27-28. There are differences: the rich man in the parable does not
propose to go himself, but asks Abraham to send Lazarus, and he
does not envisage necromancy. But the resemblance is close enough
to make the possibility suggested in Luke 16:27-28 one which could
have been familiar to Jesus' hearers from a traditional Jewish story.
We cannot be sure that the story in this form was available to them,
and there can be no question of identifying the story as a source of
the parable. But as a parallel to the parable, it confirms that the motif
employed in Luke 16:27-28 could easily have been current in Jewish
storytelling.

The question arises whether the return of Lazarus which is envisaged in Luke 16:27-31 is a return to earthly life after temporary death
or a temporary visit by the dead Lazarus as a ghost or in a dream. It
should be noted that in most stories of temporary death the subject
does not actually enter on his eternal destiny before being sent back.
Either he is treated as a mere visitor, who views the sights, or else he
gets no farther than the judgment at which his fate would be assigned. This weighs against, but does not rule out the possibility that
the suggestion is that Lazarus be sent back to resume his earthly life.
On the other hand, although the language of verse 30 (ἀπὸ νεκρῶν
πορευθῇ) would be consistent with an appearance in a dream or as a
ghost, ἐκ νεκρῶν ἀναστῇ (v 31) is not. Not only is ἀνίστημι regularly
used of resurrection;[56] it could not here naturally mean anything else,
since the image of getting up from a prone position requires the rising
of the dead body,[57] not the mere ascent of the soul from Hades.

---

[55] Pietersma and Lutz in Charlesworth ed., *The Old Testament Pseudepigrapha*, 2.435;
Pietersma, *The Apocryphon*, 56-57, 61-63.

[56] A. Oepke in TDNT 1.369-371.

[57] Cf. C. F. Evans, *Resurrection and the New Testament* (SBT 2/12; London: SCM
Press, 1970) 22-25.

Tanghe has argued persuasively that the reading ἀπελθῃ should be preferred to ἀναστῃ in verse 31.[58] The latter can be explained as a later attempt to give a christological reference, like the reading ἐγερθῃ in both verses 30 and 31 in P[75]. In that case we should probably take the reference throughout verses 27-31 to be to a temporary visit by Lazarus' shade. But if the reading ἀναστῃ is preferred, there is no need to suppose that it represents a more remarkable possibility than had been envisaged in verses 27-30,[59] still less that it refers to the resurrection of Jesus.[60] Resurrection after temporary death was a well recognized form in which the request of verses 27-28 could be fulfilled; ἀναστῃ would simply define more closely what had been left open in verses 27-30. Of course, it is possible that ἀναστῃ belongs to the Lukan redaction of the parable and is intended to carry a secondary overtone of reference to the resurrection of Jesus, but if so the overtone is not only secondary but artificial. The risen Jesus did not appear to unbelieving Jews to reveal the fate of people like them in the afterlife.

The possibility which is discussed and rejected in Luke 16:27-31 is not a miraculous sign which the rich man thinks his brothers will require in order to believe. To link this second part of the parable with discussion of the desire for and needlessness of signs to confirm religious truth is mistaken.[61] The purpose of Lazarus's proposed visit to the rich man's brothers is to reveal the fate of their brother in Hades (as well as perhaps Lazarus's own fate, by contrast) as a powerful warning that, unless they reform their lives, they will share their brother's fate. Such a proposal would not be surprising to the hearers of a story of this kind. The motif is one with which they would be familiar. What would come as a surprise is the refusal of the rich man's request. Since it is often the points at which the stories take an unexpected turn which prove peculiarly illuminating as to the meaning of Jesus' parables, Abraham's refusal to send Lazarus to the rich man's brothers deserves our close attention.

Before we discuss that point, however, a comment may be appropriate on the often remarked fact that Lazarus, uniquely among the characters in the Gospel parables, has a name. The explanation may lie purely in the exigencies of the telling of the story. Since the theme of the reversal of fortunes requires us no longer to regard the rich

---

[58] Tanghe, 'Abraham.'

[59] *Contra* Jeremias, *The Parables of Jesus,* 186.

[60] *Contra,* e.g., Mealand, *Poverty and Expectation in the Gospels,* 48.

[61] *Contra* Jeremias, *The Parables of Jesus,* 186; Bultmann, *The History of the Synoptic Tradition,* 196 and n.1.

man as rich after his death or the poor man as poor after his death, they cannot be designated as 'the rich man' and 'the poor man' after verse 22. The nature of the narrative after v. 22 makes any designation for the erstwhile rich man unnecessary (apart from Abraham's addressing him as τέκνον [v 25] corresponding to his addressing Abraham as πάτερ). But some way of referring to the erstwhile poor man becomes necessary (vv 23, 24, 25), and very cumbersome expressions would be required if he had not been given a name.

However, it may also be relevant to notice that in stories of the return of a dead person he or she is almost always named. This is because they either purport to be true anecdotes about known people or else are fictional imitations of such true anecdotes. The name Lazarus would assist the impression that the parable belongs to the category of such stories, in which a revelation from the world of the dead to the living may be expected to occur. It would increase the surprise that such a revelation, though requested, is refused.

IV ABRAHAM'S REFUSAL

By comparison with stories that are in some way comparable, the parable is unusual in two respects: (1) Among stories which tell of the fate of particular individuals after death, the parable is unusual[62] in not describing a process by which this fate became known to the living people in the story. (2) Among stories which use the motif of the return of a dead person with a message for the living, the parable is unique in not telling the story of such a return, but only of a request for such a return which is refused.

At first sight these two unusual features seem to belong respectively to the first (vv 19-26) and the second parts (vv 27-31) of the parable. On closer consideration, however, they can be seen to belong very closely together and to constitute the unity of the parable. The motif of the return of a dead person is one way in which the fate of particular individuals after death can be made known to the living. It was a wellknown alternative to the visit of the living to Hades which fulfils this function in the Egyptian story of Setme and Si-Osiris. The unusual character of the story in the parable, therefore, is that it describes the fate of particular individuals after death, proposes a way in which this fate could have become known to the living, but then

---

[62] Other examples are Lucian, *Cataplus*, which has no pretension to be anything but a satirical fiction, and EcclRab 1.15.1, which tells a parabolic story in which two men go to differing fates after death and the wicked man, seeing the other, asks about the difference in their fates. In this latter case, the lack of a name for either man shows there is no intention of referring to historical individuals.

rejects it. A hearer or reader familiar with the way the folkloric motifs in the story were generally used would already before verse 26 be expecting to be told of some means by which the fates of the rich man and Lazarus became known to the living, would recognize the rich man's request in verses 26-27 as proposing a well recognized means for this purpose, and would expect the request to be granted, the revelation to be made by Lazarus to the rich man's brothers, and most likely the brothers to repent. The story reflects the strength of these expectations in the rich man's persistence with his request (v 30) and deliberately diverges from them in the careful emphasis of Abraham's two-part response (vv 29, 31).

What Abraham refuses to grant the rich man's brothers is an apocalyptic revelation of the fate of the dead, such as Si-Orisis gave to Setme, or Jambres to Jannes. But in that case the parable's own account of the fates of the rich man and Lazarus (vv 22-26) is deprived of the status of such a revelation. The means of revelation which the reader expects it to acquire as the story proceeds are denied it. The story in effect deprives itself of any claim to offer an apocalyptic glimpse of the secrets of the world beyond the grave. It cannot claim eyewitness authority as a literal description of the fate of the dead. It has only the status of parable. It is part of a story told to make a point. The point is no more than the law and the prophets say—and that no more than the law and the prophets say is required.

The first part of the parable is a comment on the situation sketched in verses 19-21. It uses the popular motif of eschatological reversal to express the stark contradiction between that situation of flagrant injustice and the justice of God to which the poor look for remedy. If it is close to the religious folklore of the poor, it is also close to 'Moses and the prophets' (i.e. the Hebrew Bible), which hold out the ideal of relative material equality among the people of God, denounce the rich who live in luxury while the poor are destitute, and maintain the expectation of God's justice as the hope of the poor in the face of the arrogant complacency of the rich and powerful. To perceive the situation of the rich and the poor as radically unjust the rich need only listen to Moses and the prophets. If they refuse to see how the situation contradicts God's justice on the evidence of the scriptures, no purported revelation of the fate of the dead will convince them. By refusing an apocalyptic revelation from the world of the dead, the parable throws the emphasis back onto the situation with which it began. The second part of the parable, like the first, is also a comment on that situation. After the excursion into the hereafter, it brings us back to the world in which the rich coexist with the destitute because they do not listen to Moses and the prophets.

In conclusion, it may be seen that the true significance of the parable emerges when attention is given to all available parallels, not restricted to one, and when attention is given to the parable's differences from, as well as its resemblances to the parallels. Comparison with the story of Setme and Si-Osiris, its Jewish derivatives, and Lucian's *Cataplus,* shows the parable's use of the theme of reversal of fortunes to be different from theirs in highlighting the injustice of gross material inequality as such. Comparison with the story of Si-Osiris, its Jewish derivatives, along with examples of the return of a dead person to reveal the fate of the dead to the living, shows that the parable's unity hinges on Abraham's unexpected refusal of the rich man's request, directing attention away from an apocalyptic revelation of the afterlife back to the inexcusable injustice of the coexistence of rich and poor.

CHAPTER FIVE

THE TONGUE SET ON FIRE BY HELL (JAMES 3:6)

James 3:6 is a notoriously difficult verse. The problems usually discussed concern the middle part of the verse (ὁ κόσμος τῆς ἀδικίας ἡ γλῶσσα καθίσταται ἐν τοῖς μέλεσιν ἡμῶν ἡ σπιλοῦσα ὅλον τὸ σῶμα).[1] In this chapter we shall not be concerned with these, but rather with the last two phrases of the verse (καὶ φλογίζουσα τὸν τροχὸν τῆς γενέσεως καὶ φλογιζομένη ὑπὸ τῆς γεέννες), which are commonly regarded as relatively unproblematic.

Whatever the meaning of the middle part of the verse, it is clear that the two concluding phrases continue the image of the tongue as a destructive fire which was introduced in verses 5b-6a. Omitting the problematic middle part of verse 6, we have:

> ἰδοὺ ἡλίκον πῦρ ἡλίκην ὕλην ἀνάπτει·
> καὶ ἡ γλῶσσα πῦρ·
> ...
> καὶ φλογίζουσα τὸν τροχὸν τῆς γενέσεως
> καὶ φλογιζομένη ὑπὸ τῆς γεέννες.

> See how small a fire sets alight so large a forest!
> The tongue is a fire.
> ...
> setting on fire the wheel of existence
> and being set on fire by Gehenna.

By contrast with the extensive debates about the meaning of much of verse 6, most commentators are agreed on the meaning of its last four words. They think it obvious that these words refer to the source of the tongue's power for evil. The tongue derives its dangerous power from the devil or the forces of evil, here symbolized by or located in

---

[1] In my view there is much to be said for correcting the text in accordance with the Peshitta, inserting ὕλη after ἀδικίας (so J. Adamson, *The Epistle of James* [NICNT; Grand Rapids: Eerdmans, 1976] 158-159, who correctly refutes Mayor's argument against this). Vv 5b-6a can then be translated: 'See how small a fire sets alight so large a forest [wood]! The tongue is a fire, the sinful world wood.' The first sentence states the image, which the second interprets by identifying the two elements in the allegory. The image is then picked up again in v 6b ('setting on fire the wheel of existence...'), where τὸν τροχὸν τῆς γενέσεως is synonymous with ὁ κόσμος τῆς ἀδικίας.

hell (Gehenna).[2] In Moo's words: 'The power of Satan himself, the chief denizen of hell, gives to the tongue its great destructive potential.'[3]

To this, the usual interpretation there are two insuperable objections: (1) In first-century Jewish and Christian thought Gehenna is not the location of the devil or of the forces of evil. It is the place where the wicked are punished, either after the last judgment or (a view which seems to have been emerging during the first century) after death. Its angels, terrifying and cruel as they are, are servants of God, executing God's judgment on sin.[4] They are not the evil angels who rebel against and resist God. These evil angels, with Satan or the devil at their head, will at the end of history be sent to their doom in Gehenna, but they are not there yet. Rather, they inhabit the terrestrial area from the earth to the lowest heavenly sphere. (It is with this area that James associates them when he contrasts the wisdom that comes from heaven with the false wisdom that is earthly [ἐπίγειος] and demonic [δαιμονιώδης] [3:15].) (2) The fire of Gehenna is always a means or an image of God's judgment. Thus, even if James were supposing that the devil is already being punished in hell, it would make no sense to speak of the fire of Gehenna as the source from which human evil is inspired.

Some of the commentators do claim to provide evidence for locating the devil in Gehenna, but it is not evidence which bears careful examination. Thus Dibelius, who knows that the issue has been contested and realises at least that it was not common to regard Gehenna as the dwelling of Satan,[5] claims: 'That Satan dwells there is expressly stated for the first time in the *Apocalypse of Abraham*. Jas 3:6 is therefore evidence of great significance for the history of religions.'[6] He refers

---

[2] E.g. J. B. Mayor, *The Epistle of St James* (2nd edition; London: Macmillan, 1897) 114; J. Chaine, *L'Épître de Saint Jacques* (Paris: Gabalda, 1927) 83; C. L. Mitton, *The Epistle of James* (London: Marshall, Morgan & Scott, 1966) 128-129; M. Dibelius, *James* (revised by H. Greeven; trans. M. A. Williams; Hermeneia; Philadelphia: Fortress, 1975) 198; S. Laws, *A Commentary on the Epistle of James* (London: A. & C. Black, 1980) 151-152; P. Davids, *The Epistle of James* (NIGTC; Exeter: Paternoster, 1982)143; R. P. Martin, *James* (WBC 48; Waco: Word Books, 1988) 116; L. T. Johnson, *The Letter of James* (AB 37A; New York: Doubleday, 1995) 259-256.

[3] D. J. Moo, *The Letter of James* (TNTC; Leicester: IVP/Grand Rapids: Eerdmans, 1985) 126; cf. W. R. Baker, *Personal Speech-Ethics in the Epistle of James* (WUNT 2/68; Tübingen: Mohr [Siebeck], 1995) 128: 'what is conveyed here is tht [*sic*] the person who does not control his tongue makes his tongue an agent for Satan's harmful designs on the individual and society.'

[4] On the angels of hell, see chapter 8 below, section III.8.

[5] Dibelius, *James*, 199 n. 87.

[6] Dibelius, *James*, 198. This comment is echoed by J. Marty, *L'épître de Jacques: Étude critique* (Paris: Librairie Félix Alcan, 1935) 130.

to passages in Apocalypse of Abraham 14(:5) and 31(:5). These passages are also cited by Davids[7] and Martin.[8] Both passages concern Azazel, who is the chief spirit of evil in the Apocalypse of Abraham (his role as the chief of the fallen Watchers, taken from 1 En 8:1; 9:6; 10:4, 8 [cf. ApAb 14:4, 6], has been extended by identifying him with the serpent in the garden of Eden [ApAb 23:7-12]). In chapter 13 Azazel attempts to dissuade Abraham from ascending to heaven with the angel who has been sent to take him there. Rebuking him, the angel reminds Azazel that, whereas Abraham's portion is in heaven, Azazel's portion is on earth, the dwelling-place he himself has chosen and God has therefore allotted him (13:8). Abraham is told to curse Azazel, using the words: 'May you be the firebrand of the furnace of the earth! Go, Azazel, into the untrodden parts of the earth!' (14:5) The command reflects the association of Azazel with the desert (Lev 16:21-22, 26; 1 En 10:4). The curse ('May you be...') presumably invokes the doom for which Azazel is destined at the day of judgment, when he will be thrown into Gehenna for ever (1 En 10:6; 54:5-6). There is no need to suppose that he is presently in Gehenna. That the reference is to his fate at the last judgment is confirmed by 31:5, which predicts the judgment of Israel's enemies at the end of history: 'they shall putrefy in the belly of the crafty worm Azazel, and be burned by the fire of Azazel's tongue.' Despite Davids' claim that Azazel is here the inhabitant of hell in the present, not the future,[9] the future eschatological reference is entirely clear. That the devil is here depicted as the instrument of the punishment of the wicked in hell is unprecedented. It seems to result from identifying Azazel with (a) the image of a great serpent whose belly is Gehenna (PistSoph 4:126) or Hades (3 Bar G4:3-6; 5:3; cf. Sl5:3), and (b) the worm which often appears in depictions of hell as a result of exegesis of Isaiah 66:24 (where the worm is singular).[10] But even in this unusual passage, Azazel's presence in (or as) hell is in the eschatological future, and the fire he produces is for the punishment of sinners, not the source of evil on earth. The Apocalypse of Abraham offers no real support for the usual interpretation of our phrase in James 3:6.

Davids, following Laws, also refers to b. 'Arak. 15b,[11] but the 'Prince of Gehinnom' who appears there and elsewhere in rabbinic

---

[7] Davids, *The Epistle of James*, 143.

[8] Martin, *James*, 116. Martin refers to ApAb 14:6-8, but must mean 14:5-8.

[9] Davids, *The Epistle of James*, 143.

[10] M. Himmelfarb, *Tours of Hell: An Apocalyptic Form in Jewish and Christian Literature* (Philadelphia: University of Pennsylvania Press, 1983) 116-119.

[11] Laws, *A Commentary*, 152, has the correct reference (15b), which becomes 15a in Davids, *The Epistle of James*, 143.

literature (e.g. b. Sanh. 52a; b. Shab. 104a) is not a power of evil, but the angelic servant of God who rules hell on God's behalf. In the Gedulat Moshe, he escorts Moses on his tour of the punishments in Gehenna,[12] and in some versions he is called Nagarsiel (cf. also b. 'Abod. Zar. 17a).[13] In some early Christian literature he is known as Tartarouchos (the one in charge of Tartarus) (ApPet 13:5; ApPaul 16; 18; 34; 40).

Mitton attempts to support the idea that Gehenna was considered Satan's base of operation, by citing the phrase 'child of Gehenna' (υἱὸν γεέννης) in Matthew 23:15 as though it meant 'child of Satan.'[14] But the phrase actually means 'someone destined for Gehenna' (cf. 'the son of perdition': John 17:12), and diverges not a bit from the usual view of hell as the place of punishment of the wicked. There are two other texts to which the commentators could have appealed for evidence of the location of the devil in Gehenna: Ascension of Isaiah 1:4 and Testament of Dan 5:11. But the first of these can be understood differently,[15] while the second is a Christian text of uncertain date. The location of the devil in Gehenna and his role as its ruler seem to be unknown in ancient Jewish literature and developed only slowly in Christian thought after the second century.[16] To interpret James 3:6 in a way that presupposes these ideas, as most of the commentators do, is clearly indefensible.

This was already seen, among the commentators, by Adolf Schlatter,[17] whose valid objection to the usual interpretation was merely dismissed by Dibelius[18] and thereafter ignored by other commentators. Schlatter also saw, in essence, the correct interpetation of the phrase: that it must refer to the punishment of the sinner in

---

[12] M. Gaster, *Studies and Texts* vol. 1 (London: Maggs, 1925-28) 133-137 (HebVis I 33-49); L. Ginzberg, *The Legends of the Jews*, vol. 2 (Philadelphia: Jewish Publication Society, 1910) 310-313; A. Netzer, 'A Midrash on the Ascension of Moses in Judeo-Persian,' in S. Shaked and A. Netzer ed., *Irano-Judaica II: Studies Relating to Jewish Contacts with Persian Culture Throughout the Ages* (Jerusalem: Ben-Zvi Institute, 1990) 105-143.

[13] Ginzberg, *The Legends of the Jews*, vol. 2, 310-313; Netzer, 'A Midrash,' 134-137 (§§19-30). On the name, see Ginzberg, *The Legends of the Jews*, vol. 5 (Philadelphia: Jewish Publication Society, 1925) 418 (n. 118).

[14] Mitton, *The Epistle of James*, 129.

[15] See the full discussion in chapter 2 above, section VIII.

[16] J. A. MacCulloch, *The Harrowing of Hell* (Edinburgh: T. & T. Clark, 1930) 227-234, 345-346.

[17] A. Schlatter, *Der Brief des Jakobus* (2nd edition; Stuttgart: Calwer, 1956) 223-224.

[18] Dibelius, *James*, 199 n. 87. He rejects Schlatter's own interpretation of the words with bluster rather than argument: 'it cannot be seriously considered that this hell-fire is the fire of punishment such as is inflicted at the judgment of the world' (198).

Gehenna. He refers to Luke 16:24, where the rich man, in agony in the fires in Hades, asks for water to cool his tongue. Accordingly, James means that the destructive power of the tongue will incur God's judgment in the form of the burning thirst of the damned in hell. Schlatter's essentially correct insight can be further supported, amplified and refined by reference to other features of Jewish and early Christian thought about the punishments in hell, such as can be found in those apocalypses which depict them.

We should first observe that the last two phrases of James 3:6 are an instance of a very common way of thinking about eschatological judgment: the eschatological *ius talionis*.[19] The punishment, in other words, fits the crime: the tongue which *sets on fire* (φλογίζουσα) the wheel of existence will itself *be set on fire* (φλογιζομένη) by hell.[20] This verbal correspondence between the crime and its punishment is reinforced by the pun which aligns the object of the crime (τῆς γενέσεως) with the agent of its punishment (τῆς γεέννες). While the pun is purely verbal, it aids the impression of a perfect correspondence between crime and punishment which the sense of strictly just judgment expressed in the concept of *ius talionis* requires.[21] Other examples[22] of the eschatological *ius talionis* expressed by verbal correspondence between the crime and the punishment[23] are:

If anyone destroys (φθείρει) God's temple, God will destroy (φθερεῖ) that person (1 Cor 3:17).

[The time has come] to destroy (διαφθεῖραι) those who destroy (διαφθείροντας) the earth (Rev 11:18).

---

[19] On the *ius talionis* in general, see D. Winston, *The Wisdom of Solomon* (AB 43; New York: Doubleday, 1979) 232-233; I. A. Massey, *Interpreting the Sermon on the Mount in the Light of Jewish Tradition as Evidenced in the Palestinian Targums of the Pentateuch* (Studies in the Bible and Early Christianity 25; Lewiston/Queenston/Lampeter: Edwin Mellen Press, 1991) chapter 3. On the eschatological *ius talionis* in particular, see D. D. Fiensy, 'Lex Talionis in the Apocalypse of Peter,' *HTR* 76 (1983) 255-58; Himmelfarb, *Tours*, chapter 3; chapter 8 below, section III.7 (b).

[20] There is no difficulty in giving the present participle φλογιζομένη a future meaning. The future participle is not used in the Greek of the New Testament.

[21] For the *ius talionis* as the principle of divine justice, see Isa 3:11; Joel 3:6-8; Obad 15-16; 2 Thess 1:6; LAB 44:10; Tg. Neof. Gen 38:25.

[22] Old Testament examples of verbal correspondence in statements of *ius talionis* as the principle of God's justice (though not, in their OT context, eschatological) are Isa 33:1; Hos 4:6.

[23] Several of these are classified as 'sentences of holy law' by E. Käsemann, 'Sentences of Holy Law in the New Testament,' in idem, *New Testament Questions of Today* (London: SCM Press, 1969) 66-81, but Käsemann uses more restrictive formal criteria. Cf. the discussion of Käsemann's form-critical argument in D. E. Aune, *Prophecy in Early Christianity and the Ancient Mediterranean World* (Grand Rapids: Eerdmans, 1983) 237-239.

Because they shed the blood (αἷμα) of saints and prophets, you have given them blood (αἷμα) to drink. It is what they deserve! (Rev 16:6)

And the angels who did not keep (τηρήσαντας) their own position, but left their proper dwelling, he has kept (τετήρηκεν) in eternal chains in deepest darkness for the judgment of the great day (Jude 6).

Whoever is ashamed (ἐπαισχυνθῇ) of me and of my words in this adulterous and sinful generation, of that person the Son of man will also be ashamed (ἐπαισχυνθήσεται) when he comes in the glory of his Father with the holy angels (Mark 8:38).

I warn everyone who hears the words of the prophecy of this book (τοῦ βιβλίου τουτοῦ): if anyone adds to them (ἐπιθῇ ἐπ' αὐτά), God will add to that person (ἐπιθήσει ... ἐπ' αὐτὸν) the plagues described in this book (τῷ βιβλίῳ τουτῳ); if anyone takes away (ἀφέλη) from the words of the book (τοῦ βιβλίου) of this prophecy, God will take away (ἀφελεῖ) that person's share in the tree of life and in the holy city, which are described in this book (τῷ βιβλίῳ τουτῳ) (Rev 22:18-19).

The one who takes vengeance (ἐκδίκων) will suffer vengeance (ἐκδίκησιν) from the Lord (Sir 28:1).

The one who expresses anger to any person without provocation will reap anger in the great judgment (2 Enoch 44:3a).

There is even another example in the letter of James itself:

For judgment will be without mercy (ἀνέλεος) to the one who has shown no mercy (ἔλεος) (Jas 2:13a).

As well as the negative *ius talionis* (the sinner will receive a punishment equivalent to the crime committed) there is a corresponding positive principle of just reward (the righteous person will receive a reward equivalent his or her good deed). This too can expressed by verbal correspondence:

Do not turn your face away (ἀποστρέψῃς τὸ πρόσωπον σου) from anyone who is poor, and the face of God will not be turned away (ἀποστραφῇ τὸ πρόσωπον τοῦ θεοῦ) from you (Tob 4:7; cf. 13:6).[24]

James has an example of this too:

A harvest of righteousness in peace (εἰρήνη) is sown for those who make peace (εἰρήνην) (Jas 3:18).

Thus the way in which the eschatological *ius talionis* is expressed in James 3:6 corresponds closely to a common way of expressing God's eschatological justice, one which James himself uses elsewhere in his letter.

---

[24] In this case the reward is not eschatological.

There is more to be said, however, about the fact that in James 3:6 it is the *tongue* which has sinned and will be punished. One way of making the punishment correspond to the crime—both in thinking about God's providential justice in this life and God's eschatological justice in the next—was to say that the part of the body which sinned is the part which shall be punished. Two forms of this principle are relevant. One way in which it could be stated is: 'The limb which began the transgression, from it will begin the punishment' (Sifre Num 18). An example which relates to eschatological judgment is: 'A man shall not let his ears hear idle chatter, for they will be burnt first of all his limbs' (b. Ket. 5b). An example which relates to judgment in this life is worth mentioning because it concerns the tongue. The punishment of Doeg, who sinned with his tongue when he informed on David and Ahimelech, is that 'a fiery worm will go up into his tongue and make him rot away' (LAB 63:4).

A simpler form of the principle occurs in the apocryphal Epistle of Titus, following its quotation from the Apocalypse of Elijah in which the punishments in hell are described: 'In the member with which each man has sinned, in the same also shall he be tormented' (ApElfrag).[25] One specific form of punishment in hell, frequently described in the apocalyptic 'tours of hell,' is the hanging punishments, in which sinners are suspended by the limb with which they committed their sin. Suspension by the tongue is a regular instance of this, usually inflicted on those guilty of slander or false witness (ApElfrag; ApPet 7:2; ActsThom 56; Gedulat Moshe [Gaster §36; Ginzberg p.

---

[25] There is a remarkable modern literary appropriation of this theme in William Golding's novel *Free Fall*, which explores in psychological narrative the traditional theological themes of predestination, free will, sin and damnation. The narrator, Sammy, whose sin has been his callous seduction of Beatrice, amounting to a kind of torture, experiences retribution in hell when, following his interrogation in a German prisoner of war camp, he is locked in a small, pitch dark cell. The torment is purely mental as he imagines that the Nazis would be clever enough to assign to him precisely the torment that suited his particular case: 'they were psychologists of suffering, apportioning to each man what was most helpful and necessary to his case' (W. Golding, *Free Fall* [London: Faber & Faber, 1968] 173). In effect, therefore, his imagination designs for himself the torture he himself judges precisely appropriate to his own case. This torture, 'the sum of all terror,' must, he deduces, lie in the unexplored centre of the cell. When he eventually detects an object there, he identifies it as a severed penis, placed there as a warning to torment him (p. 182). (In fact, the object is merely a wet rag left on the floor by mistake [p. 253]: Sammy's torment is self-inflicted.) The narrative achieves with consummate psychological realism what the apocalyptic accounts of hell portrayed less subtly: the punishment of men guilty of sexual offences is to be eternally suspended by the genitals (Himmelfarb, *Tours*, 87-90).

311; Netzer §21[26]]; HebVis V 7 [= ChronJerah 14:4]; HebVis V 16 [= ChronJerah 16:2]; GkApMary).[27] Another punishment for those who have sinned with their tongues is being obliged to chew the tongue (ApPet 9:3; 11:8; ApPaul 37).

These punishments of the tongue do not involve fire,[28] and so, while they parallel the specific punishment of this member of the body in James 3:6, they do not parallel the statement in this text that the tongue will be set on fire. Fire, of course, is a traditional image of God's judgment and associated very specifically with Gehenna.[29] General statements of the punishment of the wicked in hell commonly speak of fire. But specific punishments for specific sins also frequently feature fire. For example, of the twenty-one specific punishments in the description of hell in the Apocalypse of Peter, fourteen involve fire. This general background would sufficiently explain the reference in James 3:6. But there is in the literature a form of punishment in hell which involves specifically the burning of the tongue by fire. In this case, it has a scriptural basis in the words of Psalm 120:3-4:

> What shall be given to you?
> And what more shall be done to you, you deceitful tongue?
> A warrior's sharp arrows,
> with glowing coals of the broom tree (נחלי רתמים).

The very distinctive phrase נחלי רתמים (coals of broom or juniper)[30] occurs in tours of hell which describe people obliged to eat coals of juniper in hell in punishment for various sins of the tongue: blasphemy (HebVis V 7 [= ChronJerah 14:4]), talking in synagogue (*Darkhei Teshuvah*[31]) and an extensive list of sins of speaking and eating (Gedulat Moshe [Netzer §31]). In addition, several rabbinic passages specifically cite Psalm 120:4 with reference to the punishment of slanderers in Gehenna (b. 'Arak. 15b; Tanhuma Buber, quoted in Strack-Billerbeck 2.765; Seder Eliyyahu Rabbah 18 [p 108]). Since this punishment is found in tours of hell only in the Hebrew visions of a relatively late date, it may be a later modification of the tradition of punishments in hell, influenced by the rabbinic interpretation of

---

[26] In this version of the Gedulat Moshe, which typically expands the lists of sins for which the damned are punished, those hanging by the tongue are guilty of eating carrion and non-kosher food as well as of slander.

[27] Cf. Himmelfarb, *Tours*, 86-89.

[28] 2 Enoch 63:4 refers to the burning of the tongue in the fire of hell, but the words are found in only one MS.

[29] Cf. Himmelfarb, *Tours*, 108-110.

[30] Only here in the Hebrew Bible.

Psalm 120:4. On the other hand, these visions certainly preserve early material, and so the punishment may be old.

However, the best parallel to our passage in James, surprisingly unnoticed by the commentators, is in the twelfth Psalm of Solomon:

1 Lord, save my soul from the criminal and wicked man,
from the criminal and slandering tongue
that speaks lies and deceit.

2 The words of the wicked man's tongue (are) twisted in many ways;
(they are) as a fire among a people which scorches its beauty.

3 His visit fills homes with a false tongue,
cuts down trees of joy, inflaming criminals;
by slander he incites homes to fighting.

4 May God remove the lips of the criminals in confusion far from the innocent, and (may) the bones of the slanderers be scattered far from those who fear the Lord.
May he destroy the slanderous tongue in flaming fire far from the devout.[32]

The passage echoes several of the Psalms of the Old Testament in which the destructive power of the slanderous and deceitful tongue is the theme (cf. especially v 1 with Ps 120:2; v 4a with Ps 12:3[4]; v 4b with Ps 140:10[11] and Ps 120:3-4). It is unfortunate that the text of verses 2b-3 is hopelessly corrupt,[33] such that even a plausible reconstruction of the original Greek or its Hebrew *Vorlage* seems impossible. In one manuscript (H) verse 2b reads: 'like fire burning up stubble on a threshing-floor.' Editors regard this as a secondary correction of the very difficult text of the other manuscripts, which is supported by the Syriac, but it remains an attractive correction.[34] What is in any case clear enough for our purposes, however, is that verses 2b-3 in some way compare the effect of the slanderous tongue with the destructive effect of fire (... πῦρ ἀνάπτον ... φλογισούσης ...). This means that when the punishment of the slanderers (v 4), which includes also the fate of

---

[31] See the translations of the tour of hell in J.-M. Rosenstiehl, 'Les révélations d'Élie: Élie et les tourments des damnés,' in A. Caquot ed., *La Littérature Intertestamentaire: Colloque de Strasbourg (17-19 Octobre 1983)* (Bibliothèque des Centres d'Études Supérieures Spécialistes; Paris: Presses Universitaire de France, 1985) 104; S. Liebermann, 'On Sins and their Punishments,' in idem, *Texts and Studies* (New York: Ktav, 1974) 40.

[32] Translation by R. B. Wright in J. H. Charlesworth ed., *The Old Testament Pseudepigrapha*, vol. 2 (London: Darton., Longman & Todd, 1985) 662.

[33] See J. Viteau, *Les Psaumes de Salomon* (Documents pour l'Étude de las Bible; Paris: Letouzey et Ané, 1911) 316; S. Holm-Nielsen, *Die Psalmen-Salomos* (JSHRZ 4/2; Gütersloh: Mohn, 1977) 87.

[34] ὥσπερ ἐν ἁλῷ πῦρ ἀνάπτον καλάμην αὐτοῦ instead of ὥσπερ ἐν λαῷ πῦρ ἀνάπτον καλλόνην αὐτοῦ.

their lips (cf. Ps 12:3[4]) and their bones (cf. Ps 53:5[6]), culminates in the destruction of their tongues by fire (ἐν πυρὶ φλογὸς γλῶσσα ψιθυρὸς ἀπόλοιτο ἀπὸ ὁσίων), this is an instance of the eschatological *ius talionis*.

The probable allusion to Psalm 120:4 in this passage (PsSol 12:4), together with the use of this verse in the later Jewish literature mentioned above, suggests that it may be to that biblical verse in particular that James 3:6 alludes when it warns that the tongue will be set alight by hell. Like the twelfth Psalm of Solomon, its version of the eschatological *ius talionis* depends on representing the tongue as a fire which itself sets things alight: 'See how small a fire sets alight so large a forest! The tongue is a fire... setting on fire the wheel of existence.' For this image there is some precedent in the Hebrew Bible

(Scoundrels concoct evil,
and their speech is like a scorching fire [Prov 16:27]),

and especially in Ben Sira:

[The tongue] has no power over the godly;
they will not be burned in its flame.
Those who forsake the Lord will fall into its power;
it will burn among them and will not be put out (28:22-23a; cf. also 11-12).[35]

James most likely knew this image in the midst of Ben Sira's lengthy reflection on the wellnigh universal destruction wrought by slander (28:13-26).[36] If so, then as usual he does not simply reproduce the wisdom of his wise predecessor, but is inspired by it to create his own wise saying.[37]

To some readers, accustomed to distinguish 'apocalyptic'—with its eschatological worldview—from 'wisdom' literature—with its this-worldly perspective, it may seem incongruous that James here combines an image of the tongue as destructive fire whose precedents lie in the wisdom tradition with an image of the tongue burning in

---

[35] Cf. also LevRab 16:4: The tongue is one of those bodily members which are placed horizontally in the body. 'Yet see how many conflagrations it has caused! How much the more then had it been in an upright [vertical] position!' (The meaning is perhaps that in the case of the whole body the horizontal position is one of rest, the vertical of activity.) Other references given in Martin, *James*, 113; Johnson, *The Letter of James*, 259, are not relevant to the image of the tongue as a destructive fire.

[36] For the power of the slanderous tongue to wreak destruction universally, which is asserted, however hyperbolically, in James 3:6 ('setting on fire the wheel of existence'), see also b. Ber. 15b.

[37] For James as a wisdom teacher who, like Ben Sira himself, draws creatively on the wisdom of his predecessors, see R. Bauckham, *James* (NT Readings; London: Routledge, forthcoming).

Gehenna, an eschatological image whose parallels are to be found primarily in apocalyptic descriptions of hell. But the distinction is misleading. By the end of the Second Temple period, wisdom paraenesis and apocalypse remained distinct literary genres, but did not embody radically divergent worldviews. Wisdom themes can be found in the apocalypses, and eschatology in wisdom texts. In particular, the old conviction of the wisdom tradition (which survived until Ben Sira) that wise and foolish, good and evil lives incur their appropriate rewards and punishments within this life gave way in the Second Temple period to the notion of eschatological judgment. Wisdom after Ben Sira, as we can now see in the wisdom texts from Qumran (4Q185, 298, 415-418, 424, 525), as well as in the Wisdom of Solomon, now teaches eschatological judgment as a central feature of its perspective on the world. The difference between wisdom paraenesis and apocalypses is that the latter contain revelations of the judgment and the fate of the dead, depicting these mysteries which are unveiled to the seer in visions, whereas wisdom is paraenetic in form, addressing wise counsel to its readers and hearers, and referring to eschatological judgment as the sanction for its injunctions. Apocalypses describe the eschatological secrets, wisdom alludes to them.

Thus the eschatological orientation in James is not in contradiction with the letter's wisdom character: such an orientation is entirely to be expected in a Jewish wisdom writing from the first century C.E. James is neither an 'apocalyptic' text which subordinates wisdom to eschatology, nor a wisdom text without eschatological expectations. It is, as we should expect a wisdom text of this date to be, a wisdom text which frequently alludes, for paraenetic purposes, to the eschatological themes that are expounded much more fully in the apocalypses. The eschatological *ius talionis* of 3:6, as well as the other examples of the form in James (2:13a; 3:18), are very appropriate for this purpose. The depiction of divine justice as *ius talionis* was traditional in wisdom tradition (Prov 21:13; Sir 27:26; 28:1-2; Tob 4:7) as well as in prophetic tradition (Isa 3:11; 33:1; Hos 4:6). The 'eschatologizing' of both traditions in Second Temple tradition, which reinterpreted the judgments to which both refer as eschatological judgments, brought these two traditions together, so that statements of eschatological *ius talionis* become a paraenetic form at home both in apocalypses and in other literary genres (see the examples of such statements given above). Thus our interpretation of James 3:6b as such a statement, which can be illuminated from the traditions about punishments in hell to be found in apocalyptic literature, is wholly appropriate to the kind of Jewish literature James is.

A final suggestion on the interpretation of James 3:6b is no more than a possibility. The phrase ὁ τροχὸς τῆς γενέσεως ('the wheel of existence') and its equivalent ὁ κύκλος τῆς γενέσεως ('the circle of existence') had become hellenistic commonplaces, known also to Jews of the hellenistic period (SibOr 2:87 = Ps-Phoc 27; Philo, *Somn.* 2.44; cf. ExodRab 31:3; b. Shab. 151b). James appears to use the phrase to mean 'little more than "life"'[38] or 'the whole course of life,'[39] without the overtones of fate or necessity or reversal of fortunes that it commonly carried. If the phrase seems not entirely suitable for James' use, the explanation for his choice of it certainly lies, in part at least, in the punning correspondence it creates between τῆς γενέσεως and τῆς γεέννες. As we have seen, the pun is not mere verbal decoration, but has a serious theological purpose: it assists the depiction of the judgment as *ius talionis*. But it may be that James was also attracted to the phrase—and chose the specific and less common form ὁ τροχὸς τῆς γενέσεως[40] rather than ὁ κύκλος τῆς γενέσεως—because it could suggest, as a kind of punning overtone, the phrase ὁ τροχὸς τῆς γεέννες ('the wheel of Gehenna'). One of the traditional punishments in the Greek Hades, first ascribed to a mythological individual, later understood as exemplary of the fate of many of the dead (cf. Virgil, *Aen.* 6.616-617), was the wheel to which Zeus bound Ixion, so that he should endlessly revolve on it. Remarkably, the philosopher Simplicius (writing c. 300 C.E.), refers to the myth and gives it an allegorical interpretation in terms of Orphic beliefs: the wheel, he says, is 'the wheel of fate and becoming' (τῷ τῆς εἱμαρμένης τε καὶ γενέσεως τροχῷ) (*In Aristot. de caelo comm.* 2.168b).[41] James may not have known this Orphic interpretation of the myth, but he could have been aware of the wheel as a punishment in hell depicted in Jewish apocalyptic descriptions, which had borrowed it, like various other infernal punishments,[42] from the Greek Hades (ApPet 12:4-6;

---

[38] Dibelius, *James*, 198.

[39] Davids, *James*, 143; cf. Johnson, *The Letter of James*, 260.

[40] However, we should note that the Jewish Greek writers (SibOr 2:87 = Ps-Phoc 27; Philo, *Somn.* 2.44) use τροχός, perhaps to avoid the specifically Orphic-Pythagorean doctrine of an endless cycle of birth, death and reincarnation, for which κύκλος was almost always used (examples in J. H. Ropes, *A Critical and Exegetical Commentary on the Epistle of St. James* [Edinburgh: T. & T. Clark, 1916] 238-239; Dibelius, *James*, 196-197).

[41] Quoted in Dibelius, *James*, 197.

[42] E.g. the punishments of Tantalus (Himmelfarb, *Tours*, 92-93) and the Danaids (Himmelfarb, *Tours*, 94-96). Cf. S. Reinach, 'Sisyphe aux enfers et quelques autres damnés,' *Revue archéologique* 1 (1903) 154-200.

SibOr 2:294-296; ActsThom 55;[43] Apocalypse of the Seven Heavens 7-8[44]).

---

[43] These Christian texts are continuous with the Jewish apocalyptic tradition of depictions of the punishments in hell.

[44] See the commentary in chapter 12 below.

CHAPTER SIX

THE CONFLICT OF JUSTICE AND MERCY: ATTITUDES TO THE DAMNED IN APOCALYPTIC LITERATURE

I INTRODUCTION

In Book V, chapter 5, of *The Brothers Karamazov*, in which Ivan Karamazov tells his story of the Grand Inquisitor, the following passage forms part of Ivan's 'literary introduction' to the story:

> There is for example one minor monastic poem (translated from the Greek, of course), *The Virgin among the Damned*, which in its descriptive power and daring can be compared with Dante. The Mother of God visits hell and the Archangel Michael acts as her guide. She sees the sinners and their torments. There is by the way one particularly curious category of sinners in a burning lake; some of these have been plunged into this lake and can never escape from it, even God has forgotten these—a conception of remarkable depth and power. The Virgin, devastated and weeping, falls to her knees before the throne of God and begs mercy for all in hell, for all those she has seen there, without favour. Her conversation with God is interesting in the extreme. She begs, she insists, and when God shows her the marks of the nails on the hands and the feet of her son and asks, "How can I forgive his torturers?" she calls upon all the saints, all the martyrs, all the angels and archangels to kneel with her and to plead for mercy for all, without distinction. It ends with her winning from God an annual cessation of tortures from Good Friday to Pentecost, and the sinners from hell thank Him there and then, crying out to Him, "You are just, O Lord, in your judgment of us."[1]

Dostoevsky has here summarized accurately the contents of a Slavonic version[2] of the Greek Apocalypse of the Virgin,[3] a work of

---

[1] F. Dostoevsky, *The Brothers Karamazov*, tr. I. Avsey (The World's Classics; Oxford: Oxford University Press, 1994) 309-310.

[2] E. Kozak, 'Bibliographische Übersicht der biblisch-apokryphen Literatur bei den Slaven,' *Jahrbücher für protestantische Theologie* 18 (1892) 127-158, lists printed texts of the Slavonic versions. Cf. also A. de Santos Otero, *Die handschriftliche Überlieferung der altslavischen Apokryphen*, vol. 1(Berlin/New York: de Gruyter, 1978) 188-195; H. Müller, '"Die Offenbarung der Gottesmutter über die Höllenstrafen": Theologischer Gehalt und dichterische Form,' *Die Welt der Slaven* 6 (1961) 26-39.

[3] Recent writers on the Greek Apocalypse of the Virgin (A. Yargro Collins, 'The Early Christian Apocalypses,' *Semeia* 14 [1979] 91-92, 116; M. Himmelfarb, *Tours of Hell* [Philadelphia: University of Pennsylvania Press, 1983] 23-24, 179) seem to know

uncertain date,[4] no literary merit,[5] but evidently, to judge by the number of extant Greek manuscripts[6] and versions,[7] very popular. It is one of the least interesting of a series of apocalypses which feature the seer's prayers for mercy for the damned (see section III below), but Dostoevsky's use of it shows his awareness that it at least poses a serious issue: that of eschatological justice and mercy, which has been Ivan Karamazov's own theme in his famous argument about theodicy in the preceding chapter. Although ostensibly Ivan's account of the apocalypse forms a purely 'literary introduction' to the story of the Grand Inquisitor, in reality it also forms a conceptual link between this story and the preceding argument. It takes up the question of eschatological forgiveness for the torturers,[8] which Ivan

---

only the Greek text published from a Bodleian MS by M. R. James (*Apocrypha Anecdota* [Texts & Studies 2/3; Cambridge: Cambridge University Press, 1893] 107-126). In fact, however, several other, variant texts have been published: C. Gidel, 'Étude sur une apocalypse de la Vierge Marie,' *Annuaire de l'Association pour l'encouragement des études grecques* 5 (1871) 92-113 (Paris MS Gr. 390); A. Vassiliev, *Anecdota Graeca-Byzantina* (Moscow: Imperial University Press, 1893) xxxii-xxv, 125-134 (a Rome MS, with variant readings from a Vienna MS); H. Pernot, 'Descente de la Vierge aux Enfers d'après les manuscrits grecs de Paris,' *Revue des Études Grecques* 13 (1900) 233-257 (reprints Gidel's text, together with three more MSS: Paris Gr. 395, Paris Suppl. Gr. 136, and a MS from Pyrghi). See also, for references to other MSS of the work, C. Tischendorff, *Apocalypses apocryphae* (Leipzig: Mendelssohn, 1866) xxvii-xxix; James, *Apocrypha*, 110; Vassiliev, *Anecdota*, xxxv. See further, chapter 13 below, section I. Dostoevsky's account does not correspond precisely to any one of these published Greek texts, which vary considerably. But each of the elements of his account is found in at least one of them: the sinners in the lake whom God forgets are in James §23; God's inability to forgive the Jews who inflicted the wounds of persecution is in Pernot §21 (which shows James §26 to be defective at this point); the period of rest granted to sinners corresponds to that in Pernot §25 (C text) and in Vassiliev (p. 132), better than to that in James §29; other elements are found in all the texts except those which break off before the end of the work.

[4] It might be as early as the sixth century or as late as the ninth. Its probable dependence on the Apocalypse of Paul is the only real clue (Himmelfarb, *Tours of Hell*, 159-160). Other literary relationships (suggested by James, *Apocrypha*, 111-113) cannot be properly assessed until a critical edition is available See also the more general considerations which point to the early medieval period, in Gidel, 'Étude,' 99-102, 108.

[5] Cf. James, *Apocrypha*, 111: 'extremely monotonous, quite contemptible as literature, and even positively repulsive in some parts'!

[6] Cf. James, *Apocrypha*, 109: 'Hardly any collection of Greek manuscripts is without one or more copies of it.' Cf. E. Patlagean, 'Byzance et son autre monde: Observations sur quelques récits,' in *Faire croire: Modalités de la diffusion at de la réception des messages religieux du XIIe au XVe siècle* (Collection de l'École Française de Rome 51; Palais Farnèse: École Française de Rome, 1981) 219.

[7] There are versions in Armenian, Georgian, Old Slavonic and Rumanian: see chapter 13 below, section I.

[8] The unpleasantly anti-Semitic nature of the discussion of this question in the Greek Apocalypse of the Virgin is ignored by Dostoevsky.

has rejected[9] and Alyosha has already related to the crucified Christ.[10]

This echo of an early medieval Christian apocalypse in one of the most penetrating modern discussions of theodicy may begin to indicate that the apocalyptic literature was a vehicle for some profound theological concerns in relation to divine justice and mercy, though in a popular and dramatic, rather than discursively theological way. This chapter aims to trace these concerns through the whole tradition of the Jewish and Christian apocalypses, a literary and theological tradition spanning more than a millennium. The continuity and, in many respects, conservative nature of the tradition will justify a method of identifying stock themes which recur in apocalyptic literature, without paying much attention to the still very debatable issues of the dates and literary relationships of many of the sources discussed.

II The justice of hell

The apocalyptic idea of the punishment of the wicked in hell owes its origin and popularity to a problem of theodicy. The typical *Sitz im Leben*, at least of the early texts, is persecution, and the damned are concretely the persecutors of God's faithful people and/or the apostates who have escaped persecution by denying their faith. A situation in which God's faithful people suffer and their enemies triumph demands a vindication of God's justice, in the deeply rooted Old Testament sense of justice *for* the oppressed which has to be at the same time justice *against* the oppressors. Hell is then fundamentally a triumph for God's righteousness.

This sense of the absolute moral *rightness* of hell comes to vivid expression in two recurrent stock themes of the apocalypses. One is the idea that the damned themselves will acknowledge the justice of their punishment. Sometimes, as in 1 Enoch 63:8-9 and Apocalypse of Peter 13:4-6, this happens after their pleas for mercy have been rejected.[11]

The second theme is the idea that the righteous will rejoice to see the punishment of the wicked in hell. An important source of this notion is Isaiah 66:24, a text which contributed much to the doctrine

---

[9] Dostoevsky, *The Brothers*, 306-307.
[10] Dostoevsky, *The Brothers*, 308.
[11] For other instances of this theme, see ChrJerah 15:8; Hippolytus (?), *De universo*; G. W. Buchanan, *Revelation and Redemption* (Dillsboro, North Carolina: Western North Carolina Press, 1978) 545.

of hell. The final phrase, 'an abhorrence (דראון) to all flesh,'[12] appears in the Septuagint as 'a spectacle (ὄρασιν) to all flesh.' The Septuagint may here follow a variant Hebrew text which had חזון for דראון, or, more probably, the translator incorrectly derived דראון from ראה. In either case the Hebrew text has been understood in the same way in 1 Enoch 27:3[13] and 62:12, according to which the wicked at the last judgment will be a 'spectacle' for the righteous. Such a meaning for the final phrase of the verse would have seemed natural in view of the beginning of the verse ('they shall go out and look at the dead bodies of the people who have rebelled against me'), which is quoted in the Hebrew Apocalypse of Elijah (Buttenweiser, p. 66; Buchanan, p. 439). According to 1 Enoch 62:12, the righteous 'will exult over (their oppressors), because the wrath of the Lord of spirits rests upon them, and his sword will be drunk from them.'[14] Isaiah 66:24 is explicitly quoted in 2 Clement 17:5-7, which explains how, at the last judgment, Christians will give glory to God when they see the punishment of those who have apostatized in order to avoid suffering in this life. Other texts in which the righteous rejoice over the eschatological punishment of the wicked are Jubilees 23:30; Testament of Moses 10:10; Apocalypse of Abraham 31:4; and Apocalypse of Peter 13:2. The language of these texts suggests that the Psalms may have played a part in inspiring the idea (cf. Ps 52:8; 38:10; 59:10; 118:7).

A further development, in line with the apocalyptic geography which locates Paradise and Gehenna within sight of each other (1 En 108:14-15; 4 Ezra 7:36-38; ApEl 5:27-28), makes the spectacle of the wicked in hell a matter of *eternal* satisfaction for the blessed in heaven. Perhaps this is intended in Apocalypse of Abraham 31:4, and it is rather more clearly intended in a passage in the Arabic Apocalypse of Peter (Book of the Rolls):

> I will place them in the mansions of heaven which overlook the sufferings of the abyss, in order to double in that day their joy and their pleasures (Mingana p. 141).

But there are very few apocalyptic texts which press the notion so far.[15] Rather it was the Fathers and the theologians of the medieval church who, from this apocalyptic starting-point, developed 'the

---

[12] This is already interpreted as referring to an eternal fate after resurrection in Dan 12:2.

[13] The Ethiopic must here be preferred to the Greek: M. Black, *The Book of Enoch or 1 Enoch* (SVTP 7; Leiden: Brill, 1985) 174.

[14] Trans. Black, *The Book of Enoch*, 60. Cf. also the idea that God (1 En 94:10) and the angels (1 En 97:2) will rejoice at the destruction of the wicked.

[15] In 1 En 62:11-13 it is explicitly not the case.

abominable fancy,' as Dean Farrer called it in 1877,[16] that the eternal
happiness of the blessed will be enhanced by their consciousness of
the torments of the damned in hell.[17]

It is important to realise that, difficult though it may be to exclude
altogether a desire for personal vengeance from the motives of the
apocalyptists, the essential motive was the wish to see God's justice
done. If hell is a triumph for God's justice, setting to rights the injustice of this world, then the righteous *ought* to rejoice to see it. In
situations of serious injustice what Max Horkheimer calls 'the longing
that the murderer should not triumph over his innocent victim'[18] has
an ethical priority and must make first claim on the kind of
eschatological theodicy with which the apocalypses are concerned. In
such situations an easy universalism which extends benevolent mercy
equally to the oppressors and the oppressed would be an affront both
to the oppressed and to the divine righteousness for which they
long.[19] Hence this first claim on theodicy—which is also Ivan
Karamazov's[20]—is emphatically acknowledged by the apocalyptic
tradition. To the credit of the tradition, however, it also sought ways
to transcend the first claim without denying it, as we shall see.

III INTERCESSION BY THE SEERS

As well as approbation of hell by the righteous who rejoice to see
God's justice done, the apocalyptic literature lays considerable stress
on another reaction to hell by the righteous. It frequently recognizes
that a genuinely good man or woman who faces the real horror of the
torments of the damned will be moved to compassion and will im-

---

[16] F. W. Farrer, *Eternal Hope* (London: Macmillan, 1878) 66.

[17] Patristic and medieval references in R. Joly, 'Le contemplation des supplices
infernaux,' in idem, *Christianisme et Philosophie* (Brussels: Éditions de l'Université de
Bruxelles, 1973) 174-177; M. Landau, *Hölle und Fegfeuer in Volksglaube, Dichtung und
Kirchenlehre* (Heidelberg: Carl Winter, 1909) 188-192; W. J. P. Boyd, 'Apocalyptic and
Life after Death,' *Studia Evangelica* 5/2 = *TU* 103 (1968) 51 n.1. For the disappear-
ance of the doctrine in the seventeenth century, see D. P. Walker, *The Decline of Hell*
(London: Routledge & Kegan Paul, 1964) 29-32.

[18] Quoted in J. Moltmann, *The Crucified God* (London: SCM Press, 1974) 223; but
cf. also Moltmann's qualification of this on p. 178.

[19] J. H. Cone, *The Spirituals and the Blues* (New York: Seabury Press, 1972) 104,
quotes a negro spiritual which, out of a situation of oppression comparable to those
of the apocalypses, provides a close parallel to the apocalyptic theme of this section:
    Then they'll cry out for cold water
    While the Christians shout in glory
    Saying Amen to their damnation
    Fare you well, fare you well.

[20] Dostoevsky, *The Brothers* , 306-308.

plore God's mercy for the damned. Simply because the horrors of hell are so deliberately contemplated in apocalyptic literature, because the apocalyptists set out to portray the torments for their readers in the most vivid terms, they were bound to give expression to this natural compassionate reaction, which sometimes becomes a genuine protest in the name of divine and human mercy against the notion of hell.

Prayers for mercy for the damned occur in the apocalypses in a number of different contexts, but the most common situation is that in which the pseudonymous seer himself or herself sees in a vision the punishments of the damned in hell and is moved to intercede for them. This is the case with

— Zephaniah in the Apocalypse of Zephaniah (2:8-9);
— Ezra in the Greek Apocalypse of Ezra (*passim*) and the (Latin) Vision of Ezra (8a, 11, 18, 22, 33, 42, 47, 55, 57c, 61)
— Baruch in the Slavonic version of 3 Baruch (16:7-8);
— Peter in the Apocalypse of Peter (3:3-4);
— Paul in the Apocalypse of Paul (33, 40, 42, 43);
— the apostles in the Didascalia of our Lord Jesus Christ (Nau §30); and
— the Virgin Mary in the Greek Apocalypse of the Virgin (James §§25-28), the Ethiopic Apocalypse of the Virgin (Chaine p. 68), and the Syriac Transitus Mariae (Lewis p 67).[21]

Similar cases in which the seer intercedes for the damned, but does not actually see them in hell, are those of Ezra in the Questions of Ezra A7, Sedrach in the Apocalypse of Sedrach (5:7; 8:10; 16:2), and Bartholomew in the Questions of Bartholomew (4:49).

It is very significant that compassion for the damned is thus attributed to ideal, exemplary figures in Jewish and Christian piety. Though the divine reaction to their intercession varies in the various texts, there can be no doubt that the apocalyptists approve this compassion. They are allowing the compassion which they and their readers feel for the damned an authoritative mode of expression. It is not a sentiment they consider disallowed by dogma, but one voiced

---

[21] Abraham's intercession in TAb A14 does not quite come into this category. For cases of intercession for the damned where the intercessor is not the pseudonymous seer but the righteous dead, see ApZeph 11 (Abraham, Isaac, Jacob, and all the righteous dead); ChrJerah 17:3 (the righteous dead in general); and the instances at or after the Last Judgment discussed in section IV below. Sometimes the pseudonymous seer is joined in his or her intercession by other saints and angels, as in ApPaul 43-44; GkApMary (James §§25-29). In 2 En 41, Enoch weeps, but does not explicitly intercede, for the damned.

by the greatest saints in direct dialogues with God, in which God at
any rate listens. The notion is probably based on extending to the
dead the biblical tradition of intercession for living sinners by righteous people such as Abraham and Moses (Gen 18:22-33; Exod 32:7-
14, 31-34; cf. TMos 11:17; 12:6; 4 Ezra 7:106-111; QuesEzra
A39-40).

In the manner of apocalyptic literature, the points which the
apocalyptic seers make in their pleas for mercy for the damned become conventional, as do some elements in the divine response.
Much of the material goes back to Ezra's penetrating debate on
theodicy with God and his angelic representative Uriel in 4 Ezra. In
that apocalypse, Ezra does not view the punishments of the damned
(although 7:78-87 recounts the torments of the intermediate state),
but his concern about the fact that damnation awaits the majority of
people, including the majority of Jews, is a prominent element in his
debate with God. Ezra frequently expresses a kind of protest against
the theological orthodoxy voiced by Uriel, and although his protests
are always rebuffed, they are by no means always adequately answered. In this way the book keeps open some of the tensions inher-
ent in its subject-matter, and its genre allows the author to give free
rein to Ezra's arguments without exactly endorsing them. It must
have been this feature of 4 Ezra which appealed to the writers of a
series of later Ezra apocalypses, which clearly to some degree imitate
the genre of 4 Ezra, though often focusing the debate more narrowly
on hell. These are the Greek Apocalypse of Ezra, the Apocalypse of
Sedrach,[22] the Latin Vision of Ezra, and the Questions of Ezra.[23]
Also of considerable interest is the Armenian version of 4 Ezra, which
Stone plausibly suggests is based on a Greek revision of 4 Ezra.[24] One
effect of the additional and rewritten material in this version is to
soften the harsh theodicy voiced by Uriel in 4 Ezra. The reviser
seems to have felt that Ezra's persuasive arguments for mercy de-
served a less uncompromising response from God. Finally, it should
be mentioned that Ezra's concern for the damned in 4 Ezra probably

---

[22] The name Sedrach in this work is best explained as a corruption of Ezra: so
(most recently) M. E. Stone, 'The Metamorphoses of Ezra: Jewish Apocalypses and
Medieval Vision,' *JTS* 33 (1982) 6.

[23] Recension A of the Questions of Ezra is a composite work, of which vv 16-30 (to
which nothing in the abbreviated Recension B corresponds) are probably an insertion into the original Ezra apocryphon.

[24] M. E. Stone, *The Armenian Version of IV Ezra* (Missoula, Montana: Scholars Press,
1979) ix; idem, 'Jewish Apocryphal Literature in the Armenian Church,' *Mus* 95
(1982) 292; idem, *A Textual Commentary on the Armenian Version of IV Ezra* (SBLSCS 34;
Atlanta: Scholars Press, 1990) ix-xiii.

also had some influence on the other major group of apocalypses which concern us in this section: those of Peter, Paul and the Virgin Mary.[25]

The following five arguments are those most commonly adduced by the apocalyptic seers in pleading for mercy for the damned:

(1) *It would have been better for them/us not to have been born* (4 Ezra 4:62-64; 7:116-117; [cf. 4:12]; 7:45, 116; ApPet 3:4; ApPaul 42; GkApMary [James §11]; ApSedr 4:2; GkApEzra 1:6, 21; 5:9, 14; 2 En 41:2).

This was already a conventional expression (cf. Eccl 4:2-3; Mark 14:21; 2 Bar 10:6), used of the damned in 1 Enoch 38:2 without any kind of pity. But in the contexts we are considering it conveys a sense of compassion and tragedy, and sometimes, at least, an element of implied protest: that the very creation of sinners should become regretable directs a question at God's purpose and providence.

(2) *The irrational animals, which expect no life after death and therefore need fear no punishment after death, are better off than humans* (4 Ezra 7:65-69; 4 EzraArm 5:14B; QuesEzra A5; B3; GkApEzra 1:22; VisEzra 62).

Again this highlights the tragedy of human existence, if most can expect only damnation. Humanity's special destiny, conventionally thought to raise us above the level of the animals, is in fact an intolerable burden which makes us envy the animals.

(3) *All are sinners* (4 Ezra 7:46, 68; 8:35; ApPaul 42; QuesEzra A4; GkApEzra 5:26; EthApMary [Chaine p. 68]).

This is the presupposition which makes the tragedy of (1) and (2) so oppressive. The seers argue that sin is endemic to humanity and that hardly any escape it. Typically they include themselves among sinners destined for hell. In this way the authors are attributing to the most righteous of people, the seers, a kind of solidarity with all of sinful humanity, by contrast with the religious exclusivism of the elect, permitting no concern for the damned majority, which is recommended to Ezra in 4 Ezra (e.g. 8:51, 55). Sometimes the solidarity goes a step further: Sedrach (ApSedr 5:7) and the Virgin (GkApMary: James §§125-126) ask to be punished with the damned in hell, while Ezra (GkApEzra 1:11; VisEzra 89) and the Virgin (GkApMary: James §126) ask to be punished *instead of* the damned, following in the tradition of Moses' request (Exod 32:32).

---

[25] On the relations between the apocalypses mentioned in this paragraph, the fullest study is now Himmelfarb, *Tours of Hell.*

(4) *Humanity is God's own creation, made in his image* (4 Ezra 8:7-14, 44-45;
    ApPaul 43; ApSedr 4:3; GkApEzra 1:10; 2:23; 5:16; GkApMary:
    Pernot §21; cf. ApPet 3:6; VisEzra 63).
    If most people are to perish, for what purpose has God made
    humanity, not as some trivial creation fit for destruction, but re-
    sembling himself? 'For what reason,' asks Sedrach, 'did you labor
    with your spotless hands and create man, since you did not desire
    to have mercy upon him?' (4:3).
(5) *God is good and merciful* (4 Ezra 7:132-140; 8:31-36; ApPaul 44;
    ApSedr 15:1; GkApEzra 1:10, 15; 5:18; cf. ChrJerah 17:3).
    The seers' appeal to God's own revealed nature, as merciful, is
    essential to their plea. In 4 Ezra 7:132-140—a passage so impres-
    sive as to be in danger of overbalancing the whole debate, Greek
    Apocalypse of Ezra 1:10 and Apocalypse of Sedrach 15:1, the
    appeal echoes the classic Old Testament revelation of the divine
    nature in Exodus 34:6-7.

A corresponding set of conventional themes recur as the divine arguments for rejecting the appeal for mercy:

(1) *Only the righteous few are precious to God, who is unconcerned about the loss
    of the wicked majority* (4 Ezra 7:52-61; 8:1, 38).
    The later apocalypses influenced by 4 Ezra evidently baulked at
    putting this extreme view into the mouth of God.
(2) *You cannot be more loving than God* (4 Ezra 5:33; 8:47; 4 EzraArm
    7:19; ApPet 3:6; ApPaul 33; 40; cf. 4 Ezra 7:19).
    The point seems to be: God loves his own creation more than you
    do, but even so does not deliver the damned from hell. Since his
    greater love is not a basis for mercy for the damned, your lesser
    love should not be. It is an odd argument!
(3) *God did not intend the destruction of the wicked* (4 Ezra 8:59; 4 EzraArm
    8:62H).
(4) *They knew God's law and disobeyed it* (4 Ezra 7:21-24, 72-73; 4
    EzraArm 8:1B-D, 61I-O; GkApEzra 5:19; VisEzra 63).
(5) *They have freely chosen evil* (4 Ezra 7:127-130; 8:56; 4EzraArm 8:1B).
(6) *God has already been patient with them* (4 Ezra 7:74; 4 EzraArm 7:74;
    8:41B; ApPaul 33).
(7) *Opportunities for repentance have been rejected* (ApPaul 44; ApSedr 15:5;
    cf. GkApMary: James §29).

Arguments (3)—(7) are the main arguments in the classic freewill
defence of hell and amount to claiming that hell is no more than the
wicked deserve. They get a good hearing in most of our apocalypses,
and in most cases it seems that our authors accept that these argu-

ments justify the existence of hell. On the other hand, these apocalypses do not normally represent their seers as wholly satisfied by these arguments. In the face of the assertion that the wicked have no excuse, the seers persist in trying to excuse them. For example, when Sedrach has been assured that God does save those who repent, but cannot save hardened sinners who refuse to repent, he begs that God should

> make a concession (συγχώρησον) also to those who have sinned against you even to the end of their life (ἐπ᾽ ἐσχάτων), O Lord, for life is very hard and unrepentant (ἀμετανόντος) [i.e. allows no time for repentance?].
> The Lord said to Sedrach, 'I made humanity in three stages of life. When they were young, I overlooked their mistakes, but again when they were adult I observed their mind, and again when they grow old, I observe them until they repent.'
> Sedrach said, 'Lord, you know and understand all these things; only do sympathize (συμπάθησαι) with sinners' (ApSedr 15:5-16:2).[26]

Thus against the claims of justice the apocalyptic seers continue to urge mercy. There remains a tension between a quite cogent defence of hell, in which a sound traditional theological position is stated, and the nevertheless persistent compassion for the damned on the part of the seers. In most cases, the tension is unresolved. Either the seer's pleas are rebuffed or no result is mentioned at all.

Sometimes the tension is resolved by a concession from God. For example, although God had told Sedrach that sinners will be saved if they repent for forty days, in response to Sedrach's pleas the period is reduced to twenty days (ApSedr 16:3). The most famous of these is the Sunday rest of the damned, a day's respite each week from the pains of hell, secured by Paul's intercession (joined by that of Michael and the angels) in the Apocalypse of Paul (44) and by the Virgin Mary in the Ethiopic Apocalypse of the Virgin (Chaine p. 68).[27] As Dostoevsky correctly reported,[28] the Greek Apocalypse of the Virgin adds a (presumably additional) period of respite for the fifty days from Easter to Pentecost each year (Pernot §25), a period also found in the Coptic version of the Apocalypse of Paul (Budge p. 1070). But the most remarkable case of a positive divine response to the seer's plea for mercy is in the fourth recension of the Armenian version of the

---

[26] My translation.
[27] On the Sabbath rest of the damned, which originated in Judaism, see I. Lévi , 'Le repos sabbatique des âmes damnées,' *REJ* 25 (1892) 1-13; 26 (1893) 131-135; T. Silverstein, *Visio Sancti Pauli* (Studies and Documents 4; London: Christophers, 1935) 79-81. For the period in the Ethiopic Apocalypse of the Virgin, see Himmelfarb, *Tours of Hell*, 20.
[28] Dostoevsky, *The Brothers* , 310.

Apocalypse of Paul, in which the prayers of Paul and the Virgin Mary secure the release of all sinners from hell and the actual abolition of hell (Leloir §35). This demonstrates that there was a real tendency in the whole tradition pressing towards *apokatastasis*, though only in this case had it the freedom to attain this conclusion. The *apokatastasis* in question, it should be noted, is not at all of an Origenist kind, since it does not rest on conceiving hell as purificatory. Rather the apocalyptists assume the purely retributive justice of hell and base their hope on mercy: human compassion finding a corresponding divine compassion.[29]

IV INTERCESSION AT THE LAST JUDGMENT

In the previous section we have considered cases where the apocalyptic seer, contemplating the punishments of the damned (whether in vision or simply in thought), intercedes for them. A somewhat different, though connected theme in the apocalypses is a prediction of the intercession of the righteous for the damned on or after the Day of Judgment, when they will have received their final condemnation to hell.

In the first place, a significant series of texts display a concern to deny that such intercession will be possible or efficacious, in view of the finality of the divine verdict at the Last Judgment, which will irrevocably fix the fate of both classes of people. Whereas before that time prophets and holy people have interceded for sinners (2 Bar 85:1-2), then there will be no

> opportunity to repent anymore,
> nor a limit to the times,
> nor a duration of the periods,
> nor a change to rest,
> nor an opportunity to prayer,
> nor sending up petition,
> nor giving knowledge,
> nor giving love,
> nor opportunity of repentance,
> nor supplicating for offences,
> nor prayers of the fathers,
> nor intercession of the prophets,
> nor help of the righteous (2 Bar 85:12-13).

---

[29] TIsaac 5:32 states that the wicked are punished in hell until God has mercy on them. In this case there is no reference to human intercession.

When Ezra asks

> whether on the day of judgment the righteous will be able to intercede for
> the ungodly or to entreat the Most High for them—fathers for sons or
> sons for parents, brothers for brothers, relatives for their kindred, or
> friends for those who are most dear (4 Ezra 7:102-103),

he receives the reply that

> no one shall ever pray for another on that day.... for then all shall bear
> their own righteousness and unrighteousness (7:105).

But Ezra persists, recalling at length how throughout the history of
God's people the great righteous men prayed for the wicked, and
requesting to know why this will not be so on the Day of Judgment:

> If therefore the righteous have prayed for the ungodly now, when corrup-
> tion has increased and unrighteousness has multiplied, why will it not be
> so then as well? (7:111)[30]

The reply is emphatic: the Day of Judgment is different; it will be
final and decisive (7:112-115). The emphasis with which the possibility of intercession at or after the Last Judgment is denied in these
passages (and cf. also TAbr A13:7; 1 En 38:6; 2 En 53:1; Hippolytus,
De universo 3)[31] suggests that the possibility was being canvassed and
needed to be denied.[32]

Variations on the same theme can be found in one of the conclusions to the Greek apocryphal Apocalypse of John, which predicts
that the angels, the Virgin and all the saints will lament for the
damned, but 'will do them no good' (Tischendorff p. 94), and in the
Hebrew Apocalypse of Elijah, which, having allowed the righteous to
see the downfall of the wicked, then predicts that God

> will move the temple a great distance away from the eternal destruction,
> so that the godly will not hear the voice of the lamentation of the ungodly
> and implore mercy for them. They will become as though they had never
> existed (Buchanan p. 440; Buttenweiser p. 66).

This interesting passage—which runs quite counter to the thinking
behind the 'abominable fancy'—acknowledges that the blessed in
heaven could not contemplate hell without being moved to compas-

---

[30] Cf. the same argument by the 'merciful' Christians reported by Augustine, *De
civ. Dei* 21.18.

[31] Cf. also Origen, *Hom. in Ezek.* 4.8; Gregory, *Dial.* 4.46.

[32] Other passages stress that God will not listen to the pleas for mercy which the
wicked themselves will make to him at the time of the Judgment (1 En 62:9-10;
SibOr 2:309-310), or simply that God's mercy comes to an end at the Judgment (1
En 60:5-6; 4 Ezra 7:33-34).

sionate intercession, and anticipates a certain kind of modern response, which attempts to protect the blessed from such consciousness of the horrors of hell.[33] The passage shows rather clearly that the 'general change in the attitude to other people's suffering,' to which Walker attributes the modern obsolescence of the 'abominable fancy,' did not begin *de novo* in the seventeenth century,[34] but has much earlier roots.

Such texts become more intelligible in the light of others which assert that intercession for the damned on the Day of Judgment *will* take place and will succeed. A medieval Christian and a medieval Jewish example will show how the same category of intercessors—the great saints of the biblical history—who feature in the material examined in section III can also play this role. In the Anglo-Saxon version of the Apocalypse of Thomas, the pleas of the Virgin Mary, Peter and the archangel Michael[35] each secure the reprieve of a third of sinners.[36] In the Hebrew Story of Daniel, it is the three patriarchs, the traditional intercessors for sinful Israelites,[37] who, standing at the three gates of Gehenna on the Day of Judgment, will remind God of his covenant. As a result God will forgive the sinful Israelites and 'will give to Abraham all those who have come from the true seed.'[38]

These medieval works may well embody ancient traditions, but the most ancient work now extant in which sinners are delivered from hell by the intercession of the righteous on or after the Day of Judgment is the Apocalypse of Peter. A most interesting feature of this work is its inclusion of all the major themes considered in this chapter. In chapter 3, Peter is granted a proleptic vision of the final judgment of sinners, so appalling that 'all who saw it with their eyes weep, whether the righteous or the angels or even [Christ] himself' (3:3).[39] Moved by their plight, Peter expresses his compassion in a standard form ('it would have been better for them if they had never been created'), whose standard function is a plea for mercy, but he is rebuked with some of the conventional responses (perhaps here drawn directly from 4 Ezra 8:44, 47) and told that he will appreciate the justice of the judgment on sinners when he knows their sins. In a

---

[33] Cf. C. S. Lewis, *The Problem of Pain* (London: Bles, 1940) 114-115; P. Geach, *Providence and Evil* (Cambridge: Cambridge University Press, 1977) 123-149.

[34] Walker, *Decline*, 30.

[35] For Michael's role in interceding for and releasing the damned, see ApPaul 43-44; GkApMary: James §§25-29; CopApJn: Budge p. 1022-1029.

[36] M. R. James, *The Apocryphal New Testament* (Oxford: Clarendon Press, 1924) 562.

[37] Cf. ApZeph 11; TJac 7:11.

[38] Buchanan, *Revelation*, 476.

substantial part of the apocalypse (chapters 7-12), Peter then sees—in a form adapted from the conventional tour of hell—how each type of punishment fits each particular crime. The prominence here of perse-cutors of Christians and Christian apostates and informers among the damned reflects the situation of persecution in which the work was written.[40]

The justice of hell is emphasized by the traditional themes in chap-ter 13: the righteous see the punishment of their persecutors; the latter beg for mercy, but when told by the angel in charge of the torments that the time for repentance is over, they acknowledge the justice of their punishment. It is not clear to whom the prayer for mercy is directed, but the natural implication is that it is to the right-eous in paradise. In that case it is the response of the righteous which is mentioned at the beginning of the next chapter (14), where the Greek text of the Rainer fragment, as emended by James,[41] must be preferred to the Ethiopic version.[42] This crucial passage reads:

> Then I will grant to my called and elect ones whomsoever they request from me, out of the punishment. And I will give them [i.e. those for whom the elect pray] a fine (καλόν) baptism in salvation from the Acherousian lake (which is, they say, in the Elysian field), a portion of righteousness with my holy ones.

(Noteworthy is the parallel between the opening words and those of the Hebrew Story of Daniel, quoted above: God 'will give to Abraham all' the Israelites condemned to hell.)

The Acherusian lake is a feature of the Greek Hades (Plato, *Phaedo* 113A-C, 114A-B) which appears elsewhere in Jewish and Christian apocalyptic literature (ApMos 37:3; ApPaul 22-23; GBart: Budge p. 208), there as here with a purificatory function.[43] Just as the 'Elysian plain' is used as a Greek equivalent for the Jewish paradise, so the

---

[39] That Christ himself should weep on seeing the final fate of the damned is an unusual feature.

[40] See chapter 8 below.

[41] M. R. James, 'The Rainer Fragment of the Apocalypse of Peter,' *JTS* 32 (1931) 270-279. His emendation of θεον εαν στεσωνται to ὃν ἐὰν αἰτήσωνται must be accepted because it has the support of SibOr 2:330-334, which is here paraphrasing the Apocalypse of Peter.

[42] The reference to the salvation of sinners from hell has perhaps been deliberately suppressed in the Ethiopic version.

[43] On the whole subject, see E. Peterson, 'Die "Taufe" im Acherusischen See,' in idem, *Frühkirche, Judentum und Gnosis* (Rome/Freiburg/Vienna: Herder, 1959) 310-332. For further Coptic material, cf. V. MacDermot, *The Cult of the Seer in the Ancient Middle East* (Berkeley/Los Angeles: University of California Press, 1971) 619-623.

Acherusian lake may be used as a Greek equivalent for the river of
the water of life in the Jewish paradise.[44]

Thus Peter's desire for mercy, so severely rebuked in chapter 3, is
granted eventually, when taken up by the elect on the Day of Judgment and after the justice of hell has been carefully demonstrated.
Although the Apocalypse of Peter is largely a compilation of traditional material, it is a deliberately redactional compilation, and so it is
worth asking how the traditional themes in this case can be combined. There is a kind of logic in the sequence. The justice of the
puishment of the persecutors is a justice owed primarily to the persecuted. But in that case it is a punishment that can be remitted if the
martyrs themselves desire mercy for their persecutors. No one else
has the right to forgive oppressors, but those whom they have oppressed do have this right. So if it is for his people's sake that God
must punish their oppressors, then *for his people's sake* (as SibOr 2:355,
interpreting ApPet 14, states) he can save those for whom they desire
mercy. In this way the conflict of justice and mercy is resolved. One
obstacle to universal salvation—that of which the apocalyptic tradition, because of its origins in situations of injustice and persecution,
was most aware—is effectively removed by the compassion and forgiveness of the saints. Other obstacles are not considered, and it is
not, of course, actually stated that salvation will be universal,[45] but as
extensive as the compassion of the elect.

Some part in the origin of this idea must have been played by
Plato, *Phaedo* 114A-B,[46] according to which a certain class of sinners,
who have committed serious crimes but are curable, can escape from
torment into the purifying waters of the Acherusian lake only by
seeking and obtaining forgiveness from those they have injured.[47]
Certainly the underlying concept of justice here is the same. But it is
tempting to guess that the idea found a home in a Christian apocalypse because of its coherence with the Christian tradition of forgiveness for enemies and especially of the martyrs' forgiveness for their
persecutors. If the martyrs, instead of predicting their persecutors'

---

[44] See Peterson, 'Die "Taufe,"' 318, 323-324. The point is supported by the fact
that in the Greek geography the Acherusian lake is not on the Elysian plain.

[45] E. Lupieri, '*Poena aeterna* nelle più antiche apocalissi cristiane apocrife non
gnostiche,' *Augustinianum* 23 (1983) 369, thinks it is probably intended.

[46] On the general question of Greek influence on the Apocalypse of Peter, see R.
Bauckham, "The Apocalypse of Peter: An Account of Research," in *Aufstieg und
Niedergang der römischen Welt*, Part II, vol. 25/6, ed. W. Haase (Berlin/New York: de
Gruyter, 1988) 4712-4750.

[47] In this case, the injured are in the Acherusian lake, being purified, whereas in
the Apocalypse of Peter they are in paradise.

punishment in hell (4 Macc 10:11; 12:12; cf. 1 En 47:1-4), prayed for their forgiveness (Acts 7:60; Eusebius, *Hist. Eccl.* 5.2.5),[48] then surely (it would have been thought) they will do so all the more when their erstwhile persecutors beg their forgiveness and intercession on the Day of Judgment. In fact, precisely this argument is reported by Augustine as the view of some Christians who may have been influenced by the Apocalypse of Peter (*De civ. Dei* 21.18).[49]

The theme reappears in only a few other texts, probably influenced by the Apocalypse of Peter.[50] Sibylline Oracle 2:330-338 is

---

[48] For a later example, see A. Hamman, *Early Christian Prayers* (Chicago: H. Regnery/London: Longmans, Green, 1961) 55.

[49] See the next chapter.

[50] Mention should also be made of the two works with which the Apocalypse of Peter is connected in the Ethiopic version (in both of the only two manuscripts of the Ethiopic). The first of these is called 'The second coming of Christ and the resurrection of the dead,' and the Apocalypse of Peter itself forms the first part of this work, but is readily distinguishable from the secondary continuation which has been attached to it and which begins: 'Peter opened his mouth and said to me, "Listen, my son Clement." This pseudo-Clementine form is that of the many later Petrine apocrypha which are presented as revelations of Christ communicated by Peter to his disciple Clement. The work is evidently inspired by the Apocalypse of Peter, but is also dependent on the Arabic Apocalypse of Peter (Book of the Rolls) or on the Ethiopic version of this in Qalementos. It cannot therefore be earlier than the eighth century and could be much later. The second work is called 'The mystery of the judgment of sinners,' and, although it is a distinct work, it seems to have been written with knowledge of the first, and in many ways continues the same style and themes. These two continuations of the Apocalypse of Peter were most probably written and attached to it in Arabic, and then translated with it into Ethiopic. Their relevance in the present context is that both refer to the secret mystery, revealed by Christ to Peter, of the divine mercy to sinners secured by Christ's intercession for them at the Last Judgment. In particular this is the central theme of the first work, 'The second coming of Christ and the resurrection of the dead,' and was presumably inspired by the passage about the salvation of the damned in ApPet 14, though, curiously, the meaning of this latter passage is obscured by the corrupt text of the Ethiopic in both the manuscripts. The teaching seems to be universalist, since only the devil and the demons are envisaged as finally damned, but the sinners who will be saved by Christ's intercession at the end are described as sinners who have believed in Christ and have participated in the Eucharist. (In this respect the argument resembles that of the 'compassionate Christians' in Augustine, *De civ. Dei* 21.19-21, whose concern is to extend the scope of salvation to people who profess Christian faith or participate in the Christian sacraments, but who have lived wicked lives [see chapter 7 below], rather than those of *De civ. Dei* 21.18, who, like the Apocalypse of Peter itself, envisage the salvation of unbelievers and persecutors of the church through the intercession of the saints.) Perhaps the failure to refer to unbelievers reveals a Christianized society as the context of composition. The other prominent feature of the teaching is the emphatic insistence on the need to keep the eschatological mercy of God for sinners hidden from sinners in this life, since this would rob the threat of damnation of its essential deterrent function in their lives. (This argument about secrecy and deterrence also features in Origenist discussion of universal salvation and in the

certainly dependent on the Apocalypse of Peter.[51] The following
rather cryptic passage in the Coptic Apocalypse of Elijah becomes
quite clear in the light of the Apocalypse of Peter:

> Those who belong to the righteous and ... will see the sinners and those
> who persecuted them and those who handed them over to death in their
> torments. Then the sinners [in torment] will see the place of the right-
> eous. And thus grace will occur. In those days, that which the righteous
> will ask for many times will be given to them (ApEl 5:27-29).

The passage is very probably dependent on the Apocalypse of Peter.[52] Finally, a passage in the Epistle of the Apostles looks like another echo of the Apocalypse of Peter:

> And we [the apostles] said to him [Jesus], "O lord, we are truly troubled
> on their [the damned] account." And he said to us, "You do well, for so
> are the righteous anxious about the sinners, and they pray and implore
> God and ask him." And we said to him, "O Lord, does no one entreat
> you?" And he said to us, "Yes, I will hear the requests of the righteous
> concerning them" (EpApp 40: Ethiopic).

That the notion had some currency in the early church is indicated
both by these passages and by Augustine (*De civ. Dei* 21.18), but it
came under the suspicion of Origenism, as the refutation inserted at
Sibylline Oracle 2:331 in manuscript Ψ indicates:

> Plainly false. For the fire which tortures the condemned will never cease.
> Even I would pray that this be so, though I am marked with very great
> scars of faults, which have need of very great mercy. But let babbling
> Origen be ashamed of saying that there is a limit to punishment.[53]

---

argument of the 'compassionate Christians' in Augustine, *De civ. Dei* 21.18 [see chapter 7 below], though in these cases it is closely linked with exegesis of Ps 30:20, and
fulfils the apologetic function of explaining why universal salvation is not clearly
taught in Scripture.) Thus this text reveals in its own way the tension of justice and
mercy: the threat of damnation is required to promote righteousness, but in view of
God's mercy it cannot be his last word. The tension here is only sustainable through
strict insistence on an esoteric revelation which it is vital remains secret, known
presumably only by those whose love of God's righteousness does not need the threat
of hell to sustain it.

[51] M. R. James, 'A New Text of the Apocalypse of Peter,' *JTS* 12 (1911) 39-44,
51-52.

[52] D. Frankfurter, *Elijah in Upper Egypt: The Apocalypse of Elijah and Early Egyptian
Christianity* (Studies in Antiquity and Christianity; Minneapolis: Fortress, 1993) 38-39,
fails to note the parallel with ApPet 14 when he judges the evidence insufficient to
establish dependence. For the view that the Apocalypse of Elijah is dependent on the
Apocalypse of Peter, see D. D. Buchholz, *Your Eyes Will Be Opened: A Study of the Greek
(Ethiopic) Apocalypse of Peter* (SBLDS 97; Atlanta, Georgia: Scholars Press, 1988) 58-61.

[53] J. H. Charlesworth ed., *The Old Testament Pseudepigrapha*, vol. 1 (London: Darton,
Longman & Todd, 1983) 353 n. c3.

CHAPTER SEVEN

AUGUSTINE, THE 'COMPASSIONATE' CHRISTIANS, AND THE APOCALYPSE OF PETER

In book 21 of the *City of God* Augustine has to defend his doctrine of hell, as the everlasting punishment of the damned in fire, on two fronts: against non-Christian Platonists (chapters 1-16) and against fellow-Christians (chapters 17-27). These are either Christians who hold a doctrine of universal salvation (and so do not believe in hell in the sense of final damnation) or Christians whose criteria for salvation are laxer than Augustine's, with the result that they extend the scope of salvation more widely than Augustine, without being universalists. In this chapter we shall be concerned with Augustine's debate with these fellow-Christians, and more especially with one particular group of them, the universalists to whom Augustine devotes chapters 18 and 24.

We need to distinguish carefully, as Augustine himself does, the various groups of Christians with whom Augustine debates in chapters 17-27. Previous treatments of our subject have been inclined to confuse them. There are in fact seven distinct views, and Augustine's procedure is to set out first the argument of each of the seven groups in turn (chapters 17-22) and then to reply to each in turn (chapters 23-27). In most cases Augustine had already discussed the view in question in an earlier work, and he borrows considerably from these earlier discussions. The earlier discussions confirm for us the distinctness of the various groups, because he had usually dealt with only one group in any one context previously. Only in the *City of God* does he bring them all together, in order to provide both a conspectus of views on the subject and a comprehensive refutation. Another feature of the groups as Augustine describes them is that, apart from the first two, each adduces a particular biblical text or group of texts in its support. The exegesis of these texts is an important feature of the debate. The fact that each group cites different texts is a useful aid to identifying them in other contexts.

The following table lists the seven groups, their doctrinal position, the biblical texts they cite according to *De civ. Dei* 21, places in his earlier works where Augustine had already discussed the same group or argument, and (where relevant) the biblical texts discussed in those earlier contexts:

(1) Origen: All, including the devil and his angels, will be saved, after purgatorial punishments.

De civ. Dei 21.17; reply: 21.23.

Also *Ad Orosium* 5-7 (415 c.e.)

(2) All human beings (but not devils) will be saved, after punishments of varying duration.

De civ. Dei 21.17; reply: 21.23.

Also *Ad Orosium* 5-7 (415 c.e.)

(3) All human beings (but not devils) will be saved by the intercession of the saints on the Day of Judgment. Thus no one will be punished at all. Hell is a threat of what the wicked deserve, but mercy will overrule it. Scripture is largely silent on this in order to promote the repentance of those who fear hell.
   Texts: Psalm 76:10(77:9); Jonah 3; Psalm 30:20(31:19); Rom 11:32.

De civ. Dei 21.18; reply: 21.24.

Also *Enchiridion* 29 (112) (421 c.e.)
   Text: Psalm 76:10(77:9)
and perhaps *Serm.* 75.9 (? 400 c.e.)

(4) All who participate in the Christian sacraments, including heretics, will be saved.
   Text: John 6:50-51.

De civ. Dei 21.19; reply: 21.25.

(5) All who participate in the Catholic eucharist will be saved.
   Text: 1 Corinthians 10:17.

De civ. Dei 21.20; reply: 21.25.

(6) All who remain in the Catholic church (hold the Catholic faith) will be saved, those who lived wickedly after temporary punishment.
   Text: 1 Corinthians 3:11-15.

De civ. Dei 21.21; reply: 21.26.

Also *De fide et operibus* 15 (24-26) (413 c.e.)
   Text: 1 Corinthians 3:11-15.

   Enchiridion 18 (67-69) (421 c.e.)
   Text: 1 Corinthians 3:11-15.

De octo Dulcitii quaestionibus 1 (423-5 C.E.)
    Texts: Matthew 5:26; 1 Corinthians 3:11-15.

(7) All who perform works of mercy will be saved.
    Texts: James 2:13; Matthew 23:34-46; 6:12, 14-15.

De civ. Dei 21.22; reply 21.27.

Also *Enchiridion* 19-20 (70-77) (421 C.E.)
    Text: Luke 11:41.

By contrast with the pagans with whom he has been arguing in chapters 1-16, Augustine in chapter 17 calls his Christian opponents *misericordi nostri*—'our own compassionate ones,' 'the compassionate Christians'—and, although this description refers immediately to the second group, it is plainly also the way Augustine regards all of the groups. With the exception of Origen, whose position on the salvation of the devil[1] had been condemned by the church,[2] Augustine does not regard these Christians as heretics, but simply as mistaken and misguided, motivated for the most part, apparently, by a misplaced compassion for the damned. In chapter 24 he calls the third group 'these perversely compassionate people' (*isti in perversum misericordes*). But he does introduce a less friendly polemical note in chapter 18, where (again with regard to the third group, members of which he had met and debated with in person) he accuses them of arguing for universal salvation because of their own evil lives. Moreover, Augustine's motive for discussing Origen is not that he is in debate with anyone who holds Origen's position insofar as it has been condemned by the church, but because he wishes to argue that the second and third groups ought, if they were to carry through their principle of compassion consistently, to hold Origen's heretical position on the salvation of devils. They avoid heresy only by inconsistency, he claims. Thus Augustine's assertion, at the outset of chapter 17, that this is to be a friendly debate among fellow-Christians does not mean that he is pulling any punches.

We turn to the identification of the various groups of Christians with whom Augustine is arguing. The second group are clearly mod-

---

[1] The evidence in Origen's own works as to whether Satan and the devils are to be finally saved is inconsistent, but he was widely thought to teach the final salvation of the devils: see H. Crouzel, 'L'Hadès et la Géhenne selon Origène,' *Gregorianum* 59 (1978) 326-328; B. E. Daley, *The Hope of the Early Church; A Handbook of Patristic Eschatology* (Cambridge: Cambridge University Press, 1991) 58-59.

[2] Cf. A. Lehaut, *L'Éternité des Peines de l'Enfer dans Saint Augustine* (Études de Théologie Historique 4; Paris: Beauchesne, 1912) 53-54.

erate Origenists.[3] They hold an Origenist doctrine of *apokatastasis*, but without the salvation of the devils. Augustine knew something about Origen himself and about eastern Origenism from Jerome,[4] but here he has in mind the Spanish Origenism about which he knew from his protégé Orosius, who in 415 consulted Augustine about Priscillianism and Origenism, the two doctrinal perils then menacing the Spanish church. A certain Avitus had brought a volume of Origen (probably the *Peri Archōn*) back from Jerusalem to Spain, and Origen's views on universal salvation were being propagated in Spain.[5] But the salvation of devils seems not to have been adopted by the Spanish. There is no reason to suppose that Augustine knew anything more about group (2) than what he learned from Orosius, whereas in the case of most, if not all, of the other groups he seems to have personally met members of them.

If the second group are clearly Origenists, there is no strong reason to think that any of the remaining five groups had anything much to do with Origenism. Though one certainly cannot rule out Origenist influence on group (6), they are explicable in terms simply of a plausible exegesis of 1 Corinthians 3:11-15. The text was a favourite with Origen and the principal text on which he based his doctrine of purificatory punishment after death,[6] but one did not have to be directly influenced by Origen in order to find a reference to a purgatorial fire for Christians in 1 Corinthians 3. None of the other groups (3-5, 7) is said to believe in temporary, purgatorial punishments after death, while group (3) are explicitly said to hold that noone goes to hell at all, not even temporarily. According to this group, the wicked are rescued from hell by the prayers of the saints immediately on being consigned to hell at the Day of Judgment. Their punishment is revoked, not implemented at all, whereas for Origenists the punishment of the wicked in hell must take place for an appropriate period until they can emerge from it fitted for eternal blessedness. Thus the universalism of group (3) is not Origenist at all, but wholly opposed to

---

[3] On the eternity or non-eternity of hell, Origen's own works are not wholly consistent (cf. Crouzel, 'L'Hadès,' 310-329, who interprets Origen as hesitant on the point, and viewing *apokatastasis* as a hope rather than a dogmatic assertion; Daley, *The Hope*, 56-58, who sees universal salvation as an essential component of Origen's eschatology). Those whom I call Origenists based their teaching on Origen's bolder and clearer statements about universal salvation (of humans).

[4] Lehaut, *L'Éternité*, 6-8.

[5] Lehaut, *L'Éternité*, 9-11.

[6] Crouzel, 'L'Hadès,' 302; J. Gnilka, *Ist 1 Kor 3,10-15 ein Schriftzeugnis für das Fegfeuer?* (Düsseldorf: M. Triltisch, 1955) 20-25. For the notion of punishment as necessarily purificatory and educational in Origen, see Daley, *The Hope*, 57-58.

Origenist eschatology. It should be clear that the two properly universalist groups (2 and 3) are quite distinct and different. Their universalism has a different basis in each case, an Origenist basis only in the case of group (2).

Ntedika asserts, in general terms, that the biblical texts in Augustine's debate with the *misericordes* are those which Origen and Origenists had popularized in this connexion.[7] He gives no evidence. The only such evidence known to me is in a brief passage in Jerome's Isaiah commentary (410 c.e.). Jerome refers to 'those who wish the punishments to be at some time finished and the torments to have a limit, even if only after many ages.' They hold that this doctrine must be kept secret in this life from those whom the fear of hell deters from sin. Jerome cites six biblical texts as the texts they adduce for their teaching (Rom 11:25; Gal 3:22/Rom 11:32; Mic 7:9; Isa 12:1; Isa 7:4; Ps 30:20[31:19]) (Jerome, *In Esaiam* 18, on Isa 66:24). Two of these texts are also used by the third group in Augustine's classification. Jerome's second text is actually a conflation of two similar texts (Gal 3:22 and Rom 11:32), the latter of which is used by Augustine's group (3). It is an obvious text to cite in support of universal salvation, and the coincidence by itself would not be significant. More significant however is the occurrence of Psalm 30:20 in both lists. Although Jerome does not explicitly say so, this verse ('How great is your kindness, O Lord, which you have kept secret from those who fear you'[8]) is plainly the basis for the doctrine of secrecy which Jerome reports and which is very similar to that which Augustine ascribes to his third group in connexion with this biblical text. The correspondence cannot be mere coincidence.

The doctrine of secrecy and the use of Psalm 30:20 to prove it are found in Origen's own work, though not with explicit reference to universal salvation.[9] They are used as an exegetical principle to explain scriptural references to the wrath and judgment of God which seem overly harsh or negative. Commenting on Romans 7:18, Origen says that God makes known his wrath. which is not his true nature, and conceals his kindness, which *is* his true nature, because he

---

[7] J. Ntedika, *L'évolution de la doctrine du purgatoire chez St Augustine* (Publications de l'Université Lovanium de Léopoldville 20; Paris: Études Augustiniennes, 1966) 19-20.

[8] Jerome: *Quam grandis multitudo bonitatis tuae, Domine, quam absondisti timentibus te;* Augustine: *Quam multa multitudo dulcedinis tuae, Domine, quam absondisti timentibus te.* The interpretation goes back to LXX (ἧς ἔκρυψας τοῖς φοβουμένους σε).

[9] But for Origen's caution about suggesting too openly that the pains of hell will not be eternal, because this would undermine their effectiveness as a deterrent, see Daley, *The Hope,* 57.

knows that humanity is weak and easily inclined to fall into sin
through negligence. So it is better for people to fear his wrath than to
become slack through hoping for his kindness (*Comm. in Rom.* 7:18
[PG 14:1150-1151]; cf. also 2:4 [PG 14:879]; 2:8 [PG 14:890-891];
5:2 [PG 14:1025]; *Comm. in Matt.* 15:11 [GCS 40:379-380]). This
interpretation of Psalm 30:20 by Origen must be the source of its use
not only by those to whom Jerome refers but also by those described
by Augustine as his third group. They could have known it through
Rufinus' translation of Origen's Commentary on Romans.

Those whose views Jerome reports are certainly Origenists, believing in temporary infernal punishments which may last for many ages.
Should we therefore conclude that Augustine's third group, with
whom they share a distinctive use and interpretation of Psalm 30:20,
are also Origenists? Decisively against such a conclusion is the fact
that three of the texts Jerome cites (Mic 7:9; Isa 12:1; Isa 7:4) *could not*
have been used by Augustine's third group. These texts speak of
experiencing God's mercy *after* experiencing his wrath and punishment. They are texts selected to support the Origenist notion of temporary punishments in hell, whereas Augustine's third group do not
believe the wicked will be punished at all. Their universalism is based
on a wholly non-Origenist argument.

It is possible that, in citing Psalm 30:20 and in the theme of secrecy, Augustine has mistakenly attributed to his third group material
which in fact belongs to his second group. But this explanation is
unlikely, since everything else Augustine knows about his second
group had been told him by Orosius, whereas he knew members of
the third group personally and had discussed the issue with them. It is
more likely that his third group had appropriated one Origenist argument. No doubt it was the apologetic need to defend their non-
Origenist brand of universalism in the face of the silence of Scripture
about it that led them to make use of an Origenist argument well
designed for this purpose. In order to answer the question why Scripture only hints at the possibility that the threat of hell may not be
carried out, they argue that Scripture maintains this silence so that
the threat of hell may be effective in bringing people to repentance.
Origen's exegesis of Ps 30:20 is used to make this point. But this
apologetic appropriation of one Origenist argument does not make
the group Origenists.

Thus Augustine's third group are not Origenists, but the background to their ideas has yet to be explained. Before doing so, we
may pay brief attention to the remaining four groups (4-7), which
require less explanation. Augustine is concerned about them because
he is anxious to insist that a moral life is necessary to salvation. Views

similar to those he combats were held by prominent Latin theologians (Jerome,[10] Ambrose,[11] Ambrosiaster), but it is not likely that he had them in mind.[12] To explain these groups we probably need not look much further than to a generous desire to extend Christian salvation to as many as possible of those who profess Christian faith. Perhaps a certain reaction against Pelagianism could also be at work.[13]

Among all the groups it is group (3) that stands out as a genuinely universalist position (unlike groups 4-7) which is not Origenist but is nevertheless a well-defined, distinctive point of view. The background to this group has not been properly investigated, in part because its distinctiveness has been overlooked in general discussions of the *misericordes*. [14]

This is how Augustine reports the argument of his third group:

> For they say that what has been divinely predicted concerning the wicked and the unbelievers is true, because they deserve (it); but that when it comes to the judgment, mercy is to gain the upper hand. For the merciful God, they say, will grant them to the prayers and intercessions of his saints (*Donabit enim eos, inquit, misericors Deus praecibus et intercessionibus sanctorum suorum*).[15] For if they prayed for them when they endured suffering from them as enemies, how much more (will they pray for them) when they see them prostrated as humble supplicants!
>
> For it is incredible, they say, that the saints should lose their bowels of mercy at the time when they will be of the fullest and most perfect sanctity, so that those who prayed for their enemies when they themselves were not without sin, will not pray for their supplicants when they (themselves) have begun to have no sin. Or will God not hear them—so many of his children and such children, when in such great sanctity as they have he will find no hindrance to their prayers? (*De civ. Dei* 21.18)[16]

This group of people, then, envisage that at the Day of Judgment (a) the damned will implore the saints to pray for them, (b) the saints will indeed pray for them, and (c) God 'will grant them to the prayers and intercessions of his saints.' It is clear that this expectation must derive from the apocalyptic tradition about the intercession of the saints for the damned at the Last Judgment which was discussed in section IV

---

[10] Daley, *The Hope*, 103-104.

[11] Daley, *The Hope*, 97-99.

[12] Lehaut, *L'Éternité*, 25-38, 39-40.

[13] Cf. Lehaut, *L'Éternité*, 40.

[14] Lehaut, *L'Éternité*, 16-40; Ntedika, *L'évolution*, 19-22.

[15] This sentence is mistranslated in Augustine, *Concerning the City of God against the Pagans*, tr. H. Bettenson, ed. D. Knowles (Harmondsworth: Penguin, 1972) 996: 'For God, they say, will in his mercy grant them the prayers and intercessions of his saints.'

[16] My translation from the text in CCL 48:784.

of the last chapter. The oldest source in which tradition is now extant is the Apocalypse of Peter, which contains all three points (a, b, c) in Augustine's report of what the Christians he knew expected: (a) in 13:4; (b) and (c) in 14:1, which reads: 'I will give to my called and elect ones whomsoever they request from me, out of the punishment' (Rainer fragment). The phraseology is strikingly close to Augustine's: God 'will grant them to the prayers and intercessions of his saints.'

Other extant passages containing this theme which can be dated before the *City of God* are, as we argued at the end of the last chapter, certainly or probably dependent on the Apocalypse of Peter (SibOr 2:330-338; ApEl 5:27-29; EpApp 40). They are less plausible sources for the teaching of Augustine's interlocutors than the Apocalypse of Peter because none of them contain (a) the supplication of the saints by the damned. The Apocalypse of Peter is the only extant text which says precisely what Augustine's interlocutors said. Of course, they could have known a no longer extant work which shared the same tradition with the Apocalypse of Peter, or they could have known the Apocalypse of Peter's teaching at secondhand through a text or texts dependent on it. But it is not at all unlikely that the Apocalypse of Peter itself was known to them. It seems to have been a popular work in the second, third and fourth centuries.[17] Its presence in the West is not only attested by the disputed evidence of the Muratorian Canon (lines 91-93): 'Also of the apocalypses we accept only those of John and Peter, which (latter) some of our people do not wish to have read in church.' It is also well attested by an allusion to it in an anonymous Latin sermon on the parable of the ten virgins, probably from North Africa and perhaps from the fourth century,[18] and a quotation from it in another Latin sermon of uncertain date (perhaps c. 300), again most likely from North Africa: Pseudo-Cyprian, *Adv. Aleatores* 8.[19] If a Latin version of the Apocalypse of Peter existed, its disappearance may be attributable precisely to Augustine's attack on this feature of its teaching, as well as to the western reaction against apocryphal works in the wake of Priscillianism and to the increasingly greater popularity of the Apocalypse of Paul as the most popular source of apocalyptic revelations of the hereafter. The latter apocalypse was dismissed by Augustine as mere fables (*Tractatus in Joannem* 98.8), but

---

[17] R. Bauckham, 'The Apocalypse of Peter: An Account of Research,' in *Aufstieg und Niedergang der römischen Welt*, 2.25/6, ed. W. Haase (Berlin/New York: de Gruyter, 1988) 4739-4741; D. D. Buchholz, *Your Eyes Will Be Opened: A Study of the Greek (Ethiopic) Apocalypse of Peter* (SBLDS 97; Atlanta, Georgia: Scholars Press, 1988) 20-80.

[18] M. R. James, 'A New Text of the *Apocalypse of Peter*,' *JTS* 12 (1911) 383; Buchholz, *Your Eyes*, 38-39.

[19] James, 'A New Text,' 50, 383; Buchholz, *Your Eyes*, 62-63.

he did not accuse it of false doctrine such as universal salvation.

Augustine's report also contains an argument for supposing that the saints will intercede for the damned:

> If they prayed for them when they endured suffering from them as enemies, how much more (will they pray for them) when they see them prostrated as humble supplicants! For it is incredible, they say, that the saints should lose their bowels of mercy at the time when they will be of the fullest and most perfect sanctity, so that those who prayed for their enemies when they themselves were not without sin, will not pray for their supplicants when they (themselves) have begun to have no sin.

This argument is not stated in the Apocalypse of Peter, but could easily occur to a reader of that work, especially in view of its references to persecution. But the argument also recalls 4 Ezra 7:106-111, where Ezra adduces the examples of the righteous men of the Old Testament who interceded for sinners (Abraham, Moses, Joshua, Samuel, David, Solomon, Elijah, Hezekiah), leading to the question:

> So if now, when corruption has increased and unrighteousness has multiplied, the righteous have prayed for the ungodly, why will it not be so then [at the Day of Judgment] as well? (7:111)

Ezra is told why it will not be so then, but it is not uncommon for readers of 4 Ezra to find Ezra's arguments more compelling than the answers he receives.

Augustine's report of the group's views continues, after the passage cited above, with explanation of how they support them with biblical texts. This kind of scriptural exposition has no parallel in the Apocalypse of Peter or elsewhere in the apocalypses that include the idea of mercy for the damned. The appeal to Scripture must be understood as defence of a doctrine Augustine's interlocutors had derived from extra-canonical apocalyptic literature but now needed to defend in a period when apocryphal literature was being increasingly discredited.[20] The reaction against Priscillianism, which valued apocryphal literature[21] and was therefore seen as demonstrating the dangers to which reading of such literature could lead, produced suspicion about

---

[20] Cf. M. Starowieyski, 'Les apocryphes chez les écrivains du IVᵉ siècle,' in *Miscellanea Historiae Ecclesiasticae VI: Congrès de Varsovie 25 Juin—1ᵉʳ Juillet 1978, Section I* (Bibliothèque de la Revue d'Histoire Ecclésiastique 67; Warsaw: Polska Akademia Nauk/Louvain-le-Neuve: Bureau de la R.H.E.; Brussels: Éditions Navwelaerts, 1983) 132-141.

[21] Some scholars may have exaggerated this. Evidence for Priscillianist use of apocrypha seems secure only for 4 Ezra and the various apocryphal Acts: H. Chadwick, *Priscillian of Avila and the Charismatic in the Early Church* (Oxford: Oxford University Press, 1976) chapter 2.

the reading even of admittedly orthodox apocrypha. In such an atmosphere Augustine's interlocutors would be obliged to buttress their
argument with canonical scriptural authority. It is worth observing
that a similar phenomenon can be observed in the apocalyptic literature itself, also as a symptom of the waning authority of apocryphal
apocalypses. Apocalypses from an earlier period almost never cite
Scripture,[22] but from this period onwards both Christian and Jewish
apocalypses (e.g. the Greek apocryphal Apocalypse of John, the Hebrew Apocalypse of Elijah) introduce scriptural quotations, as though
the apocalyptic revelation no longer carries sufficient authority itself,
without appealing to canonical Scripture to support its statements.

Finally, we should notice the theological difference between Augustine and these 'compassionate Christians' whose views he is so
concerned to refute. His major theological (as distinct from exegetical
argument is this:

> [T]he reason which now prevents the Church from praying for the evil
> angels, whom she knows to be her enemies, is the same reason which will
> then prevent her at that time of judgement from praying, however perfect
> her holiness, for the human beings who are to be tormented in eternal
> fire. Her reason for praying now for her enemies among mankind is that
> there is time for fruitful penitence... In fact, if the Church had such
> certain information about people as to know who were already predes-
> tined, although still under the conditions of this life, to go into eternal fire
> with the Devil, then the Church would pray as little for them as it does
> for him. But she has not this certainty about anyone; therefore she prays
> for all her enemies, her human enemies, that is, while they are in the
> bodily state; but that does not mean that her prayers for all of them are
> heard and answered. In fact her prayers are heard only when she prays
> for those who, although they oppose the Church, are predestined to
> salvation so that the Church's prayers for them are answered and they
> are made sons of the Church. But if any of them keep their heart impeni-
> tent up to their dying day, if they are not transformed from enemies into
> friends, are we to suppose that the Church still prays for them, that is, for
> the spirits of such men when they have departed this life? Of course not!
> And this is simply because anyone who has not been transferred to the
> side of Christ while he lives in the body is thereafter reckoned as belong-
> ing to the Devil's party (*De civ. Dei* 21.24).[23]

In the debate between Augustine and these 'merciful Christians' there
is a serious clash of theological principles. On the side of the apocalyptic tradition taken up by the 'merciful Christians' there are two key
principles. The first is the solidarity of the human race, such that the

---

[22] ApPet 4:7 is a (perhaps unique) exception.
[23] Augustine, *Concerning the City of God against the Pagans*, tr. H. Bettenson, 1002-
1003.

compassion of the saints extends to all humans, however wicked, since they understand themselves to be bound up with them, to some extent even in their sin. Therefore they feel bound to plead the case of the damned with God. The second principle is an understanding of prayer in which the saints persist in prayer even against the apparent will of God. They plead God's mercy against God's justice and, as it were, win God over. On Augustine's side of the debate, the overriding principle is the sovereign will of God. As a result the solidarity of the human race is radically severed by God's will in the form of predestination. Even in this life the church prays for the reprobate only through ignorance. If she knew who the elect were, she would pray only for them. Prayer, in Augustine's understanding, is wholly subordinated to God's will. Therefore, once the will of God with regard to the reprobate is known, as it will be at the Last Judgment, the perfection of the saints will show itself in their absolute concurrence with that divine will.

CHAPTER EIGHT

THE APOCALYPSE OF PETER: A JEWISH CHRISTIAN APOCALYPSE FROM THE TIME OF BAR KOKHBA

I Introduction

1 *Why study the Apocalypse of Peter?*

The Apocalypse of Peter deserves to be rescued from the extreme scholarly neglect it has suffered. It deserves to be studied for the following reasons:

(1) It is probably the most neglected of all Christian works written before 150 c.e. It has, of course, suffered the general stigma and neglect accorded to apocryphal works by comparison with those in the canon of the New Testament or even those assigned to the category of the Apostolic Fathers. But whereas other Christian apocryphal literature of the earliest period—such as apocryphal Gospels or the Ascension of Isaiah—have very recently been studied in some depth and are beginning to be rescued as significant evidence of the early development of Christianity, the Apocalypse of Peter has been given very little serious scholarly attention. Surely for those who are interested in Christian origins any Christian work from the first century or so of Christian history deserves the closest study.

(2) In section II of this chapter I shall argue that the Apocalypse of Peter derives from Palestinian Jewish Christianity during the Bar Kokhba war of 132-135 c.e. This makes it a very rare example of an extant work deriving from Palestinian Jewish Christianity in the period after the New Testament literature. It deserves an important place in any attempt to consider the very obscure matter of what happened to Jewish Christianity in Palestine in the period after 70 c.e.

(3) Outside Palestinian Jewish Christianity, the Apocalypse of Peter evidently became a very popular work in the church as a whole, from the second to the fourth centuries.[1] It seems to have been

---

[1] R. Bauckham, 'The Apocalypse of Peter: An Account of Research,' in W. Haase ed., *Aufstieg und Niedergang der römischen Welt*, vol. 2/25/6 (Berlin/New York: de Gruyter, 1988) 4739-4741; D. D. Buchholz, *Your Eyes Will Be Opened: A Study of the*

widely read in east and west. In some circles at least it was treated as Scripture. Along with the *Shepherd* of Hermas, it was probably the work which came closest to being included in the canon of the New Testament while being eventually excluded. After an early period of popularity, however, it almost disappeared. This must have been largely because in its major function—as a revelation of the fate of human beings after death—it was superseded by other apocalypses: in the Latin west and in the Coptic and Syriac speaking churches of the east by the Apocalypse of Paul, in the Greek east by the Greek Apocalypse of the Virgin Mary. For a number of reasons these proved in the long run more acceptable, and the Apocalypse of Peter very nearly perished altogether. But the fact that for two or three centuries it seems to have appealed strongly to the Christian religious imagination makes it an important historical source.

(4) The Apocalypse of Peter preserves Jewish apocalyptic traditions. Because of the prevalent artificial distinction between the Jewish apocalypses and the Christian apocalypses, this is the respect in which the Apocalypse of Peter has been neglected even more than in other respects. But there is in fact relatively little that is distinctively Christian about the Apocalypse of Peter. Much of its content reproduces Jewish apocalyptic traditions. It can therefore be used, of course with appropriate caution, as a source for Jewish apocalyptic ideas of the early second century c.e. And it reminds us how very much Judaism and Christianity had in common at that period.

As these four reasons for studying the Apocalypse of Peter suggest, our study of the work in this chapter will focus on the original work in the context in which it was first written. This is only one aspect of the way in which the Christian apocryphal literature needs to be studied. Many Christian apocryphal works (and the same is true of Jewish apocryphal literature) are best understood as developing literature: works which developed as they were transmitted over many centuries in a variety of cultural contexts. They were translated, expanded, abbreviated, adapted. In some cases the attempt to reconstruct an original text may be quite impossible or inappropriate. However, in the case of the Apocalypse of Peter we may fairly confidently assign it a date and place of origin, and also, despite the fact that most of the text does not survive in its original language, we may be fairly confi-

---

Greek (Ethiopic) Apocalypse of Peter (SBLDS 97; Atlanta, Georgia: Scholars Press, 1988) 20-80.

dent of the content of the original work. There are places where we may not be able to be sure of the original text, but by and large we can know what the first readers read. So in the case of the Apocalypse of Peter, the historical exercise of placing the work in its original context is a justifiable one and will yield significant historical results.

2 *The Text of the Apocalypse of Peter*

The Apocalypse of Peter was probably written originally in Greek and certainly was known in Greek to the Church Fathers. (Whether a Latin version was known in the Latin-speaking churches in the early centuries is less certain.) Unfortunately, because, after an initial period of popularity the Apocalypse of Peter fell out of favour in most of the church, very little of it survives in Greek. We have only two small manuscript fragments (the Bodleian and Rainer fragments) and a few quotations in the Fathers. (For details on these fragments and quotations, see the Bibliographical Notes at the end of this chapter.) In addition, there is one lengthy fragment in Greek (the Akhmim fragment), but this is a secondary, redacted form of the text, which cannot be relied on as evidence of the original form of the Apocalypse of Peter (see below). For our knowledge of the apocalypse we are therefore largely dependent on the Ethiopic version. This version, which contains the full contents of the original second-century Apocalypse of Peter, is the only version of the Apocalypse of Peter known to be extant. It was probably, like most Ethiopic versions of apocryphal works, translated from an Arabic translation of the Greek, but an Arabic version has not been discovered. Any study of the Apocalypse of Peter must therefore depend heavily on the Ethiopic version. Probably this is one reason why, since the identification of the Ethiopic version by M. R. James in 1911, the Apocalypse of Peter has received very little scholarly attention. Scholars have been dubious whether the Ethiopic version can be trusted to give us reliable access to the second-century Apocalypse of Peter. Those who have studied the matter with some care, such as M. R. James himself and, more recently, D. D. Buchholz, have not shared such doubts. But some indication of the reasons for trusting the Ethiopic version must be given here, in order to justify our use of it in this chapter.

Only two, closely related manuscripts of the Apocalypse of Peter are known. (For details, see the Bibliographical Notes at the end of this chapter.) In both manuscripts the Apocalypse of Peter is the first part of a longer work ('The second coming of Christ and the resurrection of the dead'), the rest of which was clearly inspired by the Apocalypse of Peter. This continuation of the ancient apocalypse, which probably originated in Arabic, would be of considerable interest if we were studying the later history of the Apocalypse of Peter. But for our present intention of studying the Apocalypse of Peter in its original, early second-century context, the important point is that we can be sure that the text of the Apocalypse of Peter itself has not been affected by this later continuation of it. The section of the Ethiopic work which is the ancient Apocalypse of Peter can be distinguished from the rest with no difficulty. Whereas the Apocalypse of Peter itself is written as though by Peter in the first person, the later continuation begins by introducing Peter's disciple Clement, who writes in the first person and reports what Peter said to him (according to a literary convention of the later Pseudo-Clementine literature). Moreover, Buchholz has demonstrated that the writer responsible for the continuation of the Apocalypse of Peter which we have in the Ethiopic text did not tamper with the content of the Apocalypse of Peter itself. He merely added; he did not modify.[2]

The general reliability of the Ethiopic version as faithful to the original text of the Apocalypse of Peter can be demonstrated by four main points:

(1) There is the general consideration that the Ethiopic translation of apocryphal texts seems, as a general rule, to be faithful translation, and such works were not usually adapted or modified in the Ethiopic tradition. This contrasts with some other languages in which apocryphal works have been transmitted—such as Slavonic and Armenian—where creative development of the text has often taken place in those traditions. Of course, the Ethiopic may well include erroneous translations and textual corruptions—and in the case of the Apocalypse of Peter these are certainly present—but deliberate adaptation of the text is rare.

(2) The general reliability of the Ethiopic version is confirmed by the two small Greek fragments and the patristic quotations.[3]

(3) There are passages in the second *Sibylline Oracle*, probably from the late second century, which are clearly closely dependent on the Apocalypse of Peter as we know it from the Ethiopic version and confirm the reliability of the Ethiopic version.[4]

---

[2] Buchholz, *Your Eyes Will Be Opened*, 376-386. Buchholz argues for some minor changes, but I do not find his argument that these are due to the author of the continuation at all compelling.

[3] M. R. James, 'A New Text of the Apocalypse of Peter,' *JTS* 12 (1911) 367-375, 573-583; K. Prümm, 'De genuino Apocalypsis Petri textu: Examen testium iam notorum et novi fragmenti Raineriani,' *Bib* 10 (1929) 62-80; Buchholz, *Your Eyes Will Be Opened*, 145-152, 418-422.

[4] James, 'A New Text,' 39-44, 51-52.

(4) Detailed study of the Apocalypse of Peter repeatedly confirms that the content of the work in the Ethiopic version belongs to the period in which the ancient Apocalypse of Peter was written. All the parallels with other literature show this. There is hardly a single idea in the Ethiopic Apocalypse of Peter which can only be paralleled at a date much later than the early second century.

These reasons for confidence in the general reliability of the Ethiopic version do not mean that it is reliable in every detail. The translation is clearly sometimes erroneous and was apparently made by a translator whose command of Ge'ez was very limited,[5] so that the Ethiopic text is frequently obscure. But such obscurities can often be clarified by careful use of parallels in ancient Jewish and Christian literature.

As well as thus justifying our predominant reliance on the Ethiopic version in this chapter, it may be necessary also to justify the fact that little reference will be made to the Akhmim Greek fragment. This fragment is part of a manuscript, probably of the eighth or ninth century, which also contains a section of the *Gospel of Peter* (the only substantial section of this work which has survived) and parts of *1 Enoch*, and which was placed in the grave of a Christian monk. It is clear that the manuscript is a small collection of texts about the other world, and was placed in a grave in accordance with the traditional Egyptian practice of providing the dead with a guide to what they will encounter after death.[6] The problem with the fragment of the Apocalypse of Peter is that it differs significantly in several ways from the Ethiopic version. But some of its important differences from the Ethiopic version are at points where the patristic quotations and the Bodleian fragment confirm the originality of the form of the text in the Ethiopic version.[7] So it has now come to be universally accepted by those who have examined the issue carefully that the Akhmim fragment is a deliberately edited form of material from the Greek Apocalypse of Peter. It may not even be, as such, a fragment of the Apocalypse of Peter itself: it may well be a fragment of another work which utilized the Apocalypse of Peter as a source. There is still a case to be made for the view of some earlier scholars that it is actually another section of the *Gospel of Peter*.[8] In any case, although it may sometimes help us to clear up an obscurity in the Ethiopic version of

---

[5] This is the judgment of P. Marrassini.

[6] M. Tardieu, 'L'Ardā Vīrāz Nāmāg et l'eschatologie grecque,' *Studia Iranica* 14 (1985) 20.

[7] See references in n. 3 above.

[8] See Bauckham, 'The Apocalypse of Peter: An Account of Research,' 4719-4720.

the Apocalypse of Peter, it must be used with great caution in studying the Apocalypse of Peter. Priority must be given to the Ethiopic
version.

3 Outline and Summary of the Apocalypse of Peter

The Apocalypse of Peter can be divided into three main sections,
whose contents can be briefly outlined as follows:

i *Discourse on the Signs and the Time of the Parousia*

1:1-3	The disciples' enquiry
1:4-8	The parousia will be unmistakable
2	The parable of the fig tree: the false Messiah and the martyrs of the last days

ii *Vision of the Judgment and its Explanation*

3	Picture of the judgment and Peter's distress
4	The resurrection
5	The cosmic conflagration
6:1-6	The last judgment
6:7-9	The judgment of the evil spirits
7-12	The punishments in hell
13	The punishments confirmed as just
14:1	The prayers of the elect save some
14:2-3	The elect inherit the promises
14:4-6	Peter's earthly future

iii *Visions of the Reward of the Righteous*

15	Vision of Moses and Elijah
16:1-6	Vision of Paradise
16:7-17:1	Vision of the true Temple and Audition about the true Messiah
17:2-7	The ascension

For readers coming fresh to the Apocalypse of Peter, a fuller summary of its contents may be helpful:

i *Discourse on the Signs and the Time of the Parousia (chapters 1-2)*
[Although it is not made clear by the opening of the work, the events
take place after Jesus' resurrection.] Jesus and his disciples are on the
Mount of Olives. They ask him about the signs and the time of his
parousia and the end of the world. Jesus warns them not to believe

the false claimants to messiahship who will come. His own coming to judgment will be in unmistakable glory.

In order to indicate the time of the end, Jesus gives them the parable of the fig tree: when its shoots become tender, the end of the world will come. When Peter asks for explanation, Jesus tells another parable of a fig tree: the barren fig tree which will be uprooted unless it bears fruit. The fig tree in both parables is Israel. The sprouting of the fig tree will take place when a false messiah arises and Israel follows him. When they reject him, he will put many to death. They will be martyrs. Enoch and Elijah will show them that he is not the true messiah.

ii *Vision of the Judgment and its Explanation (chapters 3-14)*
Jesus shows Peter a vision of the judgment of all people at the last day. Peter is distressed at the fate of sinners, but his claim that it would have been better for them not to have been created is rejected by Jesus, who promises to show Peter the sinners' deeds (in order to enable him to appreciate the justice of their condemnation).

A long prophecy (by Jesus) of the judgment of sinners follows. It begins with an account of the resurrection, which must take place so that all humanity may appear before God on the day of judgment. God's word will reclaim all the dead, because for God nothing is impossible. Then will follow the cosmic conflagration, in which a flood of fire will consume the heavens and the sea and drive all people to judgment in the river of fire. Then Jesus Christ will come and be enthroned and crowned as judge. All will be judged according to their deeds, which will appear in order to accuse the wicked. The river of fire through which all must pass will prove their innocence or guilt. The angels will take the wicked to hell. The demons will also be brought to judgment and condemned to eternal punishment.

There follows a long description of the punishments in hell. A specific, different punishment is described for each of twenty-one types of sinner. The types of sinner and their punishments are:

(1) those who blasphemed the way of righteousness—hung by tongues;
(2) those who denied justice—pit of fire;
(3) women who enticed men to adultery—hung by necks;
(4) adulterers—hung by genitals;
(5) murderers—poisonous animals and worms;
(6) women who aborted their children—in a pit of excrement up to the throat;
(7) infanticides—their milk produces flesh-eating animals;

(8) persecutors and betrayers of Christ's righteous ones—scourged and eaten by unsleeping worm;

(9) those who perverted and betrayed Christ's righteousness—bite tongues, hot irons in eyes;

(10) those who put the martyrs to death with their lies—lips cut off, fire in mouth and entrails;

(11) those who trusted in their riches and neglected the poor—fiery sharp column, clothed in rags;

(12) usurers—in pit of excrement up to the knees;

(13) male and female practising homosexuals—fall from precipice repeatedly;

(14) makers of idols—scourged by chains of fire;

(15) those who forsook God's commandmants and obeyed demons— burning in flames;

(16) those who did not honour their parents—roll down fiery precipice repeatedly;

(17) those who disobeyed the teaching of their fathers and elders— hung and attacked by flesh-eating birds;

(18) girls who had sex before marriage—dark clothes, flesh dissolved;

(19) disobedient slaves—bite tongues continuously;

(20) those who gave alms hypocritically—blind and deaf, coals of fire;

(21) male and female sorcerers—on wheel of fire in the river of fire.

The elect will be shown the punishments of the damned. The latter cry for mercy, but the angel in charge of hell, Tartarouchos, tells them it is now too late for repentance. The damned acknowledge the justice of their punishment. But when the righteous intercede for the damned, Jesus Christ the judge will grant their prayers. Those for whom they pray will be baptised in the Acherusian lake and will share the destiny of the elect. The elect will enter Jesus Christ's eternal kingdom, with the patriarchs, and his promises to them will be fulfilled.

Concluding the prophecy of judgment, Jesus now addresses Peter personally about his future. He is to spread the Gospel through the whole world. He is to go to Rome, where he will die a martyr 'at the hands of the son of the one who is in Hades.'[9]

iii *Visions of the Reward of the Righteous (chapters 15-17)*

Jesus and the disciples go to 'the holy mountain,' where the disciples are granted five revelations. The first is of Moses and Elijah, appearing in resplendent beauty as heavenly beings. When Peter asks where

---

[9] Rainer fragment.

the other patriarchs are, they are shown the heavenly paradise. Jesus says that this destiny of the patriarchs is also to be that of those who are persecuted for his righteousness.

When Peter offers to construct three tents for Jesus, Moses and Elijah, he is severely rebuked by Jesus, but promised a vision and an audition (the third and fourth of the five revelations) to enlighten him. The vision is of the tent which the Father has made for Jesus and the elect. The audition is of a voice from heaven declaring Jesus to be God's beloved Son who should be obeyed. Finally, the disciples witness the ascension of Jesus, with Moses and Elijah, through the heavens. Jesus takes with him 'people in the flesh.' The disciples descend the mountain, glorifying God, who has written the names of the righteous in the book of life in heaven.

II THE LITERARY AND HISTORICAL CONTEXTS

1 *Literary Context*

We cannot be sure whether the title Apocalypse of Peter is original. It does not occur in the Ethiopic version, which has a lengthy title or prologue which certainly does not belong to the original text. But the title Apocalypse of Peter is already used by the Muratorian Canon and by Clement of Alexandria, and so it may well be original. It is true that many of the works which now bear the title Apocalypse came to be so called only at a later date (quite apart from those which have been so called only by modern scholars), but the period in which the Apocalypse of Peter must have been written—the early second century C.E.—is one in which it is plausible to hold that the term ἀποκάλυψις could be being used as the description of a literary work containing the account of a revelation given by a supernatural being to a prophet or visionary.

But whether or not its title is original, the Apocalypse of Peter certainly belongs to that rather broad genre of ancient literature which we call apocalypses. Indeed, its date—in the early second century C.E.—places it in a golden age, perhaps the golden age of Jewish and Christian apocalyptic literature. The period between the two great Jewish revolts (between 70 and 132 C.E.) produced the greatest of all the Jewish and Christian apocalypses: the Book of Revelation, 4 Ezra and 2 Baruch—works in which the genre of apocalyptic became the vehicle for truly great literature and truly profound theology. A considerable number of other extant Jewish and Christian apocalypses also date from the late first and early second centuries: the Apocalypse of Abraham, the Ladder of Jacob, the Ascension of

Isaiah, the Greek Apocalypse of Baruch (3 Baruch), the Shepherd of Hermas, and quite probably also the Parables of Enoch, the Slavonic Apocalypse of Enoch (2 Enoch), and so-called 5 Ezra. It is hard to be sure whether this period really was exceptionally productive of apocalypses, or whether that impression is due to the accidents of survival. There certainly were more Jewish apocalypses in earlier periods, such as the early first century c.e., than have survived, and it is always very important to remember that all extant ancient Jewish apocalypses, with the exception of Daniel and the apocalyptic works found at Qumran, have been preserved by Christians. Many which were not congenial to Christian use may not have survived. With due allowance for these factors, however, it does seem probable that the writing of apocalypses especially flourished in the period from 70 c.e. to about the middle of the second century. The reasons will be partly that the destruction of Jerusalem and the temple in 70 c.e. posed for Judaism issues of theodicy and eschatology which were most suitably wrestled with or answered in the literary genre of apocalypse, and partly that much of early Christianity remained during this period a strongly eschatological religious movement which therefore found one of its most natural forms of expression in the apocalypse. I do not make the mistake of considering eschatology the sole content of apocalypses,[10] but most of the apocalypses I have mentioned do in fact focus especially on matters of eschatology, as the Apocalypse of Peter also does. Of course, during the same period—the second century—the genre apocalypse was also adopted and adapted by Christian Gnostics as a vehicle for the kind of revelations they wished to present.

The Apocalypse of Peter has some close links, by way of themes and traditions, with some of the Jewish apocalypses of its period: 4 Ezra, 2 Baruch, the Parables of Enoch. If, as I shall argue, the Apocalypse of Peter is a Palestinian Jewish Christian work, these links with contemporary Palestinian Jewish apocalypses are especially interesting. They help to explain the preservation of these Jewish works by Christians, by showing us the context of Palestinian Jewish Christian apocalyptic in which these Jewish apocalypses would have been of interest. It was doubtless in such Christian circles as those from which the Apocalypse of Peter comes that Jewish apocalypses such as 4 Ezra were read and then passed on to the wider church which later preserved them.

---

[10] This mistake has been corrected especially by C. Rowland, *The Open Heaven* (London: SPCK, 1982).

That there is actual literary dependence by the Apocalypse of
Peter on any extant Jewish apocalypse is much less certain. The links
which exist are explicable as common apocalyptic tradition, current
in Jewish and Christian apocalyptic circles of that period. It is an
important general feature of the apocalypses of this period that they
are all dependent on blocks of traditional apocalyptic material.[11] The
more one studies the way the same traditions reappear in various
apocalypses, the more it becomes impossible to suppose that literary
borrowing from one apocalypse to another can fully explain the recurrence of traditional material. Apocalyptic traditions must have
existed in some form, oral or written, independently of the
apocalypses in which such traditions are now incorporated. (Of
course, such traditional material is also sometimes preserved in works
which are not apocalypses, such as the Biblical Antiquities of Pseudo-
Philo or the letters of Paul.) We do not know the sociological context
in which these apocalyptic traditions were handed on, whether as oral
traditions in circles of apocalyptists or as written notes passed between learned individuals. But certainly what passed from one
apocalyptist to another was not just ideas, but blocks of tradition.

Every apocalypse is therefore a mixture of tradition and originality. The truly great apocalypses—Revelation and 4 Ezra, for example—are works of remarkable creativity, in both literary and
theological terms. The traditional material they certainly incorporate
is used in highly creative ways. In these works the use of tradition is
consistent with considerable originality and with very carefully studied composition. In other cases, traditional material has been put
together by a much less gifted writer and a much less profound
thinker. In one sense, the Apocalypse of Peter is one of the least
original of the apocalypses. Blocks of traditional material seem to be
incorporated often more or less as they stand. Virtually all the contents of the Apocalypse of Peter probably already existed in some
form, some as Gospel traditions, most as Jewish apocalyptic traditions. Probably no passage of more than a few verses was freely composed by the author. But this does not mean that the author is a mere
compiler of traditions. The combination and redaction of his material
has been done with a certain real skill. His creative redactional activity has made of the traditional material he used a particular whole
with a coherent message. While the Apocalypse of Peter is not a great
example of the genre, while its literary and theological merit is small,
it is nevertheless a literary work in its own right. If we are to appreci-

---

[11] Cf., e.g., M. E. Stone, *Fourth Ezra* (Hermeneia; Minneapolis: Fortress Press,
1990) 21-22, on such blocks of traditional material in 4 Ezra.

ate what it meant to its contemporaries and later readers, we must study its traditional components not only as blocks of tradition, but as they relate to each other in this particular literary whole.

So the Apocalypse of Peter turns out to have a double interest. Because of its very conservative preservation of apocalyptic traditions, it is actually a source of knowledge of *Jewish* apocalyptic traditions. It has rarely been treated in this way, because of the artificial distinction which is prevalent between the apocalypses which belong to the so-called Old Testament Pseudepigrapha and those which belong to the so-called New Testament Apocrypha. So far as apocalypses go, this distinction between Old Testament Pseudepigrapha and New Testament Apocrypha is wholly artificial. The Christian tradition of writing apocalypses was almost entirely continuous with the Jewish tradition. In the second century, as I have indicated, even Jewish apocalypses recently written were read and imitated by Christians. The Jewish and Christian apocalypses of the period must be studied together. Moreover, there is no useful distinction between Christian apocalypses written under the name of Old Testament figures such as Ezra and those written under the name of New Testament figures such as Peter. The latter are no less closely related to Jewish apocalypses than are the former.[12]

So the Apocalypse of Peter is of interest for its preservation of those apocalyptic traditions which were common to Christian and non-Christian Jews of the period. But it is also of interest as a work in its own right, with a message of its own. As such, it was no doubt read mostly by Christians, though it may also have functioned as missionary literature used by Christian Jews in their mission to non-Christian Jews. In any case, it reached not only its immediate readership of Jewish Christians but a wide Christian readership throughout the church for a century or more after it was written. Something about it evidently proved popular and relevant.

One important literary feature does distinguish the Apocalypse of Peter as a Christian apocalypse from the Jewish apocalypses to which it is closely akin. It is a revelation of Jesus Christ to the apostle Peter. In being pseudonymous, it differs from the Johannine Apocalypse and the *Shepherd* of Hermas, whose authors broke with Jewish apocalyptic tradition by not hiding behind an ancient pseudonym but writing in their own names as recipients of revelation, as Christian prophets. But like those Christian apocalypses, it is a revelation given by Jesus Christ. The Apocalypse of Peter is probably the earliest

---

[12] On this point, see R. Bauckham, 'The Apocalypses in the New Pseudepigrapha,' *Journal for the Study of the New Testament* 26 (1986) 105-106, 111-113.

extant Christian apocalypse which uses an apostolic pseudonym. The difference which this makes to its literary form is that the narrative framework—which most apocalypses have—is in this case a Gospel narrative framework. It begins with Jesus and the disciples on the mount of Olives; it ends with Jesus' ascension to heaven. The revelation is thus placed within the Gospel story of Jesus, specifically within the period of the resurrection appearances. It purports in fact to record Jesus' final revelatory teaching to his disciples prior to his departure to heaven. In a sense this gives it the character of a testament of Jesus, but it would be a mistake to make too much of this testamentary character of the Apocalypse of Peter: apart from revelation of the future, it shares none of the standard features of the Jewish testament literature. It is better to think of it as an apocalypse set at the end of the Gospel story of Jesus.

As an apocalypse set at the end of the Gospel story of Jesus, the Apocalypse of Peter is an example of a genre of Christian apocalypses which seems to have become very popular in the second and third centuries: the revelatory discourse of Jesus to one or more disciples or the revelatory dialogue of Jesus with the disciples after the resurrection. Like the Apocalypse of Peter, such works are often set on the mount of Olives or some other mountain;[13] they often end with an account of the ascension.[14] Unlike the Apocalypse of Peter they usually begin with an account of the risen Jesus' appearance to the disciples; in this respect, the Apocalypse of Peter is rather peculiar. The way it does open makes it unlikely that an account of an appearance of Jesus has been lost at the beginning, but means that there is no clear way of knowing that the scene is set after the resurrection until one reaches the account of Jesus' ascension at the end of the work.

The genre of the post-resurrection revelatory dialogue is often thought of as a Gnostic literary genre. It did indeed become very popular with the Gnostics. But it did not originate with them. Non-Gnostic examples of the genre—such as the Apocalypse of Peter, the Epistle of the Apostles, the Testament of our Lord and the Questions of Bartholomew—are not imitations of the Gnostic use of the genre. They show that the genre itself originated before Gnostics adopted it. Those who wished to attribute to Jesus Christ further revelations additional to those known from the Gospel traditions evidently found

---

[13] 1ApJas (CG V,3) 30:18-31:2; EpPetPhil (CG VIII,2) 133:14-17; SophJesChr (CG III,4) 90:14-20 (cf. 91:18-20); PistSoph; QuesBart 4:1; ApPaul (Coptic conclusion); HistJos 1.

[14] ApocrJas (CG I,2) 15:5-16:2; EpApp 51; TLord 2:27; cf. SophJesChr (CG III,4) 119:10.

it appropriate to place such revelations in the period of the resurrection appearances. This was because these additional revelations presupposed the teaching of Jesus already given in the Gospel traditions. They interpreted and developed the teaching of Jesus that was already known. They often refer back to the teaching Jesus had given before his death and offer further explanation of what Jesus had meant or further information on subjects that Jesus' earlier teaching had not sufficiently covered. Such further revelation may be eschatological, as it is in the Apocalypse of Peter, in a large part of the Epistle of the Apostles, and in the oldest, apocalyptic part of the Testament of our Lord. The Gnostics then found this genre the obvious literary vehicle for conveying the esoteric, Gnostic meaning of Jesus' teaching.

In the Apocalypse of Peter there is one very explicit reference back to the earlier teaching of Jesus in the Gospel traditions, whose full meaning is now revealed to Peter by further revelation. This is in 16:5-6. Jesus has given Peter a vision of paradise, which is said to be a revelation of 'the honour and glory of those who are persecuted for my righteousness' (16:5). Peter comments: 'Then I understood that which is written in the scripture of our Lord Jesus Christ.' The reference is certainly to Matthew's Gospel, evidently the only written Gospel the author of the Apocalypse of Peter used,[15] and to the beatitude in Matthew 5:10: 'Blessed are those who are persecuted for righteousness' sake, for theirs is the kingdom of heaven.' The Matthean saying, and the subsequent reference to reward in heaven, leaves the nature of the heavenly reward undeveloped. The apocalyptic revelation of paradise in the Apocalypse of Peter, precisely the kind of apocalyptic revelation which is notably absent from the Gospel traditions, is thought by the author of the Apocalypse of Peter to be needed to fill out the mere hints given in the pre-resurrection teaching of Jesus.

We should understand the way the Apocalypse of Peter begins in a rather similar way:

> And while he was sitting on the Mount of Olives, his own came up to him. And we bowed down and besought him each alone. And we asked him, saying to him, 'Tell us, what will be the signs of your coming and of the end of the world, that we might know and understand the time of your coming and instruct those who will come after us, to whom we shall preach the word of your gospel and whom we shall put in charge of your

---

[15] See Bauckham, 'The Apocalypse of Peter: An Account of Research,' 4723-4724.

church, so that they also, having heard it, might keep watch and be alert to the time of your coming' (1:1-3).[16]

Ostensibly this does little more than reproduce, with a little expansion and adaptation, the opening of the eschatological discourse of Jesus in Matthew 24. But the author is not intending to give, as it were, a version of that eschatological discourse, moving it from its Matthean place before the resurrection to a post-resurrection setting. Rather he is intending to represent Jesus, in response to the disciples' questions, as taking up the same subject again and this time going into much more detail on many aspects of the eschatological events. The whole of Jesus' discourse, which continues to chapter 14, is intended to develop what is undeveloped and to add what is lacking in the Matthean eschatological discourse. The way in which this is done, of course, is by resort to Jewish apocalyptic traditions.

Just as the eschatological discourse of Jesus in chapters 1-14 is not a version of the Matthean eschatological discourse, but another post-resurrection eschatological discourse, intended to supplement the first, so the narrative of chapters 15-17, which is modelled on the Matthean account of the transfiguration of Jesus should not be mistaken for a version of the transfiguration narrative.[17] It gives no support to the idea that the transfiguration was originally a post-resurrection tradition, transferred in our Synoptic Gospels into the ministry of Jesus. Chapters 15-17 of the Apocalypse of Peter actually do not describe a transfiguration of Jesus at all. It is the glorious appearance of Moses and Elijah which is featured, not the glory of Jesus. The point is that the author is simply using material from the transfiguration narrative in order to develop a new account of an apocalyptic revelation of the glorious destiny of the elect. He saw in the Matthean transfiguration narrative hints which could be developed further in a post-resurrection setting. Again he draws on Jewish apocalyptic traditions in order to develop them.

In summary we can say that the Apocalypse of Peter is a revelation by the risen Christ to Peter and the disciples, set within a post-resurrection Gospel narrative framework. It borrows materials from the Gospel traditions which were especially susceptible to development in an apocalyptic direction. It develops them by means of Jewish apocalyptic traditions, which form the greater part of its content.

---

[16] Translation adapted from Buchholz. Quotations from the Apocalypse of Peter (Ethiopic version) are from the translation by Buchholz unless otherwise stated.

[17] Bauckham, 'The Apocalypse of Peter: An Account of Research,' 4735-4736.

Apocalypse of Peter 1-2

¹ And while he was sitting on the Mount of Olives, his own came up to him. And we bowed down and besought him each alone.

² And we asked him, saying to him, 'Tell us, what will be the signs of your coming and of the end of the world, that we might know and understand the time of your coming and instruct those who will come after us,

³ to whom we shall preach the word of your gospel and whom we shall put in charge of your church, so that they also, having heard it, might keep watch and be alert to the time of your coming.'

⁴ And our Lord answered us, saying to us, 'Take heed that they do not lead you astray and that you do not become doubters, and that you do not to worship other gods.

⁵ Many will come in my name, saying, "I am the Messiah." Do not believe them and do not go near them.

⁶ For the coming of the Son of God will not be revealed, but like lightning which appears from the east to the west, so shall I come on a cloud of heaven, with great power in my glory, with my cross going before me.

⁷ I shall come in my glory, shining seven times more brightly than the sun. I shall come in my glory with all my holy angels, when my Father will set a crown on my head, so that I may judge the living and the dead

⁸ and so that I may repay everyone according to his deeds.

2¹ But you are to learn from the fig tree its parable. As soon as its shoot has gone out and its branches have sprouted, then will be the end of the world.

...

Matthew 24

³ When he was sitting on the Mount of Olives, the disciples came to him, privately, saying, 'Tell us, when will this be, and what will be the sign of your coming and of the end of the age?'

⁴ Jesus answered them, "Beware that noone leads you astray.

⁵ For many will come in my name, saying, 'I am the Messiah!'...²³,²⁶ ...do not believe it...

²⁷For

as the lightning comes from the east and flashes as far as the west, so will be the coming of the Son of man. ³⁰ᵇ...and they will see the Son of man coming on the clouds of heaven with power and great glory. ³⁰ᵃ Then the sign of the Son of man will appear in heaven...

[16²⁷ For the Son of man is to come with his angels in the glory of his Father,

and then he will repay everyone for what has been done.]

³² From the fig tree learn its lesson: as soon as its branch becomes tender and puts forth its leaves, you know that summer is near.

7 ...when its branches have sprouted at the last time false Messiahs will come, 8and they will promise, "I am the Messiah, who has come into the world"

...

11 ...Many will die and become martyrs.
12 For Enoch and Elijah will be sent to teach them that this is the deceiver who is to come into the world and who will perform signs and wonders in order to deceive.

24 For false messiahs and false prophets will appear...5 saying, 'I am the Messiah!' ...

24 ...and produce great signs and omens, to lead astray, if possible, even the elect.

2 *Historical Context*

It is unusual to be able to give a precise date and place of origin for an ancient apocalypse, but I think that in the case of the Apocalypse of Peter we can do so with considerable confidence. In this section I shall argue that the Apocalypse of Peter can be dated during the Bar Kokhba war, i.e. during the years 132-135 C.E., and that it was written in Palestine, deriving from the Jewish Christian churches. If this is correct, it makes the Apocalypse of Peter a very significant document for the history of Palestinian Jewish Christianity. It is perhaps the only work of second-century Palestinian Jewish Christianity which survives in its complete and original form.

The argument for the date and place of the Apocalypse concerns especially the first two chapters and the last two chapters of the work.[18] In chapters 1-2 the author has adapted and expanded parts of the Synoptic apocalyptic discourse as found in Matthew 24. The wording of the Apocalypse of Peter in these chapters is in several places very close to the specifically Matthean redaction of the Synoptic apocalyptic discourse, and so we can be sure that the author knew the text of Matthew 24 itself. But he has used Matthew 24 very selectively: he has in fact drawn on only eight verses of that chapter— or, to put it another way, he has used only two sections of Matthew 24: vv 3-5 and vv 24-32. To these borrowings from Matthew 24 he has added additional traditional material from other sources in order to develop those themes in Matthew 24 in which he was interested.

---

[18] Most of the following argument so far as it concerns chapters 1-2 was presented in more detail in R. Bauckham, 'The Two Fig Tree Parables in the Apocalypse of Peter,' *JBL* 104 (1985) 269-287.

So by observing his selection and expansion of material from Matthew 24 we can see how his apocalyptic expectations were focussed. As we shall see, they are focussed, in these first two chapters of the apocalypse, on just two themes.

The first three verses of the Apocalypse of Peter are the disciples' question, to which the rest of the first two chapters are Jesus' response:

> And while he was sitting on the Mount of Olives, his own came up to him. And we bowed down and besought him each alone. And we asked him, saying to him, 'Tell us, what will be the signs of your coming and of the end of the world, that we might know and understand the time of your coming and instruct those who will come after us, to whom we shall preach the word of your gospel and whom we shall put in charge of your church, so that they also, having heard it, might keep watch and be alert to the time of your coming' (1:1-3).[19]

The setting and question follow closely Matthew 24:3, except that in the apocalypse the disciples ask about the time of the parousia, not simply so that they themselves should understand it, but also so that their successors should understand it. Clearly the author writes in a post-apostolic period: the generation of the apostles has passed and it is now a subsequent generation which needs to be able to recognize the signs that the parousia is imminent. Moreover, whereas Matthew refers to the time of the destruction of Jerusalem and the temple, as well as to the time of the parousia, in the Apocalypse of Peter it is only the time of the parousia that is of interest. Evidently the author lives after c.e. 70, and he is not interested in providing *post eventum* prophecies of events, such as the fall of Jerusalem, which lay between the time of Jesus, the supposed date of the prophecy, and his own time. He is interested only in his readers' immediate situation and the events which he believes to lie in their immediate future.

The rest of the material he derives from Matthew 24 readily falls into three categories:

(a) There is the warning about false Messiahs. This subject occurs twice in the apocalyptic discourse in Matthew: 24:3-5 (where it is the opening subject of the discourse) and 24:23-26 (where the subject recurs immediately before the description of the parousia itself). The author of the Apocalypse of Peter has drawn on both these passages and ignored everything that comes in between them in Matthew. He has therefore rightly identified a major theme of the Matthean discourse, and he has also, as we shall see, rightly understood the way

---

[19] Translation adapted from Buchholz.

this theme of false Messiahs is connected in Matthew 24 with the
parousia. But as far as Matthew's account of the events that will
precede the parousia is concerned, he has selected only this one
theme. It must have been the prominence of this theme in Matthew
24 which drew him to this chapter and led him to make it the basis of
the opening of his Apocalypse. The theme of the false Messiahs and
the warning against being led astray by these imposters who make
deceptive claims is one of his main interests.

But there are two further, very important points about the way he
uses this material from Matthew 24, which we can see if we look
closely at the texts in the Apocalypse of Peter. The words of Jesus in
the Apocalypse of Peter, as in Matthew 24, begin with this theme:

> And our Lord answered us, saying to us, 'Take heed that they do not lead
> you astray and that you do not become doubters, and that you do not to
> worship other gods. Many will come in my name, saying, "I am the
> Messiah." Do not believe them and do not go near them' (1:4-5).[20]

But he then returns to the theme in 2:7-8:

> ... false Messiahs will come, and they will promise, 'I am the Messiah,
> who has come into the world'[21]

And again towards the end of chapter 2:

> Enoch and Elijah will be sent to teach them that this is the deceiver who
> is to come into the world and who will perform signs and wonders in
> order to deceive[22] (2:12: the reference to the deceptive signs and wonders
> is taken from Matthew 24:24).

In those passages the false messianic claim and the false Messiah's
potential to deceive, of which Christians must beware, derive from
Matthew 24. But we should notice, first, that whereas Matthew 24:24
speaks of false Messiahs *and false prophets* (ψευδόχριστοι καὶ ψευδοπροφῆται), the Apocalypse of Peter speaks only of false Messiahs. The
author is not interested in people who claimed to be the
eschatological prophet, but only in those who claimed to be Messiah.
But, notice also, secondly, that whereas Matthew speaks throughout
of false Messiahs, in the plural, the Apocalypse of Peter, while it
begins by following Matthew in this respect and warning against *many*
false Messiahs (1:5), goes on in chapter 2 to focus on a single
messianic pretender. In the Ethiopic text as it stands the transition is
very awkward and abrupt: the end of 2:7 speaks of false Messiahs, in

---

[20] Translation adapted from Buchholz.
[21] Translation adapted from Buchholz.
[22] Translation adapted from Buchholz.

the plural, but 2:8 speaks of 'his evil deeds,' and although verse 9 is very obscure, from verse 10 onwards it is quite clear that only one false messianic claimant is being spoken of. It may be that the text of v 7 should be corrected to refer to only a single false Messiah. But even if we accept such an emendation of the text, there is a transition from the several false Messiahs of chapter 1 to the single false Messiah of chapter 2. Moreover, in 2:12, the phrase which the author has borrowed from Matthew ('signs and wonders in order to deceive': Matt 24:24) applies in Matthew to the false Messiahs, but in the Apocalypse of Peter has been applied to the single false Messiah.

It seems clear that the author of the Apocalypse of Peter is interested in Matthew's predictions of false Messiahs mainly because they provide a startingpoint from which he can narrow the focus to the single and last false Messiah, who is his real concern. I shall be arguing that this is because at the time of writing there was a particular, single messianic claimant—by whom the Apocalypse's readers were in danger of being misled. However, we should not too easily jump to this conclusion. The expectation of a single final Antichrist who would deceive people with his false claims and who would persecute the people of God, as the false Messiah in chapter 2 of the Apocalypse of Peter does, was after all a common feature of much early Christian apocalyptic expectation. The coming of Enoch and Elijah to expose him as a deceiver (2:12) was probably also already a traditional apocalyptic feature.[23] May not the author simply be putting together Matthew 24's predictions of the false Messiahs and other traditional material in which a single Antichrist was expected? No doubt, he is doing this. But we still need to explain why his interest in the events preceding the parousia is so selective, so overwhelmingly focussed on the figure of the false Messiah. That this is because an actual messianic claimant threatened the church of his time and place will become clearer as we proceed.

(b) The second of the three categories of material that our author has drawn from Matthew 24 is the prediction of the manner of the parousia:

> For the coming of the Son of God will not be revealed, but like lightning which appears from the east to the west, so shall I come on a cloud of heaven, with great power in my glory, with my cross going before me. I shall come in my glory, shining seven times more brightly than the sun. I

---

[23] See R. Bauckham, 'The Martyrdom of Enoch and Elijah: Jewish or Christian?,' *JBL* 95 (1976) 447-458; K. Berger, *Die Auferstehung des Propheten und die Erhöhung des Menschensohnes* (SUNT 13; Göttingen: Vandenhoeck & Ruprecht, 1976) Part 1.

shall come in my glory with all my holy angels, when my Father will set
a crown on my head, so that I may judge the living and the dead (1:6-
7).[24]

Here the author depends on Matthew 24:27, 30, and perhaps also on
Matthew 16:27, but he has both selected from the Matthean depiction of the parousia and expanded it with other traditional material.
The elements here which do not come from Matthew can all be
shown to be very probably already traditional in Christian depiction
of the parousia. Nothing here is original,[25] but the author has both
selected from Matthew and added from other apocalyptic tradition in
order to make very emphatically two points about the parousia. One
is that Christ will come with divine authority to exercise judgment:
'when my Father will set a crown on my head, so that I may judge
the living and the dead, and I will repay everyone according to his
deeds' (1:7b-8). This is the point at which the author introduces the
central theme of the Apocalypse of Peter, which will be expounded at
length in chapters 3-14. But of more immediate interest to us is the
second point about the parousia: that it will be unmistakably the
parousia of Jesus Christ. This is how the depiction of the parousia in
v 6 connects with the warning against false Messiahs in v 5. The
coming of the true Messiah will be evident to all people. The disciples
should not be deceived by the claims of the false Messiahs, because
the coming of the true Messiah will be unmistakable. This point the
author has taken from Matthew, who also places the saying about the
lightning immediately after the misleading claims about the false
Messiahs in order to make the point that the parousia, like the lightning which flashes across the sky from east to west, will be evident to
all (24:27). Matthew contrasts this with the misleading claim that the
Messiah is out in the desert or is in the inner rooms (24:26): the
Apocalypse of Peter drops this point. Evidently the false Messiah who
concerns this author is not gathering his followers in the desert (like
some of the messianic claimants before 70 c.e.) or hiding in secret in
houses. But his appearance can be easily distinguished from the unmistakable character of the parousia of Jesus Christ, as expected in
Christian tradition.

As well as the simile of the lightning, the Apocalypse of Peter
labours the unmistakableness of the parousia by emphasizing the

---

[24] Translation adapted from Buchholz.
[25] For the parallels, see Bauckham, 'The Two Fig Tree Parables,' 273-275; idem,
Jude and the Relatives of Jesus in the Early Church (Edinburgh: T. & T. Clark, 1990) 101-
102.

glory of the coming Christ, of course a well-established traditional aspect of the parousia. Three times Jesus says 'I shall come in my glory' (1:6-7), and this is reinforced, the first time, with 'on a cloud of heaven, with great power'; the second time, with 'shining seven times more brightly than the sun'; the third time, with 'with all my holy angels.' These details make the parousia an unmistakably supernatural, transcendent occurrence. But one further detail makes it unmistakably the parousia of Jesus Christ: 'my cross going before me' (1:6). This appearance of the cross at the parousia—perhaps an interpretation of Matthew's 'sign of the Son of man' (24:30), certainly a stock feature of early Christian expectation (EpApp 16; ApEl 3:2; SibOr 6:26-28; Hippolytus, *In Matt.* 24:30; cf. Did 16:6)—serves here to make it clear that, by contrast to any other messianic claim, the only appearance of the Messiah which Christians can expect is unmistakably the coming of Jesus, the crucified, in glory. So we can see that the author's depiction of the manner of the parousia is very closely connected with his interest in the figure of the false Messiah. It is designed to counter the false Messiah's potential to deceive those of the Apocalypse's readers who were evidently tempted to accept his claim to messianic status.

(c) The third and final category of material which the author has taken from Matthew 24 is the parable of the fig tree, which 2:1 borrows from Matthew 24:32:

> But you are to learn from the fig tree its parable. As soon as its shoot has gone out and its branches have sprouted, then will be the end of the world.

It is in this parable that the author of the Apocalypse of Peter finds the real answer to the disciples' question about the time of the parousia. The end of the world will come when the fig tree sprouts. But what is the meaning of the sprouting of the fig tree? Peter is understandably puzzled and has to ask for an interpretation (vv 2-3).

Peter's request for an interpretation shows that for the author of the Apocalypse of Peter the meaning of the parable of the budding fig tree is not to be found within Matthew 24 itself. He does not accept the indication in Matthew 24:33 that by the sprouting of the fig tree is meant simply 'all these things'—all the events which Matthew 24 has depicted as preceding the parousia. The author of the Apocalypse of Peter requires a more specific interpretation. The sprouting of the fig tree must be some specific sign of the end. So he seeks the interpretation elsewhere and finds it in another Gospel parable about a fig tree, which he reproduces in 2:5-6. This is the parable of the barren fig tree, elsewhere found only in Luke's Gospel (13:6-9). I have argued elsewhere that the author has drawn this parable not from Luke, but from some independent tradition of the parable.[26] The important point, however, is that the author is doing what other early Christian interpreters of the parables also sometimes did: he is assuming that the imagery common to the two parables must have a common meaning. Therefore one parable can be used to interpret the other.

The second parable, the barren fig tree, tells how for many years the fig tree failed to produce fruit. The owner proposes that it be rooted out, but the gardener persuades him to allow it one more chance of fruiting. This fruiting of the fig tree is treated by our author as equivalent to the sprouting or budding of the fig tree in the parable of Matthew 24. He correctly perceives that in the parable of the barren fig-tree the fig tree represents Israel, and the contribution which this parable makes to the interpretation of the other is that it establishes that the fig tree is Israel. Jesus' interpretation of the parable begins: 'Did you not know that the fig tree is the house of Israel?' (2:4). Then after quoting the parable of the barren fig tree, he repeats: 'Did you not understand that the fig tree is the house of Israel?' (2:7). So it is the house of Israel which must sprout as the final sign of the end. But we still do not know what the sprouting or fruiting of the fig tree is. To explain this the author returns to the theme of the false Messiah, who (we are now told) will put to death those who refuse to accept his claim to messiahship. The sprouting of the fig tree represents the many martyrs of the house of Israel who will die at the hands of the false Messiah.

So finally we see that the author's third principal interest in these chapters—along with the false Messiah and the unmistakable manner of the coming of the true Messiah—is martyrdom. This is the theme which dominates the second half of chapter 2, where we are repeatedly told of the many martyrs who will die at the hands of the false Messiah. Like the other two themes, this theme of the martyrs of the last days is anchored in Matthew 24, by means of the author's interpretation of the parable of the fig tree. By means of skilful selection of material from Matthew 24 and expansion of this material from other traditional sources, the author has found dominical authority for a very clearly focussed apocalyptic expectation. He depicts a situation in which a false Messiah puts to death those who are not deceived by his claims because they know that the true Messiah, Jesus Christ, will

---

[26] Bauckham, 'The Two Fig Tree Parables,' 280-283.

come in unmistakable glory. The deaths of many martyrs of the house of Israel at the hands of the false Messiah will be the last sign that the end of the world and the parousia of Jesus Christ as judge of the world are imminent.

We could reduce the dominant concerns of these first two chapters of the Apocalypse of Peter to two closely connected concerns: (a) the question of the true and false Messiahs, and (b) martyrdom. The two concerns are closely connected because those who are not deceived by the claims of the false Messiah are to be put to death by him. This means, of course, that those who heed the warning against believing and following false Messiahs with which Jesus' words begin (1:4-5) are going to incur martyrdom. By contrast with Matthew 24, where martyrdom is mentioned (24:9) but is not a major theme and is not connected with the false Messiahs, in the Apocalypse of Peter martyrdom at the hands of the false Messiah completely dominates the expectation of what must happen before the parousia. We have to conclude that the author envisaged his readers having to discern and resist the claims of a false Messiah and facing martyrdom as a result. The question arises: Are the readers already in this situation—has the false Messiah appeared, is he already persecuting Christians—or is his appearance and persecution still future? This is the familiar problem of identifying the point at which an apocalyptic prediction moves from the present into the future.

The writer's exclusive concern with the false Messiah and the persecution he carries out must indicate that this persecution is already under way. If these were simply features of a traditional apocalyptic scenario which the author reproduces as expectation for the future, the exclusion of all other features of such traditional apocalyptic scenarios would be inexplicable. The false Messiah must be already a threat; the Apocalypse's readers must be already tempted to believe his claim; some of those who, out of loyalty to the Messiah Jesus, refuse to follow him must have already been put to death. This impression given us by the first two chapters is confirmed by the evidence which the rest of the Apocalypse of Peter provides that it was written in a situation of persecution. There are two main pieces of evidence of this kind:

(a) In the account of the punishments in hell after the last judgment. As we shall see later (in our section III, subsection 7, below), the Apocalypse of Peter, in the long account of the many categories of sinners and the specific punishments each receives in hell (chapters 7-12), is certainly taking over traditional apocalyptic material. We have many other similar accounts of the punishments in hell, which derive

from common streams of apocalyptic tradition. The literary relationships among these so-called 'tours of hell' are debatable and complex,
but there can be no doubt that, here as elsewhere, the Apocalypse of
Peter takes over traditional material. The other tours of hell show us
the kind of material which was the Apocalypse of Peter's source for 7-
12. By this means we can be confident that most of the categories of
sinners which the Apocalypse of Peter depicts in hell were traditional.
By and large, the author did not decide which sins to mention in his
account of hell: he took them over from apocalyptic tradition. But
there are three categories of sinners in hell in the Apocalypse of Peter
which cannot be paralleled in other tours of hell and which occur in
succession as a group of three in 9:1-4. The first group are 'the
persecutors and betrayers of my righteous ones'—i.e. those who put
the martyrs to death. The second group are 'the blasphemers and
betrayers of my righteousness'—probably those who apostatized in
order to escape martyrdom. The third group are 'those who put to
death the martyrs with a lie'—presumably those who informed on the
martyrs. The unique[27] inclusion of these three categories of sinners in
an account of the punishments in hell must indicate a situation of
persecution and martyrdom as the *Sitz im Leben* of the Apocalypse of
Peter.

(b) In chapter 16, when the disciples are given a vision of paradise,
Peter is told by Jesus that 'this is the honour and glory of those who
will be persecuted for my righteousness' sake' (16:5).[28] This makes it
clear that the concern with paradise in the latter part of the Apocalypse of Peter is primarily a concern for the reward that awaits the
martyrs in the next life.

If chapter 2 therefore refers to a persecution by a false Messiah which
has already begun, we may note two further points about the martyrs.
In the first place, they are Jews, as 2:11 insists ('So then the branches
of the fig tree will sprout. This is the house of Israel only. There will
be martyrs by his hand'). Secondly, the persecution can only have
begun. Presumably v 12 refers to an event still in the future: 'Enoch
and Elijah will be sent to make to teach them that this is the deceiver

---

[27] The only parallel I know is in GedMos (Gaster §43): 'they have delivered up
their brother Israelite to the Gentile.'

[28] This translation is from C. D. G. Müller, 'Apocalypse of Peter, in W.
Schneemelcher, *New Testament Apocrypha*, vol. 2, trans. R, McL. Wilson (Cambridge:
James Clarke/Louisville: Westminster/John Knox, 1992) 635.

who is to come into the world...' Unless we suppose that the author identified two of his contemporaries as Enoch and Elijah, of which he gives no hint, we must suppose that the enlightenment as to the falsity of the false Messiah's claim which Enoch and Elijah will bring to many of those who are to be martyred still lies in the future. Probably, a few of the author's fellow Jewish Christians have already been martyred: they are those who, because of their faith in Jesus as Messiah, already recognize the deception of the false Messiah. But the author expects many more Jews—those who are not yet believers in Jesus—to reject the false Messiah when Enoch and Elijah expose him. These will be the majority of the martyrs and their martyrdom lies still in the immediate future. Thus 2:13 explains: 'This is why [i.e. because Enoch and Elijah have demonstrated that the false Messiah is the deceiver] those who [then] die by his hands will be martyrs, and will be reckoned with the good and righteous martyrs who have pleased God in their life [that is, with those who have already died as martyrs].' This means that the currently unbelieving Jews who, enlightened by Enoch and Elijah, will die at the hands of the false Messiah in the future, are going to be numbered with the Jewish Christian martyrs who have already suffered death at his hands.

Who then is the false Messiah who is already persecuting Jewish Christians and who can be expected to turn against other Jews if they too reject his messiahship? The historical situation of the early church and other early Christian literature suggests only two possibilities: a Roman emperor or a Jewish messianic pretender. Against the first possibility, we may note that the author's quite explicit limitation of horizon to Jewish Christians and Jews would be very surprising if a *Roman* persecution of Christians were in view. But more decisively, when early Christian apocalyptic associates the persecuting Antichrist figure with the Roman imperial power there is always allusion to the Roman imperial cult. The Antichrist is then said to claim divinity and to require worship. The false Messiah of the Apocalypse of Peter merely claims to be the Messiah, and all the emphasis is put specifically on the issue of who is the true Messiah (1:5; 2:7-10). This points to an inner-Jewish context: a debate between the Christian claim that Jesus is Messiah and the claims of a Jewish messianic claimant.

If then, the false Messiah of the Apocalypse of Peter is a Jewish messianic pretender of the period after 70 C.E. (since the Apocalypse of Peter must be dated later than 70), there are only two possible identifications:

In the first place, we cannot neglect the possibility that the false Messiah is the leader of the Jewish revolt in Egypt and Cyrenaica in the years 115-117 in the reign of Trajan.[29] Though we know very little about it, it is clear that this revolt was on a considerable scale. Of its leader we know (from Eusebius) only his name Lucuas and the fact that Eusebius calls him 'their king' (*Hist. Eccl.* 4.2.4). A major Jewish revolt against Rome at this period must have had a messianic character, and a leader of such a revolt described as king must have been seen as a messianic figure. Our meagre sources tell us nothing of any persecution of Christians during this revolt, and we may note that Eusebius, had he known of such persecution, would certainly have mentioned it. But on the other hand, we know that the rebellious Jews massacred Gentiles in large numbers. It is likely enough that Jewish Christians who refused to join the revolt would also have suffered.

One feature of the Apocalypse of Peter could support a suggestion that it originated among Jewish Christians in Egypt during the revolt of 115-117. In 10:5, one category of the sinners in hell are the manufacturers of idols. The idols they made are described as 'the idols made by human hands, the images which resemble cats, lions and reptiles, the images of wild animals.' This has often been taken to refer specifically to Egyptian religion and therefore to point to an origin for the Apocalypse of Peter in Egypt. Images of gods in the form of animals were of course especially characteristic of ancient Egypt, and of the specific animals mentioned the first, cats, would infallibly suggest Egyptian religion. Other Jewish texts which certainly or probably originated in Egypt have similar references to animal images (Wis 12:24; 15:18; SibOr 5:278-280; Philo, *Decal.* 76-80; *De vita contemp.* 8; *Leg.* 139; 163), often specifying cats and reptiles (LetAris 138; SibOr 3:30-31; SibOr Frag 3:22, 27-30).

Since the Apocalypse of Peter may have reached Ethiopia via Egypt, it is possible that the reference to idols in the form of animals is a later gloss introduced into the text of the Apocalypse of Peter in Egypt. The reference is missing in the parallel passage of the Akhmim text. On the other hand, there are few other points in the Ethiopic version of the Apocalypse of Peter where there is any very good reason to suspect a gloss, so that we should be very cautious about resorting to this explanation. In fact, there is no real difficulty in supposing that this description of idols could have been written by a

---

[29] On this revolt and its messianic character, see especially M. Hengel, 'Messianische Hoffnung und politischer "Radikalismus" in der "jüdisch-hellenistischen Diaspora,"' in D. Hellholm ed., *Apocalypticism in the Mediterranean World and the Near East* (Tübingen: Mohr [Siebeck], 1983) 655-686 (with references to other literature).

Palestinian Jew (cf. TMos 2:7; LAB 44:5, for references to animal idols in a Palestinian context). Paul in Romans 1:23 refers to idols as 'images resembling mortal man or birds or animals or reptiles,' and Justin refers to the worship of animals in a general discussion of idolatry, evidently using specifically Egyptian forms of idolatry as an instance of idolatry in general (*1 Apol.* 24). A Jewish Christian opponent of idolatry might well have considered the worship of animal forms the most degrading form of idolatry (as later Christian writers did)[30] and singled it out for mention for this reason. At this period Egyptian cults were practised outside Egypt, and the Egyptian veneration of cats must have been very well known.[31]

That the Apocalypse of Peter originated in Egypt during the Jewish revolt under Trajan is a possibility which perhaps cannot be entirely excluded. However, there are stronger grounds for identifying the false Messiah of the Apocalypse of Peter with the leader of the Jewish revolt in Palestine in the years 132-135 C.E., the leader whose real name we now know to have been Shim'on bar Kosiva, but who is still generally known by his messianic nickname Bar Kokhba. The arguments for seeing a reference to Bar Kokhba in the Apocalypse of Peter and therefore for the origin of the work in Palestine during the Bar Kokhba revolt, are as follows:

(a) First, it is necessary to defend the view that Bar Kokhba was seen by many of his supporters as the Messiah, since this view has been contested by some recent writers.[32] For our purposes we do not need to know whether Bar Kokhba himself made a messianic claim, only that such a claim was made on his behalf by his supporters.[33] In favour of this, there is, first, the rabbinic evidence, most importantly

---

[30] E.g. Aristides, *Apol.* 12.1; Theophilus, *Ad Autol.* 1.10; Tertullian, *Ad Nat.* 2.8; Cyril of Jerusalem, *Catech.* 6.10.

[31] For the general reputation of Egypt for animal worship, see K. A. D. Smelik and E. A. Hemelrijk, "'Who knows not what monsters demented Egypt worships?": Opinions on Egyptian animal worship in Antiquity as part of the ancient conception of Egypt,' in *Aufstieg und Niedergang der römischen Welt*, 2/17/4, ed. W. Haase (Berlin/New York: de Gruyter, 1984) 1852-2000.

[32] L. Mildenberg, *The Coinage of the Bar Kokhba Revolt* (Aarau/Frankfurt am Main/Salzburg: Sauerländer, 1984) 75-76; and cf. B. Isaac and A. Oppenheimer, 'The Revolt of Bar Kokhba: Ideology and Modern Scholarship,' *Journal of Jewish Studies* 36 (1985) 57; A. Rheinhartz, 'Rabbinic Perceptions of Simeon bar Kosiba,' *Journal for the Study of Judaism* 20 (1989) 173-174, for references to others who deny that Bar Kokhba was seen in messianic terms.

[33] Rheinhartz, 'Rabbinic Perceptions,' argues that the claim was made during the war, as an explanation of Bar Kokhba's success, by some of his supporters, though not by all.

the well-known tradition (y. Ta'an. 68d)[34] that Rabbi Aqiva declared
Bar Kokhba to be the King Messiah, and connected his name with
the prophecy of the star *(kokhav)* that will come forth from Jacob
(Num 24:17), a favourite messianic text of the period. Whether this
view of Bar Kokhba is correctly attributed to Aqiva is unimportant
for our purpose. What is significant is that such a view of Bar Kokhba
could certainly not have originated after Bar Kokhba's defeat and
death. The tradition must preserve an identification of Bar Kokhba
as the Messiah and the star of Jacob which was made during the
revolt.[35] Second, from Christian sources, beginning with Justin, who
was writing only twenty years after the revolt, we know that Bar
Kosiva must have been quite widely known as Bar Kokhba ('son of
the star').[36] This pun on his real name is explicable only as an identification of him as the messianic star of Jacob (Num 24:17) and thus
corroborates the rabbinic tradition attached to the name of Aqiva.
Thirdly, rabbinic traditions which explicitly deny that Bar Kokhba
was the Messiah and Christian sources which depict him as a false
messianic pretender indirectly confirm that during the revolt he was
regarded by many as the Messiah. If it is unlikely that Christian
writers would represent as a false Messiah a Jewish leader for whom
messianic claims had never been made, it is even less likely that
rabbinic traditions hostile to Bar Kokhba would have invented a
messianic claim for him in order to deny it.[37] Fourthly, the fact that
in the recently discovered Bar Kokhba documents he is treated as a
purely human military and political leader is not, as some have supposed, in contradiction to the claim that he was regarded as Messiah.
Messianic expectations of the time certainly included the purely human figure who would restore Jewish national sovereignty by force of
arms.

(b) Turning to more detailed correlations between what we know of
Bar Kokhba and the Apocalypse of Peter, we know from Justin (*1
Apol.* 31.6) that Bar Kokhba ordered that Christians who would not
deny Jesus as the Messiah should be punished severely. This is very
early evidence of persecution of Jewish Christians by Bar Kokhba
and there is no reason at all to doubt it. The Bar Kokhba letters show

---

[34] On this tradition, see P. Schäfer, *Der Bar-Kokhba-Aufstand* (TSAJ 1; Tübingen:
Mohr [Siebeck], 1981) 55-57; P. Lenhart and P. von den Osten-Sacken, *Rabbi Akiva*
(ANTZ 1; Berlin: Institut Kirche und Judentum, 1987) 307-317.
[35] So Rheinhartz, 'Rabbinic Perceptions,' 176-177.
[36] The treatment of this evidence by Mildenberg, *Coinage*, 79-80, is irresponsible.
[37] Rheinhartz, 'Rabbinic Perceptions,' 177.

that the rebel government took strong action against Jews who failed to support the revolt, and it is therefore intrinsically likely that Jewish Christians, who could not acknowledge Bar Kokhba's political authority without accepting his messiahship, would suffer. It is true that there is not much evidence that the revolt extended to Galilee,[38] where probably the majority of Jewish Christians who lived west of the Jordan at this time were to be found. But there is no difficulty in supposing that there were also Jewish Christians in Judaea, while our interpretation of the Apocalypse of Peter does not require there to have been very large numbers of Jewish Christians killed by Bar Kokhba's troops. A small number of martyrs would sufficiently explain the expectation that many more martyrdoms would soon follow.

(c) Apocalypse of Peter 2:12 calls the false Messiah 'the deceiver who is to come into the world and who will perform signs and wonders in order to deceive.' This is a traditional expectation of the Antichrist, taken here from Matthew 24:24. The author may have understood the signs and wonders as Bar Kokhba's military success which no doubt persuaded many to regard him as the Messiah. But it is also noteworthy that later Christian tradition about Bar Kokhba attributed to him the deceptive miracles expected of the Antichrist. Eusebius, in a statement that may well be based on Aristo of Pella and may therefore preserve Palestinian Jewish Christian tradition, says that Bar Kokhba claimed to be 'a star which had come down from heaven to give light to the oppressed by working miracles' (*Hist. Eccl.* 4.6.2). Jerome (*Ad Rufin.* 3.31) says that Bar Kokhba pretended to breathe fire by means of a lighted straw in his mouth. These statements cannot, of course, be taken as evidence that Bar Kokhba really claimed to work miracles, but they do reveal a Christian tradition of identifying Bar Kokhba with the false Messiah who works miracles, a tradition which may well go back to the Apocalypse of Peter, written during the revolt itself.

(d) There seem to have been two punning variations on Shim'on bar Kosiva's name. One was the messianic nickname Bar Kokhba ('son of the star'). The other was a derogatory nickname, denying his messianic claim. This derogatory version is formed by spelling his name not with a *samek* but with a *zayin:* bar Koziva ('son of the lie'

---

[38] Schäfer, *Der Bar-Kokhba-Aufstand*, 102-134; Isaac and Oppenheimer, 'The Revolt of Bar Kokhba,' 53-54.

[kozav]), that is, 'liar.' This spelling (Koziva) is consistently used in rabbinic literature. It has sometimes recently been regarded as no more than an alternative spelling,[39] but the Bar Kokhba letters consistently spell the name either with a *samek* or, occasionally, with a *sin*, and so it is likely that the spelling with a *zayin* originated as a derogatory pun.[40] The fact that rabbinic traditions use it even in positive statements about Bar Kokhba, such as that attributed to Aqiva, merely indicates that it had become the only designation of Bar Kokhba in rabbinic tradition. From the rabbinic evidence we cannot tell whether this derogatory pun on the leader's name originated only after his defeat and the general discrediting of his messianic claim or whether it was already in use during the revolt by those Jews who refused to support him. But there is one statement in the Apocalypse of Peter which would gain particular force if the derogatory pun Bar Koziva was already in use. 2:10 declares: 'this liar was not the Messiah.' The word in the Ethiopic is different from 'deceiver' in 2:12, and presumably translates the Greek ψεύστης. The idea of the Antichrist as a deceiver was, of course, thoroughly traditional in early Christian apocalyptic traditions, and 1 John 2:22 may well indicate that the Antichrist was sometimes known specifically as 'the liar' (ὁ ψεύστης). But the statement in the Apocalypse of Peter would certainly be peculiarly apposite if it could be understood to allude also to the derogatory pun on the false Messiah's name: 'this Bar Koziva is not the Messiah.'

(e) For the last indication that the Apocalypse of Peter was written in specific opposition to Bar Kokhba's messianic movement, we must turn to a passage towards the end of the book, in chapters 16-17. The two issues of the identity of the true Messiah and the fate of those who are loyal to him—the issues which dominate the first two chapters of the apocalypse—are the issues to which the apocalypse returns in its closing chapters. In 16:7-17:1 we read:

> I said [Peter] to him [Jesus], 'My Lord, do you wish me to make three tabernacles here, one for you, one for Moses, and one for Elijah?' [8] He said to me, in wrath, 'Satan is fighting you and has veiled your mind! The manner of life of this world is defeating you. [9] But your eyes will be uncovered and your ears will be opened, [to perceive] that there is one tabernacle, not made by human hand, which my heavenly Father has made for me and for my elect.' We saw [it], rejoicing. 17[1] And behold, a

---

[39] E.g. Rheinhartz, 'Rabbinic Perceptions,' 191.
[40] Schäfer, *Der Bar-Kokhba-Aufstand,* 51-52; Lenhart and von den Osten-Sacken, *Rabbi Akiva,* 312-313.

voice came suddenly from heaven, saying, 'This is my Son, whom I love and with whom I am well pleased. Obey him!'[41]

This is a crucially important passage. Its inspiration is the Matthean account of the transfiguration of Jesus, from which our author has drawn the beginning and the end of this passage: Peter's proposal to build three tents for Jesus, Moses and Elijah (16:7) and the voice from heaven declaring Jesus to be God's beloved son (17:1). But the material in between (16:8-9) is the author's addition. In 16:8 Peter is very severely rebuked by Jesus. Although reminiscent of Jesus' rebuke of Peter in Matthew 16:23, this sharp rebuke of Peter for his proposal to build the three tents is rather surprising. Why is Peter's proposal evidence that his mind is veiled by Satan, who has conquered him with matters of this world? We shall see. But following the rebuke, Peter is promised a revelation: specifically, a two-part revelation consisting of a vision ('your eyes will be uncovered') and of an audition ('your ears will be opened'). The vision is of the one tent, not made with human hands, which God has made for Jesus and his elect (16:9). The audition is the voice declaring Jesus to be God's beloved son, whom the disciples must obey (17:1). By this double revelation— of the tent not made with hands and of Jesus as God's son—the veil Satan has cast over Peter's mind is removed and he is shown the truth.

The importance of the audition (the words of the heavenly voice) is clearly that it makes clear the identity of the true Messiah. Whereas in chapter 1 we were told only that the parousia of Jesus Christ will make his identity as the Messiah unequivocally clear, here at the climax of the whole book Jesus' messiahship is already declared by the divine voice. Clearly we are back in the same context of issues as chapters 1 and 2 presuppose.

Less obvious is the significance of the vision: the one tent, not made with human hands, contrasted with the three tents Peter proposes to make. The tent not made with human hands (the Greek must have been σκηνὴ ἀχειροποίητη) reminds us of Mark 14:58, where Jesus' prophecy of the destruction of the temple contrasts the present temple, made with hands, and the eschatological temple, not made with hands. It also resembles Hebrews 9:11, which contrasts the earthly tent (the tabernacle), made with hands, and the heavenly sanctuary: 'the greater and perfect tent, not made with hands, that is, not of this creation.' Our text is not dependent on either of these passages but moves in the same world of ideas. The tent not made

---

[41] Translation adapted from Buchholz.

with human hands which the Father has made for Jesus and his elect is the heavenly temple. It is God's heavenly dwelling-place in which he will dwell with his people in the eschatological age, when God's dwelling—God's σκηνή—will be with his people (Rev 21:3). In Jewish and Jewish Christian Greek σκηνή was used as equivalent to *mishkan* because of the correspondence of the consonants of σκηνή with the Hebrew root *shakan*. So it really meant, not so much 'tent,' as 'dwelling-place': the tabernacle or the temple as the divine dwellingplace. (In Tob 13:11 σκηνή is used for the temple which is to be rebuilt in the eschatological age.) So the connexion is easily made between the three tents or dwellings which Peter proposes to build for Jesus, Moses and Elijah, and the heavenly temple which is to be the real eschatological dwelling-place of Jesus and his elect with God. Peter's error is to propose to build earthly tents himself, instead of the heavenly temple, not made with human hands, which God has made.

But why is Peter so severely rebuked for this error, and why is it corrected, not simply by the vision of the heavenly temple, but also by the voice which makes clear the identity of the false Messiah? Peter's proposal is taken to show that Satan has blinded his mind both to the identity of the true Messiah and to the nature of the eschatological temple. The point must be that the proposal to build earthly tents, made with human hands, associates Peter with the false Messiah. The whole passage makes excellent sense and connects with the concerns of the opening chapters if we assume that the messianic pretender whom the Apocalypse of Peter opposes was intending to rebuild the temple in Jerusalem. The author understands Peter's proposal to build the three tents as, so to speak, endorsing this project of the false Messiah. By contrast, the temple in which God will dwell with the true Messiah Jesus and his people is not an earthly temple, constructed by human hands, but the heavenly temple, made by God himself. Thus the distinguishing of the true Messiah from the false is closely linked with understanding the kind of temple that each promises to his people. The climactic revelation of the Apocalypse of Peter, by revealing both the true Temple and the true Messiah, counters the satanically inspired temptation to follow the false Messiah in his proposal to build an earthly temple.

This interpretation of the passage is further confirmed and reinforced when we notice the location of the scene. For this we must go back to 15:1. The first fourteen chapters of the Apocalypse of Peter were located, like Matthew's eschatological discourse, on the Mount of Olives. But in 15:1, there is a change of location: Jesus says to Peter: 'Let us go to the holy mountain.' The last three chapters of the apocalypse are thus located on the holy mountain. Which mountain is meant? It is true that 2 Peter (1:18) locates the transfiguration on the holy mountain, and the author of the Apocalypse of Peter probably knew 2 Peter.[42] But this does not mean that he would not have intended a specific mountain. He would probably have understood, in 2 Peter's reference to the transfiguration, the deliberate allusions to Psalm 2, where God says: 'I have set my king on Zion, my holy mountain.'[43] Moreover, he would have known that the only mountain which the Old Testament ever calls 'the holy mountain' is mount Zion, the temple mount. So in Apocalypse of Peter 15:1, Jesus is proposing that he and the disciples cross the Kidron valley from the Mount of Olives to the Temple mount. Thus the visions that follow are located where, for example, in the Syriac Apocalypse of Baruch (13:1), Baruch receives revelations from God about the eschatological future—revelations which answer Baruch's anguish and perplexity about the destruction of Jerusalem and the Temple (cf. also 3 Bar: introduction). Baruch received his revelations amid the ruins of the Temple (cf. 2 Bar 8-9). The author of the Apocalypse of Peter, of course, knew that at the fictional time at which his own work is set the second Temple was still standing, but he passes over it in silence. He thus allows the implication that it is actually on the site of the temple that Peter proposes to erect the three tents. In this climax of his work, our author is actually offering his own answer to the issue that preoccupied the Jewish apocalyptists of his time: in the divine purpose what is to replace the second temple? Like some of them—for his answer is distinctively Christian only in making a connexion with the messiahship of Jesus—he turned from all thought of a human attempt to rebuild the earthly temple in favour of a transcendent temple provided by God.

This argument about the meaning of Apocalypse of Peter 16:7-17:1 really requires that the rebuilding of the temple in Jerusalem was a central policy of the messianic movement the apocalypse opposes. From the coins of the Bar Kokhba revolt we know that this was indeed the case with Bar Kokhba's campaign. There is no need for us to decide the debated question of whether the rebels succeeded in capturing Jerusalem.[44] In any case, the intention to liberate Jerusalem was undoubtedly the central proclaimed intention of the revolt. But this carried with it the intention to rebuild the temple.[45] From the

---

[42] See chapter 11 below.

[43] R. Bauckham, *Jude, 2 Peter* (WBC 50; Waco, Texas: Word Books, 1983) 219-221.

[44] Cf. Isaac and Oppenheimer, 'The Revolt of Bar Kokhba,' 54-55.

[45] Isaac and Oppenheimer, 'The Revolt of Bar Kokhba,' 47-48.

beginning of the revolt, a representation of the temple featured on all the tetradrachma coins of the regime. Various objects associated with the worship of the temple featured on other coins.[46] The temple and its worship seem to have been one of, perhaps *the* central symbol of the revolt. Anyone asking the purpose of the revolt might well have been told: to liberate Jerusalem, to rebuild the temple, to restore the temple worship. It was this central religious as well as political purpose which united most Palestinian Jews in support of Bar Kokhba[47] and presumably encouraged them to see him as the Messiah anointed by God to fulfil this purpose.

Understood against this background, the Apocalypse of Peter very interestingly reveals to us that the Jewish Christians of Palestine—or, at least, those who took the same view as our author—not only could not acknowledge Bar Kokhba as Messiah, but also that they had no sympathy for his central aim of rebuilding the temple. For them an earthly temple had no further place in the divine purpose. To any who were tempted to join their fellow-Jews in this aim of rebuilding the temple, the Apocalypse of Peter says that Satan has veiled their minds. Its apocalyptic revelation of the true Messiah and the true Temple is designed to open their eyes and uncover their ears, as it did Peter's.

III Judgment

The dominant theme in the Apocalypse of Peter is the eschatological judgment. The concern with this theme of judgment relates to the situation which the Apocalypse of Peter addresses, as we considered it in the last section. It is a situation in which a false Messiah is putting to death those who refuse to support him out of their loyalty to the true Messiah. The persecutors and apostates flourish, while those who follow the way of righteousness suffer persecution and martyrdom. It is the classic apocalyptic situation, which we can trace right back to the book of Daniel. It is the classic apocalyptic problem of theodicy. It is precisely the context in which the classic early Jewish expectation of the resurrection and judgment of the dead, the achievement of justice in the end by means of eschatological rewards and punishments, had taken shape. Thus the author of the Apocalypse of Peter was heir to a long tradition which had addressed precisely such a situation as his and had developed a scenario of eschatological judgment which he was able to re-present by means of a series of highly

---

[46] Cf. Isaac and Oppenheimer, 'The Revolt of Bar Kokhba,' 49.
[47] Mildenberg, *Coinage,* 31-48.

traditional themes. Nothing in the Apocalypse of Peter's account of eschatological judgment is specifically Christian except the identification of the divine judge as Jesus Christ in his parousia. The interest of the account lies in its exceptionally detailed and complete compilation of traditional apocalyptic themes on this subject.

In this section we shall study the various themes connected with eschatological judgment in the first fourteen chapters of the Apocalypse of Peter. For the most part, we shall consider them in the order in which the occur in the text.

1 *"Each according to his deed"*

This is a highly significant phrase which occurs five times in the Apocalypse of Peter, each occurrence of it strategically placed. The first occurrence is in the initial description of the parousia in 1:7-8. Jesus the true Messiah will come in glory with his angels and his Father will place a crown on his head, giving him authority to exercise divine judgment on the living and the dead, so that he may 'pay back everyone according to his deed' (v 8). The phrase encapsulates the theme of eschatological judgment which will dominate chapters 6-13.

Then there are two further occurrences of the phrase, "each according to his deed" in chapter 6 (vv 3 and 6). Chapter 6 is the detailed account of the last judgment itself, in which the wicked and the righteous are distinguished and the wicked assigned to their punishment. In 6:3 the point of the phrase, "each according to his deed," is that each will be confronted, in the judgment, with his or her own deeds that he or she did during his or her lifetime, and will be judged accordingly. In 6:6 the point is that appropriate punishment for the wicked will follow: in other words, the punishment of each will fit his or her particular crimes.

The use of the phrase in 6:6—with reference to the eternal punishment of "each according to his deed"—is really programmatic. It states the theme for chapters 7-12 in which the punishment appropriate to each sin is described. In all, twenty-one specific sins and the punishments allotted to each are listed in those chapters. The point of this description of hell is mainly to make precisely this point: that each particular kind of sin will receive its appropriate punishment. Thus although the phrase, "each according to his deed," is not actually used within those chapters (7-12), it is in fact the theme of them, already stated in 6:6. (The way in which the punishments are designed to fit the crime in each case is a topic we shall consider in subsection 7 below.)

Finally, the phrase is again used twice in the chapter which follows the description of hell: chapter 13. In 13:3 it again states the principle by which the punishments which have been described are allotted. It indicates the justice of the punishments in hell. The point is then reinforced in v 6, where the damned themselves, suffering their punishments, finally acknowledge the justice of their punishments: 'Righteous is the judgment of God.... For we have been paid back each one according to our deed.'

Thus the positioning of the phrase in each of its five occurrences is very significant. It occurs first in the programmatic description of the parousia as Jesus Christ's coming to exercise divine judgment. Then it occurs twice in each of the two chapters (6 and 13) which frame the long description of the punishments in hell. It states the principle of strict justice by which the punishments in hell are allotted. Repeated statement of the principle that each should be punished strictly in accordance with his or her own deeds makes it clear that the eschatological judgment is concerned with nothing but the wholly impartial judgment of individuals on their merits.

As a standard statement of the principle of divine justice, this phrase was utterly traditional in the Jewish and Christian tradition. It occurs most often in the longer form which the Apocalypse of Peter uses in 1:8 and 13:6: '*to pay back* each according to his deed.' (In Greek the wording is most often ἀποδιδόναι ἑκάστῳ κατὰ τὰ ἔργα αὐτοῦ, but there are variations.) The expression goes right back into the Old Testament tradition (Ps 62:12 [LXX 61:13]; Prov 24:12; Job 34:11; Jer 17:10) and continues in early Judaism down to the time of the Apocalypse of Peter (Sir 16:14; LAB 3:10). In post-biblical Jewish writings it can be used of God's eschatological justice at the last judgment, as in Pseudo-Philo, LAB 3:10, where it occurs in a catena of traditional apocalyptic phrases describing the eschatological events of resurrection, judgment and new creation. This standard current Jewish way of referring to God's eschatological judgment is reflected also in early Christian writers (Rom 2:6; 1 Pet 1:17; Rev 20:13; 2 Clem 11:6), but most often in early Christian literature it is Jesus Christ who will render to each according to his deeds, for early Christianity commonly transferred to Jesus Christ, as the one who will execute the judgement, all the traditional language about God's eschatological judgment (e.g. Rev 2:23).

It is important to notice that the precise contexts in which the Apocalypse of Peter uses the phrase were in some cases at least already traditional. In the first place, the phrase was a standard, almost credal, formula in descriptions of the parousia (Matt 16:27; Rev 22:12; 1 Clem 34:3; 2 Clem 17:4; Did 16:8; Hegesippus, *ap.* Eusebius,

Hist. Eccl. 2.23.9; 3.20.4; Hippolytus, *Dan.* 4.10.1-2; QuEzra B14), so much so that it later occurs in a number of actual creeds. The author of the Apocalypse of Peter certainly knew one of these texts: Matthew 16:27, which may well have been in his mind, especially in view of its proximity to the Matthean transfiguration narrative. But he certainly also knew the phrase, "to render to each according to his deed," as part of common traditional formulations about the parousia, along with other phrases which he uses in 1:6-8.

Secondly, the phrase is also found with reference to the last judgment itself and Christ's judicial activity there (Barn 4:12; EpApp 26, 29; *De Universo* 3), as in Apocalypse of Peter chapter 6. Thirdly, the phrase is used in visions of the punishments in hell, with reference to the various punishments allotted to various sins. Thus it is found in chapters 56 and 57 of the Acts of Thomas, which certainly is not dependent on the Apocalypse of Peter (as has sometimes been alleged), but on the same tradition as some of the Apocalypse of Peter's description of the punishments in hell. Furthermore, in the Hebrew Apocalypse of Elijah, Elijah says: 'I saw there [in Gehenna] spirits undergoing judgment in torment, each one according to his deed.'[48] This is most probably a relic of the ancient Apocalypse of Elijah, and should be connected with the Latin Elijah fragment (preserved in the apocryphal Epistle of Titus)[49] which actually describes the various punishments for various sins, again in a way that shows common tradition with the Apocalypse of Peter and the Acts of Thomas. Similarly, in the fragment *De universo*, which used to be ascribed to Hippolytus,[50] the angels in Hades distribute the various punishments according to each one's deeds.[51] Thus the author of the Apocalypse of Peter almost certainly already knew the phrase, "each according to his deed," already used in connection with a description of various kinds of punishments for various sins, such as he reproduces in chapter 7-12.

The already traditional use of the phrase in these three contexts is what has enabled the author of the Apocalypse of Peter to connect

---

[48] M. Buttenwieser, *Der hebräische Elias-Apokalypse und ihre Stellung in der apokalyptischer Litteratur des rabbinischen Schriftthums und der Kirche* (Leipzig: Pfeiffer, 1897) 15.

[49] M. Stone and J. Strugnell, *The Books of Elijah: Parts 1-2* (SBLTT 18; Missoula, Montana: Scholars Press, 1979) 14-15. On the connexion between this text and the Hebrew Apocalypse of Elijah, see R. Bauckham, 'Early Jewish Visions of Hell,' *Journal of Theological Studies* 41 (1990) 362-365 = chapter 2 above.

[50] According to C.E. Hill, 'Hades of Hippolytus or Tartarus of Tertullian? The Authorship of the Fragment De Universo,' *VC* 43 (1989) 105-126, it should be attributed to Tertullian.

[51] K. Holl, *Fragmente vornicänische Kirchenväter aus der sacra Parallela* (TU 5/2; Leipzig: Hinrichs, 1899) 138, lines 7-9.

the various parts of his portrayal of the judgment by means of this phrase, "each according to his deed." It is the catchphrase which he found connected the parousia, the judicial activity of the day of judgment and a description of the various punishments in hell. Actually, the Apocalypse of Peter is the only ancient Christian work in which the parousia of Jesus Christ is connected with an account of the different punishments allotted to different sins in hell. But the connection was, so to speak, waiting to be made in the traditional association of the phrase "each according to his deed" with both themes.

2 *The cosmic conflagration*

The chapter on the resurrection (chapter 4), which we must pass over quickly, is a compilation of apocalyptic traditions about the eschatological resurrection of the dead.[52] But this material is integrated into the theme of judgment by the strong emphasis throughout the chapter on the fact that the resurrection takes place *on the day of judgment* (the phrase 'day of judgment' occurs four times in the chapter, as well as the equivalent phrases 'day of God' and 'day of punishment'). The author is interested in resurrection as the prelude to the judgment of the dead.

The end of chapter 4 forges a link with the following chapter: 'On the day of judgment the earth will give back everything [i.e. in resurrection], for then it [the earth] will have to be judged at the same time, and heaven with it' (4:13). The judgment of the heaven and the earth is evidently the cosmic conflagration—the burning of the whole creation—which takes place in chapter 5. But from chapter 5 it does not seem that the author attributes an independent significance to the judgment of the heaven and the earth as such. The cosmic conflagration seems to be envisaged as the means of bringing human beings to judgment. Chapter 5 opens: 'And (this) will happen on the day of judgment to those who pervert the faith of God and to those who have committed sin...'

The description of the conflagration in verses 2-6 of chapter 5 is rather obscure in its details. But the picture seems to be of flowing cataracts of fire, apparently flowing down from the sky, which burn, consume and melt everything: the firmament, the stars, the oceans and the earth. This is the flood of fire which some Jewish expectation envisaged as the second destruction of creation, a parallel to the

---

[52] For a study of one of these traditions, see chapter 10 below.

universal Flood of water in Genesis (LAE 49:3; Josephus, *Ant.* 1.70).[53] Descriptions of the eschatological conflagration which are quite closely parallel to that in the Apocalypse of Peter occur in Jewish texts: the Qumran Thanksgiving Hymns (1QH 3:19-36), the Sibylline Oracles (SibOr 3:54-87; 4:173-181), and the Pseudo-Sophoclean verses (*ap.* Clement of Alexandria, *Strom.* 5.14.121.4; 5.14.122.1; Ps.-Justin, *De Mon.* 3). Such descriptions may owe something to Iranian eschatology—more likely than to the Stoic idea of the conflagration—but there can be no doubt that the author of the Apocalypse of Peter is immediately indebted for his description to Jewish apocalyptic tradition. In such tradition the cosmic conflagration was related to certain Old Testament texts about judgment by fire (such as Mal 3:19: 'the day [of the Lord] is coming, burning like an oven') and especially to Isaiah 34:4, which describes the destruction of the sky and the stars on the day of the Lord. The Hebrew text of this verse appears to have no reference to fire, but the Septuagint has: 'all the powers of the heavens shall *melt*' (and cf. 2 Clem 16:3). Apocalypse of Peter 5:4 ('the stars will melt in a flame of fire'; and cf. v 6) is certainly an allusion to that interpretation of Isaiah 34:4.

Following the description of the physical destruction of the world by fire, in 5:7-8 we are told the effect of the conflagration on people:

> The children of men who are in the east will flee to the west; they (in the west) will flee into the east. And those in the south will flee the north, and those (in the north) to the south. Everywhere the awesome wrath of tfire will find them... (5:7-8).

This is a vivid description of the terror of sinners, fleeing in all directions to escape the flood of fire. In whichever direction they flee the fire pursues them and finds them. This passage is an interesting example of the way apocalyptic tradition works. For the image has not been invented by the author of the Apocalypse of Peter. It was a traditional apocalyptic topos, as we can see from a parallel in the Book of Thomas from Nag Hammadi, which is unlikely to be dependent on the Apocalypse of Peter. It describes in the following terms the fate of the soul imprisoned after death in Tartarus:

> If he flees westward, he finds the fire.
> If he turns southward, he finds it there as well.
> If he turns northward, the threat of seething fire meets him again.
> Nor does he find the way to the east so as to flee there and be saved, for

---

[53] On the eschatological conflagration in Jewish and Christian literature, see R. Bauckham, *Jude, 2 Peter* (Word Biblical Commentary 50; Waco, Texas: Word Books, 1983) 300-301.

he did not find it in the day he was in the body, so that he may find it in
the day of judgment (BkThom 143:2-8).

It is quite clear that this picture originally applied, as it does in the
Apocalypse of Peter, to the fire of judgment that engulfs the world on
the day of judgment. The Book of Thomas has transferred it to hell,
in the other world, appropriately in the sense that hell is also charac-
terized as fire, but inappropriately in that the points of the compass
are hardly relevant to Tartarus. But the form of the tradition in the
Book of Thomas is also interesting in that it does not treat all four
points of the compass equally, as the Apocalypse of Peter does. The
east is evidently a direction in which the fire of judgment will not be
found, it is the direction of salvation from the fire, which the sinner
fails to find. Perhaps the idea is that east, the land of Israel, is the
place where God's people are protected from the fire that consumes
the wicked. If the author of the Apocalypse of Peter knew the tradition in this form, he found it an inappropriate image, because, as we
shall see, he seems to envisage the fire as an ordeal of judgment
through which all must pass, though the righteous will pass through it
unharmed.

Verse 7 is therefore an example of the kind of traditional apocalyptic image which was probably transmitted orally. Many similar
examples can easily be found. It was from a stock of such traditions
that apocalyptic writers composed their prophetic accounts of the last
days. This was the accepted way of writing and readers would not be
surprised to find such familiar images constantly reappearing: they
would expect it. Of course, the more creative apocalyptists doubtless
added new images of their own to those they drew from the common
stock of apocalyptic traditions. But even so unoriginal writer as the
author of the Apocalypse of Peter could give vividness and liveliness
to his work by reusing traditional apocalyptic images such as this one.

He uses this particular image in order to portray the fire that
consumes the world as serving, so to speak, to round up sinners and
drive them to the judgment of wrath in the river of fire:

> Everywhere the awesome wrath of fire will find them (and) while it pur-
> sues them, the flame which does not go out will bring them to the judg-
> ment of wrath in the river of fire which does not go out, a fire which
> flames as it burns. And the waves having separated, while boiling, there
> will be much gnashing of teeth for children of men (5:8-9).

The river of fire, as will become clear in chapter 6, is the means of
judgment. It is a kind of ordeal through which all must pass. It is not
clear whether this river of fire actually is the same flood of fire which
has flowed down from the sky and burned and melted the whole

creation. In any case, the author has brought together two rather different traditions about the fire of judgment: the fire which judges by burning the heavens and the earth, and the fire which tests all people as they pass through it. (We shall consider the latter in subsection 5 below.)

3 Jesus Christ the Judge

Before describing the judgment itself, the Apocalypse of Peter must describe the judge. This is the apocalypse's second description of the parousia:

> And all of them will see as I come on a shining cloud which is eternal. And the angels of God who are with me will place[54] the throne of my glory at the right hand of my heavenly Father. And he will place a crown on my head. Then, the nations having seen (this), each of their nations will weep (6:1-2).

Like the first description of the parousia (in 1:6-8), this one is composed of already traditional formulae. The allusions to Daniel 7:13; Psalm 110:1; and Zechariah 12:10-14; 14:5 are those which Christians had already brought together in various combinations to portray the coming of Jesus Christ as the eschatological judge. (The image of Christ's coronation by the Father, not found elsewhere in early Christian literature, may derive from Ps 21:3. For the crown itself, worn by Christ as judge, see Rev 14:14.)

Some of the imagery is common to both of the Apocalypse of Peter's two descriptions of the parousia, but there is also a major difference. Whereas the first description (1:6-8) is designed primarily to represent the parousia as the unmistakable appearance of Jesus Christ in glory, and only secondarily to emphasize his role as judge, this second description (6:1-2) is exclusively concerned with depicting Christ's status as judge, exercising his Father's divine authority to judge the world. All the images are selected for that purpose. So again we have a good illustration of the way very little of the content of the Apocalypse of Peter is original, but, on the other hand, how the traditional images are carefully selected and combined to fulfil the author's purpose. He composes from a stock of tradition, but his composition is nonetheless deliberate and careful.

---

[54] This follows the correction of the text proposed by Buchholz, *Your eyes*, 302.

4 *Deeds as Witnesses*

After the judge, the witnesses at the trial are introduced: 'each one's deeds will stand before him, each according to his deed' (6:3). In this, at first sight rather curious image, the deeds of each individual, what he has done in his lifetime, are personified. The deeds of each stand there before him or her. The reference in fact seems to be only to the wicked and their evil deeds, because the next verse distinguishes, as a separate category, 'the elect, those who have done good.'

The significance of this image of the evil deeds of the wicked standing before them at the judgment will be clearer if we compare some occurrences of the same image in other literature, for here again we are dealing with a traditional image. One parallel is Wisdom 4:20. At the eschatological judgment, the wicked 'will come with dread when their sins are reckoned up, and their lawless deeds will convict them to their face' (ἐξ ἐαντιας, equivalent to 'before him' in the Apocalypse of Peter).

Even more illuminating is a parallel in 6 Ezra 16:65. The context is the impossibility of sinners' hiding their sins from God at his eschatological judgment:

> Let no sinner say he has not sinned... Behold, the Lord knows all the works of men, their imaginations and their thoughts and their hearts... [63]Woe to those who sin and want to hide their sins! Because the Lord will strictly examine all their works, and will make a public spectacle of all of you. And when your sins come out before men, you will be put to shame; and your own iniquities will stand as your accusers in that day. What will you do? Or how will you hide your sins before God and his angels? (6 Ezra 16:53-54, 63-66)

The significance of the image is clearly that the evil deeds are personified as witnesses against the sinner, accusing him. We should remember that in Jewish judicial practice the witnesses were the accusers. It was they who accused the person on trial of the crimes which they had witnessed. So the idea in these apocalyptic passages is that whereas human justice is imperfect—because people can be convicted only of crimes which have been witnessed and because witnesses may not always be reliable—in the eschatological judgment of God sinners will not be able to escape condemnation for every sin, because the sins themselves will be the witnesses accusing them. Even sins witnessed by no other human being, sins done in secret, will come to light and will be undeniable. If the evidence presented against the sinner is his sins themselves appearing to accuse him, then the evidence against him will be irrefutable.

The image is thus a way of presenting the idea—which we have seen to be the dominant idea—of eschatological judgment according to the deeds of each person. It has the same function in the depiction of the last judgment as another, parallel image: the opening of the books in which all the deeds of every person are recorded. This may be a more familiar image, because it occurs in biblical depictions of the last judgment, especially Revelation 20:12: 'the dead were judged according to their works, as recorded in the books.' But the alternative image used in the Apocalypse of Peter is a peculiarly powerful one. In the eschatological judgment sinners will be confronted by their own sins. Their condemnation will not be an external—and therefore always disputable—judgment passed on them by the judge. Their own evil will condemn them. The justice of their condemnation will be indisputable.

5 *The Ordeal of Fire*

The motif of the sins as witnesses, taken literally, would hardly cohere very well with the image with which it is combined in Apocalypse of Peter 6:2-4: the river of fire through which all must pass. But of course both are images and need not be literally compatible.

The river of fire is the ordeal which tests people's guilt. The righteous pass through unharmed, the wicked are burned. (As it stands the text might seem to suggest that the righteous do not pass through the river at all, but v 4 is obscure in the Ethiopic and probably corrupt. From parallels elsewhere to this kind of judgment scene, the meaning must be that the righteous are unharmed by the flames which devour the wicked.) Like the accusing witnesses, this feature also derives from ancient judicial practice: the notion of a judicial ordeal which distinguishes the innocent from the wicked. The judicial ordeal was, of course, actually used in cases which could not be decided by the evidence of witnesses, as in the one example in the Pentateuch: Numbers 5:11-31. This provides for the case of a wife suspected by her husband of adultery, although there are no witnesses to give evidence against her. So the woman is subjected to an ordeal (drinking 'the water of bitterness') in order to prove her innocence. This example makes clear why the image of the ordeal in the river of fire is strictly incompatible with the image of the deeds of the sinners as witnesses accusing them: in terms of judicial practice no ordeal should be necessary when the evidence of witnesses is conclusive.

An ordeal by plunging in a river was actually an ancient judicial practice: it occurs in the code of Hammurabi, for example. The idea of an eschatological ordeal by a river of fire is an ancient Zoroastrian idea. Unlike some of the ideas which Jewish apocalyptic is sometimes said to have borrowed from Zoroastrian tradition, which in fact can-

not be securely traced back to Zoroastrian sources old enough to
have influenced Jewish apocalyptic, this idea of the eschatological
river of fire which distinguishes the righteous from the wicked is a
genuinely old Iranian one, which is found already in the *Gathas*. The
Apocalypse of Peter seems to be the earliest Jewish or Christian text
in which it occurs, but it presumably was already to be found in
Jewish apocalyptic tradition.

6 *The Judgment of Evil Spirits*

Although chapter 6:6 could very well lead straight into the description of the various different punishments in hell which begins in chapter 7, in fact there is a further passage relating to the last judgment
itself:

> The angel of God, Uriel, will bring the soul of those sinners who perished
> in the Flood and of all of them who existed in every idol (and) in every
> poured metal work [i.e. molten image], in every love [i.e. fetish], and in
> imitation [i.e. statue], and those who lived on the hills [i.e. high places]
> and in the stones and in the road, (who) have been called gods. And they
> will be burned up with them in eternal fire. And after all of them and the
> places where they dwell have come to an end, they will be punished
> forever (6:7-9).[55]

This passage must be related to the traditions found in the Enoch
literature and in Jubilees about the origin of the evil spirits. According
to 1 Enoch and Jubilees, evil is to be traced back to the fallen angels,
the Watchers, the sons of God of Genesis 6, who before the Flood
mated with women and corrupted the earth. Their offspring by their
human wives were the giants, the Nephilim. The Watchers themselves were punished at that time by being chained in the underworld, awaiting the last judgment but no longer perpetrating evil in
the world. But their children the giants became demons: when the
giants died, their spirits continued to live in the world as evil spirits,
the demons who are henceforth responsible for the evil in the world.

In Apocalypse of Peter 6:7, 'the souls of those sinners who perished
in the Flood' cannot be the human sinners who died in the Flood. For
one thing, to introduce this particular category of humans after the
universal judgment of the dead has already been apparently concluded would be odd. For another, since the dead have been presented as resurrected in bodily form, one would have to ask why it is
only the spirits of these sinners who are brought to judgment by
Uriel. These sinners who died in the Flood must be the giants, the

---

[55] Translation adapted from Buchholz, *Your eyes,* 197.

sons of the fallen angels, and their spirits are therefore the demons. Admittedly, in the Enoch traditions the giants did not actually die in the Flood. They slaughtered each other prior to the Flood. So the Apocalypse of Peter must reflect a slightly variant version of the tradition.

But that these spirits are the demons is confirmed by the following verses which associate them with those who have lived in every idol and have been called gods. In the Enoch literature there is only a brief reference associating the spirits of the giants with idolatry (1 En 19:1), but in early Christian writers who took over the same tradition about the origin of the demons—Justin (*2 Apol.* 5) and Athenagoras (*Apol.* 24-26)—there is considerable development of this theme. These writers make it quite clear that it is the spirits of the dead giants, the demons, who have inspired idolatrous religion and who are actually worshipped in pagan religion under the names of the pagan gods.

That the Apocalypse of Peter in this passage is referring to the demons who inspire the idolatry of pagan religion is confirmed by a later passage in the book. One of the categories of sinners punished in hell is that of people who manufacture idols (10:5-6). Then the very next category of sinners (10:7) is that of people who have forsaken the commandment of God and have followed the will of demons. These must be pagan religious worshippers: people who worship idols and follow the will of the demons who inspire idolatrous religion.

So our passage in chapter 6 describes the final judgment of the demons who have been responsible for all idolatrous religion. It is a version of a traditional feature of the expectation of eschatological judgment: that not only wicked people will be judged, but also the powers of supernatural evil.

7 *The Punishments in Hell*

The centrepiece of the whole depiction of judgment in the Apocalypse of Peter is chapters 7-12, where we are given a description of twenty-one different forms of punishment allotted to twenty-one different categories of sinner. (Presumably the number twenty-one [3 x 7] is the sort of number that appealed to apocalyptists. It may indicate completeness, suggesting that the twenty-one punishments are, not all the punishments in hell, but representative of all the punishments in hell. But the number seems to have no further significance: the punishments do not fall into three groups of seven or seven groups of three.)

a *Relationship to other 'tours of hell'*

This account of the punishments in hell is clearly very closely related to a whole series of other Jewish and Christian apocalyptic texts which describe the various punishments for various sinners in hell. These include later Christian apocalypses, such as the Apocalypse of Paul and the Greek Apocalypse of the Virgin Mary, and medieval Hebrew visions of hell. The same sins and the same punishments often recur, with variations, in these texts. We are clearly dealing with an apocalyptic tradition which continued for many centuries and in which the latest texts frequently preserve very old traditional material. Most of these various texts and their relationships have been studied by Martha Himmelfarb in the book she devoted to them: *Tours of Hell: An Apocalyptic Form in Jewish and Christian Literature* .[56] I reached rather similar conclusions to hers, at first independently,[57] and I have tried to develop some aspects of her work in more detail.[58] Here I shall make a number of points about Himmelfarb's work and with specific reference to the Apocalypse of Peter.

First, Himmelfarb called these texts 'tours of hell' because in almost all of them a visionary (such as Paul or Elijah) is given, as it were, a guided tour of the punishments in hell, usually by an angel or some other figure from the otherworld. She pointed out a particular feature of the literary form of these texts. On seeing a particular group of sinners undergoing punishment, the visionary usually asks, 'Who are these?,' and receives from his guide an answer beginning, 'These are...' (e.g. 'these are those who have committed adultery' or 'these are people who used to gossip in church'). The statements beginning 'These are...'—which explain what sort of sinners are being punished—Himmelfarb calls the 'demonstrative explanations.' They characterize almost all the texts which describe the various punishments in hell. But there is another feature of these texts to which Himmelfarb does not draw any particular attention: it is that almost all of them are describing the punishments suffered by the wicked now, immediately after death, before the day of judgment at the end of history. This is why someone like Paul or Rabbi Joshua ben Levi can be taken on a tour of the punishments—because they are actually taking place already. So the texts are an expression of the belief in the active punishment of the wicked immediately after death, before the last judgement. This belief only developed and gained adherence in both Judaism and Christianity over the course of the

---

[56] Philadelphia: University of Pennsylvania Press, 1983.
[57] Bauckham, 'The Apocalypse of Peter: An Account of Research,' 4726-4733.
[58] Bauckham, 'Early Jewish Visions of Hell,' 355-385 = chapter 2 above.

first and second centuries C.E. The literary genre of the tours of hell within Jewish and Christian apocalyptic most probably originated in the first century C.E., along with the belief in punishments for the wicked immediately after death.

The account of the punishments in the Apocalypse of Peter, however, is quite exceptional among the tours of hell, in that it is not really a *tour* of hell at all. That is, Peter is not shown around the punishments in hell that are already taking place when the revelation is made to him. Rather the account is a prophecy by Christ to Peter of what will happen to the wicked after the last judgment. For this reason, the question-and-answer literary form of the tours of hell is absent. Peter does not see the damned and ask 'who are these?' The demonstrative explanations, however, are usually present. Without being asked to explain, Christ, having described each punishment, then identifies the sinners in a sentence beginning 'These are they who...' or 'These people...' It seems clear that the tradition which the author of the Apocalypse of Peter used was a genuine tour of hell, in which some visionary saw the punishments, asked questions and received explanations. But the author wished to use this traditional material to describe, not the intermediate state, but the eternal punishments which follow the last judgment. So he has transformed a description by a visionary of his experiences into a prophecy put on the lips of Christ. He has eliminated the questions and retained the demonstrative explanations.[59]

One reason for this is no doubt the author's imminent expectation. We do not know what he thought of the intermediate state, whether he retained, as some other contemporary apocalypses still did, the old belief that the wicked after death are not yet actively punished, but are merely detained in the underworld awaiting punishment at the last judgment; or whether he did hold the newer belief in the active punishment of the wicked immediately after death. In either case, the intermediate state was of no great concern to him, because he clearly expected the end of history and the last judgment to occur within the very near future.

Secondly, Martha Himmelfarb has done probably almost as much as can be done to sort out the literary relationships between the texts which she calls the tours of hell, including the Apocalypse of Peter. We cannot be sure of the literary relationships because there were

---

[59] The Akhmim text of the Apocalypse of Peter, which is a secondary, redacted version, restores the form of a vision (cf. A21, A25, A26), but that this is secondary can be seen from the fact that Peter asks no questions and the 'demonstrative explanations' are not ascribed to Christ, his guide, but are simply part of the narration.

certainly other texts, especially in the early period, which have not survived, and also because there were probably oral traditions as well as literary relationships involved. What is clear is that the Apocalypse of Peter was not the first such description of the punishments in hell, nor are many of the later tours of hell to be regarded as indebted to the Apocalypse of Peter. The view, which was propounded by M. R. James and once rather commonly held, that the Apocalypse of Peter was the source of this whole tradition of descriptions of the punishments in hell has proved to be untenable. The Apocalypse of Peter is simply one product of a tradition which antedated it and which continued after it independently of it. We have at least one tour of hell which is almost certainly older than the Apocalypse of Peter and is also Jewish rather than Christian: the Elijah fragment preserved in the apocryphal Epistle of Titus, which is almost certainly a fragment of the original Apocalypse of Elijah of the first century C.E. So, once again, we must see the Apocalypse of Peter as taking over and adapting traditional material from the existing traditions or literature of Jewish apocalyptic.

Thirdly, Martha Himmelfarb claims to have disproved the influential older view of Albrecht Dieterich[60] as to the source of the Apocalypse of Peter's account of hell. Dieterich (who knew only the Akhmim Greek text, not yet the Ethiopic version of the Apocalypse of Peter) argued that the Apocalypse of Peter borrowed directly from an Orphic *katabasis:* one of the accounts of a descent to the underworld, describing the rewards and the punishments of the dead, which were popular in the Greco-Roman world, allegedly in a tradition of popular Orphic-Pythagorean religion. In opposition to this, Himmelfarb has convincingly shown that the Jewish and Christian apocalyptic tradition of tours of hell developed within the Jewish apocalyptic tradition. Probably her best evidence for this is the literary form of question by the seer followed by demonstrative explanation from the supernatural guide. This literary form was already well-established in the Jewish apocalyptic tradition, where it occurs in many cases with reference to symbolic visions or to features of the other world other than the punishments in hell. The tour of hell most probably developed as a special category of the cosmic tour apocalypses.

But if Himmelfarb has shown that the tour of hell as an apocalyptic genre developed within the Jewish apocalyptic tradition, she has probably played down too much the extent to which this develop-

---

[60] A. Dieterich, *Nekyia: Beiträge zur Erklärung der neuentdeckten Petrus Apokalypse* (1st edition 1893; 3rd edition: Stuttgart: Teubner, 1969).

ment was indebted to Greek ideas. The *idea* of describing a variety of punishments going on now in the underworld may well have come from the Greco-Roman *katabasis* literature. Certainly, specific punishments were borrowed by Jewish and Christian apocalyptists from the Greco-Roman tradition, as also occasionally from Egyptian tradition. We need to remember both that Jewish apocalyptic was a literature which freely borrowed images and ideas from other cultural traditions, and also that especially in this area of eschatology—the expectation of rewards and punishments after death—the various cultures and religious traditions of the ancient Mediterranean world had very similar concepts, so that it was easy for particular images and ideas to move from the apocalyptic of one religion to that of another.[61]

So, with reference to the Apocalypse of Peter, it is important to be clear on two points and on the difference between them: (1) that the immediate sources of the Apocalypse of Peter's description of the punishments in hell were certainly in Jewish apocalyptic; but also (2) that these Jewish apocalyptic traditions may very well include images and ideas which ultimately derive from the Greek *katabasis* literature.

b *The concept of justice*

With this introduction to the background and literary context of this section of the Apocalypse of Peter (chapters 7-12) we can turn to examine more specifically the ideas of divine judgment that this account of the twenty-one infernal punishments expresses. The most important thing that needs to be to be appreciated about this account is that it is designed to vindicate God's justice. To modern readers it is grotesque and cruel in the extreme. But in order to understand its very different impact on ancient readers and hearers we must recognize that the idea of justice which it presupposes has certain features which we no longer easily appreciate.

First, its concept of justice is, of course, purely retributive. It is putting wrongs to right by inflicting on the offender suffering which corresponds to his offence. The idea of purificatory or reformatory punishments, which appears in some strands of Greek thought about the afterlife and occasionally makes an appearance in Jewish and Christian apocalyptic, has no place here at all. The punishments described are justified as pure retribution.

Secondly, it is probably not easy for us to understand why the punishments should be eternal in duration, since, even assuming a

---

[61] Cf. C. Kappler ed., *Apocalypses et Voyages dans l'Au-delà* (Paris: Cerf, 1987) 15, 18, 44.

purely retributive notion of punishment, the eternal duration of the punishments seems to us to make them grossly disproportionate to the seriousness of the crimes. However, the Apocalypse of Peter insists that the punishments are eternal. In the Ethiopic version of the account of the various punishments, it is explicitly stated eleven times that they are eternal, and this point is also very emphatically made made in each of the chapters which frame the account of the punishments (chapters 6 and 13). (However, there is a problem about these references to the eternity of the punishment in the Ethiopic version. It is an interesting and consistent difference between the Ethiopic and the Akhmim Greek fragment that the latter, in the eight places where it parallels statements about the eternity of the punishments in the Ethiopic version, has none of these statements. Moreover, the Akhmim fragment is supported in this respect [though not in others] by the Bodleian fragment of 10:6-7. Comparison of the latter with the Ethiopic version suggests that the Ethiopic has so translated the Greek in 10:6 as to turn a reference to unceasing punishment into a reference to eternal punishment, while in 10:7 it has added a reference to eternal punishment which was not in the Greek. However, we should not too quickly conclude that none of the references to the eternity of punishment in the Ethiopic are original. The editor of the Akhmim fragment probably had his own reason for not depicting the punishments as eternal, since he understood them [differently from the original apocalypse] as the punishments of the wicked in the intermediate state, taking place contemporaneously with the disciples' vision of them, not the eternal punishments which follow the last judgment. It therefore seems probable that in the Ethiopic version references to eternal punishment have been increased, but not that there were none in the original text of the apocalypse.)

If we are to understand the eternity of the punishments, I think we should have to suppose that for apocalyptic writers, eternity is not so much a kind of continuation of this life, but rather a kind of establishment of the real truth of this life. Eschatological judgment is when the real truth of this life is revealed and receives what is finally due to it. This is final justice. Of course, the idea no doubt has also a kind of paraenetic function. Everything is really decided already in this life; repentance and good deeds cannot be put off to the next life; and so the need to live well in this life is absolute.

Thirdly, the impetus to a description of a whole series of different punishments for different sins, such as we find here and in other apocalyptic texts, is the notion that each sin ought to have a specific kind of punishment. Although we have not entirely lost this idea, modern people think more often and more naturally in terms of the relative severity of punishments. The punishment should fit the crime in the sense that it should be more or less severe according to the relative severity of the offence. But our text operates with a different idea of the sense in which the punishment should fit the crime. It is that each crime should have a specific kind of punishment appropriate to it.

This idea is found sporadically in ancient legal systems, which sometimes prescribe quite specific punishments exclusively for a specific kind of crime.[62] For example in the old Roman law parricides were punished with the sack: that is, they were put into a sack along with four animals: a dog, a cock, a snake and a monkey. The four animals were probably supposed to represent the vices which had led to the crime. Thus the idea was not just that this particularly heinous crime should be punished with exceptional cruelty, but also that it should incur a specific kind of punishment symbolically appropriate to it. In general, of course, ancient legal systems—including Jewish law—did not have a different punishment for each crime. But doubtless the thinking behind accounts of hell such as that in the Apocalypse of Peter was that the ideal justice which earthly legal systems cannot achieve will be realised in God's eschatological judgment. He will be able to allot a punishment precisely appropriate to each kind of crime. The idea is not necessarily peculiarly Jewish. For example, at the end of one of Lucian's satirical dialogues about the other world (the *Cataplus*), Rhadamanthus the judge in Hades and a Cynic philosopher who has come blameless out the judgment together consider what kind of punishment would be most appropriate for the tyrant Megapenthes. They reject some of the usual punishments of Hades in favour a novel idea, devised by the Cynic especially for Megapenthes' case: unlike the rest of the dead, he will not be allowed to drink of the waters of Lethe and so will never be able to forget the luxury and power he enjoyed on earth.

In the Apocalypse of Peter the idea of a different punishment for each sin is seen as the outworking of the principle of the judgment of each person according to his works. However, it does raise a difficulty. Surely most sinners are guilty of more than one of the twenty-one sins catalogued in the Apocalypse of Peter and should therefore incur more than one of the twenty-one punishments? There seems to be no provision for suffering more than one punishment either simultaneously or successively. Perhaps this is an indication that we should

---

[62] Cf. J.-P. Callu, 'Le jardin des supplices au Bas-Empire,' in *Du Châtiment dans la Cité: Supplices corporels et peine de mort dans le monde antique* (Collection de l'École Française de Rome 79; Rome: École Française de Rome, 1984) 341-342.

not take the description of hell too literally. It is perhaps more concerned to drive home imaginatively the principle of eschatological justice than to offer literal description of hell. Despite the vivid descriptions of actual people suffering each punishment, we should perhaps think of the account as more in the nature of an eschatological law code, setting out what is in strict justice due to each sin.

Fourthly, the general idea that each sin ought to have its own punishment becomes more specific in the idea of 'measure for measure' punishments. Martha Himmelfarb gives to a specific category of the punishments in hell the description 'measure for measure' punishments, because the principle is described in rabbinic literature as 'measure for measure' (e.g. b. Sanh. 90a)—or more fully: 'By the measure a person measures out, so it is measured out to him' (e.g. Tg Neof Gen 38:25; m. Sot. 1:7).[63] (In the Gospel tradition the saying is used rather differently: Matt 7:2; Mark 4:24; Luke 6:38.) The basic idea that the suffering one inflicts is what one should suffer oneself as retribution was common in the ancient world: Aristotle quotes the Pythagoreans as attributing to Rhadamanthus, the judge of the dead in Hades, the maxim, 'If one suffers what one did oneself, it is true justice' (*Nichomachean Ethics* 5.5.3; the same maxim also appears in Pindar, *Nemean Odes* 4.32). In Jewish legal tradition the principle was enshrined in the famous *lex talionis* of the Torah: 'an eye for an eye, and a tooth for a tooth' (Exod 21:24; Lev 24:20). If one knocks out someone else's tooth, one should lose a tooth oneself.

For the vast majority of crimes the principle in that simple form makes little if any sense. But the conviction that the *lex talionis* is how justice *ought* to operate leads to attempts to conform to it somehow. Ancient legal practice sometimes exhibits the notion that somehow the kind of punishment should *correspond* to the crime.[64] An obvious case is that of burning to death as the punishment for arsonists. A more indirect kind of correspondence can be seen in a story which is told of the emperor Alexander Severus who condemned his friend Vircunius Tirinus to die by choking in smoke. Tirinus had been in the habit of making false promises which he did not fulfil, and the Latin idiom for such behaviour was 'to sell smoke' *(fumum vendere)*. The emperor condemned him with the words: 'he who has sold smoke is punished by smoke' *(fumo punitur qui vendidit fumum) (Hist. Aug.*

---

[63] For this saying in the Targums and rabbinic literature, see M. McNamara, *The New Testament and the Palestinian Targum to the Pentateuch* (AnBib 27; Rome: Pontifical Biblical Institute, 1966) 138-142; H. P. Rüger, "'Mit welchem Mass ihr messt, wird euch gemessen werden,'" *ZNW* 60 (1969) 174-182.

[64] Cf. Callu, 'Le jardin,' 340 n. 112, 342-343.

Alex. Sev. 35.5-36.3). Even though this is by no means *lex talionis* in the strict and literal sense, there was felt to be a kind of obvious justice when the punishment corresponded in some such way to the crime.

In Jewish tradition what is most important is the conviction that the *lex talionis* must be the principle of *divine* justice. This seems to have been applied originally more with reference to divine judgments within history, and then later applied also to eschatological punishment. Occasionally, the application is obvious: what the criminal has done to others is done to him (2 Macc 5:9-10; Philo, *Flaccus* 170). Sometimes, the correspondence is the kind of loose appropriateness we have just considered. In Pseudo-Philo, LAB 44:10 we read:

> And the race of men will know that they will not make me [God] jealous by their inventions that they make, but to every man there shall be such a punishment that in whatever sin he shall have sinned, in this he will be judged. If they have lied before me, I will command the heaven and it will deny them rain. And if anyone wished to covet the wife of his neighbour, I will command death and it will deny them the fruit of their womb. And if they will make a false declaration in my name, I will not hear their prayers. And when the soul is separated from the body, then they will say, "Let us not mourn over these things that we suffer; because whatever we ourselves have devised, these we will receive."

There the principle is applied first to judgments in this life and then extended to the next. The measure-for-measure character of the punishments given as examples is quite vague and not too easy to discern, but it is quite clear that this is intended—and, furthermore, it is quite clear that this measure-for-measure character gives the punishments a kind of obvious justice which the damned themselves in hell will have to acknowledge. To receive something corresponding to what one has done oneself is to find, as it were, one's own sin boomeranging back at one.

A modern newspaper story may help to make this point. A local medical centre was troubled by young vandals putting bricks through the windows, and so they had toughened glass put in the windows. Soon afterwards a woman came into the centre to complain about what had happened to her son. He had suffered a cut on the head when he threw a brick at a window and it bounced back and hit him on the head. Probably most people's instant reaction is to feel that that is justice of the sweetest kind: the sin itself rebounding on the sinner. That is the kind of effect which measure-for-measure punishments must have had on the ancient mind, however artificial they may sometimes seem to us.

In their attempt to understand divine justice in terms of the *lex talionis,* Jewish writers tried to refine the principle in various ways.

One form of the principle, which is stated as a principle of divine punishment both in Jubilees 4:32 and in Wisdom 11:16, is that the instrument of sin should be the *instrument* of punishment. For example, Cain killed Abel with a stone, and so he himself was killed by the stones of his house when his house fell on him (Jub 4:31). The Egyptians worshipped animals, and so, among the plagues of Egypt, they were punished by plagues of animals (Wis 11:15; 12:27; 15:18-16:1). Many examples could be given (cf. Jub 48:14; LAB 44:9; Wis 11:6; 18:4-5; Rev 16:6; b. Giṭṭ. 57a; GenRab 1:18): but I do not know of this form of the principle being applied to judgments after death.

Another way of making the punishment correspond to the crime is to say that the *part of the body* which sinned is the part which should be punished. Biblical examples could again be found: e.g. Samson sinned by following the desire of his eyes, and so the Philistines put his eyes out (LAB 43:5; m. Sot. 1:8); Absalom gloried in his hair, and so was hanged by his hair (m. Sot. 1:8). The principle can be stated in three slightly different ways, and we should note that all three forms are applied to punishments in Gehenna:

(i) 'The limb which *began* the transgression, from it will begin the punishment' (Sifre Num 18). So, for example, say the rabbis, according to this principle, the divine punishment of the adulterous woman in Numbers 5 *begins* in her sexual parts (Sifre Num 18; cf. m. Sot. 1:7). But the Babylonian Talmud provides an eschatological example: 'A man shall not let his ears hear idle chatter, for they will be burnt first of all his limbs' (b. Ket. 5b).

(ii) 'The limbs that committed the sin are punished in Gehenna *more than* the other limbs' *(Darkhei Teshuvah)*. This statement occurs in one of the medieval Hebrew visions of the punishments in hell which belong to the same genre and include many of the same punishments as the account in the Apocalypse of Peter.[65] After providing descriptions of punishments in which people are punished by the sinful limb, the account says that these punishments are 'to show that the Holy One, blessed be he, is a righteous judge. The limbs that committed the sin are punished in Gehenna *more than* the other limbs.' Notice that, once again, this correspondence of punishment to sin is said to demonstrate the justice of the punishments.

---

[65] See the translation and discussion in J.-M. Rosenstiehl, 'Les révélations d'Elie: Elie et les tourments des damnés,' in *La Littérature Intertestamentaire: Colloque de Strasbourg (17-19 Octobre 1983)* (Bibliothèque des Centres d'Etudes Supérieures Spécialistes; Paris: Presses Universitaires de France, 1985) 99-107.

(iii) The third statement comes from the Christian apocryphal Epistle of Titus, which quotes a vision of the punishments in Gehenna attributed to Elijah. The quotation probably comes from the ancient Apocalypse of Elijah, which was older than the Apocalypse of Peter. In fact, this quotation is most likely the oldest extant Jewish account of the punishments in hell, the oldest example of the genre of the tours of hell. The statement of the principle is not actually given in the quotation, but is part of the Christian writer's introduction to the quotation. But it seems very likely he was drawing on his source when he says: 'You know that different judgments must be passed on sinners. In the member with which each man has sinned, in the same also shall he be tormented.' This is the simplest form of the principle.

c *Types of punishment in the Apocalypse of Peter*
If we now turn to the series of infernal punishments in the Apocalypse of Peter, we find that there are certainly four and probably five punishments which are designed according to the principle that it is the part of the body which sinned that should be punished. Three of them are in the category of 'hanging punishments' which frequently occur in the tours of hell. In many of the tours of hell there are a group of these hanging punishments, usually consisting of people hung up by the part of the body which sinned.[66] So in the Apocalypse of Peter, there are, first, those who blasphemed the way of righteousness, suspended by their tongues (7:2). Then there are women suspended by their necks and hair (7:5): these are adulteresses, who adorned their hair in order to seduce men into adultery with them. Finally. in 7:7, there are the men who committed adultery with them. They are suspended by their thighs, according to the Ethiopic version: certainly a euphemism for the sexual organ. (Other tours of hell represent people guilty of sexual sin as hanging by their sexual organs.)

The origin of the idea of these hanging punishments is somewhat debatable. Hanging was used in the ancient world both as a form of non-lethal torture and also as a means of lingering and very painful death, as in crucifixion. Hanging women by their hair seems to have been actually used as a form of torture in the Roman world.[67] The notion of hanging may have appealed to those who imagined punishments after death because it was a form of punishment which could easily be imagined as eternal: it could be prolonged as a form of

---

[66] See, especially, Himmelfarb, *Tours* , 82-92.

[67] S. Lieberman, 'On Sins and their Punishments,' in *Texts and Studies* (New York: Ktav, 1974) 43 n. 86.

unending pain without destroying its victims. But who originated the idea of hanging in hell? Himmelfarb tends rather to discount the idea that Jewish apocalyptic borrowed it from Greek ideas of the underworld, but the evidence for a Greek origin is probably stronger than she allows. We should remember that the popular descriptions of the underworld which certainly existed and from which Jewish apocalyptists would most likely have borrowed have not survived. We can only gather their contents from sources indebted to them—the philosophers, the poets, the parodists. Given this limitation of the sources, the evidence that hanging in Hades was a feature of traditional Greek descriptions of punishments in Hades is quite good. As early as Plato's *Gorgias* (525C), we are told that the worst sinners are hanging in Hades. A reference to a lost account of Pythagoras' descent to the underworld says that he saw the soul of Homer hanging from a tree as punishment for his sacrilegious stories about the gods (Diogenes Laertes, *Lives* 8.21). Virgil's *Aeneid* speaks of people hanging in Hades (6.740-741). Most interesting of all is Lucian's account of a hanging punishment in his parody of popular descriptions of Hades in his *True History* (2.26). He sees the adulterer Cinyras hanging by his genital organ. This is precisely the same punishment for the same sin as we find in the Apocalypse of Peter and in some of the other tours of hell. It is of course possible that Lucian knew Jewish apocalyptic tours of hell or Greek sources influenced by Jewish apocalyptic tours of hell. In the intercultural world of eschatological imagery there is no reason why borrowings should all have been in one direction. But on the other hand, in view of the much earlier evidence for hanging in the Greek Hades, it seems more likely that the more specific idea of hanging by the part of the body that had sinned had also developed within the Greek tradition and was borrowed from it by Jewish apocalyptists. It is worth noting that this kind of measure for measure punishment is also evidenced by another passage of Lucian, not relating to punishment after death: he has Heracles threaten a slave who had disguised himself as a philosopher that he will punish him by hanging him by his beard (the beard with which he pretended to be a philosopher) (*Fugitivi* 31).

The fact that the hanging punishments are measure-for-measure punishments does not prove that they were of Jewish origin. As we have already noticed, the measure-for-measure principle was not confined to Judaism. However, the fact that the hanging punishments are measure-for-measure punishments does explain why Jewish apocalyptists intent on depicting hell as perfect justice should have borrowed them and given them a greater prominence in Jewish accounts of hell than they probably had in Greek ones. Certainly, since they occur in Jewish and Christian tours of hell which are not dependent on the Apocalypse of Peter, the Apocalypse of Peter did not borrow them direct from a pagan source but from Jewish apocalyptic tradition. Their prominence in the Apocalypse of Peter, as the first, third and fourth punishments in the series of twenty-one, is no doubt due to the fact that they embodied the measure-for-measure principle so clearly and vividly.

As well as the three hanging punishments, there are two other punishments in the Apocalypse of Peter which embody the principle that the part of the body which sinned should suffer. The first occurs in 9:4, where we are told of those who bore false witness—whose lies have led to the deaths of the martyrs—that their lips are cut off and fire is put into their mouths and intestines. So the lips and the mouth which uttered the lies are punished, and presumably the intestines too because the deceit comes from within the liar.

The other example is not so obvious. In 11:6-7 the punishment of girls who did not keep their virginity before marriage is described. They are dressed in black clothes and their flesh is torn in pieces or dissolved. The idea of the flesh dissolving may be borrowed from the punishment of the adulterous wife in Numbers 5:27 ('her thigh shall fall away'). In that case, the 'flesh' of the young women is a euphemism for their sexual parts, and it is that part of their body which sinned that is punished. The black clothes indicate shame, as we can see from the Mishnah's discussion of the case of the suspected adulteress in Numbers 5: her husband shames her by exchanging her white garments for black (m. Sot. 1:6-7).

We have so far identified five measure-for-measure punishments in the Apocalypse of Peter: those in which the guilty limb is punished. Other measure-for-measure punishments, in which the punishment is merely in some way appropriate to the sin, are not always so easy to identify. I think we can probably identify at least six:

(i) In 8:8-9 is described the punishment of mothers who killed their infants at birth, presumably by the common ancient practice of exposure: 'The milk of their mothers flows from their breasts and congeals and rots. From in it (are) flesh-eating animals and they come out and return, and they are punished for ever with their husbands.' Clement of Alexandria, who quoted and commented on this punishment (Eclog. 49), rightly saw it as a measure-for-measure punishment. The milk which the mothers denied to their children becomes the instrument of their torture.

(ii) This account of the punishment of infanticides is preceded by an account of the punishment of those guilty of abortion. Here part of the punishment (8:1) is that they stand up to their necks in a pit of excrement—or, perhaps, as Buchholz's translation suggests: menstrual discharge. Probably the meaning is that they treated their foetuses as mere excrement.

(iii) In 9:5-7, we have the punishment of those who trusted in their riches and neglected charity to the poor. Part of their punishment is that they are clothed in filthy rags. This seems to be the only case in the Apocalypse of Peter of *lex talionis* principle in its most basic and straightforward form: these people suffer what they made others suffer.

(iv) In 11:8-9, slaves who disobeyed their masters chew their tongues eternally. This may be a measure-for-measure punishment, if the idea is that they disobeyed verbally: they answered back.

(v) The next group of sinners are hypocrites: 'men and women (who are) blind and deaf, and their clothing (is) white. And then they push one another and fall onto coals of fire which never goes out. These are those who do a charitable deed and say, "Righteous (are) we to God." (And yet) righteousness they have not sought' (12:1-2). Presumably these people are wilfully ignorant—blind to their own motives—and so their punishment is to be blind and deaf.

(vi) Finally, the murderers (in 7:9) are put in a fire full of poisonous reptiles. Perhaps these are intended to represent the murderers' evil desires that led them to murder. In that case, this would be a sort of measure-for-measure punishment.

These are the only punishments—eleven in all, out of the full catalogue of twenty-one—in which I have been able to discover a measure-for-measure element, at least. Other people's ingenuity may be able to identify a few other measure-for-measure punishments in the Apocalypse of Peter. But it is clear that by no means all the punishments are measure-for-measure. Perhaps the authors of the traditions and the author of the Apocalypse of Peter itself were simply unable to devise measure-for-measure punishments for every sin they wished to include. But if the measure-for-measure principle does not explain all the punishments, how can we explain the origin of the ideas for the other specific punishments? Three other considerations will account for most of the punishments in the Apocalypse of Peter.

The first is the reproduction in hell of punishments used in human justice on earth. We have already noticed that hanging is a case of this. Others are burning (10:7), equivalent to the practice of burning people to death; and scourging with whips and flogging with chains (9:2; 10:6). Scourging was widely practised as a punishment, usually as non-lethal, but sometimes as deliberately flogging to death (e.g. Suetonius, *Gaius* 27.7). From earthly use it had long ago entered the Greek Hades, where it was a thoroughly standard feature of the punishment of the dead (e.g. Virgil, *Aen.* 6.556-557; Lucian, *Men.* 14; *Vera hist.* 2.29) and so must have migrated to the Jewish hell from the Greek. The wheel, on which sorcerers are stretched in 12:5-6, was an exotic form of human punishment, but famous as a feature of the Greek Hades. Ixion, punished by being fixed to a wheel, was one of the famous individual sinners featured in descriptions of the Greek Hades, along with Sisyphus, Tityos, Tantalus and others. The punishments of these famous mythological individuals had long come to be seen as representative punishments, which other sinners could also expect to suffer (cf. Virgil, *Aen.* 6.616-617). Ixion's is the only one which appears in the Apocalypse of Peter.

Before leaving the category of infernal punishments modelled on earthly punishments, we should notice two interesting variations on the punishment of precipitation: that is, killing someone by throwing them off a high cliff, usually into the sea (e.g. Suetonius, *Tib.* 62.3). First, male and female homosexuals are punished thus:

> Other men and women from a height throw themselves headlong. And again they return and run, and demons force them.... And they force them to the end of existence [or to the brink of the precipice], and they throw themselves over. They do this continually in the same way. They are punished forever (10:2-3). [Probably the words 'these are idol worshippers' in v 2 are a mistaken intrusion into this text, since v 4 identifies these sinners as homosexuals.]

Then also those who fail to honour their parents suffer a punishment which, despite a rather corrupt text, is probably similar to that of the homosexuals:

> And another place, very high ... and ... fire that burns over the edge. Men and women who fall [into it], rolling. They go down into where the fear was. And again, when what has been made flows, they go up and go down and repeat like that, rolling. In this way they are punished forever (11:1-2: the gaps represent unintelligible parts of the Ethiopic text).

In both cases, people fall to their death from a high precipice, but are then obliged to repeat the exercise continually for eternity. This is a way of turning an earthly punishment which ends with someone's death into a means of eternal torment. This device is one which recurs in the apocalyptic accounts of hell in a variety of ways. Another example (which is found both in TIsaac 5:6-16 and in the

medieval Hebrew vision of Joshua ben Levi)[68] is an eternalized version of the punishment of being thrown to the lions: the damned are
eaten by the lions, but then reconstituted so that they can be eaten
again, and so on eternally.

As well as punishments which reflect earthly punishments, there
are also, secondly, a few punishments which reflect what happens to
corpses on earth. The flesh-eating birds who attack the damned in
11:4 are presumably modelled on the vultures and other birds that
feed on corpses. (These people are said to be hung up while flesh-
eating birds attack them: the image of hanging here perhaps derives
from the hanging up of corpses, rather than of living people.) The
numerous worms of 7:9 are also a feature of what happens to corpses,
although Jewish tradition had also delighted to recount stories of
notorious sinners being consumed by worms while still alive (2 Macc
9:9; LAB 44:9; 63:4; Acts 12:23; b. Soṭ. 35a).

Thirdly, there are the traditional features of the Jewish Gehenna,
notably darkness and fire, darkness original to Sheol, fire to Gehenna.
Darkness is mentioned in just one of the punishments (in 9:1; cf. also
6:5), but fire is all-pervasive. No less than fourteen of the twenty-one
punishments in the Ethiopic version include some form of fire (7:4, 7,
9; 8:4; 9:1, 3, 4, 5; 10:5-6, 7; 11:1, 8; 12:1; 12:4-7; cf. also 6:5). The
Akhmim text actually has fire in two punishments in which it does
not appear in the Ethiopic (A22, A24), but the more interesting contrast between the Ethiopic text and the Akhmim Greek fragment is
that three times the Akhmim text refers to the mire in which the
damned are sunk (A23, A24, A31). The Ethiopic has none of these
references to mud. Immersal in mud was an important ancient feature of the Greek Hades, whereas fire, though present in the torches
of the Furies (e.g. Ps.-Plato, *Axiochus* 372) and the fiery river
Pyriphlegethon (e.g. Lucian, *Cat.* 28), was probably rather less prominent. So it is worth noticing that the Apocalypse of Peter is thoroughly Jewish in the pervasiveness of fiery punishments in its hell,
while the Akhmim fragment's additional references to mud probably

---

[68] See M. R. James, *The Testament of Abraham* (Texts and Studies 2/2; Cambridge:
Cambridge University Press, 1892) 159. The repetition is not found in the text
translated by M. Gaster, 'Hebrew Visions of Hell and Paradise,' reprinted from
Journal of the Royal Asiatic Society (1893) 571-611, in M. Gaster, *Studies and Texts,* vol. 1
(London: Maggs, 1928) 158-159. For other punishments involving continual restora-
tion and repetition, see Gaster, ibid., 136, 148-149, 161; W. Leslau, *Falasha Anthology*
(Yale Judaica Series 6; New Haven/London: Yale University Press, 1951) 86 (Apocalypse of Gorgorios).

reflect a further approximation to Greek pictures of the underworld by the author who adapted this text. Fire, of course, was not only the traditional content of Gehenna, but also more broadly a deeply traditional Jewish image of divine judgment.

One Old Testament text played an important part in the development of the doctrine of hell: the last verse of Isaiah: 'They shall go out and look at the dead bodies of the people who have rebelled against me; for their worm shall not die, their fire shall not be quenched...' (Isa 66:24). We can be sure of the influence of this text on descriptions of hell wherever the fire is inextinguishable or undying, and wherever the worm is singular (as in the Hebrew of Isaiah) and also undying or unsleeping. The inextinguishable fire appears in Apocalypse of Peter 12:1 (coals of fire which never go out) and the unsleeping worm appears in 9:2 (where those who are flogged by a spirit of wrath also have their entrails eaten by an unsleeping worm).

These remarks may help us to begin to understand the kind of imagination which produced the apocalyptic accounts of the manifold punishments in hell. They are not just products of a diseased imagination run riot. They are based on certain principles and use recognizable forms of imagery. Certainly they are evidence of an age when justice was generally thought to require considerable cruelty. It is the cruelty of contemporary human justice which is here reflected in hell and refined in such a way as to make it, not less cruel, but, to authors and readers of the time, recognizably more just. The overriding concern is that the wicked should face the truth of their own evil and suffer it.

8 Angels of judgment

The account of the eschatological judgment in the Apocalypse of Peter features four named angels, as well as unnamed angels of punishment. We look first at the named angels: Uriel, Ezrael, Tartarouchos and Temelouchos.

Uriel appears three times in the Ethiopic version: (a) At 4:9, where (according to the most probable interpretation) it is Uriel, described as 'the great Uriel,' who supplies the soul and spirit to the bodies that have been resurrected. It is then explained that 'God has set him over the resurrection of the dead on the day of judgment.' (b) At 6:7, it is 'the angel of God, Uriel,' who 'will bring the souls of those sinners who perished in the Flood'—who I have argued above are the demons—to the judgment. (c) At 12:5 he sets up the wheel of fire in the river of fire in which sinners are punished.

Uriel appears frequently in early Jewish and early Christian literature,[69] often listed as the third in a list of the four archangels: Michael, Gabriel, Uriel, Raphael (e.g. ApMos 40:2; 3 Bar [Sl] 4:7; cf GkApEzra 6:1-2; cf 1 En 9:1 [Gk], where he comes second; SibOr 2:215, where he comes last; and 1 En 20:1, where he comes first in a list of seven; PrJos also implies he is one of seven archangels). Although the expression 'God has set him over the resurrection of the dead' is in accordance with the general way in which particular angels are frequently said, in the literature of this period, to be 'over' some aspect of the world and God's governance of it, this particular sphere of authority for Uriel is not attested elsewhere. However, the functions and spheres of authority of the archangels seem to vary constantly from one text to another. Uriel's role in 6:7, of bringing the demons to judgment, corresponds roughly to the statement in the Greek of 1 Enoch 20:1 that he is 'over Tartarus.' Finally, the mention of Uriel at 12:5 comes as rather a surprise, since it is Ezrael who has previously been mentioned throughout the account of the punishments in hell (7:10; 9:1; 10:5; 11:4; 12:3) and has in fact only just appeared at 12:3. The Ethiopic's reference to Uriel in 12:5 may therefore be a mistake for Ezrael. On the other hand, since one interpretation of Uriel's name could be 'flame of God' (from 'ûr, 'flame,' rather than 'ôr, 'light'), he may have been thought the most appropriate archangel to set up the wheel of fire in the river of fire.

Ezrael, who is mentioned five times in chapters 7-12, described like Uriel as 'the angel of God' (12:3), but also more specifically as 'the angel of his wrath' (9:1), is otherwise unknown by this name. But he is probably, as Buchholz suggests,[70] the archangel Sariel,[71] whose name appears to be corrupted to Ἰστραηλ in one Greek manuscript of 1 Enoch 10:1, and to 'Asre'elyer in one Ethiopic manuscript of the same verse. Sariel occasionally appears as one of the four archangels in place of Uriel (1QM 9:14-15; 4QEn[b]1:3:7 = 1 En 9:1; and in Manichean sources which reflect the Enochic Book of Giants), but he also appears along with Uriel in the list of seven archangels in 1

---

[69] On Uriel, see J. T. Milik, *The Books of Enoch: Aramaic Fragments of Qumrân Cave 4* (Oxford: Clarendon Press, 1976) 172-174; M. Dando, 'L'archange Ouriel,' *Cahiers d'Etudes Cathares* 34/3 (1983) 3-11.

[70] Buchholz, *Your Eyes*, 316.

[71] On Sariel, see G. Vermes, 'The Archangel Sariel: A Targumic Parallel to the Dead Sea Scrolls,' in J. Neusner ed., *Christianity, Judaism and Other Greco-Roman Cults: Part III: Judaism before 70* (SJLA 12/3; Leiden: Brill, 1975) 159-166; Milik, *The Books of Enoch*, 172-174; J. Z. Smith in J. H. Charlesworth ed., *The Old Testament Pseudepigrapha*, vol. 2 (London: Darton, Longman and Todd, 1985) 708-709.

Enoch 20. In Targum Neofiti (Gen 32:25) he is the angel who wrestles with Jacob, although this angel is Uriel in the Prayer of Jacob. In the Ladder of Jacob, as the angel 'in charge of dreams' (3:2), he interprets Jacob's dream at Bethel. The similarity of his name to Jacob's new name Israel (noted in LadJac 4:3) probably accounts for his association with Jacob stories. In 1 Enoch 20:6, Sariel is said in the Ethiopic version to be 'in charge of the spirits of human beings who cause the spirits to sin,' while the Greek has 'over the spirits which sin in the spirit.' Clearly, something is wrong with both versions and it is impossible to reconstruct the original with certainty. It may have represented Sariel as in charge of the spirits of human sinners, in which case his role here would accord with the role the Apocalypse of Peter gives him, of bringing the damned to their punishments. But more probably 1 Enoch 20:6 originally put Sariel in charge of the demonic spirits which lead human beings astray.

In the Apocalypse of Peter Ezrael seems to be mainly concerned with moving people around in Gehenna. In 9:1 he brings a particular group of sinners, the persecutors of the righteous, to their place of punishment. In 7:10 he brings the victims of murder to view the punishment of their murderers. In 11:4, according to the Ethiopic version, he seems to bring children to view the punishment of other children who have disobeyed their parents. Perhaps the text originally meant that he brought the children who were to be punished to their punishment. If the point is to show the punishment of guilty children to other children, then it cannot be as a warning, since the scene is set after the last judgment, but presumably to increase the satisfaction of the righteous who see what would have happened to them had they disobeyed their parents. Finally, in 12:3 Ezrael brings another group of sinners, the hypocrites, out of the flame which constitutes part of their punishment: again the text is rather obscure. It seems this is not the end of their punishment, but only of one phase of their punishment. From these four references, we might think Ezrael has the exclusive function of bringing people from one place to another in hell, but in 10:5 he has a role in the punishments themselves: he makes the place of fire in which the makers of idols and their idols burn.

The other two angels are Tatirokos, who in 13:5 rebukes the damned when they cry for mercy, telling them it is now too late to repent, and Temlakos, to whom, in 8:10, the victims of infanticide are committed, after they have seen the punishment of their parents. These are the angels called in Greek Ταρταροῦχος and Τεμελοῦχος (or Τημελοῦχος), who occur in a considerable number of apocalyptic texts about hell, Tartarouchos more often than Temelouchos. They have been thoroughly studied in a definitive study by J.-M. Rosenstiehl.[72]

Tartarouchos is the angel in charge of Tartarus, which is what his name means (compare God as οὐρανοῦχος in SibOr 8:430). The word is sometimes used as an adjective which can describe more than one angel: the angels who preside over the punishments in hell. In the Apocalypse of Peter it seems to be the proper name of a single angel.

Temelouchos is more problematic. But since in chapter 34 of the Apocalypse of Paul he wields a three-pronged fork, surely modelled on the trident of the Greek god Poseidon, Rosenstiehl convincingly argues that his name must derive from an epithet which was occasionally used of Poseidon: θεμελιοῦχος ('in charge of the foundation'). He also conjectures, plausibly, that originally Tartarouchos and Themeliouchos (Temelouchos) corresponded respectively to Pluto, the god of the underworld, and Poseidon, the god of the ocean. They were used in Jewish apocalyptic to designate respectively the angelic ruler of the subterranean underworld—Hades or Tartarus—and the angelic ruler of the submarine abyss. As the underworld and the abyss coalesced in the concept of hell, they became two of the angels of hell, and Temelouchos, whose name was no longer understood, became rather redundant, appeared less often and was sometimes replaced by Tartarouchos.

In the Apocalypse of Peter and also the Apocalypse of Paul (40)—the latter probably dependent not on the Apocalypse of Peter itself, but on a common source—Temelouchos has a special role, not as an angel responsible for the punishments of the wicked in hell, but as the angel to whose care the children who are victims of infanticide are delivered. When Clement of Alexandria (*Eclog.* 48) and Methodius (*Symp.* 2.6) allude to this passage of the Apocalypse of Peter, they spell the word with a long ē: τημελοῦχος, which associates it with the verb τημελέω, 'to care for, to look after.' Methodius in fact uses it as an adjective applied to more than one angel who look after aborted infants. This seems to be a case of a word whose real derivation had been forgotten, being given a new derivation which was highly appropriate to the role Temelouchos plays in chapter 8 of the Apocalypse of Peter. Rosenstiehl thinks it was Clement, who, in the interests of giving the word this meaning, changed Τεμελοῦχος into Τημελοῦχος. But since Methodius, who also uses this form, seems dependent on the Apocalypse of Peter independently of Clement, it is more likely that the spelling Τημελοῦχος is original to the Greek text of the

---

[72] J.-M. Rosenstiehl, 'Tartarouchos-Temelouchos: Contribution à l'étude de l'Apocalypse apocryphe de Paul,' in *Deuxième Journée d'Etudes Coptes: Strasbourg 25 Mai 1984* (Cahiers de la Bibliothèque Copte 3; Louvain/Paris: Peeters, 1986) 29-56.

Apocalypse of Peter. This would help to explain the abruptness of the text which simply says that the children will be given to the angel Temelouchos, with no indication of the purpose for which they are given to him. If his name itself implied his role as one who looks after these infants, explanation was not needed. So it may be that already in the Apocalypse of Peter any other role for the angel Temelouchos has been forgotten: his name is understood to give him this special role of taking care of those who died in infancy.

In addition to the four named angels, there are also four references to unnamed angels of judgment. (a) In 6:6, 'the angels of God' prepare for the wicked 'a place where they will be punished forever, each one according to his guilt': this means that they prepare hell with its variety of punishments for each specific sin. (b) In 7:4, 'angels of punishment' (A23 has ἄγγελοι βασανισταί, but cf. also A21: οἱ κολάζοντες ἄγγελοι) ignite the fire in which a particular group of the damned are punished. This term is also used in the Parables of Enoch (1 En 53:3; 56:1; 62:11; 63:1) for the angels who punish the wicked in hell (cf. also *De universo* 1; GkApMary [James §23]). (c) In 9:2 a group of the damned are scourged by a 'spirit of wrath.' Here 'spirit,' as commonly in early Jewish literature, means an angel, and the wrath is God's: the angel's function is be the agent of God's wrath punishing the sinner.

(d) Finally, and more problematically, in 10:2 the Ethiopic refers to 'demons.' The damned here are being punished by throwing themselves headlong from a precipice, and then forced by 'demons' to return and to repeat the exercise, and so on eternally. The reference to 'demons' is problematic because only in much later Christian literature do the demons become the agents of punishment in hell. In Jewish and early Christian apocalyptic literature, the agents of punishment in hell are righteous angels, who obey God's will in carrying out his judgment on sinners. They may be described as 'merciless' (e.g. 2 En 10:3; cf. TAbr 12:10) and of horrifying appearance (ApZeph 4:2-4), but this is not because they are evil, but because they carry out divine justice in all its unqualified rigour. So we must suspect the originality of the reference to 'demons' in the Ethiopic of 10:2. Fortunately, this is a rare case where the Akhmim text probably preserves the original wording which has been lost in the Ethiopic translation: it refers to the agents of punishment here as 'those set over [them]' (τῶν ἐπικειμένων). This is a standard way of referring to angels put in charge of something by God (cf. 4:9: 'God has set [Uriel] over the resurrection of the dead'; and especially TIsaac 5:28, which describes Temelouchos [Sah.: Abdemerouchos; Boh.: Abtelmolouchos] as 'in charge of the punishments'; cf. also GkApMary

[James §15]). In 10:2 the reference is to the angels in charge of this particular punishment.

Thus the general picture that emerges is that two named angels—Ezrael and Tartarouchos—are in overall charge of hell and its inhabitants, while numerous subordinate angels of punishment take charge of the specific punishments of specific groups of the damned. However, this picture is not at all systematically presented: it emerges from incidental and sporadic references to the various angels of judgment. The roles of angels in hell were no doubt an assumed feature of the traditions taken over by the Apocalypse of Peter. The use of divergent traditions may account for the ambiguity as to whether it is Ezrael or Tartarouchos (whose name ought to mean that he is in overall charge of hell) who is *the* angel in charge of hell.

The function of the references to the angels, within the general theme of judgment, is that, as angels of God, they make it clear that what the wicked suffer in hell is God's judgment.

9 *Those who did not believe they would be punished after death*

This is a theme which appears twice in chapter 7. About one category of sinners being punished in hell, as it happens the adulterers, this is said: 'They will say to each other, "We did not know that we had to come into eternal punishment"' (7:8). The same theme—or a similar theme—is repeated with reference to the next category of sinners, the murderers, who say to each other, "God's sentence was just and right, because we heard that we would come to this eternal place of punishment, but we did not believe it" (7:11).[73]

The adulterers say they did not know they would be punished after death. The murderers say they heard but did not believe they would be punished after death. The meaning is most likely much the same in both cases. The adulterers no doubt had the opportunity to know that adultery will be punished in hell, but they would not listen and therefore did not know. The murderers were told their crimes would incur punishment in hell, but they did not believe it. The attachment of this theme to these particular categories of sinners is probably arbitrary. They are taken as representative of any sinners in hell. This is confirmed in chapter 13, where all the sinners in hell voice the same idea: 'Have mercy on us, for now we know the judgment of God, which he told us beforehand, and we did not believe [it]' (13:4).

The idea that the wicked do not believe that there will be retribution after death, with the implication that if they did they would not

---

[73] Translation adapted from Buchholz, *Your eyes*, 203.

sin, is again a traditional topos. In 4 Ezra 7:126, Ezra, who is there identifying himself as one of the damned, says: 'While we lived and committed iniquity we did not consider that we should suffer after our death.' 2 Clement 10:4 says of those who prefer the iniquitous pleasures of the present to the promises of the future: 'For they do not know how great torment the pleasures of the present entail, and what is the joy of the promised future.'[74] We could also recall the long passage in chapter 2 of the book of Wisdom about the attitude of the wicked who think this life is all there is and therefore indulge in wickedness: we are not specifically told that they disbelieved in punishment after death, but we are told that they did not expect the righteous to be rewarded after death (2:22) and the correlative fate of the wicked is certainly implied. As a literary motif, it is likely that this idea derives originally from Proverbs 24:12, which says, in effect, that it is no use the wicked saying, 'Look, we did not know this,' for God knows the heart and repays each according to his deed. When this judgment according to deeds is interpreted as post-mortem judgment, then the words of the wicked can be given the interpretation we find in the texts we have just cited. It is noteworthy that the motif of the wicked not believing there will be retribution is closely associated in the Apocalypse of Peter with the theme of judgment according to each one's deeds (13:3-6).

Where the Apocalypse of Peter differs from the parallels we have cited is in putting this view in the mouths of the wicked when they are actually suffering in hell the punishment they did not expect during their lifetimes. The motif, of course, serves to give a strong paraenetic thrust to the portrayal of retribution in hell: it warns those who may be sceptical about the afterlife of the foolish risk they are running and it makes clear the moral function of teaching about post-mortem punishments: to deter people from sin.

This repeated motif in the Apocalypse of Peter—which it may well have taken over from traditional apocalyptic portrayals of hell—raises the interesting question of the extent of popular scepticism about judgment after death. It would be a mistake to focus this question exclusively on the Palestinian Jewish context in which the Apocalypse of Peter originated, since in this respect as in many others that context was not isolated from the whole Mediterranean world. Belief in retribution after death was a common feature of Jewish and pagan religions. Images of reward and punishment after death were among those religious ideas which passed quite easily from one religious context to another. The notion that a belief in retribution after death

---

[74] Cf. also 2 Clem 17:5; Theophilus, *Ad Autol.* 1.14; *Kerygma Petrou*, fragments 3, 4.

was morally necessary in order to deter people from evil was wide-spread.[75] Scepticism about such retribution no doubt also crossed specific religious and cultural boundaries.

Franz Cumont (in his book on the *After Life in Roman Paganism*) argues that belief in retribution after death had been very seriously weakened by the period of the late republic and early empire, not only among intellectuals but also among the populace at large.[76] But his case is at least somewhat exaggerated. He is able to quote Roman writers who claim that noone is any longer childish enough to believe the traditional pictures of Hades and Tartarus. 'That there are Manes,' says Juvenal (for example), 'a subterranean kingdom, a ferry-man armed with a pole, and black frogs in the gulfs of the Styx, that so many thousands of people can cross the dark water in a single boat'—these are fables only small children believe (*Sat.* 2.149-152). But the waning credibility of the traditional pictures of the under-world does not necessarily imply that people had ceased to believe in post-mortem retribution as such. Platonists, for example, while partly demythologizing the images, were strongly insisting on the reality of reward and punishment after death, as Plutarch does, by way of refuting the Epicureans (especially in *De sera*).[77]

However, to mention the Epicureans is to remember the availabil-ity of eschatological scepticism through the popularization of Epicu-rean views.[78] The Epicureans denied any kind of survival after death, and saw this as a liberating truth, delivering people from the fear of retribution in the next life. Their scornful attacks on the stories of punishment in Hades were wellknown. Of course, serious Epicurean philosophers did not regard this teaching as a licence for immorality, but those who upheld the common view of the need for supernatural deterrence treated the Epicureans as providing such licence and so did a kind of vulgar Epicureanism of the 'eat, drink and be merry, for tomorrow we die' character. The most interesting evidence for the spread of the Epicurean denial of post-mortem retribution among ordinary people comes from epitaphs: not only many which declare death to be the end of existence, but also those which go out of their

---

[75] Cf. H. D. Betz, 'The Problem of Apocalyptic Genre in Greek and Hellenistic Literature: The Case of the Oracle of Trophonius,' in D. Hellholm ed., *Apocalypticism in the Mediterranean World and the Near East* (Tübingen: Mohr [Siebeck], 1983) 595.

[76] F. Cumont, *After Life in Roman Paganism* (New Haven: Yale University Press, 1922) 17-18, 83-84. He rather underplays the contrary evidence he cites on pp. 84-87.

[77] Betz, 'The Problem of Apocalyptic Genre,' 593-595; H. D. Betz ed., *Plutarch's Theological Writings and Early Christian Literature* (SCHNT 3; Leiden: Brill, 1975) 181-182.

[78] Cumont, *After Life*, 7-12.

way to say that their authors die without fear because they are not
taken in by the fables about the next life: 'I do not let myself be taken
in by the Tityi and the Tantali whom some represent in Hades'[79]
(Tityus and Tantalus were subjected to specific well-known punishments in Hades and by this time often treated as representative cases
of retribution after death), or 'There is no boat of Hades, no ferryman
Charon, no Aeacus as doorkeeper, no dog Cerberus. All we, whom
death sends down to the earth, become bones and ashes and no
more.'[80]

Of course, not all scepticism about the afterlife need be Epicurean
in origin. But the widely known Epicurean position—or at least a
caricature of it—provided an available category both for those inclined to be sceptical to identify with and for those wishing to counter
such scepticism to oppose. Jewish scepticism about judgment after
death never speaks to us with its own voice in the extant literature:[81]
its expression is always attributed to it by its opponents, who sometimes at least cast it in Epicurean terms. The sinners whose attitudes
are described in detail in the early chapters of Wisdom are certainly
cast in the popular image of Epicureanism: they regard death as the
end of existence and see this belief as leaving them free to live as
wickedly as they choose.

More immediately relevant to the Apocalypse of Peter, if we are
right to locate it in Palestine, is a tradition that occurs in the Palestinian Targums.[82] Such traditions are, of course, very difficult to date,
but this one has been quite plausibly argued to go back to our
period.[83] It occurs at Genesis 4:8 and describes a dispute between
Cain and Abel following the acceptance of Abel's sacrifice and the
rejection of Cain's. Cain takes this as evidence that the world is not
governed justly, i.e. good deeds are not rewarded as they should be.
But the denial of providential justice is then extended to a denial of
eschatological justice in another world. Cain says:

> There is no judgment, there is no Judge,
> there is no other world,

---

[79] Cumont, *After Life*, 9.
[80] Cumont, *After Life*, 10.
[81] A possible exception is the inscription on the tomb of Jason, probably a
Sadducean aristocrat, in Jerusalem: see M. Hengel, *Judaism and Hellenism*, vol. 1
(London: SCM Press, 1974) 124.
[82] On this tradition, see J. H. Neyrey, *The Form and Background of the Polemic in 2 Peter*
(unpublished diss., Yale University, 1977) 221-230 (references to extensive further
literature: 221-222 n.18); Bauckham, *Jude, 2 Peter*, 79-80.
[83] G. Vermes, *Post-Biblical Jewish Studies* (SJLA 8; Leiden: Brill, 1975) 116; S.
Isenberg, 'An Anti-Sadducee Polemic in the Palestinian Targum Tradition,' *HTR* 63
(1970) 433-444.

there is no gift of good reward for the just
and no punishment for the wicked.

Abel's reply affirms that there is each of these things.

There has been discussion of whether Cain is here represented as a Sadducee or as an Epicurean.[84] A decision is perhaps not really necessary, for opponents of the Sadducees would very likely have associated the Sadducees' denial of reward and punishment after death with the Epicurean position. The tradition is not just polemic against Sadducees by attributing their views to Cain. By representing Cain the archetypal sinner as denying eschatological judgment, it condemns all eschatological scepticism as antinomian. Similarly, when the term *'appīqōrōs* became a rabbinic term for those who live dissolutely and deny reward and punishment after death,[85] the usage need not imply that the people so categorized were professed followers of Epicurus, though some may have been. It simply means that Epicurus was popularly conceived as representing the association between eschatological scepticism and licence for immorality.

So the motif we are considering in the Apocalypse of Peter belongs to a tradition of considering retribution after death as a necessary deterrent to scare people into avoiding evil. It asserts this tradition in the face of current scepticism about eschatological judgment, which is not very likely at this date to have been Sadducean in inspiration but may in part at least have been influenced by vulgar Epicureanism. It hardly needs a philosophical influence for those intent on disregarding current standards of morality to ignore and scoff at religious doctrines of judgment after death. But awareness that there was a popular philosophical position that could justify such attitudes may well have helped. It is likely that scepticism about judgment after death made fewer inroads into Palestinian Jewish culture than into some others, but the evidence shows that Jewish Palestine was certainly not immune from wider currents of Mediterranean culture, in this as in other respects.

10 *No more time for repentance*

The motif we have just considered is linked, on its last occurrence, with a plea for mercy by the damned: 'Have mercy on us, for now we have learned the judgment of God, which he told us beforehand, and

---

[84] Cf. Neyrey, *The Form and Background*, 226-230.

[85] Neyrey, *The Form and Background*, 234-237; cf. M. Hengel, *The 'Hellenization' of Judaea in the First Century after Christ* (London: SCM Press/Philadelphia: Trinity Press International, 1989) 32.

we did not believe [it]' (13:4). But the plea for mercy is rejected: 'The angel Tartarouchos will come and rebuke them with punishment increasingly, saying to them, "Now you repent, when there is no time for repentance, and life is past"' (13:5).[86]

Although I do not know another instance where the unavailability of repentance after the judgment is dramatized in this way, the idea that the opportunity for repentance is available only in this life is a common one. In connexion with the theme of final judgment it is found especially in the Jewish apocalypses contemporary with the Apocalypse of Peter: 2 Baruch and 4 Ezra. 2 Baruch 85:12 is a verse which piles up phrases to express the finality of the last judgment: not only does the list begin, 'there will not be an opportunity to repent anymore,' it also repeats the point later in the list: 'nor opportunity of repentance.' 4 Ezra 7:82 says of the spirits of the wicked in the intermediate state after death, when their final fate at the last judgment is already sealed, that one of the causes of their grief will be that 'they cannot now make a good repentance that they may live.'

The idea that after the judgment it is too late to repent is closely connected in the literature with the conviction that at the last judgment there can no longer be mercy, only strict justice, and that there can be no intercession of one person for another.[87] This complex of ideas is rooted in the sense that the last judgment is the moment when the truth of each person's life is finally exposed and given what is due to it in justice. This moment of eschatological truth must seal a person's destiny with finality.

As we shall see, the Apocalypse of Peter in chapter 14 introduces a major qualification of this absolute finality of the judgment. But this does not alter the fact that the tradition used in 13:4-5 was designed to express it.

11 *The damned acknowledge God's justice*

Following Tartarouchos's merciless rebuttal of their plea for mercy, the damned acknowledge the justice of the punishments they suffer: 'And all of them will say, "Righteous (is) the judgment of God ... For we have been paid back, each according to our deed"' (13:6). Actually this theme was already anticipated in 7:11, where those suffering punishment for murder say to one another: 'Justice and righteousness (are) the judgment of God.'

---

[86] Translation adapted from Buchholz, *Your eyes*, 227.
[87] Cf. M. E. Stone, *Fourth Ezra* (Hermeneia; Minneapolis: Fortress Press, 1990) 150 and n.41.

This is a traditional theme. For example, in one of the medieval Hebrew visions of hell which certainly preserve ancient traditions, the wicked, receiving punishment, 'acknowledge the justice of their punishment and say: "Thou hast rightly sentenced us and rightly judged us. With thee is righteousness and with us shame, as it is with us today."'[88] Or in 1 Enoch 63:8-9, the kings who have been the oppressors of the righteous, having, like the damned in the Apocalypse of Peter, begged for mercy and been denied it, then acknowledge the justice of God's condemnation of them.

The function of this theme, of course, is to provide the final confirmation of the justice of the punishments in hell.

12 Mercy for the damned

The most remarkable aspect of the Apocalypse of Peter's treatment of the destiny of the wicked comes only after all the themes we have so far considered. After their plea for mercy has been rejected, apparently definitively, by Tartarouchos and the justice and finality of their punishment confirmed (13:4-6), the prospect of their salvation from hell is introduced at the beginning of chapter 14. Since the meaning is obscured in the Ethiopic, we are very fortunate that at this point we have access to the original Greek in the Rainer fragment:

> Then I will grant to my called and elect ones whomsoever they request from me, out of the punishment. And I will give them [i.e. those for whom the elect pray] a fine (καλόν) baptism in salvation from the Acherousian Lake (which is, they say, in the Elysian field), a portion of righteousness with my holy ones (14:1, translating the text as corrected by M. R. James and confirmed by SibOr 2:330-338).

Thus, those of the damned for whom the righteous intercede are delivered from hell and admitted to paradise. It is Christ who effects this release of the damned from hell, because he is the eschatological judge who has condemned them to hell.

This theme of the mercy of the righteous for the damned is not an afterthought. In fact the whole account of the judgment is framed by two references to this theme: first in chapter 3, secondly in chapter 14. In chapter 3 it is Peter himself who pleads for mercy for the damned, when he sees their suffering in the vision of judgment given him by Christ. His plea is then rejected by Christ. But when the

---

[88] Gaster, 'Hebrew Visions of Hell and Paradise,' 22; cf. also G. W. Buchanan, *Revelation and Redemption: Jewish Documents of Deliverance from the Fall of Jerusalem to the Death of Nahmanides* (Dillsboro, North Carolina: Western North Carolina Press, 1978) 545.

righteous intercede for the wicked after the last judgment, in chapter 14, Christ grants their prayers. We shall see that this contrast makes sense precisely because the lengthy account of judgment intervenes between the two occurrences of the theme of mercy.

Chapter 3 employs a theme which recurs in many of the apocalypses which deal with hell: that the righteous when confronted with the suffering of the wicked in hell will be moved to compassion.[89] The point is strongly expressed: the disciples 'saw how the sinners will weep in great affliction and sorrow, until all who saw (it) with their eyes weep, whether the righteous or the angels or even himself [Christ]' (3:3). Peter's expression of compassion—'It would have been better for them if they had never been created' (3:4)—was traditional in such a context in the apocalypses (cf. especially 2 En 41:2; 4 Ezra 7:62-64, 116-117; cf. 4:12), but he is able to call it 'your [Christ's] word concerning these sinners' (3:4), because it occurs in the Gospel saying about Judas (Matt 26:24). In spite of this attempt to ascribe this expression of compassion to Jesus Christ himself, Peter is then rather severely rebuked by Christ, who criticizes the expression as opposition to God (3:5). The point is that Peter seems to be implying that if God were truly compassionate he would not have created those who will be damned. But Peter cannot be more compassionate towards God's creation than the Creator himself is (3:6). This response to a plea for mercy to the damned is also found elsewhere (4 Ezra 5:33; 8:47; ApPaul 33; 40). It is possible that the Apocalypse of Peter is here dependent on 4 Ezra, but also possible that both works draw on common tradition. But most important is the way Christ concludes the dialogue: 'When you saw the lament which will be for sinners in the last days, on account of this your heart became sad. But those who have done wrong against the Most High, I will show you their works' (3:7).

Peter's compassion is rejected at this stage because it is cheap. It takes no account of the demands of justice. The chapters which follow (4-13), with their account of the judgment itself and the punishment of each sinner specifically for his or her particular sin, are designed to demonstrate to Peter that hell is required by God's justice. Only when this has been made abundantly clear, by means of a whole series of traditional themes, can mercy be allowed a voice which does not detract from justice. There can be no suggestion that the wicked do not deserve hell or that they themselves can secure

---

[89] Cf. R. Bauckham, 'The Conflict of Justice and Mercy: Attitudes to the Damned in Apocalyptic Literature,' *Apocrypha* 1 (1990) 181-196 = chapter 6 above.

their release from it by repentance. The claims of justice must therefore be vindicated and admitted even by the damned themselves before those claims can be waived at the impulse of compassion. This is why chapter 13 insists on the irrevocable finality of the judgment immediately before chapter 14 revokes it.

But we have still to understand why it is in response to the prayers of the righteous that the damned are released from hell. After all, according to the vision of 3:3, Christ himself weeps to see the suffering of the damned, so that we should expect his release of the damned to spring from his own compassion and not be simply a concession to the righteous. The key to this issue is to appreciate that the justice of hell is a justice owed to the righteous, because they have been the victims of the wicked. This can be seen in those descriptions of punishments where it is said that the victims of the crimes in question are brought to see the punishment of those who have injured them: the victims of murder see the murderers being punished (7:10), aborted children not only see but are actually instruments of their mothers' punishment (8:3-4), and victims of infanticide condemn their parents (8:5-7). More generally, in 13:2 the righteous view the just punishment of the wicked. We should also remember the overriding context of persecution, so that especially in the author's mind is the justice due to the martyrs against those who have persecuted and betrayed them (cf. 9:2-4). But if the punishment of the wicked is in this sense owed to their victims, it can be remitted only if the victims themselves request mercy for their oppressors. Noone else has the right to forgive oppressors, but those whom they have oppressed do have this right. So if it is for his people's sake that Christ must judge their enemies, for his people's sake he can save those for whom they desire mercy.

It may be surprising to discover that this idea must have entered Jewish apocalyptic from the Greek Hades. In the Greek underworld, the Acherusian lake, into which the river Acheron, one of the four rivers of Hades, flows, is not in the Elysian fields (paradise), where the Apocalypse of Peter apparently locates it, but is a place of purificatory punishment in Hades. According to Plato (*Phaedo* 114), a certain class of sinners, who have committed crimes but are curable, must spend a year in Tartarus and are then brought to the Acherusian lake. But they cannot leave the lake until they persuade those they have killed or injured to let them out. If they fail to obtain the forgiveness of their victims, they must return to Tartarus and suffer further, until at last their victims permit their release from punishment. The major difference between this concept and that in the Apocalypse of Peter is Plato's notion of purificatory punishment after death. For the Apocalypse of Peter punishment is purely retributive: the wicked cannot escape hell because the punishment has purged them of their sin, but the punishment can be remitted through the sheer mercy of their victims. (This also distinguishes the Apocalypse of Peter from Origenist universalism, which interpreted hell according to the Platonic idea of purificatory punishment.) But Plato's picture does share with the Apocalypse of Peter the idea that the victims of injustice should have a say in the punishment or release of the perpetrators of injustice, and it must be the ultimate source of the tradition the Apocalypse of Peter takes up.

It may be the fact that the Acherusian lake has been dissociated from any idea of purificatory *punishment,* and assimilated instead to the Jewish and Christian idea of purificatory batheing in water (it is also a means of purification after death, though not for those condemned to hell, in ApMos 37:3; ApPaul 22-23), that accounts for its location, in the Apocalypse of Peter, in the 'Elysian field.' Just as the latter no doubt functions as a Greek name for the Jewish paradise, so the Acherusian lake is perhaps identified with the water of life, a traditional feature of the Jewish paradise.[90]

Finally, although the text provides no explicit basis for this, it is tempting to think that the idea of the salvation of the damned by the intercession of the righteous appealed to the author of the Apocalypse of Peter because of its congruence with the Christian tradition of praying for enemies and persecutors (Matt 5:44). If the martyrs, instead of predicting their persecutors' punishment in hell (4 Macc 10:11; 12:12; cf. 1 En 47:1-4), prayed for their forgiveness (Acts 7:60), surely (it could have been thought) they will do so all the more when their erstwhile persecutors beg their forgiveness and intercession on the day of judgment. In fact, precisely this argument is reported by Augustine as the view of some of those 'merciful' Christians who were probably influenced by the Apocalypse of Peter *(De civ. Dei* 21.18).[91]

IV THE DESTINY OF THE ELECT

In the central section on the eschatological judgment (chapters 3-14), the focus is on the fate of the wicked and the destiny of the elect is only briefly mentioned (3:2; 6:4; 13:1; 14:2-3). A full treatment of the latter is reserved for the third main section of the apocalypse: the

---

[90] One wonders whether this baptism of the dead after the Last Judgment has any connexion with the ritual 'baptism on behalf of the dead' to which 1 Cor 15:29 refers.

[91] See chapter 7 above.

series of revelations which are given to Peter and the disciples on mount Zion in chapters 15-17. But, in order fully to understand chapters 15-17, we need first to return to the question of the historical context in which the Apocalypse of Peter was written and to explore an aspect of this context which we have not yet considered.

1 *The* Birkat ha-Mînîm

The major aspect of the historical context of the Apocalypse of Peter which we have so far considered is the Bar Kokhba revolt. But another significant factor which must have considerably affected the relationship between Palestinian Jewish Christians and their fellow-Jews already before the Bar Kokhba revolt was the so-called *birkat ha-mînîm* ('the benediction of the *mînîm*,' i.e. the benediction [of God] for cursing the *mînîm* [heretics or sectarians]). This is the twelfth benediction of the daily *ʿAmidah* or Eighteen Benedictions. In the version known from the Cairo Genizah manuscripts it reads:

> For the apostates *(mĕšummadîm)* let there be no hope, and uproot the kingdom of arrogance *(malkūt zadôn)*, speedily and in our days.
> May the Nazarenes *(nôṣĕrîm)* and the sectarians *(mînîm)* perish as in a moment.
> Let them be blotted out of the book of life, and not be written together with the righteous [Ps 69:28].
> You are praised, O Lord, who subdues the arrogant *(zedîm)*.

As we shall see, it cannot be taken for granted that this text of the *birkat ha-mînîm* goes back to our period.

The *birkat ha-mînîm* and its significance for the split between Judaism and Christianity has been a subject of quite extensive recent discussion,[92] the details of which we cannot enter here. For our purposes the following points will indicate its significance for the context of the Apocalypse of Peter:

---

[92] My account is indebted to the following: P. Schäfer, 'Die sogenannte Synod von Jabne: Zur Trennung von Juden und Christen im ersten/zweiten Jh. n. Chr.,' *Judaica* 31 (1975) 54-64; R. Kimelman, '*Birkat Ha-Minim* and the Lack of Evidence for an Anti-Christian Jewish Prayer in Late Antiquity,' in E. P. Sanders and A. I. Baumgarten ed., *Jewish and Christian Self-Definition*, vol. 2: *Aspects of Judaism in the Graeco-Roman Period* (London: SCM Press, 1981) 226-244; W. Horbury, 'The Benediction of the Minim and the Early Jewish-Christian Controversy,' *JTS* 33 (1982) 19-61; S. T. Katz, 'Issues in the Separation of Judaism and Christianity after 70 c.e.: A Reconsideration,' *JBL* 103 (1984) 43-76; R. A. Pritz, *Nazarene Jewish Christianity* (SPB 37; Jerusalem: Magnes Press/Leiden: Brill, 1988) 102-107; P. S. Alexander, '"The Parting of the Ways" from the Perspective of Rabbinic Judaism,' in J. D. G. Dunn ed., *Jews and Christians: The Parting of the Ways A.D. 70 to 135* (WUNT 66; Tübingen: Mohr [Siebeck], 1993) 1-25.

(1) According to two different traditions in the Babylonian Talmud (b. Ber. 28b-29a) and the Palestinian Talmud (y. Ber. 4:3 [8a]), the *birkat ha-mînîm* was added to the *'Amidah* by the rabbis at Yavneh in the late first century C.E. Only the bavli tradition connects this with a rabbinic editing of the *'Amidah* as a whole ('Shim'on ha-Paqoli arranged the Eighteen Benedictions in order'). The use of the *birkat ha-mînîm* in the second century is confirmed by Justin's references to Jews cursing Christians in synagogue (*Dial.* 16; 96).

(2) In this period the *wording* of the *'Amidah* was not fixed. What the rabbis must have prescribed was that there should be a cursing of *mînîm* in one of the benedictions, not an obligatory form of words for cursing *mînîm*. Thus none of the varied formulations of the *birkat ha-mînîm* which we have in later liturgical texts can be taken as the authoritative text of our period. Some may represent forms of wording which go back to our period, but they have to be treated with great caution as evidence for the precise content of the *birkat ha-mînîm* in our period.

(3) The institution and promotion of the *birkat ha-mînîm* by the rabbis should be seen as an attempt to establish *rabbinic* Judaism as orthodox Judaism in the synagogues. The aim was to exclude all forms of non-rabbinic Judaism from the synagogues. This aim was not accomplished quickly. The mere institution of the *birkat ha-mînîm* at Yavneh would certainly not in itself have secured its widespread use. Its introduction into synagogue worship must have been part of the slow process—continuing throughout the second century—by which rabbinic Judaism made itself normative Judaism in Palestine.[93]

(4) The *mînîm* envisaged in the benediction are all forms of non-rabbinic Judaism, which the rabbis wished to label sectarian and to exclude from the synagogue. The term does not refer exclusively to Jewish Christians, but includes them. (Whether it also refers to Gentile Christians, as Justin seems to assume, is more debatable, but need not concern us here.) However, it is probable that in many parts of Palestine Christians would be the principal target of the *birkat ha-mînîm*. Jewish Christianity was rabbinic Judaism's major rival in its attempt to win Palestinian Jews to its own interpretation of Judaism. Thus it is quite possible that in particular places the usefulness of the

---

[93] Cf. M. Goodman, *State and Society in Roman Galilee, A.D. 132-212* (Oxford Centre for Postgraduate Hebrew Studies Series; Totowa, New Jersey: Rowan and Allanheld, 1983) 93-118, 178-181.

birkat ha-mînîm as an instrument for excluding Jewish Christians from the synagogue was sharpened by specific reference to Nazarenes *(nôṣĕrîm)* in the words of the benediction. Some extant texts of the *birkat ha-mînîm* include the word *nôṣĕrîm*, and the evidence of Jerome and Epiphanius suggests that by the fourth century explicit reference to the *nôṣĕrîm* was common.

(5) In texts of the twelfth benediction, the cursing of the *mînîm* is remarkably closely linked with prayer for the downfall of 'the kingdom of arrogance,'[94] i.e. the Gentile oppressors of God's people, the Roman empire. Although rabbinic tradition consistently refers to this benediction as that of the mînîm, it has been fairly pointed out that in the extant texts it is aimed just as much against 'the kingdom of arrogance' as it is against Jewish apostates and sectarians. The explanation for this feature is debated. It has been suggested that the rabbis at Yavneh added the curse on the *mînîm* to an already existing prayer against the Gentile enemies of Israel, or that the *birkat ha-mînîm* was originally a distinct benediction, later combined with another on the 'the kingdom of arrogance.' Most likely, the twelfth benediction is conceived as a prayer for the judgment of all the enemies of Israel, including both Jewish sectarians and Gentile oppressors. The aim of excluding the *mînîm* from the religious community would have been aided by associating them with the Roman oppressors.

(6) We should note the nationalistic and eschatological thrust of the whole *'Amidah*. God is the 'God of our fathers, God of Abraham, God of Isaac, and God of Jacob,' who will soon restore Jewish national sovereignty, Jerusalem and the Temple. It is in this context that the mînîm are to perish along with the Gentile oppressors, and are to be excluded from the eschatological people of God who will inherit the promises. Appropriately, the Genizah text quotes Psalm 69:28: 'Let them be blotted out of the book of life, and not be written together with the righteous.' It is in agreement with the implications of this that rabbinic tradition places the *mînîm* in Gehenna (t. Sanh. 13:5; ExodRab 19:4).

(7) The effect of the *birkat ha-mînîm* on Jewish Christians in Palestine in the early second century will no doubt have varied. In many synagogues it will not yet have been in use. But where it was used its effect will have been serious. Where *mînîm* were understood as those who did not accept rabbinic halakhah or where *nôṣĕrîm* were perhaps even

---

[94] With this term for Rome, cf. 4 Ezra 11:43.

specifically named in the benediction, then the *birkat ha-mînîm* will have effectively excluded Jewish Christians from the religious community defined by the synagogue.

Thus, as well as the Apocalypse of Peter's specific context in the Bar Kokhba revolt, in which Christians were suffering for their refusal to accept Bar Kokhba as Messiah and to participate in the revolt, we have to reckon also with the broader context of the rabbinic attempt to exclude Jewish Christians from the religious community of Israel. The former context no doubt exacerbated the latter and brought to a head the developing crisis of Jewish Christian identity in Palestine. Christians who were already in many places being excluded and ostracized by the success of the rabbinic attempt to establish rabbinic orthodoxy now found themselves further threatened by the wave of triumphant nationalism that supported Bar Kokhba's movement for the liberation of Jerusalem. In this context, the association of *mînîm* with the gentile oppressor in the *birkat ha-mînîm* would gain greater force: Jewish Christians who failed to support Bar Kokhba could be seen as renegades who were taking the side of 'the kingdom of arrogance' against God's people Israel. The crisis for Jewish Christians was therefore not simply the actuality and the threat of martyrdom. It was also their fellow-Jews' exclusion of them from the religious community of the people of God who would inherit the eschatological promises of God.

Thus, while, as we have seen, Bar Kokhba and his intention of rebuilding the Temple raised for the author of the Apocalypse of Peter and his readers the question of the true Messiah and the question of the true Temple, the *birkat ha-mînîm* raised the further, closely connected question of the true people of God. Are Christians excluded from the number of God's chosen ones to whom his promises to Abraham, Isaac and Jacob belong? Have their names been blotted out of the book of life in which the members of the eschatological people of God are recorded in heaven?

As a preliminary indication that the *birkat ha-mînîm* lies consciously in the background to the Apocalypse of Peter, we may note that the very first category of sinners in hell are those who 'have blasphemed the way of righteousness' (7:2). 'The way of righteousness' is here a designation for Christianity, considered as a way of life (as in 2 Pet 2:21; Barn 5:4). Those who have blasphemed it could be precisely those who pronounce the *birkat ha-mînîm*. We may note that a term for Christianity which characterizes it as an ethical way of life would be especially appropriate if what is in mind is the rabbinic accusation of *mînût* against those who did not accept rabbinic halakhah.

But it is for the Apocalypse of Peter's account of the post-mortem destiny of the righteous that the *birkat ha-mînîm* will provide the most enlightening context.

2 *The Visions on Mount Zion (15:1-17:1)*

The brief reference to the final destiny of the elect in 14:2-3 already adumbrates the main concerns of the visions which follow in chapters 15-16:

> I will go away, I and my elect ones rejoicing with the patriarchs, into my eternal kingdom. And with them I shall carry out the promises I have promised them, I and my Father who is in heaven (14:2-3: Rainer fragment).

The two points especially to notice here are that Jesus Christ's elect will inherit God's promises and that they will do so in company with the patriarchs. Thus, Jewish Christians are not disinherited from the eschatological destiny of Israel, as the *birkat ha-mînîm* pronounced them to be. The God of the patriarchs, Abraham, Isaac and Jacob, is the Father of Jesus Christ, and so Jewish Christians are assured of the glorious destiny promised by God to the patrairchs and their descendants. This theme, announced in 14:2-3, is developed at greater length and validated by visionary revelations in chapters 15-16.

A major transition in the apocalypse is marked by 15:1, where the disciples accompany Jesus to mount Zion, praying. Their prayer is the appropriate preliminary to a visionary revelation, which takes the form, first, of two men of dazzling splendour and indescribable beauty (15:2-7), whom Jesus then identifies as Moses and Elijah (16:1). The idea of an appearance of Moses and Elijah derives, of course, from the transfiguration narrative, but is here put to a use quite different from its function in the Synoptic transfiguration tradition. The account in the Apocalypse of Peter is not of a transfiguration. Jesus is not transfigured: his appearance is not mentioned and the account has, in fact, at this point no christological interest at all. (A christological concern appears only at 17:1.) But whereas the Synoptic transfiguration tradition has no interest in what Moses and Elijah looked like, for the Apocalypse of Peter this is the content of the revelation. Moses and Elijah appear in their glorious heavenly forms. The descriptions are composed of features traditional in descriptions of the appearance of heavenly beings: most can be paralleled in other such descriptions (cf., e.g., 1 En 14:20; 71:10; 106:2; 2 En 1:5; 19:1; 4 Ezra 7:97; ApAb 11:2-3; ApZeph 6:11; TAb A7:3; Rev 1:14-16; 10:1). What is notable is the relatively lengthy description, designed to convey a strong impression of the glory and beauty of the two figures. The point that they enjoy the glory of heaven is very emphatically made.

The reason for this emphasis is not clear until Peter and the disciples have been given a second revelation. Not content with this vision of the glory of Moses and Elijah, Peter asks, 'Where are Abraham and Isaac and Jacob and the other righteous fathers?' (16:1). In response to this request, the disciples are granted a revelation of paradise (16:2-3). From 16:4 it is clear that they saw the patriarchs in paradise, but the account of the revelation exclusively describes the place, not the people in it. (The editor who revised the text in the form we have it in the Akhmim version noticed this lack and supplied it: A17-19.) The inhabitants of paradise are not described because it is taken for granted that the patriarchs will have the same glorious heavenly appearance as Moses and Elijah. The elaborate description of the glory of the elect after death need not be repeated. Instead, a brief description of paradise itself is now given: a large garden, full of fragrant and very fruitful trees. Again, these features are wholly traditional (cf., e.g., 1 En 24:3-5; 32:3-4; 2 En 8:1-8; ApAb 21:6; Rev 22:2; 3 En 23:18), but the account is perhaps rather surprisingly brief. The author is evidently content briefly to evoke the well-known features of paradise, in order to make his real point: that it is in paradise that the patriarchs rest (16:4) in their heavenly glory.

The purpose of both revelations—that of the glorious appearance of Moses and Elijah and that of paradise—now becomes apparent in Jesus' words at 16:4-5: '"You have seen the patriarchs, and their rest is like this." And I rejoiced and believed that this (is) "the honour and the glory of those who are persecuted for my righteousness."'[95] The phrase 'honour and glory' may be a reminiscence of 2 Peter's transfiguration account (2 Pet 1:17), while 'those who are persecuted for my righteousness' certainly alludes to the Matthean beatitude, 'Blessed are those who are persecuted because of righteousness, for theirs is the kingdom of heaven' (Matt 5:10). This is clear from Peter's subsequent comment: 'I understood what is written in the book of my Lord Jesus Christ' (16:6). In other words, the heavenly reward for Jesus' persecuted followers, which the Gospel of Matthew specifies only as 'the kingdom of heaven,' is now more fully revealed to Peter: it is to be glorified like Moses and Elijah and to rest in paradise with the patriarchs.

---

[95] Translation adapted from Buchholz, *Your eyes*, 238.

As well as the obvious motive of providing encouragement for readers who may be faced with martyrdom for their discipleship of Jesus, the emphasis on the patriarchs is notable. Moses and Elijah, as representatives of the glorified elect, were given by the transfiguration tradition. But the author has chosen to emphasize that it is also with Abraham, Isaac and Jacob and 'the other righteous fathers' that those who are persecuted for Jesus Christ's sake will share heavenly glory. Moreover, as in 14:2-3, participation in the destiny of the patriarchs is here identified with the promise that Jesus Christ has made to his elect, i.e. with the beatitude of Matthew 5:10. This emphasis makes excellent sense against the background of the rabbinic attempt, by means of the *birkat ha-mînîm*, to exclude Jewish Christians from the religious community of Israel and its eschatological promises.

Thus, 15:2-16:6 answers the question: do Jewish Christians belong to the true people of God? As we have already seen in our section I.2, the subsequent section of the text, 16:7-17:1, goes on, by means of two further revelations—a vision of the heavenly temple and a declaration of Jesus' messiahship, to answer the related questions of the identity of the true temple and the true Messiah.

3 *The Ascension (17:2-6)*

The series of four revelations in 15:2-17:1 is completed by a fifth: Jesus' ascension into heaven. This completes the series and unites the answers to the three issues that the other four revelations have given. It does so because it reveals the true Messiah leading his people into the heavenly temple.

17:2-6 reads:

> A large, very white cloud came over our head and it lifted up our Lord and Moses and Elijah. I trembled and was terrified. And we watched and this heaven opened, and we saw men who were in the flesh. They came and went to meet our Lord and Moses and Elijah, and they went into the second heaven. And the word of scripture was fulfilled: "This generation seeks him and seeks the face of the God of Jacob." [Ps 23:6 LXX] And there was great fear and great amazement in heaven. The angels flocked together, that the word of scripture might be fulfilled, which said: "Open the gates, princes!" [Ps 23:7, 9 LXX] And then this heaven which had been opened was closed.

The cloud, of course, has been borrowed from the transfiguration narrative, and like the other elements borrowed from the transfiguration narrative in chapters 15-17 it has been given a quite different function from that in the Synoptic tradition. But, unlike the ascension narrative in Acts 1, the disciples do not just see the cloud bear Jesus (with Moses and Elijah) up into the sky. They see the heavens opened; that is, they are allowed to see into the lowest of the heavens above the firmament. The rest of the account is given in two stages, each as a fulfilment of words from Psalm 23(24). Evidently this psalm is the author's principal means of interpreting the ascension. There is other second-century evidence of the application of this psalm to the ascension (Justin, *1 Apol.* 51; *Dial.* 36; 85; Irenaeus, *Dem.* 84; *Adv. Haer.* 4.33.13), although the Apocalypse of Peter is earliest text in which the psalm is so used and the only one in which verse 6 is interpreted with reference to the ascension. Justin and Irenaeus refer only to verses 7-10.

In the first of the two stages of the account (17:3), Jesus, Moses and Elijah are joined, in the first heaven, by 'people in the flesh,' and proceed, accompanied by them, into the second heaven. These 'people in the flesh' are then identified as the people to whom Psalm 23:6 (LXX) refers. The importance of this reference lies in the fact that in the psalm the reference is to the people who are able to enter God's presence in the temple (v 3). The author of the Apocalypse of Peter has taken this to be the heavenly sanctuary, in which God dwells in the highest heaven. The 'people in the flesh' therefore join Jesus on his ascent through the heavens, in order to accompany him into the heavenly sanctuary.

Precisely what interpretation the author gave to the psalm's words, 'seeks him, and seeks the face of the God of Jacob' (cf. LXX: ζητούντων αὐτον, ζητούντων τὸ προσώπον τοῦ θεοῦ Ἰακοβ), it is impossible to be sure. He may have taken 'him' to be Jesus, so that their seeking him is shown by their meeting Jesus in the first heaven, while their seeking the God of Jacob refers to their ascent with Jesus through the heavens to God's presence in the heavenly temple. Probably it is a happy coincidence that the psalm's reference to the 'God of Jacob' continues the apocalypse's emphasis on the patriarchs.

In the second stage of the account, Jesus' ascent, with his retinue, through the heavens is greeted with fear and astonishment, and the angels gather together in order to fulfil the words of the psalm (repeated in verses 7 and 9 of Ps 23 LXX): 'Lift up the gates, you princes' (LXX: Ἄρατε πύλας οἱ ἄρχοντες ὑμῶν). Either the angels gather in order to cry out this command to the doorkeepers, who are the ἄρχοντες of the psalm, or else the angels are themselves the ἄρχοντες who hurry to open the gates. In any case, the gates are those of the heavenly sanctuary, opened in order to let 'the king of glory' enter (Ps 23:7-9).

He enters, of course, along with the 'people in the flesh.' Whereas Justin and Irenaeus, who quote only vv 7-10 of the psalm, speak only

of the angelic doorkeepers of heaven admitting Jesus the king of glory
into heaven, the author of the Apocalypse of Peter, by referring also
to verse 6 of the psalm, finds in it a depiction of Jesus' taking with him
those who are permitted to ascend to God's heavenly sanctuary. In
this way his portrayal of the ascension is able to bring together all
three themes of the earlier revelations on mount Zion: the true people
of God who will be glorified with the patriarchs (15:2-16:6), the true
temple in heaven which the Father has made for Jesus and his elect
(16:7-9), and the true Messiah Jesus (17:1). In his ascension, the Messiah takes his people with him into the heavenly temple.

But who are the 'people in the flesh' who meet Jesus in the first
heaven? They must be righteous people of the past whom Jesus in his
descent to Hades and his resurrection delivered from death. Other
second-century texts attest the view that many of the righteous dead
left Hades with Christ at his resurrection (OdesSol 42:11) and ascended to heaven with him at his ascension (AscenIs 9:17; cf. Origen,
Comm. in Rom. 5:10). According to a saying which occurs quite widely
in patristic literature, he descended alone but ascended with a great
multitude (Acts of Thaddeus, *ap.* Eusebius, *Hist. Eccl.* 1.13.20; Melito,
New frag. 2.17; Cyril of Jerusalem, *Catech. Lect.* 14.18; Ps.-Ignatius,
Trall. 9; Armenian *Acts of Callistratus* 9). Moreover, there is good evidence that originally the conception was of an actual resurrection of
dead people with Christ. Language normally reserved for bodily
resurrection is used (Ignatius, *Magn.* 9.2; Melito, *Peri Pascha* 101;
New frag. 2.12, 15; Origen, *Comm. in Rom.* 5:10; Irenaeus, frag. 26,
which connects this resurrection of the saints with Matt 27:52). So
the Apocalypse of Peter's reference to 'people in the flesh' is entirely
in line with this tradition. Presumably they are envisaged as having
risen from the dead with Christ at his resurrection, and then, during
the period of his resurrection appearances to the disciples, waiting
in the first heaven until they can ascend with him through the heavens.

These 'people in the flesh' would then be pre-Christian Jews, but
they would function in the Apocalypse of Peter as representative of
the whole of the Messiah's people whom he takes into heaven. If it is
Jesus who leads these righteous people of the past into heaven, then
Jesus' own followers in the present can be assured of the same destiny. But a problem arises as to the relation between these 'people in
the flesh' and the patriarchs whom Peter and the disciples have just
seen in paradise (16:1-4). We might have expected the latter to have
been among the righteous dead that Jesus delivered from Hades and
took with him at his ascension. We can dismiss at once the possibility
that the paradise of 16:2-3 is only their temporary abode, prior to

their ascension with Jesus to the heavenly sanctuary.[96] Such a temporary paradise, no longer (since the ascension) inhabited, would certainly not be portrayed as the destiny of the Christian martyrs (16:4-5). It is possible that 16:1-4 should be understood as a proleptic vision of the paradise which the patriarchs and the Christian elect will enter together after the last judgment (cf. 14:2-3). Alternatively, we should have to suppose that before Jesus' resurrection and ascension the patriarchs were already in paradise, but other righteous Israelites were in Sheol. Only the latter rise and ascend with Jesus. This rather anomalous view is found in the *Ascension of Isaiah,* which makes a distinction between, on the one hand, 'the holy Abel and all the righteous' (9:8; cf. 9:9, 28), who in Isaiah's time have already received their 'robes' (their heavenly bodies) and are in the seventh heaven, and, on the other hand, 'many of the righteous' (9:17), whom Christ plunders from the angel of death (9:16) at his descent into Hades and who only receive their robes when they ascend with him to the seventh heaven (9:17-18).

(We should note that in any case the Apocalypse of Peter seems to have no very consistent view about resurrection. Chapter 4 portrays all the dead, righteous and wicked, raised at the end of history prior to the last judgment. But it is only after the last judgment, in 13:1, that the righteous 'put on the garments of the life above.' Eschatological imagery is not always used consistently, especially in a work compiled from a variety of traditions, as the Apocalypse of Peter is.)

4 *Written in the Book of Life (17:7)*

The Apocalypse of Peter concludes with the statement that the disciples 'descended from the mountain, praising God who has written the names of the righteous in the book of life in heaven' (17:7). This is a highly significant statement, confirming that the major concern of the visions on mount Zion was with assuring Jewish Christians of their eschatological destiny. The 'book of life' is the heavenly register of the members of the people of God. To have one's name written in it was to be assured of a share in the eschatological future of God's people, whereas to have one's name blotted out of it was to be deprived of that share.

The image derived from the Old Testament (especially Ps 69:28, the only OT text to use the actual term 'book of life'; cf. also Exod 32:33, and, for the eschatological reference, Dan 12:1) and was com-

---

[96] In *De universo* 1, Abraham's bosom is a temporary abode for 'the fathers and the righteous' until the Last Judgment.

monly used. It was commonly said that the names of the elect were in
the book of life (JosAsen 15:4; Phil 4:3; Rev 13:8; 17:8; 20:15; 21:27)
or written in heaven (JosAs 15:4; Luke 10:20; Heb 12:23; cf. 1 En
104:1), and that the names of the wicked (wicked or apostate members of the people of God) were blotted out of the book of life (Jub
30:22; 1 En 108:3; Rev 3:5; cf. JosAsen 15:4). Thus the terminology
of Apocalypse of Peter 17:7 is not surprising. But it should be noticed
that, in referring to 'the righteous,' this text is verbally closer than any
other to Psalm 69:28 ('Let them be blotted out of *the book of life*, and
not be *written* together with *the righteous*'), suggesting that this text may
be consciously in mind and that the possibility of being blotted out of
the book of life is being deliberately countered. (Also very close to the
Apocalypse of Peter is JosAsen 15:4, which likewise rejects that possibility: 'your name was written in the book of the living in heaven...
and it will not be erased.')

Such a deliberate allusion to Psalm 69:28 may be significant when
we remember that the version of the *birkat ha-mînîm* in the Cairo
Geniza manuscripts quotes this verse against the *mînîm*. We cannot be
sure that this usage goes back to the early second century, but if it
does the conclusion of the Apocalypse of Peter could be read as a
deliberate reassurance to its readers that God will not enact that curse
against Jewish Christians.

V PETER

Our author's choice of Peter as his apostolic pseudonym is not in the
least surprising. Peter in the apocalypse takes the role of leader or
spokesman among Jesus' disciples, as he does in the Synoptic traditions generally and especially in the Gospel of Matthew, which seems
to be the only written Gospel our author used. No doubt, our author
shared the Palestinian Jewish Christian reverence for James the
Lord's brother, but the latter's role was never understood as in competition with the preeminence of Peter among the twelve. The two
were preeminent in different ways: James as the leader of the mother
church in Jerusalem, Peter as leader of the twelve in their apostolic
mission to preach the Gospel throughout the world.

Also influential in the author's choice of Peter may have been
Peter's special role in the transfiguration narrative, which the apocalypse reflects in 16:7 (Peter's proposal to construct tents for Jesus,
Moses and Elijah). But the principal passage in which traditions specifically about Peter himself feature is one we have not yet considered: 14:4-6. These verses are really an appendix to the second major
part of the apocalypse (chapters 3-14). With the words, 'I have told

you, Peter, and I have informed you' (14:3b), the revelation of the judgment which began with chapter 3 is at last concluded. But Jesus now addresses, in 14:4-6, some words of personal relevance to Peter himself. They concern his eventual martyrdom and his commission to preach the Gospel throughout the world. The inclusion of this material may be largely due to the appropriateness of these themes in a post-resurrection setting, in which the commissioning of the apostles to preach the Gospel is standard (Matt 28:16-20; Mark 16:15-18; Luke 24:47-48; Acts 1:8; EpApp 19; 30; EpPetPhil [CG VIII,2] 137:23-25; cf. TLord 1:14) and in which the Johannine tradition also knew a specific commissioning of Peter and a prophecy of his martyrdom (John 21:15-19).

For the text of this passage the Rainer fragment provides the Greek of verse 4 and five words only of verse 5, but since the Ethiopic of verse 4 is clearly very corrupt the Rainer fragment is extremely valuable here. It reads in translation:

> Go now to the city that rules over the west, and drink the cup that I have promised you, at the hands of the son of the one who is in Hades, so that his disappearance (ἀφάνεια) may receive a beginning. ⁵And you, chosen (correcting δεκτός to ἐκλεκτός) of the promise...

The Ethiopic from verse 5 onwards has:

> You have been chosen by [for?] the promise which I promised you. And send out, therefore, into all the world my story in peace, ⁶since it is full of joy. The source of my word is the promise of life, and suddenly the world will be snatched away.[97]

Unfortunately, verse 6 is probably corrupt beyond recovery. But the whole passage is of considerable interest for two reasons: its evidence and understanding of the martyrdom of Peter, and its view of Peter as the apostle to the Gentiles. It is also the only passage in the Apocalypse of Peter which looks beyond the sphere of Jewish Christianity in Palestine, and so gives us a rare glimpse of the attitude to the wider Christian mission held by second-century Palestinian Jewish Christians.

As far as Peter's martyrdom is concerned, our passage needs to be placed alongside a roughly contemporary passage in the Ascension of Isaiah, which refers to Nero as responsible for Peter's death: 'a lawless king, a matricide, who himself, this king, will persecute the plant which the twelve apostles of the Beloved have planted, and one of the twelve will be delivered into his hands' (AscenIs 4:2-3). Here the

---

[97] Translation adapted from Buchholz, *Your eyes*, 232.

reference to Nero and the Neronian persecution of the church is unequivocal, because of the term 'matricide,' which was frequently used to identify the figure of Nero without naming him (e.g. SibOr 4:121; 5:363; 8:71; cf. Philostratus, *Vit. Apoll.* 4.32). This makes it likely that Peter's martyrdom is located in Rome, but the point is not made explicitly. By contrast, in the Apocalypse of Peter the identity of Peter's murderer would not be clear unless we had other evidence to connect Peter's martyrdom with Nero, but the location of the martyrdom at Rome is unequivocal. The 'city which rules over the west' is certainly Rome.[98] The expression might actually reflect the time of writing during the Bar Kokhba war, when Rome's rule in the east (Palestine) was contested, but more probably it reflects a Palestinian sense of place, according to which the Roman empire lay to the west and the Parthian empire to the east.

These two texts, in the Ascension of Isaiah and the Apocalypse of Peter, in fact provide together the earliest unequivocal evidence of Peter's martyrdom at Rome during the reign of Nero. 1 Clement 5:4 cannot really bear the weight which has usually been placed upon it as evidence for this event,[99] and so the Ascension of Isaiah and the Apocalypse of Peter are actually much more important historical evidence for the date and place of Peter's death than has usually been realised. (Oscar Cullmann's highly influential discussion of the evidence[100] draws unwarranted conclusions from 1 Clement 5:4, plays down the significance of AscenIs 4:2-3, and takes no account at all of the Apocalypse of Peter.) Moreover, both texts, as we shall see in the case of the Apocalypse of Peter, probably preserve early tradition, in that they reflect an apocalyptic understanding of the significance of Peter's martyrdom which must have originated in the years immediately after the event.

Nero was the first Roman emperor to persecute the church, and, although the persecution was confined to Rome, it must have seemed of major significance for the whole church, especially if Peter, regarded as the leader of the apostles, was martyred during it or soon afterwards. Nero's attack on the church could easily have been seen as the Antichrist's final onslaught on the people of God. The civil

---

[98] Ignatius, *Rom.* 2.2; cf. 1 Clem 5:6-7.

[99] See R. Bauckham, 'The Martyrdom of Peter in Early Christian Literature,' in *Aufstieg und Niedergang der römischen Welt*, 2.26/1, ed. W. Haase (Berlin/New York: de Gruyter, 1992), 539-595, which contains a full discussion of all references to Peter's death in Christian literature before 200 C.E.

[100] O. Cullmann, *Peter: Disciple—Apostle—Martyr*, trans. F. V. Filson (London: SCM Press, 1953) 70-152.

wars which threatened the very survival of the empire at the time of Nero's death and later could have seemed the final internecine strife in which, according to some apocalyptic expectations, the enemies of God's people were to slaughter each other immediately before the end (e.g. Zech 14:13; 1 En 56:7; 100:1-4). A Christian apocalyptic tradition which identified Nero as the Antichrist would have been able to maintain this identification by accepting the widespread rumour that Nero had not really died and would return from hiding in the east. Some early Christian writings (Rev 17:7-14; AscenIs 4:2-14) therefore expect the Antichrist in the form of the returning Nero.

That such an identification of Nero as the Antichrist belonged to the tradition which the Apocalypse of Peter uses is suggested by the description of Nero as 'the son of the one who is in Hades' (14:4). Admittedly, the expression is a little odd. If it means that Nero is the son of the devil, this would be a quite appropriate description of the Antichrist (cf. John 8:44) and there is some later Christian evidence for the idea that Antichrist will be the son of the devil.[101] But in Jewish and Christian literature of this period, the devil is not usually located in Hades, the place of the dead. Only from the fourth century onwards does the concept of Satan as the ruler of the dead become common.[102] Perhaps a mistranslation of the Semitic idiom, 'the son of perdition' (which describes the Antichrist in 2 Thess 2:3; cf. John 17:12), lies behind our passage. Alternatively, we would have to regard it as a rare early instance of the location of the devil in Hades (along with TDan 5:11; perhaps AscenIs 1:3).

Also rather puzzling are the following words: 'so that his destruction (or disappearance) may receive a beginning.' The Ethiopic translator apparently took 'his destruction' (αὐτοῦ ἡ ἀφάνεια: literally 'his disappearance') in an active sense: 'his work of destruction.' But ἀφάνεια can scarcely bear this meaning. It must refer to God's destruction (in judgment) of the one who has put Peter to death. The antecedent of αὐτοῦ could be either τοῦ υἱοῦ (i.e. Nero) or τοῦ ἐν "Αιδου (i.e. the devil): Peter's death brings about the beginning either of Nero's destruction or of the devil's. Probably the former is meant. The Jewish martyrological idea that the death of the martyr brings down divine judgment on his persecutor and thus brings about his destruction is probably in mind.

---

[101] W. Bousset, *The Antichrist Legend*, trans. A. H. Keane (London: Hutchinson, 1896) 140.

[102] J. A. MacCulloch, *The Harrowing of Hell* (Edinburgh: T. & T. Clark, 1930) 227-234, 345-346.

The choice of the word ἀφάνεια, though it can mean simply destruction, may be more significant: it may allude to the widespread belief that Nero had not really died at all, but fled secretly to the east, where he was awaiting in hiding the moment when he would return to conquer the Roman Empire.[103] This expectation was taken up into Jewish apocalyptic in the Jewish Sibylline Oracles, where the returning Nero was identified with the eschatological adversary, and was also echoed in early Christian apocalyptic in the Ascension of Isaiah and in the book of Revelation. Allusions, in this connexion, to Nero's disappearance (at his supposed death) or invisibility during his flight to the east or sojourn in the east, are quite common (SibOr 4:120; 5:33; 5:152; John of Antioch, frag. 104; Commodian, *Carmen de duobus populis* 831; Lactantius, *De mort. pers.* 2.7). It seems to have been a stock theme of the legend of Nero's return, and so it is quite probable that ἀφάνεια in Apocalypse of Peter 14:4 alludes to it. In that case, the statement that Nero's disappearance will receive *a beginning* (ἀρχήν), may mean that Nero's supposed death, as judgment for his putting Peter to death, was only the beginning of his disappearance, because his final disappearance (destruction) will happen only when he returns as the final Antichrist and is judged by Christ at his parousia. (It is possible that the word ἀρχήν is also a play on the idea of Peter as the ἀρχή of the church, as in, e.g., NHApPet 71:19.)

A later passage which spells out the ideas to which Apocalypse of Peter 14:4 briefly alludes is Lactantius, *De mortibus persecutorum* 2.5-8:

It was when Nero was already emperor that Peter arrived in Rome; after performing various miracles—which he did through the excellence of God Himself, since the power had been granted to him by God—he converted many to righteousness and established a faithful and steadfast temple to God. This was reported to Nero; and when he noticed that not only at Rome but everywhere great numbers of people were daily abandoning the worship of idols and condemning the practice of the past by coming over to the new religion, Nero, abominable and criminal tyrant that he was, leapt into action to overturn the heavenly temple and to abolish righteousness, and, first persecutor of the servants of God, he nailed Peter to the cross and slew Paul. For this he did not go unpunished; God took note of the way in which His people were troubled. Cast down from the pinnacle of power and hurtled from the heights, the

---

[103] On the legend of Nero's return, see R. H. Charles, *The Ascension of Isaiah* (London: A. & C. Black, 1900) lvii-lxxiii; R. H. Charles, *A Critical and Exegetical Commentary on the Revelation of St. John*, vol. 2 (ICC; Edinburgh: T. & T. Clark, 1920) 76-87; J. J. Collins, *The Sibylline Oracles of Egyptian Judaism* (SBLDS 13; Missoula, Montana: Scholars Press, 1974) 80-87; A. Yarbro Collins, *The Combat Myth in the Book of Revelation* (HDR 9; Missoula, Montana: Scholars Press, 1976) 176-183.

tyrant, powerless, suddenly disappeared; not even a place of burial was to be seen on the earth for so evil a beast. Hence some crazed men believe that he has been borne away and kept alive (for the Sibyl declares that "the matricide, though an exile, will come back from the ends of the earth" [SibOr 5:363]), so that, since he was the first persecutor, he may also be the last and herald the arrival of Antichrist...

The first sentence of this passage corresponds to the narrative in the second-century Acts of Peter, but the later part about Nero's punishment, disappearance and expected return does not correspond to anything in the extant text of the Acts of Peter. Though Lactantius was writing in the early fourth century, he frequently made use of early sources, especially of an apocalyptic character. It is notable that the passage seems to be really about Peter: the mention of Paul's martyrdom under Nero is an afterthought, quite possibly Lactantius' own addition to his source. It is credible that Lactantius is echoing an old tradition about Peter's death in Rome and the subsequent fate of Nero. Certainly he makes the same connexion between the two as is made in Apocalypse of Peter 14:4.

The idea of the return of Nero as the eschatological adversary was probably not part of the eschatological expectation of the author of the Apocalypse of Peter himself. As we have seen, he himself identified Bar Kokhba as the Antichrist, and his apocalyptic scenario in chapters 1-2 scarcely leaves room for another, Roman Antichrist. But, as we have frequently noted, most of his work is compiled from already existing traditional material. There is no difficulty in supposing that, for his prophecy of Peter's martyrdom, he took up a Christian apocalyptic tradition, similar to that in the Ascension of Isaiah,[104] which had connected Peter's martyrdom under Nero with the expectation of Nero's eschatological return.

Apocalypse of Peter 14:5 indicates that Peter's martyrdom will come at the end of a ministry of preaching the Gospel throughout the world and probably suggests that he has been chosen by Christ as the apostle to the Gentiles. The reference to the promise Christ has made to Peter is most likely an allusion to Matthew 16:18 and interprets this promise of Jesus to build his church on Peter as fulfilled by Peter's worldwide preaching of the Gospel. If we compare the passage in the Apocalypse of Peter with the eulogy of Paul's ministry and martyrdom in 1 Clement 5:5-7 ('...After he ... had preached in the East and

---

[104] The argument of E. Peterson, 'Das Martyrium des hl. Petrus nach des Petrus-Apokalypse,' in *Miscellanea Giulio Belvedere* (Vatican City: Società "Amici delle Catacombe," 1954) 130, for a literary connexion between *Apocalypse of Peter* 14:4 and AscenIs 4:2-3 is not convincing.

in the West, he won the genuine glory for his faith, having taught righteousness to the whole world and having reached the farthest limits of the West...'), Apocalypse of Peter 14:4-5 looks rather like a Petrine alternative to Clement's view of Paul. However, we should be cautious about concluding that it is a deliberately polemical rejection of Pauline Christianity by Jewish Christians who transferred the image of the apostle to the Gentiles from Paul to Peter. Some Palestinian Jewish Christians rejected Paul and his mission and in their literature (notably the so-called *Kerygmata Petrou* source of the Pseudo-Clementines) polemicized against him, but others approved of the Pauline mission from a distance (as can be seen from Jerome's quotations from a Jewish-Christian targum to Isaiah).[105] The Apocalypse of Peter ignores Paul and evidently knows nothing of the Pauline literature: this should probably be interpreted as the attitude of a group which was remote from contact with Pauline Christianity, but need not imply explicit hostility to Paul.

In any case, the idea of Peter as apostle to the Gentiles certainly has roots of its own, independent of polemical rivalry with Pauline Christianity's image of Paul. At least from the late first century, Jewish Christianity developed the idea of the twelve apostles as commissioned to preach the Gospel to the Gentile world as well as to Israel (Matt 28:19-20; cf. Luke 24:47; Acts 1:8), and this idea became common in the early second century in literature which ignores Paul (AscenIs 3:17-18; Mark 16:15-18; *Kerygma Petrou, ap.* Clement of Alexandria, *Strom.* 6.5.43; 6.6.48; Acts of John 112) as well as in works which take account of Paul's Gentile mission (EpApp 30; cf. 31-33). This tradition must have some basis in actual Jewish Christian mission to Gentiles, independent of the Pauline mission. Since Peter was widely regarded as having a position of special eminence among the twelve and since he was known to have gone to Rome, the capital of the empire, the idea of Peter as preeminently the apostle to the Gentiles arises naturally out of the idea of the twelve as apostles to the Gentiles. Again there is almost certainly some basis in fact.[106] The traditions in Acts represent Peter as actually the pioneer of the Gentile mission (10:1-11:18). According to the agreement of Galatians 2:7-9, Peter's mission outside Palestine—in Antioch and Rome—would have been primarily to diaspora Jews. But just as Paul also

---

[105] See R. A. Pritz, *Nazarene Jewish Christianity* (SPB 37; Jerusalem: Magnes Press/ Leiden: Brill, 1988) 64-70.

[106] Cf. M. Hengel, *Acts and the History of Early Christianity*, trans. J. Bowden (London: SCM Press, 1979) 92-98.

preached the Gospel to Jews, so Peter can hardly have regarded himself as forbidden to preach to Gentiles. In Antioch he seems to have associated himself with the Antiochene church's enthusiastic outreach to and inclusion of Gentiles (Gal 2:12). 1 Peter shows him associated in Rome with men who had been connected both with the Jerusalem church and with Paul's Gentile mission (1 Pet 5:12-13). As a letter sent from the church of Rome to churches (Pauline and non-Pauline) of Asia Minor, but sent in the name of Peter, as the most eminent among the Roman church leadership, 1 Peter shows that Peter during his last years (or perhaps only months) in Rome was not associated merely with a narrow Jewish Christian group, but with the Roman church as such, a church which probably at that stage combined close links with Jerusalem and strong commitment to the Gentile mission.

Thus the Apocalypse of Peter's portrayal of Peter as the apostle to the Gentiles, who spread the Gospel throughout the world before ending his ministry at Rome, is an idealization and exaggeration with some basis in fact. Moreover, it shows us that probably the mainstream of Palestinian Jewish Christians in the early second century, while themselves preoccupied with mission to their compatriots and increasingly isolated from developments in the wider church, nevertheless retained a positive view of the Gentile mission and the wider church whose foundation they attributed primarily to Peter.

Finally, we may ask whether this passage about Peter has any particular relevance to the overall message of the Apocalypse of Peter in its historical context. In a document concerned to encourage those faced with the possibility of martyrdom, clearly reference to Peter's own martyrdom is appropriate. In the sequence of material in the apocalypse, Peter, now knowing that he himself is going to face martyrdom, has a personal interest in the revelation in chapters 15-17 of the 'honour and glory of those who are persecuted for my righteousness' (16:5). However, there may also be a special significance in the fact that Peter, unlike the Jewish Christian martyrs of the Bar Kokhba period, was put to death by the imperial power of Rome. We noted in connexion with the *birkat ha-mînîm* that Jewish Christians who did not support Bar Kokhba would probably have been regarded as collaborators with the Roman oppressors. Such an accusation is implicitly countered by recalling that the leader of the apostles himself died in Rome as a victim of Roman power.

VI Bibliographical Notes

1 *Texts and Translations*

a *Ethiopic version*

The Ethiopic version of the Apocalypse of Peter was probably made from the Arabic (though no Arabic version is now known to be extant), which in turn would have been translated from the original Greek. The Ethiopic version is now known in two manuscripts: D'Abbadie 51 (Paris) and Hammerschmidt Lake Tana 35 (photographed in 1969 by E. Hammerschmidt). These two manuscripts are closely related. R. W. Cowley, who was the first to discuss the Lake Tana manuscript's text of the Apocalypse of Peter in print ('The Ethiopic Work Which is Believed to Contain the Material of the Ancient Greek Apocalypse of Peter,' *JTS* 36 [1985] 151-153) thought D'Abbadie 51 was a copy of Lake Tana 35, but D. D. Buchholz (see below) thought that either D'Abbadie 51 was an ancestor (but not the immediate ancestor) of Lake Tana 35, or both shared a common ancestor. This last position is supported (in an unpublished communication) by P. Marrassini. Unfortunately, the text in both manuscripts is frequently corrupt.

In both manuscripts the ancient Apocalypse of Peter does not appear as a distinct work but forms the first part of a larger work, called 'The second coming of Christ and the resurrection of the dead,' which is followed by another, closely related work called 'The mystery of the judgment of sinners.' Both works have been inspired by the Apocalypse of Peter and were most probably composed in Arabic before being translated into Ethiopic. However, once the section corresponding to the ancient Apocalypse of Peter has been identified, it is readily distinguishable from the secondary continuation of it.

The text of these two Ethiopic works was first published, with French translation, by S. Grébaut from MS D'Abbadie 51. Under the title, 'Littérature Ethiopienne: Pseudo-Clementine,' he first published 'The mystery of the judgment of sinners' (*Revue de l'Orient chrétien* 12 [1907] 139-151, 285-297, 380-392; 13 [1908] 166-180, 314-320), and then 'The second coming of Christ and the resurrection of the dead' (*Revue de l'Orient chrétien* 15 [1910] 198-214, 307-323, 425-439). Grébaut himself did not recognize that the latter contained the ancient Apocalypse of Peter (198-214, 307-323), but this was immediately pointed out by M. R. James ('A New Text of the Apocalypse of Peter,' *JTS* 12 [1911] 36-54, 157, 362-367). Grébaut's remains the only edition of the whole Ethiopic text of 'The second coming of Christ and the resurrection of the dead' and 'The mystery of the judgment of sinners,' the only complete translation of both of these works in any modern language (though Erbetta provides an Italian translation of 'The second coming of Christ and the resurrection of the dead': see below), and the only French translation of the Ethiopic version of the Apocalypse of Peter. Unfortunately the translation is full of mistakes.

For the Apocalypse of Peter itself, a new critical edition of the Ethiopic text, based, for the first time, on both manuscripts, has been published in D. D. Buchholz, *Your Eyes Will be Opened: A Study of the Greek (Ethiopic) Apocalypse of Peter* (SBLDS 97; Atlanta, Georgia: Scholars Press, 1988). This book is Buchholz's 1984 Claremont Graduate School Ph.D. dissertation (published unaltered). It is the fullest monograph study of the Apocalypse of Peter to date, including a study of introductory questions and a brief commentary on the text. But it is most important for the edition of the Ethiopic text, two new English translations of the Ethiopic (one literal, one free), and the demonstration of the reliability of the Ethiopic version as witness to the original Apocalypse of Peter. (Buchholz also divided the chapters into verses for the first time. His verse divisions should be adopted as standard.)

The new German edition of the New Testament Apocrypha includes a translation of the Ethiopic (along with the Greek fragments and patristic quotations): W. Schneemelcher ed., *Neutestamentliche Apokryphen in deutscher Übersetzung*, vol 2 (5th edition; Tübingen: Mohr [Siebeck], 1989) 562-578 (English translation in *New Testament Apocrypha*, vol. 2, trans. R. McL. Wilson [Cambridge: James Clarke/ Louisville:Westminster/John Knox Press, 1992] 620-638). Unfortunately, the translation is that of H. Duensing, which was made from Grébaut's edition of the text, was first published in 1913 ('Ein Stücke der urchristlichen Petrus-Apokalypse enthaltender Traktat der Äthiopischen Pseudoklementinischen Literatur,' *ZNW* 14 [1913] 65-78), appeared in earlier editions of Hennecke-Schneemelcher, and is here reproduced with hardly any changes. The editor (C. Detlef G. Müller) makes no reference to the Lake Tana manuscript, and appears to know no literature on the Apocalypse of Peter published after 1952.

M. Erbetta, *Gli Apocrifi del Nuovo Testamento*, vol. 3 (Casale Monferrato: Marietti, 1981) 209-233, gives an Italian translation of Grébaut's text of the whole of 'The second coming of Christ and the resurrection of the dead,' including the Apocalypse of Peter (as well as of the Greek fragments and patristic quotations).

b *Patristic quotations*

In the absence of a complete Greek text of the Apocalypse of Peter, the patristic quotations from the work are important, both for verifying the content of the original apocalypse and also for giving us some access to the original Greek. There are five or six quotations in Greek:

(1) Clement of Alexandria, *Eclog.* 41a and 48 [the only words actually quoted from the Apocalypse of Peter are the same in both these texts and correspond to ApPet 8:10];
(2) Clement of Alexandria, *Eclog.* 41b [corresponding to ApPet 8:4];
(3) Clement of Alexandria, *Eclog.* 49 [corresponding to ApPet 8:8-9];
(4) Methodius, *Symp.* 2.6 [corresponding to ApPet 8:6, 10];
(5) Macarius Magnes, *Apocrit.* 4.6 [corresponding to ApPet 4:13];
(6) Macarius Magnes, *Apocrit.* 4.7 [this has been taken to be a quotation from the Apocalypse of Peter, but, although it corresponds roughly to ApPet 5:4, it is in fact a quotation of Isa 34:4 and should probably be understood as no more than that].

The Greek texts of these quotations can be found in J. A. Robinson and M. R. James, *The Gospel according to Peter, and the Revelation of Peter* (London: C. J. Clay, 1892) 94-96 (with English translations: 71-79); E. Preuschen, *Antilegomena* (2nd edition; Giessen: Töpelmann, 1905) 87-88 (with German translations: 191-192); E. Klostermann, *Apocrypha 1. Reste des Petrusevangeliums, der Petrusapokalypse und des Kerygma Petri* (2nd edition; Bonn: Marcus & Weber, 1908) 12-13; Buchholz, *Your Eyes Will Be Opened* (see above) 22-36 (with English translations).

There are also two patristic quotations in Latin:

(1) The first, which explicitly mentions the Apocalypse of Peter, is from an anonymous sermon on the parable of the ten virgins, perhaps from the fourth century. The Latin text is given in M. R. James, 'A New Text of the Apocalypse of Peter,' *JTS* 12 (1911) 383; Buchholz, *Your Eyes Will Be Opened*, 38-39 (with English translation). In fact, it is not so much a quotation as a reference to the river of fire as depicted in ApPet 6:2.
(2) The second, which should certainly be identified as a quotation from the Apocalypse of Peter, although the source is not named, is in a sermon of uncertain date (perhaps c. 300): Pseudo-Cyprian, *Adv. Aleatores* 8. It corresponds to ApPet 12:5. The Latin text is given in M. R. James, 'A New Text of the Apocalypse of Peter,' *JTS* 12 (1911) 50, 383; Erbetta, *Gli Apocrifi* (see above), 223; Buchholz, *Your Eyes Will Be Opened*, 62-63 (with English translation).

c *Bodleian fragment*

This small fragment of an Egyptian manuscript (in the Bodleian Library, Oxford) contains the Greek text, in fragmentary condition, of Apocalypse of Peter 10:6-7. The Greek text is given in M. R. James, 'A New Text of the Apocalypse of Peter,' *JTS* 12 (1911) 367-369; Buchholz, *Your Eyes Will Be Opened* (see above) 146 (but he gives only James' reconstruction, with English translation).

d *Rainer fragment*

This fragment (in the Rainer collection in Vienna) of a third- or fourth-century manuscript contains the Greek text of Apocalypse of Peter 14:1-5a. It was first published (with a French translation) by C. Wessely, 'Les plus anciens monuments du christianisme écrits sur papyrus (II),' *Patrologia Orientalis* 18/3 (Paris: Firmin-Didot, 1924) 482-483, but Wessely thought it must be a fragment of the Acts of Peter. It was first identified as part of the Apocalypse of Peter by K. Prümm, 'De genuino Apocalypsis Petri textu: Examen testium iam notorum et novi fragmenti Raineriani,' *Bib* 10 (1929) 62-80 (including the text with Latin translation: 77-78). The Greek text, with emendations which have been widely accepted, and English translation are given in M. R. James, 'The Rainer Fragment of the Apocalypse of Peter,' *JTS* 32 (1931) 270-274; and Buchholz, *Your Eyes Will Be Opened* (see above) 228. James argued that the Bodleian and Rainer fragments are of the same manuscript (*JTS* 32 [1931] 278).

e *Akhmim fragment*

In 1887 the French Archeological Mission discovered, in a cemetery near Akhmim (Panopolis) in Upper Egypt, a small vellum book, probably of the eighth or ninth century, which is now in the Museum of Egyptian Antiquities in Cairo. The manuscript contains the now well-known fragment of the Gospel of Peter in Greek and some fragments of 1 Enoch in Greek, as well as a Greek text which, when it was discovered, was identified as part of the Apocalypse of Peter. It became the main basis for study of the Apocalypse of Peter until the identification of the Ethiopic version in 1911. But in the light of the Ethiopic version, the Bodleian and Rainer fragments it became clear, and is now accepted by all who have worked in detail on the Apocalypse of Peter, that the Akhmim text is not of the Apocalypse of Peter in its original form, but a heavily redacted version in which the text has been abbreviated and otherwise considerably modified in both major and minor ways. It cannot, like the Ethiopic version, the Bodleian and Rainer fragments, and the patristic quotations, be used as evidence of the original, second-century Apocalypse of Peter as such.

It was first published (with a French translation) in 1892 by U. Bouriant, 'Fragments du texte grec du livre d'Enoch et de quelques écrits attribués à saint Pierre,' *Mémoires publiés par les membres de la mission archéologique française au Caire* 9 (1892-93) 142-146; and photographs of the manuscript are in A. Lods, 'Reproduction en héliogravure du manuscrit d'Enoch et des écrits attribués à saint Pierre,' in the same volume, 224-228, with Plates VII-X. The text has frequently been edited: see especially J. A. Robinson and M. R. James, *The Gospel according to Peter, and the Revelation of Peter* (London: C. J. Clay, 1892) 89-93 (with English translation: 48-51); A. Harnack, *Bruchstücke des Evangeliums und der Apokalypse des Petrus* (TU 9/2; Leipzig: Hinrichs, 1893) (with German translation, and establishing the division into 34 verses which is now generally used); E. Preuschen, *Antilegomena* (2nd edition; Giessen: Töpelmann, 1905) 84-87 (with German translation: 188-191); E. Klostermann, *Apocrypha 1. Reste des Petrusevangeliums, der Petrusapokalypse und des Kerygma Petri* (2nd edition; Bonn: Marcus & Weber, 1908) 8-12. For translations, see also W. Schneemelcher, *Neutestamentliche Apokryphen in deutscher Übersetzung*, vol 2 (5th edition; Tübingen: Mohr [Siebeck], 1989) 570-577; W. Schneemelcher ed., *New Testament Apocrypha*, vol. 2, trans. R. McL. Wilson (Cambridge: James Clarke/Louisville: Westminster/John Knox Press, 1992) 628-635; M. Erbetta, *Gli Apocrifi del Nuovo Testamento*, vol. 3 (Casale Monferrato: Marietti, 1981) 216-218.

f *Slavonic version*
The possibility of a Slavonic version of the Apocalypse of Peter is raised and a reference to a Moscow manuscript which may contain it is given by A. de Santos Otero, *Die handschriftlichen Überlieferung der altslavischen Apokryphen*, vol. 1 (PTS 20; Berlin/New York: de Gruyter, 1978) 212-213, but the existence of such a version has not yet been verified.

2 *Secondary Literature*

A detailed history of research on the Apocalypse of Peter up to c. 1982 and an exhaustive bibliography up to 1987 will be found in R. Bauckham, 'The Apocalypse of Peter: An Account of Research,' in W. Haase ed., *Aufstieg und Niedergang der römischen Welt*, vol. 2.25/6 (Berlin/New York: de Gruyter, 1988) 4712-4750.

CHAPTER NINE

A QUOTATION FROM 4Q SECOND EZEKIEL IN THE APOCALYPSE OF PETER

The Apocalypse of Peter is an early second-century Christian work, whose complete text survives only in an Ethiopic version.[1] I have argued in the previous chapter[2] that it is a Palestinian Jewish Christian work which can be dated rather precisely during the Bar Kokhba war (132-135 C.E.). It contains only one explicit citation of scripture, at 4:7-9. I give these verses in the two recent English translations of the Ethiopic, by Dennis D. Buchholz and Julian Hills:

> **7** For everything is possible for God and therefore thus it says in scripture: the son of man prophesied to each of the bones. **8** 'And you said to the bone, "Bone (be) to bones in limbs, tendons and nerves, and flesh and skin and hair on it." **9** And soul and spirit the great Uriel [and] will give at the command of God,' for him God has appointed over his resurrection of the dead at the day of judgment. (Buchholz)[3]

> **7** because everything is possible for God: as it says in the scripture: 'Son of man, prophesy over the bones, **8** and say to each bone, "(Let) bone (be) with bones at their joints, and tendons and muscles, flesh and skin, and hair upon it, and soul and spirit."' **9** Then great Uriel will deliver (them) over to the command of God, for God set him over the resurrection of the dead on the day of judgment. (Hills)[4]

Although the original Greek version of the Apocalypse, known to the Church Fathers, is not extant at this point, we do have a poetic

---

[1] For a full account of research on all aspects of the work, see R. Bauckham, 'The Apocalypse of Peter: An Account of Research,' in *Aufstieg und Niedergang der römischen Welt*, Part II, vol. 25/6, ed. W. Haase (Berlin/New York: de Gruyter, 1988) 4712-4750.

[2] See also R. Bauckham, 'The Two Fig Tree Parables in the Apocalypse of Peter,' *JBL* 104 (1985) 269-287.

[3] D. D. Buchholz, *Your Eyes Will Be Opened: A Study of the Greek (Ethiopic) Apocalypse of Peter* (SBLDS 97; Atlanta, Georgia: Scholars Press, 1988) 183, 185. Buchholz's edition and translation are the first to be based on both of the two known Ethiopic MSS. He provides both a literal and a free translation, of which the former is quoted here, as more useful for the present purpose.

[4] This translation by Julian Hills, which I use with his permission, will be published in A. Yarbro Collins and M. Himmelfarb ed., *New Testament Apocrypha*, vol. 2 (Sonoma, CA: Polebridge Press, forthcoming).

paraphrase of most of the Apocalypse in Sibylline Oracle 2:194-338,[5] which while it certainly cannot be relied on to reproduce the contents of the Apocalypse of Peter exactly, can be used cautiously as a check on the accuracy of the Ethiopic version. Lines 221-226 correspond to our passage:

καὶ τότε νερτερίοις ψυχὰς καὶ αὐδήν
δώσει ὁ ἐπουράνιος, καὶ τ᾽ ὀστέα ἁρμοσθέντα
ἁρμοῖς παντοίοις [...?] σάρκες καὶ νεῦρα
καὶ φλέβες ἠδὲ τε δέρμα περὶ χροῒ καὶ πρὶν ἔθειραι·
ἀμβροσίως πηχθέντα, καὶ ἔμπνοα κινηθέτα
σώματ᾽ ἐπιχθονίων ἐνὶ ἤματ᾽ ἀναστήσονται.[6]

Then the heavenly One will give to those who dwell in the underworld souls and breath (spirit) and voice, and bones fitted together with every kind of joint... flesh and tendons and veins and also skin around the flesh and the former hairs. Bodies of earthly people, divinely fixed together, breathing and set in motion, will be raised in one day.

Clearly both passages are related to Ezekiel 37:1-4, but the list of the components of the resurrected people in Sibylline Oracle 2:221-224 corresponds with that in Apocalypse of Peter 4:7-8(9) rather than with Ezekiel. Sibylline Oracle 2:221-224 has the following ten components: souls, breath (spirit), voice, bones, joints, flesh, tendons, veins, skin, hairs. Of these only the following six could have derived from Ezekiel 37:4-10 LXX: breath (πνεῦμα), bones (ὀστᾶ), joint (ἁρμονίαν), tendons (νεῦρα), flesh (σάρκες), skin (δέρμα). Apocalypse of Peter 4:7-8(9), on the other hand, has a list of nine components, corresponding with all of those in Sibylline Oracle 2:221-224 with the single exception of 'voice' (αὐδήν). Thus Sibylline Oracle 2:221-224 must be dependent on the Apocalypse of Peter and confirms the accuracy of the Ethiopic version of the latter at this point.

The extent of the quotation in Apocalypse of Peter 4:7-9 is not quite clear. The quotation marks with which Buchholz delimits the quotation correspond to peculiar punctuation marks which occur here (and only here) in manuscript T. But if these are intended to indicate the quotation, as they probably are, they can tell us no more

---

[5] This was conclusively shown by M. R. James, 'A New Text of the Apocalypse of Peter,' *JTS* 12 (1911) 39-44, 51-52, but is not recognized by J. Daniélou, 'La Vision des ossements desséchés (Ezech. 37,1-14) dans les Testimonia,' *RechSR* 53 (1965) 224-225, whose study entirely neglects the Apocalypse of Peter, or by J. J. Collins in his discussion of sources and redaction in SibOr 2 in J. H. Charlesworth ed., *The Old Testament Pseudepigrapha*, vol. 1 (London: Darton, Longman & Todd, 1983) 330-333.

[6] Text from J. Geffcken, *Die Oracula Sibyllina* (GCS 8; Leipzig: Hinrichs, 1902) 38, with punctuation changed.

than an Ethiopian scribe's view of the extent of the quotation. It is much more probable that the quotation begins in v 7 with 'Son of man,' and in that case Hills's correction (following Grébaut) of *tanabay* ('prophesied'), the reading of both MSS, to *tanabaya* ('prophesy') becomes essential. The resulting opening words of the quotation, 'Son of man, prophesy over each of the bones, and say to the bone,' are to be accepted because they correspond to a frequent formula in Ezekiel ('Son of man, prophesy over ... and say': ...וֹאמרת ... עַל הַנבֵא אֶל בֶּן־אָדָם).[7]

Buchholz and Hills differ in their understandings of the end of v 8 and the beginning of v 9. Buchholz has to ignore the conjunction (*wa*) before 'the great Uriel,' but Hills has to supply an object and produces a not very satisfactory sense in verse 9a. Sibylline Oracle 2:221-224 does not really help here: it rearranges the list, bringing 'souls and spirit' to the fore and introducing God as their giver. However, the account of the resurrection in the Hebrew Apocalypse of Elijah (*Sefer Eliyahhu*) having quoted Ezekiel 37:8a ('I looked and behold there were tendons on them'), continues: 'The ministering angels will open their graves and put their breath within them, and they will live, and they will stand them upon their feet.'[8] This is an interpretation of Ezekiel 37:12, 13-14, in which the action attributed directly to God in Ezekiel is performed by the mediation of angels. It is characteristic of the literature of early Judaism to introduce angels as the agents of actions directly attributed to God in the Old Testament. Thus it is very plausible that the Apocalypse of Peter should interpret Ezekiel in the way that Buchholz translates verse 9a: 'And soul and spirit the great Uriel will give at the command of God.' This clause could belong to the quotation, while the rest of verse 9 could be the author's own explanation of the quotation's reference to Uriel. But since Uriel appears again in this role in 6:7, it is also quite possible that the quotation ends with 'hair on it' at the end of verse 8. The whole of chapter 4 of the Apocalypse of Peter is a compilation of traditions about resurrection. The author may well have quoted one account of Ezekiel's vision of resurrection in verses 7b-8, but then in verse 9 continued with another traditional interpretation of Ezekiel's vision.

---

[7] Literal translation of the Hebrew consecutive perfect וֹאמרת may also explain the Ethiopic perfect which Buchholz, *Your Eyes*, 296, insists must be translated 'and you said.'

[8] Translation by G. W. Buchanan, *Revelation and Redemption: Jewish Documents of Deliverance from the Fall of Jerusalem to the Death of Nahmanides* (Dillsboro, North Carolina: Western North Carolina Press, 1978) 439; cf. M. Buttenwieser, *Der hebräische Elias-Apokalypse und ihre Stellung in der apokalyptischen Litteratur des rabbinischen Schrifttums und der Kirche* (Leipzig: Pfeiffer, 1897) 66.

Whatever the extent of the quotation, it seems fairly clear that in verse 8, following the reference to 'joints' or 'limbs,' the quoted text has been summarized rather than quoted verbatim. The mere list of additional components of the body make no sense as part of Ezekiel's command to the bones. They must have been originally the object of further commands by Ezekiel, or at least the text must have said that they were added to the bones, as Ezekiel 37:8 does of the sinews, flesh and skin.

The source of the quotation has been hardly ever discussed, though Buchholz suggests that it may not have been 'taken directly from Ezekiel but from an apocryphal work based on Ezekiel.'[9] Oddly enough, it has not been mentioned among the various quotations in early Christian literature which might derive from the Apocryphon of Ezekiel.[10] This is probably because scholars have paid so little attention to the Apocalypse of Peter.[11] But the quotation, despite its obvious relationship to Ezekiel 37:3-14, diverges so much from that passage that the question of an apocryphal source ought to be raised, especially as it is the only formal scriptural quotation in the Apocalypse of Peter and therefore might reasonably be expected to be relatively accurate.

The source of the quotation can now be identified as the Ezekiel apocalypse (designated Second Ezekiel or Pseudo-Ezekiel) which is extant in small fragments, representing several copies of the work, from Qumran Cave 4 (4Q385-391). Not all of the fragments numbered 4Q385-391 have yet been published, and it is debated how many of them should be assigned to Second Ezekiel. However, the fragments which concern us, two fragments (2 and 3) of 4Q385, are undoubtedly fragments of Second Ezekiel and have been published in a preliminary edition and translation by John Strugnell and Devorah Dimant.[12] Fragment 2 contains (in lines 5-8) an account of Ezekiel's

---

[9] Buchholz, *Your Eyes*, 296.

[10] Cf. the discussions in M. R. James, 'The Apocryphal Ezekiel,' *JTS* 15 (1914) 236-243; idem, *The Lost Apocrypha of the Old Testament* (London: SPCK, 1920) 64-70, 87, 89, 92-93; Daniélou, 'La Vision des ossements desséchés,' 230-233; A.-M. Denis, *Introduction aux pseudépigraphes grecs d'Ancien Testament* (SVTP 1; Leiden: Brill, 1970) 187-191; K.-G. Eckart, 'Das Apokryphon Ezechiel,' in *Apokalypsen* (JSHRZ 5; Gutersloh: Mohn, 1974) 47-50; E. Schürer, *The History of the Jewish People in the Age of Jesus Christ (175 B.C.- A.D. 135)*, revised by G. Vermes, F. Millar and M. Goodman, vol. 3/2 (Edinburgh: T. & T. Clark, 1987) 793- 796; J. R. Mueller and S. E. Robinson in Charlesworth, *Old Testament Pseudepigrapha*, vol. 1, 487-490.

[11] It is typical that G. Otranto, 'Ezechiele 37,1-14 nell' esegesi patristici del secondo secolo,' *Vetera Christianorum* 9 (1972) 55-76, makes no reference to the Apocalypse of Peter.

[12] J. Strugnell and D. Dimant, '4Q Second Ezekiel,' *RevQ* 13 (1988) 45-58.

vision of the resurrection parallel to canonical Ezekiel 37:1-14, and since this passage is also represented in two overlapping fragments (4Q388 3 and 4Q386 1) the text can fortunately be reconstructed almost completely.[13] I reproduce here the text as edited by Strugnell and Dimant (continuous underlining indicates that the text is preserved in 4Q388 3, broken underlining that it is preserved in 4Q386 1), and their translation:

5 [ויאמר] בן אדם הנבה על היצממות ואמרת ה°°° 14 עצם אל עצמו ופרק

6 [אל פרקו ויה]י כן ויאמר שנבצ ויעלו עליהם נדים ויקרמו עור

7 [מלמעלה ורה]י כ[ן] ויאמר שוב אנבא על ארבע רוחחות השמים ורפחו רוח[ות]

8 [השמים בהם ויחיו] ויצמד עם רב אנשים ויברכו את יהוה צבאות אש[ר חרם]

5 [And he said:] 'Son of man, prophesy over the bones and say: [Be ye joined (?)] bone to its bone and joint
6 [to its joint.' And it wa]s so. And he said a second time: 'Prophesy and let sinews come upon them and let them be covered with skin
7 [above.' And it wa]s s[o]. And he said again: 'Prophesy concerning the four winds of heaven and let the win[ds
8 of heaven] blow [upon them and they shall revive,] and a great crowd of people shall stand up, and they shall bless Yahweh Sabaoth wh[o has given them life again.']

The quotation in Apocalypse of Peter 4:7-8 corresponds to this text in the following ways:

(1) The opening words of Yahweh in 4Q385 2 line 5 derive from three verses of Ezekiel 37: בן־אדם (37:3), הנבא על־העצמות ... ואמרת (37:4), עצם־אל־עצמו (37:7). Precisely the same words in the same sequence appear in Apocalypse of Peter 4:7-8.

(2) One effect in both cases is to produce a formula characteristic of Ezekiel ('Son of man, prophesy over the bones, and say'; cf. Ezek 6:2-3; 13:2, 17-18; 21:7-8, 14, 33; 28:21-22; 29:2-3; 30:2; 34:2; 35:2-3; 38:2-3; 39:1). This coincidence is not remarkable. In fact, some witnesses to the text of Ezekiel 37:4 itself add בן־אדם (a few manuscripts of MT, Lucianic recension of LXX, Old Latin). This is probably a secondary addition, influenced by the form of the divine address to

---

[13] Strugnell and Dimant, '4Q Second Ezekiel,' 54, suppose that Ezekiel must have seen the vision of the dry bones in the preceding column and that fragment 2 lines 1-4 also relates to it. It seems to me more probable that fragment 2 lines 5-8, which is set apart by spaces at the end of line 4 and the beginning of line 9, is a self-contained summary of Ezekiel's vision of the dry bones.

[14] Here Strugnell and Dimant, '4Q Second Ezekiel,' 53, suggest הקרבו (cf. Ezekiel 37:7: ותקרבו). E. Puech informs me that the reading ויקרבו is certain.

Ezekiel which is found so often elsewhere in the book, but it shows
not only that either or both of our texts could have been dependent
on that form of the text of Ezekiel 37:4, but also how easily the words
of Ezekiel 37:4 could be independently adapted in this way.

(3) Much more significantly, both our texts make the words 'bone to
its bone,' from Ezekiel 37:7, what Ezekiel is commanded by Yahweh
to say to the bones. This is a major variation from canonical Ezekiel.

(4) The words ופרק אל פרקו ('and joint to its joint') in 4Q385 2 lines
5-6 have no basis in the MT of Ezekiel 37:7-8, but are paralleled by
the reference to 'joints' in Apocalypse of Peter 4:8. It is true that there
is a reference to joints in Ezekiel 37:7 LXX (καὶ προσήγαγε τὰ
ἑκάτερον πρὸς τὴν ἁρμονίαν αὐτοῦ: 'and the bones approached each
one to its joint'). This is the best LXX reading, and is found in
Papyrus 967,[15] the earliest witness of the pre-hexaplaric LXX of
Ezekiel.[16] But it should probably be understood as a translation of the
Hebrew we have in the MT, with πρὸς τὴν ἁρμονίαν αὐτου translating
אל עצמו, presumably in order to render the meaning of 'its bone'
more intelligible.[17] Apocalypse of Peter 4:8, on the other hand, reproduces the whole of canonical Ezekiel's phrase עצם אל עצמו and adds
a reference to joints, as does 4Q385.

The question should be raised whether these correspondences are
best explained by the hypothesis that the Apocalypse of Peter quotes
4Q Second Ezekiel, or by the hypothesis that the Apocalypse of Peter
quotes a form of the text of canonical Ezekiel which differed from the
MT and on which 4Q Second Ezekiel was also dependent. The latter
would probably be the best explanation of points (2) and (4) above if
they stood alone. But a very considerably variant text would have to

---

[15] But with ἔκαστον for ἑκάτερον. Published in M. Fernández-Galiano, 'Nuevas
Páginas del Códice 967 del A. T. Griego (Ez 28,19-43,9) (PMatr. bibl. 1),' *Studia
Papyrologica* 10 (1971) 35. On this manuscript, see J. Lust, 'Ezekiel 36-40 in the Oldest
Greek Manuscript,' *CBQ* 43 (1981) 517-533; idem, 'The Order of the Final Events in
Revelation and in Ezekiel,' in J. Lambrecht ed., *L'Apocalypse johannique et l'Apocalyptique
dans le Nouveau Testament* (BETL 53; Gembloux: Duculot/Leuven: University Press,
1980) 179-183.

[16] MSS of the Lucianic recension which read προσήγαγε τὰ ὀστᾶ ὀστέον πρὸς ὀστέον
ἔκαστον πρὸς τὴν ἁρμονίαν αὐτοῦ have probably added a literal rendering of the MT
(ὀστέον πρὸς ὀστέον) to the existing LXX text. For Lucianic revisions of LXX Ezekiel
according to the MT, cf. J. Ziegler, *Ezechiel* (Septuaginta 16/1; Göttingen:
Vandenhoeck & Ruprecht, 1952) 48-50.

[17] It is worth noting that ἁρμονία is used in LXX only in Ezekiel 37:7 and 23:42
(where it translates המון).

be postulated to account for point (3). Manuscripts of the LXX of Ezekiel which elsewhere offer evidence of a shorter text[18] provide no support for such a hypothesis, while the fragments of Ezekiel from Qumran so far published are very close to the MT.[19]

However, the consideration which must be decisive is that the adaptation of the text of Ezekiel to which our point (3) refers is very similar to the way in which 4Q Second Ezekiel continues to adapt the text of Ezekiel in the rest of the passage quoted above. Just as Yahweh's first speech to Ezekiel (lines 5-6) uses words from the end of Ezekiel 37:7, which in Ezekiel describe what happened after the prophet had prophesied, so Yahweh's second speech (lines 6-7) is another command to Ezekiel to prophesy, using words from Ezekiel 37:8, and Yahweh's third speech (lines 7-8) takes up not only Yahweh's command to the prophet in Ezekiel 37:9, but also, once again, the description of the event in Ezekiel 37:10. The compositional technique of this section of 4Q Second Ezekiel is to transfer the canonical text's account of the resurrection into Yahweh's commands to the prophet to prophesy. This means that the Apocalypse of Peter, in the correspondence we have noted as point (3), reflects the major characteristic feature of this passage of 4Q Second Ezekiel in its rewriting of Ezekiel 37. That the Apocalypse of Peter is actually quoting 4Q Second Ezekiel seems therefore very likely.

There is, however, one problem about identifying 4Q Second Ezekiel as the source of the quotation in Apocalypse of Peter 4:7-8. The latter has, following 'joints,' these further components of the body: tendons, muscles, flesh, skin, hair. Of these, only two (tendons, skin) occur in 4Q385 2:6-7, whereas three (tendons, flesh, skin) appear in canonical Ezekiel 37:8. But Strugnell and Dimant observe that the overlapping fragment 4Q386 1 i 6-8 must have had a longer text at this point and indicates an omission of about two lines in 4Q385.[20] It seems quite possible that a reference to flesh occurred in the longer text, and even possible that muscles and hair were also mentioned. Furthermore, Strugnell and Dimant state that in general the overlapping fragments of 4Q Second Ezekiel reveal the existence

---

[18] See J. Lust, 'The Use of Textual Witnesses for the Establishment of the Text: The Shorter and Longer Texts of Ezekiel,' in J. Lust ed., *Ezekiel and his Book: Textual and Literary Criticism and their Interrelation* (BETL 74; Leuven: University Press/Peeters, 1986) 7-20.

[19] J. Lust, 'Ezekiel Manuscripts in Qumran: Preliminary Edition of 4Q Ez a and b,' in Lust ed., *Ezekiel and his Book*, 90-100.

[20] Strugnell and Dimant, '4Q Second Ezekiel,' 53.

of variant forms of the same text among the Qumran copies of the
work.[21] There is no great difficulty in supposing that Apocalypse of
Peter 4:7-8 is based upon a form of this text.

That 4Q Second Ezekiel was cited as scripture by the author of
the Apocalypse of Peter is of interest in demonstrating that this work
was not confined to the Qumran community and increases the probability that it did not originate there.[22] If, as I believe, the Apocalypse
of Peter is a Palestinian Jewish Christian work, it cannot show that
4Q Second Ezekiel was translated into Greek or circulated outside
Palestine. Thus it does not help us very much in considering whether
4Q Second Ezekiel is the same work as the Apocryphon of Ezekiel,[23]
of which we have three Greek fragments of a papyrus copy (Chester
Beatty papyrus 185)[24] and several quite certain quotations in the
Fathers,[25] as well as a few other possible quotations.[26] From what we
know of the Apocryphon of Ezekiel and what we so far know of 4Q
Second Ezekiel, their identity seems very plausible, as Ben G. Wright
has now argued in some detail, though he is careful to point out that
our present evidence cannot unequivocally prove that the
Apocryphon of Ezekiel and 4Q Second Ezekiel were the same
work.[27]

However, there are two quotations in the Fathers which have
sometimes been attributed to the Apocryphon of Ezekiel[28] and which
do seem to bear some relationship to the text of 4Q Second Ezekiel
which we have just examined:

[21] Strugnell and Dimant, '4Q Second Ezekiel,' 46.

[22] Cf. Strugnell and Dimant, '4Q Second Ezekiel,' 57-58. M. Kister, 'Barnabas
12:1, 4:3 and *4Q Second Ezekiel*,' *RB* 97 (1990) 63-67, argues that Barn 12:1 derives
from the words at the end of 4Q385 2.

[23] Strugnell and Dimant, '4Q Second Ezekiel,' 47 n. 8, do no more than raise the
question.

[24] Text in C. Bonner, *The Homily on the Passion by Melito, Bishop of Sardis with Some
Fragments of the Apocryphal Ezekiel* (Studies and Documents 12; London: Christophers/
Philadelphia: Philadelphia University Press, 1940) 183-190; M. Black ed., *Apocalypsis
Henochi Graeca* and A.-M. Denis, *Fragmenta Pseudepigraphorum quae supersunt Graeca*
(PVTG 3; Leiden: Brill, 1970) 125-128.

[25] Mueller and Robinson in Charlesworth, *Old Testament Pseudepigrapha*, vol. 1, 492-
495.

[26] See the references in n. 10 above especially to the discussions by James and
Daniélou.

[27] B. G. Wright, 'The Apocryphon of Ezekiel and 4QPseudo-Ezekiel: Are They
the Same Work? How Do We Know?,' forthcoming in the proceedings of the 1997
Jerusalem congress *The Dead Sea Scrolls—Fifty Years After Their Discovery: Major Issues and
New Approaches*. I am grateful to Ben Wright for discussing the issue with me and
providing me with a copy of his paper in advance of publication.

[28] Cf. James, 'Apocryphal Ezekiel,' 243; idem, *Lost Apocrypha*, 92-93; Daniélou, 'La
Vision des ossements desséchés,' 232-233.

Justin, *1 Apol.* 52.5-6:

ἐρρέθη δὲ διὰ Ἰεζεκιὴλ τοῦ προφήτου οὕτως· Συναχθήσεται ἁρμονία πρὸς ἁρμονίαν καὶ ὀστέον πρὸς ὀστέον, καὶ σάρκες ἀναφυήσονται. καὶ πᾶν γόνυ κάμψει τῷ κυρίῳ, καὶ πᾶσα γλῶσσα ἐξομολογήσεται αὐτῷ.

It was said through Ezekiel the prophet: 'Joint shall be joined to joint and bone to bone, and flesh shall grow again. And every knee shall bow to the Lord, and every tongue shall confess him.'

Tertullian, *De Res.* 32.1:

Habes scripturam: Et mandabo piscibus maris et eructuabunt ossa quae sunt comesta, et faciam compaginem ad compaginem et os ad os.

You have the scripture: 'And I will command the fish of the sea and they shall vomit up the bones that are consumed, and I will put joint to joint and bone to bone.'

Both quotations are typical of the testimonia in early Christian literature in being combined quotations, and this makes it unlikely that either of them as such is from the Apocryphon of Ezekiel. The words that resemble Ezekiel 37:7-8 are followed in Justin's quotation by words from Isaiah 45:24, while the first part of Tertullian's quotation resembles 1 Enoch 61:5 and Apocalypse of Peter 4:3-5 (cf. also SibOr 2:233-237, dependent on the latter).[29] But the correspondence between the two quotations in the phrase 'joint to joint and bone to bone' is striking.[30] Whereas Ezekiel 37:7 MT has only 'bone to its bone' (עֶצֶם אֶל עַצְמוֹ) and Ezekiel 37:7 LXX only 'the bones each to its joint' (τὰ ὀστᾶ ἑκάτερον πρὸς τὴν ἁρμονίαν αὐτοῦ), 4Q385 2 5-6 has precisely the double phrase 'bone to its bone and joint to its joint' (עצם אל עצמו ופרק אל פרקו) which appears in reverse order in Justin's and Tertullian's quotations. Unless we postulate a variant text of canonical Ezekiel, to which both the quotations and 4Q Second Ezekiel were indebted, it seems likely that this phrase in Justin's and Tertullian's quotations derives ultimately from 4Q Second Ezekiel. The words which follow in Justin (καὶ σάρκες ἀναφυήσονται) may reflect Ezekiel 37:7 LXX (νεῦρα καὶ σάρκες ἐφύοντο), but might also be based on the variant text of 4Q Second Ezekiel which we postulated above lay behind Apocalypse of Peter 4:7-8 and referred to 'flesh.' The indebtedness of these quotations to 4Q Second Ezekiel would be easy to understand if the latter was the same as the Apocryphon of

---

[29] I discuss these texts in chapter 10 below.

[30] O. Skarsaune, *The Proof from Prophecy* (NovTSup 56; Leiden: Brill, 1987) 436, suggests that Justin's lost treatise *De Resurrectione* was the source of Tertullian's quotation.

Ezekiel, which evidently circulated quite widely in the second-century church,[31] to which Justin probably owed another quotation (*Dial.* 47.5),[32] though evidently without knowing its source, and from which Tertullian explicitly quotes (*De Carne Christi* 23.2, 6).[33]

---

[31] See the evidence of writers who cite it in Mueller and Robinson in Charlesworth, *Old Testament Pseudepigrapha*, vol. 1, 494-495.

[32] He attributes it to 'our Lord Jesus Christ,' but it is attributed to Ezekiel in Evagrius' Latin translation of Athanasius' *Life of Antony*. See the collection of parallels in W. D. Stroker, *Extracanonical Sayings of Jesus* (SBL Resources for Biblical Study 18; Atlanta, Georgia: Scholars Press, 1989) 73-74.

[33] On this quotation see K.-G. Eckart, "Die Kuh des apokryphen Ezechiel," in W. Sommer and H. Ruppel ed., *Antwort aus der Geschichte: Beobachtungen und Erwägungen zum geschichtlichen Bild der Kirche* (FS Walter Dress; Berlin: Christliche Zeitschriftenverlag, 1969) 44-48.

I am grateful to Dr George Brooke for acute and helpful criticism of this paper in an earlier draft, And to Professoir E. Puech for most useful comments on the paper.

CHAPTER TEN

RESURRECTION AS GIVING BACK THE DEAD

I

The relationship between the Apocalypse of John and the extra-canonical Jewish apocalypses has been variously understood. At one extreme are those who see Revelation as a typical Jewish apocalypse, whose admittedly Christian authorship makes little significant difference,[1] while at the other extreme are those who distinguish sharply between prophecy and apocalyptic and minimize Revelation's resemblances to the Jewish apocalypses in order to classify it as a Christian prophecy in continuity with Old Testament prophecy.[2] This discussion has often not sufficiently recognized the diversity of the Jewish apocalypses, both in themes and in literary forms. Nor has it sufficiently distinguished the various dimensions of Revelation's possible relationship to them. Thus one could ask whether John is indebted to Jewish apocalyptic for the literary forms he uses, for theological ideas, for symbolic images, for the ways in which he interprets Old Testament scriptures. In each of these aspects he may be more or less distinctive while also being indebted to apocalyptic tradition. His distinctiveness may be comparable to that of one Jewish apocalypse in relation to others[3] or it may be due to his deliberately Christian

---

[1] J. Massyngberde Ford, *Revelation* (AB 38; New York: Doubleday, 1975) offers one version of the view, which was more popular in a past era of source criticism, that Revelation in fact originated as a Jewish apocalypse (among the followers of John the Baptist, according to Ford), to which some Christian additions have been made. The rather common view that Revelation is 'more Jewish than Christian' (cf. R. Bultmann's famous statement: 'The Christianity of Revelation has to be termed a weakly christianized Judaism': *Theology of the New Testament*, vol. 2 [London: SCM Press, 1955] 175) rests on the untenable presupposition that early Christianity was something different from Judaism, whereas in fact first-century Christianity was a distinctive form of Judaism.

[2] Most recently, F. D. Mazzaferri, *The Genre of the Book of Revelation from a Source-critical Perspective* (BZNW 54; Berlin/New York: de Gruyter, 1989). His case for Revelation's continuity with OT prophecy is excellent, but unfortunately his account of Jewish apocalyptic is a caricature. E. Schüssler Fiorenza, *The Book of Revelation: Justice and Judgment* (Philadelphia: Fortress Press, 1985) chapter 5, rightly refuses the alternative of prophecy or apocalyptic.

[3] I pointed out some rarely noted differences between Revelation and the major Jewish apocalypses in 'The *Figurae* of John of Patmos,' in A. Williams ed., *Prophecy and Millenarianism: Essays in Honour of Marjorie Reeves* (London: Longman, 1980) 109-111 = R. Bauckham, *The Climax of Prophecy: Studies on the Book of Revelation* (Edinburgh: T. & T. Clark, 1993) 174-177.

prophetic consciousness and message. We should probably reckon with both types of distinctiveness.

One aspect of Revelation's relationship to the Jewish apocalypses which has been little enough explored is Revelation's use of specific items of apocalyptic tradition which also appear in Jewish apocalypses and sometimes also in later Christian apocalypses. Where these have been noticed they have often been taken to show that John was actually borrowing from a particular Jewish apocalyptic work, such as 1 Enoch.[4] Although it is *a priori* quite likely that John had read some of the Jewish apocalypses which we know, it seems to me impossible to prove his specific literary dependence on any such work. The traditions in question usually turn out to be attested in a variety of works, Jewish and Christian, in such a way that a chain of literary dependence is very difficult to reconstruct and it seems more plausible to think of traditions which were known, independently of their use in particular apocalypses, in circles, Jewish and Christian, which studied and produced apocalyptic literature. One such tradition, which occurs in Revelation, will be studied in this chapter.[5] It is a way of describing the general resurrection, which in Revelation 20:13a takes this form: 'And the sea gave up the dead which were in it, and Death and Hades gave up the dead which were in them.'

The study of the tradition to which Revelation 20:13a belongs will not only illuminate this verse's relationship to that tradition and illustrate Revelation's use of apocalyptic traditions. It will also be a contribution to the study of ideas of resurrection in early Judaism and early Christianity. For most Jews and Christians, including most of those who wrote the extant literature, such ideas were embodied in conventional ways of speaking about resurrection: words, phrases, images, and scriptural allusions. Some of these, such as the image of resurrection as a waking from sleep, are well-known. But study of the full range of conventional ways of speaking of resurrection in the literature of this period has only begun.[6] It is important that it be pursued

---

[4] E.g. R. H. Charles, *A critical and exegetical commentary on the Revelation of St John* (ICC; Edinburgh: T. & T. Clark, 1920) vol. 1, lxv, lxxxii-lxxxiii; and for discussion, cf. Mazzaferri, *Genre*, 48-49.

[5] For other examples, see Bauckham, *The Climax*, chapter 2.

[6] Significant studies of the language of resurrection include M. E. Dahl, *The Resurrection of the Body* (SBT 36; London: SCM Press, 1962) 98-100, 121-125; C. F. Evans, *Resurrection and the New Testament* (SBT 2/12; London: SCM Press, 1970) 20-27; J. F. A. Sawyer, 'Hebrew words for the resurrection of the dead,' *VT* 23 (1973) 218-234; J. Chmiel, 'Semantics of the Resurrection,' in E. A. Livingstone ed., *Studia Biblica 1978: I. Papers on Old Testament and Related Themes* (JSOTSS 11; Sheffield: JSOT Press, 1979) 59-64.

if we are to advance our understanding of the context in which the New Testament writers spoke of resurrection. In this chapter, we shall explore one traditional image of resurrection: that the place of the dead will give back the dead.

II

In this section we present the collection of texts which will be discussed in the rest of the chapter:

(A) 1 Enoch 51:1:

> And in those days the earth will return that which has been entrusted to it,
> and Sheol will return that which has been entrusted to it, that which it has received,
> and destruction [Abaddon] will return what it owes.[7]

(B) 4 Ezra 7:32:

> *Et terra reddet qui in eam dormiunt*
> *et pulvis qui in eo silentio habitant*
> *et promptuaria reddent quae eis commendatae sunt animae.*
>
> And the earth shall give back those who sleep in it,
> and the dust those who dwell silently in it,
> and the chambers shall give back the souls which have been committed to them.

(C) Revelation 20:13:

> καὶ ἔδωκεν ἡ θάλασσα τοὺς νεκροὺς τοὺς ἐν αὐτῇ,
> καὶ ὁ θάνατος καὶ ὁ Ἅιδης ἔδωκεν τοὺς νεκροὺς τοὺς ἐν αὐτοῖς....
>
> And the sea gave up the dead which were in it,
> And Death and Hades gave up the dead which were in them....

---

[7] Translation by M. A. Knibb, *The Ethiopic Book of Enoch*, vol. 2 (Oxford: Clarendon Press, 1978) 135. E. Isaac in J. H. Charlesworth ed., *The Old Testament Pseudepigrapha*, vol. 1 (London: Darton, Longman & Todd, 1983) 36, prefers a form of the Ethiopic text with only two main clauses:

> In those days, Sheol will return all the deposits which she had received
> and hell [Abaddon] will give back all which it owes.

Isaac discusses the textual variants in this verse in 'New Light Upon the Book of Enoch from Newly-Found Ethiopic MSS,' *JAOS* 103 (1983) 408, where he argues that the three-clause form of the text is a secondary scribal harmonization with 4 Ezra 7:32 (our text B). However, the three-clause form of the text of 1 Enoch 51:1 is closer to LAB 3:10 (our text D), with which it shares the same three terms for the place of the dead (the earth, Sheol, Abaddon). Since LAB is not extant in Ethiopic, this correspondence cannot have originated within the Ethiopic textual tradition. Therefore most probably the three-clause form of the text of 1 Enoch 51:1 is original.

(D) Pseudo-Philo, *Liber Antiquitatum Biblicarum* 3:10:

> ...*Et vivificabo mortuos, et erigam dormientes de terra.*
> *Et reddet infernus debitum suum*
> *et perditio restituet paratecen suam....*

> ...And I will give life to the dead, and raise from the earth those who
>   sleep,
> and Sheol will give back what it owes,
> and Abaddon will restore what has been entrusted to it....

(E) 2 Baruch 21:23:

> Therefore, reprove the angel of death, and let your glory appear, and let
>   the greatness of your beauty be known,
> and let the realm of death [Sheol] be sealed so that it may not receive the
>   dead from this time,
> and let the treasuries of the souls restore those who are enclosed in them.[8]

(F) Apocalypse of Peter 4:3-4:

> He will command Gehenna that it open its bars of adamant and to give
>   back all which is his in it.
> **4** He will command the beasts and the birds, [and] he will command that
>   they give back all the flesh they have eaten,
> because he requires human beings to make their appearance.[9]

(G)   Apocalypse of Peter 4:10-12:

> **10** See and understand the seeds which were sown in the ground. Like a
> dry thing which is without soul it is sown into the ground, and it lives and
> bears fruit. **11** And the earth will give back in accordance with (its) pledge
> what has been entrusted to it. That which dies, the seed sown in the
> ground, and revives and is given life (is) the human race. **12** How much
> more (will he not revive) those who believe in him, and his elect ones, for
> whose sake he made (the earth). God will raise them up on the day of
> judgment.[10]

(H) Apocryphal quotation in Tertullian, *De Res.* 32.1:

> *Et mandabo piscibus maris*
> *et eructuabunt ossa quae sunt comesta,*
> *et faciam compaginem ad compaginam et os ad os.*

---

[8] Translation by A. F. J. Klijn, in Charlesworth, *Old Testament Pseudepigrapha*, vol.
1, 628.
[9] Translation by D. D. Buchholz, *Your Eyes Will Be Opened: A Study of the Greek
(Ethiopic) Apocalypse of Peter* (SBLDS 97; Atlanta, Georgia: Scholars Press, 1988) 181,
183.
[10] Translation by Buchholz, *Your Eyes*, 185, 187.

And I will command the fish of the sea,
and they shall vomit up the bones that were consumed,
and I will bring joint to joint and bone to bone.

(I) 2 Baruch 42:8:

And dust will be called, and told,
'Give back that which does not belong to you
and raise up all that you have kept until its own time.'[11]

(J) 2 Baruch 50:2:

For the earth will surely give back the dead at that time;
it receives them now in order to keep them, not changing anything in
their form.
But as it has received them so it will give them back
And as I have delivered them to it so it will raise them.[12]

(K) 4 Ezra 4:41b–43a:

In inferno promptuaria animarum matrici adsimilata sunt.
42 *Quemadmodum enim festinavit quae parit effugere necessitatem partus,
sic et haec festinat reddere ea quae commendata sunt* **43** *ab initio.*

The chambers of the souls in Sheol are like the womb.
42 For just as a woman in travail hastens to escape the pains of
childbirth,
so also do these places hasten to give back what has been entrusted to
them **43** from the beginning.

(L) Pseudo-Philo, *Liber Antiquitatum Biblicarum* 33:3:

*...infernus accipiens sibi deposita non restituet nisi reposcetur ab eo qui
deposuit ei....*

...Sheol which has received what has been entrusted to it will not restore
it unless it is reclaimed by him who entrusted it to it....

(M) Midrash on Psalms 1:20:

R. Berechiah taught: It was the wilderness which said, *I am the rose of
Sharon* (Cant 2:1): 'I am the one beloved by the Holy One, blessed be He,
for all the good things of the world are hidden within me, and God has
bestowed his blessing upon me, for He said, *I will plant in the wilderness the
cedar, the Shittah tree, and the myrtle, and the oil-tree; I will set in the desert the fir-
tree, and the pine, and the box-tree together* (Isa 41:10). And when the Holy One,
blessed be He, requires it of me, I shall return to God what He laid away
with me, and I shall again blossom as the rose, and shall sing a song to

---

[11] Translation by A. F. J. Klijn, in Charlesworth, *Old Testament Pseudepigrapha*, vol.
1, 634.
[12] Translation by Klijn, in Charlesworth, *Old Testament Pseudepigrapha*, vol. 1, 638.

Him, for it is said, *The wilderness and the parched land shall be glad; and the desert shall rejoice, and blossom as the rose* (Isa 35:1).'

The Rabbis taught that it was the earth which said *I am the rose of Sharon:* 'I am the beloved one in whose shadows all the dead of the world are hidden. But when the Holy One, blessed be He, requires it of me, I shall return to Him what He laid away with me, as it is said *Thy dead shall live, my dead bodies shall arise—Awake and sing ye that dwell in the dust* (Isa 26:19), and I will blossom as the rose, and sing a song to God, as it is said *From the uttermost part of the earth have we heard songs: "Glory to the Righteous"* (Isa 24:16).'[13]

(N) Midrash Rabbah on Canticles 2:1:2:

R. Berekiah said: This verse (Cant 2:1) is spoken by the wilderness. Said the wilderness: 'I am the wilderness, and beloved am I, for all the good things of the world are hidden in me, as it says, *I will plant in the wilderness the cedar, the acacia tree* (Isa 41:19); God has placed them in me for safe keeping, and when God requires them from me, I shall return to Him His deposit unimpaired. I also shall blossom with good deeds, and chant a song before Him, as it says, *The wilderness and the parched land shall be glad* (Isa 35:1).' In the name of the Rabbis it was said: This verse is said by the land [of Israel]. It says: 'I am it, and I am beloved, since all the dead are hidden in me, as it says, *Thy dead shall live, my dead bodies shall arise* (Isa 26:19). When God shall require them from me I shall return them to Him, and I shall blossom forth with good deeds like a rose, and chant a new song before Him, as it says, *From the uttermost parts of the earth have we heard songs* (Isa 24:16).'[14]

(O) Pirqe de R. Eliezer 34:

Rabbi Ishmael said: All the bodies crumble into the dust of the earth, until nothing remains of the body except a spoonful of earthy matter. In the future life, when the Holy One, blessed be He, calls to the earth to return all the bodies deposited with it, that which has become mixed with the dust of the earth, like the yeast which is mixed with the dough, improves and increases, and it raises up all the body. When the Holy One, blessed be He, calls to the earth to return all the bodies deposited with it, that which has become mixed with the dust of the earth, improves and increases and raises up all the body without water.[15]

---

[13] Translation by W. G. Braude, *The Midrash on Psalms,* vol. 1 (YJS; New Haven: Yale University Press, 1959) 28-29. Braude's note explains the first paragraph as referring to the generation that died in the wilderness wanderings and were buried in the desert, but another possibility is suggested by 1 Enoch 61:5, quoted and discussed in section IV below.

[14] Translation by M. Simon in H. Freedman and M. Simon ed., *Midrash Rabbah,* vol. 9 (London: Soncino Press, 1939) 92.

[15] Translation by G. Friedlander, *Pirkê de Rabbi Eliezer* (2nd edition; New York: Hermon Press, 1965) 258.

(P) Pesiqta Rabbati 21:4:

> Another comment [on Ps 76:9]: R. Phinehas taught in the name of R. Johanan: If the earth is said to have *feared*, why *still*? And if *still*, why *feared*? The explanation of the earth's fear is in what the earth said: 'It may be that the time of the resurrection of the dead has come and the Holy One, blessed be He, requires of me what He has deposited with me, as it is written *The earth also shall disclose her blood and shall no more cover her slain* (Isa 26:21).' But then when she heard God say *I*, she grew still.[16]

(Q) b. Sanh. 92a:

> R. Tabi said in R. Josia's name: What is meant by, *The grave; and the barren womb; and the earth that is not filled by water* (Prov 30:16): now, what connection has the grave with the womb? But it is to teach thee: just as the womb receives and brings forth, so does the grave too receive and bring forth. Now, does not this furnish us with an *a fortiori* argument? If the womb, which receives in silence, yet brings forth amid great cries [of jubilation]; then the grave, which receives the dead amid cries [of grief], will much more so bring them forth amid great cries [of joy]![17]

III

It will be useful to preface our consideration of the texts given in section II with a brief distinction between two basic ideas of resurrection in Jewish tradition, which we may call unitary and dualistic. The simplest and doubtless the earliest Jewish notion of resurrection was that the dead would return from the place of the dead to life on earth. It presupposed the existence of the dead as shades in Sheol and imagined these shades returning from Sheol to real life. Because ancient Israelite thought made no sharp distinctions between Sheol and the grave or between the dead person in Sheol and the body in the grave, such distinctions did not belong to the original notion of resurrection. The dead person was conceived as returning from Sheol and of course resuming a fully corporal existence, but this did not necessarily mean that the shade from Sheol was reunited with his or her corpse, resuscitated from the grave. Since death was not conceived as the separation of the person from her body, but as the death of the bodily person, so resurrection was not the reunion of person and body, but the resurrection of the bodily person. The notion is not the resurrection of the body so much as the bodily resurrection of the dead.

---

[16] Translation by W. G. Braude, *Pesikta Rabbati* (YJS 18; New Haven: Yale University Press, 1968) 419.

[17] Translation by H. Freedman in I. Epstein ed., *The Babylonian Talmud: Sanhedrin* (London: Soncino Press, 1935) 618.

Reflection on and apologetic defence of this idea could easily produce a more dichotomous anthropology in which death is seen as the separation of the shade which descends to Sheol from the body which is laid in the grave, and resurrection is therefore understood as the reunion of the two. Such a development is quite comprehensible even without hellenistic influence, though hellenistic influence may have had some part to play in it. In any case, its dualism is not a truly Greek dualism, but preserves in its own way the Jewish conviction that human life is essentially corporeal. If the shade and its body are sharply distinguished in death, then precisely because the body is integral and essential to the person's life, his return to life must mean the return of his body to life just as much as the return of his shade to life. It must mean the reunion of shade and body in restored bodily life. When the words soul or spirit are used in this conception to refer to the shade in Sheol,[18] they should not be taken in the fully Platonic sense of the real person who never dies but escapes from the body into eternal life. Both the soul in Sheol and the body in the grave are *dead*; both come back to life in the resurrection when they are re-united. The more soul and body were distinguished in *death*, the more it was necessary to preserve the Jewish unitary view of human *life* by insisting that this earthly body is raised to eternal life.[19] While the older view was content to think of the dead returning (of course, to bodily life), many Jews and Christians of the first and second centuries c.e. increasingly insisted on the resurrection (as well as, of course, transformation) of *this* body which has been buried in the grave. They did not all do so, but often it was precisely those who were most aware of hellenistic anthropological dualism who guarded against it by stressing the resurrection of *this* body, and who entered on a rather detailed apologetic for this somewhat difficult notion.

However, what we need especially to recognize in the present context is that older ways of thinking and speaking of resurrection, simply as the return of the dead from Sheol, persisted alongside newer, more dualistic ideas of a reunion of soul and body. The former were enshrined in various *traditional ways of speaking* about resurrection, of which the tradition we shall study was one. It is probably correct to suppose that many writers had, not so much a concept of resurrection, but rather a number of conventional ways of speaking of resurrection. Older and newer ways of speaking of resurrection

---

[18] For the usage of these terms, see D. S. Russell, *The Method and Message of Jewish Apocalyptic* (London: SCM Press, 1964) 357-360.

[19] Of course, there were also forms of Jewish expectation which did not expect bodily resurrection: e.g. Jubilees, Wisdom.

were not necessarily perceived as contradictory and may both be used by the same writer. Armed with these preliminary observations we may be better able to appreciate the tradition embodied in the series of texts collected in section II, whose basic image of resurrection is that *the place of the dead will give back the dead*.

With the exception of the rabbinic texts (M-Q), in which the tradition survives at later dates, all of the texts given (A-L) probably date from the period c. 50-150 c.e. However, we should remember that this is a period from which a great deal of Jewish and Christian apocalyptic literature survives. It may be an accident of the survival of sources that the tradition is not attested earlier.[20] In any case, it seems clear that the recurrence of this tradition in a variety of Jewish and Christian works cannot be explained purely by literary relationships among these works.[21] We must be dealing with a rather widespread traditional formula.

Since a great deal of Jewish thinking about resurrection seems to have derived from reflection on Old Testament texts which could be interpreted as referring to resurrection, it is possible that our tradition originated as a paraphrase of the end of Isaiah 26:19 ('the earth will cast forth the shades,' or 'the earth will give birth to the shades'). Apart from Isaiah 26:21, if this is interpreted of resurrection, Isaiah 26:19 is the only Old Testament text which makes the place of the dead (here the earth) the subject of the act of resurrection, just as our tradition does. Modern scholarship usually takes תפיל to mean 'will give birth to' (i.e. let [the young] drop). The earth gives birth to the dead who are at present in her womb. This image of resurrection as birth is rare in later Jewish literature, but texts K (4 Ezra 4:41-42) and text Q (b. Sanh. 92a) both compare the place of the dead with the womb and the act of resurrection with childbirth. Isaiah 26:19 may lie behind these passages. It is worth noting that text Q (included at the end of our collection of texts because it uses the idea, though not the actual language of *giving back* the dead) understands childbirth as a matter of giving back what has been received. Just as the womb

---

[20] Therefore it is rather doubtful whether the correspondence between 1 Enoch 51:1 and examples of our tradition in 2 Baruch, 4 Ezra and LAB can itself be taken as an indication of a late first-century c.e. date for the Parables of Enoch, as G. Stemberger, *Der Leib der Auferstehung: Studien zur Anthropologie und Eschatologie des palästinischen Judentums im neutestamentlichen Zeitalter (ca. 170 v. Chr—100 n. Chr.)* (AnBib 56; Rome: Biblical Institute Press, 1972) 29, proposes.

[21] M. Black, *The Book of Enoch or I Enoch: A New English Edition* (SVTP 7; Leiden: Brill, 1985) 214, regards LAB 3:10 as 'a clear allusion' to 1 Enoch 51:1, but the full range of parallels makes common tradition at least as likely.

receives and brings forth, so the grave receives the dead and brings them forth.

However, if our tradition originated from interpretation of Isaiah 26:19, the Jewish reader of Isaiah 26:19 who originated it missed or did not appreciate the image of childbirth. Instead, he paraphrased the last three words of the verse in terms of a legal metaphor: 'the earth will return that which has been entrusted to it.'[22] This statement occurs in this form in text A (1 Enoch 51:1), which may well preserve the most original form of our tradition, and the same idea recurs in many of our texts (see texts B, D, G, I, K, L, M, O, P). The full legal terminology is clearest in text L (LAB 33:3). The idea is that God has entrusted the dead to the place of the dead for safekeeping. The place of the dead does not therefore own them, but owes them to God and must return them when he reclaims them at the time of the resurrection. The point of the metaphor is that Sheol has no absolute right to the dead so that it may retain them for ever. It has only a temporary right, a kind of custodianship of the dead, granted it by God. The dead actually belong to God; he entrusts them to Sheol for safekeeping, but retains the right to reclaim them. The idea therefore represents a powerful step beyond the old idea that in death a person falls out of the sphere of God's sovereignty into the power of Sheol. The metaphor of God's entrusting the dead to Sheol for safekeeping is an assertion of God's sovereignty over the realm of the dead, and therefore of his power to demand that Sheol surrender the dead back to life.

The three lines of text A (1 Enoch 51:1) repeat the same thought in synonymous parallelism. The three terms 'earth,' 'Sheol,' and 'Abaddon,' are used synonymously for the place of the dead. The thought of the whole verse is simply that the place of the dead will give back the dead who have been entrusted to it. Some have interpreted this text (as well as other texts in our collection) according to the dualistic understanding of resurrection, according to which the body must be recovered from one place, the soul from another, in order to be reunited. The earth restores the body, Sheol and Abaddon the soul. But in that case one would have expected two lines rather than three. R. H. Charles thought that Sheol and Abaddon represent two different places from which the righteous and the wicked souls respectively come,[23] but there is no evidence of such a

---

[22] The same legal metaphor is used differently in the idea that a person's soul is entrusted to him or her by God and must be returned at death: GkApEzra 6:3, 17, 21; ApSedr 9:2; Hermas, *Mand.* 3.2.

[23] R. H. Charles, *The Book of Enoch* (2nd edition; Oxford: Clarendon Press, 1912) 99.

distinction between the terms Sheol and Abaddon in Jewish litera-ture.[24] In Old Testament texts they occur in synonymous parallelism as alternative terms for the place of the dead (Job 26:6; cf. Prov 15:11; 27:20; 1QH 3:19). It is best to interpret the whole verse in continuity with Old Testament thought, according to which the *dead person* is in the earth or Sheol or Abaddon.[25] The personification of the place of the dead is also rooted in Old Testament usage (e.g. Job 24:19; 28:22; Isa 5:14).

Comparison of text A (1 Enoch 51:1) with the following texts (B-E) shows that there was a traditional formulation, whose basic structure is three lines of synonymous parallelism expressing the thought that the place of the dead will give back the dead. The persistence of the threefold form indicates that in none of these cases are we likely to be justified in distinguishing a place of the body and a place of the soul: the idea expressed in this form remains the simple one of the return of the dead. The various terms for the place of the dead which are used in these texts can be understood, largely from an Old Testament background, as synonyms for Sheol.

As well as the three terms for the place of the dead in text A (1 Enoch 51:1)—the earth, Sheol, Abaddon—which recur exactly in text D and two of which recur individually in some other texts (earth: texts B, D, G, M, N, O, P; Sheol/Hades: texts C, E, L), the following terms are also used in these texts to describe the place or the power which gives back the dead: the dust (texts B, I), the chambers or treasuries of the souls (texts B, E, K), the sea (text C), Death (text C), the angel of death (text E), and Gehenna (text F). The last is surpris-ing, especially as the text refers to the iron gates which are elsewhere those of Sheol/Hades,[26] and must be understood as the Ethiopic translation's rendering of Hades in the original Greek of the Apoca-lypse of Peter.[27] This is confirmed by Sibylline Oracle 2:228-229 (quoted in section IV below), which is dependent on this verse of the Apocalypse of Peter and refers to 'the gates of Hades.' The references in texts F and H to animals which are commanded to give back the dead will be left aside now for discussion in section IV.

Of the remaining terms, 'the dust' is used as in Isaiah 26:19 and Daniel 12:2, two key passages for the Jewish concept of resurrection,

---

[24] Stemberger, *Leib der Auferstehung*, 46. In AscenIs 10:8, Abaddon is the lowest part of the underworld, below Sheol, but there is no indication that it contains a distinct class of the dead.

[25] For the earth as synonymous with Sheol, see 1 Sam 28.13.

[26] Isa 38:10; Wis 16:13; 3 Macc 5:51; PsSol 16:2; Matt 16:18; cf. Ps 107:16; OdesSol 17:10.

[27] Cf. Buchholz, *Your Eyes*, 293.

as well as in other Old Testament passages (e.g. Job 17:16; 20:11; Pss 22:29; 30:10), for the place of the dead. 'The angel of death' in text E (2 Bar 21:23) may be Abaddon, who is 'the angel of the abyss' in Revelation 9:11. The personification of Abaddon in Job 28:22 could have led to the idea that he is the angel in charge of the underworld and therefore the angelic power to whom God entrusts the dead.

In Revelation 20:13 the three places of the dead are the sea, Death and Hades. The personified Death may be this author's substitute for Abaddon, since he has used the latter name for the king of the demons (rather than the ruler of the dead) in 9:11 (cf. also 4QBer^a 2:7). Death and Hades are a standard pair in Revelation (1:18; 6:8; 20:13-14; cf. also LAB 3:10b) and may represent the Old Testament pair Sheol and Abaddon, though there is also Old Testament precedent for the pair Death and Sheol (Hos 13:14). More problematic is the sea. It is not plausible to introduce a distinction between body and soul into this verse, so that sea is the place from which the bodies of those who have died at sea are recovered, while Death and Hades surrender their souls.[28] In this case, the earth as the place where the bodies of other people are to be found would surely have to be mentioned too. But in any case, the object of both clauses is 'the dead' (τοὺς νεκρούς). The language is clearly not intended to distinguish soul and body, but simply to speak of the return of the dead. There seem then to be two possible explanations for the reference to the sea. It may be the place for a special category of the dead: those who have died at sea.[29] Whereas those who are buried in the earth are thought of as being in Sheol/Hades, those who die at sea are thought of as being in the subterranean ocean. But there seems to be no other evidence for this distinction.[30] So more probably, and in the light of

---

[28] J. Daniélou, *The Theology of Jewish Christianity* (trans. J. A. Baker; London: Darton, Longman & Todd/Philadelphia: Westminster Press, 1964) 24-25, suggests that according to the original text of 4 (5) Ezra 2:31 God will bring the dead from the 'depths of the earth' and 'the depths of the sea': but this reconstruction of the original text is highly conjectural. Cf. also SibOr 2:233 (quoted in section IV below): but here those who die at sea are only one category of several whose bodies are destroyed without burial.

[29] Charles, *Revelation*, vol. 2, 195-196, thinks this is the meaning of the present text, though he considers the original text to have read τὰ ταμεῖα rather than ἡ θάλασσα.

[30] Cf. H. B. Swete, *The Apocalypse of St John* (2nd edition; London: Macmillan, 1907) 273; M. Kiddle, *The Revelation of St John* (MNTC; London: Hodder & Stoughton, 1940) 406; G. B. Caird, *The Revelation of St John the Divine* (BNTC; London: A. & C. Black, 1966) 260. These writers depend on a passage in Achilles Tatius (fifth century C.E.), cited by Wetstein, to the effect that those who die at sea have no access to Hades. I do not know the basis for the claim by Ford, *Revelation* 359, that 'there was a tradition that only those who died on dry land would rise from the dead.'

several Old Testament passages which closely associate the subterranean ocean with Sheol (e.g. 2 Sam 22:5-6; Job 26:5; Ps 69:15; Jon 2),
the sea is here simply another synonym for Sheol. Thus Revelation
20:13 preserves the synonymous parallelism exhibited by the tradition
as found elsewhere.

There remains the term: the chambers of the souls. This term
occurs frequently in 4 Ezra, twice in 2 Baruch (21:23; 30:2), once in
Pseudo-Philo (LAB 32:13; cf. 21:9), and occasionally in the Rabbis, to
designate the place where the righteous dead await the resurrection.
(LAB 15:5 also speaks of the 'chambers of darkness' where the wicked
are kept.) It may have originated as an interpretation of Isaiah
26:20.[31] Whether or not the original text of 4 Ezra 4:41 (text K)
explicitly located the chambers of the souls in Sheol, there can be
little doubt that both 2 Baruch and 4 Ezra imply that the chambers
are in Sheol. So the phrase 'the chambers of the souls' is another
equivalent to Sheol, the place of the dead, at least with reference to
the righteous dead.

In this context 'souls' *need* mean no more than the dead in Sheol,
the shades. It need not imply the distinction of body and soul in death
and resurrection as the reunion of the two. Certainly, this dichotomous view of death and resurrection seems not to be found in 2
Baruch, which can describe the resurrection either as the coming
forth of the souls from the chambers (chapter 30) or as the restoration
of the dead by the earth in the same bodily form in which they died
(chapter 50). These are surely not two distinct aspects of resurrection,
but alternative ways of describing the same event: the return of the
dead to bodily life. 2 Baruch never speaks of death as the separation
of soul and body or of resurrection as the reunion of the two.

4 Ezra, however, does explicitly speak of death as the separation of
soul and body (7:78, 88-89, 100).[32] Presumably, therefore, for this
author resurrection must be the reunion of body and soul, and
Stemberger argues that he actually describes it in those terms in 7:32
(our text B), though his use of the traditional formulation hampers
him in doing so. According to Stemberger, the first two lines of this
text are intended to describe the return of the body from the earth,

---

[31] This is how the chambers (ταμεῖα) of Isa 26:19 are understood in 1 Clem 50:4,
which gives a composite quotation of Isa 26:19 and Ezek 37:12. (On this quotation,
see Daniélou, *Theology of Jewish Christianity*, 95; and idem, 'La Vision des ossements
desséchés (Ezech. 37,1-14) dans les *Testimonia*,' *RechSR* 53 [1965] 221, 225.) That the
chambers of Isa 26:19 are in Sheol could have been concluded by comparison with
Prov 7:27, according to the midrashic technique of *gᵉzērā šawā*.

[32] On 4 Ezra's anthropology, see Stemberger, *Leib der Auferstehung*, 79-81.

the third line the return of the soul from the chambers.[33] He argues
that the third line is set apart from the first two by the change from
the simple pronoun (*qui*) to 'the souls which' (*animae quae*).[34]

However, it remains more plausible to interpret all three lines as
synonymous parallelism, as elsewhere in this tradition. In each line
the author uses a traditional description of the dead which is appropriate to the place of the dead as specified in that line. Thus in the
first line, the earth gives back those who sleep in it, because 'those
who sleep in the earth' is a traditional description of the dead (Dan
12:2; 2 Bar 11:4; 21:24), while in the second line the dust gives back
those who dwell silently in it, because 'those who dwell in the dust' is
another traditional description of the dead (Isa 26:19; cf. Job 7:21;
Dan 12:2; 1QH 6:34).[35] When in the third line the author uses 'souls'
to describe the dead, this is not meant to distinguish this line from the
first two, but simply to correspond to the conventional phrase 'the
chambers of the souls.' When 'the chambers' is used for the place of
the dead, the appropriate term for the dead is 'souls,' just as when
'the earth' is used for the place of the dead, the appropriate term for
the dead is 'those who sleep in it.' Thus 4 Ezra has not broken the
rule that the three lines of the traditional form are synonymous, and
although the author himself probably understood resurrection as the
reunion of soul and body, the language of the traditional form he uses
in itself expresses no more than the simple idea of the return of the
dead from the place of the dead.

In 4 Ezra 7:32 we see the persistence of the traditional form in a
context where it is no longer strictly appropriate. If this form is to be
interpreted consistently with a dichotomous view of death and resurrection, it becomes necessary to regard the dead whom Sheol restores
as *either* souls who return from the place of souls *or* bodies which are
brought up from their graves. If the author of 4 Ezra himself interpreted 7:32 in line with his own dichotomous view, he must have
taken it to refer to the return of souls rather than bodies. In other
writers, however, the language of bringing back the dead was adapted
to the dichotomous view in the alternative manner, i.e. it is used of
the return of bodies from their graves. This is the case in text O, a
late rabbinic passage, which is clearly concerned with the physical
continuity of the old body and the resurrection body, and interprets
the traditional language to mean that the earth receives and restores
the corpse. It therefore exhibits an apologetic concern with the prob-

---

[33] Stemberger, *Leib der Auferstehung*, 75, 82.
[34] Stemberger, *Leib der Auferstehung*, 74.
[35] For Sheol as a place of silence, cf. Pss 94:17; 115:17.

lem of the decay of the corpse, which is foreign to the older way of speaking represented by the majority of our texts. It is worth noticing that although the Rabbis in general held a dichotomous view of death and resurrection, the other rabbinic texts in our collection (N, P, Q) still speak of the earth receiving and restoring *the dead*, not their bodies. This is a striking example of the persistence of conventional language about resurrection.

A particularly interesting use of our tradition occurs in 2 Baruch 50:2 (text J). Like Paul in 1 Corinthians 15:35, the author is here concerned to answer the question, 'In what form will the dead rise?' (cf. 49:2-3). The answer is a kind of two-stage resurrection: the dead are first raised in exactly the form in which they died (50:2) and then transformed into glory. The first stage is necessary so that the dead can be recognized. This seems to be in answer to an apologetic problem which is explicitly raised in rabbinic literature (e.g. GenRab 95:1; EcclRab 1:4:2): how will it be possible to know that it is really the dead who are raised? The answer is that they will initially be recognizable as the same people who died.[36] But in order to maintain that the dead will initially be raised in exactly the form in which they died, 2 Baruch does not, as has often been said,[37] appeal to the notion of resurrection as resuscitation of the corpse. At any rate, the passage need not be read as concerned with the material identity of the body. Essentially what it does is to press the implications of the notion that the place of the dead will restore the dead who were committed to it. In strict law, this legal notion requires that Sheol restore *exactly* what was entrusted to it. Therefore the dead will return from Sheol exactly as they went to it.

Finally in this section, some further observations on the form the tradition takes in our various texts will be appropriate. The tradition appears in its pure form only in texts A and B: three lines each of which states that the place of the dead will give back the dead who were entrusted to it. Text C (Rev 20:13) has abbreviated the form: it has three terms for the place of the dead, but couples the last two in one line. It has also dropped the legal metaphor, and with this omission the idea of giving *back* the dead has receded from prominence. Text D retains the legal metaphor and the same three terms for the place of the dead as are found in text A. However, the first line no longer speaks of the earth returning the dead but of God raising them. This change has probably been made in order to adapt the form to its context here in a divine speech and to emphasize the

---

[36] For recognition in the resurrection, cf. also LAB 62:9.
[37] E.g. Evans, *Resurrection and the New Testament*, 16.

divine initiative in the act of resurrection. A similar motivation may account for the more drastic modification in text E, which is in the context of a prayer to God. Here the idea of the place of the dead restoring the dead is found only in the last clause, but the three terms (angel of death, Sheol, treasuries of the souls) may indicate that the threefold formula still lies behind this text.

Another group of texts (I-O) do not preserve the threefold formula, but use only one term for the place of the dead. However, they employ the same image of resurrection: the place of the dead restores the dead who have been committed to it. It should be noted that most of the texts in this group make explicit what the standard formula (found in the threefold form in texts A-E) does not: that Sheol restores the dead *when and because* God requires it to do so (texts I, L-P). These texts are evidently concerned to stress that resurrection is God's act. The same concern is found in texts F and H, which also, in referring to animals which have eaten the dead, constitute a special variation of the whole tradition, which raises problems to be considered separately in the next section.

Text G (ApPet 4:10-12) is anomalous in that the deposit with which the earth is entrusted and returns is here the seeds which are sown in it and grow out of it as plants. The Apocalypse of Peter is using the rather widespread analogy of the seed for the process of death and resurrection (cf. 1 Cor 15:36-38; John 12:24; 1 Clem 24:4-5; Justin, *1 Apol.* 19.4; 3 Cor 3:26-27; Theophilus, *Ad Autol.* 1.13; b. Ket. 111b; b. Sanh. 90b; EcclRab 5:10:1; Pirqe de R. Eliezer 33).[38] The two traditions about resurrection are combined in such a way that our tradition retains its original reference—to the earth giving back *the dead*—only indirectly, as it were, by way of the seed which is an image for the dead.

IV

The two texts F and H in our collection of texts in section II are distinguished from the others by their common use of the idea that God will command *animals* which have eaten the dead to give back the dead. There are two other texts (1 Enoch 61:5; SibOr 2:227-237) which were not included in the collection in section II because they do not belong to the tradition represented by that collection, but which do share with texts F and H an interest in the resurrection of

---

[38] The whole of chapter 4 of the Apocalypse of Peter is a collection of traditions about resurrection. Although the work itself is Jewish Christian, this collection is of purely Jewish traditions.

the dead that have been consumed by animals. Since these will be relevant to our discussion of texts F and H, it will be useful to give them here, along with texts F (extended) and H:

1 Enoch 61:5:

> And these measurements will reveal all the secrets of the depths of the
> earth,
> and those who were destroyed by the desert,
> and those who were destroyed by the fish of the sea and by the animals,
> that they may return and rely on the day of the Chosen One;
> for no one will be destroyed before the Lord of Spirits,
> and no one can be destroyed.[39]

Sibylline Oracle 2:227-237:

> καὶ τότ᾽ ἀμειλίκτοιο καὶ ἀρρήκτου ἀδάμαντος
> κλεῖθα πέλωρα πυλῶν τε ἀχαλκεύτου Ἀίδαο
> ῥηξάμενος Οὐριὴλ μέγας ἄγγελος εὐθὺ βαλεῖται,
> καὶ πάσας μορφὰς πολυπενθέας εἰς χρίσιν ἄξει
> εἰδώλον τὰ μάλιστα παλαιγενέων Τιτήνων
> ἠδ᾽ ὁπόσας θῆρες καὶ ἑρπετὰ καὶ πετεηνά
> θοινήσαντο, ὅλας ταύτας ἐπὶ βῆμα καλέσσει·
> καὶ πάλιν, ἅς ἔφθειρεν ἐνὶ φλογὶ σαρκοφάγον πῦρ,
> καὶ ταύτας ἐπὶ βῆμα θεοῦ στήσειεν ἀγείρας.[40]

> Then Uriel, the great angel, will break the gigantic bolts,
> of unyielding and unbreakable steel, of the gates
> of Hades, not forged of metal; he will throw them wide open
> and will lead all the mournful forms to judgment,
> especially those of ancient phantoms, Titans
> and the Giants and such as the Flood destroyed.
> Also those whom the wave of the sea destroyed in the oceans,
> and as many as wild beasts and serpents and birds
> devoured; all these he will call to the tribunal.
> Again, those whom the flesh-devouring fire destroyed by flame,
> these also he will gather and set at the tribunal of God.[41]

Apocalypse of Peter 4:3-5, 7-8:

> He will command Gehenna that it open its bars of adamant and to give
> back all which is his in it.
> **4** He will command the beasts and the birds, [and] he will command that
> they give back all the flesh they have eaten,

---

[39] Translation by Knibb, *Enoch*, 148-149.

[40] Text from J. Geffcken, *Die Oracula Sibyllina* (GCS 8: Leipzig: Hinrichs, 1902) 38-39.

[41] Translation by J. J. Collins in Charlesworth, *Old Testament Pseudepigrapha*, vol. 1, 350-351.

because he requires human beings to make their appearance.
5 For there is nothing which perishes for God,
and there is nothing which is impossible for him....
7 ...thus it says in the scripture: the son of man prophesied to each of the
bones,
8 saying to the bone, "Bone (be) to bones in limbs, tendons and nerves,
and flesh and skin, and hair on it."[42]

Apocryphal quotation in Tertullian, *De Res.* 32:1:

Et mandabo piscibus maris
et eructuabunt ossa quae sunt comesta,
et faciam compaginem ad compaginam et os ad os.

And I will command the fish of the sea,
and they shall vomit up the bones that were consumed,
and I will bring joint to joint and bone to bone.

The second of these texts occurs within a passage (SibOr 2:196-338)
which is largely a poetic paraphrase of the Apocalypse of Peter.[43] The
passage quoted is dependent on Apocalypse of Peter 4:3-4, 9; 6:7. It
is possible that lines 233-237, with their references not only to those
eaten by animals, but also to those destroyed by sea and fire, reflect a
longer text of Apocalypse of Peter 4:4 than is preserved in the
Ethiopic version. But Sibylline Oracle 2 frequently expands on its
source in the Apocalypse of Peter.

The relationship of the other texts is more problematic. The
Apocalypse of Peter has in common with 1 Enoch 61:1 not only the
reference to animals who have devoured the dead (animals and birds
in one case, fish and animals in the other), but also an explanatory
statement to the effect that God allows noone to be permanently
destroyed:

'For there is nothing which perishes for God' (ApPet 4:5)

'For no one will be destroyed before the Lord of Spirits' (1 En 61:1).

The apocryphal quotation which Tertullian cites as Scripture agrees
with 1 Enoch against the Apocalypse of Peter in referring to 'the fish
of the sea'.[44] But both the Apocalypse of Peter and Tertullian's quo-

---

[42] Translation by Buchholz, *Your Eyes*, 181, 183, 185.

[43] This was conclusively shown by M. R. James, 'A New Text of the Apocalypse of
Peter,' *JTS* 12 (1911) 39-44, 51-52, but is not recognized by Daniélou, 'La Vision des
ossements desséchés,' 224-225, whose study entirely neglects the Apocalypse of Peter,
or by Collins in his discussion of sources and redaction in SibOr 2 in Charlesworth,
Old Testament Pseudepigrapha, vol. 1, 330-333.

[44] In the comment which follows the quotation (32:2), Tertullian refers also to 'the
other animals and carnivorous birds.'

tation, unlike 1 Enoch, state that *God will command* the animals in question to restore what they have eaten, which is in one case said to be flesh and in the other bones (whereas in 1 Enoch the reference is to persons destroyed). This makes it less likely than has usually been thought[45] that Tertullian himself or his quotation is directly dependent on 1 Enoch 61:1. It is possible that the Apocalypse of Peter is dependent on 1 Enoch 61:1 (which would make it the earliest evidence of the existence of the Parables of Enoch), but most likely that all three texts are dependent on a common tradition. In the Apocalypse of Peter this tradition in 4:4 occurs in a form exactly parallel to 4:3 and so becomes a variant of the tradition that the place of the dead will give back the dead. This is also, though less clearly, the case in Tertullian's quotation (where the more graphic 'vomit up' takes the place of 'give back'). The idea of *God commanding* the place of the dead to give back the dead is found elsewhere in the texts we have collected in section II (see texts E, I, M, N, O, P).

In Tertullian's quotation the specification that it is 'bones' that are eaten and restored by the fish is appropriate to the last line of the quotation, which alludes to Ezekiel 37:7, but in a particular form that is also found in Justin (*1 Apol.* 52.5: 'Joint shall be joined to joint, and bone to bone, and flesh shall grow again...').[46] Both Tertullian's quotation and Justin's (which is attributed to Ezekiel but continues with words from Isa 45:24) are the kind of composite and adapted quotations typical of the early Christian *testimonia*.[47] At first sight it looks as though Tertullian's quotation may be dependent on the Apocalypse of Peter, since the latter has not only a parallel to the first two lines of the former in 4:4 but also a quotation from scripture in 4:7-8 which includes words similar to the last line of Tertullian's quotation. But this line is in fact closer to Justin's quotation than it is to ApPet 4:7-8,[48] whereas the latter can now be seen to be, not a free quotation from canonical Ezekiel, but a more exact quotation from the recently published apocryphal Ezekiel text from Qumran (4Q385 Second Ezekiel[a] 2:5-7).[49]

---

[45] E.g. E. Evans, *Tertullian's Treatise on the Resurrection* (London: SPCK, 1960) 266; J. Daniélou, *The Origins of Latin Christianity*, tr. J. A. Baker (London: Darton, Longman & Todd/Philadelphia: Westminster Press, 1977) 166-167.

[46] For later patristic citations of the text in this form, see Daniélou, 'La Vision des ossements desséchés,' 222.

[47] Cf. Daniélou, 'La Vision des ossements desséchés,' 222-224.

[48] O. Skarsaune, *The Proof from Prophecy* (NovTSup 56; Leiden: Brill, 1987) 436, suggests that Justin's lost treatise *De Resurrectione* was the source of Tertullian's quotation.

[49] See chapter 9 above.

More important than the precise literary relationships are the
views of resurrection expressed in these texts. 1 Enoch 61:5 deals with
a problem in the old concept of resurrection as the return of the dead
from Sheol. Since Old Testament thought did not distinguish sharply
between the grave and the underworld, those who are in Sheol are
those who have been buried. But the question may then arise: what of
those who are not buried? 1 Enoch 61:5 mentions three examples:
those who die in the desert where there is noone to bury them, those
who die at sea and are eaten by fish, those who are eaten by wild
animals. (SibOr 2:236-237, perhaps with Christian martyrdoms by
burning in mind, adds another such category: those consumed by
fire.) Can these people too 'return' and 'rely on the day of the Chosen
One' (the day of resurrection)? The author states that they too are in
Sheol ('the depths of the earth'). They appear to be destroyed, but in
God's sight ('before the Lord of Spirits') noone can be destroyed. It is
noteworthy that although the problem behind this passage is the destruction of the corpse, it deals not with bodies but with dead people.
The people, not just their bodies, were destroyed and are in Sheol,
waiting to return. There is no trace of the concern, to be found in
later patristic writers,[50] to explain how the matter which has been
consumed by the animals can be recovered and reconstituted as the
resurrection body.

Both the Apocalypse of Peter and Tertullian's quotation seem concerned (with their references, respectively, to 'flesh' and 'bones')
rather with the resurrection of the body as such, whereas the passage
in the Sibylline Oracle, despite its dependence on the Apocalypse of
Peter, speaks, like 1 Enoch 61:5, simply of the dead. Of course, the
notion that the animals will return the flesh or the bones they had
devoured could hardly have been intended literally. Tertullian himself, though very much a literalist in his views of resurrection, anticipates the objection that if his quotation be taken literally the animals
themselves would have to be resurrected first in order to spew up
their human victims (*De Res.* 32.2). Clearly the images in Apocalypse
of Peter 4:4 and Tertullian's quotation are not meant to explain how
the corpses of those consumed by animals could be restored in resurrection; they are simply a vivid means of asserting that they will be.

---

[50] E.g. Athenagoras, *De Res.* 3-7; Augustine, *De Civ. Dei* 21.12, 20.

V

In conclusion we return to John's use of the tradition in Revelation 20:13. In the context of an account of the last judgment (20:12-13), the tradition functions to evoke the resurrection of the dead for judgment. Since there is no interest here in the form of resurrection, the tradition, which asserted simply that the dead will return from death, served John's purpose well. The tradition's three lines of synonymous parallelism he has reduced to two, making 'Death and Hades' the joint subject of the second verb, but the remaining repetition serves to emphasize the universality of resurrection so that all may be judged. It was perhaps because John always refers to 'Death and Hades' together (1:18; 6:8; 20:14) that he wished to keep them together in 20:13, in parallel with 'the sea,' but it may also be that he wanted to state the resurrection in two clauses in order to make the climactic third clause of the sentence the statement about the judgment.

The use of the term 'the sea' for the place of the dead (or probably better understood, in parallel with 'Death and Hades,' as the power which holds the dead in death) was probably not in the tradition as John knew it. It reflects his image of the sea as the primeval chaos from which opposition to God derives (13:1). By referring to it in 20:13 he prepares the way for the reference to it in 21:1. As Death and Hades are destroyed (20:14), so in the new creation there will be no more sea. Thus by varying the tradition's terms for the place of or power over the dead, John has integrated the tradition into his own work.

CHAPTER ELEVEN

2 PETER AND THE APOCALYPSE OF PETER

I HISTORY OF SCHOLARSHIP

The relationship between 2 Peter and the Apocalypse of Peter, though much discussed in the older literature, has never been satisfactorily clarified. It was the publication of the Akhmim Greek fragment in 1892 which first provided evidence for postulating a literary relationship between the two works.[1] At this time, before the Ethiopic text of the Apocalypse of Peter was known, the Akhmim fragment could be treated as a reliable witness to the original Greek text of the Apocalypse. Resemblances between it and 2 Peter were detected by James, who listed fifteen resemblances,[2] and Harnack.[3] Some concluded that 2 Peter was dependent on the Apocalypse of Peter,[4] some

---

[1] Even before this, some scholars conjectured such a relationship: A. von Harnack, Review of A. Hilgenfeld in *TLZ* 9 (1884) 337-343; T. Zahn, *Geschichte des Neutestamentlichen Kanons*, vol. 2/2 (Erlangen/Leipzig: Deichert, 1892) 819-820.

[2] J. A. Robinson and M. R. James, *The Gospel according to Peter and the Revelation of Peter* (London: C. J. Clay, 1892) 52-53.

[3] A. von Harnack, *Bruchstücke des Evangeliums und der Apokalypse des Petrus* (TU 9/2; Leipzig: Hinrichs, 1893) 54-55 n.1, 71-72. See also E. Bratke, 'Studien über die neu entdeckten Stücke der jüdischen und altchristlichen Literatur,' *Theologische Literaturblatt* 14 (1893) 113; J. M. S. Baljon, 'De Openbarung van Petrus,' *Theologische Studiën* 12 (1894) 45; G. Salmon, *A Historical Introduction to the Study of the Books of the New Testament* (7th edition; London: John Murray, 1894) 591; G. Krüger, *History of Early Christian Literature in the First Three Centuries* (tr. C. R. Gillett; New York: Macmillan, 1897) 37-38; A. Rutherford, in A. Menzies ed., *Ante-Nicene Christian Library: Additional Volume* (Edinburgh: T. & T. Clark, 1897) 143.

[4] A. von Harnack, *Die Chronologie der altchristlichen Litteratur bis Eusebius*, vol. 1 (Leipzig: Hinrichs, 1897) 471-472; followed by A. Jülicher, *An Introduction to the New Testament* (tr. [from 2nd German edition, 1900] by J. P. Ward; London: Smith, Elder, 1904) 239; H. Weinel, 'Die Offenbarung des Petrus,' in E. Hennecke ed., *Handbuch zu den Neutestamentlichen Apokryphen* (Tübingen: Mohr [Siebeck], 1904) 212 (this view no longer appears in the 1924 edition of this work); G. Hollmann, 'Der Brief Judas und der zweite Brief des Petrus,' in J. Weiss ed., *Die Schriften des Neuen Testaments*, vol. 2 (2nd edition; Göttingen: Vandenhoeck & Ruprecht, 1907) 573; R. Knopf, *Die Briefe Petri und Judä* (KEK; 7th edition; Göttingen: Vandenhoeck & Ruprecht, 1912) 255; and J. Moffatt, *An Introduction to the New Testament* (3rd edition; Edinburgh: T. & T. Clark, 1918) 367. This view is still maintained by J. H. Elliott, in R. A. Martin and J. H. Elliott, *James, I/II Peter, Jude* (Augsburg Commentary on the NT; Minneapolis: Augsburg, 1982) 130.

that the two works derive from the same circle,[5] while Sanday suggested common authorship.[6] However, the view which prevailed generally was that argued by first by Simms[7] and then more influentially by Spitta:[8] that the author of the Apocalypse of Peter borrowed from 2 Peter. The general acceptance of this view,[9] without further examination, is rather surprising. It was the only view to be argued on the basis of detailed examination of the issue, but Spitta's conclusion was based only on a comparison of the first seven of the thirty-four verses of the Akhmim fragment (in Harnack's numeration) with 2 Peter 1:16-2:3,[10] while Simms, although he examined the full list of resemblances which had been proposed by James, found few of them very convincing. On the basis of the Akhmim text alone the relationship between the two works seems in fact rather tenuous.

In fact, Spitta's article was out of date as soon as it appeared, because the publication (in 1910) and recognition (in 1911) of the Ethiopic text of the Apocalypse of Peter should have put the question of the relationship between the Apocalypse of Peter and 2 Peter in a quite new light. In the first place, if, as detailed study has repeatedly shown, the Ethiopic text represents the order and content of the

---

[5] M. R. James, *The Second Epistle General of Peter and the General Epistle of Jude* (Cambridge: Cambridge University Press, 1912) xxviii; F. H. Chase, 'Peter, Second Epistle of,' in J. Hastings ed., *A Dictionary of the Bible*, vol. 3 (Edinburgh: T. & T. Clark, 1900) 815-816.

[6] W. Sanday, *Inspiration* (London: Longmans, Green, 1893) 347-348, 384. Against this view, see Chase, 'Peter, Second Epistle of,' 815; J. B. Mayor, *The Epistle of St. Jude and the Second Epistle of St. Peter* (London: Macmillan, 1907) cxxxii-cxxxiii. E. Kühl, *Die Briefe Petri und Judae* (KEK; 6th edition; Göttingen: Vandenhoeck & Ruprecht, 1897) 375-376, thought that 2 Peter 2, which he regarded as a later interpolation in 2 Peter, might have the same author as the Apocalypse of Peter.

[7] A. E. Simms, 'Second Peter and the Apocalypse of Peter,' *Expositor* 5/8 (1898) 460-471.

[8] F. Spitta, 'Die Petrusapokalypse und der zweite Petrusbrief,' *ZNW* 12 (1911) 237-242; cf. idem, 'Die evangelische Geschichte von der Verklärung Jesu,' *ZNW* 12 (1911) 131.

[9] E.g. O. Bardenhewer, *Geschichte der altkirchlichen Literatur,* vol. 1 (2nd edition; Freiburg im Breisgau: Herder, 1913) 613 (following Spitta). The same view was argued (independently of Simms and Spitta) by C. Bigg, *A Critical and Exegetical Commentary on the Epistles of St. Peter and St. Jude* (ICC; Edinburgh: T. & T. Clark, 1901) 207-209; Mayor, *The Epistle of St. Jude,* cxxx-cxxxiv; P. J. Dillenseger, 'L'authenticité de la II^a Petri,' *Mélanges de la Faculté Orientale de l'Université Saint Joseph* (Beirut) 2 (1907) 197-199 (refuting Harnack).

[10] E. Repo, *Der "Weg" als Selbstbezeichnung des Urchristentums* (Suomalaisen Tiedeakatemian Toimituksia/Annales Academiae Scientiarum Fennicae B132/2; Helsinki: Suomalainen Tiedeakatemia, 1964) 96; and D. D. Buchholz, *Your Eyes Will Be Opened: A Study of the Greek (Ethiopic) Apocalypse of Peter* (SBLDS 97; Atlanta, Georgia: Scholars Press, 1988) 96, criticize Spitta for this reason.

original Apocalypse of Peter much more faithfully than the Akhmim
fragment, which is a considerably redacted version, then the latter's
resemblances to 2 Peter could be due to the redactor rather than to
the original author of the Apocalypse of Peter. Especially suspicious,
for this reason, are the close resemblances between the first two verses
of the Akhmim fragment and 2 Peter 2:1-3. Secondly, however, the
Ethiopic version of the Apocalypse of Peter provides much more
material for comparison with 2 Peter, including some even more
striking points of contact than those detected in the Akhmim fragment. It is therefore astonishing to find that most scholars have continued to accept the work of Simms and Spitta as conclusive, and to
base the judgment that the Apocalypse of Peter is dependent on 2
Peter solely on the evidence of the Akhmim fragment.[11] As Buchholz
comments, with Spitta's essay the 'whole discussion ground virtually
to a halt.'[12]

Rather few attempts[13] have been made to compare the Ethiopic
version of the Apocalypse of Peter with 2 Peter in order to determine
their relationship.[14] Loisy found the Ethiopic version consistent with
Harnack's view that 2 Peter (especially its account of the transfiguration) is dependent on the Apocalypse,[15] although (a concession in
reality fatal to his theory) he had to regard the material derived from

---

[11] E.g. J. Chaine, *Les épîtres catholiques* (Études Bibliques; 2nd edition; Paris:
Gabalda, 1939) 3-4; C. Maurer, 'Apocalypse of Peter,' in E. Hennecke, W,
Schneemelcher and R. McL. Wilson ed., *New Testament Apocrypha*, vol. 2 (London:
Lutterworth, 1965) 664; M. Green, *The Second Epistle General of Peter and the General
Epistle of Jude* (TNTC; Leicester: Inter-Varsity Press, 1968) 14 n.1; J. N. D. Kelly, *A
Commentary on the Epistles of Peter and Jude* (BNTC; London: A. & C. Black, 1969) 236;
D. Guthrie, *New Testament Introduction* (3rd edition; London: Inter-Varsity Press, 1970)
859; J. A. T. Robinson, *Redating the New Testament* (London: SCM Press, 1976) 177-
179; C. D. G. Müller, 'Apocalypse of Peter,' in E. Hennecke, W, Schneemelcher and
R. McL. Wilson ed., *New Testament Apocrypha*, vol. 2 (revised edition; Cambridge:
James Clarke/Louisville: Westminster/John Knox, 1992) 622.

[12] Buchholz, *Your Eyes*, 94-95.

[13] But Buchholz, *Your Eyes*, 96-97, is ignorant of most of them.

[14] In 'The Apocalypse of Peter: An Account of Research,' in *Aufstieg und Niedergang
der römischen Welt*, Part II, vol. 25/6, ed. W. Haase (Berlin/New York: de Gruyter,
1988) 4722-4723, I referred to a study of my own on this issue, and indicated its
main conclusion. The present chapter is an updated version of that study, hitherto
unpublished.

[15] A. Loisy, *Remarques sur la Littérature Épistolaire du Nouveau Testament* (Paris: Librairie
Émile Nourry, 1935) 131-137; idem, *The Birth of the Christian Religion* (tr. L. P. Jacks;
London: Allen & Unwin, 1948) 37-39; idem, *The Origins of the New Testament* (tr. L. P.
Jacks; London: Allen & Unwin, 1950) 52, 281. This view of the relationship was also
held by E. J. Goodspeed, *A History of Early Christian Literature* (Chicago: University of
Chicago Press, 1942) 54.

the Synoptic Gospels in the Apocalypse of Peter's transfiguration narrative as later interpolations.[16] Blinzler, on the other hand, discussed the relation of the transfiguration traditions in Apocalypse of Peter E15-17 and 2 Peter 1:16-18, but concluded that a literary relationship cannot be regarded as certain.[17] Repo refuted Spitta's case and argued once again that 2 Peter is dependent on the Apocalypse of Peter, but his argument is spoiled by his erroneous view that the Akhmim text is much better evidence than the Ethiopic for the original Apocalypse, as a result of which he still paid insufficient attention to the Ethiopic version.[18] Schmidt observed that most of the points of resemblance noted by James between the Akhmim fragment and 2 Peter do not occur in the Ethiopic version, and rightly held that a relationship between the Apocalypse of Peter and 2 Peter must be established primarily from the Ethiopic rather than from the Akhmim text. Since he found very few points of contact between the Ethiopic and 2 Peter, he concluded that there was insufficient evidence to demonstrate any relationship.[19] Unfortunately, he overlooked some of the most important resemblances between the Ethiopic and 2 Peter. Smith provided a fairly full survey of points of contact between the Apocalypse (both the Akhmim fragment and the Ethiopic) and 2 Peter, and reached the conclusion that dependence by the Apocalypse on 2 Peter is the most probable explanation.[20] The only important omission from Smith's discussion is the consideration of contacts between the Rainer Greek fragment of the Apocalypse of Peter and 2 Peter, which will emerge as important in our own discussion below. Finally, Buchholz, writing without knowledge of Smith's work and noting some previously unnoticed points of contact,[21] concluded that: 'A thorough investigation of the relationship of the Ethiopic text to 2 Peter is much to be desired... The desired investigation is still awaited.'[22]

---

[16] Loisy, *The Origins*, 53-54.

[17] J. Blintzler, *Die neutestamentlichen Berichte über die Verklärung Jesu* (NTAbh 17/4; Münster i. W.: Aschendorff, 1937) 73-76.

[18] Repo, *Der "Weg"*, 95-107.

[19] D. H. Schmidt, 'The Peter Writings: Their Redactors and their Relationships' (dissertation, Northwestern University, 1972) 112-116. Similarly A. Yarbro Collins, 'The Early Christian Apocalypses,' *Semeia* 14 (1979) 72.

[20] T. V. Smith, *Petrine Controversies in Early Christianity* (WUNT 2/15; Tübingen: Mohr [Siebeck], 1985).

[21] Buchholz, *Your Eyes*, 97 n. 3.

[22] Buchholz, *Your Eyes*, 96-97.

II PARALLELS

The following list of parallels between the Apocalypse of Peter and 2 Peter is intended to include all significant parallels (omitting some trivial resemblances which have sometimes been suggested), using the evidence of all the witnesses to the text and content of the original Apocalypse. The parallels from all witnesses are given in the order required by the Ethiopic version, which (unlike the Akhmim text) preserves the original order of material.[23]

(1) E1:4:

> 'that you do not become doubters, and that you do not worship other gods.'

This passage (inserted into material otherwise derived from Matt 24:4-5) could allude to 2 Peter 3:3-4, but recalls even more strongly 1 Clement 23:3 = 2 Clement 11:2; and Hermas, *Vis.* 3:4:3, which refer to those who doubt the parousia.

(2) A1:

> πολλοί ἐξ αὐτῶν ἔσονται ψευδοπροφῆται ('many of them shall be false prophets'); cf. 2 Peter 2:1: ἐγένετο δὲ καὶ ψευδοπροφῆται ('but there were also false prophets').

A1-2 is clearly a much abbreviated form of the opening section of the Apocalypse of Peter, which is preserved more fully in E1-2. E2:7 refers to 'false christs' rather than to 'false prophets,' and is clearly dependent on Matthew 24:24, which refers to the future coming of both 'false christs' and 'false prophets.' Thus, even if ψευδοπροφῆται was in the original Apocalypse, which must be very doubtful, it would more likely derive from Matthew 24:24 than from 2 Peter 2:1, where the false prophets belong to the past. The word is most probably due to the Akhmim text's redactor's memory of Matthew 24:24.

---

[23] The Greek texts of the Akhmim fragment (A) and the patristic quotations are from Robinson and James, *The Gospel*, 89-96, but the verse divisions of A are Harnack's (now the standard ones). The Greek text of the Bodleian fragment (B) is from M. R. James, 'A New Text of the Apocalypse of Peter,' *JTS* 12 (1911) 367-369, and that of the Rainer fragment (R) is from M. R. James, 'The Rainer Fragment of the Apocalypse of Peter,' *JTS* 32 (1931) 271. The translation of the Ethiopic (E) is from Buchholz, *Your Eyes*, and that of the Akhmim fragment from E. Hennecke, W. Schneemelcher and R. McL. Wilson ed., *New Testament Apocrypha*, vol. 2 (London: Lutterworth, 1965) 668-683.

(3) A1:

> ὁδοὺς καὶ δόγματα ποικίλοι [i.e. ποικίλα] τῆς ἀπωλείας ('ways and diverse doctrines of destruction'); cf. 2 Peter 2:1: αἱρέσεις ἀπωλείας ('heresies that lead to destruction').

Again this phrase is not in the Ethiopic and so is unlikely to come from the original Apocalypse of Peter, though ὁδοὺς does belong to the characteristic terminology of both the Apocalypse of Peter and 2 Peter (see below, nos. 10 and 15). It may be the Akhmim text's redactor's reminiscence of 2 Peter.

(4) E2:9:

> 'they will deny him to whom our fathers gave praise whom they crucified..., the first Christ'; cf. 2 Peter 2:1: καὶ τὸν ἀγοράσαντα αὐτοὺς δεσπότην ἀρνούμενοι ('who will deny even the Master who bought them').

The Ethiopic text here is difficult and may not be wholly reliable. If the one who is denied (or disbelieved) is the false Messiah, to whom the preceding two verses refer, as Hills argues (translating 'they will not believe him who is called "the glory of our fathers"—[our fathers] who crucified him who was Christ from the beginning'),[24] then there is no parallel with 2 Peter 2:1. Certainly, nothing can be based on this text.

(5) E4:1:

> 'when the day of God comes'; cf. 2 Peter 3:12: τὴν παρουσίαν τῆς τοῦ θεοῦ ἡμέρας ('the coming of the day of God').

The parallel is striking because the designation 'day of God' for the day of judgment is found only in these two passages in early Christian literature before 150, though Revelation 16:14 has 'the great day of God the Almighty' (τῆς μεγάλης ἡμέρας τοῦ θεοῦ παντοκράτορος; cf. also 2 Bar 55:6).

(6) E4:5-6:

> '...because it will happen when God speaks. Everything will occur according to his way of creating: he gave his command, and the world and everything in it came to be. It will be like that in the final days'; cf. 2 Peter 3:5-7.

---

[24] J. V. Hills, 'Parables, Pretenders and Prophecies: Translation and Interpretation in the *Apocalypse of Peter* 2,' *RB* 4 (1991) 566-568, 572.

The parallel between the creation of the world by God's word and the occurrence of the events of the day of judgment by God's word seems to be found only in these two passages and in 1 Clement 27:4 (which, as I have argued elsewhere, probably depends on the same Jewish apocalyptic source as 2 Pet 3:5-7[25]). In 2 Peter 3:5-7 and 1 Clement 27:4 it is used with reference to the eschatological destruction of the world, in Apocalypse of Peter E4:5-6 with reference to the eschatological resurrection of the dead. This means that my hypothesis of 2 Peter's dependence on a Jewish apocalypse which was also the source of 1 Clement 27:4 is preferable to a theory of dependence by 2 Peter on this passage of the Apocalypse of Peter.[26] It is more likely that the Apocalypse is dependent on 2 Peter or on 2 Peter's source.

(7) E4:13:

> '[the earth] must be judged at the same time, and heaven with it'; also *ap.* Macarius Magnes, *Apocritica* 4.6.16: καὶ αὐτὴ [i.e. ἡ γῆ] μέλουσα κρίνεσθαι σὺν καὶ περιέχοντι οὐρανῷ ('[the earth] itself will be judged along with the heaven that encompasses it'); cf. 2 Peter 3:7, 10, 12.

(8) E5:2-4:

> 'Cataracts of fire will be opened up.... And the waters will be turned and will be given into coals of fire and everything which is in it will burn up and even the ocean will become fire. From under heaven (there will be) a bitter fire which does not go out and it will flow for the judgment of wrath. Even the stars will melt in a flame of fire like they had not been created'; cf. 2 Peter 3:7, 10, 12.

The Apocalypse of Peter's account of the eschatological conflagration certainly could not derive solely from 2 Peter, since it has features which are not found in 2 Peter but are paralleled elsewhere ('cataracts of fire': cf. 1QH 3:19-25; Sib 3:84; burning the sea: cf. Sib 3:85), and seems to have made independent use of Isaiah 34:4. On the other hand, a Jewish apocalypse (especially as quoted in 2 Clement 16:3) is a more plausible source than the Apocalypse of Peter for 2 Peter's account of the conflagration.[27] The resemblance between the two works is most plausibly explained from common Jewish apocalyptic traditions.

---

[25] R. Bauckham, *Jude, 2 Peter* (WBC 50; Waco: Word Books, 1983) 296-297.
[26] Against Repo, *Der "Weg"*, 103.
[27] Bauckham, *Jude, 2 Peter*, 304-305.

(9) A21:

> ἕτερον τόπον...αὐχμηρόντων [i.e. αὐχμηρότατον ?] ('another place...very gloomy'); cf. 2 Peter 1:19: ἐν αὐχμηρῷ ('in a murky place').

The word αὐχμηρός ('gloomy, murky') is rare and occurs in early Christian literature before 150 only in these two places. But the contexts are entirely different.

(10) E7:2:

> 'they blasphemed the way of righteousness'; A22: οἱ βλασφημοῦντες τὴν ὁδὸν τῆς δικαιοσύνης ('those who had blasphemed the way of righteousness'); A28: οἱ βλασφημήσαντες ... τὴν ὁδὸν τῆς δικαιοσύνης ('those who blasphemed the way of righteousness')[28]; cf. 2 Peter 2:2: δι᾽ οὓς ἡ ὁδὸς τῆς ἀληθείας βλασφημηθήσεται ('because of whom the way of truth will be blasphemed'); 2:21: τὴν ὁδὸν τῆς δικαιοσύνης ('the way of righteousness').

The use of βλασφημεῖν in 2 Peter 2:2 cannot be dependent on the Apocalypse of Peter, since it is used in 2 Peter 2:2 to make allusion to Isaiah 52:5[29] and there is no such allusion in the Apocalypse of Peter's use of the verb. Nor is the Apocalypse of Peter's use of the verb likely to be dependent on 2 Peter 2:2, since the way in which the Apocalypse uses it (with reference to apostasy from or opposition to Christianity) is common and natural (cf. Acts 26:11; Hermas, *Sim.* 8:6:4; Mart. Polycarp 9:3; Letter of the Churches of Vienne and Lyons, *ap.* Eusebius, *Hist. Eccl.* 5.1.48, where the parallel with ApPet A2 should also be noticed). The point of contact between the two works is therefore simply in the expression 'the way of righteousness.'

The 'way' terminology is characteristic of both works.[30] Besides 'the way of righteousness,' which both works use, 2 Peter also uses 'the way of truth' (2:2), 'the straight way' (2:15), and 'the way of Balaam' (2:15), while the Apocalypse of Peter also uses 'the way of God' (A34 = B) and 'ways of destruction' (A1 only). This diversity seems to indicate that probably neither work has directly borrowed this terminology from the other. It seems to belong to the natural usage of both writers and probably indicates common indebtedness to a tradition of Christian terminology. Repo has no convincing basis for arguing that the Apocalypse of Peter is closer to the original Semitic usage, whereas the terminology is less at home in 2 Peter.[31]

---

[28] The parallel to A28 in the Ethiopic is E9:3: 'the blasphemers and betrayers of my righteousness.'

[29] Bauckham, *Jude, 2 Peter*, 242.

[30] Bauckham, *Jude, 2 Peter*, 241-242.

[31] Repo, *Der "Weg"*, 104-107.

(11) A23, 31:

βορβόρου ('mire'); cf. 2 Peter 2:22: βορβόρου ('mire').

Although these are the only occurrences of the word in early Christian literature before 150, there is unlikely to be any connexion between them. The word is used in the Akhmim text of the Apocalypse of Peter (and is notably without equivalent in the Ethiopic) because it was a standard feature of descriptions of Hades in Greek literature,[32] whereas in 2 Peter it belongs to the proverb about the sow, where it was also traditional,[33] and has no reference to hell.

(12) E7:6:

'that they might capture the souls of men for destruction'; cf. 2 Peter 2:14: δελεάζοντες ψυχὰς ἀστηρίκτους ('they ensnare unstable souls'; cf. also 2:18).

The contexts are different.

(13) A24:

τῷ μιάσματι τῆς μειχίας [i.e. μοιχείας] ('the adulterous defilement'); A32: οἱ μιάναντες τὰ σώματα ἑαυτῶν ('those who defiled their bodies'); cf. 2 Peter 2:10: τοὺς ὀπίσω σαρκὸς ἐν ἐπιθυμίᾳ μιασμοῦ πορευόμενους ('those who in polluting lust defile the flesh').

The word μίασμα ('defilement') is found only in these two places in early Christian literature before 150, but the contexts are different. The language of the Apocalypse of Peter may be influenced by 1 Enoch (see 7:1; 9:8; 10:11; 12:4; 15:3, 4),[34] as is that of 2 Peter 2:10 at second-hand, via dependence on Jude 8.

(14) E7:8:

'"We did not know that we had to come into eternal punishment"'; E7:11: '"For we heard and we did not believe that we would come into this eternal punishment"' (and cf. 13:4).

This scepticism of the sinners about their future judgment may bear comparison with that of the scoffers in 2 Peter (2:3b; 3:4). Both works emphasize that judgment will nevertheless overtake such sceptics. On the other hand, the idea that the wicked do not believe that there will

---

[32] Examples in M. Aubineau, 'La thème du 'bourbier' dans la Littérature grecque profane et chrétienne,' *RevSR* 33 (1959) 186-189.

[33] Aubineau, 'La thème,' 201-202; Bauckham, *Jude, 2 Peter*, 279.

[34] Cf. Bauckham, *Jude, 2 Peter*, 56.

be retribution after death is a traditional topos (4 Ezra 7:126; 2 Clement 10:4; cf. Wis 2:22).

(15) E10:7:

> 'they who abandon the commandment of God'; B: οἵτινες κατέλιπον ὁδὸν τοῦ θεοῦ ('those who have forsaken the way of God'); A34: οἱ ἄφθαντες [i.e. ἀφέντες] τὴν ὁδὸν τοῦ θεοῦ ('those who forsook the way of God'); cf. 2 Peter 2:15: καταλείποντες εὐθεῖαν ὁδόν ('leaving the straight way').

For the use of the 'way' terminology in both works, see no. 10 above. The metaphor of 'leaving' the way is an obvious one.[35] The Ethiopic of the Apocalypse of Peter (probably here inferior to B and A) substitutes 'the commandment of God' for 'the way of God,' probably under the influence of the use of this phrase elsewhere in the Apocalypse (E8:9; A30; ap. Methodius, Symp. 2.6); cf. the use of 'the way of righteousness' and 'the holy commandment' as equivalents in 2 Peter 2:21.

(16) R (14:1):

> τοῖς κλητοῖς μου καὶ ἐκλέκτοις μου ('my called and my elect'; cf. E 14:1: 'my elect and my righteous'); cf. 2 Peter 1:10: τὴν κλῆσιν καὶ ἐκλογήν ('call and election').[36]

This resemblance could be significant only in connexion with the following parallels.

(17) R (14:2):

> εἰς τὴν αἰωνίαν μου βασιλείαν ('into my [Christ's] eternal kingdom'); E14:2: 'into my eternal kingdom'; cf. 2 Peter 1:11: εἰς τὴν αἰώνιον βασιλείαν τοῦ κυρίου ἡμῶν καὶ σωτῆρος Ἰησοῦ Χριστοῦ ('into the eternal kingdom of our Lord and Saviour Jesus Christ').

The phrase αἰώνιος βασιλεία is found in Christian literature before 150 only in these two passages,[37] and the significance of this is increased by the fact that in both cases it refers to Christ's, rather than God's, kingdom, a comparatively rare concept in early Christian literature before 150 (cf. Matt 13:41; 16:28; Luke 1:33; 22:29-30; 23:42; John 18:36-337; 1 Cor 15:24-25; Col 1:13; 2 Tim 4:1, 18; Heb 1:8; 1 Clem 50:3; 2 Clem 12:2; Barn 7:11; EpApp 39 [Ethiopic]).

---

[35] Examples in Bauckham, Jude, 2 Peter, 267.
[36] On this pair of words, see Bauckham, Jude, 2 Peter, 190.
[37] See Bauckham, Jude, 2 Peter, 192.

(18) R (14:3):

> ποιήσω μετ᾽ αὐτῶν τὰς ἐπαγγελίας μου ἅς ἐπηγγειλάμην αυητοῖς ('I will per-
> form for them my promises which I have promised them'); E14:3: 'I will
> do for them what I have promised them'; cf. 2 Peter 1:4: τὰ μέγιστα καὶ
> τίμια ἡμῖν ἐπαγγέλματα δεδώραται ('he [Christ] has bestowed on us the
> very great and precious promises').

The idea of *Christ's* promises is very rare in early Christian literature
before 150 (cf. 2 Clem 5:5).

(19) R (14:3):

> ἰδοὺ ἐδήλωσά σοι, Πέτρε ('Behold, I [Christ] have informed you, Peter');
> E14:3: 'I have told you, Peter'; cf. 2 Peter 1:14: καθὼς καὶ κύριος ἡμῶν
> Ἰησοῦς Χριστὸς ἐδήλωσέν μοι ('as our Lord Jesus Christ also informed me
> [Peter]').

The verb is a very natural one in both passages, and this correspondence could be significant only in connexion with other correspondences in the same context in the Apocalypse of Peter. In 2 Peter what
Christ has informed Peter is that he is shortly to die. In the Apocalypse of Peter (R) the object is πάντα, i.e. the preceding eschatological
prophecy, but Christ immediately goes on to prophesy Peter's death.

(20) R (14:4);

> πίε τὸ ποτήριον ὃ επεγγειλάμην σοι ('drink the cup which I [Christ] have
> promised you [Peter]'); cf. 2 Peter 1:14.

In Christian literature before 150 a prophecy of Peter's death given
him by Christ is found only in these passages and in John 21:18 (cf.
13:36).[38]

(21) E15:1:

> 'let us go to the holy mountain' ; A4: τὸ ὄρους [i.e. ὄρος]; cf. 2 Peter 1:18:
> τῷ ἁγίῳ ὄρει ('the holy mountain').

The phrase 'the holy mountain' is not found in Matthew, which
seems to be the main source of the Apocalypse of Peter's transfiguration account. In 2 Peter it derives from Psalm 2:6,[39] whereas in the
Apocalypse of Peter it serves to identify the mountain as mount Zion,

---

[38] Cf. Bauckham, *Jude, 2 Peter*, 200-201; idem, 'The Martyrdom of Peter in Early
Christian Literature,' in *Aufstieg und Niedergang der römischen Welt*, Part II, vol. 26/1, ed.
W. Haase (Berlin/New York: de Gruyter, 1992) 539-595.

[39] Bauckham, *Jude, 2 Peter*, 221.

the site of the temple.[40] Thus the use of the phrase in both works could be coincidental, but it is a striking coincidence, especially in combination with other points of contact in the same context (nos. 24, 25, 26 below).

(22) A5:

> τῶν ἐξελθόντων ἀπὸ τοῦ κόσμου ('who had departed from the world'); cf. 2 Peter 1:15: τὴν ἐμὴν ἔξοδον ('after my death').

Both expressions for death were standard,[41] and so the correspondence is insignificant.

(23) E16:1:

> 'God Jesus Christ' (the parallel in A12 has only τῷ κυρίῳ); E16:4: 'my Lord and my God Jesus Christ' (the parallel in A20 has only ὁ κύριος); cf. 2 Peter 1:1.[42]

If the use of 'God' with reference to Jesus Christ is original in the Apocalypse of Peter, it is a relatively rare parallel, at this date, to 2 Peter's usage, but we cannot be sure that it is original.

(24) E16:5:

> 'the honor and the glory of those who pursue my righteousness'; cf. 2 Peter 1:17: τιμὴν καὶ δόξαν ('honour and glory').

Although 2 Peter uses this phrase of the transfigured Christ, while in the Apocalypse of Peter it refers to Christians in paradise, it should be noted that the Apocalypse of Peter has used the transfiguration tradition in order to describe, not the glory of Christ, but the glory of Moses and Elijah (E15:2-7), who represent the destiny of the patriarchs and Christians in paradise (E16:1-6). If the author of the Apocalypse of Peter has transferred the phrase 'honour and glory' from Christ to Christians, this would be the same procedure as he has used (in E15:2-7) in transferring the description of the transfigured Christ (derived from Matt 17:2) to Moses and Elijah. Of course, τιμὴν καὶ δόξαν is a natural combination, and this point of resemblance between the two works is again significant only in the context of others.

---

[40] See chapter 8, section II.2 above.

[41] Cf. Bauckham, *Jude, 2 Peter*, 202.

[42] See Bauckham, *Jude, 2 Peter*, 168-169, for an argument that τοῦ θεοῦ ἡμῶν in this verse refers to Jesus.

(25) E17:1:

> 'a voice came suddenly from heaven'; cf. 2 Peter 1:18: ταύτην τὴν φωνὴν ...
> ἐξ οὐρανοῦ ('this voice from heaven').

In Matthew, the Apocalypse of Peter's principal source for the transfiguration tradition, the voice comes from the cloud, as it does also in Mark and Luke.[43]

(26) E17:1:

> "'This is my Son whom I love and I have been pleased with him'"; cf. 2
> Peter 1:17: ὁ υἱός μου ὁ ἀγαπητός μου οὗτός ἐστιν, εἰς ὃν ἐγὼ εὐδόκησα ('This
> is my Son, my Beloved, on whom I have set my favour').

Though the Apocalypse of Peter's form of the words of the heavenly voice could derives from Matthew 17:5,[44] it is possible that 'my Son whom I love' represents 2 Peter's unique repetition of μου with ἀγαπητός.

III CONCLUSIONS

Some of the above points of contact are unremarkable and cannot be used as evidence of a literary relationship (nos. 1, 2, 4, 9, 11, 12, 13, 14, 22). Some depend on doubtfully original readings in the Apocalypse of Peter (nos. 2, 3, 23). Some could be evidence of common theological traditions or a common context in some form of 'Petrine school' (nos. 5, 6, 7, 8, 10, 14, 15). The most impressive group of correspondences, which is impressive only when considered as a group, consists of numbers 16, 17, 18, 19, 20, 21, 24, 25. Numbers 16-20 are all correspondences between two short passages (E14:1-4 = R; and 2 Pet 1:4-15), while numbers 21, 24, 25 are correspondences between the versions of the transfiguration tradition which immediately follow in each of the two works (E15-17 = A4-20; and 2 Pet 1:16-18). The fact that these correspondences occur in close proximity in both works suggests a literary relationship between the two works. Since the Apocalypse of Peter's transfiguration narrative is almost certainly dependent on Matthew and in any case unquestionably dependent on Synoptic tradition, while 2 Peter's account of the transfiguration is probably independent of the Synoptic tradition;[45]

---

[43] For discussion of this difference between 2 Peter and the Synoptics, see Bauckham, *Jude, 2 Peter*, 205-206.

[44] See the comparison of the various forms in Bauckham, *Jude, 2 Peter*, 206-207.

[45] Bauckham, *Jude, 2 Peter*, 205-210.

and since the Apocalypse of Peter has put the transfiguration tradition to a secondary use, as a revelation of the glory of the redeemed rather than of Jesus Christ, it is clear that the dependence must be of the Apocalypse of Peter on 2 Peter, not *vice versa*. It looks as though the author of the Apocalypse of Peter turned for inspiration in writing chapter 14 (=R) to the opening section of 2 Peter, and then, in his adaptation of the transfiguration tradition, combined material from Matthew with reminiscences of 2 Peter 1:16-18.

If a literary relationship is therefore somewhat probable in the case of numbers 18, 19, 20, 21, 24, 25, it is likely that some of the other points of contact between the two works also reflect familiarity with 2 Peter on the part of the author of the Apocalypse. But in the case of the 'way' terminology (nos. 10, 15) and the ideas about the eschatological conflagration (nos. 6, 7, 8), common theological tradition, rather than direct literary relationship, may be the explanation for the resemblances.

CHAPTER TWELVE

THE APOCALYPSE OF THE SEVEN HEAVENS:
THE LATIN VERSION

I INTRODUCTION

A little known apocalyptic work, which I propose should be known as the Apocalypse of the Seven Heavens,[1] survives in an incomplete Latin text in an eighth- or ninth-century manuscript, and also in Anglo-Saxon and Middle Irish versions. It describes how the departed souls of the righteous and the wicked are conducted through the seven heavens, where a series of fiery ordeals detain the wicked in torment for periods of time, while the righteous pass through unharmed. When the souls reach the seventh heaven they are judged by God and the wicked are consigned to hell, a description of which concludes the apocalypse. The Latin text was first published in 1907 by Donatien de Bruyne, who correctly described it as 'une apocalypse inconnue'.[2] In 1919 Montague Rhodes James, always alert to the literary relationships of apocryphal works and expert in detecting the remains of ancient apocryphal literature in later contexts,[3] pointed out that the apocalypse of which de Bruyne's text is a fragment must have been the source of closely related passages in two Irish works: *The Vision of Adamnán* and the third recension of the *Evernew Tongue*.[4] The apocalypse, he judged, 'must be fairly ancient',[5] and although he did not provide the kind of detailed study which is needed to back up such a judgment, James' scholarly instinct, informed by an encyclopedic knowledge of apocryphal literature, should not be lightly disre-

---

[1] St. J. D. Seymour, *Irish Visions of the Other-World* (London: SPCK, 1930) 112, and M. McNamara, *The Apocrypha in the Irish Church* (Dublin: Dublin Institute for Advanced Studies, 1975) 141, called it simply 'The Seven Heavens'; R. Willard, *Two Apocrypha in Old English Homilies* (Beiträge zur Englischen Philologie 30; Leipzig: Tauchnitz, 1935) 1, called it the Apocryphon of the Seven Heavens.

[2] B. de Bruyne, 'Fragments retrouvés d'apocryphes priscillianistes,' *RBén* 24 (1907) 323.

[3] For James' remarkable contribution to the study of apocryphal literature see W. R. Pfaff, *Montague Rhodes James* (London: Scolar Press, 1980), especially the bibliography on pp. 427-438.

[4] M. R. James, 'Irish Apocrypha,' *JTS* 20 (1919) 14-16.

[5] James, 'Irish Apocrypha,' 16.

garded. It is hoped that the present study will vindicate, at least in a preliminary way, James' belief in the antiquity of this work.

St. John D. Seymour pointed out two other Irish versions of the work and provided useful comparative studies of the Irish and Latin versions, though his interest was in the Irish literature rather than its ancient sources.[6] Then in 1935 Rudolph Willard published an Old English version of the apocalypse, together with a comparative study of the various versions, which remains much the fullest study of the work to date.[7] However, like Seymour, Willard did not attempt to study the work's relationship to ancient and early medieval apocalyptic literature in general. More recently, Martin McNamara included a brief account of our apocalypse in his very useful catalogue of apocryphal literature in Ireland,[8] while David Dumville discussed the way in which it may have reached Ireland.[9]

The principal aims of the present chapter are to provide a detailed study of the Latin text of the apocalypse, which has been even more neglected than the Anglo-Saxon and Irish versions, and on the basis of this study to place the work in the context of ancient Jewish and Christian apocalyptic literature. It will be argued that the Latin text, abbreviated and somewhat corrupted though it is, provides a more reliable means of access to the original work than do the Anglo-Saxon and Irish versions, which will be used here mainly for the light they can throw on the Latin text. The material peculiar to them could certainly not be neglected in a full study of this work, but the question of its originality presents problems which require more extensive discussion than is possible in the present context. It must also await the availability of a full edition of all the Irish texts and a full study of the relationships between them and with other Irish literature. However, in order to justify the present study's approach to the Latin text, a preliminary discussion of its relationship to the other versions will be provided.

---

[6] St. J. D. Seymour, 'The Seven Heavens in Irish Literature', *Zeitschrift für Celtische Philologie* 14 (1923) 18-23; idem, 'Notes on Apocrypha in Ireland', *Proceedings of the Royal Irish Academy* 37C (1927) 107-117; idem, *Irish Visions*, 112-119.

[7] Willard, *Two Apocrypha*, 1-30.

[8] McNamara, *Apocrypha*, 141-143 (no. 108).

[9] D. N. Dumville, 'Biblical Apocrypha and the Early Irish: A Preliminary Investigation,' *Proceedings of the Royal Irish Academy* 73C (1973) 325-28. Another recent study is J. Stevenson, 'Ascent through the Heavens, from Egypt to Ireland,' *Cambridge Medieval Celtic Studies* 5 (1983) 21-35. She notes some of the ancient parallels, but concentrates far too exclusively on the NHApPaul, and is therefore misled into considering the content of our apocalypse to be Gnostic in origin.

II THE TEXTS

In this section the available texts in all three languages are listed, with some brief details of them. For convenience I have retained the sigla already used by Willard.[10]

Latin

K   Karlsruhe MS Augiensis CCLIV, fol. 156[r-v].
     Latin text: D. de Bruyne, 'Fragments retrouvés d'apocryphes priscillianistes,' *RBén* 24 (1907) 323; reprinted in PL, *Supplementum* II (1960-62) 1510.
     Free English Translation: St. J. D. Seymour, 'The Seven Heavens in Irish Literature,' *Zeitschrift für Celtische Philologie* 14 (1923) 22-23.

Our text occurs in the third (fols. 153-213) of the three manuscript books which comprise MS Augiensis CCLIV.[11] This third manuscript derives from Reichenau, where it was written at the end of the eighth or the beginning of the ninth century,[12] when the monastery of Reichenau had strong Irish connections.[13] De Bruyne printed the first six items of this manuscript (fols. 153[r]-172[v]) and regarded them as a collection of Priscillianist texts, but these six items should not be detached in this way from the rest of the manuscript, with which they have links.[14] De Bruyne's only substantial evidence for the Priscillianist origin of the texts he prints is their frequent quotations from apocryphal sources, including the fragment of our apocalypse quoted in the second item,[15] but the Irish origin of the manuscript[16]

---

[10] See his list: *Two Apocrypha*, 6-7.

[11] See A. Holder, *Die Handschriften der grossherzoglich Badischen Hof- und Landesbibliothek in Karlsruhe. V. Die Reichenauer Handschriften. Erster Band. Die Pergamenthandschriften* (Leipzig: Teubner, 1906) 575-577; Dumville, 'Biblical Apocrypha,' 326-327.

[12] Cf. Holder, *Handschriften*, 579; Dumville, 'Biblical Apocrypha,' 326.

[13] This is played down by L. Gougard, *Christianity in Celtic Lands* (London: Sheed and Ward, 1932) 158, 161, but for evidence for it, cf. *ibid.*, 265, 308; L. Gougard, *Gaelic Pioneers of Christianity* (Dublin: Gill, 1923) 101, 105; and especially J. F. Kenney, *The Sources for the History of Ireland* (New York: Columbia University Press, 1929) 550-551.

[14] Dumville, 'Biblical Apocrypha,' 327.

[15] de Bruyne, 'Fragments,' 318-320.

[16] For the contacts between this Reichenau MS and Pseudo-Isidore, *Liber de numeris* (PL 83, cols. 1293-1302), an Hiberno-Latin work of the eighth century, see R. E. McNally, *Der irische Liber de numeris: Eine Quellenanalyse des pseudo-isidorischen Liber de numeris* (dissertation, Munich, 1957) 205 (references to Karlsruhe MS Aug. CCLIV). For the Irish origin of items 5 and 6 in de Bruyne's text, see Dumville, 'Biblical Apocrypha,' 327.

more immediately accounts for this feature, since apocryphal works little known or unknown in the rest of Europe were well known in the Irish church at this period,[17] and specifically two of the works quoted, the Apocalypse of Thomas[18] and our apocalypse, were known in Ireland. It remains a plausible, but distinct, hypothesis that such apocryphal works reached Ireland from Spain where Priscillianism assisted their preservation.[19]

Thus the work in which the fragment of our apocalypse occurs is best regarded as an Hiberno-Latin homily. The quotation is followed by a paragraph of woes addressed to sinners who are bound for hell (fols. 156^v-157^r; de Bruyne, pp. 323-324), and it is clear that it is in order to reinforce his warning of hell that the homilist has included the quotation. That he has abbreviated the text he quotes with a view to this particular purpose seems likely.

Irish

Our apocalypse is known in Ireland both as a separate tract, pre-served in a fifteenth-century manuscript (LF below), and as incorp-orated into three other works of Middle Irish literature: the *Vision of Adamnán (Fís Adamnáin)*, the *Adventure of Columcille's Clerics (Echta clérech Choluim Cille)* and the *Evernew Tongue (Tenga Bith-núa)*. The *Vision of Adamnán* probably originated in the tenth century,[20] and if the passage (§§ 15-20) derived from our apocalypse is not an original part of the

---

[17] See especially McNamara, *Apocrypha*; Dumville, 'Biblical Apocrypha,' 299-338.

[18] The quotation from the Apocalypse of Thomas, not identified by de Bruyne, was pointed out by James, 'Irish Apocrypha,' 16. It is on de Bruyne p. 325, lines 54-64.

[19] See J. N. Hillgarth, 'The East, Visigothic Spain and the Irish,' *Studia patristica* 4/2 (= *TU* 79; Berlin: Akadamie-Verlag, 1961) 443-456; idem, 'Visigothic Spain and Early Christian Ireland', *Proceedings of the Royal Irish Academy* 62C (1962) 1647-1694; idem, 'Old Ireland and Visigothic Spain', in R. McNally ed., *Old Ireland* (Dublin: Gill, 1965) 200-227. In these three articles, Hillgarth argues that contacts between Spain and Ireland from the sixth to the eighth centuries provided the channel for much literature to reach Ireland, and that the Irish church's special links with the Christian East were thus mediated by Spain. Dumville, 'Biblical Apocrypha,' 321-329, applies this argument more particularly to the transmission of apocryphal works to Ireland. The link with Priscillianism must be treated with some caution, since Priscillian's own use of apocrypha seems to have been limited to the apocryphal Acts: see E.-Ch. Babut, *Priscillien et le Priscillianisme* (Paris: H. Champion, 1909) 231-240. But that Priscillianist influence in Spain provided a more congenial context for the survival of apocryphal works than in many other parts of the Western Church is plausible.

[20] See J. D. Seymour, 'The Eschatology of the Early Irish Church,' *Zeitschrift für Celtische Philologie* 14 (1923) 180; McNamara, *Apocrypha*, 165.

work,[21] it must at least have been incorporated at an early date. The
corresponding material in one fourteenth century manuscript of the
Adventure of Columcille's Clerics (Y below) is borrowed from the *Vision of
Adamnán* but that in the *Evernew Tongue* must derive from our apocalypse independently of the *Vision of Adamnán*. It is certainly not part of
the original, probably tenth-century,[22] Irish version of the *Evernew
Tongue*, but occurs in a recension which has unfortunately been published only in a manuscript of 1817 (M below). Finally, a text which
has not been published (N below) is said by Seymour to belong to a
version of the *Evernew Tongue*, but differs considerably from M.

It seems likely that some of these Irish versions are independent
translations of somewhat varying Latin texts, but this question has still
to be investigated.

Finally, it is worth noting that a trace of dependence on our apocalypse is almost certainly to be found in the Epilogue to the *Martyrology
of Oengus (Félire Óengusso Céli Dé)*, an Irish work of c. 800.[23] This takes
the knowledge of the apocalypse in Ireland back to approximately the
same date as the writing of K at Reichenau. Further study may well
bring to light other evidence of its influence on the eschatological
beliefs and literature of the Irish church.[24]

Seven Heavens
LF   Liber Flavus Fergusiorum (Royal Irish Academy MS 23 0 48) II
     fol. 20[v].
     Irish text: G. Mac Niocaill, 'Na Seacht Neamha,' *Éigse* 8 (1955-
     57) 239-241.
     English summary: Seymour, 'The Seven Heavens,' 20-21.

Vision of Adamnán 15-20/17-25[25]
LU   Lebor na hUidre (Royal Irish Academy MS) pp. 28[b]-29[b].
     Irish text: E. Windisch, *Irische Texte* (Leipzig: S. Hirzel, 1880)
     179-184.

---

[21] cf. Seymour, 'Eschatology,' 181.
[22] McNamara, *Apocrypha*, 115.
[23] W. Stokes, *Félire Óengusso Céli Dé: The Martyrology of Oengus the Culdee* (London:
Henry Bradshaw Society, 1905) 269; epilogue, lines 119-120, describe the soul of the
righteous after death 'on the hills of the seven heavens, having been borne past
torments.'
[24] For introductions to Irish eschatology, see Seymour, 'Eschatology'; idem, *Irish
Visions*; B. Grogan, 'Eschatological Teaching in the Early Irish Church', in M.
McNamara ed., *Biblical Studies: The Medieval Irish Contributions* (Proceedings of the Irish
Biblical Association 1; Dublin: Dominican Publications, 1976) 46-58.
[25] For other MSS of the *Vision of Adamnán*, see Kenney, *Sources*, 444-445.

Irish text and English translation: W. Stokes, *Fis Adamnáin slicht Libair na Huidre: Adamnán's Vision* (Simla, privately printed, 1870) 8-13.

English translations: C. S. Boswell, *An Irish Precursor of Dante* (London: D. Nutt, 1908) 35-38; M. Herbert and M. McNamara, *Irish Biblical Apocrypha* (Edinburgh: T. & T. Clark, 1989) 141-143.

LBr Leabhar Breac (Royal Irish Academy MS) pp. 254b-255a.

Irish text: Windisch, *Irische Texte*, 179-184.

P Paris MS (Bibliothèque Nationale, Fonds celtique 1) fols. 96r-97r.

Irish text and French translation: J. Vendryes, 'Aislingthi Adhamnain d'après le texte du manuscrit de Paris,' *Revue Celtique* 30 (1909) 367-371.

Adventure of Columcille's Clerics (3rd recension)[26]

Y Yellow Book of Lecan (Trinity College Dublin MS 1318), cols. 711-712.

Irish text and English translation: W. Stokes. 'The Adventure of St Columba's Clerics,' *Revue Celtique* 26 (1905) 148-153.

Evernew Tongue (3rd recension)[27]

M Modern Version (1817).

Irish text and French translation: G. Dottin, 'Une rédaction moderne du *Teanga Bithnua*,' *Revue Celtique* 28 (1907) 294-297.

Evernew Tongue

N Royal Irish Academy MS 23 L 29.

English summary: Seymour, 'The Seven Heavens,' 22.

Anglo-Saxon

C Corpus Christi College Cambridge MS 41, pp. 292-95.

Anglo-Saxon text: R. Willard, *Two Apocrypha in Old English Homilies* (Beiträge zur Englischen Philologie 30; Leipzig: B. Tauchnitz, 1935) 4-6.

---

[26] The material in question is borrowed from the *Vision of Adamnán* and is found only in one MS of this recension: see Kenney, *Sources*, 447-448.

[27] For other MSS of this recension see R. Flower, *Catalogue of Irish Manuscripts in the British Museum*, Vol. 2 (London: British Museum, 1926) 558-559; McNamara, *Apocrypha*, 116-117.

The manuscript is from the late eleventh or early twelfth century, but the homily in which our apocalypse is incorporated originated at an earlier date.[28] Another substantial quotation from the final part of the apocalypse is found in another homily, existing in two manuscripts (Cotton Faustina A IX; Corpus Christi College Cambridge 302): Willard, *Two Apocrypha*, pp. 24-25 gives the text.

III The Latin Text compared with other versions

In order to illustrate how the Latin text (K), though corrupt, tends to be preferable to the Anglo-Saxon and Irish versions, we shall discuss two examples. The first is the description of the wheel which the Latin text locates in the sixth heaven, though the equivalent material in the other versions is placed in the fifth heaven (in M in the fourth heaven). We need to compare the Latin text here not only with the Anglo-Saxon and Irish versions of our apocalypse, but also with the description of a wheel in the Latin redactions IV, V, VIII and X of the Apocalypse of Paul and with the description of a wheel in the Coptic Apocalypse of John.

K (vv 7-9: see section IV below)
In medio eius rotam et angelo tartarucho cum uirgis ferreis percutientis rotam et inde uoluitur in gyru et flumine tres; ponitur homo peccatur super rotam, XII annis tormentatur. Centum scintille procedit de rotam & centum pondus in uno scindule & centum anime percremant.

C (translation from text in Willard, p. 5)[29]
There is an encircling river (whirlpool?) and a fiery wheel turning in the midst of the river, and it thrusts the sinners downwards into the fiery river. When our Creator wishes to release the souls from the flowing fire, he sends his angels with hard rods that are heavier in weight than stones. The angel strikes with them on the burning river and hews the souls up out of the river. At each blow a hundred sparks burst forth, in each is the weight of a man. A hundred sinful souls die and come to naught because of the sparks.

LU (Boswell, p. 37; cf. Herbert and McNamara, p. 142; Stokes, p. 11)
In that place is a fiery river, which is unlike all other rivers, for in the midst of it is a strange kind of whirlpool, wherein the souls of the wicked keep turning round and round, and there they abide for the space of sixteen years; the righteous, however, win through it straightway, without any hindrance. So soon as the due time cometh for the sinners to be released thereout, the angle strikes the water with a rod, hard as though

---

[28] Willard, *Two Apocrypha*, 2.
[29] I am very grateful to the late Ms A. de la Portas for translations of the Anglo-Saxon.

it were of stone, and uplifts the spirits with the end of that rod.
(P and Y show only minor variations from LU.)

M (Dottin, pp. 295, 297)
Il y a un fleuve de feu à cette porte-là et il est différent des autres fleuves
et les âmes des pécheurs y restent pour être tourmentées par le feu et
quand Dieu pense le moment venu de le délivrer des pécheurs, un ange
de Dieu vient vers eux avec une vierge d'épine de fer à la main et ainsi est
cette verge: chaque épine a cent parties, en sort que chaque épine
donnerait cent blessures sur la face de chaque pécheur.

LF (summarised Seymour, p. 21)
A whirlpool (as in LU). When it is time for release an angel comes with a
spiky rod. This has one hundred points to the end of it, and a hundred
drops of poison on each point or thorn, which wound the face of the
sinner.

Apocalypse of Paul Redaction IV (Meyer, p.366)
in quo est rota ignea habens mille orbitas, mille vicibus in uno die ab
angelo tartareo percussa, et in unaquaque vice mille anime cruciantur.

Apocalypse of Paul Redaction IV (PL 94, col. 501)
in quo rota ignea mille vicibus: in illo die ab angelo tartareo in
unaquaque vice mille animae concremantur.

Apocalypse of Paul Redaction IV (Brandes, *Visio*, p. 76; 'Quelle', p.45)
in quo est rota ignea habens mille orbitas. Mille vicibus uno die ab angelo
tartareo volvitur, et in unaquaque vice mille anime cruciantur in ea.

Apocalypse of Paul Redaction V (Silverstein, pp. 197-198)
in quo est rota ignea que semper ardet et habet mille orbitas, mille
vicibus in uno die ab angelo tartareo, et in unaquaque vice mille anime
cremantur

Apocalypse of Paul Redaction VIII (Silverstein, p. 209)
in quo rota ignea habens [mille orbitas], mille vicibus in uno die ab
angelo tartareo percussa; et in una die mille vicibus anime cruciantur et
refigerantur.

Apocalypse of Paul Redaction X (Silverstein, p. 224)
in quo est rota ignea habens mille orbitas, mille vicibus in una hora
percussa rota, dico, ab angelo tarthareo, et in unaquaque vice mille
anime cremante.

Hypothetical original text of Redaction IV behind all these Apocalypse of
Paul texts:[30]
in quo est rota ignea habens mille orbitas. Mille vicibus in uno die ab

---

[30] The reconstruction takes into account the derivation of redactions V, VIII and
X from Redaction IV: see the stemma in T. Silverstein, 'The vision of Saint Paul:
new links and patterns in the Western tradition,' *Archives d'Histoire Doctrinale et Littéraire
du Moyen Age* 34 (1959) 225.

angelo tartareo percussa (volvitur), et in unaquaque vice mille anime concremantur.

Coptic apocryphal Apocalypse of John (Budge, p. 1023)
And there was a wheel, and thousands of thousands, and tens of thousands of tens of thousands of fiery lightnings leaped forth, and shot down into the chaos of Tartarus, that burned with fire..... The wheel of fire which thou hast seen beareth down the sinners who are on it, and it submergeth them for three hundred days.

Comparing K first with the Coptic apocryphal Apocalypse of John, we notice that these two texts share two main features of the wheel: that it revolves with sinners on it, and that it emits sparks in very large numbers. Since a literary relationship between these two works is scarcely conceivable, except in the form of common dependence on an ancient work, it is clear that these two features of the wheel in K must be original. In these respects, then, K is more original than C, in which the sparks do not come from the wheel, and the Irish versions, in which there is no wheel at all. However, another feature of the wheel that is found in C, but not in K, is also to be found in the Coptic apocryphal Apocalypse of John: that the wheel carries the sinners down into the fire. This must be an original feature which has dropped out of K, and we may guess that the meaningless words *et flumine tres* are the remnant of it.

The description of the wheel in the Latin redactions of the Apocalypse of Paul[31] is in places so close to K (*ab angelo tartareo percussa volvitur ..... mille anime concremantur*) that a literary relationship seems very likely. But K cannot have derived its description from Apocalypse of Paul, because the latter lacks features which K shares with the Coptic apocryphal Apocalypse of John: that the sinners are on the wheel (though this may be understood in the Apocalypse of Paul[32]) and that sparks come from it. It is therefore likely that Apocalypse of Paul Redaction IV borrowed this description from our text. (It is characteristic of the Latin redactions of ApPaul to add details borrowed from other sources.) In that case, the Apocalypse of Paul texts are witnesses to the originality of a further feature of K, which they share but which differs in both the Anglo-Saxon and the Irish versions: that the angel strikes the wheel.

---

[31] It was mainly through the great popularity of redaction IV of the Apocalypse of Paul, and its vernacular versions (see T. Silverstein, *Visio Sancti Pauli: The History of the Apocalypse in Latin* [Studies and Documents 4; London: Christophers, 1935] 52), that the wheel became a widely known feature of hell in the later Middle Ages.

[32] Cf. the illustration of the Apocalypse of Paul mentioned in Willard, *Two Apocrypha*, 20 n. 107.

Of the versions of our apocalypse, C is closest to K. The most important differences are that in C two elements of the description – the angel(s) striking with rods, and the hundred sparks which consume a hundred sinners – are no longer related to the wheel, but are given a function in relation to the removal of souls from the fiery river. But the resulting picture is very odd. It looks as though a text which said that the angel strikes the burning *wheel* and at each blow a hundred sparks burst forth, was miscopied, such that the angel strikes the burning *river*. The notion of the removal of the souls from the river would then have been a scribe's attempt to explain why the angel strikes the river.

A version something like C must lie behind the Irish versions, but further corruption has also occurred. The wheel has been replaced by a whirlpool, presumably through some misunderstanding of *rota*. The thorns or spikes (of M and LF) may result from reading *scintille* (sparks) as *spinule* (thorns) or *spicula* (spikes).

Thus it seems clear that on the whole C and the Irish versions result from attempts to make sense of Latin texts more corrupt than K. On the other hand, C has preserved one feature which has dropped out of K (the wheel submerges sinners in the river). One feature of LU, P and Y (the righteous pass on without delay) may also be an original feature, which K has omitted through its general tendency to concentrate on the fate of the wicked.

Our second illustration of the relative superiority of K to the other versions concerns the contents of the sixth heaven. K has no account of the fifth heaven, but the contents of its sixth heaven are assigned to the fifth heaven in C and the Irish versions (except M). These versions give the following accounts of the sixth heaven:

C (translation from text in Willard, p. 5)
there is not here any torment spoken of or enumerated, but instead there shines the light of the most glorious of precious stones.

LU (cf. Stokes, p. 13; Boswell, p. 37; Herbert and McNamara, p. 142)
No punishment or torment is enumerated for the souls in that gate, but they are illumined there by the light and radiance of precious stones.
(LBr and P are the same)

Y (cf. Stokes, p. 151)[33]
No punishment is enumerated there.

LF (summarized Seymour, p. 21)
No torment, but light from precious stones.

---

[33] Stokes has not here translated the text of Y which he prints on p. 150, but the text of LU.

N (summarized Seymour, p. 22)
No pain is there but souls are bathed in the well of healing.

It should also be noted that M has inadvertently conflated the contents of the third and fourth heavens (by homoioteleuton omitting everything between the '12,000 cubits' of the third heaven and the '12,000 cubits' of the fourth heaven), places the contents of K's sixth heaven in its fourth heaven, and then mentions no more heavens below the seventh.

The evidence is further complicated by the fact that K's account of the seventh heaven begins with a description of the throne of God, which is not found in the other versions: *dominus habitat super lapidem preciosum unde venit lux et ignis de lapide* (v 10). This can scarcely be unconnected with the 'light from precious stones' which C, LU, P and LF place in the sixth heaven. Willard therefore concludes that the numbering of the heavens and the contents of the sixth heaven in these texts is original, while K has conflated the sixth and seventh heavens.[34] However, this is very unlikely, because K's description of the throne of God closely resembles common apocalyptic descriptions of the divine throne (see note on v 10 in section V below) and therefore certainly belongs in the seventh heaven.

The best explanation is as follows. The numbering of the heavens in K is correct, but the account of the fifth heaven has been lost through the mistake of a scribe who, misled by the mention of the fifth heaven in v 5, passed on to the account of the sixth heaven. Later scribes therefore renumbered K's sixth heaven as the fifth, but were faced with nothing to record about the sixth heaven. The statement in Y and the first statement in C and LU simply state this situation ('here no punishment is recounted'). To this purely negative comment, a later scribe added the second statement in C and LU, which borrows part of K's account of the seventh heaven, so as not to leave the sixth heaven empty. The scribe who originated the second statement in N may have known only the negative statement or may not have been satisfied with LU's second statement. In either case, he decided to give the sixth heaven a clear function in the passage of the souls through the heavens by borrowing the well of healing from the second heaven (where the other Irish texts locate it). It is just possible that M follows a text in which no attempt had yet been made to fill the gap at the sixth heaven.

Once again, therefore, it seems that the Anglo-Saxon and Irish versions derive originally from a Latin text no less corrupt than K,

---

[34] Willard, *Two Apocrypha*, 22.

and their differences from K result from an ingenious but mistaken attempt to remedy the defects of a corrupt text.

These two examples imply not that the Anglo-Saxon and Irish versions are of no value in recovering the original text, but that they must be used with great caution. Some of their contents which are not found in K may be original, but others are secondary elaborations. Further progress in distinguishing the two may be possible when all the Irish texts are published and studied by an expert in Irish language and literature. For the time being, priority must be given to K, and the other versions used with great caution to elucidate K.

IV LATIN TEXT AND ENGLISH TRANSLATION

I reproduce here de Bruyne's text, adding verse numbers for ease of reference. No attempt is made to correct either the execrable grammar and spelling of the text or its evident corruptions. The translation attempts to render the text as it stands. Some corrections of the text are suggested in the next section.

> **1** Omnis roris qui discendit de austro super faciem terrae, sursum ascendit in celom cum ipsum. **2** Abottem tertium celum in medio eius fornacem ardentem. Ita constitutum est altitudo flamme: XII milia cupitis; **3** anima sanctorum & peccatorum per illum ueheuntur, anima sanctorum in momento pertransit, anima uero peccatorum XII annis habitant in medio fornacem ardentem. **4** Tunc venit angelus, baiulat illius usque ad quartum celum qui uocatur iothiam, ubi habitat flumini igneo & muro flumini; **5** altitudo flumini XII milia cubitis & fluctus eius exalatur usque ad quintum celum & ubi peccatoris morantur XII annis in medio fluminis. **6** Tunc angelum adfert illum usque ad sextum celum qui appellatur seloth. **7** In medio eius rotam et angelo tartarucho cum uirgis ferreis percutientis rotam et inde uoluitur in gyru et flumine tres; **8** ponitur homo peccatur super rotam, XII annis tormentatur. **9** Centum scintille procedit de rotam & centum pondus in uno scindule & centum anime percremant. **10** Deinde, tradatur homo peccator ad celum septimum qui uocatur theruch, ubi dominus habitat super lapidem preciosum, unde venit lux et ignis de lapide. **11** Dominus iudicat de illo homo peccator & tradator hunc ad angelum tartarucho. **12** Et angelum dimergit eum in infernum, ciuitas ferreas & muros & muros ferreos igneos, et XII turres & XII dracones in uno turres & XII penis & XII flagellis ardentis.

> **1** Every dew which descends from the south wind onto the face of the earth ascends up to heaven with it. **2** Abottem [is] the third heaven: in the midst of it [there is] a burning furnace. The height of the flame is fixed thus: 12,000 cubits. **3** The souls of saints and sinners are carried through it. The souls of saints pass through it in a moment, but the souls of sinners dwell twelve years in the midst of the burning furnace. **4** Then the angel comes, and carries him up to the fourth heaven, which is called

Jothiam, where dwells a fiery river and the wall of the river (?). **5** The height of the river is 12,000 cubits, and its wave is raised up to the fifth heaven. There sinners remain for twelve years in the midst of the river. **6** Then the angel takes him up to the sixth heaven, which is called Seloth. **7** In the midst of it [there is] a wheel, and an angel of Tartarus striking the wheel with iron rods. By this means (?) he turns it around, and three rivers (?). **8** The person who is a sinner is put on the wheel and is tormented for twelve years. **9** A hundred sparks come from the wheel, and a hundred pounds in each splinter, and a hundred souls are burnt up. **10** Then the person who is a sinner is handed over to the seventh heaven, which is called Theruch, where the Lord dwells on a precious stone, whence comes light and fire [comes] from the stone. **11** The Lord judges concerning that person who is a sinner and hands him over to an angel of Tartarus. **12** And the angel plunges him into hell, an iron city and walls and fiery iron walls, and twelve towers and twelve dragons in each tower and twelve punishments and twelve burning whips.

V COMMENTARY

v 1. The location of the sources of meteorological phenomena in one or more of the heavens is a feature of several ancient accounts of the heavens, and since dew was thought in antiquity to come down from the sky like rain (cf. 1 En 60:20), it was often included in these phenomena. Such accounts show no consistency as to which heaven contains which phenomena. In 2 Enoch 6, the treasuries of the dew are the last mentioned contents of the first heaven, which also contains the angels who rule the stars, the treasuries of snow and ice, and the treasuries of the clouds. 3 Baruch 10 locates the heavenly lake, which is the source of rain, in the fourth heaven. The so-called α text of Testament of Levi 3:2 locates the harmful meteorological phenomena—fire, snow and ice—in the first of its series of only three heavens, but the β text places them in the second of its seven heavens. In b. Ḥag. 12b the harmful meteorological phenomena, including 'harmful dews', are stored in the sixth heaven, as they are also in Visions of Ezekiel (Jacobs p. 31). The Syriac History of the Virgin (Budge pp. 128-29) locates the treasuries of snow, rain, dew, winds and other phenomena in the second of its three heavens (cf. also SyrTransMar: Smith Lewis p. 65). The Mysteries of John (Budge p. 247) locates the fountain which pours dew on the earth in the seventh heaven. Sepher ha-Razim distributes meteorological phenomena through the second, third and fourth heavens, locating the treasuries of dew in the fourth (Morgan p. 67). It is therefore plausible to suppose that v 1 of our text is the conclusion of a more extensive account of the meteorological phenomena of the second heaven, which may (as in 2 En 4-5) have described other phenomena before the dew.

The association of dew with the wind recalls 1 Enoch 34:2-3; 36:1; 75:5; 76:1-14, passages which represent the apocalyptic interest in meteorology at an early stage, before the development of the scheme of the seven heavens. Our text's evident interest in speculative meteorology is paralleled especially in 3 Baruch 10:8-9, while the particular theory that dew derives from the *south* wind is found in Aristotle (*Meteor.* 1:10) and the idea of a cycle of descent and return is not unlike Aristotle's (*Meteor.* 1:9).

This detail about the dew preserved in K is of a purely meteorological interest and cannot relate directly to the main theme of the rest of the text: the passage of souls through the heavens. However, in C the second heaven contains a fiery river in which souls are purified and another river called *Fons Roris* in which souls are bathed and healed of their wounds. In the Irish texts the Latin phrase has not survived and there is no mention of dew, but instead a well or spring (a better translation of *fons* than C's *flod*) performs the healing function for righteous souls, while scalding sinners. It seems clear that K's material of purely meteorological interest, which is quite characteristic of ancient apocalyptic texts, is original, but it has dropped out of the later versions, which found it of no relevance to the theme of the passage of the souls through the heavens. But C's term *fons roris* is a relic of the meteorological interest of the original text, which evidently described a heavenly source of dew, like the fountain of dew in the seventh heaven in the Mysteries of John (Budge p. 247) or the lake in the fourth heaven which is the source of rain in 3 Baruch 10. The parallel with the Mysteries of John is all the stronger in that this text also associates winds from heaven with the descent of the dew to earth (p. 253). Whether the *fons roris* in our apocalypse originally also performed a function in relation to the souls or whether this is the elaboration of a later editor is hard to tell. Something of a parallel could be found in Questions of Ezra A16, which integrates the meteorological phenomena of the lower heavens into the theme of the souls' ascent through the heavens by making them hazards through which the souls must pass.[35]

v 2. *Abottem* is the name of the third heaven. Our text also gives the name Jothiam to the fourth heaven (v 4), the name Seloth to the sixth heaven (v 6) and the name Theruch to the seventh heaven (v 10). These names bear no resemblance to the names in rabbinic literature (b. Ḥag. 12b; GenRab 6:6) and Merkabah literature (3 En 17;

---

[35] Cf. also 3 Bar 10:5 (G), probably a secondary addition in our Greek text, which introduces the souls of the righteous into the description of the source of the rain.

VisEzek), or to those found elsewhere in apocryphal literature (2 En 20:3; 21:6; 22:1 in the longer recension; EthBkMyst pp. 3-6). Like many names in Christian and Gnostic literature originating in Greek, these names may be Semitic-sounding inventions, or they may be very corrupt. Just possibly *Abottem* is a corruption of *Abaddon* (Job 26:6 etc.; Rev 9:11), which is the name of one of the compartments of hell in Hebrew Vision VII 2.

In the Anglo-Saxon and some of the Irish versions (LF, M, N) the equivalent names in the course of the account are given as the names of the *doors* of each heaven,[36] while these same versions introduce the whole account with a list of names of the seven heavens, which are more in the nature of descriptions than strictly names.[37] Lists identical or similar to the latter are found elsewhere in Hiberno-Latin and Irish literature,[38] and may therefore represent an Irish addition to the text of our apocalypse. It is possible, however, that these versions are more original than K in mentioning and giving names to the doors of the heavens. Certainly, doors and doorkeepers are a feature of ancient accounts of the seven heavens (e.g. AscenIs 10:24-27; 3 Bar 2:2; 3:1; 11:2; 14:1; 15:1 NHApPaul 20:10-11; MystJn: Budge p. 242).

v 2. *tertium celum.* Hell is located in the third heaven in 2 Enoch 10; Questions of Ezra A20; 3 Baruch 4:3-6; 5:3 (G, but cf. Sl); and apparently in the first heaven in Greek Apocalypse of Ezra 1:7, while in Testament of Isaac 5:4-32 the punishments of hell are located generally in the heavens.[39] Our text seems peculiar in that it narrates successive punishments through which the wicked souls pass in the third, fourth, (fifth?) and sixth heavens, before being judged by God in the seventh heaven and then consigned to hell. But something similar seems to be in view in the abbreviated account in Questions of Ezra A20, where not only is hell in the third heaven, but all of the lower heavens are hazardous, up to the fifth heaven, in which the soul is investigated and its fate determined. The Nag Hammadi Apocalypse of Paul places the investigation at the entrance to the fourth heaven (20:5-21:22), while in the fifth heaven angels whip the souls

---

[36] See the comparative table in Willard, *Two Apocrypha*, 9.

[37] See the comparative table in Willard, *Two Apocrypha*, 7.

[38] Seymour, 'Seven Heavens,' 28-29; Stokes, *Félire Óengusso*, 464; Pseudo-Isidore, *Liber de numeris* 7.38; McNally, *Der irische Liber*, 122-124.

[39] On these texts, see H. Bietenhard, *Die himmlische Welt im Urchristentums und Spätjudentum* (WUNT 2; Tubingen: J. C. B. Mohr, 1951) 205-209. On the relocation of Hades in the lower heavens in hellenistic thought, see F. Cumont, *Lux Perpetua* (Paris: P. Geuthner, 1949) 191-196, 208; idem, *After Life in Roman Paganism* (New Haven: Yale University Press, 1922) 79-83, 103, 168.

towards their judgment (22:2-10). Acts of John 114 envisages that the departed soul must encounter the dangers of hell on its way to God. The elaborate scheme of post-mortem punishments in Pistis Sophia 103; 111; 127; 139-140; 144-147 envisages a long series of punishments in Amente, Chaos and the Way of the Midst, prior to the examination and judgement of the soul by the Virgin of Light and its reincarnation, while the severest and ultimate hell, in the dragon of outer darkness (126), lies beyond this scheme. Behind this gnosticized account probably lies an apocalyptic one similar in conception to that in our text, as further similarities will confirm.

v 2. *fornacem ardentem.* Gehenna is described as a fiery furnace in Matthew 13:42, 52; 1 Enoch 54:6; Targum Neofiti Genesis 15:17; Genesis Rabbah 6:6 (referring to Mal 3:19; Isa 31:9); cf. also Acts of John 114. Furnaces appear as one form of infernal punishment among others in Vision of Ezra 48, 50, 51; Barlaam 30:281; and the Latin redactions of the Apocalypse of Paul.[40]

v 2. *XII milia cupitis* [i.e. *cubita*]. Measurements of this kind are common in apocalyptic descriptions of heaven and hell: cf. Apocalypse of Paul 32 (P: the depth of the pit of hell is 3,000 cubits; StG: 30,000 stadia); Coptic Apocalypse of Paul (Budge p. 1058: pits of various depths); Coptic apocryphal Apocalypse of John (Budge p. 1022: smoke from the abyss rises 300 stadia); Vision of Ezra 23 (L: height of the burning cauldron is 200 cubits). For the figure 12,000, cf. Revelation 21:16; Hebrew Vision II 2.

v 3. The account presumes that all souls, good and evil, ascend through all the heavens to the throne of God in the seventh, as in Questions of Ezra 19-21, but whereas the latter focuses on the good souls, our text focuses on the wicked, and mentions the good only at this point. However, the information that the righteous pass quickly through the punishment is repeated in the next heaven in C and in the next two heavens in LU, P and Y, and may therefore have been omitted in our text, which has been abbreviated partly, it seems, in accordance with a predominant interest in the fate of the wicked. In any case, one must assume that the righteous souls pass quickly and

---

[40] Silverstein, *Visio*, 72-75. But this feature certainly does not prove that our text is dependent on ApPaul, as A. Ruegg, *Die Jenseitsvorstellungen vor Dante und die übrigen literarischen Voraussetzungen der "Divina Commedia"* I (Einsiedeln/Koln: Benzinger, 1945) 344, thinks.

unharmed through the perils of the upper heavens, as they do
through the third.

The idea that the righteous pass through the same fiery punishments as the wicked, but without harm, is also found in Vision of
Ezra 4-7, 23-26, 58; Testament of Isaac 5:24; Questions of Ezra 22;
and Pistis Sophia 103; 112; 115; 147. In the latter two works the
context, of preliminary punishments prior to judgement, is the same
as in our text. This makes the punishments really a form of trial by
ordeal, and this concept of probative punishments explains their
place preceding the judgement which determines the soul's eternal
destiny.

The most ancient form of this kind of fiery ordeal was probably
the river of fire, which functioned in this way at the day of judgement
(ApPet 6:2-5; SibOr 2:252-55; 8:411; Lactantius, *Div. Inst.* 7:21) and
also immediately after death (TIsaac 5:24-25; GBart: Budge p. 207;
EncJnBapt: Budge pp. 346-347; SahLifeMary IV 116; BohDorm-
Mary 11:14; SahDormMary II 2:16-17;[41] BohHistJos 13:9; SahHist-
Jos III 22:1).[42]

v 3. *XII annis.* Few of the apocalyptic accounts of the post-mortem
punishments refer to periods of punishment, since the common notion is that the sinner suffers the punishment assigned to him for ever;
but cf. Testament of Isaac 5:17-20; Acts of Thomas 57; Hebrew
Vision V 23. But the best parallels to our text in that they give lengths
of time spent in preliminary punishments, prior to judgement, are in
Pistis Sophia 139-140; 144-147.

v 4. *flumini igneo.* The fiery river is a common feature of apocalyptic
depictions of the last judgement (ApPet 6:2; SibOr 2:252-55; 8:411)
and of the punishments in hell (Virgil, *Aen.* 6.550-551; 2 En 10:2;
TIsaac 5:21; QuesEzra A17; ApPaul 31; 32; 35; 36; GkApMary 5;
EthApMary: Chaine p. 61/72; PistSoph 102; 144; 147; GkApJn 24;
SyrHistMary: Budge p. 131; CopLifePach 88). The image of flowing
fiery liquid probably originated from the observation of volcanic lava
flows. For our text, the best parallels are those in which the fiery river

---

[41] For other parallels in versions of the Transitus Mariae, see C.-M. Edsman, *Le
baptême de feu* (Acta Seminarii Neotestamentici Upsaliensis 9; Leipzig: Lorentz/
Uppsala: Lundequistska, 1940) 70.

[42] See also M. R. James, *The Lost Apocrypha of the Old Testament* (London: SPCK,
1920) 90-91; V. MacDermot, *The Cult of the Seer in the Ancient Middle East* (Berkley/Los
Angeles: University of California Press, 1971) 619-620, 622; Edsman, *Le baptême*, 66-
87.

is an ordeal through which righteous and sinners pass (see note on v 3 above).

v 4. *muro flumini.* It seems that C and the Irish versions which retain this wall (LU, P, Y) read something like this text, and C, LU and P explain it by making the wall surround the river. According to LU, P and Y the wall itself is fiery, a detail which may be original, but may be only a natural supposition by analogy with everything else in these fiery heavens.

The function of the wall is unclear, but in Apocalypse of Paul 37 (P) there is a wall which apparently surrounds a confined space containing fire,[43] in which certain sinners suffer. In our text, the wall is perhaps to prevent the sinners escaping from the river. It is less likely that we have here the idea of a wall of fire as itself an ordeal through which sinners must pass (cf. Dante, *Purg.* 27).

v 5. *altitudo flumini XII milia cubitis.* C may be correct in making this measurement the *breadth* of the river: *altitudo* would be a mistake for *latitudo*, perhaps influenced by v 2. This is supported by LU, P and Y, which make the measurement the breadth of the *wall*, but with the improbable consequence that in those versions the sinners remain twelve years in the wall.

v 5. *fluctus eius exal[t]atur usque ad quintum celum.* Cf. the following descriptions of the waves of the fiery river: 'its waves were like a wild sea over the sinners, and when the waves rose, they sank over 10,000 cubits' (GkApMary 23); 'its waves rising to about thirty cubits' (TIsaac 5:21); 'tossing its waves exceedingly, and its waves are higher than any mountain' (SahDormMary II 2:16). In the first two of these texts it is because the river is boiling that it throws up waves to a great height.

v 6. *sextum celum.* Probably owing to the mention of the fifth heaven in v 5, the account of the fifth heaven has been accidentally omitted (see section III above).

v 7. *angelo tartarucho* (cf. v 11). ταρταρούχος is an adjective used to describe angels who control Tartarus (plural in Hippolytus, *Dan.* 2.29.11; *Haer.* 10.34). In translations of apocalypses originally written in Greek, it was often retained and sometimes understood as the

---

[43] But in StG the sinners are in a fiery wall.

proper name of a particular angel (ApPet 13:5; BkThom 142:41; ApPaul P16).[44] The same thing happened to the word τημελοῦχος (ApPet 8:10 and *ap*. Clement Alex., *Eclog.* 41; 48; Methodius, *Symp.* 2.6, and the versions of the Apocalypse of Paul that treat the two angels Tartarouchos and Temelouchos as interchangeable). But in the Latin of Vision of Ezra 2; 19; 40, where the best reading is *angeli tartaruci*,[45] the word must be understood as an adjective describing a class of angels. It is also used in this way in a prayer in an eighth century Hiberno-Latin manuscript (*angelis tartarucis et angelis sathanae*),[46] which brings us close to the linguistic context in which our text was transmitted. Probably our text depends on a Greek Vorlage in which ταρταροῦχος was certainly adjectival and the two angels so described (vv 7, 11) would be two different angels. Probably the translator, like the translator of the Vision of Ezra, intended his Latin to mean the same.

v 7. *uirgis ferreis*: cf. Nag Hammadi Apocalypse of Paul 22:4.

v 7. *et flumine tres.* As they stand in the context these words make no sense, but an indication of what lay behind them in the original form of the text may be gathered from C: 'a fiery wheel turning in the midst of the river, and it thrusts the sinners downwards into the fiery river.' This is confirmed by Apocalypse of Peter 12:4-6 and the passage dependent on it in Sibylline Oracle 2:294-96, which also contain, rather obscurely, the idea of a revolving wheel whose lower part is submerged in fire, and especially by Coptic apocryphal Apocalypse of John (Budge p. 1023): 'The wheel of fire which thou hast seen beareth down the sinners who are on it, and it submergeth them for three hundred days; only with the greatest difficulty can a man remain fast in the lower part thereof, [for] afterwards they are cast up again, like a wheel, in the third year. All those who are to be punished are bound thereto, and the path of all of them leadeth to the bottom of that pit.' This seems to mean that the wheel took three

---

[44] Even in the ending of GkApJn, in MS E, the word, reduced to ταροὐχ has become the proper name of an angel, along with τεμελούχ (p. 94).

[45] MS B has *tartar*[...] in v 2, *tartaruti* in v 19, and *tartaruci* in v 40. MS L has *tartarici* in v 40. On ταραροῦχος and τημελοῦχος, see now the definitive study: J.-M. Rosenstiehl, 'Tartarouchos-Temelouchos: Contribution à l'étude de l'Apocalypse de Paul,' in *Deuxième Journée d'Etudes Coptes: Strasbourg 25 Mai 1984* (Cahiers de la Bibliothèque Copte 3; Louvain/Paris: Peeters, 1986) 29-56.

[46] P. David, 'Un receuil de conférences monastiques irlandaises du VIIIᵉ siècle. Notes sur le manuscrit 43 de la bibliothèque du chapitre de Cracovie', *RBén* 49 (1937) 64.

years to revolve, and since the lowest part was submerged (presumably in fire), a sinner bound to the wheel spent three hundred days submerged. Our text may originally have said that the angel revolved the wheel in the river of fire either every three years or three times in the twelve-year period of punishment (v 8).

v 8. *ponitur homo peccatur super rotam*: cf. Coptic apocryphal Apocalypse of John (Budge p. 1023): 'All those who are to be punished are bound [to the wheel]'; Apocalypse of Peter 12:5: 'men and women hanging in it [the wheel] by the power of its turning'; Acts of Thomas 55 (G): 'souls were hung on those wheels.' One most naturally thinks of them bound to the rim of the wheel (as in medieval illustrations of this feature in hell[47]), but in Virgil, *Aen.* 6.616-617 they seem to be stretched out on the spokes of the wheel.

v 9. *Centum scintille procedit de rotam.* There is a close parallel in Coptic apocryphal Apocalypse of John (Budge p. 1023): 'there was a wheel, and thousands of thousands, and tens of thousands of tens of thousands of fiery lightnings leaped forth.' It is in this sense that the wheel is described as *ignea* in Apocalypse of Paul Redactions IV, V, VIII, X, probably dependent on our text (see section III above). There are wheels of fire also in Acts of Thomas 55 (G, Syr); Apocalypse of Peter 12:5; Sibylline Oracle 2:294-96.

v 9. *centum pondus in uno scindule* makes poor sense. Very likely *uno scindule* should be amended to *una scintilla*, but even if there were some point in the information that each spark weighed a hundred pounds, the phrase is an odd way to convey it. The text translated in C probably had *centum pondus* (or *pondo*), which C has converted to 'the weight of a man.' But *pondus* may have resulted from misreading σπινθῆρες (sparks) as στάθμια (weights). The original sense would then have been: 'A hundred flashes of fire come from the wheel, and in each flash of fire there are a hundred sparks, and a hundred sinners are burnt up [by each spark?].'

With these emendations, this description of the wheel conforms to a standard type of apocalyptic description in accounts of hell and

---

[47] See the fifteenth century illustration in D. D. R. Owen, *The Vision of Hell: Infernal Journeys in Medieval French Literature* (Edinburgh/London: Scottish Academic Press, 1970) Plate 1; and another medieval illustration described in Willard, *Two Apocrypha*, 20 n. 107.

paradise: cf. 2 Baruch 29:5 ('on one vine will be a thousand branches, and one branch will produce a thousand clusters, and one cluster will produce a thousand grapes, and one grape will produce a cor of wine'; the variant of this saying in Papias, *ap.* Irenaeus, *Adv. Haer.* 5.33.3-4, adds a similar description of wheat; and cf. further variants in ApPaul 22; EncJnBapt: Budge pp. 348-349); Gedulat Moshe (Gaster §42: 'each scorpion has 70,000 mouths, and each mouth 70,000 stings, and each sting has 70,000 vesicles filled with poison and venom, and with these are the sinners imbued and thus they are tortured'); Hebrew Vision V 24 ('there are seven compartments in hell, and in each of them are 6,000 rooms, in each room 6,000 windows, in each window there are 6,000 vessels filled with venom, all destined for slanderous writers and iniquitous judges'); Apocalypse of Paul Redaction I 2 ('a fiery dragon having a hundred heads on its neck, and a thousand teeth in each head, and each tooth glowed like a lion'; cf. Red VII); Hebrew Apocalypse of Elijah (Buchanan p. 436: '40,000 camps. Every camp [will have] 400,000 towers, and for every tower, 40 ladders').

v 10. *super lapidem preciosum*: cf. Ezekiel 1:26; 10:1.

v 10. *lux et ignis*: cf. Daniel 7:10; 1 Enoch 14:18-19; Apocalypse of Abraham 18:13; 2 Enoch 20:1; Questions of Ezra A21; Nag Hammadi Apocalypse of Paul 22:17-19, 27-30; Sepher ha-Razim (Morgan p. 82). The description of the divine throne is brief in the extreme, but consists of standard features of such descriptions. The river of fire flowing from the divine throne (Dan 7:10; 1 En 14:19)[48] was probably originally a distinct motif from that of the river of fire which judges and punishes sinners, but later the two concepts were fused (b. Ḥag. 13b; 3 En 33:4-5).[49] Our text could have understood the fire from the throne to flow through the lower heavens (cf. 3 En 33:5) in which the fiery ordeals take place, but there is no indication that this is the case.

v 11. The Irish version in LBr (Windisch, p. 183) here retains from its Latin Vorlage the words of God to the angels of heaven: *Hanc animam multo peccantem angelo Tartari tradite et demergat eam in infernam.* The correspondence with our text is close, but it is not possible to tell whether the narrative form (in K) or the divine speech (in LBr) is the

---

[48] Cf. Bietenhard, *Die himmlische Welt*, 75.
[49] Cf. Edsman, *Le baptême*, 19-31.

more original. Cf. also Apocalypse of Paul 16; 18, where God judges souls and hands them over to an angel of Tartarus (ταρταροῦχος) to be consigned to hell (16P: *tradatur ergo angelo tartarucho*; StG: *tradatur angelo Tartari*); and Book of Thomas 142:40-41 ('will deliver them over to the angel Tartarouchos'); 142:33-34 ('cast him from heaven down to the abyss').

v 12. *infernum* probably translates ᾅδης and refers to a subterranean hell. For a description of the subterranean hell after an account of the seven heavens, cf. perhaps 2 Enoch 40:12. In the extant versions of 3 Baruch, the seer gets no further than the fifth heaven, but 16:4-8 (Sl) promises further sights – of the glory of God, the restingplace of the righteous, and the punishments of the wicked – which the original apocalypse surely went on to describe.[50] The glory of God would be in the seventh heaven, and the restingplace of the righteous could be in the seventh or sixth heaven (cf. QuesEzra A20). It is possible (though unparalleled) that Baruch saw hell in the sixth heaven, but perhaps more likely that he was taken to a hell located, as in our text, altogether outside the seven heavens.

v 12. *civitas ferreas*. The idea of hell as a fortified city is found in Virgil's *Aeneid* (6.549 ff.), but I know no exact parallel to the description of Hades as an iron city (but cf. next note on Dante). The idea could have been suggested by the well-known motif of the iron and bronze gates of Hades (Ps 107:16; OdesSol 17:10; ApPet 4:3; GNic 21:1; QuesBart 1:20; Tertullian, *De Res.* 44; and cf. ApZeph 5:5-6, where it is not clear whether the gates are those of Hades or heaven). The gate of Virgil's hell has columns of adamant and an iron tower above it (*Aen.* 6.552, 554), while the fortified walls (*moenia*) come from the forges of the Cyclops (630-31).

v 12. *muros ferreos igneos*: cf. the iron walls of the city of Dis, whose buildings glow with fire, in Dante, *Inferno* 8.70-78 (78: *le mura ni parean che ferro fosse*). Though Dante's city is modelled on Virgil's (*Aen.* 6.549 ff.), the latter has only an iron gatetower (554), while the walls, though certainly metallic (630-631), are not explicitly said to be iron. It is tempting to guess that, directly or indirectly, our text influenced

---

[50] The Apocalypse of Baruch known to Origen (*De princ.* 2.3.6) described seven heavens. See further R. Bauckham, 'Early Jewish Visions of Hell,' *JTS* 41 (1990) 371-374 = chapter 2 above, section V.

Dante,[51] but it would have been easy for a reader of Virgil independently to draw the conclusion that the walls of hell are iron.[52]

v 12. *XII dracones in uno turres* presumably means that there are twelve dragons (serpents) in *each* of the twelve towers, or possibly that there is one dragon in each of the twelve towers. The picture in C seems to be of twelve walls in concentric circles, and a dragon in each of the regions between the walls.

A parallel might be found in Pistis Sophia 126, where the ultimate hell, the dragon of outer darkness, contains twelve chambers (ταμεῖα) in each of which an archon inflicts punishments.

The Anglo-Saxon and Irish versions explain how the dragons torture the souls: each dragon in turn eats the soul and then spews or passes it out; in the Irish versions, the last dragon then passes the soul into the devil's stomach. The possibility that this explanation is original is suggested by (a) a parallel kind of torture in Testament of Isaac 5:10-15, in which successive groups of lions eat and spit out a sinner, and in the Coptic Apocalypse of Paul (Budge p. 1044), where the same thing is done by 'powers of darkness' with the faces of wild beasts; (b) a phrase in the homiletical sequel to our text in K, which describes hell as a place where lions and dragons kill sinners (*ubi leones & dracones interficiunt impiis & peccatoris*: de Bruyne, p. 325 line 33) and may reflect the author's knowledge of the fuller text he has summarised in v 12.

v 12. *XII penis* [i.e. *poenas*]. Both Greek Apocalypse of Ezra 4:21 and the Greek apocryphal Apocalypse of John (Tischendorff p.94: MS B) refer to the δωδεκάπληγος (twelvefold wound) of the abyss, and the latter text associates it with the wild beasts and reptiles of hell. But since our text repeatedly uses the number twelve, the resemblance may be coincidental.

v 12. *XII flagellis ardentis.* For the fiery scourges, with which angels whip the damned in hell, cf. Apocalypse of Zephaniah 4:4; Testa-

---

[51] This guess could be supported by the points of contact which Ruegg, *Jenseitsvorstellungen*, 341-344, finds between our text, in the form in which it is found in the *Vision of Adamnán* 15-20, and Dante's *Purgatorio*. He compares the seven heavens and their angelic doorkeepers with Dante's seven *gironi* and their angelic guardians.

[52] For the influence of Virgil on the Christian image of hell, see P. Courcelle, 'Les Pères de l'Église devant les enfers virgiliens,' *Archives d'Histoire Doctrinale et Littéraire du Moyen Age* 30 (1955) 5-74.

ment of Abraham A12:1; Book of Thomas 142:42-143:1; Sibylline
Oracle 2:288; Vision of Ezra 13; Coptic Life of Pachomios 88; Pistis
Sophia 144.

VI Conclusions

The commentary has brought to light a wide range of parallels to our
text, both in indubitably ancient Jewish and Christian sources and in
sources so far removed, in geographical and cultural context, from
our text that the contacts are explicable only via ancient sources.[53]
Naturally, this demonstrates only that the contents of our apocalypse
derive from ancient sources, not necessarily that the apocalypse itself
is an ancient work. However, the demonstrably ancient contents of
our text could not have been derived from other apocalyptic works
which we know to have been available in early medieval Europe,
such as the Apocalypse of Paul. Rather than postulate unknown ancient sources behind our apocalypse, it is a more economical hypothesis to suppose that our apocalypse is itself an ancient work.
Certainly the text contains nothing that could not be as old as the
second century C.E. The slight indications that the Latin text is translated from Greek (the word *tartaruchus*, though this is not an infallible
sign of a Greek Vorlage [see note on v 7], and the possibility of
mistranslation in v 9) also provide some support for this conclusion.

The place of our text in the tradition of Jewish and Christian
apocalyptic literature can be better understood if we note its affinities
with three (overlapping) categories of such literature:

(1) Accounts of the seven heavens in which the contents of the heavens are miscellaneous and include both meteorological phenomena
and punishments: 3 Baruch, 2 Enoch,[54] and Questions of Ezra A16-
30.[55] There are also accounts which include meteorological and astronomical phenomena but not punishments: Apocalypse of
Abraham 19; Testament of Levi 3 (β text); b. Ḥag. 12b; Mysteries of
John; Didascalia of our Lord Jesus Christ 21; Sepher ha-Razim;

---

[53] Note especially the striking parallels with the Armenian text QuesEzra, and
with the Coptic works CopApJn, MystJn and PistSoph.

[54] The extension of the scheme of seven heavens to include three more heavens, in
the longer recension of 2 En 20-22, is secondary.

[55] The meteorological phenomena occur in v 16 and could describe the region
through which the soul has to pass before reaching the first heaven (cf. QuesBart
4:30-35). But in view of v 19, it is more likely that v 16 is a general description of the
heavens, which are then relics of an apocalyptic scheme which located meteorological phenomena and punishments in several heavens.

Gedulat Moshe (Gaster §§ 8-25); Visions of Ezekiel.[56] Although most of these accounts locate many angels in the heavens, controlling the meteorological and astronomical phenomena, conducting souls through the heavens, and engaged in the worship of God, their miscellaneous contents distinguish them from another category of accounts of the seven heavens in which the heavens are populated exclusively by various ranks of angels (AscenIs; QuesBart 4:30; Irenaeus, *Dem.* 9; probably ApZeph [Clem]).

Of the former category of accounts, both 3 Baruch and 2 Enoch are tour apocalypses, in which the seer is conducted through the seven heavens to view their contents. It seems that this type of apocalypse originated from adapting the genre of the cosmic tour, found in the oldest parts of 1 Enoch (17-36, 72-82), to the later cosmological conception of the seven heavens. The various sights which Enoch saw in distant parts of the earth, including the sources of meteorological phenomena and the places of post-mortem punishments, were relocated in the seven heavens. Other accounts, such as our text, Questions of Ezra A16-30 and b. Ḥag. 12b, which are not in the form of tour apocalypses, share the same kind of concept of the heavens.

The scheme of seven heavens, whether with miscellaneous or with purely angelological contents, seems to have flourished in Jewish and Christian apocalyptic in the period c. 100 C.E. to c. 200 C.E., to which the texts which can be fairly securely dated belong (3 Bar; AscenIs; ApAb; Irenaeus, *Dem.* 9).[57] Thereafter it was not very popular in Christianity,[58] and was little known in Latin Christianity outside Ireland. Its popularity in Irish Christian literature[59] is probably due to the survival of ancient apocalyptic works in Ireland, including our apocalypse and also the *Evernew Tongue*, which seems to be a form of an ancient Philip apocryphon[60] and in all recensions contains an

---

[56] TIsaac 5, which places hell in the heavens, but does not enumerate seven heavens or describe other contents, should perhaps also be loosely associated with these texts, as dependent on the same kind of tradition.

[57] Other second-century texts which mention seven heavens are EpApp 13; Aristo of Pella, *apud* Maximus, *Scholia in Dion. Areop.* 1. J. Daniélou, *The Theology of Jewish Christianity* (London: Darton, Longman and Todd, 1964) 174, claims that the scheme of seven heavens is not Jewish, but peculiarly Jewish Christian, but this claim is refuted by 3 Bar; ApAb 19; ApMos 35:2; b. Ḥag. 12b; SephRaz; VisEzek.

[58] It may have been in part discredited by Gnostic speculation about the seven heavens: cf. Charles in W. R. Morfill and R. H. Charles, *The Book of the Secrets of Enoch* (Oxford: Clarendon Press, 1896) xliv-xlvi.

[59] See Seymour, 'Seven Heavens'; and especially McNally, *Der irische Liber*, 122-124; more briefly, R. E. McNally, *The Bible in the Early Middle Ages* (Westminster, Maryland: Newman Press, 1959) 27.

[60] James, 'Irish Apocrypha,' 9-13.

account of the seven heavens with astronomical, meteorological and angelological contents.[61] Even in Irish literature, however, our apocalypse is alone in locating punishments in the seven heavens.

(2) Accounts of the ascension of the souls of the righteous and the wicked dead, conducted by angels, through the heavens. The best parallel to our text is Questions of Ezra A14-20, which, though focusing on the fate of the righteous souls, clearly envisages that wicked souls are also taken at least as far as the fifth heaven (v 20). A somewhat similar concept is found in the Nag Hammadi Apocalypse of Paul, which must be based on a Jewish or Christian scheme of seven heavens (note especially the throne of the Jewish God in the seventh heaven: 22:24-30), which it has extended to include three more heavens, superior to the Jewish God.[62] The righteous ascend to the eighth, ninth or tenth heaven (24:1-7), while the souls of the wicked are brought by angels from earth to the fourth heaven, where their guilt is investigated (20:5-21:22), and angels whip souls through the fifth heaven on their way to judgement (22:2-10). The many accounts, in the latter part of the Pistis Sophia (103-147), of the ascent of souls, good and bad, through the realms of the archons, until they are judged by the Virgin of Light, are probably also based on an apocalyptic scheme of ascent through the heavens, similar to that in our text. Apocalypse of Paul 11-18 describes how angels bring both good and bad souls up to the throne of God to be judged, but does not enumerate seven heavens (cf. also TAb A10-14; B8-11).[63] By contrast, the Ascension of Isaiah envisages the ascent only of righteous souls through the seven heavens.

(3) Accounts of the post-mortem punishments of the wicked. In distinction from texts such as 2 Enoch 10, in which hell is described in very general terms, our text distinguishes a series of different punishments, in several heavens, as well as indicating further punishments in

---

[61] For the first recension, see W. Stokes, 'The Evernew Tongue,' *Ériu* 2 (1905) 109-110; Herbert and McNamara, *Irish Biblical Apocrypha*, 114; and for the second recension, see U. Nic Énrí and G. Mac Niocaill, 'The Second Recension of the Evernew Tongue,' *Celtica* 9 (1971) 18-19.

[62] Stevenson, 'Ascent through the Heavens,' fails to distinguish between the Gnostic character of NHApPaul itself and the Jewish or Christian apocalyptic scheme of seven heavens on which it is based. She therefore mistakenly postulates a Gnostic origin for our Apocalypse of the Seven Heavens.

[63] Elsewhere (19, 21) ApPaul envisages a scheme of three heavens, with paradise in the third heaven, owing to its dependence on 2 Cor 12:4, but although the third heaven is unlikely to be the highest, the scheme is not further developed.

hell. This brings it closer to works which describe a whole series of punishments in hell, and some of the particular forms of punishment in our text can be paralleled in such works. However, most of these accounts, unlike our text, describe different categories of punishments for different classes of sinners (ApZeph 10:4-9; ApPet; ActsThom 55-57; ApPaul and the group of Christian apocalypses dependent on it; TIsaac 5; GkApEzra; VisEzra; GkApJn; ApElfrag). [64] Our text is distinguished from these works by the fact that the various punishments it describes in the heavens are experienced successively by all sinners, as well as by the fact that these punishments are primarily ordeals, prior to judgement and eternal punishment in hell. Only two other detailed accounts of post-mortem punishments seem to fit this pattern: Pistis Sophia 103-147 and Questions of Ezra A16-30. The former not only relates a whole series of punishments, which affect souls in proportion to their spiritual state, tormenting some only a little and others not at all (cf. 103, 112, 115, 147); it also allots specific time periods to each of the successive punishments (cf. 139-147), as in our text. Judgment is pronounced only after these ordeals (cf. 103, 111, 144). In Questions of Ezra A16-30 the fire of hell and ice is located in the third heaven (20; cf. 2 En 10), but all the lower heavens are described as dangerous ordeals through which good and evil souls must pass (20, 22; cf. 16-17) before definitive judgment is pronounced on them in the fifth heaven. It should be noted that the idea of post-mortem punishments as ordeals which bring to light the wickedness or righteousness of the souls has also survived in the Vision of Ezra (combined with the notion of punishments appropriate to each class of sinners) and in Testament of Isaac 5:24, but the pattern of successive ordeals prior to judgment is lacking in these works.

From this study of the categories of apocalyptic literature to which our text is related, it becomes clear that its greatest overall affinity is with Questions of Ezra A16-30. This section of recension A of the Questions of Ezra, which does not correspond to anything in recension B, is plausibly attributed by Stone to a distinct source document, which has been incorporated into the Questions of Ezra owing to its relevance to the topic of the fate of the soul after death. [65] The

---

[64] On these works see the full study in M. Himmelfarb, *Tours of Hell: An Apocalyptic Form in Jewish and Christian Literature* (Philadelphia: University of Pennsylvania Press, 1983), and further discussion of the origin of this type of apocalypse in chapter 2 above.

[65] M. E. Stone in J. H. Charlesworth ed., *The Old Testament Pseudepigrapha*, vol. 1 (London: Darton, Longman & Todd, 1983) 592-593. Vv 14-15 may constitute the overlap between two sources, containing material from both.

Questions of Ezra itself belongs to the category of apocalyptic works inspired by 4 Ezra (GkApEzra, VisEzra, ApSedr, and the Armenian expansion of 4 Ezra), whose common characteristic is a dialogue about divine judgment and mercy in relation to the fate of sinners. But the section A16-30 has no particular affinity with 4 Ezra [66] or with this group of works, and need not have been associated with Ezra before its incorporation in the Questions of Ezra. Its contents, however, are certainly ancient in character and must derive from an ancient source, which in view of the absence of any distinctively Christian features in A16-30, may have been Jewish, but, of course, may also have been a Christian work in the Jewish tradition. [67]

The similarity between our apocalypse and Questions of Ezra A16-30 supports the independence of the latter and the antiquity of both, since an Hiberno-Latin text and a medieval Armenian text [68] are not likely to be related at any stage later than Christian antiquity. Both texts give the appearance of being somewhat abbreviated accounts, and it may be that Questions of Ezra A16-30, whose interest now focuses on the fate of the righteous, originally dealt more fully with the fate of the wicked, while our apocalypse, whose interest now focuses on the fate of the wicked, originally dealt more fully with the fate of the righteous.

Neither work is the kind of apocalypse in which a seer is conducted through the seven heavens to view their contents. Questions of Ezra A16-30 is presented as a revelation by the angel who conducts souls through the heavens (cf. also TLevi 3 [β text], for an account of the seven heavens by an angel). It is possible that our text also belonged originally on the lips of a heavenly revealer. Like Questions of Ezra A16-30, our apocalypse lacks any distinctively Christian features, and so the question of Jewish or Christian origin must similarly be left open.

---

[66] The resemblance between vv 19-21 and 4 Ezra 7:80-98 is quite superficial.

[67] For a general account of apocryphal literature in Armenian, which gives some indication of the sources from which such literature reached the Armenian church, see M. E. Stone, 'Jewish Apocryphal Literature in the Armenian Church,' *Muséon* 95 (1982) 285-309.

[68] Recension A of QuesEzra is known in a MS written in 1208: Stone in Charlesworth, *Pseudepigrapha*, 591.

CHAPTER THIRTEEN

THE FOUR APOCALYPSES OF THE VIRGIN MARY

There are four Apocalypses of the Virgin Mary, which are among the most neglected of the Christian apocalypses, even though one of them (the Greek Apocalypse of the Virgin) has been arguably, along with the Apocalypse of Paul, one of the two most influential of the extra-canonical Christian apocalypses. The aim of this chapter is to take the basic and preliminary steps towards placing them within the tradition of Jewish and Christian apocalyptic literature, in particular in the tradition of apocalypses concerned primarily with the fate of the dead.

In all four of these apocalypses the Virgin (in some accompanied by the apostles) is shown hell and the damned and intercedes for them. In two (the Greek Apocalypse and the Obsequies Apocalypse) this is all or most of the content. In two others (the Ethiopic Apocalypse and the Six Books Apocalypse) it is part of a larger tour of the other world, especially the places of the dead. Two of the four apocalypses (the Obsequies Apocalypse and the Six Books Apocalypse) form the concluding parts of versions of the *Transitus Mariae* (the story of the dormition or assumption of the Virgin), and, although they are complete apocalypses in themselves, they are not known to have circulated as independent works. The other two (the Greek Apocalypse and the Ethiopic Apocalypse) are known only as independent works. None of these four apocalypses is dependent on any of the others, but two of them (the Greek Apocalypse and the Ethiopic Apocalypse) are certainly inspired by and dependent on the Apocalypse of Paul, and so belong to the Apocalypse of Paul Family, as Martha Himmelfarb calls the works she regards as descendants of the Apocalypse of Paul.[1] (Other members of the family are the Ethiopic Apocalypse of Baruch, the Apocalypse of Gorgorios, and the various Latin Redactions of the Apocalypse of Paul.) The third of our apocalypses (the Obsequies Apocalypse) is closely related to the Apocalypse of Paul, but it may have been a source used by the latter rather than depending on it. The fourth of our four apocalypses (the

---

[1] M. Himmelfarb, *Tours of Hell* (Philadelphia: University of Pennsylvania Press, 1983) 19-24, 171.

Six Books Apocalypse) is certainly not dependent on the Apocalypse of Paul, though again it may have been a source for the latter, and it will be shown to be probably a considerably earlier work than the Apocalypse of Paul. It is a distinctive early Christian apocalypse which has not hitherto been recognized as such.

I THE GREEK APOCALYPSE OF THE VIRGIN

Bibliography[2]

E. Cothenet, 'Marie dans les Apocryphes,' in H. du Manoir ed., *Maria: Études sur la Sainte Vierge,* vol. 6 (Paris: Beauchesne, 1961) 117-130.

R.M. Dawkins, 'A Cretan Apocalypse of the Virgin,' *Byzantinische Zeitschrift* 30 (1929-30) 300-304.

R.M. Dawkins, 'Κρητικὴ Ἀποκάλυψις τῆς Παναγίας,' *Κρητικά Χρονικά* 2 (1948) 487-500 (Cretan version).

A. Delatte, *Anecdota Atheniensia,* vol. 1 (Bibliothèque de la Faculté de Philosophie et Lettres de l'Université de Liège 36; Liège: H. Vaillant-Carmanne/Paris: E. Champion, 1927) 272-288.

M. Erbetta, *Gli Apocrifi del Nuovo Testamento,* vol. 3 (Casale Monferrato: Marietti, 1981) 447-454 (Italian translation)

M. van Esbroeck, 'Gli apocrifi georgiani,' *Augustinianum* 23 (1983) 145-159.

M. Geerard, *Clavis Apocryphorum Novi Testamenti* (CC; Turnhout: Brepols, 1992) 211-212 (no. 327).

C. Gidel, 'Étude sur une apocalypse de la Vierge Marie,' *Annuaire de l'Association pour l'encouragement des études grecques* 5 (1871) 92-113. (Reprinted, without the Greek text, in C. Gidel, *Nouvelles Études sur la Littérature Grecque Moderne* [Les Littératures de l'Orient 3; Paris: Maissonneuve, 1878] 312-330.)

F. Halkin ed., *Bibliotheca Hagiographica Graeca,* vol. 3 (3rd edition; Subsidia Hagiographica 8a; Brussels: Société des Bollandistes, 1957) 128-130 (nos. 1050-1054). (BHG)

F. Halkin ed., *Novum Auctarium Bibliothecae Hagiographicae Graecae* (Subsidia Hagiographica 65; Brussels: Société des Bollandistes, 1984) 294-295 (nos. 1050-1054). (BHG)

B.P. Hasdeu, *Cuvente den Bătrîni II: Cărtile Poporane ale Romănilor în secolul XVI în legătură cu literatura poporană cea nescrisă* (Bucharest: Editura Didactică și pedagogică, 1984; anastatic reprint of 1879) 229-293 (= §§301-402) (Rumanian, Old Slavonic and Greek texts).

L. Heuzey, 'Les Supplices de l'Enfer d'après les Peintures Byzantines,' *Annuaire de l'Association pour l'encouragement des études grecques* 5 (1871) 114-119.

---

[2] This bibliography and that for section II have been augmented with information generously passed to me by Johan L. de Jong (Amsterdam). I am very grateful to him for sharing with me the fruits of his extensive bibliographical search.

M. Himmelfarb, *Tours of Hell* (Philadelphia: University of Pennsylvania Press, 1983).

M. R. James, *Apocrypha Anecdota* (TextsS 2/3; Cambridge: Cambridge University Press, 1893) 109-126. See also his notes in *Apocrypha Anecdota: Second Series* (TextsS 5/1; Cambridge: Cambridge University Press, 1897) 141.

E. Kozak, 'Bibliographische Übersicht der biblisch-apokryphen Literatur bei den Slaven,' *Jahrbücher für protestantische Theologie* 18 (1892) 127-158.

J. Matl, 'Bulgarien,' in K. Algermissen, L. Boër et al., ed., *Lexicon der Marien-kunde*, vol. 1 (Regensburg: Pustet, 1967) 997-1001.

J. Matl, 'Hölle und Höllenstrafen in den volksreligiösen Vorstellungen der Bulgaren und Serben,' *Vorträge auf der Berliner Slawistentagung (11.-13. November 1954)* (Berlin: Akademie-Verlag, 1956) 162-175.

D. Milošević, *The Last Judgment* (Pictorial Library of Eastern Church Art 3; Vaduz: Catholic Art Book Guild, 1964).

S. Mimouni, 'Les *Apocalypses de la Vierge:* état de la question,' *Apocrypha* 4 (1993) 101-112.

H. Müller, '"Die Offenbarung der Gottesmutter über die Höllenstrafen": Theologischer Gehalt und dichterische Form,' *Die Welt der Slaven* 6 (1961) 26-39.

E. Patlagean, 'Byzance et son autre monde: Observations sur quelques récits,' in *Faire croire: Modalités de la diffusion at de la réception des messages religieux du XIIe au XVe siècle* (Collection de l'École Française de Rome 51; Palais Farnèse: École Française de Rome, 1981) 201-221.

L. M. Pereto, 'L'Apocalisse della Madre del Signore,' *Marianum* 18 (1956) 227-231.

H. Pernot, 'Descente de la Vierge aux Enfers d'après les manuscrits grecs de Paris,' *Revue des Études Grecques* 13 (1900) 233-257.

M. Ruffini, *L'Apocalisse della Madre del Signore* (Florence: Edizione Fussi, 1954) 42-71 (Rumanian version and Italian translation).

A. Rutherford, in A. Menzies ed., *Ante-Nicene Christian Library*, Additional Volume (Edinburgh: T. & T. Clark, 1897) 167-174 (English translation).

A. de Santos Otero, *Die handschriftliche Überlieferung der altslavischen Apokryphen*, vol. 1 (Berlin/New York: de Gruyter, 1978) 188-195.

I. Sreznevskij and G. S. Destunis ed., 'Choždenie presvatija bogorodica po mukam,' *Izvestija Imperatorskoj Akademii Nauk po otdeliniju russkago jazyka i slovesnnosti* [= Transactions of the Imperial Academy of Letters...] 10/5 (1861/1863) 551-578 (Old Slavonic and Greek texts).

F. Stegmüller, *Repertorium Biblicum Medii Aevi*, vol. 1 (Madrid: Instituto Francisco Suárez, 1950) 238-239 (no. 273).

F. Stegmüller, *Repertorium Biblicum Medii Aevi*, vol. 8 (Madrid: Instituto Francisco Suárez, 1976) 206-207 (no. 273).

F. Tailliez, 'La Vierge dans la littérature populaire roumaine,' in H. du Manoir ed., *Maria: Études sur la Sainte Vierge*, vol. 2 (Paris: Beauchesne, 1952) 273-323.

F.J. Thomson, 'Apocrypha slavica,' *Slavonic and East European Review* 58 (1980) 265-268.

C. Tischendorf, *Apocalypses apocryphae* (Leipzig: H. Mendelssohn, 1866) xxvii-xxx.

R. Trautmann, *Altrussisches Lesebuch*, vol. 1 (Leipzig: Harrassowitz, 1949; reprinted Wiesbaden: Harrassowitz, 1968) 26-38 (Old Slavonic version).

D. Tschiżewskij, *Paradies und Hölle: Russische Buchmalerei* (Recklinghausen: A. Bongers, 1957) 20-21.

A. Vassiliev, *Anecdota Graeca-Byzantina* (Moscow: Imperial University Press, 1893) 125-134.

Mère Marie de la Visitation, 'Marie et le Purgatoire,' in H. du Manoir ed., *Maria: Études sur la Sainte Vierge*, vol. 5 (Paris: Beauchesne, 1958) 887-917.

M. Vloberg, *La Vierge: notre Médiatrice* (Grenoble: Arthaud, 1938) 210-219.

S. J. Voicu, 'Gli Apocrifi armeni,' *Augustinianum* 23 (1983) 161-180.

S. Weil, 'Observations critiques sur une Apocalypse de la Vierge Marie,' *Annuaire de l'Association pour l'encouragement des études grecques* 6 (1872) 26-27.

A. Wenger, 'Foi et Piété Mariales à Byzance,' in H. du Manoir ed., *Maria: Études sur la Sainte Vierge*, vol. 5 (Paris: Beauchesne, 1958) 956-963.

The Greek Apocalypse of the Virgin (whose most common title in the manuscripts is 'The Apocalypse of the all-holy Mother of God concerning the Punishments'[3]) is known in a large number of Greek manuscripts, which vary quite considerably. (At least seven edited texts have been published: Sreznevskij and Destunis[4] [Vienna Theol. 333 (Lambec. 337)], reprinted in Hasdeu; Gidel [BHG 1052: MS Paris BN gr. 390]; James [BHG 1050: MS Oxford Bodl. Misc. gr. 56, fol. 342-350]; Vassiliev [MSS Rome Casanatense G VI 1; Vienna Theol. 333 (Lambec. 337)]; Pernot [BHG 1051-1054: MSS Paris BN Suppl. gr. 136; Paris BN gr. 390; Paris BN gr. 395; and a Pyrghi MS]; Delatte [BHG 1052, 1054i: MSS Paris BN gr. 316, 352]; Dawkins 1948 [Cretan version]. For unpublished MSS, see also Mimouni 105 n. 32; Tischendorf; BHG 1050-1054 [Halkin 1957, pp. 128-130; 1984, pp. 294-295].) There are also versions of the work in Armenian (Voicu p. 177), Old Slavonic (Sreznevskij and Destunis, reprinted in Hasdeu; Kozak pp. 151-152; Trautmann; de Santos Otero; Thomson pp. 265-266; Müller; Tschizewskij; Matl), Georgian (Geerard no. 331; van Esbroeck 158-159) and Rumanian (Hasdeu; Ruffini; Pereto; Tailliez). It was evidently a very popular work, especially in monastic circles, in the Byzantine and Slavic worlds.

Although there are few precise verbal echoes, it is almost certainly inspired by and dependent on the Apocalypse of Paul (31-44),[5] which Piovanelli has now convincingly argued dates in its entirety (i.e. chap-

---

[3] Ἀποκάλυψις τῆς ὑπεραγίας Θεοτόκου περὶ τῶν κολάσεων.

[4] In this chapter bibliographical references in parenthesis in the text refer to items in the Bibliography at the head of each section.

[5] The closest parallels are James §5 cf. ApPaul 31; James §11 cf. ApPaul 42; James §23 cf. ApPaul 41; James §29 cf. ApPaul 44.

ters 1-51 in the full Latin text) from c. 400 C.E.[6] This therefore provides a *terminus a quo* for dating the Greek Apocalypse of the Virgin. The earliest manuscript for which a date is given in the literature is from the eleventh or twelfth century (Oxford Bodl. Misc. gr. 56). Until more comprehensive editions of the texts are published and the work's literary relationships further clarified,[7] it is hardly possible to be more precise about its date.

It is one of the later works in a tradition of apocalypses in which a seer is given a conducted tour of the torments of the damned in hell and intercedes for them (others include the Apocalypse of Zephaniah, the Apocalypse of Paul, the Greek Apocalypse of Ezra, the Latin Vision of Ezra).[8] Most of these works include the tour of hell in a larger cosmic tour or tour of the places of the dead, but in some later works, notably the Latin Vision of Ezra and some of the Latin Redactions of the Apocalypse of Paul, the focus is exclusively on hell. Similarly, in most manuscripts, the Greek Apocalypse of the Virgin consists only of a tour of hell, though in some a brief visit to paradise is appended (Vassiliev, p.132; Pernot §26; cf. James 1897). The archangel Michael conducts Mary the Mother of God through hell and explains the punishments to her. Each punishment corresponds to a particular kind of sin, according to a pattern which is standard in such apocalypses. In this case the sins have strongly ecclesiastical (e.g. James §§12, 13, 16, 19) and anti-Semitic features (James §§23, 26). Unlike many other apocalyptic tours of hell, there is rarely an intelligible relationship between the form of punishment and the specific sin. (A rare example is that those hanging by their tongues are guilty of sins of the tongue [James §14].) Most of the punishments, though probably inspired by those in the Apocalypse of Paul, seem to be, in their specific form, the author's inventions, and the sins, many of which do not occur in earlier tours of hell, the author's choices, but the author seems content to assign specific punishments to specific

---

[6] P. Piovanelli, 'Les origines des l'*Apocalypse de Paul* reconsidérées,' *Apocrypha* 4 (1993) 25-64. He refutes theories which hypothesize an earlier form of the work, and argues for a *terminus a quo* in 395 (death of Theodosius I) and a *terminus ad quem* in 416 (when Augustine refers to it), though an earlier terminus ad quem of 402 would be required if Prudentius (*Cathemerinon* 5.125-136) refers to it. But it is unlikely that Prudentius does, since the respite from the pains of hell which he depicts is not for twenty-four hours weekly, but for one night (the Paschal night) annually (cf. 137-144).

[7] Whether it is dependent on the Apocalypse of Peter, the Greek Apocalypse of Ezra and the Apocalypse of Sedrach, as S. Mimouni, 'Les *Apocalypses de la Vierge*: état de la question,' *Apocrypha* 4 (1993) 107, thinks, is quite uncertain. Whether other Byzantine apocalypses, such as the Apocalypse of Anastasia, are dependent on it, also needs investigation.

[8] See Himmelfarb, *Tours of Hell* ; and chapters 2 and 3 above.

sins fairly arbitrarily. Even by comparison with other apocalyptic tours of hell, the work is crude and unimaginative, but the account of the punishments was presumably valued for its paraenetic function of scaring readers from the sins listed.

But, in common with other such works, it also gives voice—in this case the highly authoritative voice of the all-holy Mother of God—to a natural compassion for the sufferings of the damned (James §§11, 15, 25-28). The climax comes when Mary's prayer for mercy for the damned (which is explicitly limited to Christians and excludes Jews: James §26), in which she is joined by Michael and various saints, is granted in the form of a respite from punishment for fifty days each year (the period from Easter to Pentecost). Perhaps this is intended to be additional to the weekly Sunday rest which Paul's intercession, in the Apocalypse of Paul, had already secured or would subsequently secure for the damned (in chapter 44 of ApPaul, on which GkApMary James §29 is clearly modelled). However, later readers, at a time when this Apocalypse of the Virgin had displaced the Apocalypse of Paul in most areas of the church in which it circulated, would not know of the concession granted to Paul. It is odd that in the Coptic version of the Apocalypse of Paul God's response to the plea for mercy to the damned is to grant them both the weekly Lord's Day rest and the annual fifty days from Easter to Pentecost (Budge p. 1070). There is no Coptic version of the Greek Apocalypse of the Virgin, but perhaps the redactor of the Coptic version of the Apocalypse of Paul knew the Greek Apocalypse.

Mimouni (p. 108) has argued that the Greek Apocalypse of the Virgin was originally attached to an early version of the *Transitus Mariae*. But this argument seems to be based on a failure to recognize that this apocalypse and the two apocalypses which are attached to versions of the *Transitus Mariae* (the Obsequies Apocalypse and the Six Books Apocalypse: see below) are all quite distinct works.[9] The extant Greek Apocalypse of the Virgin has certainly not developed out of one of the other two. The existence of an independent Apocalypse of the Virgin, as the Greek Apocalypse is in all known manuscripts, needs no special explanation. Generically it belongs to a long tradi-

---

[9] Mimouni, 'Les *Apocalypses de la Vierge*,' 108, following A. Wenger, 'Foi et Piété Mariales à Byzance,' in H. du Manoir ed., *Maria: Études sur la Sainte Vierge*, vol. 5 (Paris: Beauchesne, 1958) 958, refers, plausibly, to the title, in some MSS, of the Discourse on the Dormition by John of Thessalonica, as indicating that an apocalypse like those in the Syriac and Ethiopic versions of the *Transitus Mariae* originally existed in a Greek version also. But the proper inference is that either the Obsequies Apocalypse or the Six Books Apocalypse in an original Greek version filled this role, not that the quite different Greek Apocalypse of the Virgin did so.

tion of apocalyptic works of this kind,[10] and even in its limitation to a
tour of hell it is not, as we have noted, unique, but exemplifies a trend
in later representatives of this tradition. (Thus, the supersession, in the
East, of the Apocalypse of Paul by the Greek Apocalypse of the
Virgin has its parallel in the West in the Latin Redactions of the
Apocalypse of Paul which reduce its subject-matter largely or exclusively to hell.) A tour of hell which featured the seer's plea for mercy
for the damned was already traditional—and known especially in
Apocalypse of Paul 31-44, which provided the model for the Greek
Apocalypse of the Virgin—and given both the Virgin Mary's
preeminence in Byzantine Christianity[11] and her growing reputation
as the mother of mercy (Wenger p. 956), the attribution of such a tour
to her is a natural choice.

Mimouni (pp. 102, 109) also argues, following Wenger, that the
Virgin's visit to hell in this apocalypse and in those which conclude
versions of the *Transitus Mariae* (which, again following Wenger, he
does not clearly distinguish) was created as a kind of equivalent to
Jesus' descent to Hades, so that the *Transitus Mariae* literature would
parallel the *Descensus ad Inferos* literature. But the parallel is forced.
Christ delivered the righteous people of the Old Testament period
from their detention in Hades; his Mother gains an annual respite in
the punishment of those condemned to eternal punishment.[12]

II THE ETHIOPIC APOCALYPSE OF THE VIRGIN

Bibliography

K. Berger, 'Der Streit des guten und des bösen Engels um die Seele:
   Beobachtungen zu 4QAmr^b und Judas 9,' *JSJ* 4 (1973) 1-18.
E.A.W. Budge, *Legends of Our Lady the Perpetual Virgin and her Mother Hannâ*
   (Oxford; Oxford University Press, 1922) 245-278 (English translation).
M. Chaîne, *Apocrypha de Beata Maria Virgine* (CSCO 39-40; Rome: de Luigi,
   1909; reissued Louvain: Secrétariat du CSCO, 1962) (Text and Latin
   translation).
M. Chaîne, 'Le Cycle de la Vierge dans les apocryphes éthiopiens,' *Mélanges
   de la Faculté Orientale de l'Université Saint-Joseph (Beyrouth)* 1 (1906) 189-196.

---

[10] It is significant that Mimouni does not refer to Himmelfarb, *Tours of Hell*.

[11] Note that the role of Michael, though taken over in part from the Apocalypse of
Paul, also corresponds to his prominence in Byzantine Christianity.

[12] The term Hades is used (James §3), as in Luke 16:23, because the punishments
occur in the intermediate state, not after the Last Judgment. They are certainly not
purgatorial punishments from which the souls will later be delivered, as Wenger, 'Foi
et Piété,' 960-961, thinks.

M. Erbetta, *Gli Apocrifi del Nuovo Testamento*, vol. 3 (Casale Monferrato: Marietti, 1981) 455-470 (Italian translation).

M. Himmelfarb, *Tours of Hell* (Philadelphia: University of Pennsylvania Press, 1983).

P. Peeters, 'Apocrypha de B. Maria Virgine,' *AnBol* 29 (1910) 197-199.

This work, though quite distinct from the Greek Apocalypse, belongs to the same type, but (like the Apocalypse of Zephaniah and the Apocalypse of Paul) is concerned with the other world of the dead, rather than exclusively with the punishments in hell. Mary is taken up into heaven, sees the fate of good and bad souls as they leave the body at death and are judged, paradise and its inhabitants, and the punishments of hell and their victims, and pleads for mercy for the damned. Much of the content is closely related to the Apocalypse of Paul (12-16, 19-20, 23-31, 34-41, 43-44), from which it has been borrowed and freely adapted. There are quite extensive additions to the material drawn from the Apocalypse of Paul (e.g. Chaîne pp. 48, 49, 52-57, 58-59, 60-61). Material specific to Paul has of course been omitted or altered, but not much of special appropriateness to Mary has been added. Since the Apocalypse of Paul itself is not extant in Ethiopic, it could be regarded as in effect the Ethiopic version of that apocalypse.[13] It is certainly much closer to that work than is the Greek Apocalypse of the Virgin or the Obsequies Apocalypse, the other two apocalypses of the Virgin related to the Apocalypse of Paul.

There are some undoubtedly late features: one category of sinners in hell are Muslims (Chaîne p. 66). There are also specifically Ethiopian features: the weekly period of respite for the damned, granted at Mary's intercession, lasts from the evening of the sixth day to the morning of the second (Chaîne p. 68), in line with the Sabbath observance of the Ethiopian church. Piovanelli argues that this, along with the punishment in hell of a patriarch who did not maintain the orthodox form of trinitarian belief (Chaîne p. 63), places the Ethiopic version of the work in the controversies of fourteenth and fifteenth-century Ethiopia.[14] But he also supposes that, like other Ethiopic apocrypha of that period, it was translated from Arabic,[15] and that it

---

[13] An account of the departure of souls from their bodies, such as is found in the Apocalypse of Paul, occurs in the Ethiopic Book of the Angels (W. Leslau, *Falasha Anthology* [Yale Judaica Series 6; New Haven/London: Yale University Press, 1951] 50-56).

[14] Piovanelli, 'Les origines,' 37 n.39.

[15] P. Piovanelli, 'Les aventures des apocryphes en Éthiopie,' *Apocrypha* 4 (1993) 215, places it among the apocrypha translated from Arabic in the period from the 13th to the 18th centuries.

probably had a Greek original.[16] It would then be comparable with the Greek Apocalypse of the Virgin—as a Byzantine transference of material from Paul to Mary—though a closer adaptation of material from the Apocalypse of Paul than the latter is. Why one became so popular in the Byzantine world, while the other survived only in Ethiopia, is puzzling. Another closely related work is the Ethiopic Apocalypse of Baruch,[17] which seems to be dependent on both the Ethiopic Apocalypse of the Virgin and on the Apocalypse of Paul (cf. Himmelfarb, pp. 22-23).

An interesting feature of the Ethiopic Apocalypse of the Virgin, not to be found in the Apocalypse of Paul or in the other Apocalypses of the Virgin, is the abundance of biblical quotations. Explicit quotations of Scripture are rare in the older apocalypses,[18] but are found in later apocalyptic works, such as the Greek apocryphal Apocalypse of John and the medieval Hebrew apocalypses, where they serve to give canonical support to non-canonical revelations. This feature does not seem to be found in other Ethiopic versions of such works, and so may be a further indication that the Ethiopic Apocalypse of the Virgin derives from a Greek original.

III THE OBSEQUIES APOCALYPSE OF THE VIRGIN

Bibliography

V. Arras, *De Transitu Mariae Apocrypha Ethiopice*, vol. 1 (CSCO 342-343: Aeth 66-67; Louvain: Secrétariat du CSCO, 1973). (Ethiopic text in CSCO 342: Aeth 66; Latin translation in CSCO 343: Aeth 67). Bibliography and notes are in V. Arras, *De Transitu Mariae Apocrypha Ethiopice*, vol .2 (CSCO 352: Aeth 69; Louvain: Secrétariat du CSCO, 1974) 72-105.

C. Donahue, *The Testament of Mary: The Gaelic Version of the Dormitio Mariae together with an Irish Latin Version* (Fordham University Studies, Language Series 1; New York: Fordham University Press, 1942).

M. van Esbroeck, 'Apocryphes géorgiens de la Dormition,' *AnBol* 91 (1973) 55-75.

M. van Esbroeck, 'Les textes littéraires sur l'Assomption avant le Xe siècle,' in F. Bovon ed., *Les Actes Apocryphes des Apôtres* (Publications de la Faculté de Théologie de l'Université de Genève 4; Geneva: Labor et Fides, 1981) 265-285.

---

[16] Piovanelli, 'Les origines,' 37, 55.

[17] Leslau, *Falasha Anthology*, 57-76. Leslau translates the Falasha text of this work, but refers (164 n.17) to other manuscripts which are probably of the Christian version, from which the Falasha version is adapted.

[18] Rare examples are ApPet 4:7; ApPaul 21.

J. Gribomont, 'Le plus ancien *Transitus* marial et l'encratisme,' *Augustinianum* 23 (1983) 237-247.

M. Herbert and M. McNamara ed., *Irish Biblical Apocrypha* (Edinburgh: T. & T. Clark, 1989) 129-131 (translation of Irish).

St J. D. Seymour, 'Irish Versions of the Transitus Mariae,' *JTS* 23 (1922) 36-43.

St J. D. Seymour, *Irish Visions of the Other World* (London: SPCK, 1930) 34-37.

E. Testa, 'L'origine e lo sviluppo della Dormitio Mariae,' *Augustinianum* 23 (1983) 250-262.

A. Wenger, *L'Assomption de la T. S. Vierge dans la Tradition Byzantine du VIe au Xe Siècle* (Archives de l'Orient Chrétien 5; Paris: Institut Français d'Études Byzantines, 1955) 258-259 (Latin text).

H. Willard, 'The Testament of Mary: The Irish Account of the Death of the Virgin,' *Recherches de théologie ancienne et médiévale* 9 (1937) 341-364.

W. Wright, *Contributions to the Apocryphal Literature of the New Testament* (London: Williams & Norgate, 1865) 47-48 (translation of Syriac).

Two of the most neglected of the early Christian apocalypses are those which are found within the *Transitus Mariae* literature (which tells the story of the dormition or assumption of the Virgin Mary). Those scholars who have laboured to unravel the complexities of this literature, as well as to understand the origin and significance of its themes. have rarely paid more than the most cursory attention to these apocalypses, while those who study the apocalyptic literature have rarely even noticed their existence. (Thus, for example, despite the fact that one includes 'a tour of hell' while the other includes a vision of hell closely related to the tradition of tours, neither is noticed in Martha Himmelfarb's generally comprehensive study of this apocalyptic genre.[19] Despite the resemblances, in different ways, of both these apocalypses to the Apocalypse of Paul, studies of the latter never refer to them.) When the existence of these apocalypses is noticed, the fact that they are two quite different and independent apocalypses is rarely appreciated.

Tracing the relationships among the many surviving texts, in at least nine languages, of the narrative of the dormition/assumption is a complex task, not yet complete. But van Esbroeck's classification of almost all the early texts into two families serves very well our present purpose. He calls them the 'Palm of the Tree of Life' type and the 'Bethlehem and Censings' type, after distinctive features of the narrative in each, and provides a family tree of the texts in each family (1981, pp. 270, 273). In some of the earliest texts, which are closest to the putative original of each type, an apocalypse in which the Virgin

---

[19] Himmelfarb, *Tours of Hell*.

Mary (after her body has been carried to Paradise and her soul reunited with it) is shown the places of the dead occurs towards the end
of the whole work. There are two quite different apocalypses of this
kind, each limited to one of the two families identified by van
Esbroeck. We shall call them the Obsequies Apocalypse and the Six
Books Apocalypse, because the early Syriac version in each case is
called respectively the Obsequies of the Virgin Mary and the Six
Books.[20] The presence of these apocalypses in texts which are the
earliest or among the earliest in each family makes it very likely that
they were original to the prototype of each type, and that the absence
of the apocalypses from almost all later forms of the texts shows that
they were subsequently dropped in most of the textual traditions.
One reason may be that they could not compete with the growing
popularity of the independent Greek Apocalypse of the Virgin, in
which there is a much more extensive tour of the punishments in hell
and in which the Virgin's intercession for the damned is more effective.

The Obsequies Apocalypse is best preserved in the Ethiopic *Liber
Requiei* (Arras §§90-102), which seems to be closest to the original,[21]
and in the Irish Testament of Mary (Donahue, pp. 50-55 [MS Bodl.
Laud Misc. 610]; Herbert and McNamara, pp. 129-131, §§50-55
[MS Royal Irish Academy 23 0 48 (*Liber Flavus Fergusiorum*)]),[22] which
abbreviates the text. There is a Syriac fragment, in a fifth-century
manuscript (Wright),[23] which corresponds closely with the Ethiopic,
and a very abbreviated Latin version (MS Paris BN lat. 3550: text in
Wenger). The apocalypse also appears in a Georgian version of the
Transitus Mariae (which has not been translated). (In van Esbroeck's
stemma of the 'Palm of the Tree of Life' family [1981, p. 270], these
texts appear as E1, H1/H2, S1, Latin N[L2]. The fragments of a
Georgian *Transitus Mariae* of this type [I1-3] break off before the
apocalypse would have appeared [van Esbroeck 173]. Thus, of the
early forms of this type, the apocalypse is demonstrably lacking only

---

[20] Cf. W. Wright, 'The Departure of my Lady Mary from the World,' *Journal of
Sacred Literature* 6 (1865)160: 'the six books of the Departure of my Lady Mary from
the world.' In some forms of the work it is divided into six books, in others into five.

[21] On its importance, cf. V. Arras, *De Transitu Mariae Apocrypha Ethiopice*, vol .1
(CSCO 343: Aeth 67; Louvain: Secrétariat du CSCO, 1973)v-viii; M. van Esbroeck,
'Apocryphes géorgiens de la Dormition,' *AnBol* 91 (1973) 56.

[22] There is also a partial translation in St J. D. Seymour, *Irish Visions of the Other
World* (London: SPCK, 1930) 35-37.

[23] This fragment of the apocalypse is one of several fragments of the Syriac Obsequies, from the same manuscript. On their relationship to the text in the Ethiopic
version, see J. Gribomont, 'Le plus ancien *Transitus* marial et l'encratisme,'
Augustinianum 23 (1983) 237 n.3.

in the Coptic [C1] and in one form of the Latin [Latin M[L2].) These
various versions must all go back to a now lost Greek redaction of the
Transitus Mariae, the original of the 'Palm of the Tree of Life' family.[24]
That the apocalypse did exist in Greek in a Greek text of the *Transitus
Mariae* of the 'Palm of the Tree of Life' type is confirmed by the fact
that some manuscripts of the discourse on the dormition by John of
Thessalonica bear the title: 'This is the book of the repose of Mary
and *what was revealed to her*, in five books.'[25] The title preserves a
reference to the apocalypse which has dropped out of the text. If this
apocalypse is dependent on the Apocalypse of Paul (see below), written c. 400 (see section I above), then, in view of the date of the Syriac
manuscript, the apocalypse must date from the fifth century. If, on
the other hand, the Apocalypse of Paul is dependent on it, then it
could be earlier.

The narrative is as follows: When the soul and body of the Virgin
Mary have been reunited in paradise, the apostles, who have been
brought to paradise with her body, remind Jesus of his promise to
show them the punishments in hell. So they and Mary and the archangel Michael are transported, with Jesus, to the far west, where the
entrance to hell is located.

When it is opened for them, the damned in hell remind Michael of
his daily intercession for them and complain that he seems to have
forgotten them. The apostles and Mary are overcome by the sorrow
of the damned. Michael replies, explaining that he constantly intercedes for all creatures, including the damned. At each of the twelve
hours of the day and of the night, when prayers are offered to God,
he intercedes to God for every creature and every human soul, and
he is joined by the angels of the waters, the winds and the clouds who
pray God to bless the earth with the means of sustenance for creatures. But seeing the torment of the damned, Michael is moved to ask
Jesus for rest for them now. Jesus replies that Michael cannot love the
damned more than he and his Father do. He gave his life for them,
and his blood continuously intercedes with the Father for them. The
Father desires to be merciful but those who spurn his Son's blood
cannot be pardoned.[26]

The apostles are now shown the specific punishments[27] of three
individual sinners (in the Ethiopic version) or four categories of sin-

---

[24] M. van Esbroeck, 'Virgin, Assumption of,' in D. N. Freedman ed., *The Anchor
Bible Dictionary*, vol. 6 (Garden City, New York: Doubleday, 1992) 856.

[25] Αὕτη ἡ βίβλος τῆς ἀναπαύσεως Μαρίας καὶ ὅπερ αὐτῇ ἀπεκαλύφθη, ἐν πέντε
γράμμασιν: Wenger, 'Foi et Piété,' 958; Mimouni, 'Les *Apocalypses de la Vierge*,' 108.

[26] This seems to be the sense of the very obscure text (Arras §94).

[27] These do not appear in the Latin.

ners (in the Irish version). All are ecclesiastical office-holders (Ethiopic: reader, deacon, priest; Irish: doctors, priests, elders, judges).[28]

The damned now see Mary and the apostles and beg them to intercede for them to be granted a little respite from their sufferings. Jesus again points out to them that they have been justly punished for their refusal to heed what was taught them. But, on account of the prayers of Michael and the apostles and his mother Mary, he grants them a respite of three hours every Sunday.

The Ethiopic version then records a visit of the apostles to paradise, which is lacking in the Irish,[29] but probably original, since the Irish version abbreviates and since the tendency in the transmission and adaptation of such apocalyptic works was to reduce tours of the places of the dead to tours of hell only. In paradise the apostles see the Old Testament saints, brought there from Hades by Christ, and all the righteous dead reclining in the bosom of the three patriarchs. They also see Enoch with the olive tree from which the branch brought by the dove to Noah came. (The tradition that the olive branch came from Eden is found in rabbinic literature: GenRab 33:6; LevRab 31:10; CantRab 1:15:4; 4:1:2. That Enoch was in Eden at the time of the Flood, from which it was protected, is found in Jubilees 4:23-24. Our text seems to be unique in connecting these traditions.)

There is a close relationship between this apocalypse and the Apocalypse of Paul. The parallels are almost entirely with Apocalypse of Paul 34-36, 43-44. In chapters 34-36, the Apocalypse of Paul depicts the punishment of four individual sinners, who, like those in the Obsequies Apocalypse (who in the Ethiopic version are individuals, not groups), are all ecclesiastical office-bearers (priest, bishop, deacon, reader). The sins and punishments do not correspond exactly to those of the three or four in the Obsequies Apocalypse, but they are related. In chapters 43-44 of the Apocalypse of Paul, the damned beg Michael for mercy, and the intercession of Paul, Michael and the angels gains from Christ the weekly respite for the damned. The corresponding narrative in the Obsequies Apocalypse is divided in two parts (Arras §§90-94, 99-100) between which are placed the four

---

[28] The view of C. Donahue, *The Testament of Mary: The Gaelic Version of the Dormitio Mariae together with an Irish Latin Version* (Fordham University Studies, Language Series 1; New York: Fordham University Press, 1942) 9-10, that the punishments are a gloss in the Irish version, is refuted by their occurrence in the Ethiopic.

[29] At the end of the Irish version the apostles leave Mary with Jesus in paradise and return to the lands of their mission, but nothing is said about their seeing the righteous dead in paradise, as in the Ethiopic.

punishments (Arras §§95-98) which correspond to Apocalypse of Paul 34-36.[30] Besides these five chapters of the Apocalypse of Paul (34-36, 43-44), the only point of clear correspondence is with chapter 31, where Paul is taken 'towards the setting of the sun' to see the punishments in hell, just as in the Obsequies Apocalypse Christ takes the apostles and Mary and Michael 'to the setting of the sun' in order to see hell.

Comparison of the parallel passages strongly suggests literary dependence between the two works, but it is not easy to decide in which direction the dependence lies. For example, Michael's address to the damned is longer in the Obsequies Apocalypse (Arras §§91-93), shorter in the Apocalypse of Paul (43), though covering the same themes. The additional details about Michael's intercessory role in the Obsequies Apocalypse (prayers at each of the twelve hours of day and night, the role of the angels of the waters, the wind and the clouds) have parallels elsewhere,[31] but it is not clear whether they are expansions of a shorter text or whether the more concise text is an abbreviation.

However, some arguments can be brought in favour of the priority of the Obsequies Apocalypse: (1) The four clerical sinners in Apocalypse of Paul 34-36 are the only instances, among the many punishments Paul sees, of individual sinners rather than groups.[32] This may indicate that they have come, as a set of four, from a source. (2) In the Obsequies Apocalypse, Jesus responds to Michael's plea for mercy for the damned: 'Cease your weeping. Surely you do not love them more than he who created them, or pity them more than he who gave them breath?' (Arras §94; Irish similar). This resembles what Paul is twice told by the angel when he weeps over the damned: 'Why do you weep? Are you more compassionate than God? For since God is good and knows that there are punishments, he bears patiently the race of men, permitting each one to do his own will ...' (ApPaul 33); 'Why are you weeping? Are you more compassionate than the Lord God ... who has appointed judgment and allowed every man to choose good or evil...?' (ApPaul 40) The evidence of other texts shows that the form of this rebuke in the Obsequies Apocalypse, with its appeal to

---

[30] In recension 1 of the Armenian Apocalypse of Paul the material corresponding to chapters 43-44 of the Latin (§§46, 49-51, 55) is twice interrupted by additional punishments (§§47-48, 52-54).

[31] Testament of Adam 1-2 (Horarium) and related texts; Coptic apocryphal Apocalypse of John (Budge p. 1027); Mysteries of John (Budge pp. 242-243, 253).

[32] The occurrence of groups rather than individuals in the Irish version of the Obsequies Apocalypse is clearly secondary: these punishments have been assimilated to the more usual form of punishments in tours of hell.

the fact that the sinners are God's own creation, is the traditional form (4 Ezra 5:33; 8:47; ApPet 3:6), while the form in the Apocalypse of Paul is innovatory, though the two works agree in the reference to weeping and the phrasing as a question. It is possible that the Obsequies Apocalypse is dependent on the Apocalypse of Paul and on the traditional form known independently, but it is somewhat easier to suppose that the Apocalypse of Paul is dependent on the Obsequies Apocalypse. (3) In the Apocalypse of Paul the respite granted to the damned is a day and a night (Sunday) each week, whereas in the Obsequies Apocalypse it is three hours every Sunday. It seems odd that, if the concession in the Apocalypse of Paul were already known and used by the author of the Obsequies Apocalypse as his source, he should attribute to the intercession of Mary and the apostles only three hours out of the twenty-four granted to Paul's intercession. (By contrast, the annual period of fifty days granted to Mary's intercession in the Greek Apocalypse of the Virgin makes sense as an addition to the weekly day of rest granted in the Apocalypse of Paul.)

These arguments are not conclusive, and the issue must be left open. Further study of the literary relationships of the Apocalypse of Paul may clarify it.

IV The Six Books Apocalypse of the Virgin

Bibliography

E. A. W. Budge, *The History of the Blessed Virgin Mary and The History of the Likeness of Christ which the Jews of Tiberias made to mock at* (London: Luzac, 1899).

M. Chaîne, *Apocrypha de Beata Maria Virgine* (CSCO 39-40; Rome: de Luigi, 1909; reissued Louvain: Secrétariat du CSCO, 1962) (Ethiopic text and Latin trans.).

M. Enger, *Ahbār Yūhannā as-salīh fī naqlat umm al-masīh, id est Ioannis Apostoli de Transitu Beatae Mariae Virginis Liber* (Elberfeldae: Friderichs, 1854) (Arabic text and Latin trans.).

A. Smith Lewis, *Apocrypha Syriaca: The Protevangelium Jacobi and Transitus Mariae* (Studia Sinaitica 11; London: C. J. Clay, 1902) (Syriac text and trans.).

W. Wright, 'The Departure of my Lady Mary from the World,' *Journal of Sacred Literature* 6 (1865) 417-448; 7 (1865) 110-160 (Syriac text and trans.).

This apocalypse, probably the most interesting of the four, occurs in the final section (fifth and/or sixth book) of the Syriac *Transitus Mariae* (edited from different manuscripts by Smith Lewis [translation pp. 64-69] and Wright [translation pp. 156-160]; cf. also incomplete text in Budge p. 131), which in its present form probably dates from the fifth century. It is also found in Arabic (Enger [translation pp. 88-107]) and Ethiopic versions (Chaîne [translation: Latin section pp. 39-42]). There are considerable variations between the various texts. Smith Lewis's text of the Syriac has the fullest text, with some unique material and some which does not appear in Wright's text but does appear in the Arabic and Ethiopic versions. In one case Wright's text agrees with the Arabic and the Ethiopic in a section absent from Smith Lewis's text. The Arabic and the Ethiopic are relatively close, but the Arabic text we have is not the Arabic text which must have been the immediate *Vorlage* of the Ethiopic. Probably Smith Lewis's text has preserved material omitted for the sake of abbreviation in the others; sometimes it may contain secondary elaborations of the text. The two are not always easy to distinguish, but in many cases there seems good reason to suppose that the longer texts are original and the textual tradition tended to abbreviation rather than expansion.

Unlike the Obsequies Apocalypse, the revelations in this apocalypse are given by Christ to Mary alone, after the apostles have departed and he has raised Mary from the dead in paradise. Also unlike the Obsequies Apocalypse, she is not only shown paradise and hell, but is given a fuller cosmic tour, ascending through the heavens to the throne of God.

Jesus promises to show Mary 'the glory of my Father's house,'[33] but before being taken up to the divine palace above the heavens she is shown paradise ('the Paradise of Eden' which is the earthly paradise). Elijah, Enoch, Moses and (in the Syriac version) Peter (!) come to paradise. Jesus shows her what he has prepared 'for the just who love me.' She sees the dwellings of the righteous, and the sweet-smelling trees of paradise, and samples their fruit. Probably, as in Wright's text, she does not see the righteous themselves, who (it appears from later in the apocalypse) are not yet there. (The other texts contain obscure references to the righteous in paradise which are probably confusions.)

She is taken up through the heavens with Christ in a chariot, apparently accompanied by Elijah, Enoch, Peter and John.[34] There

---

[33] Quotations from the Six Books Apocalypse in this section are from Smith Lewis unless otherwise indicated.

[34] In Smith Lewis's text they are accompanied also by Enoch and Elijah, to whom Wright's text adds Simon Cephas and John the young. The latter may have been added to explain his presence at the end of the narrative. (The Arabic and the Ethiopic lack any reference to the chariot or those who accompany Mary.) But at a later point, in a passage unique to Smith Lewis's text, John and Peter are both present along with Enoch and Elijah.

appear to be three heavens, which in the Arabic and Ethiopic versions are numbered, while the Syriac speaks of 'the lower heaven,' the 'heaven of heavens' (a designation of the highest heaven [1 Enoch 71:5], or of the second heaven in some Jewish texts which count seven heavens[35]), above which are 'the waters above the heavens.' The heavenly Jerusalem, in which God dwells, is above the waters.

In the lower heaven Mary sees the storehouses of meteorological phenomena such as rain, snow, dew, and storms. Also in the lower heaven she sees the place where Elijah stands and prays.[36] In the heaven of heavens she sees hosts of angels singing the trisagion.[37] Above the heaven of heavens she comes to the heavenly Jerusalem in which God dwells. It has twelve walls, which must be understood as concentric, and twelve gates, one in each wall, each gate bearing the name of one of the apostles. One of the apostles stands at each gate, accompanied by angels and archangels praising. At the outermost gate, there are also, along with innumerable angels, Abraham, Isaac, and Jacob, and David, worshipping. Mary passes into the city through the twelve gates, and at each gate she is shown reverence by a category of heavenly beings, thus:[38]

> at the first gate by angels,
> at the second gate by cherubim,
> at the third gate by seraphim,
> at the fourth gate by the family of the archangels (?),
> at the fifth gate by lightnings and thunders,
> at the sixth gate by those who cried 'Holy, holy, holy' before her,
> at the seventh gate by fire and flame,
> at the eighth gate by rain and dew,
> at the ninth gate by Gabriel and Michael,
> at the tenth gate by the heavenly lights (sun, moon, stars),
> at the eleventh gate by all the apostles,
> at the twelfth gate by her Son.

(The presence of the apostles both at each of the twelve gates and all reverencing Mary at the eleventh gate is problematic, since the apostles are not yet dead and had returned to their various mission fields

---

[35] VisEzek (Jacobs p. 29); SephRaz (Morgan p. 43). The expression itself is biblical (Deut 10:14; 1 Kgs 8:27; 2 Chr 2:5; 6:18; Neh 9:6; Ps 148:4).

[36] With Elijah's place in the lower heaven, cf. b. Sukk. 5a.

[37] In Smith Lewis's text she sees such hosts of angels first in the heaven of heavens, then more standing above the waters when she rises above the heaven of heavens. This may represent a secondary expansion of the simpler text of the Arabic and Ethiopic which lack the first description of angels and place the second in the second heaven. Wright's text lacks the whole section.

[38] There are some variations among the texts. The following list gives the readings most likely to be original.

prior to Mary's resurrection in paradise. Moreover, Peter and John, according to the Syriac texts, are accompanying her. The Arabic version solves the problem by not referring to Peter and John, by placing guardians, not apostles, at each of the twelve gates, which merely bear the names of the apostles, and by describing those who reverence Mary at the eleventh gate as 'souls of disciples, fathers, prophets, elect, and righteous.' But since the Ethiopic agrees with the Syriac in having apostles standing at each gate and reverencing Mary at the eleventh it is likely that our Arabic text [at this point not representing the *Vorlage* of the Ethiopic] has omitted the apostles to avoid the problem.)

Entering the city, Mary worships God the Father. She sees the Trinity: 'the Father being glorified by His Son and the Son by His Father, and the Spirit by both of them.' Smith Lewis's text then uniquely has a passage describing the Merkavah-throne of God:

> And she saw a throne and a chariot, and from beneath the chariot there issued a river of fire; and it came and abode upon the whole heaven, burning nothing. And she saw the guardian angels who bore the chariots from beneath; and the seraphim who escorted it from above; and the cherubim who spread their wings and escorted it, and cried 'Holy.' And she saw the glorious throne of God; the Father sitting and His Son on His right hand; and the Spirit who was standing and hovering over them. And she saw the seraphim of fire, and the curtains of flame.

This traditional imagery of the divine throne and throne-room must surely be original, omitted in the other texts perhaps because they found the preceding statement of the mutual glorification of the Trinity (only the Arabic, which here abbreviates drastically, lacks this) an appropriate climax in itself.

All versions of the text now quote the much used traditional formula for revelations of the eschatological blessings of the righteous: Christ showed Mary 'what eye hath not seen, nor ear heard, nor hath it entered into the heart of man, what God giveth to the righteous on the day of resurrection.'[39] Smith Lewis's text connects this immediately with the revelation to Mary of the tabernacles of the righteous, but the other texts are almost certainly more original in treating it as a revelation in itself of 'hidden and secret things' (Ethiopic). Only Wright's text expands on this, in a deliberately cryptic way: Christ showed Mary 'glories that proclaim concerning miracles, and mira-

---

[39] Many occurrences of the formula are collected in M. Stone and J. Strugnell, *The Books of Elijah: Parts 1-2* (SBLTT 18; Missoula, Montana: Scholars Press, 1979) 42-73. It is used, as in the Six Books Apocalypse, of what is revealed to a visionary in an apocalypse in AscenIs 11:34 (Latin).

cles that cry out concerning glories; and hidden things that cry out
concerning revealed things, and revealed things that cry out concerning hidden things' (Wright p. 158).

In all the texts except Smith-Lewis, Mary is now shown the place
where Enoch lives and prays—'within the extreme limit of created
things' (Wright p. 158). This clearly complements the revelation of
the place in the lower heaven where Elijah lives and prays, and since
Smith Lewis's text does include the latter, we must conclude that
both are original, and that therefore probably all the material found
in the other texts but absent from Smith Lewis's at this point is
original. (We should expect Enoch's place to be in the paradise of
Eden [as in Jub 4:23-26 and as seems to be implied in the Obsequies
Apocalypse], but since Enoch had to come to Eden at the beginning
of our apocalypse, that location cannot be intended here. Rather our
text follows 1 Enoch 106:8, which places Enoch [after his final translation, if biblical chronology is followed] at the ends of the earth.)

Now follow in all texts the key revelations of the righteous dead
and the wicked dead and their respective destinies. Mary sees the
tabernacles of the righteous, and the righteous dead themselves looking at them from afar and rejoicing. They do not yet inhabit them,[40]
but will receive them as their reward on the day of resurrection. She
also sees Gehenna, a very dark place, with smoke and the smell of
sulphur and blazing fire. The wicked see it from afar and grieve,
knowing that it is reserved for them to enter on the day of judgment.
Mary hears the righteous praising God for the reward he will give the
righteous at the last day, and she hears the wicked crying to Christ to
have mercy on them at his coming to judgment. Mary adds her own
voice to this prayer for mercy for the damned. (She receives no reply.)

Another passage unique to Smith Lewis's text seems again to describe a chariot-throne or thrones carried by the cherubim, this time
one on which Christ and Mary are conveyed in glory above the
heavens. Obeying a decree that all creatures come forth to meet
them, Enoch, Elijah, John and Peter reappear and worship before
Christ and his mother. The trumpets of heaven sound for the fearful
moment when the angels are due to worship Christ, who is praised by
all heaven for taking a human mother. This elaborately described
scene of worship focuses on Mary's role in the incarnation and appropriately concludes the revelation of the hidden things of his Father's
house which Jesus has shown to his mother.

---

[40] In the Arabic and the Ethiopic they are in them, but this is clearly a change to
the sense which creates a confusion.

They return to paradise where Mary reveals to John all that Christ had revealed to her, and predicts that these things will be revealed at the time of the end. A short passage of eschatological prophecy here describes the afflictions of the end-time leading to the parousia. Jesus pronounces Mary blessed, in that in this last time when afflictions multiply, people will be able to call on her and be delivered. Another speech addressed by Mary to Jesus concludes the narrative. (In this final section both Smith Lewis's text and the Arabic have additional material peculiar to each, which seems likely to secondary expansion.)

This apocalypse deserves a detailed commentary, but we must be content here with pointing out the significance of various aspects of it:

(1) The apocalypse is a tour of the places of the dead in the other world, like the Apocalypse of Zephaniah, the Apocalypse of Paul, the Ethiopic Apocalypse of the Virgin, the Gedulat Moshe, and the Apocalypse of the Seven Heavens. Unlike those apocalypses which focus exclusively on hell or on hell and paradise with the emphasis on the former (as in the Greek Apocalypse of the Virgin and the Obsequies Apocalypse), there is an attempt at comprehensiveness, probably drawing on diverse traditional materials, which results in a certain degree of apparent incoherence, as is also the case in the Apocalypse of Paul. Thus Mary evidently sees the tabernacles of the righteous twice. She sees them first in the Paradise of Eden before she ascends through the heavens, when there is no mention of their inhabitants or prospective inhabitants, and then again after the ascent through the heavens, when she sees them, in an unnamed place, and while also viewing Gehenna (probably she is looking down on both places from a vantage-point in the heavens, like Enoch in 2 En 8:1; 10:1 or Abraham in ApAbr 21), and this time sees also the righteous dead viewing their tabernacles from afar and awaiting the time when they will inhabit them (perhaps it is only from this vantage-point that she can see the righteous dead, who could not be seen when she was herself in paradise and saw their tabernacles). The intention of depicting comprehensively the places of the dead explains why Mary is shown the place where Elijah is and the place where Enoch is, since these men, who were translated bodily, are seen as a very special category of the dead for whom special provision is made in the other world.[41] (As we shall observe further below, the attention to Enoch and Elijah may also be due to the fact that they are analogous to

---

[41] Elijah and Enoch appear, with rather different functions, in the other world in ApPaul 20; AscenIs 9:9.

Mary who herself is in a unique category of the dead.) In contrast to the tendency of apocalyptic revelations of the fate of the dead to focus particularly on hell and its punishments, this apocalypse is more concerned with the eschatological destiny of the righteous, as is appropriate for a revelation whose purpose is for Jesus to show his mother 'the glory of My Father's house'[42] (in which, if the reference is to John 14:2, there are many mansions for the righteous). The character of the work as a tour of the places of the dead may also explain why there are two major passages which are probably original but appear only in Smith Lewis's text: the description of the Merkavah-throne of God and the description of the praise of Christ with his mother by all the heavenly beings. Since these do not describe places of the dead they were considered dispensable by copyists wishing to abbreviate.[43]

(2) As we have argued in chapters 2 and 3 above, tours of the places of the dead in the other world developed out of the older and more comprehensive cosmic tours, which they in many ways resemble, differing only in focusing more exclusively on the places of the dead. The focus is not always entirely exclusive. In particular some such apocalypses, with a strong emphasis on the places of the dead, contain an ascent through the heavens in which some of the kinds of contents usually viewed by an apocalyptic seer on a tour of the heavens are mentioned without excluding those not relevant to the fate of the dead (Gedulat Moshe, Questions of Ezra, Apocalypse of the Seven Heavens). Mary's ascent through the heavens climaxes in the revelation of the secret, unimaginable things that have been prepared for the righteous, but on the way to this revelation she sees some of the usual sights: the meteorological storehouses (e.g. 2 En 6; TLevi 3:2; SephRaz [Morgan pp. 43, 61, 67]; b. Ḥag. 12b; VisEzek [Jacobs,

---

[42] Smith Lewis's text refers to this house at both the beginning and the end of the revelation, but the first reference is lost in the Arabic and the Ethiopic, and the second in all three of the other texts. The term would be most easily understood to mean the throne-room of God at the centre of the heavenly Jerusalem (Wright's text uniquely refers to 'the decorated Jerusalem, the palace of my Father in which He dwells,' while the Arabic refers to 'the holy house' in the third heaven), but seems to be used in a broader sense, including the tabernacles of the righteous in paradise.

[43] On the other hand it is possible that the latter passage, along with the probably secondary passage unique to Smith Lewis's text after Mary's ascent from the lower heaven, both of which passages extol Mary as Jesus' mother in a scene of heavenly worship of Christ, are secondary additions to the text designed to bring out more fully the preeminence of Mary as the mother of Christ and the vehicle of his incarnation. Both refer to Mary as 'the mother of their Lord' (alluding to Luke 1:43), but the title 'Mother of God' (Theotokos) is not used in these passages or in any other part of the apocalypse.

p. 31]; cf. 1 En 60:11-22; LAB 19:10; 32:7; 2 Bar 10:11),[44] the angels ceaselessly singing praises to God (e.g. 2 En 17; AscenIs 8; SephRaz [Morgan p. 77]; b. Ḥag. 12b), the chariot-throne of God with its angelic attendants and fiery surroundings in the heavenly throne-room/sanctuary (e.g. 1 En 14:8-25; 2 En 20-22; QuEzra A21, 26-30; ApAbr 17-18; SephRaz [Morgan pp. 81-82]).[45] Less usual, and so deserving of special comment below, are the heavenly Jerusalem and Mary's passage through its twelve walls and gates to the dwelling-place of God in the centre, and the vision of God as the three trinitarian Persons glorifying each other. The broad structure of as-cent through the heavens, followed by views of paradise and hell, is common to our apocalypse, 3 Baruch[46] and the Gedulat Moshe, and is modified here primarily by the fact (given by the dormition/as-sumption story to which the apocalypse is attached) that the whole revelation begins in paradise.

(3) The description and function of the heavenly Jerusalem in the Six Books Apocalypse are quite unlike those in any other apocalyptic description. The city is located in the highest heaven, evidently above the waters above the heavens. It is where God dwells. It has twelve concentric walls, and one gate in each wall, each gate named after one of the twelve apostles. The apostles themselves stand at their gates (as gatekeepers? or simply to welcome Mary?) along with angels and archangels singing praises. Also mentioned are Abraham, Isaac and Jacob, and David.[47] The city is called 'the heavenly Jerusalem' and (only in Smith Lewis's text) 'the city of the great King' (Ps 48:2; Matt 5:35). Whether or not original, this biblical phrase sums up the concept of the city: it is the city in which God the great ruler of heaven and earth has his palace. Mary enters the city in order to

---

[44] Following these meteorological storehouses, Smith Lewis's text uniquely has: 'and she saw there wrath and concord, which when they are ordered go forth to mankind.' For parallels to these, in association with the meteorological phenomena, cf. TLevi 3:2: 'fire, snow and ice, ready for the day determined by God's righteous judgment;' VisEzek (Jacobs, p. 31): 'the treasurehouses of blessing...the storehouses of peace, the dreadful punishments reserved for the wicked and rewards for the right-eous'; b. Ḥag. 12b: 'the treasures of peace and the treasures of blessing;' GedMosh (Gaster §§ 19-20): Moses sees anger and wrath (two angels).

[45] Parallels to specific details in the Six Books Apocalypse account are: the throne and the chariot distinguished (ApAbr 18:3, 12-13); the river of fire (Dan 7:10; 1 En 14:19; 71:2, 6; SephRaz [Morgan p. 82]; 3 En 36:1-2); guardian angels (1 En 71:7; QuEzra A26, 30); curtains of fire (cf. the *pargod* in 3 En 45:1).

[46] See chapter 3, section V above.

[47] Smith Lewis's text also has 'all the prophets;' the Arabic also has 'all since Adam up to the rest of the prophets.'

come into God's presence and worship before his throne. It does not seem to be where the righteous dead in general live or will live, for paradise, where their tabernacles await them, is not in the city (nor in the heavens, but at the distant edge of the world). Perhaps particularly eminent people are there: the patriarchs, David the psalmist who leads the heavenly worship, and the apostles. Perhaps the righteous in general visit (or will visit) the city in order to worship God in his presence. Why the gates are named after the apostles is not clear, nor is what the apostles do at their gates. Perhaps the notion of the apostles ruling with Christ lies behind this (Matt 9:28). The twelve walls indicate security, just as, in a different way, the very high wall in Revelation 21:17 does.

The description is not at all influenced, as the cities in Revelation 21 (11-13, 18-21)[48] and the Qumran New Jerusalem text (4QNJ[a] 1:1:13-22; 1:2:7-10; 2:2:15) are, by Ezekiel's city, with its twelve gates in a single wall named after the twelve tribes of Israel (48:30-34), nor by the new Zion of Isaiah, built of precious stones (Isa 54:11-12; cf. Tob 13:16). It seems to be quite independent of the biblical traditions on which other descriptions of the heavenly or new Jerusalem are modelled. The only Jerusalem described in an apocalypse which it resembles at all is 'the city of Christ,' also once called Jerusalem, in the Apocalypse of Paul (22-24, 29). This also has twelve concentric walls[49] and twelve gates (23), and in it David leads the singing of praise to God (29), but there the resemblance ends. The city in the Apocalypse of Paul is not in heaven[50] but at the edge of the world. God does not dwell in it, but the righteous dead (or some of them or some of the time?) do. Christ, it seems, will come to the city in the eschatological future (29). The description in the Apocalypse of Paul is as independent of biblical traditions as that in the Six Books Apocalypse, and the resemblances suggest some degree of common tradition behind the two works. A direct literary relationship seems unlikely, but it is not impossible that the Apocalypse of Paul is dependent on the Six Books Apocalypse.

A few other traces of such a tradition can be found. A medieval Jewish eschatological midrash has seven concentric walls around the

[48] The account of the heavenly Jerusalem in ArApPet (Mingana pp. 145-147) seems dependent solely on Rev 21.

[49] In the Anglo-Saxon version of the Apocalypse of the Seven Heavens, hell has twelve concentric walls (see chapter 12 section V above), a feature probably borrowed from the Apocalypse of Paul.

[50] The reference to David singing before God in the seventh heaven (29) is problematic.

new Jerusalem.[51] The tenth-century Irish *Vision of Adamnán (Fís Adamnáin)*, has seven concentric walls around the heavenly city, and, like the twelve walls of the city of Christ in the Apocalypse of Paul, 'Each is higher than the next' (12; cf. ApPaul 23).[52] It is the home of the righteous dead, but, unlike the city in the Apocalypse of Paul, it is the royal seat of God in which he sits enthroned (8-11).[53] This is the closest parallel I know to the heavenly Jerusalem of the Six Books Apocalypse: a heavenly city which is the present heavenly dwelling place of God. 2 Enoch 55:2 identifies the highest heaven with the heavenly Jerusalem, as in the Six Books Apocalypse, but only in one manuscript.

References to the heavenly Jerusalem are usually to the Jerusalem which is now in the heavens and will be revealed as the eschatological Jerusalem in the future (2 Bar 4:2-6; 32:4; 4 Ezra 7:26; 8:52; 10:52; 13:36; b. Ḥag. 12b [where Jerusalem and the Temple are in the fourth of the seven heavens, whereas the throne of God is in the seventh];[54] VisEzek [Jacobs pp. 30-31: here Jerusalem and the Temple are in the fifth of the seven heavens]; cf. Rev 3:12; 21:10; Gal 4:26; Heb 12:22; 13:14; Commodian, *Inst.* 1.44.1-5). It is not where God dwells or where his heavenly throne is located (in b. Ta'an. 5a, God says: 'I shall not enter the Jerusalem which is above until I enter the Jerusalem which is below'). Although God's dwelling in the seventh heaven is regularly represented as the throne-room of his heavenly palace and/or the inner sanctuary of his heavenly temple, this palace or temple is not usually depicted as the centre of a heavenly Jerusalem in the highest heaven, as the Six Books Apocalypse presents it.

(4) The Virgin Mary's vision of the Trinity—'the Father being glorified by His Son and the Son by His Father, and the Spirit by both of them' (the phrase in this form is found in both Smith Lewis's text and the Ethiopic; Wright's text has 'and the holy Spirit between the two

---

[51] G. W. Buchanan, *Revelation and Redemption* (Dillsboro, North Carolina: Western North Carolina Press, 1978) 544.

[52] In the ending unique to the Coptic version of the Apocalypse of Paul, three concentric walls of gold, silver and gold respectively, surround paradise (Budge p. 1079), while in a medieval Jewish midrash on the Garden of Eden, it is surrounded by three concentric walls of fire (Buchanan, *Revelation and Redemption*, 556-559).

[53] M. Herbert and M. McNamara, *Irish Biblical Apocrypha* (Edinburgh: T. & T. Clark, 1989) 139-140.

[54] In the Gedulat Moshe (Gaster § 13) the Temple is in the fourth heaven, but the city is not mentioned.

of them'; the Arabic abbreviates drastically here)[55]—is highly distinctive. Visions of God as Trinity are rare in the Christian apocalypses, but one other example is in the Ascension of Isaiah, in which Isaiah sees the Son ('the Lord') and the Holy Spirit ('the angel of the Holy Spirit') worshipping the Father ('the Great Glory') (AscenIs 9:37-40). For this subordinationist vision of the Trinity worshipping our apocalypse substitutes (possibly deliberately) one more appropriate to co-equal trinitarian Persons.

The mutual glorification of the Father and the Son is no doubt drawn from the Fourth Gospel (John 13:31-32; 17:1, 4-5), which does not, however, say that the Father and the Son glorify the Spirit (according to John 16:14, the Spirit glorifies the Son). The explanation for the precise words of our text should be sought in a particular context of the development of trinitarian theology, namely, the controversy about the deity of the Spirit in the late fourth century. Basil the Great's controversy with the "Pneumatomachi" centred on the appropriateness—denied by the "Pneumatomachi," vigorously defended by Basil—of a doxology addressed to the Holy Spirit along with the Father and the Son. Such a doxology implies that all three Persons are equally worthy of the ascription of honour and glory to them. It was in these terms that Basil's defence of the co-equal deity of the Spirit was echoed by the Creed of the Council of Constantinople (381), which says that the Holy Spirit 'with the Father and the Son is worshipped and glorified.' The debate was about the human ascription of glory to the Spirit, but in the course of his *De Spiritu Sancto* (375) Basil related this contested issue of the glorification of the trinitarian Persons by humans to the glorification of each other by the trinitarian Persons:

> The Lord said of Himself: 'I have glorified Thee on earth, having accomplished the work which Thou gavest me to do' [John 17:4], and concerning the Spirit He said, 'He will glorify me, for He will take what is mine and declare it to you' [John 16:14]. The Son is also glorified by the Father, when the Father says, 'I have glorified Thee, and I will glorify Thee again' [cf. John 12:28]. The Spirit is glorified by His communion with the Father and the Son, and by the testimony of the Only-Begotten: 'Every sin and blasphemy will be forgiven men: but the blasphemy against the Spirit will not be forgiven' [Matt 12:32] (*De Spiritu Sancto* 18.46).[56]

---

[55] In Smith Lewis's text only there is also an earlier parallel statement: 'the Jerusalem which is in heaven, wherein the Father is adored by His Son, and the Spirit by both.'

[56] Translation from St Basil the Great, *On the Holy Spirit*, trans. D. Anderson (New York: St Vladimir's Seminary Press, 1980) 73-74.

Here is asserted the mutual glorification of the Son and the Father, the glorification of the Son by the Spirit, and the glorification of the Spirit by the Father and the Son. Our text in the Six Books Apocalypse concisely expresses all these, with the exception of the glorification of the Son by the Spirit. In the late fourth-century controversial context this did not need to be asserted, whereas the glorification of the Spirit by the Father and the Son, without which the Spirit would be regarded as inferior, did need to be asserted. In that context the words of our text are a clear and unequivocal way of describing the three Persons of the one Godhead as fully and co-equally divine.

The variant reading in Wright's text ('and the holy Spirit between the two of them') might be an older version of the text, whose wording has been adapted in Smith Lewis's text to the needs of the issue in debate in the late fourth century. But since Smith Lewis's text is supported by the Ethiopic, it is easier to attribute Wright's text to a later scribe to whom the idea that the Spirit is glorified by the Father and the Son was unfamiliar and seemed strange.

If we could be sure that this statement of the mutual glorification of the trinitarian Persons belonged to the original text of the Six Books Apocalypse, it would be a strong indication of the approximate date of the work. But there is reason to think it is an addition to the original text. In Smith Lewis's text there follows a description of the divine throne and chariot and the angelic beings who attend it, followed by another description of the Trinity as seen by Mary: 'she saw the glorious throne of God; the Father sitting and His Son on His right hand; and the Spirit who was standing and hovering over them.' This could easily be a much older way of describing a vision of the Trinity, and its place in the description is what we should expect: following the account of the throne and its attendants. It seems likely that the account of the Trinity in mutual glorification was prefaced to the original account of what Mary saw in the divine throne-room. Then scribes responsible for the form of the text in witnesses other than Smith Lewis's text recognized that the account of the divine throne and the second description of the Trinity to which it leads were redundant and omitted them.

(5) The prominence of Enoch and Elijah in this apocalypse is striking. Not only, as we have already noticed, is Mary shown the place in the other world where each of them is, but also they meet her in paradise at the beginning of the apocalypse (along with Moses, who, however, is never mentioned again thereafter) and accompany her on her ascent through the heavens. They reappear in the final scene of worship in heaven which is unique to Smith Lewis's text. They are

more prominent in this apocalypse than in any other except those
which bear their own names. This can surely not be unconnected
with the fact that their bodily translation to the other world (unique
to them in the Old Testament, though Jewish tradition put some
other Old Testament figures into the same category) parallels Mary's
own special privilege of being taken bodily into paradise prior to the
general resurrection in the future. Moreover, to both Enoch and
Elijah were attributed cosmic tour apocalypses in which the fate of
the dead in the other world features: 1 Enoch 12-36; 2 Enoch; and
the lost ancient Apocalypse of Elijah (on which see chapter 2 section
III above). It seems highly probable that it was the parallel with
Enoch and Elijah which led to the attribution of a cosmic tour apocalypse to the Virgin Mary as the concluding part of the story of her
dormition/assumption. The cosmic tours of Enoch and Elijah provide a much more convincing generic model for the apocalypses of
the Virgin than do the narratives of Christ's descent to Hades, which
Wenger and Mimouni proposed they were intended to parallel (see
section I above). If, as our next point will support, the Six Books
Apocalypse is the oldest of the Apocalypses of the Virgin, it appears
that the cosmic tours of Enoch and Elijah provided the model for this
first Apocalypse of the Virgin, which then itself provided the model
for the others which followed.

(6) In chapters 2 and 3 above we have argued that the Jewish and
Christian apocalypses document a change in views of the intermediate state. In the older view the dead are conceived as in a state of
waiting for the last judgment and the resurrection, when the righteous will be rewarded and the wicked punished. They already know
their fate, which is determined on the basis of their lives, and they
either rejoice to know that they can expect to enter paradise or suffer
in anticipation of their assignment to Gehenna. When visionaries in
the apocalypses see paradise or hell they see them as empty of but
prepared for the human inhabitants who will be assigned to them in
the future. The later view which very gradually replaced the older
was that the righteous are already enjoying the delights of paradise
and the wicked already suffering the punishments of hell prior to the
last judgment. This view made a difference to the apocalypses, since
it made it possible for the apocalyptic seers to view the righteous
enjoying their reward and the wicked suffering, not in a vision of the
eschatological future but in an account of what can be seen in the
other world now. The effect is particularly seen in the tours of hell, in
which (as in the Greek and Ethiopic Apocalypses of the Virgin, and
to a lesser extent the Obsequies Apocalypse) the seer can now be

conducted around a large number of different punishments in hell and see the various categories of sinners already suffering the just fate due to their own particular sins. The intended paraenetic effect on the readers is thereby made much more vivid and effective. The growing prominence of the tour of hell in apocalypses concerned with the fate of the dead in the other world is closely related to the change in understanding of the intermediate state.

The Six Books Apocalypse espouses the earlier view. This does not enable a precise dating, since the two views were both current for a long period, and expressions of the earlier view can still be found in writers of the late fourth and early fifth centuries.[57] But there seems to be no other apocalypse expressing this earlier view which can plausibly be dated later than the mid-second century, and so this feature of the Six Books Apocalypse at least points towards an earlier rather than a later date.

(7) Finally, the closing conversation between Mary, John and Jesus displays a sense of living in the last period of history and the approach of the parousia, which is not evident in the other Apocalypses of the Virgin. There is a prediction of the series of woes and afflictions which will precede the parousia, and an assertion of the relevance of the apocalypse at this time (in the future from the work's fictional place in history, but present or near in the author's and first readers' perspective), when people will be able to be protected from the eschatological afflictions by invoking Mary's name. It is not accidental that, among the four Apocalypses of the Virgin, this sense of approaching eschatological crisis occurs only in the one that espouses the older view of the intermediate state. It is not possible to make simple and automatic correlations between imminent expectation of the parousia and the older view of the intermediate state, and between a lack of interest in the eschatological future of the world and the later view of the intermediate state. But there is some truth in these correlations. It is not the case that collective eschatology disappears when the dead are thought to be rewarded and punished immediately after death. The Apocalypse of Paul, for example, is not devoid of expectation of the future when Christ will come to reign and the resurrection and the judgment will occur (e.g. 15, 16, 21, 29), but it is relatively marginal. The same is true of the Obsequies Apocalypse (for the future judgment see Arras §91), whereas in the

---

[57] B. E. Daley, *The Hope of the Early Church* (Cambridge: Cambridge University Press, 1991) 100-101, 117, 160, 165-166.

Six Books Apocalypse interest in the places of the dead in the other world is still combined with interest in the coming eschatological climax of history, as it was in, for example, 1 Enoch 1-36.

V CONCLUSION

Our conclusions so far allow the following reconstruction of the history of composition of these four Apocalypses of the Virgin. Since the Obsequies Apocalypse and the Six Books Apocalypse are known only as belonging to versions of the *Transitus Mariae*, we must assume that they originated as such and never existed as independent works. The earlier of the two—dating from the fourth century at the latest, but perhaps considerably earlier—is the Six Books Apocalypse, which must have belonged to a very early form of the *Transitus Mariae*, prior to the development of the two types of text which van Esbroeck calls the 'Palm of the Tree of Life' type and the 'Bethlehem and Censings' type. It was attached to the story of the *Transitus Mariae* because, in view of Mary's bodily translation to paradise which was seen as analogous to the translations of Enoch and Elijah, it seemed appropriate to attribute to her a cosmic tour like those attributed to Enoch and Elijah. The Six Books Apocalypse remained part of both types of *Transitus Mariae* text as the two types developed in divergence from each other, but in the 'Palm of the Tree of Life' family it was soon replaced by the Obsequies Apocalypse. The reason will have been the changing view of the intermediate state. The older view, which characterizes the picture of the other world in the Six Books Apocalypse, was being superseded by the newer view, which the Obsequies Apocalypse espouses. This newer view made possible, not only the depiction of sinners presently suffering punishments in hell, but also the idea of a respite from pain granted them through the intercession of the Virgin, a theme which is lacking in the Six Books Apocalypse but prominent in all three of the later Apocalypses of the Virgin.

It is not certain whether the Obsequies Apocalypse was written in the fourth century, before the Apocalypse of Paul, which would in that case have used it as a source, or in the fifth century, after the Apocalypse of Paul and in dependence on it, but there are some reasons to suggest that the former is more probable. In either case the popularity which the Apocalypse of Paul rapidly gained in the fifth century, as a full-scale account of every aspect of the fate of the dead in the other world, depicted according to the newer view of the intermediate state, had its effect on the writing of apocalypses of the Virgin. The two which were written as independent works, not as part of a *Transitus Mariae* narrative, were both inspired by the Apocalypse of

Paul. One, the Ethiopic Apocalypse of the Virgin, is a free adaptation of much of the text of the Apocalypse of Paul, transferring the visions from Paul to Mary. The other, the Greek Apocalypse of the Virgin, is a new work, but one which has drawn its ideas very largely from the accounts of the punishments and of Michael's and Paul's intercession for the damned in the Apocalypse of Paul. We cannot be sure when they were written, but if the Ethiopic Apocalypse does derive from a Greek original, then most likely it was written after the Greek Apocalypse, with whose great popularity it failed to compete, surviving only in its Ethiopic version.

In both families of *Transitus Mariae* narratives, the apocalypse attributed to the Virgin at the end of the narrative eventually survived only rarely. In most forms of the narrative it was dropped. The reason is probably that the tendency towards shorter versions of the *Transitus Mariae* (which can be observed even within the textual traditions of the Six Books and Obsequies Apocalypses) combined with the competition from fuller, independent Apocalypses concerned with the fate of the dead to make the apocalypses within the *Transitus Mariae* dispensable. In the West, where the Obsequies Apocalypse did exist in Latin and Irish, the competition came from the massively popular Apocalypse of Paul, which in its many recensions dominated the medieval West's understanding and imagination of the other world. The Apocalypse of Paul was also dominant in the Syriac and Coptic speaking churches of the East, but in the Greek speaking churches (and later in other churches within the Byzantine cultural orbit) it was the Greek Apocalypse of the Virgin which displaced not only the two apocalypses within the *Transitus Mariae* narratives but also the Apocalypse of Paul. There is a further story yet to be told of the influence of these apocalypses, which remained influential for many centuries, on the new visions of the other world attributed in both the medieval West and the Byzantine East, no longer to characters from the biblical history, but to figures of early medieval history.

In the sequence of four Apocalypses of the Virgin we can see clearly certain tendencies which characterize the whole development of Jewish and Christian apocalypses depicting the world of the dead. There is the shift from the older to the newer view of the intermediate state. There is the development from cosmic tour apocalypses, which included, with more or less emphasis, the places of the dead but also revealed other mysteries of the other world, to apocalypses exclusively concerned with the places of the dead. There is a further development, within apocalypses predominantly concerned with the fate of the dead in the intermediate state, to focus very largely, or even exclusively on the punishments in hell, depicted in terrifying detail.

Finally, in the Ethiopic Apocalypse, we see, in a context where the authority of a claimed apocalyptic revelation to a revered biblical figure was evidently no longer sufficient to warrant its statements, the introduction of scriptural quotations to buttress the authority of the revelations of the other world.

CHAPTER FOURTEEN

THE ASCENSION OF ISAIAH:
GENRE, UNITY AND DATE

I

It is no exaggeration to say that study of the Ascension of Isaiah has been revolutionized by the work of the research team of Italian scholars brought together by Mauro Pesce in 1978. The major fruit of their work is the two volumes of texts and commentary, published as volumes 7 and 8 of the *Corpus Christianorum Series Apocryphorum* in 1995.[1] The first of these volumes contains new editions of all the texts and versions of the work or parts of it (Ethiopic, Greek, Coptic, Latin, Old Slavonic), together with a synopsis in Latin, so that the student of this work at last has relatively easy access to all the complex textual evidence for it. The second volume, which is entirely the work of Enrico Norelli, is a 600-page introduction and commentary. The scope and thoroughness of Norelli's work on the Ascension of Isaiah are such that even this large volume could not do it full justice, and so he has also published a substantial volume of essays,[2] which supplement the commentary and can be used as a companion volume to it. Norelli's work constitutes the most important study of the Ascension of Isaiah to date, and in many respects is likely to prove definitive. But it is not the only significant work to come out of Italy. In addition to several significant articles by members of the group,[3] three further books have appeared. At a conference in Rome in 1981, members of the group were joined by several other Italian scholars, and a volume

---

[1] P. Bettiolo, A. Giambelluca Kossova, C. Leonardi, E. Norelli, and L. Perrone eds., *Ascensio Isaiae: Textus* (CCSA 7; Turnhout: Brepols, 1995); E. Norelli ed., *Ascensio Isaiae: Commentarius* (CCSA 8; Turnhout: Brepols, 1995). Original members of the team who did not contribute to these volumes are A. Acerbi, P. C. Bori, A. Danti and M. Pesce himself.

[2] E. Norelli, *L'Ascensione di Isaia: Studi su un apocrifo al crocevia dei cristianesimi* (Origini NS 1; Bologna: Centro editoriale dehoniano, 1994). For a brief (100 pages) account of his conclusions, see E. Norelli, *Ascension du prophète Isaïe* (Collection de Poche de l'AELAC; Turnhout: Brepols, 1993).

[3] Especially E. Norelli, 'Il martirio di Isaia come *testimonium* antigiudaico?,' *Henoch* 2 (1980) 37-56; idem, 'La resurrezione di Gesù nell'*Ascensione di Isaia*,' *Cristianesimo nella Storia* 1 (1980) 315-366; P. C. Bori, 'L'estasi del profeta: "Ascensio Isaia" 6 e l'antico profetismo cristiano,' *Cristianesimo nella Storia* 1 (1980) 367-389.

of ten papers from the conference was published.[4] Antonio Acerbi, who was associated with the group without participating directly in the edition, has published two books, one tracing the transmission history of the Ascension of Isaiah from the second to the sixteenth century,[5] the other a study of the content and composition of the work.[6] All this material has brought the study of the Ascension of Isaiah by leaps and bounds into a completely new era of study. It is extremely unfortunate that accounts of the Ascension of Isaiah in the major reference works published in recent years[7] have been written in ignorance of it, and for the most part merely perpetuate the views of the scholars who worked at the beginning of the century (especially R. H. Charles[8] and E. Tisserant[9]). But significant contributions have

---

[4] M. Pesce, *Isaia, il Diletto e la Chiesa: Visione e esegesi profetica cristiano-primitive nell'*Ascensione di Isaia (Texte e Ricerche di Scienze Religiose 20; Brescia: Paideia Editrice, 1983). The contributors are A. Acerbi, U. Bianchi, P. C. Bori, I. P. Culianu, G. Gnoli, E. Norelli, L. Perrone, M. Pesce, M. Simonetti.

[5] A. Acerbi, *Serra Lignea: Studi sulla Fortuna della* Ascensione di Isaia (Rome: Editrice A. V. E., 1984). (For the *Ascension of Isaiah* in Ethiopia, see P. Piovanelli, 'Les aventures des apocryphes en Éthiope,' *Apocrypha* 4 (1993) 197-224.)

[6] A. Acerbi, *L'Ascensione di Isaia: Cristologia e profetismo in Siria nei primi decenni del II secolo* (Studia Patristica Mediolanensia 17; Milan: Vita e Pensiero, 1989). For critique of this work, see Norelli, *L'Ascensione*, 55-59; idem, 'Interprétations nouvelles de l'Ascension d'Isaïe,' *Revue des Études Augustiniennes* 37 (1991) 11-22.

[7] H. F. D. Sparks ed., *The Apocryphal Old Testament* (Oxford: Clarendon Press, 1984) 775-812; G. W. E. Nickelsburg in M. E. Stone ed., *Jewish Writings of the Second Temple Period: Apocrypha, Pseudepigrapha, Qumran Sectarian Writings, Philo, Josephus* (CRINT 2/2; Assen: Van Gorcum/Philadelphia: Fortress, 1984) 52-56; M. A. Knibb, 'Martyrdom and Ascension of Isaiah,' in J. H. Charlesworth ed., *The Old Testament Pseudepigrapha*, vol. 2 (London: Darton, Longman & Todd, 1985) 143-176; E. Schürer, *The History of the Jewish People in the Age of Jesus Christ (175 B. C.—A. D. 135)*, revised by G. Vermes, F. Millar, M. Goodman, vol. 3/1 (Edinburgh: T& T. Clark, 1986) 335-341; A. Dupont-Sommer and M. Philonenko ed., *La Bible: Ecrits Intertestamentaires* (Paris: Gallimard, 1987) lxxxviii-xci, 1019-1033; C. D. G. Müller, 'The Ascension of Isaiah,' in E. Hennecke and W. Schneemelcher ed., *New Testament Apocrypha*, vol. 2 (revised ed., trans. R. McL. Wilson; Cambridge: James Clarke/ Louisville: Westminster/John Knox, 1992) 603-620; J. L. Trafton, 'Isaiah, Martyrdom and Ascension of,' in D. N. Freedman ed., *The Anchor Bible Dictionary*, vol. 3 (New York: Doubleday, 1992) 507-509; C. A. Evans, *Noncanonical Writings and New Testament Interpretation* (Peabody, Massachusetts: Hendrickson, 1992) 32. Similarly oblivious of the work of the Italian scholars are E. Yassif, 'Traces of Folk Traditions of the Second Temple Period in Rabbinic Literature,' *JJS* 39 (1988) 216-220; J. D. Crossan, *The Cross that Spoke* (San Francisco: Harper & Row 1988) 82-83, 368-373; G. C. Jenks, *The Origins and Early Development of the Antichrist Myth* (BZNW 59; Berlin/New York: de Gruyter, 1991) 126-127, 176, 312-327; M. Himmelfarb, *Ascent to Heaven in Jewish and Christian Apocalypses* (New York/Oxford: Oxford University Press, 1993) 55-59.

[8] R. H. Charles, *The Ascension of Isaiah* (London: A. & C. Black, 1900).

[9] E. Tisserant, *Ascension d'Isaïe* (Paris: Letouzey et Ané, 1909).

also been made in recent years by two English speaking scholars working largely independently of the work of the Italians: Robert G. Hall[10] and Jonathan M. Knight.[11]

II

Our present concern is primarily with the issue of the unitary or composite nature of the work. Since W. Gesenius in 1821[12] almost all scholars have agreed that the Ascension of Isaiah is not the single work of a single author,[13] but a composite work whose constituent parts can be identified and distinguished from the redactional material which has united them. Until recently it was the source-critical theory of R. H. Charles which was dominant. Charles distinguished three sources which have been combined to form the present work. He called them the Martyrdom of Isaiah, the Testament of Hezekiah (3:13b-4:18) and the Vision of Isaiah (6:1-11:40). The first of these is the story of Isaiah's persecution and martyrdom in chapters 1-3 and 5, a purely Jewish work which has been taken over by the Christian redactor. Charles assigned 1:1, 2a, 6b-13a; 1:1-8, 10-3:12; 5:1b-14 to this source, but scholars who accept that there is such a source have rarely agreed on its precise extent. The most recent sustained attempt to isolate the purely Jewish text from Christian redaction, by A. Caquot in 1973,[14] well illustrates just how difficult it is to do so: the more closely one looks the more Christian redaction there seems to be. At this point scholarship since 1980 has, with complete unanimity, made a substantial advance over the older scholarship. Pesce's

---

[10] R. G. Hall, 'The *Ascension of Isaiah:* Community Situation, Date, and Place in Early Christianity,' *JBL* 109 (1990) 289-306; idem, *Revealed Histories: Techniques for Ancient Jewish Historiography* (JSPSS 6; Sheffield: JSOT Press, 1991) 137-147; idem, 'Isaiah's Ascent to See the Beloved: An Ancient Jewish Source for the *Ascension of Isaiah,*' *JBL* 113 (1994) 463-484. For a critique of Hall's work, see Norelli, *L'Ascensione,* 50-55.

[11] J. M. Knight, *Disciples of the Beloved One: The Christology, Social Setting and Theological Context of the Ascension of Isaiah* (JSPSS 18; Sheffield: Sheffield Academic Press, 1996). See also his student guide: *The Ascension of Isaiah* (GAP 2; Sheffield: Sheffield Academic Press, 1995).

[12] Reported in Norelli, *L'Ascensione,* 24-25.

[13] Rare proponents of the unity of the whole work were F. C. Burkitt, *Jewish and Christian Apocalypses* (Schweich Lectures 1913; London: Oxford University Press, 1914) 45-48; V. Burch, 'The Literary Unity of the Ascensio Isaiae,' *JTS* 20 (1919) 17-23. This comment by Burkitt (45) is worth quoting: 'I sometimes fancy that the spirit of Beliar must be dwelling in some of my friends when they use the wooden saw to dissect the Ascension of Isaiah.'

[14] A. Caquot, 'Bref Commentaire du "Martyr d'Isaïe,"' *Sem* 23 (1973) 65-93. Caquot limits the Jewish source to 1:6-11; 2:1, 4-6, 12-16; 3:6-12; 5:1b-6, 8-10.

argument, based on careful study of the extant Jewish traditions about the martyrdom of Isaiah, has largely established the case that, although the author of chapters 1-5 used Jewish haggadic traditions, there was no Jewish text which he incorporated and which can now be distinguished.[15] These chapters are entirely the work of one or more Christian authors.

It is worth noting that the title Martyrdom of Isaiah is purely modern: in ancient literature it nowhere designates either chapters 1-5 of the Ascension of Isaiah or a source. Moreover, the title Ascension of Isaiah is known—in the Ethiopic version and in references to it by Epiphanius and Jerome—only as the title of the whole work (chapters 1-11), never of chapters 6-11 alone, which bear the title Vision of Isaiah both in the Ethiopic version (which also includes chapters 1-5) and in SL[2] (the Slavonic and second Latin versions, which consist only of 6:1-11:40). The title *Martyrdom and* Ascension of Isaiah (used in Charlesworth, *Old Testament Pseudepigrapha)* is therefore misleading. Using the title Martyrdom of Isaiah is confusing (does it refer to the alleged Jewish source incorporated in chapters 1-5 or to these chapters themselves?) and pre-judges the source-critical issue. If used to refer to chapters 1-5 themselves, it assumes that these chapters once existed independently of chapters 6-11, which, as we shall see, is not necessarily the case.

From the conclusion that no non-Christian Jewish source can be isolated in chapters 1-5 it need not follow that these chapters are the work of a single author. When Charles distinguished between the Martyrdom of Isaiah and what he called the Testament of Hezekiah (3:13b-4:18),[16] his argument rested in part on the alleged awkwardness of the inclusion of the account of Isaiah's vision (3:13-4:22) within the narrative of the persecution and martyrdom of Isaiah. That this account is a manifestly Christian passage, while the narra-

---

[15] M. Pesce, 'Presupposti per l'utilizzazione storica dell' *Ascensione di Isaia,*' in Pesce ed., *Isaia,* 40-45; idem, *Il "Martirio di Isaia" Non Esiste:* L'Ascensione di Isaia *e le Tradizione Giudaiche sull'Uccisione del Profeta* (Bologna: Centro Stampa Baiesi, 1984). Cf. Acerbi, *L'Ascensione,* 254-256; Norelli, *Ascensio Isaiae: Commentarius,* 51-53; idem, *L'Ascensione,* 45-49, 229-234; Knight, *Disciples,* 28-29, 33-34. Against the thesis that the *Opus imperfectum in Matthaeum* is dependent on the purely Jewish text of the Martyrdom of Isaiah, see Acerbi, *Serra,* 95-101; Norelli, *L'Ascensione,* 69-78. According to Norelli, *Ascensio Isaiae: Commentarius,* 286, Pesce's argument from the Jewish traditions is conclusive only when supported by his own argument for the coherence of the whole of chapters 1-5 (see below).

[16] Charles thought this section is the vision of Hezekiah to which 1:2-5 refers and that the eleventh-century writer George Cedrenus knew it under the title Testament of Hezekiah. Against this particular argument about 3:13b-4:18, see Pesce, 'Presupposti,' in Pesce ed., *Isaia,* 24-28.

tive it interrupts could be regarded as Jewish, helped his argument. But if 3:13-4:22 (or part of this passage) is seen as lacking coherence with the rest of chapters 2-3, 5, then, even if the case for a purely Jewish narrative of Isaiah's martyrdom is abandoned, a distinction between two Christian sources can be made. Acerbi's theory of the composite character of chapters 1-5 rests on finding disaccord between 3:13b-31 and its context.[17] He postulates two independent works (both Christian): (1) a story of Isaiah's martyrdom with a prophecy of Antichrist and the parousia (1:1-5a, 7-3:13a; 4:2-12, 14-19, 23-5:15a; (2) Isaiah's vision (6:1-11:40). The two texts were joined by a redactor who was responsible for 1:5b-6; 3:13b-31; 4:13, 20-22; 5:15b; 11:41-43.

This new source theory is rejected by Norelli, who sees chapters 1-5 as a coherent and unified composition by one author. His argument is of considerable importance because it establishes the thematic unity of these chapters and removes the basis not only for Acerbi's recent source-critical proposal, but also for the older source-critical theories, like that of Charles. Norelli argues that both the narrative of Isaiah's persecution and martyrdom and the section of the prophetic passage in which the work's own historical context is surely depicted from the author's point of view (3:21-31) have as their central theme the conflict between true and false prophecy. In telling the story of Isaiah the author deploys a traditional narrative model, which can be seen in Jewish retellings of narratives from the books of Kings, in which a false prophet incites an evil king to persecute a false prophet. The reason the author tells Isaiah's story in this way is that he sees his own context also as a scene of conflict between true and false prophecy, i.e. between the group of prophets from which the Ascension of Isaiah derives, who have been marginalized (3:27), and the corrupt ecclesiastical authorities who are depicted as false prophets (3:32-31). Thus the story of Isaiah, persecuted at the instigation of the false prophet Belchira, is narrated as a model for the experiences which Christian prophets, opposed by church elders and pastors, are undergoing. It has been composed to meet the paraenetic and polemical needs which become explicit in 3:21-31.[18]

Norelli's case for the unity of chapters 1-5 is sound. But Norelli does not hold that all eleven chapters of the Ascension of Isaiah are a

---

[17] Acerbi, *L'Ascensione*, chapter 8.

[18] Norelli, *Ascensio Isaiae: Commentarius*, 46-49; idem, *L'Ascensione*, 58-59, 93-109; idem, 'Interprétations,' 18-22. In 'Interprétations,' 20-21, Norelli deals with the three specific respects in which Acerbi found 3:13-31 out of accord with its context in chapters 1-5.

unity. He holds that the second part, the vision of Isaiah (6:1-11:40), was composed first and circulated independently. The first part (1-5) is from another author who added it to the already existing second part (and added 11:41-43 to help bind the two parts together). The two parts reflect two successive phases of the history of the group of Christian prophets from which they come.[19] Norelli's argument for this theory about the composition of the Ascension of Isaiah is significant and raises important issues. He could be right, but I am not convinced that there are decisive reasons for preferring this view to the simpler hypothesis that the whole work is a single composition from a single author. After all, the two parts of the work share an impressive range of highly distinctive ideas and terminology, so that even Charles admitted, with reference to what he considered the two distinct sources 3:13-4:22 and 6:1-11:40, that 'there are so many similarities of thought and diction that it is not unreasonable to assume ... that they were the work of one and the same writer, or the work of two closely related writers.'[20] There is a *prima facie* case for assuming the unity of the whole work,[21] and in the next two sections I shall provide arguments for this view.

III

It is quite clear that formally the Ascension of Isaiah falls into two very distinct parts. Chapters 1-5 are a narrative about Isaiah, though containing a report of Isaiah's vision (3:13-4:22), which is predominantly in the first person (3:31-4:22). Chapters 6-11 consist of a first-person account of Isaiah's vision (7:2-11:35), with a third-person narrative framework (6:1-71; 11:36-40 [+41-43]). Norelli argues that the first part could not stand apart from the second, since it clearly refers to the contents of the second (1:5-6a; 2:9; 3:13; cf. 4:13), but that the second part contains no necessary reference to the first[22] and could be an independent text.[23] This depends on Norelli's view that the references to judgment and destruction in 8:12 and 10:12 are to the submission of the evil powers to the Beloved at the time of his ascension (11:23). We shall argue below that they are references

---

[19] Norelli, *Ascensio Isaiae: Commentarius*, 36-52; idem, *L'Ascensione*, 59-67.

[20] Charles, *The Ascension*, xlii-xliii.

[21] Knight, *Disciples*, works with this assumption, without systematically defending it.

[22] The reference to Isaiah's martyrdom in 8:12 need not presuppose chapters 1-5 as such, but only general knowledge of the story.

[23] Norelli, *Ascensio Isaiae: Commentarius*, 36-37.

rather to the eschatological judgment and destruction of the evil powers at the parousia. In that case these verses are in fact references to the first part of the work, which describes these eschatological events in full (4:14-18), just as 3:13 is a reference to the second part of the work, where the Beloved's descent and transformation are fully recounted. This makes the relationship between the two parts less one-sided, more symmetrical than Norelli allows.

The second part does actually exist as an independent text in the transmission tradition represented by the Old Slavonic version (S) and the second Latin version (L²), which contain only chapters 6-11 (and lack 11:41-43). But this cannot, of course, prove that these chapters originally existed without chapters 1-5. The textual tradition of SL², which has also adapted the text of chapters 6-11 in other ways, could have detached these chapters from the rest of the work. But the impression of formal distinctness between the two parts is increased by the fact that the second part has its own title ('The Vision which Isaiah the son of Amoz saw') which stands at its head not only in SL², but also in the Ethiopic version, which contains all eleven chapters.[24] The formal caesura marked by this (sub)title is evident also in the fact that the chronological notice with which chapter 6 begins places the narrative of chapters 6-11 at an earlier time than the narrative of chapters 1-5. The latter begins in the twenty-sixth year of Hezekiah (1:1) and is set largely in the subsequent reign of Manasseh (2-5), with the report of Isaiah's vision, which took place in the twentieth year of Hezekiah (1:6), constituting a sort of flashback (3:13b-4:22) introduced to explain Beliar's hostility to Isaiah during Manasseh's reign (3:13a; 5:1, 15-16). At 6:1 the narrative begins afresh in the twentieth year of Hezekiah.

On the other hand, there are also strong indications of formal unity between the two parts of the work. The reference in the first chapter to Isaiah's vision in the twentieth year of Hezekiah (1:6) is picked up at the beginning of the second part (6:1). The concluding three verses of the work (11:41-43) form a kind of inclusio both with the beginning of the whole work (11:42-43; cf. 1:1, 5; 2:1-2) and with the end of the first part (11:41; cf. 5:15-16). A series of interconnected references link the vision of Isaiah with both the beginning and the end of the narrative of chapters 1-5: with Hezekiah's testamentary gift to his son Manasseh and with the martyrdom of Isaiah that results from Beliar's anger (1:5-6; 3:13a; 5:1, 15-16; 11:41-43).

Most interesting is the description of Isaiah's vision given in 1:5: 'concerning the judgment of the angels, and concerning the destruc-

---

[24] The beginning of chapter 6 is not extant in other versions.

tion of this world, and concerning the robes of the saints, and concerning the going out and the transformation and the persecution and the ascension of the Beloved.'[25] The order of the items in this initial summary of Isaiah's vision is explicable only if it is designed to cover the two different accounts of the vision in 3:13b-4:22 and 7-11.[26] The order then covers the contents of the vision in the order in which their fullest treatment appears, in whichever of the two accounts this is: the judgment of the angels and the destruction of this world (4:2-19), the robes of the saints (9:24-26), the going out, the transformation, the persecution and the ascension of the Beloved (10:17-11:32). All the items occur more briefly in the other account (the judgment of the angels and the destruction of this world: 10:12; the robes of the saints: 4:16; the going out, the transformation, the persecution and the ascension of the Beloved: 3:13, 18). But if the summary in 1:5 were either of the account in 3:13b-4:22 or of the account in 7-11, the order of the items would be inexplicable. It is clear, then, that 1:5 treats the two accounts of Isaiah's vision as complementary, in that they focus on different aspects of the vision's content: 3:13a gives merely a brief summary of material which is treated extensively in 10:17-11:14; in 3:13b-20 there is a rather fuller version of what appears more briefly in 9:14-16; 11:19-22; while 3:21-4:18 deals extensively with the eschatological aspect to which there are only passing allusions in 8:12; 10:12-13 (cf. 11:37). In the text itself the two accounts of Isaiah's vision are thus presented not as alternatives or as contradictory, but as complementary.[27]

None of these formal indications of unity is inconsistent with Norelli's hypothesis. They could all be due to the author of 1-5; 11:40-43, who in this way made chapters 6-11 a coherent part of the larger unity he created by adding 1-5 and 11:40-43. (But it should be noticed that the way in which the form of the text in SL[2] concludes, in place of 11:41-43, is singularly weak: 'And he ceased speaking and went out from Hezekiah the king.' This is better understood as an attempt to round off the narrative when chapters 6-11 were separated from 1-5, and 11:41-43 had to be omitted, than as the original conclusion to the originally independent text 6:1-11:40.) What is in any

---

[25] In this quotation the Ethiopic version has been corrected in accordance with the Greek Legend 1:2 (and cf. *Ascension of Isaiah* 3:13), following Charles, *The Ascension*, 5, and Norelli, *Ascensio Isaiae: Commentarius*, 87-89.

[26] It is clear from 3:13a; 5:1, 15-16; 11:41-43 that these are two accounts of the same vision, and should not therefore be called 'the First Vision' and 'the Second Vision,' as in Knights, *Disciples*.

[27] Norelli, *Ascensio Isaiae: Commentarius*, 45, understands 1:5 rather differently.

case clear is that an adequate account of the literary character of the Ascension of Isaiah must do justice both to the indications of formal distinction between the two parts of the work and to the indications of formal unity.

This requires consideration of the genre of the work. Scholars who have studied the Ascension of Isaiah have usually been so impressed by the difference and distinction between the two parts that they have confined discussion of genre to each part separately.[28] But in order to understand the unity of the work as we have it it is necessary to ask whether there is a generic model for a work composed of two such distinct parts. In fact, there is an obvious model of this kind: the book of Daniel. When Isaiah lists the prophetic works, besides the canonical book of Isaiah, in which the contents of his vision can also be found (4:21-22), 'the words of Daniel' occur last, a position probably indicative of the importance of Daniel for the author, rather than of comparative unimportance.[29] Daniel is the only work listed here which can be classified as generically an apocalypse. The author(s) of the Ascension of Isaiah must have known other apocalypses, since the account of Isaiah's ascent through the seven heavens resembles other such accounts, but apparently only Daniel has for the author of 4:21-22 the kind of authority to deserve a place in his list of authoritative eschatological prophecies. It is the only work listed which could have provided a generic model for the literary form of the Ascension of Isaiah as a whole.

Daniel comprises six narrative chapters, relating stories about the activities of Daniel and his three friends at the courts of the kings, and six chapters of visions, in which Daniel's first-person accounts of his visions are framed by a minimal third-person narrative framework (7:1; 8:1; 10:1).[30] Similarly the Ascension of Isaiah comprises, in

---

[28] On the genre of chapters 1-5, see Pesce, 'Presupposti,' 35-40 (ostensibly about the whole work, but convincing only with reference to 1-5); Norelli, *Ascensio Isaiae: Commentarius,* 48; idem, *L'Ascensione,* 93-109, 221-227. On the genre of chapters 6-11, see Norelli, *Ascensio Isaiae: Commentarius,* 44; A. Yarbro Collins, 'The Early Christian Apocalypses,' *Semeia* 14 (1979) 84-85; M. Himmelfarb, 'The Experience of the Visionary and Genre in the Ascension of Isaiah 6-11 and the Apocalypse of Paul,' *Semeia* 36 (1986) 97-111.

[29] Though there is little explicit dependence on Daniel in the accounts of Isaiah's vision, the time period in 4:14 is a variation on the period given in Dan 12:12.

[30] Scholars commonly postulate diverse origins for the stories and the visions, and have usually thought that the stories originated earlier than and separately from the visions. However, it is the final form of the book of Daniel, comprising both the narratives and the visions, that will have been known to the author(s) of the Ascension of Isaiah, and which could function as a generic model. Whether or not the author(s) of the Ascension of Isaiah knew Daniel in a form which included the LXX Additions does not greatly affect the issue.

roughly equal proportions, a narrative about Isaiah and a first-person account of Isaiah's vision within a third-person narrative framework (6:1-7:11 11:36-40). Although there are no references to the visions of Daniel within the narrative part of the book, Nebuchadnezzar's dream and Daniel's interpretation of it in chapter 2 adumbrate the main theme (the four world empires succeeded by the kingdom of God) of the visions of chapters 7-12, and so provide a kind of precedent for the summary of Isaiah's vision (3:13-4:22) within the narrative section of the Ascension of Isaiah, anticipating the full-scale account of the vision in the second part of the book. The functions of the narrative section of each book are at least partly parallel: Daniel and his friends are models for the righteous under persecution for whom the book of Daniel was intended, just as Isaiah and his fellow-prophets are models for the persecuted Christian prophets for whom the Ascension of Isaiah was written. Finally, the fact that the second part of this work is dated prior to the narrative of chapters 1-6 should not, if Daniel provided the generic model, be regarded as surprising or problematic. The visions in Daniel are not placed chronologically subsequent to the sequence of narratives. Rather the narratives and the visions are each grouped together, each in their own chronological succession, with the result that the first and second visions are dated (7:1; 8:1) prior to the last two of the stories (5-6). Similarly in the Ascension of Isaiah the sequence of the two parts is not dictated by chronology and should not be expected to be. It conforms to the Danielic model of a narrative section followed by a visionary section.

According to Norelli, if the Ascension of Isaiah were the work of a single author, then he would have placed the vision of Isaiah at the end 'as a sort of documentary appendix.'[31] But this implies a subordination of the second part to the first which the Danielic model can enable us to avoid. In the case of Daniel, as John Goldingay observes, the book is 'as much a series of short stories to which visions are attached as a series of visions prefaced by some stories.'[32] The juxtaposition of the two generically different parts, of roughly equal length, to form a work of mixed genre does not imply the subordination of one part to the other, but that each part has its own function in itself and in relation to the other.

The Ascension of Isaiah is not the only later apocalypse which follows Daniel as its generic precedent in combining narrative and vision. The Apocalypse of Abraham, a Jewish apocalypse roughly

---

[31] Norelli, *Ascensio Isaiae: Commentarius*, 37 ('come una sorta di appendice documentaria').

[32] J. E. Goldingay, *Daniel* (WBC 30; Dallas: Word Books, 1989) 321.

contemporary with the Ascension of Isaiah , has a similar structure.[33] Chapters 1-8 tell the story of Abraham's rejection of his father Terah's idolatry in favour of the worship of the one true God. The following chapters (9-32) tell of his ascent to the presence of God in the highest heaven and the revelation of history and eschatology which he there receives from God. The two parts are linked by the theme of idolatry, and Abraham in the first part functions as the paradigm of rejection of idolatrous worship by those who worship the true God. In fact the Apocalypse of Abraham has resemblances to the Ascension of Isaiah which go beyond the Daniel model. Unlike Daniel, in which the narrative section comprises a series of discrete stories and the visionary section a series of discrete, though thematically related, visions, both the Apocalypse of Abraham and the Ascension of Isaiah have a narrative section in which a single narrative about the work's hero and seer is told, followed by a visionary section comprising a single visionary experience in which the seer ascends through the heavens to the throne of God in the seventh and receives a visionary revelation as he looks down from the highest heaven through the lower heavens to earth. In both cases the narrative section is a distinctive narrative development of an already existing and well-known legend about the hero: Abraham's rejection of idolatry and conversion to monotheism, Isaiah's martyrdom by being sawn apart on the orders of Manasseh.

Nebuchadnezzar's dream, in chapter 2 of Daniel, provides, as we have noted, a kind of parallel to the account of Isaiah's vision in Ascension of Isaiah 3:13-4:22. It resembles in broad outline the themes of the visions in Daniel 7-12, but it is not actually the same vision as any of those recounted in chapters 7-12. So it does not provide an exact parallel to the Ascension of Isaiah's two complementary accounts of the same vision, one of them within the narrative section. But the phenomenon of two different accounts which differ in ways that the reader must suppose to be complementary rather than contradictory is found, for example, in Acts, where the three differing accounts of Paul's experiences on the road to Damascus and soon after (9:1-24; 22:4-21; 26:9-18) must surely be read in this way. An example which is generically much closer to the Ascension of Isaiah can be found in 2 Enoch, where Enoch's tour of the heavens is recounted twice, first as the narrative of Enoch's ascent through the

---

[33] The Book of Watchers (1 Enoch 1-36), which may be earlier than Daniel, has, following the introduction (1-5), a narrative section and a section of visionary journeys. The structure is less clearly parallel to Daniel's, but it provides another example of the combination of narrative and apocalyptic vision.

heavens (3-36) and then as Enoch's own report of the same events given to his sons (3-36, 39-43). The two accounts differ considerably, but should be read as complementary, not as alternatives or as contradictory. There is no difficulty at all in supposing that the two versions of Isaiah's vision have been designed to complement each other. Their complementary nature is in fact quite clear in that each summarizes briefly what the other presents at greater length, as we have already observed.

The occurrence of a title ('The Vision which Isaiah the son of Amoz saw') at the beginning of the second part of the Ascension of Isaiah is quite consistent with our claim about the generic unity of the work, since this encompasses rather than ignoring the sharp distinction between the two parts of the work. We should notice that, in the canonical book of Isaiah, this form of words is used not only for the title of the whole book (1:1) but also as the superscription of a specific oracle within the book (2:1; cf. 13:1).

IV

We have argued that, once the genre of the Ascension of Isaiah as a whole is correctly identified as a composite genre consisting of a narrative section and a visionary section, as in Daniel, then the clear formal distinction between the two parts is not an impediment to recognizing the unity of the whole work, but is appropriately contained within the kind of formal unity appropriate to this genre. But Norelli's case does not rest on formal criteria alone; it also depends on stressing the difference of content and perspective between chapters 1-5 and chapters 6-11. At this point his argument has to be rather carefully balanced. In his view the author of chapters 1-5 attributed high authority to the vision of Isaiah as recounted in chapters 6-11. Indeed, he wrote to defend its authority against attacks (3:31). He attached his own work to the already existing chapters 6-11, creating a new whole. This would hardly be possible if the contents of the two parts were in blatant contradiction, though Norelli sometimes comes close to reading them as actually contradictory.[34] What he does argue is that the content and perspective of the two parts diverge so widely in emphasis and interest as to make it implausible that one author could have composed them as a single work.

As Norelli argues, there is a clear contrast between the emphasis on the temporal or 'horizontal' dimension in the first part and the

---

[34] E.g. Norelli, *Ascensio Isaiae: Commentarius*, 45.

emphasis on the spatial or 'vertical' dimension in the second part. The first part tells a story of earthly events, the struggle between true and false prophecy in which the true prophets are persecuted. Its version of Isaiah's vision, while alluding briefly to the Beloved's descent and ascent, focuses on the growth and crisis of the church on earth, and the parousia in the eschatological future. The second part recounts Isaiah's visionary ascent through the upper levels of the cosmos, and the visionary revelation in which he sees the Beloved descend and ascend. In the perspective of the first part, the powers of evil are at work in historical persons and earthly events, and will be destroyed in the future by Christ. In the second part, the interest is in the cosmological dimension, in which the powers of evil occupy the lowest level of the heavens. Christ in his ascension to heaven has already achieved their submission and restored the whole cosmos to divine rule. (While Norelli says that this does not have to mean that the author of chapters 6-11 did not expect a future parousia, he maintains that it could not have been of primary importance to him.[35]) Finally, in line with the differences already noted, the first part offers believers a collective eschatological hope for the future, while the second part sees their destiny as ascension to heaven at death, made possible by the already accomplished subjugation of the hostile powers by Christ.[36]

This characterization of the contrasting contents and concerns of the two parts of the work is broadly correct. The important question is whether the differences entail such a degree of tension between the two parts that they could not have been written as the two parts of a single work, or whether they could be understood as deliberately complementary emphases in a work which explores one aspect of its subject in the first part, another in the second.

The two dimensions which are emphasized respectively in the two parts—horizontal and vertical, temporal and spatial, historical-eschatological and cosmological—are both aspects of the worldview of the Jewish and Christian apocalypses, though the emphasis varies. It is true that there is a certain tension between them in the Ascension of Isaiah. The view that the destiny of the righteous is to ascend to heavenly glory (symbolized by their heavenly robes, thrones and crowns), surmounting the vast distance that separates this world from the divine world above, is not obviously very compatible with the eschatological hope for the coming of God's kingdom in this world.

---

[35] Norelli, *Ascensio Isaiae: Commentarius*, 38.
[36] Norelli, *Ascensio Isaiae: Commentarius*, 37-39, 44-45.

But the tension can be observed not only between the two parts of the Ascension of Isaiah, but also within the first part itself. At the parousia the saints who are already in the seventh heaven in glory descend to earth, wearing their heavenly robes (glorious heavenly bodies), with Christ. They join with the believers on earth who are alive at the parousia, and appear to spend a period on earth before ascending to heaven along with those believers, who at this point leave their earthly bodies behind on earth and acquire their heavenly robes. The resurrection, judgment and destruction of all evil follow (4:14-18).[37] This passage combines the expectation that Christ will finally eliminate evil from this world with the conviction that this material world must pass away and the righteous find their destiny in heavenly glory above. Salvation has both a temporal aspect—at the eschatological consummation of the history of this world—and a spatial aspect—in the ascent to heaven. The occurrence of both in 4:14-18 makes it possible that the emphases of the two parts of the work do not, as Norelli maintains,[38] represent a shift of emphasis within the group to which the authors of the two parts belonged, but are deliberately complementary.

To the two dimensions—spatial and temporal—there also correspond in early Christianity the beliefs that Christ has already gained the submission of all the powers, including the forces of evil, and that he will finally defeat and destroy evil at his parousia in the future. The tension between these two perspectives in the Ascension of Isaiah is by no means unique. For example, in chapter 5 of the book of Revelation, the exalted Christ is seen triumphant on the divine throne in heaven and receives the worship of every creature in the universe, but the rest of the book continues with its own version of the kind of prophetic expectation of demonic domination in the world followed by Christ's final destruction of evil at his parousia that is found also in Ascension of Isaiah 4:2-18. Norelli himself admits that the subjection of all the powers to the exalted Christ in Ephesians 1:20-22 evidently does not exclude the continuing warfare of believers with the supernatural forces of evil which is depicted in 6:10-17 (cf. also 1 Pet 3:22; 5:8).

However, we should also note that Norelli's view that chapters 6-11 of the Ascension of Isaiah make no reference at all to a future

---

[37] On the combination of earthly and heavenly eschatology in this passage, see C.E. Hill, *Regnum Caelorum: Patterns of Future Hope in Early Christianity* (Oxford: Clarendon Press, 1992) 94-95 (a discussion marred by its acceptance of Charles's source theory); Knight, *Disciples*, 241-244, 259.

[38] Norelli, *Ascensio Isaiae: Commentarius*, 52.

eschatological prospect involving the destruction of the powers of evil rests on debatable exegetical grounds. It is extremely unfortunate that in the narrative of Christ's ascent through the heavens following his resurrection a crucial passage has fallen out in all versions of the text, presumably owing to homoeoteleuton at an early stage of the transmission of the Greek text. In the text we have 11:23-24 describes the response of Satan and the (evil) angels of the firmament when Christ ascends in glory. This should be followed by an account of his ascent to the first heaven, but verse 25 continues with his ascent to the second heaven. It may be that what now reads as the response of Satan and the angels of the firmament was originally that of the angels of the first heaven, and that the response of the Satan and the angels of the firmament has dropped out of the text. Their submission to Christ must have been recorded (cf. 10:15: 'the princes and the powers of that world will worship you'), but we cannot be sure that the precise form of their response has been preserved.

Probably more important are the two passages that refer to Christ's destruction of the evil powers: 'until the one comes whom you are to see, and he will destroy him [Satan]' (8:12); 'that you [Christ] may judge and destroy the princes and the angels and the gods of that world, and the world which is ruled by them' (10:12). This latter passage closely resembles 1:5: 'concerning the judgment of the angels, and concerning the destruction of this world.' This certainly refers to what is to happen at the parousia (4:14-18), but Norelli takes 7:12 and 10:12 to refer to the submission of the powers of evil to the risen and glorious Christ at the time of his ascension.[39] However, since these powers worship Christ (10:15), they are clearly not 'destroyed' (although the Greek is not extant for these verses, it must have had καθαιρέω[40]) at that time. Norelli's attempt to evade this problem, by supposing that not the powers but their rebelliousness is destroyed,[41] is unconvincing.[42] These verses must look beyond the submission of the powers to Christ at his exaltation and envisage the

---

[39] Norelli, *Ascensio Isaiae: Commentarius*, 388, 519.

[40] Charles, *The Ascension*, 106.

[41] Norelli, *Ascensio Isaiae: Commentarius*, 519. The Ethiopic verb is the same in 7:12 and 10:12, while 1:5 has the cognate substantive.

[42] The sequence in 10:12-14 need not mean that Christ's ascension (14) follows his judgment and destruction of the powers of evil (12b) (*contra* Norelli, *Ascensio Isaiae: Commentarius*, 518; Knight, *Disciples*, 65), only that it follows God's summoning of Christ (12a). Since v 14 refers to Christ's ascension *from Sheol* to the seventh heaven ('from the gods of death to your place'), it cannot in fact follow the submission of the powers of evil which takes place when Christ ascends to the firmament. The 'afterwards' of v 14 looks back to God's summoning in v 12.

future judgment and destruction of the powers at his parousia. This means that the perspective of chapters 6-11 is not as exclusively focused on the past and present, to the exclusion of future eschatology, as Norelli maintains. In order consistently to maintain this view, he also has to take 'the end of this age (αἰών[43])' (11:37) in the unlikely sense of what Christ has already achieved in his descent and ascent.[44]

However, an argument that the different emphases of the two parts of the Ascension of Isaiah are complementary and belong to the original design of the whole work must explain why an author should have so systematically divided his subject-matter into these two aspects, each assigned to one part of his work, with no more than brief references in each case to the aspect treated in the other part.[45] The answer lies once again in giving full recognition to the genre. Already in the book of Daniel it is to some degree the case that, while the narratives adopt a 'horizontal' perspective within the course of historical events on earth, the visions enter the 'vertical' dimension of the divine world above the human. Though concerned with history and future eschatology, they give Daniel a heavenly perspective which not even his interpretation of Nebuchadnezzar's dream in chapter 2 had adopted.

By adopting the composite genre of narrative and vision, the author of the Ascension of Isaiah was able to exploit the full possibilities of exploring the two perspectives in a complementary way. The story of Isaiah's persecution and martyrdom requires a temporal and historical perspective, and it raises the issue of evil in terms of conflict in the earthly, historical sphere. From this perspective the appropriate divine revelation is of the coming defeat and destruction of evil in the eschatological future. Isaiah's visionary ascent through the heavens, on the other hand, enables the heavenly perspective which can only be had from this unique vantage-point, and it confronts and resolves the issue of evil in terms of cosmological rebellion and subjugation. From this perspective the appropriate divine revelation is of the assertion of divine rule throughout the cosmic order, from the divine throne in the seventh heaven down to Hades where the dead were held captive.

The deliberate complementarity of these two perspectives can be better appreciated if we return to the way in which the two accounts of Isaiah's vision (3:13-4:22 and 7:1-11:40) differ in complementary

---

[43] The Greek word is preserved in the Coptic version: Bettiolo et al., *Ascensio Isaiae: Textus*, 187.

[44] Norelli, *Ascensio Isaiae: Commentarius*, 593.

[45] Cf. Norelli, *Ascensio Isaiae: Commentarius*, 37.

fashion. The story of the Beloved's descent and ascent is recognizably the same story in both cases (3:13-18; 10:17-11:33; and cf. also 9:13-17; 10:8-15), but the focus of the description is quite different. In chapter 3 the focus is on the earthly, observable events, including the Beloved's exit from the tomb in the presence of eyewitnesses (3:14-17). The consequences of his resurrection are the church's mission to the nations and the charismatic life of the early church. The reader is not taken back into heaven with the Beloved, but along the temporal, historical line that leads through the decay of the church—the earthly situation in which the first readers are to recognize their own context—to the coming earthly manifestation of Beliar's power and the coming of Christ to defeat evil and to save his people here in this world. In chapters 10-11, on the other hand, the focus is on what is not observable on earth but is visible to Isaiah from his visionary place in heaven: the beloved's secret descent through the heavens, Satan's activity against him (11:19), his descent to Hades (11:20), his ascent in glory through the heavens and his enthronement at God's right hand.

This second and longer account includes, of course, the narrative of his miraculous birth (11:2-17).[46] For the most part both accounts of the Beloved's career are in 'kerygmatic summary' form,[47] but each develops a fuller narrative in just one instance: in the first account the Beloved's exit from the tomb (3:14-17), in the second his miraculous birth (11:2-17). These are parallel and complementary: the Beloved's miraculous birth is that stage of his descent from the seventh heaven to Hades at which he enters human life on earth, while his resurrection and exit from the tomb is that stage of his ascent from Hades to the seventh heaven at which he appears again in the human world. But whereas the latter is portrayed as the visible manifestation of the Beloved in his true glory in the world, the former is his hidden entry into human life (11:4, 11, 14, 16, 17). That this child is the Beloved in human form can be seen only by Isaiah from his heavenly perspective.

Both parts of the Ascension of Isaiah are concerned with the evil powers and Christ's triumph over them. In the historical world in which the readers live corruption and apostasy in the church (3:21-

---

[46] Against the view that 11:2-22 (absent in SL²) is a later interpolation, see Charles, *The Ascension*, xxii-xxiv; A. Vaillant, 'Un apocryphe pseudo-bogomile: la Vision d'Isaïe,' *Revue des Études slaves* 42 (1963) 111-112; Norelli, *Ascensio Isaiae: Commentarius*, 42-43, 535-538; idem, *L'Ascensione*, 265-269.

[47] See R. Bauckham, 'Kerygmatic summaries in the speeches of Acts,' in B. Witherington ed., *History, Literature and Society in the Book of Acts* (Cambridge: Cambridge University Press, 1996) 185-217 (191-204 on Ascension of Isaiah).

31) are preparing the way for the apparent triumph of Beliar in the world (4:1-13). Like Isaiah and his fellow-prophets faithful believers must suffer in this world at the hands of Beliar: opposition from false prophets, persecution, martyrdom and flight. But paradoxically it is Beliar's knowledge that he is doomed to destruction that incites his fury against Isaiah (3:13; 5:1, 15-16; 11:41)[48] and against those who believe and disseminate Isaiah's vision in the last days. Isaiah foresaw the destruction of Beliar by the Beloved, and so the believers can await his coming (4:13) with hope. But Isaiah's vision also has more to offer them, if as readers they follow his ascent to heaven and share his heavenly vision of the cosmic event of the Beloved's descent and ascent. From this heavenly perspective they can see that the powers of evil in their superterrestrial stronghold have already admitted defeat, the dead have already ascended with Christ from Sheol to heavenly glory, and Christ has already established his divine sovereignty over the whole cosmos. This is the 'vertical' truth of things, which can be seen only from the unique perspective of the visionary in the seventh heaven. It stands in tension with the 'horizontal' reality of suffering and apostasy, persecution and the dominion of Beliar on earth. But in the lived experience of the readers the tension is no doubt a positive, not a negative factor. The 'vertical' reality cannot cancel the 'horizontal' but it can complement it. At the end of the work, readers who have been, as it were, taken up into heaven with Isaiah and seen the achieved reality of Christ's cosmic triumph over evil are brought back into the historical world of continuing conflict. For even Isaiah cannot remain in heaven. He must return to earth and to the body, and he must suffer martyrdom at the instigation of Satan before he can ascend to share Christ's triumph in heaven (11:34-35, 41-43).[49]

---

[48] Acerbi, L'Ascensione, 259, argues that these passages are inconsistent with the idea found in chapters 6-11 that the Beloved's descent and his identity while on earth are hidden from Satan (10:17-11:24). If this is an inconsistency, it is surely an inconsistency of which a single author is capable. But it may not be. That Satan knows that Isaiah predicted the descent of the Beloved and his own destruction need not mean that he was able to recognize the Beloved when he actually descended.

[49] Knight, Disciples, 264-267, argues for the complementary nature of the different eschatological perspectives in what he calls the First and Second Visions, specifically with reference to the social function of the Second: 'The Second Vision encourages readers to persevere until the parousia by reminding them that the decisive victory over Beliar has already been secured' (267).

V

Most recent studies have dated the Ascension of Isaiah or its constituent parts and redaction in the period from the late first century to the early decades of the second century c.e.[50] The criteria used are mostly indicative only of a very approximate date. Of course, theories of the composite nature of the work can lead to attempts to date the constituent parts separately. Charles dated all three constituent parts of the work, on his view, to the first century (the two Christian parts to the end of the century), but the final redaction of the whole work in the late second or early third century.[51] Norelli dates chapters 6-11 to the end of the first century and chapters 1-5 to the beginning of the second century.[52] In this section we shall focus on only those indications of date which have the potential for being relatively precise and we shall presuppose the unity of the work, for which we have argued.

The most promising indications of date may be expected from the section of apocalyptic prophecy 3:21-4:18, which certainly provides a firm *terminus a quo* in its reference to the martyrdom of Peter (4:3) in 64 or 65 c.e.[53] However, the description of the state of the church in 3:21-30 is not especially helpful for dating, since it depicts the church as the author saw it. 3:27 does not mean that there are no longer many Christian prophets, but only that the author considers few of the Christian prophets to be true prophets. Bagatti[54] finds in 3:21-23 a reference to the struggle between Thebuthis and Simeon son of Clopas for the leadership of the Jerusalem church after the death of James (Hegesippus, ap. Eusebius, *Hist. Eccl.* 4.22.5), but this would be plausible only if there were other indications of such a context. He also sees a reference to the Jerusalem Christians' flight to Pella in 4:13,[55] but the flight of the righteous from Antichrist into the desert is

---

[50] E.g. Pesce, *Isaia*, 299-300, reporting the views of several at the 1981 Rome conference, and M. Simonetti, 'Note sulla cristologia dell'*Ascensione di Isaia*,' in Pesce, *Isaia*, 204 (1st half of 2nd century); Acerbi, *L'Ascensione*, 277-282 (100-130 C.E.); Hall, 'The *Ascension of Isaiah*,' 300-306 (early 2nd century); Knight, *Disciples*, 33-39 (112-138 C.E.).

[51] Charles, *The Ascension*, xliv-xlv.

[52] Norelli, *Ascensio Isaiae: Commentarius*, 65-66.

[53] R. Bauckham, 'The Martyrdom of Peter in Early Christian Literature,' in *Aufstieg und Niedergang der römischen Welt*, Part II, vol. 26/1, ed. W. Haase (Berlin/New York: de Gruyter, 1992) 539-595 (566-570 on the *Ascension of Isaiah*).

[54] B. Bagatti, *L'Eglise de la Circoncision* (Jerusalem: Franciscan Publishing House, 1965) 8; and cf. Norelli, *Ascensio Isaiae: Commentarius*, 263-264.

[55] So also F. Neirynck, 'Marc 13: Examen Critique de l'Interprétation de R. Pesch,' in idem, *Evangelica* (ed. F. van Segbroeck; BETL 60; Leuven: Peeters/Leuven University Press, 1982) 567.

a traditional apocalyptic motif[56] and is almost certainly still future from the author's point of view. The absence of reference to the fall of Jerusalem in 70 c.e.[57] is probably insignificant, since the author is preoccupied here with the current state of the churches he knew and their approaching encounter with Antichrist.

Two features of chapter 4 have attracted special attention as possible indications of date: the reference to Beliar's appearance in the form of Nero (4:2-4) and the apparent indication that some of those who had seen Jesus in the flesh are still living (4:13). The reference to a king who is a matricide is certainly intended to identify Nero: this most notorious of his crimes was standardly used to identify Nero, and was so used in expectations of his return (SibOr 4:121; 5:145, 363; 8:71). Some have therefore supposed that this section of the Ascension of Isaiah was written during Nero's reign, with the time-period of 4:12, 14 being reckoned from Peter's martyrdom.[58] In fact, however, the reign of Beliar in the form of Nero is an expected second reign of Nero, who was widely expected to return after his supposed death.[59] The reference back to the events of the historical reign of Nero in 4:2-3 is made in order to identify Beliar with Nero, but from verse 4 onwards the reference is to Beliar's coming (still future for the author and his readers) as the returning Nero. This coming reign of Beliar-Nero is described entirely in traditional terms from the apocalyptic tradition (4:4-12), with no further reference (after verses 2-3) to any features specific to the Nero legend. This means that, of the three forms of the legend of Nero's return which I have elsewhere distinguished in Jewish and Christian literature (especially

---

[56] W. Bousset, *The Antichrist Legend* (tr. A. H. Keane; London: Hutchinson, 1896) 212-214.

[57] Surprisingly, this argument is not used by J. A. T. Robinson, *Redating the New Testament* (London: SCM Press, 1976) 240 n.98. Knight, *Disciples*, 38-39, thinks 3:6-10 *does* refer to the fall of Jerusalem in 70 c.e., but this is to read the story of Isaiah in too allegorical a way.

[58] R. Laurence, *Ascensio Isaiae Vatis* (Oxford: Oxford University Press, 1819) 171-177; J. V. Bartlet, *The Apostolic Age* (Edinburgh: T. & T. Clark, 1900) 524; M. Guarducci, 'La Data del Martirio di San Pietro,' *La Parola del Passato* 23 (1968) 101-111; Robinson, *Redating*, 239-240 n.98; cf. discussion in Bauckham, 'The Martyrdom of Peter,' 569-570.

[59] On the legend of Nero's return, see Charles, *The Ascension*, lxvii-lxxxiii; P. Prigent, 'Au temps de l'Apocalypse: Le culte impérial au 1er siècle en Asie Mineure,' *RHPR* 55 (1975) 227-230; J. J. Collins, *The Sibylline Oracles of Egyptian Judaism* (SBLDS 13; Missoula, Montana: Scholars Press, 1974) 80-87; A. Yarbro Collins, *The Combat Myth in the Book of Revelation* (HDR 9; Missoula, Montana: Scholars Press, 1976) 176-183; L. Kreitzer, 'Hadrian and the Nero Redivivus Myth,' *ZNW* 79 (1988) 92-115; R. Bauckham, *The Climax of Prophecy: Studies on the Book of Revelation* (Edinburgh: T. & T. Clark, 1993) 407-431.

the Sibylline Oracles),[60] our passage in the Ascension of Isaiah is an example of the third form and quite closely resembles the Jewish Sibylline Oracle 3:63-74 (which also uses the name Beliar).[61]

The expectation of Nero's return originated very soon after his death (when it was widely believed that he had not died but had gone into hiding).[62] The first of the impostors who actually claimed to be Nero appeared around July 69 C.E., about a year after Nero's death. The last we hear of pagan expectations of Nero's return is a remark by Dio Chrysostom, writing around the end of the first century, who indicates that it was still lively and popular (*Orat.* 21.10). The Jewish Sibylline Oracles (the third, fourth and fifth) in which the expectation of Nero's return is prominent probably date from the period c.80 C.E. (SibOr 5)[63] to the early second century, but the material is intrinsically difficult to date, partly because the Oracles were frequently interpolated and updated. But it may be significant that in the Christian book 2, which must date from the middle to late second century, the legend is not used (despite a passage which resembles Ascension of Isaiah 4 in lines 165-169, 179-183), while in books 7 and 8 (probably later second century) it receives only brief mention (8:70-71, cf. 139-147). It remained part of the Christian apocalyptic tradition even in the third, fourth and fifth centuries (Lactantius, *De Mort. Pers.* 2.7-9; Commodian, *Carmen de duobus populis* 825-830; Augustine, *De Civ. Dei* 20.19), buts its period of vigorous life would seem to have been in the half-century or so following Nero's death. It is therefore in this period that the Ascension of Isaiah can, on this evidence, be most plausibly dated.

The use of the legend of Nero's return cannot date the work any more precisely. The three Jewish and Christian forms of the legend cannot be treated as successive phases of development. Charles' attempt to chart stages in the development of the legend,[64] suggesting that the form in Ascension of Isaiah 4 must date from a period when it would no longer have been thought that Nero was still alive, in hiding in the east, is misguided. The passage of time did not prevent

---

[60] Bauckham, *The Climax*, 414-423.

[61] Bauckham, *The Climax*, 419-421.

[62] The common term '*Nero redivivus* myth' is a misnomer: the usual belief was that Nero had not died but had gone into hiding, and this belief, with the expectation of his reappearance, persisted long after his natural span of life would have ended: see Bauckham, *The Climax*, 421-423.

[63] Bauckham, *The Climax*, 416.

[64] Charles, *The Ascension*, lxvii-lxxiii; idem, *A critical and exegetical commentary on the Revelation of St John*, vol. 2 (Edinburgh: T. & T. Clark, 1920) 76-85.

people from continuing to think of Nero as surviving alive.[65] In any
case, the real significance of the legend for the author of the Ascension of Isaiah was that it made possible the idea of Beliar's descent
and appearance on earth in human form, parallel to those of the
Beloved. Such a use of the Nero legend was probably possible at any
time after 69 C.E. The Beliar-Nero material therefore advances the
terminus a quo for the date of the work only to 69.

4:13 has often been held to provide a rough *terminus ad quem* in the
later first century C.E., since it appears to mean that some of those
who had seen Jesus are still living at the time of writing. Only the
Ethiopic version is extant:

> And of many believers and saints, when they have seen the one for whom
> they hoped, the one who was crucified, Jesus the Lord Christ—after I,
> Isaiah, have seen the one who was crucified and ascended—and also of
> those who believed in him, few will be left in those days, as his servants,
> fleeing from desert to desert and awaiting the coming of the Beloved.[66]

If we accept this rather awkward text without emendation, it apparently refers to two categories of believers: those who had seen Jesus
('many believers and saints, when they have seen the one for whom
they hoped, the one who was crucified, Jesus the Lord Christ') and
others who had not ('those who believed in him'). At the time predicted there will be few Christians of either category left. This does
not mean, as Charles supposed,[67] that at the time when the author
wrote few Christians who had seen the Lord were still alive. The text
refers to a time which from the author's perspective is in the future,
and the fact that there will then be few Christians results from the
apostasy of the majority of Christians as predicted in 4:9. It is not that
only a few of those who had seen the Lord will still be alive, but that
few of them will remain 'as his servants,' just as also few of those who
believed in Jesus without seeing him will remain faithful Christians.
Probably those who had seen the Lord are mentioned because the
author holds the early Christian expectation, not yet disappointed,
that the parousia would occur within the lifetime of the generation to
which the apostles belonged. In that case the passage—and, on our
view, the Ascension of Isaiah as a whole—must date from a time
when more than a few of this generation were still alive, i.e. before c.
80 C.E.

---

[65] Bauckham, *The Climax*, 421-422.
[66] The translation is based on Bettiolo et al., *Ascensio Isaiae: Textus*, 68.
[67] Charles, *The Ascension*, 51.

Major possibilities of interpreting the text in a different way are two. First, the text may be considered corrupt and emended. Bousset proposed the following emendation:

> And (there shall be) many believers and saints, who on seeing the one they did not expect shall flee from desert to desert awaiting coming of the Beloved.[68]

This emendation excises all reference to Jesus and inserts a negative ('the one they did *not* expect'), with the result that the person the believers have seen is not Christ but the Antichrist,[69] who has been described in the immediately preceding passage (4:2-12). Bousset argues that 'the one they did not expect' was an apocalyptic technical term for the eschatological adversary or Antichrist, citing 4 Ezra 5:6 (*regnabit quem non sperant qui inhabitant super terram:* 'one shall reign whom those who dwell on earth do not expect'[70]) and the Armenian Seventh Vision of Daniel[71] ('then the Antichrist shall rule, and men shall turn aside from the worship of God and become unbelievers, through the coming of him whom they did not seek nor expect, who is an adversary unto all'[72]). The emendation is initially attractive, since it gives a sense which fits the context well. It is easy to see how, if the negative were omitted accidentally, the rest of the text in the Ethiopic version could have arisen out of the attempt to identify 'the one they expected' as Jesus.

However, there are very serious objections to Bousset's emendation. First, the vocabulary of the parts of the text Bousset excises is typical of the Ascension of Isaiah, especially in this section: 'believers

---

[68] Bousset, *The Antichrist*, 214, cf. 138. Bousset has 'his coming,' but the problem that 'his' then has no antecedent is avoided by following those MSS of the Ethiopic which read 'the coming of the Beloved.'

[69] Bousset, *The Antichrist*, 138.

[70] The parallel to this phrase in Sir 11:5 suggests the meaning that this figure will not succeed to a throne, but will be someone noone would have expected to become a ruler.

[71] This Armenian text is a translation of a Greek original, probably of the late fifth or early sixth century CE: P. J. Alexander, *The Oracle of Baalbek: The Tiburtine Sibyl in Greek Dress* (Dumbarton Oaks Studies 10; Washington: Dumbarton Oaks Centre for Byzantine Studies, 1967) 118-119. (But S. J. Voicu, 'Gli Apocrifi armeni,' *Augustinianum* 23 [1983] 170, assigns it to the seventh century.) Such Byzantine apocalypses sometimes preserve old Jewish apocalyptic traditions (cf. P. J. Alexander, *The Byzantine Apocalyptic Tradition* [ed. D deF. Abrahamse; Berkeley: University of California Press, 1985] 133-135, 174-181).

[72] Translation in J. Issaverdens, *The uncanonical writings of the Old Testament found in the Armenian MSS. of the Library of St. Lazarus* (Venice: Armenian Monastery of St Lazarus, 1901) 344-345.

in him' (cf. 3:19; 8:26), 'in those days' (cf. 3:20, 23, 25, 27; 4:18), 'his servants' (cf. 3:28),[73] 'Jesus the Lord Christ' (cf. 9:5, 17; 10:7[74]). Secondly, it does not, on closer consideration, provide an acceptable sense in the context. In the parallels cited those who 'did not expect' the Antichrist are either people in general (4 Ezra: 'those who dwell on earth') or Christians who are taken in by the Antichrist and apostatize (Seventh Vision of Daniel), whereas in Bousset's emendation of Ascension of Isaiah 4:13 they are the Christian believers who remain faithful and flee from the Antichrist. These are precisely the people who *do* expect the Antichrist and are therefore not deceived by him. They have been forewarned of him by prophecies including this chapter of the Ascension of Isaiah itself! The Seventh Vision of Daniel clearly distinguishes the apostates who 'did not seek or expect' the Antichrist from the 'pious men' who 'will know and mark the adversary of all mankind,' since they have been forewarned of his signs.[75]

The passage in the Seventh Vision of Daniel suggests the possibility of an alternative emendation. Of those Christians who 'became unbelievers, through the coming of him whom they did not seek or expect,' it further remarks that 'their eyes shall be closed and turn no more unto him in whom before they had hoped,' i.e. Christ.[76] Perhaps the original text of the Ascension of Isaiah referred, in ironic contrast, both to the Antichrist 'for whom they did not hope' and to Christ 'for whom they had hoped before.' The following emended text could be proposed:

> And many believers and saints, when they have seen the one for whom they [did not hope, shall turn aside from him for whom before they] hoped, the one who was crucified, Jesus the Lord Christ, ... and of those who believed in him, few will be left in those days, as his servants, fleeing from desert to desert and awaiting the coming of the Beloved.

The bracketed words could have fallen out by homoeoteleuton. However, the proposal has two disadvantages. First, the emendation requires the excision of the words 'after I, Isaiah, have seen the one who was crucified and ascended' as a later interpolation, added after the bracketed words had fallen out of the text. This parenthetical

---

[73] On this term (as part of a complex of imagery derived from the parable in Luke 12:35-38 in AscenIs 3:28-4:16), see Norelli, *Ascensio Isaiae: Commentarius*, 270.

[74] In all these cases the Ethiopic version should be preferred to SL[2] which regularly change the christological terminology of the *Ascension of Isaiah*, eliminating 'Jesus' and 'Christ.' In 10:7 the Ethiopic is supported by Greek Legend 2:37, 41.

[75] Issaverdens, *The uncanonical writings*, 345.

[76] Issaverdens, *The uncanonical writings*, 344-345.

clause is admittedly awkward and may be secondary.[77] Perhaps a scribe who found the preceding words puzzling offered these words in the margin as an alternative, which then became incorporated into the text as an addition. The second disadvantage in the proposed emendation is therefore more serious. It is that this verse would then repeat, quite superfluously, the reference to apostasy which has already occurred in 4:9.

The final major proposal for interpreting this verse accepts the text as it stands and presses the parallel between the two clauses 'when they have seen the one for whom they hoped, the one who was crucified' and 'after I, Isaiah, have seen the one who was crucified and ascended.' Erbetta[78] and Norelli[79] both connect these two clauses closely, insisting on the same sense of 'see' in both cases, and both deny that the first refers to seeing the earthly Jesus during his earthly life. Erbetta thinks that the believers are Jewish Christians who had shared the Jewish messianic hope and then have 'seen' in the sense of 'recognised' the one for whom they had hoped, aided in this by Isaiah's vision of the crucified and ascended one (chapters 6-11). But, as Norelli points out, Isaiah's vision cannot be understood as 'recognition' of the one who fulfils the Jewish messianic hope. Norelli himself proposes that the believers in question are those who have seen Christ in a visionary ascent to heaven like Isaiah's. Isaiah's own vision is mentioned here as providing the model for that of Christian prophets. A possible objection to this proposal is that the Ascension of Isaiah seems to insist that Isaiah's experience is unique (8:11-12; 11:34; cf. 7:23). Strictly speaking these texts only state that noone before Isaiah had had such an experience, and so they leave open the possibility that Isaiah's experience was paralleled in the Christian prophetic circle from which the Ascension of Isaiah comes. The resemblances between the account of Isaiah's ascent and the later Hebrew Hekhalot literature[80] show that mystical experiences must lie in some way behind the Ascension of Isaiah, but it is nevertheless the case that the work itself says nothing to imply that ascents like Isaiah's

---

[77] Charles, *The Ascension*, 31-32, treats it as an interpolation, but as one made when (according to his source theory) the Testament of Hezekiah (3:13-4:18) was incorporated into its present context as a report of a vision by Isaiah. The interpolation serves 'to adapt the Testament of Hezekiah to its present context.'

[78] M. Erbetta, *Gli Apocrifi del Nuovo Testamento*, vol. 3: *Lettere e Apocalissi* (Casale Monferrato: Marietti, 1981) 190-191. I have not seen Erbetta's fuller argument in 'Ascensione di Isaia IV 3 è la testimonianza più antica del martirio di Pietro?,' *Euntes docet* 19 (1966) 427-436.

[79] Norelli, *Ascensio Isaiae: Commentarius*, 260-261.

[80] Bauckham, *The Climax*, 140-143.

were practised in the author's prophetic circle. One might ask what function a distinction between the prophets who practised visionary ascent and other believers would have in the context of 4:13. But a more decisive objection to Norelli's proposal is that the object of vision is in fact differently described in the two cases: the Christian believers have seen 'the one who was crucified, Jesus the Lord Christ' whereas Isaiah has seen 'the one who was crucified and ascended.' The two phrases distinguish the earthly Jesus seen by disciples during his earthly life and the ascended Lord seen by Isaiah in vision. The parallels later in the work to the phrase 'Jesus the Lord Christ' are 'the Lord Christ, who is to be called in the world Jesus' (9:5) and 'my Lord Christ who will be called Jesus [in this world]' (10:7).[81] These are the only three occurrences of the name 'Jesus' in the Ascension of Isaiah. They make it clear that it is the name by which the earthly Jesus is called in this world. It is not even used when Isaiah, in vision, sees him on earth (11:2-21) because Isaiah from his heavenly perspective knows him as the Lord. Only in his earthly appearance is the Beloved known in this world as Jesus. The phrase 'Jesus the Lord Christ' (4:13) therefore indicates that these believers know him to be 'the Lord Christ' but have seen him precisely in his earthly sojourn in the human form Jesus.

While it is not possible to be entirely sure that the text of 4:13 in the Ethiopic version corresponds exactly to the original text, the most probable interpretation is that the verse does refer to believers who had seen Jesus in the flesh and are still living at the time of writing. However, this interpretation can be considerably strengthened when the whole of the Ascension of Isaiah is seen as a single work, as we have argued it should be. In that case another, corresponding indication that the work was written during the first Christian generation is found in 11:37-38: 'and the end of this age and the whole of this vision will be accomplished in the last generation.'[82] It would make no sense to describe the generation in which the descent and ascent of the Beloved (10:17-11:33) occur as the last generation, unless it is also the generation in which the parousia and the end of the world occur. The 'whole of this vision' comprehends the two complementary accounts of Isaiah's vision, i.e. the account in 3:13-4:22, which reaches

---

[81] Greek Legend 2:37 probably preserves the original Greek of this verse: τῷ κυρίῳ μου καὶ Χριστῷ ὃς κληθήσεται Ἰησοῦς ἐν τῷ κόσμῳ τούτῳ.

[82] This sense is given by E and S, and supported by the Coptic fragment. L² has what is clearly a correction designed to avoid the implication that all that Isaiah saw would occur in the last generation of history: *Consummatio seculi huius et opera implebuntur in novissimis generationibus.*

as far as the parousia and the final judgment, as well as the account in 10:17-11:33 which concludes with Christ's enthronement at the right hand of God. An intelligible sense can be given to 11:37-38 only if these verses presuppose both parts of the Ascension of Isaiah and presuppose the early Christian view that the generation of those who saw Jesus in the flesh was the last generation of history,[83] in whose lifetime the parousia and the end of the age would also occur.[84]

The conclusion is that the Ascension of Isaiah most probably dates from the decade 70-80 C.E. If this is correct, it makes even more obvious what is clear even if one prefers the rather later dates which recent scholarship has proposed: that the Ascension of Isaiah is a work of very considerable relevance to the study of the New Testament and earliest Christianity.[85] Now that definitive editions of the texts and major studies of the work are available, the time has come to end the extraordinary neglect of this work by New Testament scholars.[86] Issues which deserve much more extensive study include: the affinities between the worldview of the Ascension of Isaiah and that of the Gospel of John;[87] the possibility that the Ascension of Isaiah, which is certainly not Gnostic, documents a development of the Jewish apocalyptic worldview in the direction of later Gnosticism;[88] its place in the development of trinitarian belief and of docetic

---

[83] Cf. R. Bauckham, *Jude, 2 Peter* (WBC 50; Waco: Word Books, 1983) 290-293; idem, 'The Two Fig Tree Parables in the Apocalypse of Peter,' *JBL* 104 (1985) 276-277; idem, *Jude and the Relatives of Jesus in the Early Church* (Edinburgh: T. & T. Clark, 1990) 318-326, 364. Relevant texts are Matt 16:28 par Mark 9:1 par Luke 9:27; Matt 24:34 par Mark 13:30 par Luke 21:32; John 21:22-23; 2 Pet 3:4; 1 Clem 23:2-5; 2 Clem 11:1-7; Hermas, *Vis.* 3.4.3; 3.5.1; 3.8.9.

[84] *Contra* Norelli, *Ascensio Isaiae: Commentarius,* 592-593. Norelli, *Ascensio Isaiae: Commentarius,* 38, 45, sees one indication of the different perspectives of the two parts of the Ascension of Isaiah in the fact that in chapters 6-11 the phrase 'in the last days' is used of the earthly life of the Beloved (9:13) whereas in chapters 1-5 it refers to the present period of disorder when the parousia is close at hand (3:30). But in the light of 11:37-38 there is no need to make such a distinction. The 'last days' are the final generation of history in which all the events from the descent of the Beloved to his parousia occur. The context of a third occurrence of the phrase 'in the last days' (3:15) is unfortunately very obscure: see the discussion between J. Verheyden, 'L'Ascension d'Isaïe et l'Évangile de Matthieu: Examen de AI 3,13-18,' in J.-M. Sevrin ed., *The New Testament in Early Christianity: La réception des écrits néotestamentaires dans le christianisme primitif* (BETL 86; Leuven: Leuven University Press/Peeters, 1989) 253-254, 268-270, and Norelli, *L'Ascensione,* 152-157.

[85] Examples of the value of the Ascension of Isaiah are Bauckham, 'Kerygmatic summaries,' 191-204; idem, *The Climax,* 86-88, 140-148, 425-428.

[86] The Greek fragment of the text is not even included in 'Early Christian Literature' as defined by the *Lexicon* of Bauer, Arndt and Gingrich.

[87] Cf. J.-A. Bühner, *Der Gesandte und seiner Weg im Vierten Evangelium* (WUNT 2/2; Tübingen: Mohr, 1977) 355-357.

[88] Cf. Norelli, *Ascensio Isaiae: Commentarius,* 40.

Christology;[89] the evidence it provides for the nature of early Christian prophecy;[90] its evidence of early Christian exegetical traditions, especially in the interpretation of the prophecies of Isaiah;[91] and the nature of its Gospel traditions, which are strikingly similar to some of Matthew's special traditions and to the Gospel of Peter, probably without dependence on either of these Gospels.[92]

---

[89] Cf. Bauckham, *The Climax*, 140-148; M. Simonetti, 'Note sulla cristologia dell' *Ascensione d'Isaia*,' in Pesce ed., *Isaia*, 185-209; Acerbi, *L'Ascensione*, 99-209; Norelli, *L'Ascensione*, 253-264; Knight, *Disciples*, 71-183.

[90] Cf. Bori, 'L'estasi del profeta,' 367-389; idem, 'L'esperienza profetica nell'*Ascensione di Isaia*,' in Pesce ed., *Isaia*, 133-154; Acerbi, *L'Ascensione*, 210-253; Norelli, *L'Ascensione*, 235-248; idem, 'L'*Ascensione di Isaia* nel quadro del profetismo cristiano,' *Ricerche storico bibliche* 5 (1993) 123-148; Hall, 'The *Ascension*,' 293-296. Indicative of the gross neglect of the Ascension of Isaiah in New Testament scholarship is its virtual absence from the otherwise very comprehensive work of D. E. Aune, *Prophecy in Early Christianity and the Ancient Mediterranean World* (Grand Rapids: Eerdmans, 1983).

[91] Cf. Acerbi, *L'Ascensione*, 32-82.

[92] Cf. R. Bauckham, 'The Study of Gospel Traditions Outside the Canonical Gospels: Problems and Prospects,' in D. Wenham ed., *Gospel Perspectives*, vol. 5: *The Jesus Tradition Outside the Gospels* (Sheffield: JSOT Press, 1984) 380; E. Norelli, 'La resurrezione di Gesù nell'*Ascensione di Isaia*,' *Cristianesimo nella Storia* 1 (1980) 315-366; Verheyden, 'L'Ascension,' 247-274; Norelli, *L'Ascensione*, 115-166, 213-219.

INDEX OF BIBLICAL REFERENCES

INDEX OF DEAD SEA SCROLLS

INDEX OF JEWISH AND CHRISTIAN
APOCRYPHAL LITERATURE

INDEX OF OTHER ANCIENT AND
MEDIEVAL LITERATURE

INDEX OF ANCIENT AND MEDIEVAL
PERSONS AND PLACES

INDEX OF MODERN AUTHORS

SUPPLEMENTS TO NOVUM TESTAMENTUM

ISSN 0167-9732

2. STROBEL, A. *Untersuchungen zum eschatologischen Verzögerungsproblem auf Grund der spätjüdische-urchristlichen Geschichte von Habakuk 2,2 ff.* 1961. ISBN 90 04 01582 5

6. *Neotestamentica et Patristica.* Eine Freundesgabe Herrn Professor Dr. Oscar Cullmann zu seinem 60. Geburtstag überreicht. 1962. ISBN 90 04 01586 8

8. DE MARCO, A.A. *The Tomb of Saint Peter.* A Representative and Annotated Bibliography of the Excavations. 1964. ISBN 90 04 01588 4

10. BORGEN, P. *Bread from Heaven.* An Exegetical Study of the Concept of Manna in the Gospel of John and the Writings of Philo. Photomech. Reprint of the first (1965) edition. 1981. ISBN 90 04 06419 2

13. MOORE, A.L. *The Parousia in the New Testament.* 1966. ISBN 90 04 01593 0

15. QUISPEL, G. *Makarius, das Thomasevangelium und das Lied von der Perle.* 1967. ISBN 90 04 01595 7

16. PFITZNER, V.C. *Paul and the Agon Motif.* 1967. ISBN 90 04 01596 5

17. BELLINZONI, A. *The Sayings of Jesus in the Writings of Justin Martyr.* 1967. ISBN 90 04 01597 3

18. GUNDRY, R.H. *The Use of the Old Testament in St. Matthew's Gospel.* With Special Reference to the Messianistic Hope. Reprint of the first (1967) edition. 1975. ISBN 90 04 04278 4

19. SEVENSTER, J.N. *Do You Know Greek?* How Much Greek Could the first Jewish Christians Have Known? 1968. ISBN 90 04 03090 5

20. BUCHANAN, G.W. *The Consequences of the Covenant.* 1970. ISBN 90 04 01600 7

21. KLIJN, A.F.J. *A Survey of the Researches into the Western Text of the Gospels and Acts.* Part 2: 1949-1969. 1969. ISBN 90 04 01601 5

22. GABOURY, A. *La Stucture des Évangiles synoptiques.* La structure-type à l'origine des synoptiques. 1970. ISBN 90 04 01602 3

23. GASTON, L. *No Stone on Another.* Studies in the Significance of the Fall of Jerusalem in the Synoptic Gospels. 1970. ISBN 90 04 01603 1

24. *Studies in John.* Presented to Professor Dr. J.N. Sevenster on the Occasion of His Seventieth Birthday. 1970. ISBN 90 04 03091 3

25. STORY, C.I.K. *The Nature of Truth in the 'Gospel of Truth', and in the Writings of Justin Martyr.* A Study of the Pattern of Orthodoxy in the Middle of the Second Christian Century. 1970. ISBN 90 04 01605 8

26. GIBBS, J.G. *Creation and Redemption.* A Study in Pauline Theology. 1971. ISBN 90 04 01606 6

27. MUSSIES, G. *The Morphology of Koine Greek As Used in the Apocalypse of St. John.* A Study in Bilingualism. 1971. ISBN 90 04 02656 8

28. AUNE, D.E. *The Cultic Setting of Realized Eschatology in Early Christianity.* 1972. ISBN 90 04 03341 6

29. UNNIK, W.C. VAN. *Sparsa Collecta.* The Collected Essays of W.C. van Unnik Part 1. Evangelia, Paulina, Acta. 1973. ISBN 90 04 03660 1

30. UNNIK, W.C. VAN. *Sparsa Collecta.* The Collected Essays of W.C. van Unnik Part 2. I Peter, Canon, Corpus Hellenisticum, Generalia. 1980. ISBN 90 04 06261 0

31. UNNIK, W.C. VAN. *Sparsa Collecta.* The Collected Essays of W.C. van Unnik Part 3. Patristica, Gnostica, Liturgica. 1983. ISBN 90 04 06262 9

33. AUNE D.E. (ed.) *Studies in New Testament and Early Christian Literature.* Essays in Honor of Allen P. Wikgren. 1972. ISBN 90 04 03504 4

34. HAGNER, D.A. *The Use of the Old and New Testaments in Clement of Rome.* 1973. ISBN 90 04 03636 9

35. GUNTHER, J.J. *St. Paul's Opponents and Their Background.* A Study of Apocalyptic and Jewish Sectarian Teachings. 1973. ISBN 90 04 03738 1

36. KLIJN, A.F.J. & G.J. REININK (eds.) *Patristic Evidence for Jewish-Christian Sects.* 1973. ISBN 90 04 03763 2

37. REILING, J. *Hermas and Christian Prophecy.* A Study of The Eleventh Mandate. 1973. ISBN 90 04 03771 3

38. DONFRIED, K.P. *The Setting of Second Clement in Early Christianity.* 1974. ISBN 90 04 03895 7

39. ROON, A. VAN. *The Authenticity of Ephesians.* 1974. ISBN 90 04 03971 6

40. KEMMLER, D.W. *Faith and Human Reason.* A Study of Paul's Method of Preaching as Illustrated by 1-2 Thessalonians and Acts 17, 2-4. 1975. ISBN 90 04 04209 1

42. PANCARO, S. *The Law in the Fourth Gospel.* The Torah and the Gospel, Moses and Jesus, Judaism and Christianity According to John. 1975. ISBN 90 04 04309 8

43. CLAVIER, H. *Les variétés de la pensée biblique et le problème de son unité.* Esquisse d'une théologie de la Bible sur les textes originaux et dans leur contexte historique. 1976. ISBN 90 04 04465 5

44. ELLIOTT, J.K.E. (ed.) *Studies in New Testament Language and Text.* Essays in Honour of George D. Kilpatrick on the Occasion of His Sixty-fifth Birthday. 1976. ISBN 90 04 04386 1

45. PANAGOPOULOS, J. (ed.) *Prophetic Vocation in the New Testament and Today.* 1977. ISBN 90 04 04923 1

46. KLIJN, A.F.J. *Seth in Jewish, Christian and Gnostic Literature.* 1977. ISBN 90 04 05245 3

47. BAARDA, T., A.F.J. KLIJN & W.C. VAN UNNIK (eds.) *Miscellanea Neotestamentica.* I. Studia ad Novum Testamentum Praesertim Pertinentia a Sociis Sodalicii Batavi c.n. Studiosorum Novi Testamenti Conventus Anno MCMLXXVI Quintum Lustrum Feliciter Complentis Suscepta. 1978. ISBN 90 04 05685 8

48. BAARDA, T., A.F.J. KLIJN & W.C. VAN UNNIK (eds.) *Miscellanea Neotestamentica.* II. 1978. ISBN 90 04 05686 6

49. O'BRIEN, P.T. *Introductory Thanksgivings in the Letters of Paul.* 1977. ISBN 90 04 05265 8

50. BOUSSET, D.W. *Religionsgeschichtliche Studien.* Aufsätze zur Religionsgeschichte des hellenistischen Zeitalters. Hrsg. von A.F. Verheule. 1979. ISBN 90 04 05845 1

51. COOK, M.J. *Mark's Treatment of the Jewish Leaders.* 1978. ISBN 90 04 05785 4

52. GARLAND, D.E. *The Intention of Matthew 23.* 1979. ISBN 90 04 05912 1

53. MOXNES, H. *Theology in Conflict.* Studies in Paul's Understanding of God in Romans. 1980. ISBN 90 04 06140 1

55. MENKEN, M.J.J. *Numerical Literary Techniques in John.* The Fourth Evangelist's Use of Numbers of Words and Syllables. 1985. ISBN 90 04 07427 9

56. SKARSAUNE, O. *The Proof From Prophecy.* A Study in Justin Martyr's Proof-Text Tradition: Text-type, Provenance, Theological Profile. 1987. ISBN 90 04 07468 6

59. WILKINS, M.J. *The Concept of Disciple in Matthew's Gospel, as Reflected in the Use of the Term 'Mathetes'.* 1988. ISBN 90 04 08689 7

60. MILLER, E.L. *Salvation-History in the Prologue of John.* The Significance of John 1:3-4. 1989. ISBN 90 04 08692 7

61. THIELMAN, F. *From Plight to Solution.* A Jewish Framework for Understanding Paul's View of the Law in Galatians and Romans. 1989. ISBN 90 04 09176 9

64. STERLING, G.E. *Historiography and Self-Definition.* Josephos, Luke-Acts and Apologetic Historiography. 1992. ISBN 90 04 09501 2

65. BOTHA, J.E. *Jesus and the Samaritan Woman.* A Speech Act Reading of John 4:1-42. 1991. ISBN 90 04 09505 5

66. KUCK, D.W. *Judgment and Community Conflict.* Paul's Use of Apologetic Judgment Language in 1 Corinthians 3:5-4:5. 1992. ISBN 90 04 09510 1

67. SCHNEIDER, G. *Jesusüberlieferung und Christologie.* Neutestamentliche Aufsätze 1970-1990. 1992. ISBN 90 04 09555 1

68. SEIFRID, M.A. *Justification by Faith.* The Origin and Development of a Central Pauline Theme. 1992. ISBN 90 04 09521 7

69. NEWMAN, C.C. *Paul's Glory-Christology.* Tradition and Rhetoric. 1992. ISBN 90 04 09463 6

70. IRELAND, D.J. *Stewardship and the Kingdom of God.* An Historical, Exegetical, and Contextual Study of the Parable of the Unjust Steward in Luke 16: 1-13. 1992. ISBN 90 04 09600 0

71. ELLIOTT, J.K. *The Language and Style of the Gospel of Mark.* An Edition of C.H. Turner's "Notes on Marcan Usage" together with other comparable studies. 1993. ISBN 90 04 09767 8

72. CHILTON, B. *A Feast of Meanings.* Eucharistic Theologies from Jesus through Johannine Circles. 1994. ISBN 90 04 09949 2

73. GUTHRIE, G.H. *The Structure of Hebrews.* A Text-Linguistic Analysis. 1994. ISBN 90 04 09866 6

74. BORMANN, L., K. DEL TREDICI & A. STANDHARTINGER (eds.) *Religious Propaganda and Missionary Competition in the New Testament World.* Essays Honoring DIETER GEORGI. 1994. ISBN 90 04 10049 0

75. PIPER, R.A. (ed.) *The Gospel Behind the Gospels.* Current Studies on Q. 1995. ISBN 90 04 09737 6

76. PEDERSEN, S. (ed.) *New Directions in Biblical Theology.* Papers of the Aarhus Conference, 16-19 September 1992. 1994. ISBN 90 04 10120 9

77. JEFFORD, C.N. (ed.) *The Didache in Context.* Essays on Its Text, History and Transmission. 1995. ISBN 90 04 10045 8

78. BORMANN, L. *Philippi – Stadt und Christengemeinde zur Zeit des Paulus.* 1995. ISBN 90 04 10232 9

79. PETERLIN, D. *Paul's Letter to the Philippians in the Light of Disunity in the Church.* 1995. ISBN 90 04 10305 8

80. JONES, I.H. *The Matthean Parables.* A Literary and Historical Commentary. 1995 ISBN 90 04 10181 0

81. GLAD, C.E. *Paul and Philodemus.* Adaptability in Epicurean and Early Christian Psychagogy. 1995 ISBN 90 04 10067 9

82. FITZGERALD, J.T. (ed.) *Friendship, Flattery, and Frankness of Speech.* Studies on Friendship in the New Testament World. 1996. ISBN 90 04 10454 2

83. VAN TILBORG, S. *Reading John in Ephesus.* 1996. 90 04 10530 1

84. HOLLEMAN, J. *Resurrection and Parousia.* A Traditio-Historical Study of Paul's Eschatology in 1 Corinthians 15. 1996. ISBN 90 04 10597 2

85. MORITZ, T. *A Profound Mystery*. The Use of the Old Testament in Ephesians. 1996. ISBN 90 04 10556 5
86. BORGEN, P. *Philo of Alexandria - An Exegete for His Time.* 1997. ISBN 90 04 10388 0
87. ZWIEP, A.W. *The Ascension of the Messiah in Lukan Christology.* 1997. ISBN 90 04 10897 1
88. WILSON, W.T. *The Hope of Glory*. Education and Exhortation in the Epistle to the Colossians. 1997. ISBN 90 04 10937 4
89. PETERSEN, W.L., J.S. VOS & H.J. DE JONGE (eds.). *Sayings of Jesus: Canonical and Non-Canonical*. Essays in Honour of TJITZE BAARDA. 1997. ISBN 90 04 10380 5
90. MALHERBE, A.J., F.W. NORRIS & J.W. THOMPSON (eds.). *The Early Church in Its Context*. Essays in Honor of Everett Ferguson. 1998. ISBN 90 04 10832 7
91. KIRK, A. *The Composition of the Sayings Source*. Genre, Synchrony, and Wisdom Redaction in Q. 1998. ISBN 90 04 11085 2
92. VORSTER, W.S. *Speaking of Jesus*. Essays on Biblical Language, Gospel Narrative and the Historical Jesus. Edited by J. E. Botha. 1998. ISBN 90 04 10779 7 (In preparation)
93. BAUCKHAM, R. *The Fate of Dead*. Studies on the Jewish and Christian Apocalypses. 1998. ISBN 90 04 11203 0